AS LEVEL
BIOLOGY

Phil Bradfield, John Dodds, Judy Dodds and Norma Taylor

Longman

Pearson Education Limited
Edinburgh Gate
Harlow
Essex

© Pearson Education Limited 2001

The right of Phil Bradfield, John Dodds, Judy Dodds, and Norma Taylor to be identified as the authors of this Work has been asserted by them in accordance with the Copyright, Designs and Patents Act of 1988.

Ninth impression 2007
ISBN 978-0-582-42946-8

Concept Designed by Hardlines Ltd, Charlbury, Oxford.

Designed and produced by Gecko Ltd, Cambridge.

Illustrations by Jerry Fowler, Helen Humphreys, Geoff Jones, Peter Simmonett and Raymond Turvey.

Printed in China
GCC/09

Acknowledgments

The authors would like to thank many people for their help, support and encouragement in writing this book. In particular: Steve Potter, Alan Clamp, Judy Webster and Graham Causton.

Photo acknowledgements are on page 567.

Dr Phil Bradfield is Head of Biology at Davenant Foundation School, Loughton, Essex. He is also an examiner for A-level Biology.

John Dodds is Assistant Principal and Head of Biology at The Albany College, Hendon.

Judy Dodds is Coordinator of Sixth Form Biology at Cardinal Wiseman School, Ealing and also teaches A-level Biology at The Albany College, Hendon.

Norma Taylor has retired after teaching A-Level Biology for 26 years, most recently at The Albany College, Hendon.

Contents

Introduction

This book is for any student studying Biology at AS level. It covers the core content of all the major specifications. We have used a number of different features to help you with your studies.

The summary at the end of each chapter condenses the content of the chapter into a series of bullet points, to help you with revision.

End of chapter questions test your knowledge of the whole chapter. Most are exam-style questions, to give you plenty of practice. Some of these questions also give you an opportunity to demonstrate **Key Skills**. These questions are marked with a symbol.

🔑 **C2.2** This symbol means you can fully demonstrate Communications skill 2.2 with the question.

🔑 **N3.2** This example means that you can partially demonstrate Application of Number skill 3.2 with the question.

The introduction to the chapter gives you an idea of the content of the chapter, and reminds you of some things you studied at GCSE.

This list gives you the main ideas in the chapter. It is not a full contents list - that is given on pages iii - v.

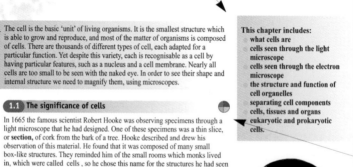

① Cells

The cell is the basic 'unit' of living organisms. It is the smallest structure which is able to grow and reproduce, and most of the matter of organisms is composed of cells. There are thousands of different types of cell, each adapted for a particular function. Yet despite this variety, each is recognisable as a cell by having particular features, such as a nucleus and a cell membrane. Nearly all cells are too small to be seen with the naked eye. In order to see their shape and internal structure we need to magnify them, using microscopes.

1.1 The significance of cells

In 1665 the famous scientist Robert Hooke was observing specimens through a light microscope that he had designed. One of these specimens was a thin slice, or **section**, of cork from the bark of a tree. Hooke described and drew his observation of this material. He found that it was composed of many small box-like structures. They reminded him of the small rooms which monks lived in, which were called cells , so he chose this name for the structures he had seen in the cork (Figure 1.1).

Hooke did not realise the importance of his find. He even thought that the cell walls were the living material, and the cells themselves were empty.

By the start of the nineteenth century light microscopes were much improved in quality, and microscopists had seen cells in a vast range of animal and plant material. In 1839 this led two biologists called Schleiden and Schwann to suggest that the cell was the basic unit of structure and function in the living organism. This became known as the **cell theory**.

What is the advantage for an organism to be made up of many tiny compartments like this? The answer lies partly in the nature of an organism s complex chemical reactions, or **metabolism**. For this metabolism to function efficiently, many different molecules must be closely associated with one another. Without cells, bounded by cell membranes, molecules would tend to disperse and be unable to react with each other. Inside a cell they remain close together, and reactions can be carried out more efficiently. This idea is called **compartmentalisation**, and is repeated *inside* cells, where internal structures called cell **organelles** separate the different metabolic processes which go on within them. It is a rather long word, but just means being divided up into compartments .

This chapter includes:
what cells are
cells seen through the light microscope
cells seen through the electron microscope
the structure and function of cell organelles
separating cell components
cells, tissues and organs
eukaryotic and prokaryotic cells.

Figure 1.1 The first drawing ever made of cells: Robert Hooke s observation of cork cells (1665)

These 'pies' tell you whether or not the section or box applies to your specification. Not all the content in the book applies to all the specifications, and some topics from the A2 part of the specification have been included in this book if they logically fit into the chapter.

Remember
An organelle is a structure inside a cell which carries out a particular process. Some organelles are surrounded by membranes, compartmentalising the metabolic reactions within (e.g. nucleus, chloroplast). Others are not surrounded by membranes (e.g. ribosomes).

1

Remember boxes include exam hints, definitions of new words or phrases, or reminders of facts that some students may find difficult to remember.

Key for label

 AQA A (AS)

 AQA A (A2)

 Edexcel (AS)

 Edexcel (A2)

 OCR (AS)

 OCR (A2)

 AQA B (AS)

AQA B (A2)

Each chapter is divided into sections. These numbers tell you which sections appear on the pages you are looking at.

Extension boxes contain material that is only in one specification but should be of interest to students studying all the specifications. The 'pie' tells you which specification the material applies to.

Cross references are provided in the main text and in extension boxes, to make it easy for you to look up related ideas.

1.19 **1.20**

Figure 1.25 Section through a leaf showing different tissues

(a) light

(b) light

Figure 1.26 Orientation of photosynthetic cells in the palisade mesophyll of a leaf: more light reaches the chloroplasts when the cells are arranged as in (a) rather than (b)

The chloroplasts can be seen to move around in the cell, with the result that they achieve maximum light absorption. Covering the surface of the leaf is a single cell layer called the **epidermis**, which functions in a protective manner, rather like the epithelia of an animal. Transport tissues such as **xylem** and **phloem** also exist, allowing movement of water and solutes through the plant (Chapter 12, page 343).

An **organ** is made up of several different tissues, forming a structure with a specific physiological function or functions. For example, the human liver is an organ composed of a number of tissues. As well as liver cells (Figure 1.8) it contains blood, connective tissue, epithelia and others. An artery and a vein are both organs: their walls contain layers of smooth muscle, elastic and fibrous connective tissue, blood vessels and an inner endothelium lining the lumen of the vessel (Section 10.8, page 292). One of the most obvious plant organs is the leaf, the organ of photosynthesis. This contains a number of tissues, such as epidermis, palisade and spongy mesophyll, xylem and phloem (Figure 1.25).

1.20 Eukaryotic and prokaryotic cells

So far we have mainly considered the structure of animal and plant cells. These cells both have a nucleus surrounded by a nuclear envelope, and are referred to as **eukaryotic** cells. Eukaryotic is derived from Greek words meaning 'true nucleus'. Fungi and protoctistans (algae and protozoa) are also **eukaryotes**, since their cells also have a nucleus (Figure 1.23). These four groups of organisms (animals, plants, fungi and protoctista) make up four of the five **kingdoms** of living organisms. The fifth kingdom consists of unicellular organisms made of a very different kind of cell: the **prokaryotes**.

Prokaryotes are all **bacteria**. The word **prokaryotic** means 'before nucleus'. This describes the main difference between eukaryotic and prokaryotic cells: prokaryotes have no nucleus or nuclear membrane. Their

> **Did You Know**
> *Escherichia coli* is a very common bacterium living in the human gut. It is normally harmless, feeding on food and breakdown products of digestion. It is estimated that the number of *E. coli* cells in your body is about 65 billion. This is greater than the total number of humans who have ever lived on the Earth! Also, *E. coli* only makes up some 0.1% of the *total* bacteria in the body: this total works out at a staggering 65 000 000 000 000!

25

Box 1.2 Calculating magnification

When you have observed a specimen through the microscope and drawn a diagram of it, it is important that you indicate the magnification of your drawing. This is best done by putting a scale bar alongside, showing a suitable length for comparison (see for example Figure 1.4).

An alternative way is to show the magnification, for example: ×200. You may be tempted to multiply the eyepiece magnification by the objective magnification, e.g. ×4 by ×10, to arrive at the answer ×40. However, this only shows the magnification of your microscope, not your drawing. To calculate the magnification of your actual drawing, you must use the formula:

$$\text{Magnification} = \frac{\text{length of drawing}}{\text{real length of specimen}}$$

Note that these measurements **must be in the same units**, such as μm.

The same principle can be used to calculate the magnification of a cell or organelle in a micrograph. The formula is now:

$$\text{Magnification} = \frac{\text{length of organelle in photo}}{\text{real length of organelle}}$$

Again it is vital that the two measurements are in the same units. For example, the nucleus of the liver cell in Figure 1.8 is 11 μm in diameter. The nucleus in the electron micrograph is 55 mm (55 000 μm) across, so its magnification is 55 000 ÷ 11, which is × 5000. (See Section 1.2, page 2 for details of inter-converting units.)

?

8 The real length of the chloroplast in Figure 1.20 is 4 μm. Measure the length of the chloroplast in the photomicrograph in mm. *(1 mark)*

Convert this into μm and calculate its magnification *(2 marks)*

1.18 Cell fractionation by differential centrifugation

An important way in which biologists have been able to investigate the functions of the various components of cells is to carry out experiments using isolated organelles. For example, much of the workings of the mitochondrion was discovered by investigations made upon mitochondria extracted from liver cells. But how can minute organelles be isolated intact from whole cells? This process, known as **cell fractionation**, can be achieved by the technique of **differential centrifugation**. First we must understand the workings of a **centrifuge**.

A centrifuge is a common piece of laboratory equipment, often available for use in school laboratories (Figure 1.21).

The job of the centrifuge is to separate suspended particulate material out of a liquid. It does this by spinning a test tube of the mixture around at very high speeds, so that the solid particles sink to the bottom of the tube, forming a **sediment** or **pellet**. When an object is spun around like this, it is accelerating, because of its constantly changing direction of movement. This acceleration is

Did You Know boxes include facts related to the chapter that we think you will find interesting!

Self-assessment questions are provided at various places within each chapter. They should help you to check your understanding of the work you have done so far. Answers to these questions are provided at the end of the chapter.

$\boxed{1}$ Cells

The cell is the basic 'unit' of living organisms. It is the smallest structure which is able to grow and reproduce, and most of the matter of organisms is composed of cells. There are thousands of different types of cell, each adapted for a particular function. Yet despite this variety, each is recognisable as a cell by having particular features, such as a nucleus and a cell membrane. Nearly all cells are too small to be seen with the naked eye. In order to see their shape and internal structure we need to magnify them, using microscopes.

This chapter includes:
- what cells are
- cells seen through the light microscope
- cells seen through the electron microscope
- the structure and function of cell organelles
- separating cell components
- cells, tissues and organs
- eukaryotic and prokaryotic cells.

1.1 The significance of cells

In 1665 the famous scientist Robert Hooke was observing specimens through a light microscope that he had designed. One of these specimens was a thin slice, or **section,** of cork from the bark of a tree. Hooke described and drew his observation of this material. He found that it was composed of many small box-like structures. They reminded him of the small rooms which monks lived in, which were called 'cells', so he chose this name for the structures he had seen in the cork (Figure 1.1).

Hooke did not realise the importance of his find. He even thought that the cell walls were the living material, and the cells themselves were empty.

By the start of the nineteenth century light microscopes were much improved in quality, and microscopists had seen cells in a vast range of animal and plant material. In 1839 this led two biologists called Schleiden and Schwann to suggest that the cell was the basic unit of structure and function in the living organism. This became known as the **cell theory**.

What is the advantage for an organism to be made up of many tiny compartments like this? The answer lies partly in the nature of an organism's complex chemical reactions, or **metabolism**. For this metabolism to function efficiently, many different molecules must be closely associated with one another. Without cells, bounded by cell membranes, molecules would tend to disperse and be unable to react with each other. Inside a cell they remain close together, and reactions can be carried out more efficiently. This idea is called **compartmentalisation**, and is repeated *inside* cells, where internal structures called cell **organelles** separate the different metabolic processes which go on within them. It is a rather long word, but just means 'being divided up into compartments'.

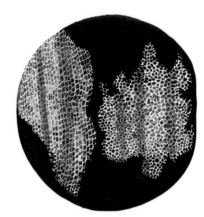

***Figure 1.1** The first drawing ever made of cells: Robert Hooke's observation of cork cells (1665)*

 Remember

An organelle is a structure inside a cell which carries out a particular process. Some organelles are surrounded by membranes, compartmentalising the metabolic reactions within (e.g. nucleus, chloroplast). Others are not surrounded by membranes (e.g. ribosomes).

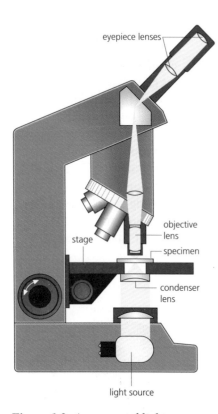

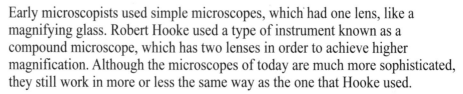

1.2 Light microscopy and cell structure

Early microscopists used simple microscopes, which had one lens, like a magnifying glass. Robert Hooke used a type of instrument known as a compound microscope, which has two lenses in order to achieve higher magnification. Although the microscopes of today are much more sophisticated, they still work in more or less the same way as the one that Hooke used.

In light (or **optical**) microscopy, the object to be examined is placed in a beam of light. The beam passes through the specimen and then through a series of lenses which produce a magnified image of the object (Figure 1.2).

The **condenser** lens focuses the light onto the specimen for maximum illumination. The lower, **objective** lens magnifies the object, and the image from this lens is further enlarged when viewed through the upper, **eyepiece** lens. The beam from the light source directly enters the observer's eye. Using this method living cells can be viewed, or thin sections which have been cut from plant or animal tissue. These specimens have to be thin enough for light to pass through them. With the exception of coloured parts of cells, such as chloroplasts (Section 1.17, page 17), most cells are transparent and virtually invisible without some kind of staining. Staining can also be used to show the location of a particular organelle or substance in the cell, such as starch granules or DNA in the nucleus. However, staining has the disadvantage that it often kills the cells. Stained and preserved material can be kept as **permanent** slides, and temporary or permanent slides can be photographed through the microscope, producing **light micrographs**. A selection of light micrographs of various plant and animal cells is shown in Figure 1.3.

Figure 1.2 A compound light microscope

💡 Remember

Notice that a scale bar is shown on the photographs of cells (e.g. Figure 1.3) so that the size of each cell or the structures within them can be estimated. The units used here are μm (micrometres). The Greek letter μ (mu) indicates one millionth (of a metre in this case). μm are usually used to describe the size of cells or their organelles. For small structures, such as the thickness of the plasma membrane, a smaller unit is needed, the nanometre (nm) which is one billionth of a metre. To summarise:

Unit	Symbol	Size in metres
1 metre	1 m	1 m
1 centimetre	1 cm	10^{-2} m
1 millimetre	1 mm	10^{-3} m
1 micrometre	1 μm	10^{-6} m
1 nanometre	1 nm	10^{-9} m

To convert μm to mm, you have to divide by 1000. For instance a cell with a length of 250 μm is (250 ÷ 1000) or 0.25 mm long.

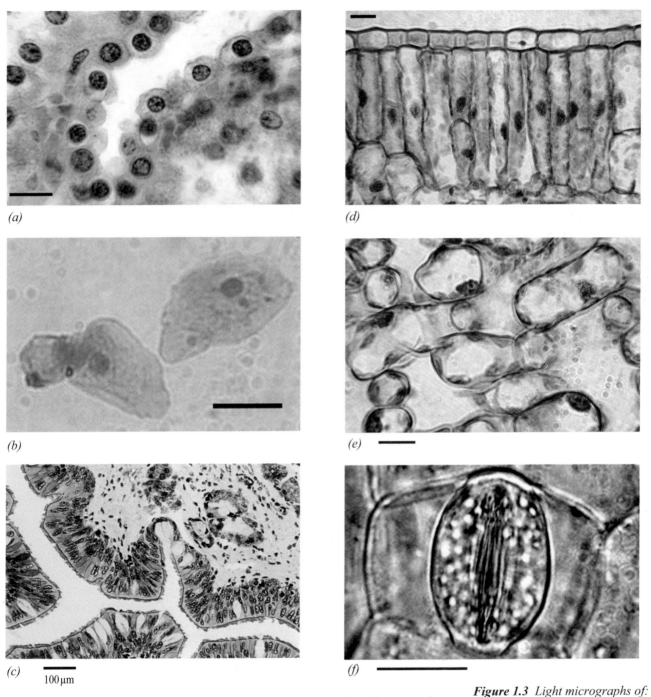

(a)

(b)

(c) 100 µm

(d)

(e)

(f)

Figure 1.3 *Light micrographs of:*
(a) kidney tubule cells
(b) cheek lining cells
(c) trachea epithelium cells
(d) leaf palisade cells
(e) leaf spongy mesophyll cells
(f) leaf guard cells
All scale bars in this book are 10 µm
unless otherwise stated.

From light microscopy images such as these it is possible to identify certain key features of a plant and animal cell (Figure 1.4).

(Note that later in this chapter (Section 1.20, page 25) we will see that animals and plants are composed of **eukaryotic** cells, whereas **bacteria** are simpler, **prokaryotic** cells. It is easier to compare these two types of cell if we first look in detail at the more complex eukaryotic cells, since you are likely to be more familiar with these from your previous study of science.)

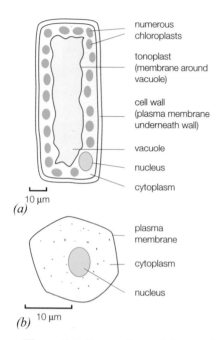

Figure 1.4 *Comparison of plant and animal cells as seen through the light microscope*

💡 **Remember**

An animal cell usually consists of a thin **cell surface membrane** or **plasma membrane** enclosing two inner compartments:
- the **nucleus** containing the genetic material and surrounded by a nuclear membrane
- the **cytoplasm**, which is everything apart from the nucleus contained within the plasma membrane. The liquid part of the cytoplasm is called the **cytosol**.

A plant cell also has these features, but in addition has:
- a **cell wall** made of cellulose, surrounding the cell membrane
- **chloroplasts** in some plant cells, where photosynthesis occurs
- a large central space called a **vacuole**, surrounded by a membrane called the **tonoplast** and filled with a liquid called **cell sap**.

❓

1 The scale bar in Figure 1.4(a) represents a length of 10 μm. What is the approximate length of the plant cell in the diagram? Give your answer in μm and m. *(2 marks)*

Membranes such as the plasma membrane are critical to the functioning of a cell. As we have seen, they allow compartmentalisation to occur, separating the numerous metabolic processes. A membrane is a thin but complex layer. In fact its actual thickness is not visible through the light microscope. Labels in text books just show the location of membranes as boundaries around organelles and the cell. The structure and functions of membranes are dealt with in more detail in Chapter 2, page 37.

1.3 Magnification and resolution: the electron microscope

Only the shape of whole cells or large organelles can be distinguished through the light microscope, which can magnify an object by a maximum of about 1500 times ($\times$1500). This enables us to see the structures shown in Figure 1.4, but as you can tell from the light micrographs (Figure 1.3) it does not let us see smaller organelles. In fact those which *are* visible lack clarity: they appear 'fuzzy'. The actual *magnification* is less important than the **resolution** of the image. A microscope with a high **resolving power** enables us to view images with a high resolution. This means that two small objects close to each other can be seen as being separate. With low resolution they will be visible as one object. Take for example the light micrograph of the cheek lining cell shown in Figure 1.3. The magnification of the photo is about $\times$1800. We could take one of these photographs, place it on an overhead projector and enlarge it to over a metre in diameter. The magnification would then be about $\times$20000, but the image on the screen would be no more detailed, *so its resolution would be the same.*

The factor which limits the resolution of images viewed through the light microscope is the wavelength of the light used. With an expensive microscope, using light of a wavelength 500 nm (0.5×10^{-6} m), the resolving power enables two points to be seen about 0.2 μm apart. To improve the resolution beyond this, 'light' of a shorter wavelength must be used. This can be achieved using the **transmission electron microscope** (Figure 1.5).

The principle behind the electron microscope is that fast-moving electrons, although they are particles, also behave like waves. If a beam of electrons is directed at a specimen, the beam can be bent and focused by **electromagnetic** lenses, in the same way that glass lenses are used in a light microscope (Figure 1.6).

The beam of electrons is produced by a heated filament, focused on the specimen by the condenser lens, and the image then magnified by the objective and projector lenses. You can see the similarity between this and the arrangement of glass lenses in the light microscope. Using electrons, wavelengths about 100 000 times shorter than visible light can be obtained, so that a modern electron microscope can resolve points down to about 0.1 nm (10^{-10} m), and can achieve magnifications of up to 1 million times. This means that a cell with a diameter of 20 μm will be enlarged to a diameter of 20 metres.

The image formed in the electron microscope is projected onto a cathode ray tube so that it is visible to the operator, looking rather like a black and white TV screen. When suitable sections are found, they are photographed to give a permanent record, called an **electron micrograph**.

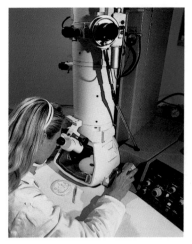

Figure 1.5 *A modern transmission electron microscope in use: it can achieve much greater resolution than the light microscope*

2 Say whether each of the following statements about the resolving power of a microscope is true or false. Explain your answers briefly:

(a) A microscope with a high resolving power will form two images of a single object.

(b) The resolving power is the ability of the microscope to reveal fine detail.

(c) If the magnification of a microscope is high, the resolving power will be high too.

(d) If the distance between two objects is small, the resolving power must be high to see them as separate objects. *(4 marks)*

The scanning electron microscope

There is a second type of electron microscope called the scanning electron microscope (s.e.m.). This is used to examine the *surface* of specimens. The surface is first coated with a thin film of metallic gold or palladium. A fine beam of electrons is then passed backwards and forwards (scanned) over the surface and electrons that are reflected from it are collected line by line and amplified to form an image on a cathode ray tube. The scanning electron microscope gives a much lower resolution than the transmission electron microscope (t.e.m.) of about 5–20 nm. However, it gives surface views with a great depth of field, so that they look three-dimensional (Figure 1.7).

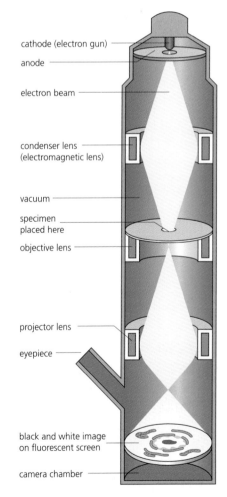

cathode (electron gun)

anode

electron beam

condenser lens (electromagnetic lens)

vacuum

specimen placed here

objective lens

projector lens

eyepiece

black and white image on fluorescent screen

camera chamber

Figure 1.6 *Image formation in transmission electron microscope*

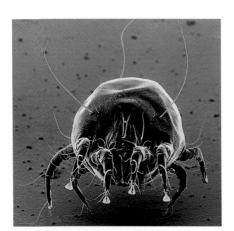

Figure 1.7 *Notice how the scanning electron microscope (SEM) reveals details of the surface of this dust mite (× 350)*

1.5 The limitations of electron microscopy

The development of the electron microscope has revolutionised our understanding of the structure and function of the cell. Many cell organelles only became visible through the electron microscope, and a knowledge of the internal organisation of the organelles has helped in our understanding of how they work. However, whereas a living specimen can be observed through the light microscope, the electron microscope can only be used with dead material. This is because there must be a vacuum inside the microscope, otherwise the electrons would be scattered in all directions by the air molecules. A living organism or cell cannot be placed in a vacuum.

There is a second major problem. The tissue to be observed through the electron microscope has to undergo several stages of preparation, each of which may alter the 'real' appearance of the cells. These procedures are often harsh, involving treatment with corrosive chemicals and physical shock (see Box 1.1). How do we know that the resulting electron micrographs are truly representative of the cell's structure? Any deviation from the 'real' appearance of a cell is known as an **artefact**. This could be a deviation in shape or structure of a cell or an organelle. Sometimes the preparation procedures even result in the creation of structures that do not really exist in the living cell.

3 Suggest how electron microscopists could use different preparation methods to find out if an unidentified structure was an artefact or not.

(2 marks)

Box 1.1 Preparation of material for viewing through the electron microscope

Extension

Tissues to be observed through the transmission electron microscope are subjected to five main preparation procedures. These are fixation, dehydration, embedding, sectioning and staining. (Similar procedures are used for making permanent slides for the light microscope, but the chemicals and methods used are less harsh, and less likely to produce artefacts.)

- **Fixation** aims to preserve the material in a life-like state. This is done by placing it in a fixative solution, usually a mixture of glutaraldehyde and osmium tetroxide (OsO_4). Osmium tetroxide also stains lipids and membranes.

- **Dehydration** removes water, allowing the tissue to be penetrated by the embedding medium. Dehydration is carried out gradually, by immersing the tissue in a series of mixtures of ethanol/water solutions of increasing concentration, finishing with 100% ethanol.

- **Embedding** the specimen in a suitable medium allows it to be cut into very thin sections. For electron microscopy the medium must be very hard to keep the specimen rigid. Usually a plastic or epoxy resin such as Araldite is used.

Box 1.1 Preparation of material for viewing through the electron microscope (cont'd)

- **Sectioning** cuts the specimen into 'slices' 20–100 nm thick, so that the electrons will pass through it. The sections are cut using a machine called an ultramicrotome, using a glass or diamond knife.

- **Staining** is completed with compounds containing heavy metals, such as osmium, lead or uranium.

It is not surprising that procedures such as these may result in damage to or distortion of the cellular structure, producing artefacts.

Electron microscopes are very expensive pieces of equipment. They are large, complex and have to be maintained under controlled conditions, such as a constant temperature, as well as needing expensive pumps to maintain their internal vacuum. Because of this their use is normally limited to universities and other research establishments. Some of the differences between the light microscope and the transmission electron microscope are summarised in Table 1.1.

Table 1.1 *Comparison of light microscope and transmission electron microscope*

Light microscope	Transmission electron microscope
uses light of wavelength 450 to 700 nm	uses electrons of wavelength 0.01 nm
light refracted by glass lenses	electron beams refracted by electromagnetic lenses
low resolution: 200 nm	high resolution: 0.1 nm
low magnification: ×1500 maximum	high magnification: ×1 000 000 maximum
image formed on the retina of the eye	projected image formed on cathode ray tube or photographic film
can be used to view living or dead specimens	can only be used to view dead specimens
less likely to produce artefacts	more likely to produce artefacts

1.6 The ultrastructure of the cell

The fine detail of the organisation of a cell is called its **ultrastructure**. The ultrastructure of each cell organelle is closely related to its function, and organelles common to different cells have a similar ultrastructure. For example, a chloroplast is easily recognisable in any photosynthetic plant cell by its shape and internal organisation. Because of this, biology text books often refer to a 'typical' animal or plant cell, which contain all the common organelles. There is really no such thing as a 'typical' cell; instead there is an enormous variety of cells adapted to perform different functions. We can see most of the organelles commonly found in an animal cell by looking at an electron micrograph of a mammalian liver cell (Figure 1.8).

Even from this relatively low magnification electron micrograph, it is obvious that the cytoplasm is not the simple 'jelly' seen by light microscopy. It is a complex arrangement of organelles, some of which are surrounded by a membrane. They are separated from other organelles by a complicated system of interconnecting membrane-bound spaces. Remember that membranes are important structures, acting as boundaries and allowing compartmentalisation within the cell.

1.7 The nucleus

The nucleus is usually the largest organelle in an animal or plant cell, appearing as a spherical structure 10–20 µm in diameter and surrounded by a double membrane called the **nuclear envelope**. The contents of the nucleus, the **nucleoplasm**, has a characteristic patchy (granular) appearance which is easy to recognise in an electron micrograph (Figure 1.8). When you are given an electron micrograph to interpret, it is usually simple to spot the nucleus, which then gives you an appreciation of the scale of the rest of the cell. The nuclear envelope is continuous with the intracellular membranes of the cytoplasm, called the **endoplasmic reticulum** (see Section 1.8, page 10). The nuclear envelope compartmentalises the chemical reactions taking place in the nucleus. It also restricts movement of materials out of the nucleus to holes, or **pores** in the envelope, allowing the nucleus to control events in the cytoplasm. The nucleoplasm contains the **chromosomes** and one or more dark structures called **nucleoli** (singular **nucleolus**). The structure of the nucleus, nucleolus and the surrounding endoplasmic reticulum is shown in Figure 1.9.

Chromosomes contain the hereditary material, the **deoxyribonucleic acid** or **DNA**, attached to proteins called **histones**. The chromosomes are only visible as the familiar separate bodies when the cell is undergoing division. Between divisions, the chromosomal material forms a diffuse granular mass called **chromatin**. Some chromatin contains densely packed DNA, and stains more darkly. This is called **heterochromatin**. More lightly staining areas of the material are called **euchromatin**. When a cell divides, the DNA coils upon itself, shortening and thickening the chromosomes so that they can be seen through the light microscope.

DNA is the chemical which contains the **genetic code**. This topic will be dealt with in full in Chapter 5, but in outline, the code controls the production of proteins, including enzymes, in the cytoplasm of the cell, and so controls the cell's development and activities.

Nucleoplasm also contains a second nucleic acid called **ribonucleic acid** or **RNA**. There are three types of RNA (Section 5.3, page 123). One of these is called **ribosomal RNA** (or **rRNA**). This is made in the nucleolus from instructions contained in the DNA. The nucleolus then combines the rRNA with protein to assemble the **ribosomes**, which are found in the cytoplasm (see below). A second type of RNA in the nucleus is **messenger RNA (mRNA)** which carries the instructions for making proteins out from the DNA to the cytoplasm. (The third type of RNA, transfer RNA or tRNA, is only found in the cytoplasm as part of the protein synthesis process described in Section 5.9, page 134).

> **Remember**
>
> The functions of the nucleus are:
> - to control the synthesis of proteins, including enzymes, in the cell, and so control the cell's activities
> - to divide at the start of cell division, ensuring that the daughter cells have exact copies of the cell's genetic material in their chromosomes
> - to assemble ribosomes.

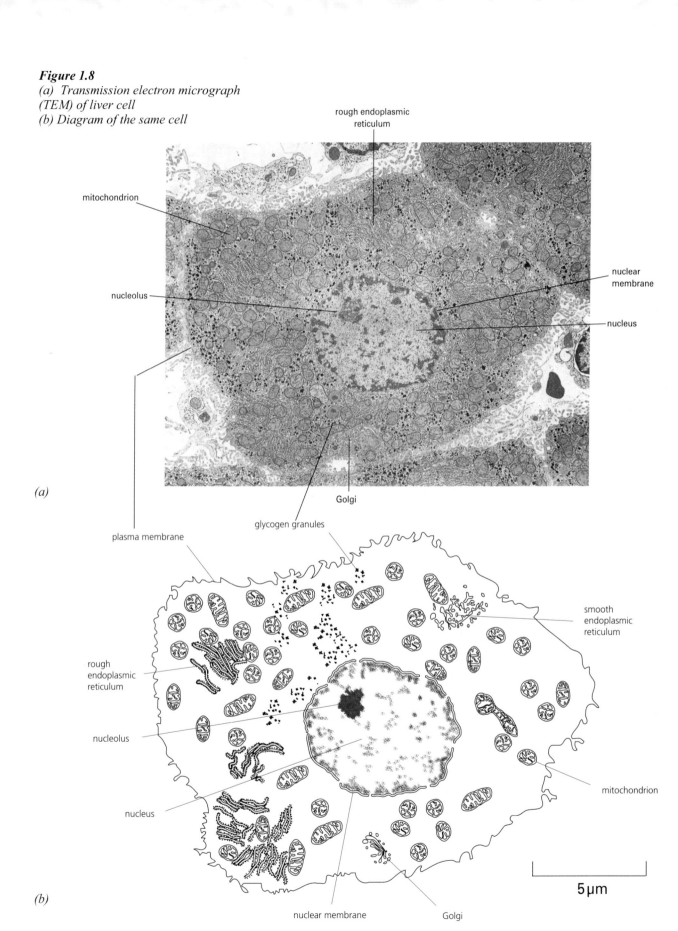

Figure 1.8
*(a) Transmission electron micrograph
(TEM) of liver cell
(b) Diagram of the same cell*

rough endoplasmic
reticulum

mitochondrion

nucleolus

nuclear
membrane

nucleus

Golgi

glycogen granules

(a)

plasma membrane

smooth
endoplasmic
reticulum

rough
endoplasmic
reticulum

nucleolus

mitochondrion

nucleus

5 μm

nuclear membrane

Golgi

(b)

Figure 1.9 *The nucleus, nuclear envelope and endoplasmic reticulum*

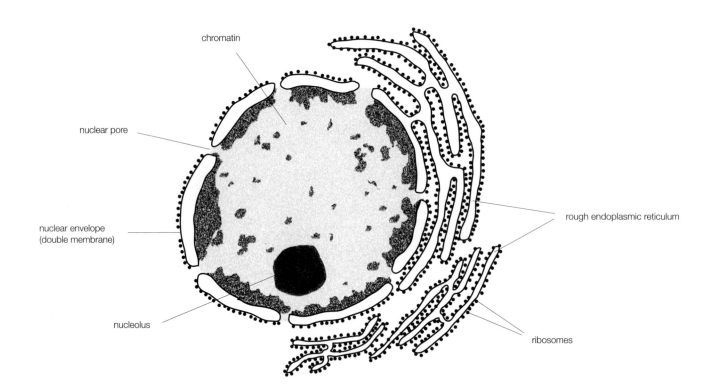

chromatin

nuclear pore

nuclear envelope (double membrane)

nucleolus

rough endoplasmic reticulum

ribosomes

1.8 The endoplasmic reticulum

The endoplasmic reticulum (ER) is formed by a complex three-dimensional system of sheet-like or tubular membranes enclosing spaces called **cisternae** (Figure 1.10). As we have seen, this system is joined to the nuclear envelope. Some of the ER is 'studded' on the outside with granules known as **ribosomes**. This type of ER is known as **rough endoplasmic reticulum** (rough ER).

Ribosomes are minute organelles about 20–25 nm in diameter, made of protein and RNA. They are also found 'loose' in the cytoplasm, where they are known as **free ribosomes**. They function as the site of the cell's protein synthesis. The 'messages' for the manufacture of proteins are encoded in the DNA of the nucleus, and carried out to the ribosomes by mRNA. At the ribosomes, the message is converted into an amino acid sequence, and ultimately a protein (Section 5.9, page 134).

Rough ER also transports the proteins around the cell after they have been made. In some cells, particular proteins are transported to the surface for secretion out of the cell. Rough ER is extensive in cells which produce a lot of protein, such as the enzyme-secreting cells of the digestive system. The rough ER gives more surface area for the proteins to be synthesised, stored and transported.

Where the ER lacks encrusting ribosomes it is called **smooth endoplasmic reticulum** (smooth ER). Smooth ER is generally more tubular than rough ER (Figure 1.10). It is concerned with the synthesis and transport of lipid molecules, rather than protein. Liver cells synthesise much lipid material, such as cholesterol, and this is reflected in the large amounts of smooth ER present in these cells.

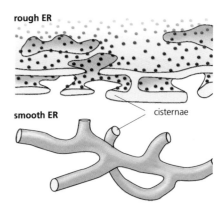

Figure 1.10 Rough and smooth endoplasmic reticulum. Apart from lacking encrusting ribosomes, smooth ER is more tubular than rough ER.

1.9 The Golgi apparatus

The Golgi apparatus, also known as the Golgi body, was discovered in 1898 by an Italian scientist called Camillo Golgi. At first it was thought by some biologists to be an artefact, until its existence and detailed structure were fully revealed by electron microscopy. We now know that Golgi bodies are present in virtually all animal and plant cells. This organelle consists of a stack of sack-like flattened membranes enclosing spaces called **cisternae**, and associated small hollow spheres of membrane, called **vesicles**. The main function of the Golgi apparatus is to chemically modify or package the proteins synthesised at the ribosomes (Figure 1.11).

Vesicles containing protein are 'pinched off' the rough ER. They fuse together to form the flattened membrane-bound cisternae of the Golgi apparatus, on its **forming face**, or side nearest the nucleus. Inside the cisternae, carbohydrates may be added to the proteins, forming **glycoproteins**. In turn, vesicles containing glycoproteins bud off from the Golgi cisternae from its **maturing face** (furthest from the nucleus). These vesicles move towards the plasma membrane of the cell and fuse with it, releasing their contents out of the cell. This process of release of materials by secretory vesicles is called **exocytosis** (see Section 2.8, page 53).

Glycoproteins form one of the main types of chemical which can be secreted by cells. An example of a substance which is produced in this way is **mucus**, which is secreted by cells lining parts of the respiratory and digestive systems.

The Golgi apparatus is also involved in joining certain sugars together to build polysaccharides for the formation of plant cell walls, and in the formation of lysosomes.

> **Remember**
>
> Ribosomes are the site of protein synthesis in the cell. Smooth ER, which lacks attached ribosomes, synthesises lipid.

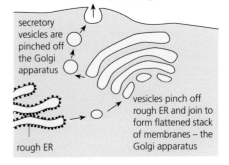

Figure 1.11 The Golgi apparatus

1.10 Lysosomes

Lysosomes are also found in most plant and animal cells, especially in animal cells which are phagocytic. These are cells which carry out the process of phagocytosis (cell 'eating') where particles from the cell's surroundings are engulfed into the cytoplasm (Section 2.8, page 54). They include certain white blood cells, and microorganisms such as *Amoeba*.

Lysosomes are formed by the inclusion of digestive enzymes, such as proteases and lipases, into vesicles from the Golgi apparatus. Lysosomes may fuse with each other, forming an organelle which consists of a 'cocktail' of digestive enzymes surrounded by a single membrane. They may then fuse with other membrane-bound vacuoles containing food particles or a 'worn out' organelle. The enzymes in the lysosome then break down its contents. (The word 'lysosome' is derived from the word 'lysis', which means 'to split'.)

It is very important that the enzymes contained within lysosomes are isolated from the rest of the cell inside the lysosome membrane, otherwise their release would result in self-digestion of the cell. In fact, this sometimes happens in certain tissues, such as the tadpole's tail when it is changing into a frog; this process is called apoptosis or programmed cell death. It can also take place in some diseases such as rheumatoid arthritis, where the cartilage of joints is attacked by the lysosome enzymes.

1.11 Mitochondria

Mitochondria are present in all plant and animal cells. Using suitable staining techniques, they are just visible through the light microscope as tiny rods in the cytoplasm, varying from about 1.5 to 10 µm in length, with a fixed diameter of about 1 µm. The number of mitochondria present in a cell is dependent on its energy demands. Cells with a high energy requirement, such as muscle or nerve cells, contain thousands of mitochondria, whereas less active cells have fewer. This gives a clue to the function of the mitochondrion, which is the release of energy during aerobic respiration, and manufacture of a source of chemical energy which can be used in the cell to drive its metabolism. This universal energy 'currency' is the chemical **adenosine triphosphate (ATP)**.

Using the electron microscope, a mitochondrion can be seen to be a sausage-shaped structure, or circular in cross-section. It has a smooth outer membrane and an inner membrane which is folded into a number of shelf-like **cristae** which increases its surface area. This inner membrane surrounds a jelly-like **matrix** (Figure 1.12).

The matrix contains enzymes and compounds involved in a series of reactions called the **Krebs cycle** (named after its discoverer, Sir Hans Krebs). This sequence of reactions is part of the aerobic breakdown of food molecules such as glucose, which eventually results in the synthesis of ATP on tiny structures called **stalked particles** on the inner mitochondrial membrane. The large surface area of the inner membrane allows for the formation of more ATP. This description of the workings of the mitochondrion is a very simplified one: the full details of the biochemistry of aerobic respiration will be dealt with in the second year of the A-level course.

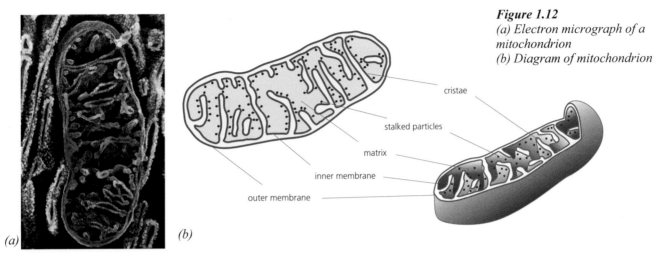

(a)   *(b)*

Figure 1.12
(a) Electron micrograph of a mitochondrion
(b) Diagram of mitochondrion

cristae

stalked particles

matrix

inner membrane

outer membrane

In the matrix of the mitochondrion there are mitochondrial ribosomes, which are smaller than the ribosomes found in the rest of the cytoplasm. The mitochondrion also contains a circular strand of DNA. The importance of these observations will be discussed later in this chapter (Box 1.3, page 28).

?

4 Explain why cells which have a high demand for energy, such as muscle, have a high number of cristae per mitochondrion.   *(2 marks)*

1.12 The cytoskeleton

One of the more recent discoveries regarding the structure of the cell is an extensive three-dimensional network of fibrous protein structures present throughout the cytoplasm. This network is called the **cytoskeleton** and it is made up of three types of fibre: microtubules, microfilaments and intermediate fibres (Figure 1.13).

Microtubules are tiny tubes, about 25 nm in diameter, made of a protein called **tubulin**. The walls of the microtubules are formed by the globular tubulin molecules arranged in a helical pattern (Figure 1.14).

The microtubules can be lengthened by addition of more tubulin sub-units, or shortened by their removal, so that the structure of the cytoskeleton can be continuously modified. **Cross-bridges** may form between nearby microtubules.

Microfilaments are solid fibres, about 7 nm in diameter. They are made mainly of a protein called **actin**, along with smaller amounts of another protein called **myosin**. Both of these proteins are found in muscle fibres, and interactions between the two are the basis of the mechanism of muscle contraction. They probably have a related function in other cells, being responsible for the movement of organelles within the cell, as well as movements of whole cells (cell **motility**). Organelles can sometimes be seen to move around the cell when viewed through the light microscope. For example, chloroplasts will move towards the end of a cell nearest to the light, and mitochondria will move to regions in the cell which need the most energy. Whole cell motility occurs in some cells, such as *Amoeba* and phagocytic white blood cells.

💡 Remember

The function of the mitochondrion is the synthesis of ATP, using the energy derived from the aerobic respiration of glucose. ATP is made on the inner mitochondrial membrane, which is greatly folded to give more surface area for ATP synthesis.

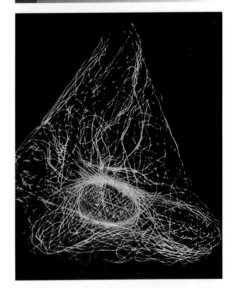

Figure 1.13 Immunofluorescence photomicrograph of microtubules in a cell

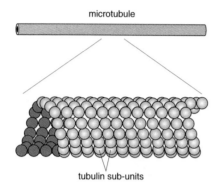

microtubule

tubulin sub-units

Figure 1.14 *Structure of a microtubule*

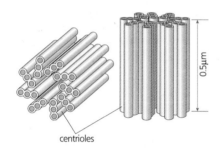

0.5 μm

centrioles

Figure 1.15 *Centrioles*

The third type of fibre in the cytoskeleton is the **intermediate filament**, which also seems to be involved in cell motility.

1.13 Centrioles

Centrioles are small hollow cylindrical organelles, present in pairs in animal cells, fungi and some algae. They are about 0.5 μm long and 0.2 μm in diameter. Each centriole is made up of nine triplets of microtubules and is arranged at 90° to the other, forming the **centrosome** (Figure 1.15).

During cell division the centrioles replicate (copy) themselves and migrate to opposite poles of the cell. They are thought to have a role in the formation of the **spindle** fibres, which are also made of microtubules. During the division of the nucleus, the chromosomes attach to the spindle fibres and are separated into the two daughter nuclei (Section 6.4, page 158).

Recently, experiments have shown that the centrioles may be the site of formation of the whole cytoskeleton network, not just the spindle. This has led to them being renamed **microtubule organising centres**.

1.14 Cilia and flagella

Cilia and flagella are organelles belonging to some animal cells and a few types of plant cells. Together, they are known as **undulipodia**. They are thin cytoplasmic threads projecting from the surface of the cell, also containing microtubules. They are similar in structure, but flagella are longer (about 100 μm, compared with 5–10 μm for cilia) and fewer in number than cilia. **Cilia** (singular **cilium**) are present in large numbers on the surface of some cells, such as the epithelia lining the trachea and the inside of the oviducts (Figure 1.16). Their function is to beat backwards and forwards in one direction, pushing extracellular fluids along. In the oviduct for example, this helps the movement of the egg. The longer **flagella** (singular **flagellum**) normally move the whole cell or organism, as in the case of the tail of the sperm cell, which is a single flagellum.

Cilia and flagella both contain a characteristic arrangement of nine outer pairs of microtubules and two central ones, all extending the length of the organelle. This is called the (9 + 2) arrangement, and is probably responsible for producing the beating movements, although the exact mechanism is not clear.

1.15 Microvilli

Microvilli are minute finger-shaped outgrowths, or folds, of the plasma membrane of some animal cells, such as the epithelium lining of the small intestine (Figure 1.17). Plant cells have a cell wall outside the plasma membrane which prevents projections of this kind, so they lack microvilli.

The fringe of microvilli can just be seen through the light microscope in a stained preparation of suitable cells, and is known as a '**brush border**'. The function of microvilli is to greatly increase the surface area of cells, allowing for increased absorption of materials. For example, in the small intestine the microvilli of the epithelium allow a faster uptake of the products of digestion.

The microvilli contain many filaments of the proteins actin and myosin (also found in muscle cells). These probably maintain the shape of the microvilli, but may also be involved in moving them from side to side, increasing contact with the fluid outside the cell.

?

5 Explain the differences (in form and function) between cilia and microvilli. *(6 marks)*

6 What cellular processes would be taking place in the following cells:

   (a) a cell in which the membrane contained many microvilli

   (b) a cell with much rough endoplasmic reticulum

   (c) a cell with much smooth endoplasmic reticulum

   (d) a cell with a large number of Golgi bodies? *(4 marks)*

1.16 The plant cell wall

One of the distinctive features of a plant cell is its cell wall. Figure 1.19 shows an electron micrograph of a mesophyll cell from the leaf of a plant.

The cell wall can be easily identified as a thick uniform layer around the cell, outside the plasma membrane. Its rigid nature allows it to support the cell. For this reason, plant cells tend to have a more fixed box-like shape than animal cells. The cell wall also allows internal pressures to build up in a plant cell as a result of the osmotic entry of water (Section 2.7, page 49). This makes the cell **turgid**, contributing greatly to the support of the plant. These internal changes of pressure are not possible in animal cells, which lack a cell wall.

The cell wall is composed of the carbohydrate **cellulose** (for a description of the chemical nature of cellulose, see Section 3.7, page 70). It is a non-living material secreted by the cell, and for this reason is not classed as an organelle. After a plant cell divides, the cellulose is laid down as **microfibrils** embedded in a matrix made of several complex polysaccharides, including **pectins** and **hemicelluloses**. Each microfibril consists of thousands of cellulose molecules cross-linked to each other in a bundle. This arrangement makes up the **primary cell wall**, where the microfibrils are orientated in many directions, allowing the wall to stretch as the cell grows. Later, when the cell has reached its maximum size, the wall may be thickened by addition of further layers of cellulose, each having the microfibrils orientated in the same direction, but at a different angle to the other layers (Figure 1.18). This is called the **secondary cell wall**. This arrangement of cellulose microfibrils within a matrix gives enormous tensile strength to the cell wall, rather like glass- or carbon fibre-reinforced plastic.

Between neighbouring cell walls is the **middle lamella**, which is a sticky jelly-like material composed of calcium and magnesium pectates, which acts as an adhesive, sticking the cells together.

The secondary cell wall can become impregnated with other substances, affecting its properties. In cork cells of bark a material called **suberin** is laid

(a)

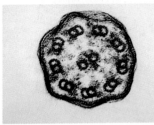

(b)

Figure 1.16
(a) Scanning electron micrograph of cilia on trachea epidermis
(b) TEM of a transverse section of a cilium showing (9 + 2) arrangement of microtubules ($\times$ 70 000)

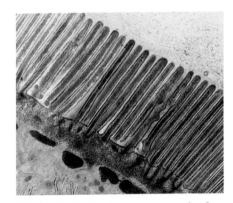

Figure 1.17 *Electron micrograph of microvilli on surface of an intestinal epithelium cell*

Figure 1.18 *Cellulose microfibrils in cell wall as seen by scanning electron microscope*

Figure 1.19
(a) Electron micrograph of leaf
mesophyll cell
(b) Diagram of same cell

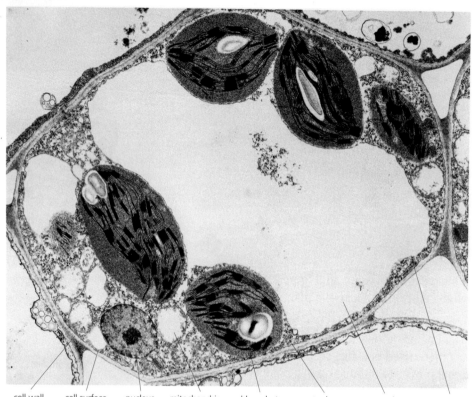

(a)

| cell wall | cell surface membrane | nucleus | mitochondrion | chloroplast | cytoplasm | vacuole | tonoplast |

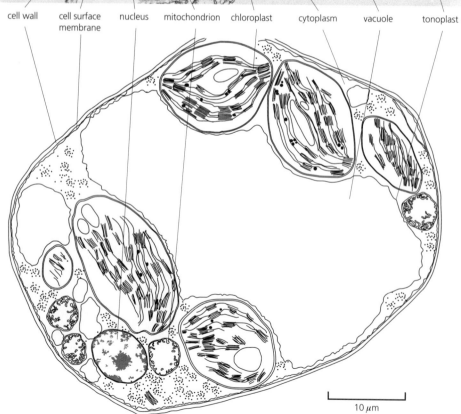

(b)

10 μm

down, making the tissue impermeable to water. In **xylem vessels** and **sclerenchyma** fibres, **lignin** is deposited, increasing the tensile strength of these **lignified** tissues. However, unless the wall has been modified by the addition of these substances, it remains freely permeable to water and other molecules: it does not act as a barrier to dissolved solutes.

A living connection is maintained between neighbouring plant cells by thin strands of cytoplasm, called **plasmodesmata** (singular **plasmodesma**), which pass through pores in the walls. This continuous system of cytoplasm allows for the transport of materials between cells.

Plants are not the only organisms with cell walls. Algae also have walls made of cellulose, and fungi and bacteria have cell walls, but they are made of other polysaccharide-based materials. Bacterial cell walls are made of **peptidoglycan** (Section 1.20, page 26) whilst the fungal cell wall contains **chitin**, the same substance that forms the exoskeleton of arthropods.

7 Explain the difference between the cell wall and the cell surface (plasma) membrane of a plant cell. *(3 marks)*

1.17 Chloroplasts

Another distinctive difference between plant and animal cells is the presence of **chloroplasts** in many plant cells. It is an important difference, because chloroplasts are the site of **photosynthesis**, the process by which plants absorb light energy and use it to make organic molecules from inorganic ones.

Chloroplasts are large organelles, 2–10 µm in diameter, and easily visible through the light microscope. They are present in large numbers in any photosynthetic tissue, such as the palisade mesophyll cells of leaves (Figure 1.19). In plants they are usually shaped like a biconvex lens, although the chloroplasts of algae are much more variable in shape. An electron micrograph and diagram of a chloroplast are shown in Figure 1.20.

The chloroplast is bounded by a double membrane or envelope, surrounding a matrix or **stroma**. In the stroma is a system of flattened sack-like membranes called **thylakoids**, arranged in stacks called **grana** (singular **granum**). The molecules of chlorophyll, which give the chloroplast its green colour, are located on the thylakoids. The chlorophyll absorbs light energy in what are called the **light-dependent** reactions of photosynthesis. This energy is converted to chemical energy. Water molecules are split into oxygen and hydrogen, and the hydrogens used to reduce carbon dioxide to carbohydrate in the **light-independent** reactions, which take place in the stroma. One product of photosynthesis can be seen in the chloroplast in the form of starch grains (Figure 1.20). Lipid droplets are usually visible in the stroma as well. Interestingly, chloroplasts, like mitochondria, contain their own DNA in a circular loop, as well as small ribosomes. This fact is discussed in Box 1.3, page 28.

Table 1.2 shows a summary of the main organelles found in eukaryotic cells.

Figure 1.20 *Internal structure of a chloroplast*
(a) Transmission electron micrograph (× 6300)
(b) Diagram

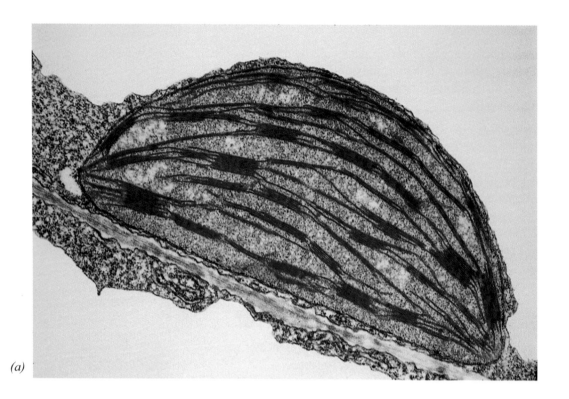

(a)

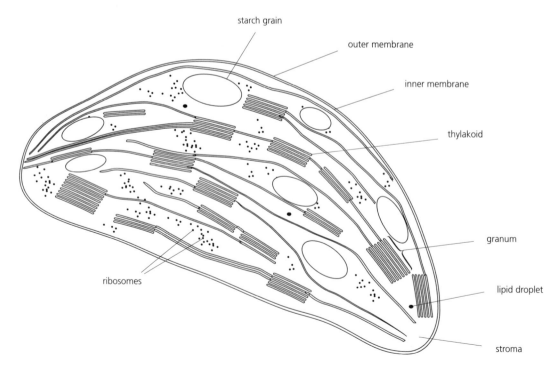

starch grain

outer membrane

inner membrane

thylakoid

granum

lipid droplet

ribosomes

stroma

(b)

Table 1.2 Summary of cell organelles

Organelle	Location and occurrence in cell	Size	Function
nucleus	usually one per cell in cytoplasm	10–20 µm	contains the hereditary material (DNA) which codes for synthesis of proteins in the cytoplasm
nucleolus	one to several in nucleus	1–2 µm	synthesises ribosomal RNA and manufactures ribosomes
rough endoplasmic reticulum	throughout cytoplasm	membranes about 4 nm thick, enclosing cisternae of varying diameter	transport of proteins synthesised on ribosomes
smooth endoplasmic reticulum	in cytoplasm. Extent depends on type of cell		synthesis of lipids
ribosomes	attached to rough endoplasmic reticulum or free in cytoplasm	20–25 nm	site of protein synthesis
Golgi apparatus	in cytoplasm	variable	synthesis of glycoproteins, packaging of proteins
lysosomes	in cytoplasm	100 nm	digestion of unwanted materials and worn-out organelles
mitochondria	in cytoplasm. Several to thousands per cell	1 µm wide and up to 10 µm in length	production of energy by aerobic respiration
microtubules and micro-filaments	throughout cytoplasm	microtubules 25 nm in diameter, micro-filaments 7 nm	form cytoskeleton and allow movement of cell organelles
centrioles	pair, in cytoplasm, usually near nucleus	0.5 µm × 0.2 µm	form the spindle fibres during cell division of animal and fungal cells
cilia and flagella	surface of some animal cells	cilia 5–10 µm in length, flagella 100 µm in length	movement of extracellular fluid (cilia) or whole cell (flagella)
microvilli	small folds in the plasma membrane of some cells	a few µm in length	increase surface area for absorption
cell wall	cellulose layer surrounding plant cells	variable, sometimes thickened by additional materials	supports the cell and maintains its shape
chloroplasts	in cytoplasm of some plant cells	2–10 µm in diameter	site of photosynthesis

Extension

Box 1.2 Calculating magnification

When you have observed a specimen through the microscope and drawn a diagram of it, it is important that you indicate the magnification of your drawing. This is best done by putting a scale bar alongside, showing a suitable length for comparison (see for example Figure 1.4).

An alternative way is to show the magnification, for example: ×200. You may be tempted to multiply the eyepiece magnification by the objective magnification, e.g. ×4 by ×10, to arrive at the answer ×40. However, this only shows the magnification of your microscope, not your drawing. To calculate the magnification of your actual drawing, you must use the formula:

$$\text{Magnification} = \frac{\text{length of drawing}}{\text{real length of specimen}}$$

Note that these measurements **must be in the same units**, such as μm.

The same principle can be used to calculate the magnification of a cell or organelle in a micrograph. The formula is now:

$$\text{Magnification} = \frac{\text{length of organelle in photo}}{\text{real length of organelle}}$$

Again it is vital that the two measurements are in the same units. For example, the nucleus of the liver cell in Figure 1.8 is 7 μm in diameter. The nucleus in the electron micrograph is 43 mm (43 000 μm) across, so its magnification is 43 000 ÷ 7, which is × 6100. (See Section 1.2, page 2 for details of inter-converting units.)

8 The real length of the chloroplast in Figure 1.20 is 4 μm. Measure the length of the chloroplast in the photomicrograph in mm. *(1 mark)*

Convert this into μm and calculate its magnification *(2 marks)*

1.18 Cell fractionation by differential centrifugation

An important way in which biologists have been able to investigate the functions of the various components of cells is to carry out experiments using isolated organelles. For example, much of the workings of the mitochondrion was discovered by investigations made upon mitochondria extracted from liver cells. But how can minute organelles be isolated intact from whole cells? This process, known as **cell fractionation**, can be achieved by the technique of **differential centrifugation**. First we must understand the workings of a **centrifuge**.

A centrifuge is a common piece of laboratory equipment, often available for use in school laboratories (Figure 1.21).

The job of the centrifuge is to separate suspended particulate material out of a liquid. It does this by spinning a test tube of the mixture around at very high speeds, so that the solid particles sink to the bottom of the tube, forming a **sediment** or **pellet**. When an object is spun around like this, it is accelerating, because of its constantly changing direction of movement. This acceleration is measured in units called 'g', which is the acceleration due to gravity. A school laboratory centrifuge may operate at up to 1000 times the value of *g* (1000*g*), but more sophisticated (and more expensive) machines can operate at *g* 'forces' of over 100 000*g*. These are called *ultra*centrifuges, and they produce **ultracentrifugation** of a suspension.

If the tube is spun around at a slow speed, large particles will sediment down first. As the speed of rotation is increased, smaller particles will sediment. This fact can be used to separate the differently sized organelles from a cell. The stages in this process are outlined in Figure 1.22.

First the cells must be broken up. Pieces of a suitable tissue, such as liver, are cut up in cold, isotonic buffer solution. These terms need explaining. A **buffer** is a solution containing a mixture of salts which maintain a constant pH. A solution which is **isotonic** has the same water potential as the cell contents, and so will prevent osmotic damage to the cells (Section 2.7, page 49). This is the purpose of the 0.25 M sucrose in Figure 1.22. If the solution has a different water potential from that of the tissue, water will either enter or leave the cells by osmosis. This will cause the cells to swell or shrink, distorting them. The tissue is kept at about 2 °C by placing the beaker in a larger one filled with ice. The temperature must not fall below freezing point, or the cells will be damaged by the water freezing and expanding. However, it is important that the tissue is kept cold.

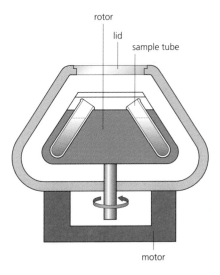

Figure 1.21
  Section through a laboratory centrifuge. An ultracentrifuge works on the same principle, but operates at much higher speeds

9 Why do you think it is important to keep the tissue cold throughout the preparation procedure? *(2 marks)*

The small pieces of tissue are then ground up in a **pestle homogeniser**. This is a ground-glass pestle driven by an electric motor, which is a close fit inside a special test tube. As the pestle is spun around and moved up and down, it grinds up the cells between the pestle and the walls of the tube. Another way that tissues can be broken up is by subjecting them to high-frequency sound waves (ultrasound); this process is called **sonification**.

The homogenised tissue is then centrifuged at slow speed for ten minutes. This results in a pellet which is rich in large organelles, such as nuclei. The liquid above the pellet (the **supernatant**) is then poured off and centrifuged at higher speeds, sedimenting smaller organelles such as mitochondria into the pellet. Finally ultracentrifugation is used, allowing the separation of the smallest organelles, such as ribosomes, attached to small pieces of endoplasmic reticulum.

The fractions collected in this way are never pure, and some damage inevitably occurs to the organelles. However, the functions of the different components can be more easily investigated when they are isolated from the other reactions taking place in intact cells.

10 If plant cells were fractionated as in Figure 1.22, which pellet do you think would contain the chloroplasts? Explain your answer.

(2 marks)

Figure 1.22 Fractionation of cell components by differential centrifugation

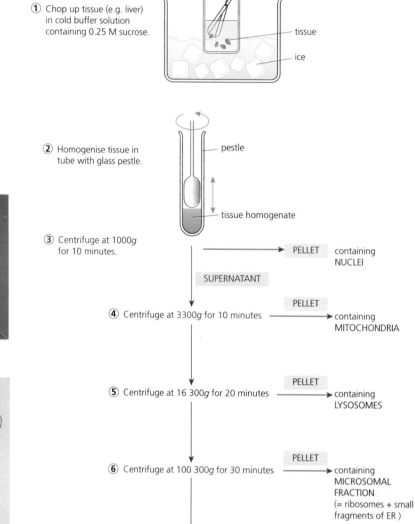

① Chop up tissue (e.g. liver) in cold buffer solution containing 0.25 M sucrose.

tissue

ice

② Homogenise tissue in tube with glass pestle.

pestle

tissue homogenate

③ Centrifuge at 1000*g* for 10 minutes.

PELLET containing NUCLEI

SUPERNATANT

④ Centrifuge at 3300*g* for 10 minutes

PELLET containing MITOCHONDRIA

⑤ Centrifuge at 16 300*g* for 20 minutes

PELLET containing LYSOSOMES

⑥ Centrifuge at 100 300*g* for 30 minutes

PELLET containing MICROSOMAL FRACTION (= ribosomes + small fragments of ER)

SOLUBLE COMPONENTS

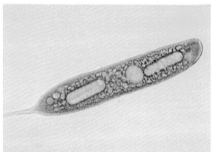

(a) Amoeba *(× 200)*

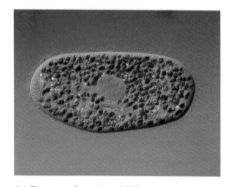

(b) Euglena *(× 400)*

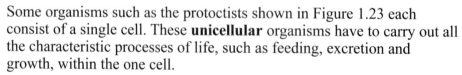

(c) Paramecium *(× 150)*

Figure 1.23 Three protoctists – these particular species are made of a single cell

1.19 Cells, tissue and organs

Some organisms such as the protoctists shown in Figure 1.23 each consist of a single cell. These **unicellular** organisms have to carry out all the characteristic processes of life, such as feeding, excretion and growth, within the one cell.

The *Amoeba*, for example, feeds and grows until it reaches a certain size, when it divides into two cells, each constituting a new organism. Other organisms are composed of many cells: they are **multicellular**. They range in complexity from colonies of similar cells, as in sponges, through to large complex organisms made up of millions of specialised cells, as in the human body. The process by which a multicellular organism, during its development, forms different types of cell specialised to perform a specific function is known as cell **differentiation**. Cells which carry out a particular function are organised into **tissues**, and tissues in turn form parts of functional units called **organs**.

A **tissue** is an aggregation of similar cells. Each cell of a particular type derives from a common origin during the growth of the organism. Take the example of blood. Mammalian blood consists of three types of cell suspended in the liquid plasma (Section 11.1, page 309). The most numerous cells, the red blood cells or **erythrocytes**, are formed from cells in the bone marrow. During their differentiation they lose their nucleus and develop the familiar **biconcave disc** shape. Their lack of nucleus, shape and the red pigment (**haemoglobin**) that they contain are all adaptations which enable them to carry out their main function: the transport of oxygen. Blood also contains several different types of white blood cells, or **leucocytes**, derived from the bone marrow, thymus gland and lymph nodes (their origin depends on the type of leucocyte). The majority of leucocytes are involved with the body's defence against disease-causing organisms, such as bacteria and viruses. A third type of cell (or part of a cell) are the **platelets**, which are membrane-bound fragments of large cells of the bone marrow, called megakaryocytes. They function in the process of blood clotting. We can see that blood is a complex tissue, consisting of a number of different cell types in a fluid matrix.

Other tissues are simpler in their structure. One such type of animal tissue is **epithelium**. Epithelia are tissues which line the outer surface of the body or an organ, the internal surface of organs, such as the gut, and tubes such as blood vessels. If the epithelium lines the inside of an organ or tube it is called an **endothelium**. Several types of epithelia consist of a single layer of cells and are called **simple** epithelia. Some are made up from several cell layers, referred to as **compound** epithelia. Figure 1.24 shows the structure of a number of types of epithelia.

Figure 1.24 Structures of different types of epithelia

(a) simple squamous

(b) cuboidal

(c) columnar

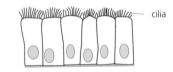

(d) ciliated

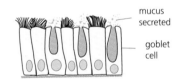

(e) glandular

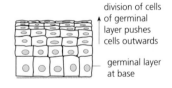

(f) compound stratified

Each layer of cells in an epithelium is firmly held together by a cement-like substance with the bottom layer resting upon a non-cellular **basement membrane** consisting of fibres of connective tissue secreted by other cells. A basic function of many epithelia is protective: they resist physical damage from abrasion and penetration by micro-organisms. However, some epithelia have evolved very particular functions. A simple **squamous** epithelium consists of thin flattened cells with little cytoplasm and a central nucleus (Figure 1.24a). This gives them a shape rather like a poached egg, except that they are joined to other cells of the epithelium by a wavy **tessellated** membrane. Squamous epithelium produces a smooth lining surface, for example the lining of arteries and veins (Section 10.8, page 292). In other locations, squamous epithelium freely allows the diffusion of materials to take place, for instance through the wall of capillaries and the lining of the alveoli of the lungs (Section 9.6, page 240). A **ciliated** epithelium (Figure 1.24d) normally consists of a layer of columnar cells with many cilia extending from their outer membrane surface. Ciliated cells of this type of epithelium are always interspersed with **goblet cells** (Figure 1.24e) which secrete **mucus**. The cilia move to set up currents in the mucus secretions. This is an advantage in such locations as the lining of the trachea, for moving particles out of the respiratory system (Section 9.5, page 238) or the lining of the oviduct, for movement of the egg after ovulation (Section 7.2, page 184).

Much of the lining of the gut, such as the stomach and intestine, consists of simple **columnar** epithelium (Figure 1.24c), with associated glandular tissue and goblet cells. In some regions of the gut, particularly the mouth and oesophagus, there is a high risk from abrasion due to the friction from recently swallowed food. In these regions a **stratified** epithelium exists (Figure 1.24f). This type of compound epithelium consists of several layers of cells, forming a tough impermeable barrier. The cells at the base of the layers divide to form the layers above, and the cells above are steadily pushed outwards. As this happens they gradually become flattened. Any cells removed by friction due to passage of the food are replaced by more cells from below. Stratified epithelium also forms the outer surface of the skin. Here the outer layers of cells become **cornified** by formation of the protein **keratin**, which turns the cells into a tough horny layer. The stratified epithelial cells of the mouth are also cornified, but those of the oesophagus are not.

The cells of plants are also differentiated into tissues. The leaf of a flowering plant contains a layer of vertically orientated cells near the upper surface of the leaf called the **palisade mesophyll** (Figure 1.25).

This tissue consists of cells which contain numerous chloroplasts and are effective in carrying out photosynthesis (see Figures 1.4 and 1.19). The arrangement of the cells, in a single layer with each cell arranged vertically, means that there are fewer cell walls for the light to penetrate (Figure 1.26).

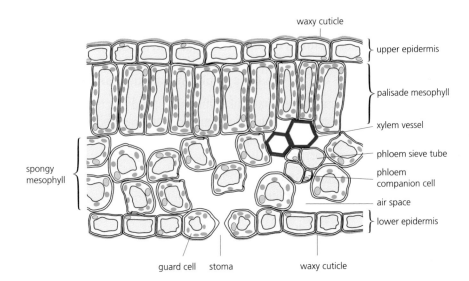

Figure 1.25 Section through a leaf showing different tissues

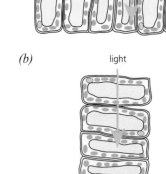

Figure 1.26 Orientation of photosynthetic cells in the palisade mesophyll of a leaf: more light reaches the chloroplasts when the cells are arranged as in (a) rather than (b)

The chloroplasts can be seen to move around in the cell, with the result that they achieve maximum light absorption. Covering the surface of the leaf is a single cell layer called the **epidermis**, which functions in a protective manner, rather like the epithelia of an animal. Transport tissues such as **xylem** and **phloem** also exist, allowing movement of water and solutes through the plant (Chapter 12, page 343).

An **organ** is made up of several different tissues, forming a structure with a specific physiological function or functions. For example, the human liver is an organ composed of a number of tissues. As well as liver cells (Figure 1.8) it contains blood, connective tissue, epithelia and others. An artery and a vein are both organs: their walls contain layers of smooth muscle, elastic and fibrous connective tissue, blood vessels and an inner endothelium lining the lumen of the vessel (Section 10.8, page 292). One of the most obvious plant organs is the leaf, the organ of photosynthesis. This contains a number of tissues, such as epidermis, palisade and spongy mesophyll, xylem and phloem (Figure 1.25).

1.20 Eukaryotic and prokaryotic cells

So far we have mainly considered the structure of animal and plant cells. These cells both have a nucleus surrounded by a nuclear envelope, and are referred to as **eukaryotic** cells. Eukaryotic is derived from Greek words meaning 'true nucleus'. Fungi and protoctistans (algae and protozoa) are also **eukaryotes**, since their cells also have a nucleus (Figure 1.23). These four groups of organisms (animals, plants, fungi and protoctista) make up four of the five **kingdoms** of living organisms. The fifth kingdom consists of unicellular organisms made of a very different kind of cell: the **prokaryotes**.

Prokaryotes are all **bacteria**. The word **prokaryotic** means 'before nucleus'. This describes the main difference between eukaryotic and prokaryotic cells: prokaryotes have no nucleus or nuclear membrane. Their

Did You Know

Escherichia coli is a very common bacterium living in the human gut. It is normally harmless, feeding on food and breakdown products of digestion. It is estimated that the number of *E. coli* cells in your body is about 65 billion. This is greater than the total number of humans who have ever lived on the Earth! Also, *E. coli* only makes up some 0.1% of the *total* bacteria in the body: this total works out at a staggering 65 000 000 000 000!

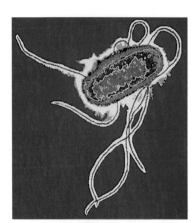

Figure 1.27 Electron micrograph of an E. coli *cell* (× 4720)

 Did You Know

There are always 'exceptions to the rule' in biology! Nearly all bacteria are very small cells, about a micrometre in length and only visible through a powerful light microscope. In the late 1980s a bacterium was discovered which is so large that it is visible with the naked eye. This organism is called *Epulopiscium fishelsoni,* and lives in the intestine of the Red Sea surgeon fish. It averages 250 by 40 μm in size, and can grow to 600 μm in length.

This record has now been broken by *Thiomargarita namibiensis*. This is a spherical bacterium which lives in marine sediments off the coast of Africa. It averages 180 μm in diameter (just about visible without a microscope) but can reach 750 μm, which is about the size of a pinhead. Its huge cell is stuffed with inorganic substances (mainly nitrates) which the bacterium uses to generate energy.

DNA is therefore not separated from the rest of the cytoplasm, but forms a single circular loop, sometimes called a **bacterial chromosome**. This DNA is not associated with proteins, unlike eukaryotic chromosomes. Bacteria also have smaller loops of DNA in the cytoplasm, called **plasmids**.

Prokaryotic cells are much smaller than eukaryotic ones, and much simpler in their structure. They lack endoplasmic reticulum and membrane-bound organelles like mitochondria and chloroplasts. An electron micrograph of a very common bacterium, *Escherichia coli*, is shown in Figure 1.27.

Notice the high magnification of Figure 1.27. Bacterial cells are just visible through the light microscope, but little can be seen of their internal structure without the use of electron microscopy. This reveals a number of other differences from eukaryotic cells. Both types of cell have a cell membrane, cytoplasm, DNA and ribosomes, but prokaryotic cells lack any complex structures such as Golgi bodies, cytoskeleton or lysosomes. A diagram of a 'generalised' bacterium is shown in Figure 1.28.

Although bacteria have a **cell wall**, it is not made of cellulose, but a substance called **peptidoglycan**, which consists of parallel polysaccharide chains cross-linked by short peptide chains. It is called **murein** in some older text books. This produces a complex three-dimensional network which is impregnated with other compounds, forming a rigid box-like structure. The wall maintains the shape of the cell, and protects it against bursting if water enters by osmosis. Outside the cell wall, some bacteria have a diffuse **slime layer** or thicker **capsule**. These are secretions of the cell which in some species act to stick the cells together in colonies. They also act to protect the cell, for example against attack by phagocytic white blood cells. Short protein rods called **pili** or **fimbriae** project from the walls of some bacteria, where they function to stick the cell to other cells or to surfaces.

Some species of bacteria have one or many **flagella**, each consisting of a single rod of protein fibres, rather than the (9 + 2) hollow microtubule structure of the eukaryote flagellum (Section 1.14, page 14). Each flagellum is rigid, and does not beat from side to side to produce movement. Instead it is shaped like a corkscrew, and propels the bacterium along by acting as a helical rotor. In this way bacteria which have flagella are able to swim through fluids.

The **cytoplasm** of the bacterial cell contains scattered **ribosomes**, but these are not attached to membranes as with the rough endoplasmic reticulum of eukaryotic cells. They are also smaller than eukaryotic ribosomes, and sediment down more easily during ultracentrifugation (see Section 1.18, page 20). They are known as 70S ribosomes, whereas those from eukaryotic cells are called 80S (the symbol S standing for a 'Svedberg' unit of sedimentation). The cytoplasm contains inclusions such as **glycogen granules** for carbohydrate storage and **lipid droplets**.

Although there are no membrane-bound organelles, bacteria often have infolds of the plasma membrane. In some bacteria, enzymes of aerobic respiration are attached to infolds known as **mesosomes**, and photosynthetic bacteria have similar **thylakoids** where bacterial chlorophyll and enzymes of photosynthesis are located. These two structures have functions which are similar to those of the internal membranes of mitochondria and chloroplasts (see Box 1.3, page 28).

The bacterial chromosome is long enough to contain several thousand genes: about 1000 have so far been identified in *E. coli*. Most bacteria also have plasmids, which are small self-replicating rings of DNA not associated with the main chromosome. The plasmid genes are not essential for the growth or metabolism of the bacterium, but are usually beneficial in some way, such as conferring resistance to antibiotics.

Plasmids are essential to **genetic engineering** (Chapter 16, page 481) because they can be modified by the addition of new genes, including genes from other organisms. They can then be used as a **vector** to introduce these genes into a host bacterium. The bacterium is allowed to multiply and produce the desired gene product in bulk.

Table 1.3 summarises the main differences between eukaryotic and prokaryotic cells.

Figure 1.28 *Diagram of a generalised bacterial cell*

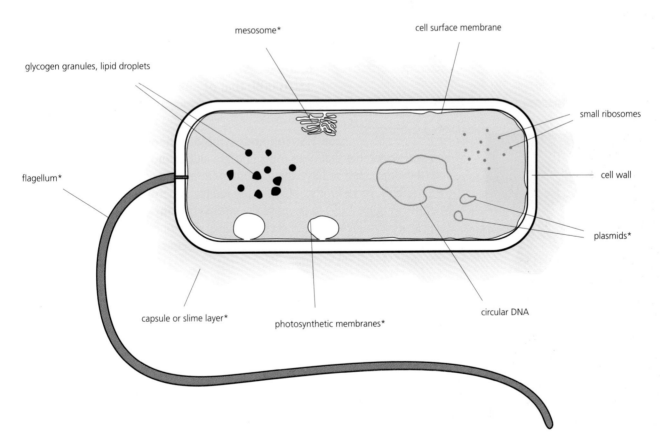

mesosome*

cell surface membrane

glycogen granules, lipid droplets

small ribosomes

flagellum*

cell wall

plasmids*

capsule or slime layer*

photosynthetic membranes*

circular DNA

* = not present in all bacteria

Table 1.3 *Differences between eukaryotic and prokaryotic cells*

Eukaryotic cells	Prokaryotic cells
true nucleus surrounded by a nuclear envelope	no true nucleus
linear DNA associated with histone proteins forming true chromosomes	circular DNA not associated with proteins. Separate loops of DNA called plasmids
cell wall, if present, made of cellulose (plants and algae) or chitin (fungi)	cell wall containing peptidoglycan
endoplasmic reticulum present	no endoplasmic reticulum or associated organelles such as Golgi apparatus
membrane-bound organelles such as mitochondria, and chloroplasts (in plants and algae)	no membrane-bound organelles. Mesosomes and thylakoids present in some bacteria
large (80S) ribosomes attached to endoplasmic reticulum	small (70S) ribosomes scattered in cytoplasm
if present, flagella have (9 + 2) arrangement of microtubules	if present, flagella are made of a single microtubule
cells are large, typically 10–100 μm in diameter, some cells can be up to 400 μm	cells are small, typically 0.5–3 μm in diameter. Volume may be as little as 1/10 000th that of eukaryotic cell

Extension

Box 1.3 The endosymbiont theory

You will remember that both mitochondria and chloroplasts contain DNA and ribosomes, and so have the machinery to manufacture some of their own proteins. In 1970, this observation led the American biologist, Lynn Margulis (Figure 1.29) to propose the **endosymbiont theory**. This suggests that mitochondria and chloroplasts were once free-living organisms (bacteria) which became, during the course of evolution, incorporated into eukaryotic cells.

Figure 1.29 *Lynn Margulis, the American biologist who proposed the endosymbiont theory*

Box 1.3 The endosymbiont theory (cont'd)

The ancestral eukaryotic cell, although having a true nucleus, must have lacked both mitochondria and chloroplasts. At some distant stage in evolution, non-photosynthetic bacterial cells established this relationship with the eukaryotic cells, resulting in a cell with both nucleus and mitochondria. Later, a similar evolutionary process incorporated photosynthetic bacteria into the eukaryotic cell, which through further evolution led to the plant cell, with nucleus, mitochondria and chloroplasts.

The hypothesis is called the 'endosymbiont' theory because symbionts are organisms which live together, both benefiting from the relationship, and 'endo' means 'inside'. With chloroplasts for example, the photosynthetic bacteria presumably gained carbon dioxide directly from the eukaryote's respiration, and the eukaryote gained sugars from the bacterium.

Apart from these organelles having their own genetic machinery, there are several other observations in support of the endosymbiont theory. Both organelles are similar to bacteria in size, they have circular, rather than linear DNA, and their ribosomes are the smaller, 70S variety found in bacteria.

The endosymbiont theory initially received little support from other biologists, but it is now widely accepted. The cells of your body may be harbouring countless billions of disguised, but useful bacteria!

Summary – ① Cells

- The cell is the basic structural unit of living organisms. Cells and their organelles allow compartmentalisation: separating chemical reactions and making metabolic processes more efficient. The structures in the cell which allow this compartmentalisation are membranes.

- Light microscopes can magnify cells up to about ×1500. Electron microscopes can achieve magnifications hundreds of times greater than this, but more importantly produce images with much greater resolution. However, the preparation procedure for the e.m. may produce artefacts in the specimen.

- The nucleus compartmentalises the cell's genetic material, contained within the chromosomes. The nucleus is bounded by a nuclear envelope, which is perforated by pores to allow exchange of materials with the rest of the cell.

- The endoplasmic reticulum consists of sheets of membranes. Rough ER is covered with ribosomes, and is the location of protein synthesis. Smooth ER lacks ribosomes, and is the site of lipid synthesis.

- The Golgi apparatus is made up of a stack of flattened membrane-bound cisternae. It chemically modifies proteins to glycoproteins, and is involved in the formation of lysosomes. Lysosomes are responsible for intracellular digestion of unwanted materials.

- Mitochondria are the source of most of the cell's ATP. This chemical, a universal energy 'currency', is synthesised on the inner membrane of the mitochondrion.

- Cells contain an intricate network of hollow protein microtubules, as well as thinner solid microfilaments. These form the cytoskeleton, involved in intracellular movement of organelles and cell motility. They are present in other organelles, such as the centrioles, as well as the (9+2) structure of cilia and flagella.

- Microvilli are extensions of the plasma membrane which serve to increase its surface area for absorption.

- Plant cells differ from animal cells in having a cell wall, and sometimes a large fluid-filled sap vacuole and chloroplasts.

- The cell wall of plants is made of cellulose, and supports the cell. It has cytoplasmic connections with other neighbouring cells by cytoplasmic strands called plasmodesmata.

- Chloroplasts are the site of photosynthesis. On their inner thylakoid membranes are located the chlorophyll molecules, which absorb light energy. This energy is used to synthesise carbohydrates from carbon dioxide and water in the stroma between the membranes.

- Cell components can be isolated by homogenisation followed by differential centrifugation.

- Cells of plants, animals, fungi and protoctista have a true nucleus, and are called eukaryotic. Prokaryotic cells (bacteria) lack a nucleus, and have just a circular loop of naked DNA. They also have no membrane-bound organelles such as mitochondria or chloroplasts.

❓ Answers

1 The cell is about 100 µm long *(1)* or 1×10^{-4} m *(1)*.

2 (a) False. If there is really only one object, the microscope should not show two, unless something is wrong with the image! *(1)*

   (b) True. The better the resolving power, the better fine detail will be seen. *(1)*

   (c) False. The magnification can be great without the resolution being high, giving a 'blurred' image. *(1)*

   (d) True. This is the definition of resolving power. *(1)*

3 Compare the appearance of the 'suspect' structure on specimens prepared by several different methods *(1)*. If the structure appears the same in all methods, it is less likely to be an artefact *(1)*.

4 The cell's energy 'currency', ATP, is made on the inner membrane of the mitochondrion *(1)*. Therefore the more cristae a mitochondrion has, the more energy it can make *(1)*. (Note that this is in addition to a higher number of mitochondria per cell.)

5 Cilia are thin threads of cytoplasm (about 5–10 µm long) extending from the surface of a cell *(1)*. They contain a (9 + 2) arrangement of microtubules *(1)* and beat backwards and forwards to move extracellular fluid along *(1)*. Microvilli are minute folds in the surface membrane of a cell *(1)* which increase its surface area *(1)*. They do not contain the (9 + 2) arrangement, but have protein filaments to move the microvilli and increase contact with the extracellular fluid *(1)*.

6 (a) Absorption of extracellular materials (the microvilli increase the surface area for absorption) *(1)*

   (b) Synthesis of much protein *(1)*

   (c) Synthesis of much lipid *(1)*

   (d) Secretion of glycoproteins *(1)*

7 The cell wall is a thick non-living layer *(1)* around the cell, made of cellulose *(1)*, whereas the plasma membrane is a thin living layer underneath the cell wall *(1)*.

8 Length = 125 mm *(1)*, which is equal to 125 000 µm *(1)*. Therefore the magnification is 125 000 ÷ 4, which is ×31 250 *(1)*.

9 It is kept at low temperatures to slow down chemical reactions/stop enzyme action *(1)*, which might cause decomposition of the tissue/changes to the cell *(1)*.

10 The first pellet, centrifuged at 1000*g* *(1)*. Chloroplasts are a similar size to nuclei and would sediment down in the first fraction *(1)*.

End of Chapter Questions

1 Figure 1.30 is a diagram of a cell from the epithelial lining of the mammalian intestine.

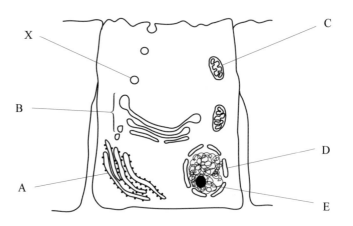

Figure 1.30

(a) Name the structures labelled A–E.   *(5 marks)*

(b) Explain the functional relationship between the structures A, B and X.
                                                                                      (4 marks)

(c) Outline the role of organelle C in the metabolism of the cell.   *(4 marks)*

                                                                       (Total 13 marks)

2 Table 1.4 refers to features of animal, plant and prokaryotic (bacterial) cells. Copy the table, then if the feature is present, place a tick (✔) in the appropriate box and if the feature is absent, place a cross (✘) in the appropriate box.

Table 1.4

Feature	Animal cell	Plant cell	Prokaryotic cell
cell wall made of cellulose			
cell membrane			
endoplasmic reticulum			
mesosome			
cytoskeleton			
ribosomes			
Golgi apparatus			
chloroplasts			

                                                                              (8 marks)

3 Explain the meaning of the following terms:

    (a) Resolving power (of a microscope)   *(1 mark)*

    (b) Artefact (in microscopy)   *(2 marks)*

    (c) Lysosome   *(4 marks)*

    (d) Middle lamella   *(3 marks)*

    (e) Plasmodesma   *(4 marks)*

    (f) Thylakoid   *(3 marks)*

    (g) Differentiation (of cells)   *(2 marks)*

    (h) Plasmid   *(2 marks)*

                                        (Total 21 marks)

4 Table 1.5 gives descriptions of organelles found in eukaryotic cells. Copy the table and write the name of each organelle in the box alongside the description.

Table 1.5

(a) rod-shaped organelle, 1 μm in diameter and up to 10 μm long. Has a double membrane, the inner membrane folded into cristae.	
(b) contains the cell's genetic material. Surrounded by a double membrane.	
(c) hollow cylindrical organelle, 0.5 μm long and 0.2 μm in diameter. Consists of nine triplets of microtubules.	
(d) a three-dimensional tubular system of membrane-bound cisternae. Responsible for synthesis and transport of lipid molecules.	
(e) finger-like extensions of the cell membrane. Present in some cells to increase the surface area for absorption.	

                                                (5 marks)

5 *Figure 1.31* shows part of a cell as seen under an electron microscope.

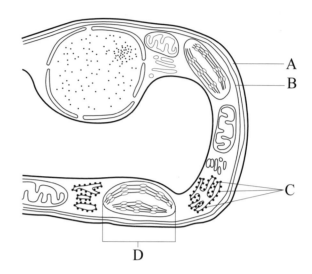

Figure 1.31

(a) Identify structures **A** to **D**. (4 marks)

(b) Describe how a sample of whole chloroplasts could be obtained from leaf tissue. (3 marks)

AQA (B) 2000 (Total 7 marks)

6 *Figure 1.32* shows the structure of a bacterial cell as seen using an electron microscope.

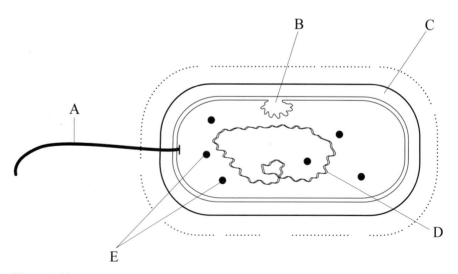

Figure 1.32

(a) Name the parts labelled A, B, C and D. (3 marks)

(b) Describe the roles of the parts labelled B, C and E. (3 marks)

Edexcel 2000 (Total 6 marks)

7 *Figure 1.33* shows the structure of a liver cell as seen using an electron microscope.

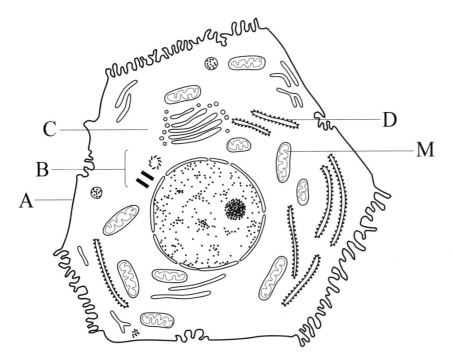

Figure 1.33

(a) Name the parts labelled A, B, C and D.   *(4 marks)*

(b) The magnification of the diagram is 12 000. Calculate the actual length of the mitochondrion labelled M, giving your answer in μm. Show your working.   *(2 marks)*

Edexcel 2000   *(Total 6 marks)*

2 Cell membranes

All animal and plant cells are surrounded by a membrane which controls the entry and exit of materials. In addition, plant cells have a cellulose cell wall around the outer membrane. The nuclear membrane keeps genetic material separated from the rest of the cell.

Diffusion is the movement of a substance from where it is in high concentration to an area where it is in lower concentration.

Osmosis is the movement of *water* from a dilute solution to a more concentrated solution, through a partially permeable membrane. Membranes can be described as both **partially permeable** and **selectively permeable**. Membranes that are permeable only to specific molecules, such as water and some solutes, are described as partially permeable. Selectively permeable membranes select and control the uptake of particular solutes. Root hair cells and the cells of the proximal convoluted tubule in the nephron demonstrate this selectivity.

This chapter includes:
- cell membrane structure
- role of membranes
- simple and facilitated diffusion
- active transport
- osmosis
- cytosis.

2.1 Cell membranes

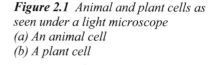

The membrane surrounding a plant or animal cell can be referred to as the **cell surface membrane,** the plasma membrane or the plasmalemma. Plants have a cellulose cell wall as well.

Figure 2.1 Animal and plant cells as seen under a light microscope
(a) An animal cell
(b) A plant cell

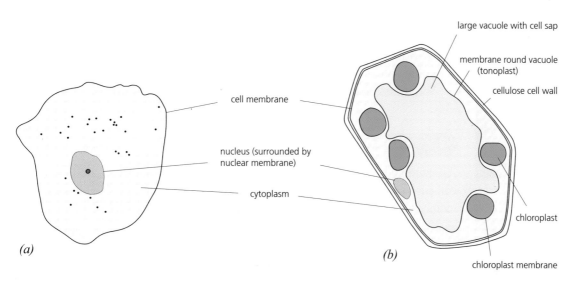

cell membrane

nucleus (surrounded by nuclear membrane)

cytoplasm

large vacuole with cell sap

membrane round vacuole (tonoplast)

cellulose cell wall

chloroplast

chloroplast membrane

(a)

(b)

Prokaryotic cells, e.g. bacteria, have the *outer* cell surface membrane only no internal membrane-bound organelles (little organs) are present.

Eukaryotic cells have both the outer cell surface membrane and membranes surrounding organelles.

Internal membranes have greatly increased the number of membranes present in the cell, allowing compartmentalisation and specialisation, thus enabling eukaryotes to become complex and highly successful. The nucleus, chloroplasts and other organelles in a eukaryotic cell each have a membrane around them, which separates them from other organelles in the cell.

Mitochondria (singular mitochondrion) have both an outer membrane and an inner one folded into finger-like projections called cristae. The cristae are the site of aerobic respiration (Figure 2.2).

The advantages of membranes in a cell include the following:

- Membranes control which substances enter and leave a cell.

- Membranes separate one organelle from another, e.g. chloroplasts are separate from the nucleus. This keeps all the reactants for a process in one organelle, so the reaction will be faster and more efficient.

- Membranes isolate harmful substances from the rest of the cell, e.g. lysosomes contain digestive enzymes that could destroy the whole cell if not isolated by membranes.

- In animal cells, folds in the cell membrane may form microvilli. This increases the surface area for diffusion and exchange of material (Figure 2.8, page 48).

1 Suggest reasons why microvilli are only possible in animal cells but not in plant cells. *(1 mark)*

2 Although prokaryotes are more numerous and widespread than eukaryotes, their level of complexity and efficiency is restricted. What has enabled eukaryotes to become more complex? *(2 marks)*

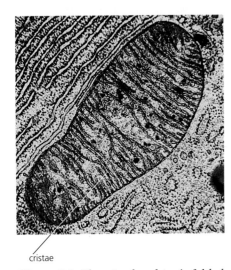

cristae

Figure 2.2 *The mitochondrion's folded inner membrane (cristae) has enzymes embedded in it. These enzymes are involved in respiration (TEM)*

2.2 Structure of membranes

All membranes have a similar structure, including the outer cell membrane (or cell surface membrane) of both prokaryotic and eukaryotic cells and the membranes around organelles in eukaryotes.

The cell surface membrane is always a single membrane. Some organelles also have a single membrane, e.g. the Golgi apparatus, but others have a double membrane, e.g. the nucleus, mitochondria and chloroplasts.

Membranes are composed of **phospholipids** with **proteins** scattered amongst them.

Phospholipids in the cell membrane

Phospholipids are molecules which are made up of phosphate 'heads' and fatty acid 'tails'. (See Section 3.13, page 79 for the structure of phospholipids.)

The surface of the membrane has a mosaic appearance as it is made up of smaller phosphate 'heads' and larger proteins producing a mosaic effect (Figure 2.3).

The phospholipids in the cell membrane are constantly moving from side to side and swapping places. This gives the name **fluid mosaic model**, as the structure moves and changes.

Phosphate is attracted to water and described as **hydrophilic** (water loving). The phosphate heads turn *towards* solutions (water). Fatty acids are repelled by water and are called **hydrophobic** (water hating). The hydrophobic fatty acid 'tails' turn *away* from solutions (water). Therefore in water, phospholipid molecules automatically orientate themselves so that the hydrophobic fatty acid tails avoid contact with water and the hydrophilic phosphate heads are attracted to water. This maintains the membrane structure with the phosphate heads on the outer part facing 'water' and the fatty acid tails pointing inwards.

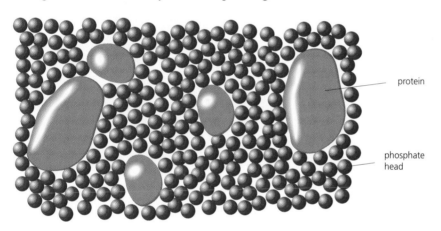

Figure 2.3 Surface view of membrane showing mosaic structure. Proteins give stability and structure to a fluid membrane

Figure 2.4 shows the basic framework of the cell membrane. Other diagrammatic models of the cell membrane can be seen in Figure 2.5. In watery solutions, the phospholipid molecules naturally form a **bilayer**, two layers of phospholipids, with the phosphates on the outside and the fatty acids pointing inwards.

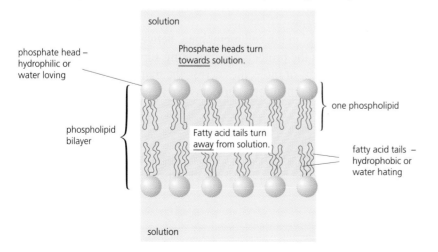

Figure 2.4 Basic framework of the cell membrane

The main purpose of the hydrophobic centre of the membrane is to prevent the free diffusion of water and polar molecules through the membrane. It acts as a barrier to free movement. The membrane exerts control over what passes through, via protein carriers and channel proteins. It is **selectively permeable**, only allowing specific molecules to pass through. This bilayer is stable and forms the basic framework for the membrane. If this structure is disrupted by molecules passing through the membrane, it easily springs back into the original position with phosphates on the outside and fatty acids on the inside.

Cell surface membranes composed of a single membrane, are formed from one bilayer, double membranes are formed from two bilayers. Under the electron microscope, a single membrane appears as two dark bands, the phosphates, separated by a lighter band, the fatty acid tails (see Figure 2.6).

Figure 2.5 *Diagrammatic models of the cell membrane*

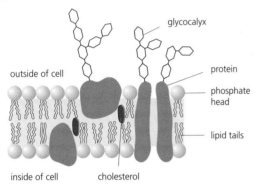

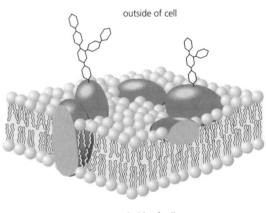

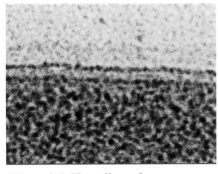

Figure 2.6 *The cell membrane (phospholipid bilayer) appears as two dark bands with a light layer inbetween*

?

3 Why is the cell membrane described as a bilayer? *(1 mark)*

4 How does the membrane structure help to keep solutions apart? *(2 marks)*

Proteins in the cell membrane

There are proteins 'floating' in the cell membrane, between the phospholipids. The two main functions of the proteins are providing support and stability in a fluid structure, and transport of molecules across the membrane. Apart from some structural proteins, the membrane proteins are mainly globular. (See Section 3.21, page 91.)

Globular proteins in the cell membrane form specific-shaped protein carriers. The specific shape determines which molecules can cross the membrane; only those of matching shape will be transported. They are able to carry **specific** substances across the membrane from a high concentration of the substance to a lower concentration of the substance by **facilitated diffusion** (see Section 2.5, page 47). Proteins also carry substances from low to high concentrations across a membrane by **active transport** (see Section 2.6, page 48).

On the **outer** part of cell surface membranes there are carbohydrates sticking out like 'antennae' from protein bases. Together, these form a **glycocalyx layer**, which allows cells to recognise each other and therefore group together to form **tissues**. A tissue is a group of similar cells working together, e.g. muscle.

Many **enzymes** (another type of protein) are found embedded in the cell membrane where they speed up reactions. Increasing the surface area of membranes means more surface for enzymes, so increasing the rate of reactions. For example, the enzymes in the membrane of the small intestine speed up the digestion of disaccharides.

Some proteins that span the membrane are called **channel proteins**. These proteins are able to transport substances quickly across the membrane by avoiding the hydrophobic centre. **Open hydrophilic channels** are permanently open, other channels are **gated**.

Open hydrophilic channels allow for rapid diffusion of molecules across the membrane, e.g. water. Although some water molecules may slip through the lipid centre, most will pass through the open hydrophilic channels which offer no resistance to the passage of water, as they avoid the hydrophobic fatty acid centre of the membrane.

Gated channel proteins are able to open and close, thus altering the permeability of a membrane to the same molecule. They can open at certain times to allow the rapid diffusion of ions, for example sodium ions across an axon membrane. This change in permeability is essential for the transmission of the nerve impulse along an axon.

Proteins in the membrane act as **receptor sites**. These globular proteins on the outside of the membrane, of specific shape, are able to combine with matching-shaped molecules to initiate a reaction. For example, the protein receptor that matches with adrenaline, found on the outside of the cell, is able to initiate a reaction inside the cell resulting in the release of glucose.

Glycoproteins and glycolipids
The cell surface membrane contains protein molecules and phospholipids. A polysaccharide chain may be attached to either.

A polysaccharide attached to a protein, forms a *glycoprotein*. A polysaccharide attached to a phospholipid, forms a *glycolipid*.

The polysaccharide is always on the outside of the cell surface membrane.

Remember

Glycoprotein is poly-saccharide plus protein. Glycolipid is polysaccharide plus phospholipid.

Function of glycoproteins and glycolipids

Both form hydrogen bonds with water molecules outside the cell, helping to stabilise the membrane. Glycoproteins and glycolipids are particularly numerous in cells exposed to hostile conditions such as the duodenum, where changes in pH and friction threaten to disturb the stability of the membrane.

Glycoproteins and glycolipids are involved in cell-to-cell recognition, enabling cells of similar type to group together to form tissues.

The varying carbohydrate chains emerging from the cell surface membrane of the red blood cells are responsible for producing the four different blood groups, A, B, AB and O.

Some glycoproteins and glycolipids act as receptor sites.

For example, there are receptor sites on liver cells into which the hormone *insulin* fits. A series of enzyme, controlled reactions follows resulting in the conversion of glucose to glycogen in the liver. As a result, the level of glucose in the blood falls.

5 Why is the glycocalyx only found on the outside of the cell surface membrane? *(1 mark)*

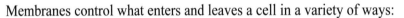

2.3 **Transport of substances across membranes**

Membranes control what enters and leaves a cell in a variety of ways:

- **diffusion** a) simple
  b) facilitated

- **active transport**

- **osmosis** – the transport of water

- **cytosis**

These transport mechanisms are summarised in Figure 2.7.

Remember

The term membrane includes both cell surface and epithelial membranes covering or lining an organ.

Membranes also surround organelles in the cells of eukaryotes.

Figure 2.7 *How substances cross the cell membrane*

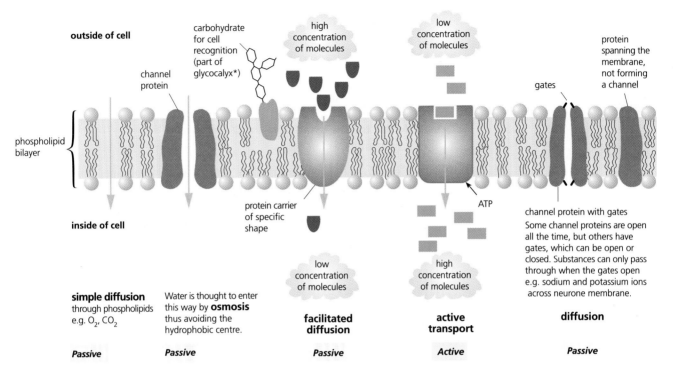

outside of cell

channel protein

carbohydrate for cell recognition (part of glycocalyx*)

high concentration of molecules

low concentration of molecules

protein spanning the membrane, not forming a channel

gates

phospholipid bilayer

protein carrier of specific shape

inside of cell

ATP

low concentration of molecules

high concentration of molecules

simple diffusion
through phospholipids
e.g. O_2, CO_2

Passive

Water is thought to enter this way by **osmosis** thus avoiding the hydrophobic centre.

Passive

facilitated diffusion

Passive

active transport

Active

channel protein with gates
Some channel proteins are open all the time, but others have gates, which can be open or closed. Substances can only pass through when the gates open e.g. sodium and potassium ions across neurone membrane.

diffusion

Passive

* glycocalyx
This is only found on the outer side of the membrane, for cell recognition letting similar cells group together to form a tissue.

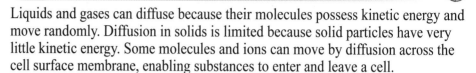

2.4 Diffusion

Liquids and gases can diffuse because their molecules possess kinetic energy and move randomly. Diffusion in solids is limited because solid particles have very little kinetic energy. Some molecules and ions can move by diffusion across the cell surface membrane, enabling substances to enter and leave a cell.

Diffusion is a passive process, not requiring energy from respiration, so metabolic poisons that inhibit respiration do not affect diffusion.

Factors affecting the rate of diffusion across a membrane
- the surface area of membrane
- the difference in concentration on either side of a membrane
- the thickness of the membrane or exchange surface
- the size and type of molecule
- the temperature.

The greater the **surface area**, the faster the rate of diffusion, as there is more surface for molecules to pass through. All membranes through which diffusion takes place in quantity are folded to increase the surface through which diffusion can take place (Figure 2.8). **Villi** (singular **villus**) are produced when a *layer of cells* folds, as in the small intestine, for increased uptake of digested food. **Microvilli** (singular **microvillus**) form when the cell surface membrane *within one cell* folds, as in the small intestine, to increase the surface area for absorption.

> **Remember**
>
> Diffusion is the movement of a substance from where it is in high concentration to an area where it is in lower concentration.
>
> High concentration → Low concentration

Figure 2.8
(a) Surface area and folding
(b) TEM of microvilli
(c) An animal cell with microvilli

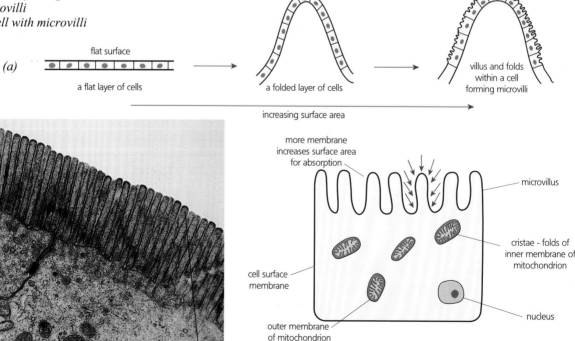

Diffusion relies entirely on the **difference in concentration** between two places and substances always diffuse down a concentration gradient, from high to low concentration. This continues until the concentrations are equal, when **equilibrium** is reached.

To maintain a difference in concentration, a transport system is often present to remove the diffusing molecules, thus keeping them at a low concentration. This ensures that diffusion continues. If there is a big difference in concentration over a short distance, this produces a steep **concentration gradient**. The greater the concentration gradient, the more rapid the rate of diffusion. Cells that can maintain a steep concentration gradient therefore have an advantage.

Within the same medium, a difference in concentration affects the rate of diffusion, but between two different media, like air and blood, it is the difference in **partial pressure** of oxygen and carbon dioxide that determines the rate of diffusion (see Section 9.6, page 241). The partial pressure of a gas is the pressure one gas contributes to a mixture of gases.

In the alveoli, a short diffusion distance is present due to the thin lining layer, or **epithelium**, lining both the alveoli and the blood capillaries. Therefore oxygen can diffuse quickly through to the blood, which carries the oxygen away from the lungs. This removal of oxygen maintains a difference in the partial pressure of oxygen between the alveoli and the blood. A steep pressure gradient is maintained, ensuring continued diffusion. (See Figure 9.10, page 240.)

The thickness of the membrane or exchange surface also affects the rate of diffusion. The distance between two concentrations of a molecule, across which diffusion takes place, is called the **diffusion distance**. The thicker the membrane, the greater the diffusion distance and the slower the rate of diffusion.

Internal exchange surfaces inside organisms where diffusion takes place, are often made up of one layer of thin, flat cells called **squamous** or pavement epithelium. This thin layer reduces the distance across which diffusion takes place; in other words, it reduces the diffusion distance, so increasing the rate of diffusion.

6 The mother's blood forms a blood space on one side of the placenta, not confined to blood vessels. Suggest how this might help in exchange of materials with the fetus. *(2 marks)*

The size and type of molecules diffusing also affect the rate of diffusion. Oxygen and carbon dioxide are small molecules. They can slip more easily through the phospholipid bilayer than larger molecules. Molecules that are soluble in lipids, e.g. alcohol, can cross the membrane faster than water-soluble ones as they can easily pass through the fatty acid centre of the membrane.

Temperature is another important factor affecting the rate of diffusion.

Increasing the temperature provides molecules with more **kinetic energy** and they move faster. Hence, a rise in temperature speeds up the rate of diffusion.

 Remember

The greater the difference in concentration between two places, the faster the rate of diffusion between them.

 Remember

Concentration gradient

$$= \frac{\text{concentration at A} - \text{concentration at B}}{\text{distance between A and B.}}$$

Remember

The shorter the diffusion distance, the faster the rate of diffusion.

Remember

Exam hint

$$ROD \propto \frac{SAD}{TOES}$$

ROD is Rate Of Diffusion.

SAD is Surface Area × Difference in concentration

TOES is Thickness of Exchange Surface.

Definition

The rate of diffusion across a cell membrane is directly proportional to the surface area of the membrane times the difference in concentration on either side. It is inversely proportional to the thickness of the exchange surface (the membrane).

Did You Know

Alcohol can diffuse quickly through the lipid bilayer as it is soluble in fat. This is why alcohol can affect people so soon after drinking.

Fick's Law shows the relationship between some of these factors that affect the rate of diffusion.

$$\text{Rate of diffusion} \propto \frac{\text{Surface area* × difference in concentration*}}{\text{Thickness of exchange surface**}}$$

* The larger these are, the faster the rate of diffusion.

** The larger this is, the slower the rate of diffusion.

For the maximum rate of diffusion, the surface area and difference in concentration must be as *big* as possible, whilst the thickness of the membrane or exchange surface must be as *small* as possible.

There are two main types of diffusion:

● **Simple diffusion** is when molecules like oxygen and carbon dioxide pass through the membrane unassisted.

Some molecules can pass straight through the phospholipid bilayer by simple diffusion, e.g. O_2, CO_2. No proteins are involved. Oxygen and carbon dioxide are both soluble in lipids and can therefore pass through the lipids forming the membrane. This is a passive process not requiring an input of energy. Some water molecules can also slip through this way, but as they are not soluble in lipids, most enter via the channel proteins spanning the membrane, also called hydrophilic pores.

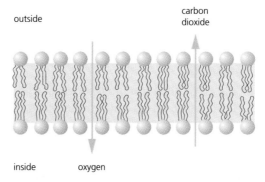

Oxygen and carbon dioxide pass through by simple diffusion.

Water passes mainly through the hydrophilic pores (channel proteins). However, some water can pass through the phospholipid bilayer by simple diffusion.

Figure 2.9 Simple diffusion of oxygen and carbon dioxide.

● **Facilitated diffusion** is when specific protein carriers in the cell membrane are needed to transport molecules like glucose across a membrane (see Section 2.5, page 47).

In both cases, molecules pass down a concentration gradient from high to low concentration, therefore it is a passive process *not* requiring external energy.

7 Smokers cough a lot and this breaks down some of the folds in the alveoli. How might this affect them? (See Section 9.5, figure 9.8.)

(2 marks)

2.5 Facilitated diffusion

Proteins of specific shape called **protein carriers** have binding sites which carry matching-shaped substances across the membrane. Molecules are carried from high to low concentration, assisted by protein carriers, so this diffusion is called **facilitated diffusion**. The exact mechanism involved is not known but proteins clearly control passage of materials across the membrane.

Figure 2.10 Facilitated diffusion

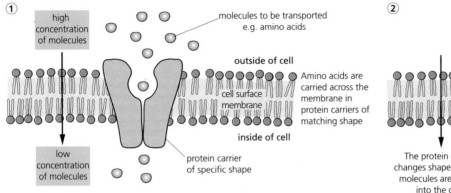

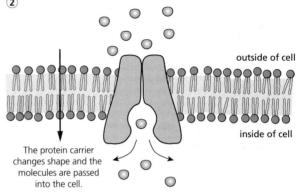

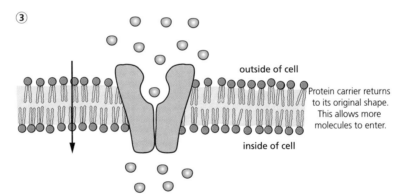

The specific shape of the protein carrier depends on the sequence of amino acids and how it is folded to form the **tertiary structure** (see Section 3.17, page 87).

Protein carriers are specific, normally carrying only one specific molecule across the membrane. For example, the **glucose protein carrier** only transports glucose, which can attach to the binding site on the protein. The possible protein shapes are almost infinite and enable a huge variety of molecules to be transported across the membrane. This is a passive process, not requiring energy from ATP.

Remember

The specific shape of the protein determines what is carried across the membrane.

8 Give two ways in which facilitated diffusion and simple diffusion are similar and one way in which they are different.
(3 marks)

Mitochondria

Lots of mitochondria indicates a high rate of respiration, resulting in the production of lots of energy in the form of ATP.

ATP is needed for **active transport**.

Therefore a large number of mitochondria in a cell indicates that active transport is taking place. The cell is described as **metabolically active**.

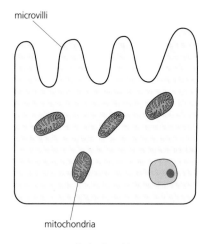

Lots of mitochondria mean a high rate of respiration and lots of ATP made. ATP is required for active transport.

Figure 2.11 *A typical cell carrying out active transport*

2.6 Active transport

Here molecules are transported across the membrane, from low concentrations to high concentrations, the opposite of diffusion.

Active transport can be likened to a pumping action, like lifting water uphill, which requires an input of energy. In cells, ions need to be pumped in a similar way from an area where they are in lower concentration to an area where they are in higher concentration. This occurs in both plants and animals. Cells where this takes place need a large supply of ATP to provide the energy required for active transport. The ATP is produced during respiration in the mitochondria. A typical cell carrying out active transport is shown in Figure 2.11. The swing door model of active transport is shown in Figure 2.12.

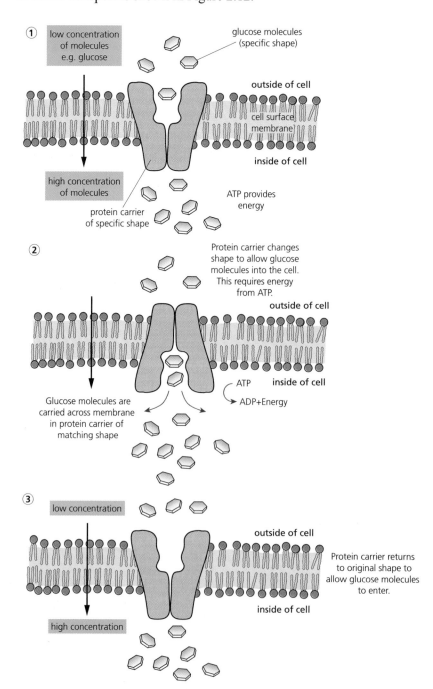

Figure 2.12 *The swing door model of active transport*

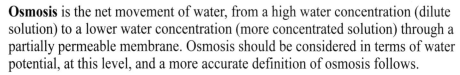

9 Why might a cell benefit from microvilli if carrying out active transport?
(2 marks)

10 How are facilitated diffusion and active transport similar? How are they different?
(2 marks)

2.7 Osmosis

Osmosis is the net movement of water, from a high water concentration (dilute solution) to a lower water concentration (more concentrated solution) through a partially permeable membrane. Osmosis should be considered in terms of water potential, at this level, and a more accurate definition of osmosis follows.

Water potential (ψ) is a measure of the **kinetic energy** of water molecules. Water molecules are constantly moving in a random fashion. Some water molecules collide with the cell membrane, creating a pressure on it known as water potential (represented by the Greek letter psi, ψ). The higher their kinetic energy, the more they move and hit the membrane and the higher their water potential. Solutes restrict the movement of water, so a strong sugar solution with lots of solute particles will lower the kinetic energy and hence the water potential of the water. Water movement is restricted due to the attractive forces that exist between the water molecules and the solute particles, causing the formation of **hydration shells** (see Figure 2.13). A dilute sugar solution with fewer solute particles will allow the water potential to be higher as fewer solute particles are present to attract and restrict the movement of the water molecules.

The highest water potential is found in pure water, where no solutes are present to restrict movement. The water potential of pure water is arbitrarily assigned a value of 0 kilo Pascals or 0 kPa. Adding solutes lowers the water potential to a negative value. The more solute particles added, the lower the water potential becomes, i.e. the more negative.

e.g.   pure water   ψ = 0 kPa   highest water potential

dilute sugar solution   ψ = −100 kPa

more concentrated sugar solution   ψ = −350 kPa   lower water potential

> ### Remember
> The nearer to 0, the higher the water potential.

Figure 2.13 Comparing the ability of water to move in different solutions

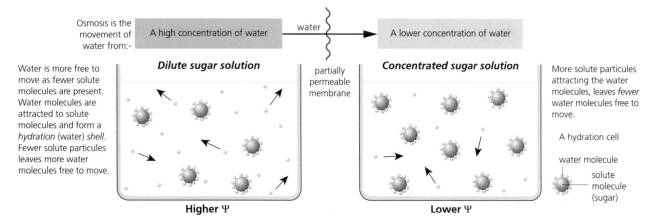

Osmosis is the movement of water from:- A high concentration of water → water → A lower concentration of water

Dilute sugar solution

Water is more free to move as fewer solute molecules are present. Water molecules are attracted to solute molecules and form a *hydration* (water) *shell*. Fewer solute particules leaves more water molecules free to move.

partially permeable membrane

Concentrated sugar solution

More solute particles attracting the water molecules, leaves *fewer* water molecules free to move.

A hydration cell

water molecule

solute molecule (sugar)

Higher ψ   **Lower ψ**

Definition

In osmosis, water moves from an area of higher water potential to an area of lower water potential through a partially permeable membrane.

 11 Why does water have a higher water potential in dilute solutions than in concentrated solutions? *(1 mark)*

When does osmosis occur?

If two solutions are separated by a partially permeable membrane and the water potential of each solution is different, osmosis will occur. All the membranes in a cell are partially permeable and allow water through by osmosis. Osmosis is a type of diffusion as water is passing from where water is in higher concentration to where it is in lower concentration. It is a passive process, not requiring an input of energy. If there is a difference in water potential between adjacent solutions osmosis will take place, it cannot be stopped.

Water molecules pass in both directions but there is a net movement of molecules from a higher to a lower water potential. Only when the water potential of two adjacent solutions is the same, will osmosis stop and there will be no further net movement of water molecules. Water will then move equally between the solutions. (See Figure 2.14.)

 12 Water enters plant cells by osmosis. Why don't the cells burst? *(1 mark)*

***Figure 2.14** Osmosis*
(a) When osmosis occurs
(b) When no osmosis occurs

(a) When osmosis occurs

(b) When no osmosis occurs

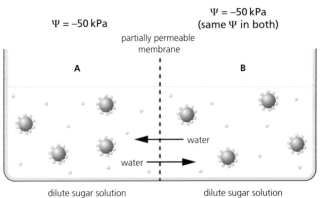

Higher Ψ   **Lower Ψ**

partially permeable membrane

original level | A   B   new level

pure water | only water is small enough to pass through the membrane | dilute sugar solution

Higher water potential (Ψ). Water more free to move as no solutes present.

Lower water potential (Ψ). Water less free to move as solute particles present.

Osmosis occurs from:-

A → B

More water molecules will move and hit the membrane from **A** and move into **B**, than **B** to **A**. The level will fall in **A** and rise in **B**

Ψ = –50 kPa   Ψ = –50 kPa (same Ψ in both)

partially permeable membrane

A   B

dilute sugar solution | dilute sugar solution

Water hits membrane *equally* from both sides, as the Ψ is the same in **A** and **B**, therefore water is equally free to move. The two cells are at *equilibrium*, they have the same water potential (Ψ).

There is *no* net movement as water passes *equally* in both directions. *Osmosis stops* as the two solutions have the same Ψ. No change in level will occur.

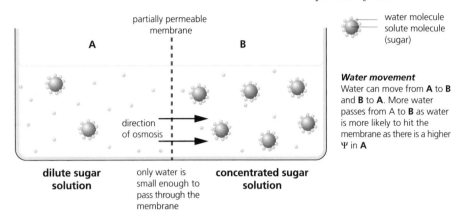

Figure 2.15 and Table 2.1 Summary of the process of osmosis

Water movement
Water can move from **A** to **B** and **B** to **A**. More water passes from A to **B** as water is more likely to hit the membrane as there is a higher Ψ in **A**

Table 2.1

Dilute sugar solution	Concentrated sugar solution
● high concentration of water	● lower concentration of water
● fewer solute particles	● more solute particles
● water more free to move as fewer solutes means less attraction to water molecules	● water less free to move as more solutes attracting them
● water has **more kinetic energy** and is more likely to hit the membrane	● water has **less kinetic energy** and is less likely to hit the membrane
● water has a **higher water potential**	● water has a **lower water potential.**
direction of osmosis ⟶	

How free the water is to move depends on three factors:

● The number of **solute** particles.

● The **pressure** in the cell.

● The **temperature**. At higher temperatures, water has greater kinetic energy and the water molecules move faster.

In plant cells water enters the vacuole and causes it to push outwards, thus increasing the pressure. A swollen plant cell is said to be **turgid**. Eventually, the pressure inside the plant cell will stop any more water entering. The water potential inside and outside the cell are equal and opposite.

Water continues to move by osmosis until the water potential of two adjacent cells is the same. At this stage the cells are at **equilibrium**, as they have the same water potential, osmosis ceases and there is no further net movement of water.

Remember

At equilibrium, the water potential of adjacent cells is the same, there is therefore no further net movement of water.

Before osmosis

In Figure 2.16 water passes from cell A to cell B, as the water in cell A has a higher water potential (nearer to 0), is more free to move and more likely to hit the membrane. Cell B has a lower water potential and the water is less free to move.

Eventually the two cells will have the same water potential at equilibrium.

After osmosis

At equilibrium, the water potential of both cells is $-200\,$kPa (the average of the two solutions).

$$\text{Water potential } \psi = \frac{(-100) + (-300)}{2} = \frac{-400}{2} = -200 \text{ kPa}$$

This is the average water potential of both cells.

The 2 cells have the same ψ. They have reached **equilibrium**. Water still crosses the membrane, but equally in both directions. There is no net movement of water. At this point osmosis will stop as they both have the same water potential and water will hit the membrane equally from both sides.

Figure 2.16
(a) Before osmosis
(b) After osmosis

(a) Before osmosis   *(b) After osmosis*

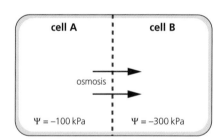
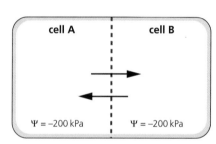
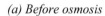

Water passes from A to B by osmosis as A has the higher ψ (closer to 0, the ψ of pure water).

13 Which way will water move by osmosis in each example in Figure 2.17?

(3 marks)

Figure 2.17 *Which way will water move by osmosis?*

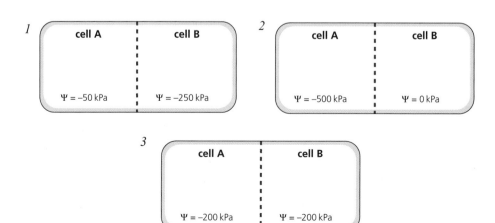

Hypotonic, hypertonic and isotonic solutions

Solutions in which cells are placed vary in concentration. The greater the solute concentration the lower the water potential, as solutes restrict the free movement of water molecules.

Hypotonic solution The solution surrounding a cell may have a lower solute concentration and therefore a higher water potential than the cell. Water passes from the solution into the cell by osmosis. Solutions with a lower solute concentration are described as **hypotonic**. Hypo means 'under' (under strength).

Hypertonic solution The solution surrounding a cell may have a higher solute concentration and therefore a lower water potential than the cell. Water will pass out of the cell by osmosis. Solutions with a higher solute concentration are described as **hypertonic**. Hyper means 'over' (over strength).

Isotonic solution If the solution surrounding a cell has the same solute concentration as the cell, water will pass equally between them. There will be no net movement of water. They have the same water potential. When a solution has the same solute concentration as the cell, it is described as **isotonic**. Iso means the 'same' (same strength).

This is only true in animals where the absence of a cell wall prevents the build-up of pressure and consequently the solute potential equals the water potential.

Solution	Solute concentration	Water potential	Direction of osmosis
Hypotonic	lower than cell	higher than cell	into cell
Hypertonic	higher than cell	lower than cell	out of cell
Isotonic	same as cell	same as cell	no net movement

The terms hypotonic, hypertonic and isotonic can also be used when comparing liquids of varying solute concentration. This is particularly useful when describing the differences in the solute concentration in the mammalian nephron.

14 Suggest why *Amoebae* living in fresh water do not burst even though water enters by osmosis.   *(2 marks)*

2.8 Cytosis

Substances can enter and leave cells through gaps in the phospholipid bilayer that arise in the cell membrane during the process of **cytosis**. Larger molecules may be broken down in a vesicle first, to facilitate cytosis. These gaps form either when the cell membrane **infolds**, allowing substances to be taken in, or when the cell membrane fuses with internal **vesicles** allowing substances to be released from the cell. Cytosis requires energy and involves breaking open the bilayer and then reforming it.

There are two types of cytosis: **endocytosis** when substances are taken in and **exocytosis** when substances are released.

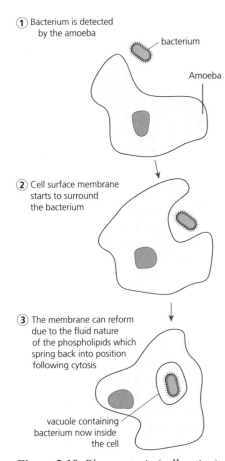

① Bacterium is detected by the amoeba

bacterium

Amoeba

② Cell surface membrane starts to surround the bacterium

③ The membrane can reform due to the fluid nature of the phospholipids which spring back into position following cytosis

vacuole containing bacterium now inside the cell

Figure 2.18 *Phagocytosis (cell eating) in amoeba*

Endocytosis

Endocytosis involves taking substances *into* the cell. The cell surface membrane infolds or **invaginates** round substances outside the cell to form a vacuole, which then enters the cell and the membrane reforms.

There are two types of endocytosis: **phagocytosis** and **pinocytosis**.

Phagocytosis, shown in Figure 2.18, is made possible due to the fluidity of the cell membrane.

Pinocytic vesicles, where the cell surface membrane starts to infold, indicate that pinocytosis is taking place (Figure 2.19).

The membrane can reform due to the fluid nature of the phospholipids, which can spring back into position following cytosis, with the phosphate heads on the outside and fatty acid tails on the inside. Figure 2.20 shows endocytosis in relation to the membrane structure.

Exocytosis

This is when solids or liquids leave the cell through gaps in the cell membrane that form when vesicles fuse with the cell membrane.

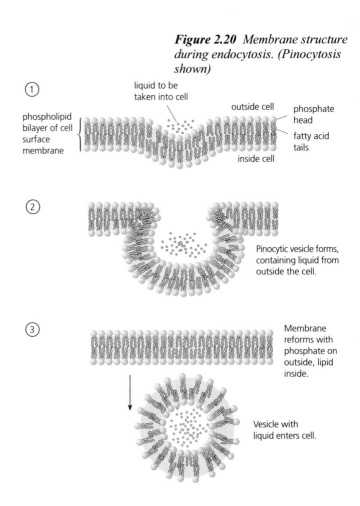

Figure 2.20 *Membrane structure during endocytosis. (Pinocytosis shown)*

① liquid to be taken into cell

phospholipid bilayer of cell surface membrane

outside cell

phosphate head

fatty acid tails

inside cell

② Pinocytic vesicle forms, containing liquid from outside the cell.

③ Membrane reforms with phosphate on outside, lipid inside.

Vesicle with liquid enters cell.

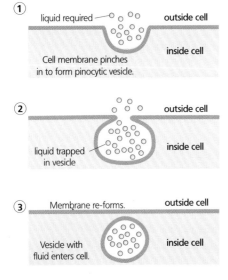

① liquid required

outside cell

inside cell

Cell membrane pinches in to form pinocytic vesicle.

② outside cell

liquid trapped in vesicle

inside cell

③ Membrane re-forms.

outside cell

Vesicle with fluid enters cell.

inside cell

Figure 2.19 *A simplified diagram of pinocytosis (cell drinking)*

Vesicles within the cell containing liquid or solids, are isolated from the rest of the cell by an internal membrane. This vesicle may have formed from pinching off part of the Golgi body (see Section 1.9, page 11). The vesicle moves towards the cell surface membrane and fuses with it, enabling the contents of the vesicle to be exported from the cell. The membrane then reforms with the typical phospholipid arrangement.

Figure 2.21 describes the process of exocytosis, the removal of solids or liquids from the cell. This process avoids the need for substances to pass through the actual membrane. Instead, they pass through temporary gaps formed by the separating of the phospholipid molecules.

Remember

Cytosis is possible due to the fluid nature of the membrane. The membrane is able to pull apart and then spring back to its original phospholipid bilayer, phosphate on the outside and fatty acid tails on the inside.

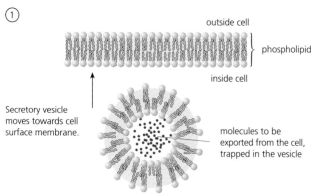

① outside cell

phospholipid

inside cell

Secretory vesicle moves towards cell surface membrane.

molecules to be exported from the cell, trapped in the vesicle

Figure 2.21 Membrane structure during exocytosis

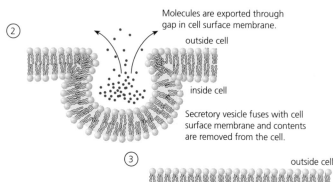

Molecules are exported through gap in cell surface membrane.

② outside cell

inside cell

Secretory vesicle fuses with cell surface membrane and contents are removed from the cell.

③ outside cell

inside cell

Cell surface membrane reforms – vesicle membrane is incorporated into the cell surface membrane as it is the same structure.

Summary – (2) **Cell membranes**

- All animal and plant cells are surrounded by a cell membrane.
- The internal membranes allow the formation of organelles in eukaryotes.
- Organelles allow for specialisation within a cell and greater efficiency.
- The structure of the cell surface membrane is the same as the membranes around organelles.
- The basic framework of the membrane is the phospholipid bilayer, with hydrophilic phosphate heads and hydrophobic fatty acid tails.
- Proteins scattered within the phospholipids serve to help in transportation across the membrane, provide structural support and form enzymes.
- Substances can cross the membrane by simple diffusion, facilitated diffusion, active transport and osmosis. Facilitated diffusion and active transport involve protein carriers.
- Active transport requires energy to carry substances from low to high concentration.
- Osmosis is the movement of water from an area of high water potential to an area of lower water potential through a partially permeable membrane. It is a passive process.
- Water potential is a measure of the kinetic energy of water molecules.
- Pure water has a water potential of $0\,kPa$ and this is the highest water potential as water is free to move with no solutes to restrict movement.
- Solutions have a lower water potential as water is less free to move due to the presence of solutes. The water potential of solutions has a negative value.
- Cytosis is the transport of substances into and out of cells through gaps in the membrane caused by movement of the phospholipids.
- Phagocytosis and pinocytosis are examples of endocytosis, when substances are taken into the cell.
- Exocytosis is when solids or liquids leave the cell in vesicles.

❓ Answers

1 The rigid cellulose cell wall prevents the membrane folding into microvilli in plant cells. *(1)*

2 Eukaryotes have membranes inside the cell which has allowed the formation of organelles and therefore specialisation to take place. *(2)*

3 The cell membrane is made up of two layers of phospholipids, a bilayer. *(1)*

4 The hydrophobic fatty acid tails stop the free movement of many water-soluble substances across the membrane, thus solutions are kept apart. *(2)*

5 The glycocalyx serves for cell recognition and therefore it needs to be on the outside of the membrane where cells are able to detect it, so allowing grouping into tissues. *(1)*

6 As the blood is not found in blood vessels, there is less distance for substances to diffuse, so reducing the diffusion distance and speeding up the rate of diffusion. The one-cell, lining layer of the capillaries across which diffusion normally takes place is not present here. *(2)*

7 Long-term coughing can break the delicate folds of the alveoli, so reducing their surface area for gas exchange and less oxygen enters the blood. *(2)*

8 Both facilitated diffusion and simple diffusion involve the movement of molecules from where they are in high concentration to where they are in low concentration, i.e. with the concentration gradient. Consequently, no input of energy is required for either process. Facilitated diffusion involves protein carriers whilst simple diffusion does not. *(3)*

9 Active transport requires protein carriers which are found in the cell membrane. If there is more membrane then more protein carriers can be present. *(2)*

10 Facilitated diffusion and active transport both require a protein carrier to transport molecules across the membrane.

They differ in that molecules move from high to low concentration during facilitated diffusion and from low to high concentration in active transport. *(2)*

11 In dilute solutions there are fewer solute particles restricting the movement of the water molecules. *(1)*

12 Plant cells have a strong cell wall which withstands the pressure caused by the entry of water. *(1)*

13 Relates to Fig. 2.17.

No.1. Water will move from A to B as A has the higher water potential; water always moves from a higher to a lower water potential.

No.2. Water will move from B to A, as B has the higher water potential. In fact this is the highest water potential, found in pure water.

No. 3. Water will move equally from A to B and from B to A. There will be no net movement in either direction as the water is equally free to move in both cells, they have the same water potential. *(3)*

14 The water that enters the *Amoeba* by osmosis must be constantly removed. It only has a cell surface membrane surrounding it which would burst if stretched too much by the entry of water. The water passes into a contractile vacuole which moves to the cell surface membrane, fuses with it and squeezes the water out by exocytosis. This process requires energy in the form of ATP. *(2)*

End of Chapter Questions

1 By what processes can substances cross the membrane? *(4 marks)*

2 Distinguish between endocytosis and exocytosis. What property of the membranes allows these processes to take place? *(3 marks)*

3 What is meant by the term 'equilibrium' in relation to the water potential of adjacent cells? *(2 marks)*

🔑 N2.2 **4** Cell A has a water potential of −500 kPa, and cell B next to it has a water potential of −800 kPa. Which way will water move by osmosis and what will the water potential be when equilibrium is reached? *(2 marks)*

5 Plants growing in a salty soil have problems getting water. Using your knowledge of osmosis, try and explain why. *(3 marks)*

6 What is the effect on water potential if starch in a cell is hydrolysed (broken down) to sugar? *(2 marks)*

7 When a respiratory inhibitor is used, the concentration of phosphate ions in the root hair cells is the same as in the soil. However, if no inhibitor is used, the concentration in the root hair cells is found to be much higher. Explain why this happens. *(3 marks)*

8 An experiment was carried out with cells of carrot tissue to determine the effect of temperature on the absorption of potassium ions.

Slices of carrot tissue were immersed in a potassium chloride solution of known concentration. The changes in concentration of potassium ions in the solution were determined at intervals for 6 hours. From these measurements, the mass of potassium ions taken in by the carrot cells was found. The experiment was carried out at 2 °C and 20 °C. The solutions were aerated continuously.

The results are shown in the graph below. Absorption of potassium ions is given as micrograms of potassium per gram of fresh mass of carrot tissue ($\mu g\ g^{-1}$).

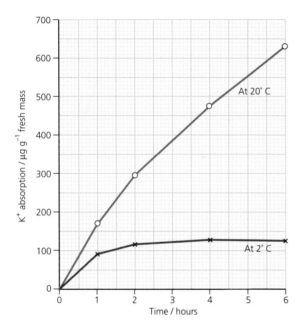

(a) During the first hour, some of the potassium ions enter the cells by diffusion. State *two* conditions which are necessary for a substance to enter a cell by diffusion. *(2 marks)*

N2.1
N3.2

(b) (i) Calculate the mean rate of absorption of potassium ions at 20 °C, between 2 and 6 hours. Show your working. *(3 marks)*

N2.1

(ii) Compare the rates of absorption of potassium ions at 2 °C and 20 °C during this experiment. *(3 marks)*

(iii) Suggest an explanation for the differences in the rates of absorption of potassium ions at the two temperatures. *(3 marks)*

(Total 11 marks)

London 1998

9 (a) Give **two** differences between osmosis and active transport. *(2 marks)*

(b) Samples of red blood cells were placed in a series of sodium chloride solutions of different concentrations. After three hours, the samples were examined to find the percentage of cells which had burst. The results are shown in the graph.

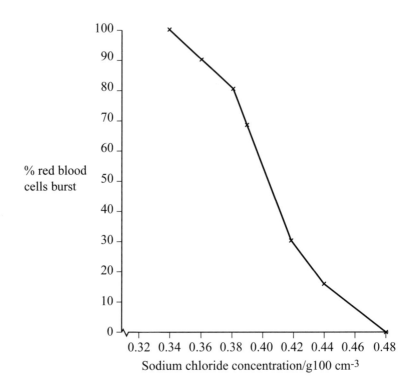

(i) Explain why all the red blood cells burst when placed in a 0.34% sodium chloride solution. *(3 marks)*

(ii) The red blood cells burst over a range of sodium chloride concentrations. Suggest a reason for this. *(1 mark)*

(c) When cells from an onion were placed in the same range of sodium chloride solutions, none of the cells burst. Explain why. *(1 mark)*

(Total 7 marks)

3 Biological molecules

Biological molecules are those which are found commonly in living organisms.

Molecules which are found inside living forms and in non-living situations may be biological but they are also considered as **inorganic**. **Water** is a very important inorganic, biological compound. Although it is found widely in non-living parts of the earth, it has special properties which make it suitable to be the main component of all living organisms. Similarly some inorganic (mineral) salts and inorganic (mineral) ions, as well as being common in the non-living world, have essential roles inside living forms.

Some molecules are produced **only** by living forms and so are found only in them, their secretions and the products of their death and decay. These molecules are large, containing mainly atoms of carbon, hydrogen and oxygen. Compounds with these types of molecules are known as **organic** compounds. As their structure differs, they are placed in different groups. Some of these groups are:

- **carbohydrates** – sugars, starch, cellulose and glycogen belong to this group. Sugars such as glucose are a main energy source in the human diet.
- **lipids** – fats and oils are important lipids. They are energy rich and are an essential part of an animal's diet. They are used for energy storage and insulation against heat loss. Lipids do not dissolve in water and can form a waterproof layer, covering some animals and plants (for example, the waxy cuticle of leaves).
- **proteins** – these make up 50% of the dry mass of living matter. The basic units of all proteins are amino acids. There are twenty common amino acids that can build up into chain-like molecules. The type of protein depends upon the order of amino acids in the chain. There are millions of different proteins and their functions are varied, ranging from acting as enzymes to being the structural substance in hair.

This chapter includes:
- the nature and role of inorganic biological molecules
  (a) water
  (b) inorganic salts and ions
- the nature and role of organic biological molecules
  (a) carbohydrates
  (b) lipids
  (c) proteins
- paper chromatography – a useful analytical technique.

Table 3.1 *Approximate composition of a slim human male*

Substance	Content as % fresh mass
water	70
lipid	15
protein	12
carbohydrate	0.5
inorganic ions	2.5

Figure 3.1 *What we are made of*

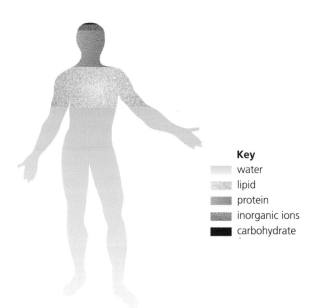

Key
- water
- lipid
- protein
- inorganic ions
- carbohydrate

Table 3.2 *Examples of water content of living organisms*

Example	Water content as % fresh mass
human	70
jellyfish	98
lettuce leaf	95
human brain	85

Water has very small molecules, each containing just two hydrogen atoms and one atom of oxygen. Other compounds with molecules of similar size, such as ammonia or methane, are gases at standard temperature (25 °C), while water is a liquid with a boiling point of 100 °C. This is just one peculiarity of water which helps to make it suitable as a biological molecule. It has many special properties which can be explained by studying the nature of the water molecule. Its importance as a biological molecule is a result of these properties.

The structures of hydrogen and oxygen atoms are shown in Figure 3.2. The outer shell of the oxygen atom can hold eight electrons and the shell of the hydrogen atom can hold two electrons. When they form a water molecule two pairs of electrons are shared, as shown in Figure 3.3. The oxygen is now linked to the hydrogen by two **covalent** bonds. As the unshared electrons of the oxygen atom repel the shared electrons, the hydrogen atoms are pushed towards each other, giving the molecule a V-shaped structure.

Figure 3.2 *Structure of oxygen and hydrogen atoms*

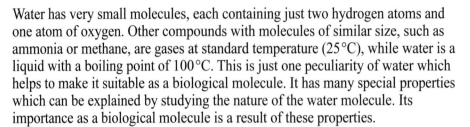

Figure 3.3 *A water molecule*

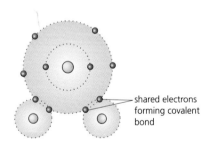

shared electrons forming covalent bond

Each electron has a negative charge and, as the oxygen nucleus attracts the electrons more than the hydrogen nuclei do, one end of the molecule is negatively charged while the other is positively charged.

A molecule with an uneven distribution of charges is called **polar**. The water molecule may be referred to as **dipolar** as one end is negative and the other is positive. There are forces of attraction between these weak negative and positive charges. The negative ends of water molecules attract the positive ends of other water molecules and **hydrogen bonds (H-bonds)** are formed between water molecules. This causes water molecules to cling to each other and form clusters.

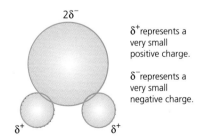

$2\delta^-$

δ^+ represents a very small positive charge.

δ^- represents a very small negative charge.

δ^+ δ^+

Figure 3.4 *The dipolar nature of the water molecule*

> 💡 **Definition**
>
> A **hydrogen bond** is a force of attraction between the small negative charge on an electronegative atom, such as oxygen, and the small positive charge on a hydrogen atom which is bonded to another electronegative atom

3.2   The role of water

It is the polar nature of water molecules and their tendency to cling to each other by hydrogen bonding that give water the special properties which make it so vital to life. Table 3.3 lists some ways in which the properties of water make it important, both as a component of living forms and as a medium for them to live in.

Table 3.3   Properties of water

Property	Significance
high specific heat capacity	it takes a lot of heat energy to raise the temperature of water (as some energy is used to break H-bonds). So water temperature is fairly stable when air temperature changes rapidly. This stability is essential for enzymes
high latent heat of vaporisation	much heat energy is needed to change liquid water into vapour (because it takes energy to break H-bonds). So, much heat energy is absorbed as water evaporates from body surfaces. This means that sweating, panting and transpiration are effective ways of cooling
high density	water has its maximum density at 4°C and expands upon freezing (as more H-bonds form a lattice in ice crystals). So ice floats on water and lakes freeze at the top first, protecting organisms below. Water is a dense liquid (as the molecules cling together). It is able to support organisms by the upthrust it exerts. For example, a whale could not support its body weight in air
cohesion	as water molecules cling together, water rises as a continuous column up the vascular tissue of plants when pulled from above by transpiration. Water molecules on the surface are attracted to those below, giving a 'skin-like' surface tension. Creatures such as pond skaters can support themselves on the surface of ponds without sinking in
good solvent	many substances have molecules with polar groups or molecules which dissociate to give polar ions. These charged particles are attracted to the polar water molecules and become dispersed among the water molecules. Such substances dissolve easily in the water. Water transports substances in solution around organisms in transport systems. Metabolic reactions take place between substances in solution
reactivity	water can take part in chemical reactions in body metabolism. It is an essential reactant in hydrolysis reactions and in photosynthesis
transparency	the penetration of light through water is essential for photosynthesis in plant cells. Photosynthesis in aquatic organisms depends upon light penetrating some distance through a body of water

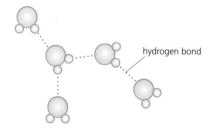

hydrogen bond

Figure 3.5   The formation of hydrogen bonds between water molecules

Box 3.1 Hot water

As the oceans are such large bodies of water, their temperature varies very little and so the seas provide an extremely stable environment for life. The animals living in the sea usually have the same body temperature as the surrounding water and so their temperature too remains stable. The importance of this was demonstrated during 1998, the warmest year on record at that time.

During that year, the temperature of the sea water of the Indian Ocean around the Maldive Islands rose by a few degrees quite quickly. A current of warm water flowed into the area as a result of the most intense outbreak for fifty years of a phenomenon known as El Niño. This warm current arrived at the same time as the area was experiencing exceptionally high air temperatures which also helped to warm up the water.

This temporary effect killed millions of the animals which build up the coral reefs. As a result vast areas of coral reefs and the life which depends on them have died.

Figure 3.6 *Damaged coral reefs in the Indian Ocean*

3.3 The nature and role of inorganic (mineral) salts and ions

Some inorganic salts are found in organisms, usually in a solid, incompressible supportive or protective role. For example, snail shells are rich in calcium carbonate and mammal bones contain a mixture of salts, including calcium phosphate and magnesium salts. In the inner ear there are tiny granules of calcium carbonate which are essential for balance.

However, many inorganic salts are soluble in water and dissociate into charged particles (ions) as they dissolve. Therefore, most inorganic salts in living organisms are found in the form of ions in solution in cytoplasm or body fluids. They play an important part in body metabolism. Many ions combine with organic molecules to form complex molecules, for example, phosphates form part of DNA molecules.

There are many different inorganic ions and their functions are too varied to discuss under one heading. Table 3.4 is meant as a guide to some of the commoner functions of inorganic ions but the importance of various ions will be covered in more detail as the study of different topics takes place.

Table 3.4 Functions of some inorganic ions

Ion	Function
calcium	needed for blood clotting and muscle contraction. Activates some enzymes
magnesium	component of chlorophyll
potassium	needed for transmission of nerve impulses
sodium	needed for transmission of nerve impulses. Common ion helping to maintain the correct water potential
chloride	common ion helping to maintain correct water potential. Needed to form hydrochloric acid in gastric juice
iodide	trace needed to make hormone, thyroxine
iron	component of haemoglobin, many enzymes and coenzymes
nitrate	needed in plants to form amino acids
phosphate	component of DNA, RNA, ATP and phospholipids

3.4 Organic biological molecules – The nature and role of carbohydrates

This group of molecules takes its name from 'hydrated (watered) carbon' which means that each molecule contains carbon together with hydrogen and oxygen in the same ratio to each other as they are in water (2H:O). Therefore the general formula for any carbohydrate molecule is $C_x(H_2O)_y$.

There are three groups of carbohydrates: monosaccharides (single sugars), disaccharides (double sugars), polysaccharides (multiple sugars).

Definition

Carbohydrates are a group of organic compounds whose molecules contain atoms of carbon, hydrogen and oxygen only. The ratio of hydrogen atoms to oxygen atoms is always 2:1

Remember

Many words used in Biology contain certain parts which have come from Greek or Latin. This does not mean that you have to be a classical scholar to understand them but you may find the following helpful.

Part of word	Meaning
mono... or uni...	one
di... or bi...	two
tri...	three
pent...	five
hex...	six
poly... or multi...	many
sacchar...	sugar
...lysis	splitting/ breakdown involved
hydro...	water involved

Remember

When a substance, such as a sugar, **reduces** another chemical, it takes oxygen, or electrons, from that chemical or donates hydrogen to it. In doing so, the sugar becomes oxidised. (Such a chemical reaction is called a redox reaction.)

3.5 Monosaccharides (single sugars)

These are the simplest types of carbohydrate and have the same number of carbon atoms as oxygen atoms in the molecule. Therefore their general formula is $(CH_2O)_n$.

They are all white, crystalline solids which dissolve in water to give sweet-tasting solutions. When they are in solution, they all readily reduce other chemicals and therefore are regarded as **reducing sugars**.

There are many different monosaccharides with different numbers of atoms and different arrangements of atoms in the molecules. These include:

- **trioses** $C_3H_6O_3$ (n = 3) e.g. glyceraldehyde
- **pentoses** $C_5H_{10}O_5$ (n = 5) e.g. ribose
- **hexoses** $C_6H_{12}O_6$ (n = 6) e.g. glucose, fructose and galactose

There are different trioses, pentoses and hexoses because the same numbers of atoms may be arranged in various ways within the molecules. Differing arrangements of the atoms give the molecules slightly different shapes and different properties.

The glucose molecule itself may vary slightly, and its two most common structures are shown below in simplified forms.

Figure 3.7 *Simplified formulae for alpha-glucose and beta-glucose*

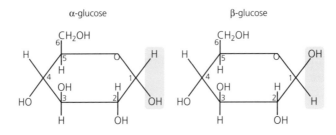

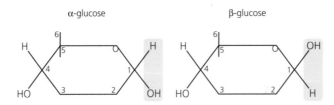

In these diagrams, the positions of carbon atoms are represented by their numbers only.
Note carefully the different arrangement of atoms around the carbon I atoms in α - glucose and β - glucose. This small difference can give the molecules different properties.

Definition

Substances such as glucose and fructose which have the same numbers, but different arrangements, of atoms in their molecules, are called **isomers** of each other. (Isomers have the same **molecular** formula but different **structural** formulae.)

Hexoses such as glucose form the main source of energy for a living organism. When they are broken down during respiration they release chemical energy which has been trapped within the molecule.

> **Remember**
>
> Before describing more complex carbohydrates, it is necessary to understand that: chemical reactions known as **condensation** and **hydrolysis** reactions play an important role in the building up and breaking down of most organic molecules.
> - A **condensation** reaction is a reaction in which two smaller molecules join together to form a larger one and release a molecule of water.
>   In a general way, this can be shown as:
> $$AOH + BH \rightarrow AB + H_2O$$
>   where AB is a generalised formula for the larger molecule.
> - A **hydrolysis** reaction is a reaction in which a large molecule reacts with water and, in doing so, is split into two smaller ones.
> $$AB + H_2O \rightarrow AOH + BH$$

3.6 Disaccharides (double sugars)

These are sugars whose molecules are formed when two hexose sugar molecules react together by means of a **condensation** reaction. (This reaction is reversible and a disaccharide molecule can be broken down into hexose sugars during a **hydrolysis** reaction.)

An overall equation representing an example of this is shown below:

(a) using molecular formulae:

condensation →

$$C_6H_{12}O_6 + C_6H_{12}O_6 \rightleftharpoons C_{12}H_{22}O_{11} + H_2O$$

← hydrolysis

glucose   glucose   disaccharide   water
                          (maltose)

(b) using simplified structural formulae:

Figure 3.8

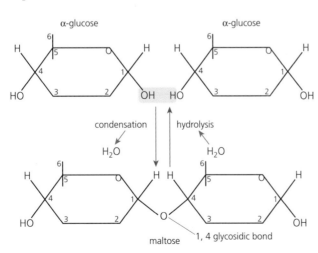

The bond formed between the two reacting sugars is called a **glycosidic bond** and as it is formed between the carbons 1 and 4 it is referred to as the **1,4 glycosidic bond**.

So all disaccharide sugars have the molecular formula $C_{12}H_{22}O_{11}$. They are also all white, crystalline solids and dissolve in water to produce sweet-tasting solutions. Although they all have the same molecular formula, they can be formed from the condensation of different hexoses and have different arrangements of atoms in the molecules. For this reason there are many different disaccharides. The commonest ones are:

- **maltose** (malt sugar) – formed when two alpha-glucose molecules condense together

- **lactose** (milk sugar) – formed when alpha-glucose condenses with galactose

- **sucrose** (cane/beet sugar) – formed when alpha-glucose condenses with fructose

The properties of these disaccharides vary. While maltose and lactose are reducing sugars, sucrose cannot reduce other chemicals and is a **non-reducing sugar**.

1 During digestion, when large molecules of organic food are broken down into smaller soluble molecules so that they can be absorbed, all the digestive reactions are hydrolysis ones. Which sugars are produced by the digestion of (a) sucrose and (b) lactose? *(2 marks)*

3.7 Polysaccharides (many sugars)

Polysaccharides are the most complex carbohydrates and have the largest molecules. The molecules are formed when many monosaccharide (usually hexose) molecules condense together to form long chains. Such molecules are known as **condensation polymers**.

Definition

A **condensation polymer** is a substance with molecules which are long chains built up by the condensation of many similar units. The basic units are known as monomers

In the case of the most common polysaccharides, glucose is the monomer. (Although alpha-glucose can be considered as a monomer of maltose, this disaccharide is considered as a **dimer** as it is only a double unit and no long chain is formed.)

Polysaccharides are insoluble in water, they are not sweet and are not 'sugars'. Their general formula is $(C_6H_{10}O_5)_n$ where n is a large variable number. The commonest examples are **starch**, **glycogen** and **cellulose**.

The properties of these three vary so much that they must be considered separately.

Starch – an energy store in plants

Starch is a polymer of alpha-glucose. It is formed in plant cells from glucose and is stored in the form of grains (see Figure 3.9). As it has compact and insoluble molecules, it is an ideal form in which to store glucose molecules and these can be reformed by hydrolysis later, when needed.

Starch is a mixture of two types of chain formed from alpha-glucose:

● **Amylose**. Many alpha-glucose molecules condense together forming 1,4 glycosidic bonds, so producing long unbranched chains. As seen in the drawing, these chains take up a coiled (helical) configuration as each monomer has a bulky side group which has to be accommodated (Figure 3.10). Amylose forms about 20% of starch.

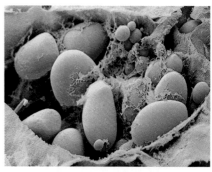

Figure 3.9 *Starch grains in a potato tuber cell (SEM × 640)*

Figure 3.10 *The structure of amylose*

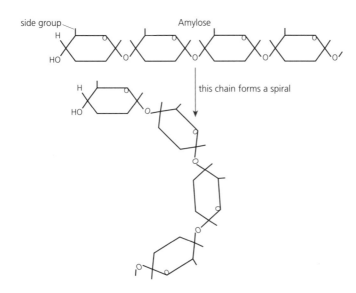

side group
this chain forms a spiral
Amylose

Remember

It is essential that storage compounds are insoluble so that they have no osmotic effects and so do not affect the movement of water in or out of the cells and also so that they cannot diffuse away

● **Amylopectin**. This is branched and consists of alpha-glucose condensed together in two ways forming 1,4 glycosidic bonds and 1,6 glycosidic bonds (Figure 3.11). The coiled chains of amylopectin may contain 1500 monomers with branches every ten units. It often forms about 80% of starch although the proportions of the two components of starch vary slightly from one species to another.

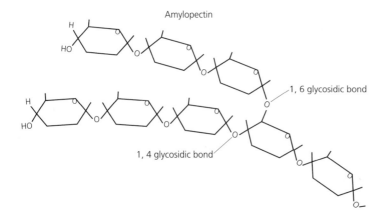

Amylopectin
1, 6 glycosidic bond
1, 4 glycosidic bond

Figure 3.11 *The structure of amylopectin*

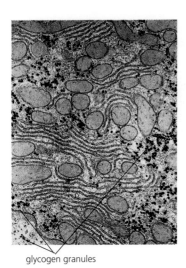

glycogen granules

Figure 3.12 *Glycogen granules in liver cells (TEM)*

Figure 3.13 *Condensation of two beta-glucose molecules forming a portion of a cellulose molecule*

Glycogen – an energy store in animals and fungi

Glycogen is also a polymer of alpha-glucose condensed to form 1,4 glycosidic and 1,6 glycosidic bonds but here the chains formed are more branched and shorter than those of amylopectin. Each chain may only be 10–20 units long. Glycogen contains no unbranched chains.

It is also produced as an insoluble storage product of glucose. It is found in animals and fungi but not in plants. It takes the form of small granules suspended in the cytoplasm of cells and can be seen especially in liver and muscle cells (Figure 3.12). As its chains are so short, it can be hydrolysed rapidly, producing glucose for an animal's urgent needs.

Cellulose – a structural compound in plants

Cellulose has very different properties from starch or glycogen. It does not form grains or small granules and its role is not storage but structural. It is fibrous and strong and is the major component of plant cell walls.

This difference reflects the fact that, unlike starch or glycogen, the monomer of cellulose is beta-glucose. As can be seen in Figure 3.13, when two beta-glucose molecules condense together forming 1,4 glycosidic bonds, alternate molecules are rotated through 180° allowing the appropriate –OH groups to react.

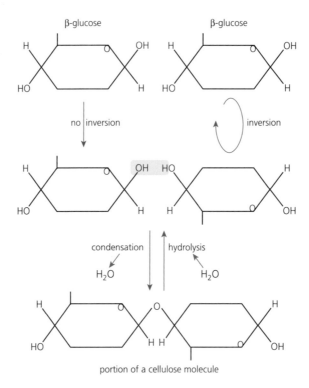

portion of a cellulose molecule

This has two effects: the unbranched chains are straighter as the bulky side groups have to be accommodated on opposite sides alternately; and also **hydrogen bonds** are formed between the –OH groups and the oxygen of adjacent straight chains (Figure 3.14). This gives cellulose a strong, fibrous structure.

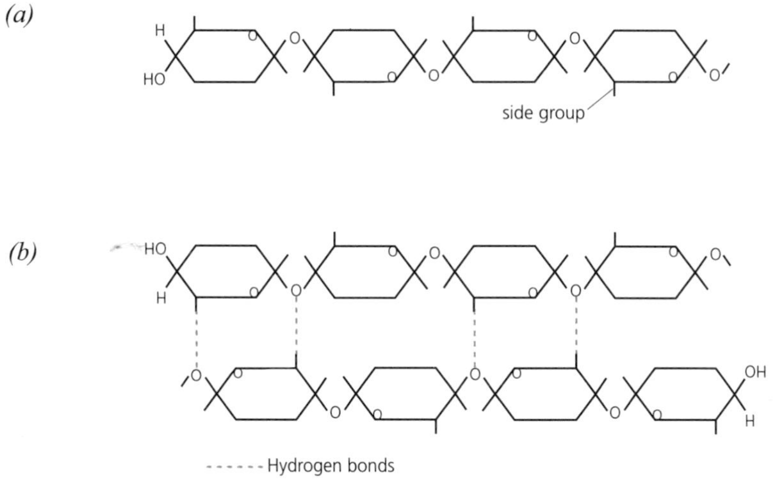

(a)

side group

(b)

------ Hydrogen bonds

Figure 3.14
(a) Alternate beta-glucose molecules invert in this way as they condense, giving the straight chain cellulose molecule, as shown
(b) Adjacent cellulose molecules form hydrogen bonds, as shown

The parallel cellulose molecules form bundles known as microfibrils and these in turn cluster into macrofibrils with immense tensile strength and stability. The bundles are arranged in a gel-like matrix of other smaller polysaccharides in plant cell walls. (see Figure 1.19, page 15)

Table 3.5 Summary of differences between starch, glycogen and cellulose

	Starch	Glycogen	Cellulose
monomer	α-glucose	α-glucose	β-glucose
bonds linking monomers	1,4 glycosidic (amylose) + 1,4 and 1,6 glycosidic (amylopectin)	1,4 and 1,6 glycosidic	1,4 glycosidic
nature of chains	amylose amylopectin 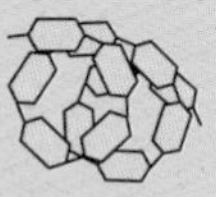 coiled unbranched 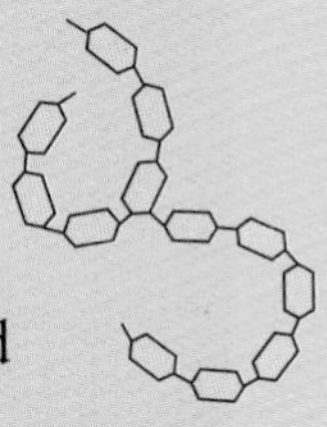 long branched chains, some coiling	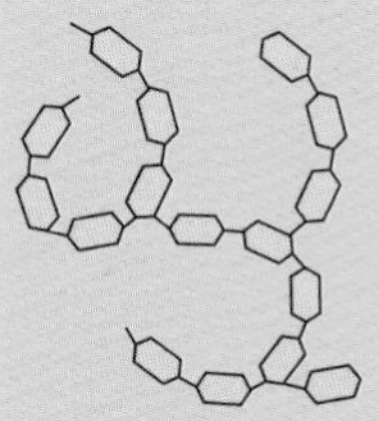 short many-branched chains, some coiling	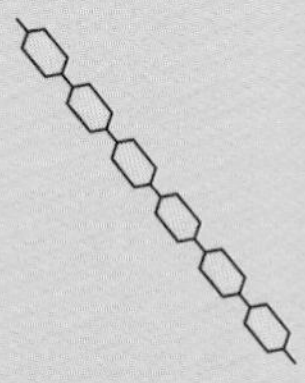 straight, long unbranched chains form H-bonds, with adjacent chains
occurrence	plants	animals and fungi	plants
function	carbohydrate energy store	carbohydrate energy store	structural
general form	grains	small granules	fibres

2 Give two differences between each of the following polymer chains:
  (i) amylose and cellulose
  (ii) amylopectin and glycogen   *(4 marks)*

Extension

Box 3.2 Useful cellulose

Although cellulose may only form 20–50% by mass of cell walls of all plant cells, it is the most abundant organic molecule on Earth and 50% of all the carbon in plants is in cellulose. Because it is so abundant and strong while being chemically and physically stable, humans have found many uses for it. Cotton and paper are almost pure cellulose, and fibres such as rayon and Lycra also contain some cellulose. It is found in a whole variety of other products such as photographic film, nail varnish and even explosives.

Recently, artificial blood vessels have been made from cellulose. Tubes of cellulose, made by bacteria, have been inserted successfully into rats and may have a future in human surgery.

Figure 3.15 *Uses of cellulose:*
(a) Scanning electron micrograph of paper (× 30)
(b) Scanning electron micrograph of toilet tissue (× 36)
(c) Artificial blood vessels made from cellulose

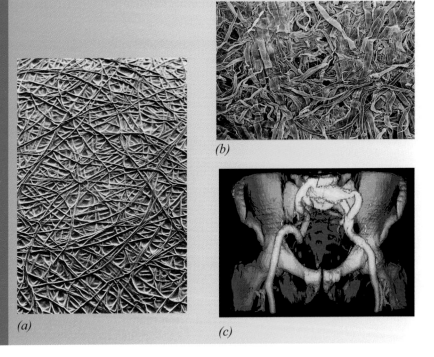

(a)

(b)

(c)

Box 3.3 Ants as farmers

As cellulose is so stable, it is difficult to hydrolyse, and the enzyme **cellulase** which speeds up its hydrolysis is only found in some micro-organisms including fungi and bacteria. However, cellulose, as it contains so much glucose, is energy rich and potentially a good food for animals, if only it could be digested!

Some animals have gone to extraordinary lengths to tap this source of food. Cows, for example, harbour millions of micro-organisms in a special stomach to digest cellulose for them.

Some types of ants collect leaves and drag them into their nests as a source of cellulose. They then collect the correct species of fungi and place them on these leaves and provide suitable conditions for the fungi to grow. The fungi digest the cellulose in the leaves along with other nutrients and the ants then live by feeding on the fungi.

Ants can be said to have lived by 'farming', fifty million years before man discovered this way of life. There are even more parallels with modern farming methods. Ants are believed to harbour bacteria, which secrete antibiotics, to prevent the growth of unwanted fungi. They also spread their own waste onto the leaves as fertiliser.

Figure 3.16 *(a) A worker ant protect by soldiers from the same colony*

(b) Leaf cutter ants cultivating their fungal garden

Box 3.4 Chitin

Chitin is a very common biological molecule, it forms the cell walls of all fungi and a major part of the exoskeletons (cuticles) of all arthropods. As three-quarters of all the animal species on Earth are arthropods (including insects, which by themselves make up more than one-half of the Earth's animal species), it follows that chitin must have some useful properties.

It is light, stable, strong, flexible, transparent and permeable to water and gases. These properties suggest similarity to cellulose and indeed the molecule is similar, but here the monomers are glucosamine which is formed when an amino group reacts with beta-glucose. As in cellulose with its monomers of pure beta-glucose, alternate molecules are inverted, leading to a fibrous structure. It is not a pure carbohydrate but is referred to as a carbohydrate derivative.

Figure 3.17
(a) Scanning electron micrograph of the chitin walls of fungal hyphae
(b) A beetle's chitin exoskeleton

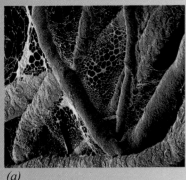

(a)

(b)

3.8 Biochemical tests for presence of types of carbohydrates

In order to find out which carbohydrates are present in small samples of food, the following tests can be carried out. In each case the food sample is crushed or dissolved in water.

The test for a reducing sugar (Benedict's test)
This test depends upon the fact that reducing sugars reduce blue copper (II) sulphate in Benedict's solution to brick red copper (I) oxide.
It is not possible to distinguish between different reducing sugars using this test.

Procedure Benedict's solution is added to the food sample and the mixture is heated at 90 °C for 4 minutes.

Result if a reducing sugar is present A brick red precipitate is formed in the original blue solution.

The amount of precipitate formed depends upon the amount of reducing sugar in the sample. Different amounts of brick red precipitate viewed in a blue solution appear different colours.

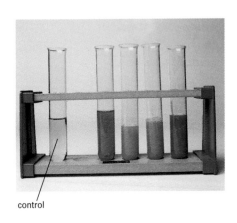

control

Figure 3.18 Range of colours produced by the Benedict's test with no reducing sugar (control) and increasing amounts of reducing sugar

Small amount ——————————→ large amount
green ——→ yellow ——→ orange ——→ brick red

The test for a non-reducing sugar (e.g. sucrose)
This test depends upon the fact that a non-reducing sugar does not reduce Benedict's solution, but it can be hydrolysed into reducing sugars which do so.

Table 3.6 *Summary of range of carbohydrates*

Type of carbohydrate	General formula	Specific example	Monomer	Role and occurrence
monosaccharides	$(CH_2O)_n$			
(a) trioses	$C_3H_6O_3$	glyceraldehyde	–	• intermediate in respiration (A2) • in all cells
(b) pentoses	$C_5H_{10}O_5$	ribose	–	• forms part of RNA molecule • in all cells
		deoxyribose $(C_5H_{10}O_4)$		• forms part of DNA molecule • in all cells
(c) hexoses	$C_6H_{12}O_6$	glucose	–	• substrate for respiration • in all cells
		galactose	–	• in milk sugar (lactose)
		fructose	–	• in sucrose
disaccharides	$C_{12}H_{22}O_{11}$	maltose	α-glucose	• intermediate in starch formation/breakdown • in germinating seeds
		lactose	α-glucose + galactose	• energy source for young mammals • sugar in milk
		sucrose	α-glucose + fructose	• form in which sugars are transported in plants • also forms energy stores in cane and beet
polysaccharides	$(C_6H_{10}O_5)_n$	starch	α-glucose	• energy storage in plant cells
		glycogen	α-glucose	• energy storage in animal or fungi cells
		cellulose	β-glucose	• structure and support • in cell walls of plant cells

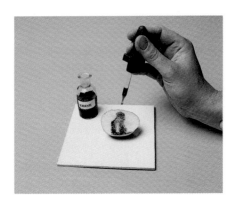

Figure 3.19 The starch in the potato causes the 'iodine solution' to go blue-black

It can only be valid when carried out on food where a previous sample has been shown to contain no (or a very small amount of) reducing sugar.

Procedure The sample is boiled in a water bath with dilute hydrochloric acid for two minutes. The mixture is then allowed to cool before being neutralised by adding dilute sodium hydroxide solution (confirmed by using Universal Indicator paper). The Benedict's test, as described above, is now carried out.

Result if non-reducing sugar present A brick red precipitate is formed.

The test for starch (the iodine/potassium iodide test)
This test depends upon the fact that iodine, dissolved in potassium iodide solution, here referred to as 'iodine solution', combines with the amylose in starch to make a complex blue-black compound.

Procedure Yellow iodine solution is added to a food sample.

Result if starch present A blue-black colour is produced.

The test for cellulose
If plant tissue is stained with chlor-zinc iodide, any cellulose cell walls stain a violet colour.

3 If sucrose were the only sugar present in a sample of food, describe and explain the results you would expect using these biochemical tests. Include a word equation in your answer. *(4 marks)*

4 Why is a blue-black colour not produced if iodine solution is added to glycogen or cellulose? *(2 marks)*

 3.9 **The nature of lipids**

Lipids, like carbohydrates, have molecules that consist of carbon, hydrogen and oxygen atoms only. However, lipid molecules have a much lower proportion of oxygen to hydrogen. The molecules are non-polar and therefore cannot dissolve in a polar solvent such as water, although they can dissolve in non-polar solvents such as alcohols or benzene.

Definition

Lipids are a group of organic compounds whose molecules contain atoms of carbon, hydrogen and oxygen only. The ratio of hydrogen to oxygen atoms is always much greater than 2:1. They are insoluble in water

The most well-known lipids are fats and oils; these are called **triglycerides**. Lipids also include waxes and steroids (including cholesterol) which, because of their everyday use or health implications, are also quite 'famous'. Other important lipid derivatives are the phospholipids which form the basis of all cell membranes.

3.10 Fats and oils (triglycerides)

All triglyceride molecules are formed when a molecule of glycerol condenses, and therefore combines, with three fatty acid molecules.

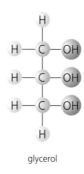

glycerol

Figure 3.20 Glycerol

A molecule of glycerol has the molecular formula $C_3H_8O_3$ and the structural formula shown.

Glycerol always has the same structure and, unlike the triglyceride it can produce, it is soluble in water because of its polar –OH groups.

Different triglycerides are produced according to which fatty acids condense with this glycerol molecule. There are over seventy different fatty acids but they all contain one **carboxyl** group which gives the molecule acid properties as it dissociates to release a hydrogen ion in water.

carboxyl group

Figure 3.21 A carboxyl group

Attached to this group is a long hydrocarbon chain which varies in different fatty acids. For example, the structural formula of the fatty acid, stearic acid $(CH_3(CH_2)_{16}COOH)$, is shown in Figure 3.22.

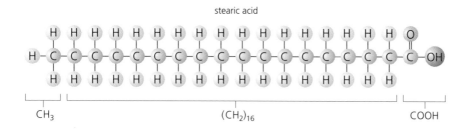

Figure 3.22 Stearic acid is a saturated fatty acid

Stearic acid is a **saturated** fatty acid because there are no double bonds in the hydrocarbon chain and so it is as saturated with hydrogen as possible. An **unsaturated** fatty acid is one where one or more double bonds between carbon atoms in the chain mean that fewer hydrogen atoms are present. For example, the structural formula of oleic acid $(CH_3(CH_2)_7-C=C-(CH_2)_7COOH)$ is shown in Figure 3.23.

Figure 3.23 Oleic acid is an unsaturated fatty acid

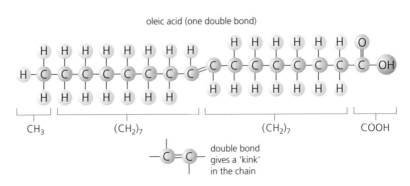

oleic acid (one double bond)

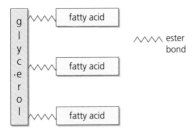

Figure 3.24 A triglyceride

The triglyceride molecule can be represented simply as an E-shape, as shown in Figure 3.24. The glycerol is linked to the fatty acids by **ester bonds**. As the polar parts of the glycerol and the fatty acid molecules are lost in the condensation process, the resulting triglyceride is non-polar and, therefore, insoluble in water.

Glycerol condenses with three fatty acids, as shown in Figure 3.25. These fatty acids may all be the same or be different from one another. They may all be saturated, all be unsaturated or there may be some of each.

Figure 3.25 Formation of triglycerides

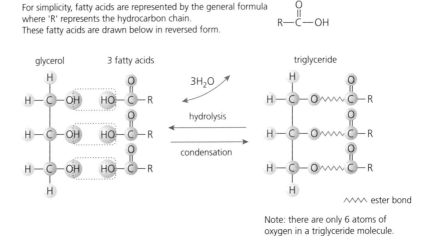

The types of fatty acid present in the triglyceride molecule affect its chemical and physical properties. If all or most of the fatty acids in the molecule are saturated, then a saturated fat is formed. If all or most of the fatty acids present are unsaturated, then a polyunsaturate is formed and it is usually an oil.

Fats are solid at room temperature and are usually produced as energy stores in animals. Fats are therefore animal products and are found in meat. Oils are liquid at room temperature and are produced in plants, very often as energy stores in seeds; for example, sunflower seeds. Fish also tend to produce oils; for example, cod liver oil.

We, as humans, are capable of making some fatty acids in our bodies from other molecules. However, there are some which we cannot make. It is essential that we eat these within triglycerides and, therefore, these are called **essential** fatty acids.

Remember

SSS – Single (bonds), **Saturated** (lipids), **Solid** (at room temperature)

DUL – Double (bonds), **Unsaturated** (lipids), **Liquid** (at room temperature)

3.11 Waxes

Waxes are lipids whose molecules have single hydrocarbon chains linked to an alcohol other than glycerol and they are not digested by animals. They are found commonly as waterproof coverings in living organisms. Insects' chitin exoskeletons are covered with a waxy layer to prevent them losing water and, so, dehydrating. For similar reasons, leaves have a waxy cuticle. Bees have glands for making wax with which they build their honeycombs.

3.12 Steroids

These are lipids with highly complex molecules. They form the basis of many hormones such as oestrogen and testosterone. Cholesterol is a well-known steroid. Although cholesterol is often thought of as a dangerous compound related to heart disease, it is, in fact, an essential molecule in living organisms. It is found in cell membranes where it has a structural role and aids phospholipids in forming a barrier to the free passage of molecules. It is made in the liver as well as being supplied in the diet.

3.13 Phospholipids

Phospholipids are lipid derivatives, as each molecule contains a phosphorus atom in addition to carbon, hydrogen and oxygen. Their structure is very similar to that of a triglyceride. However, two fatty acid molecules and one phosphoric acid molecule are condensed with a molecule of glycerol. The formation of a phospholipid is shown in the diagram.

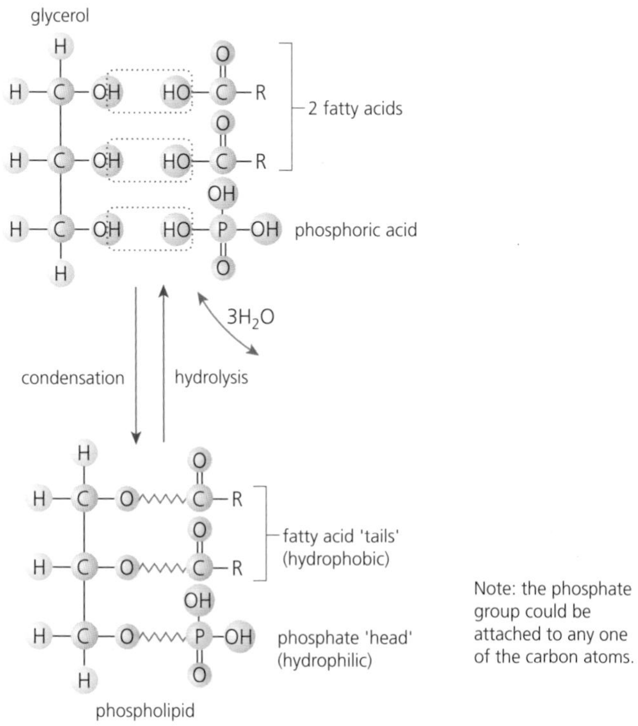

Figure 3.26 Formation of a phospholipid

glycerol

2 fatty acids

phosphoric acid

3H₂O

condensation   hydrolysis

fatty acid 'tails' (hydrophobic)

phosphate 'head' (hydrophilic)

Note: the phosphate group could be attached to any one of the carbon atoms.

phospholipid

It can be seen that the phosphate part of the molecule has polar – OH groups which are attracted to polar water molecules while the rest of the molecule is non-polar. The polar phosphate 'head' is **hydrophilic** (water-loving). The rest of the molecule including the fatty acid 'tails' is **hydrophobic** (water-hating). The phospholipid molecule is often represented as in Figure 3.27 to stress the fact that the parts of the molecules are often orientated in this way in living organisms. This is an essential property, responsible for their role in cell membranes (see Section 2.2, page 38).

Figure 3.27 Simplified diagrams of a phospholipid molecule

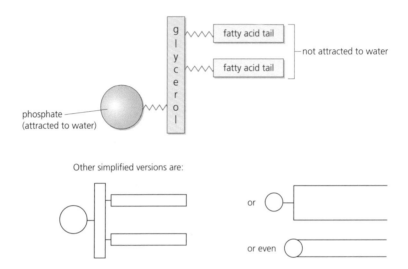

3.14 **Biochemical test for the presence of lipid (the emulsion test)**

This test depends upon the fact that lipids are insoluble in water but soluble in an alcohol, such as ethanol.

Procedure The food sample is crushed, if solid, and placed into a test tube. Ethanol is added and the mixture is shaken vigorously. After settling, the ethanol is poured into another test tube containing cold water.

Result if lipid present The mixture becomes cloudy as tiny droplets of lipid come out of solution forming an emulsion.

Figure 3.28 The emulsion test

?

5 Give two differences between the chemical structure of a triglyceride and amylose. *(2 marks)*

6 What is meant by (a) an ester bond; (b) an unsaturated fatty acid? *(2 marks)*

7 Triglycerides are large molecules formed by condensation reactions but are **not** condensation polymers. Why is this so? *(2 marks)*

3.15 The role of lipids

They are used as **high energy stores** by living organisms. 1 g of lipid can yield over twice as much energy as 1 g of carbohydrate or protein. They are insoluble and stable and yet can be readily respired to release their energy. So they are an ideal form of light energy store. Humans store fats while plant seeds may be rich in oils. (When they are respired, they release many water molecules. The camel's hump contains fat which produces useful quantities of water on respiration as well as releasing energy.)

They are used in **waterproof coverings**. They repel and are impermeable to water and so wax cuticles are found on insects and leaves to prevent water loss, while sea birds preen their feathers with oil, produced in a gland, to prevent water entering the air space between the feathers. Treatment of oil-polluted birds with detergents can remove these natural oils leading to loss of heat and loss of buoyancy. Humans have skin glands which produce the oily mixture, sebum, which prevents excessive drying of the skin.

They form an **insulating layer** against heat loss. As it is a poor conductor of heat the layer of fat under the skin of humans and especially in sea mammals such as whales (blubber) helps them to keep warm in cold climates.

They act as **shock-absorbing layers**. As they are compressible, a layer under the skin protects the internal organs against physical damage. Also fat is often deposited around delicate organs such as kidneys or the heart to give extra protection.

Phospholipids are major components of **cell membranes**. The structure of phospholipids causes them to orientate themselves into bilayers with a hydrophobic centre. This is the essential basis of cell membranes.

Steroids have various roles. Cholesterol is an important component of cell membranes and nerve fibre sheaths. Steroids form the basis of many hormones such as oestrogen, cortisone and testosterone. Vitamin D can be produced from steroids in the fat under the skin in sunlight.

Lipids form the basis of **scents**. Plant 'perfumes' are fatty acid derivatives produced by plants which attract insects for pollination.

(a)

(b)

(c)

Figure 3.29 Some of the roles of lipids:
(a) Sunflower with 'oil-rich' seeds
(b) Camel's hump (fat store)
(c) Pelican preening feathers with oil secretions
(d) Whales have blubber
(e) Fat around a kidney
(f) Perfumed flower attracting an insect

(d)

(e)

(f)

81

Box 3.5 Lipids and health

Today, when we hear about 'fats', 'cholesterol' and 'steroids', it is often in relation to our appearance, health or sporting abilities.

Clearly a diet, adequate in most respects, but over-rich in lipids means that the energy content of our food is greater than the energy we use. The excess is stored in extra fat deposits and we become overweight (obese). Obesity has its dangers. For example, it puts strain on the heart and supporting structures of the body and is considered to be a risk factor in high blood pressure, arthritis, sugar diabetes and certain cancers.

A diet which is rich in saturated fats and cholesterol may lead to a raised level of a dangerous form of blood cholesterol, leading to fats and cholesterol derivatives being deposited in the lining of arteries, narrowing the channel for blood flow (**atherosclerosis**). A small blood clot may block the channel stopping the blood, and therefore oxygen supply, to essential tissues which then die. If brain tissue dies, a stroke follows, while the death of heart tissue leads to a heart attack. Some people naturally manufacture more cholesterol than others and the risk of atherosclerosis does not depend entirely upon diet.

However, a diet which contains too little lipid also has dangers. Although some lipids can be made from other compounds such as excess carbohydrate, some essential fatty acids must be provided by the diet. Lipid in our food will also contain important fat-soluble vitamins including A, D, E and K. Young women with severe lack of lipid (e.g. as the result of anorexia nervosa) may not be able to manufacture sex hormones and their periods may stop.

Steroids are the basis of the hormone testosterone. This promotes muscle development in young men as they reach puberty. This is a fact which has led sportsmen to inject large quantities of these so-called anabolic (building up) steroids in order to enhance their muscle development. The long-term side effects of this illegal abuse are slowly becoming clear. These include heart disease, impotence and sterility (sometimes accompanied by a decrease in the size of the testes).

Box 3.6 Are you the right weight for your height?

Measure your weight (mass) in kilograms and your height in metres.

Calculate your Body Mass Index (BMI) as follows:

$$BMI = \frac{mass}{height^2}$$

For adults, the ideal BMI is between 18.5 and 24.9 kg m^{-2}.

A BMI over 30 kg m^{-2} indicates obesity.

3.16 The nature of proteins

Amino acids are the monomers of all proteins. All amino acid molecules contain atoms of carbon, hydrogen and oxygen together with nitrogen. Some amino acids contain sulphur atoms too. These amino acids condense together to form long chains known as polypeptides. A protein molecule consists of one or more than one polypeptide chain.

Definition

Proteins are a group of organic compounds whose molecules consist of carbon, hydrogen, oxygen, nitrogen and sometimes sulphur atoms. They are condensation polymers of amino acids

Amino acids have the general formula shown in Figure 3.30. Each amino acid contains a carboxyl group (as do the fatty acids). There is also an amino group present. The part of the molecule which is different in every amino acid is known as the **R-group**.

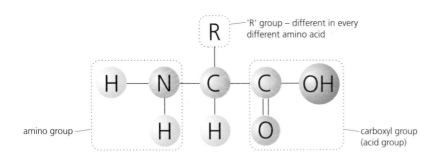

Figure 3.30 Structural formula of an amino acid

The R-group can vary enormously and some examples are shown in Figure 3.31. There is no need to memorise these, but it is important to realise the variety. For example, some R-groups are polar, some are non-polar, some contain carboxyl groups and some contain hydroxyl (–OH) groups. A few, such as cysteine, contain sulphur.

Humans can produce some amino acids in the body by conversion from others. However, some cannot be formed in this way and must be eaten as part of proteins in the diet. These are called **essential** amino acids.

Figure 3.31 Some examples of different amino acids

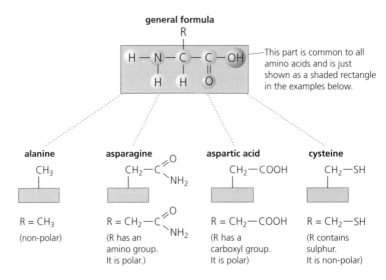

Box 3.7 Behaviour of amino acids in water

When an amino acid dissolves in water, the carboxyl group dissociates, freeing a hydrogen ion, so becoming negatively charged. Meanwhile the amino group acquires a hydrogen ion and becomes positively charged. Therefore the ion formed has both a negative and a positive charge and is called a **zwitterion**.

The ability to take up hydrogen ions from a solution enables the amino acids to take up hydrogen ions readily from an acid solution, so making the solution less acid. On the other hand, amino acids release hydrogen ions readily in alkaline conditions, so making the solution less alkaline. For this reason, the amino acid can act as a **pH buffer**. A pH buffer is a substance which can resist a change in the acidity or alkalinity of its surroundings.

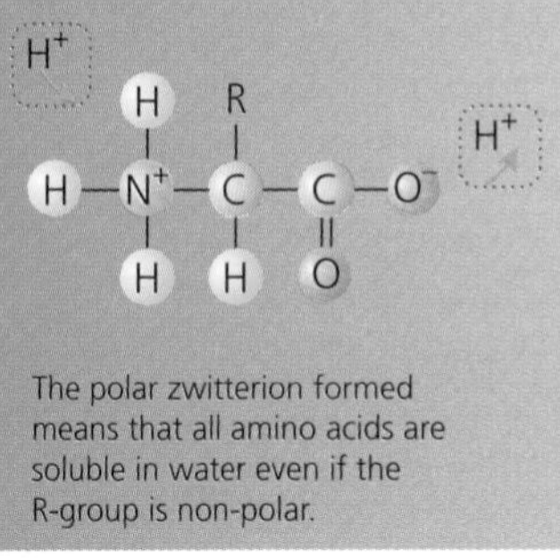

Figure 3.32 An amino acid dissolved in water forming a zwitterion

The polar zwitterion formed means that all amino acids are soluble in water even if the R-group is non-polar.

Condensation of amino acids

Two amino acids condense together, as shown, to form a **dipeptide**. The bond which is formed, linking the amino acids, is called a **peptide bond**.

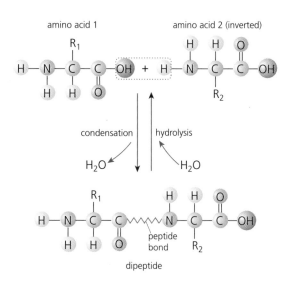

Figure 3.33 *Condensation of amino acids*

Further condensation reactions between amino acids lead to the formation of long chains called **polypeptides**. Amino acids may condense in any order and form chains of any length. All polypeptide chains formed will have similar 'backbones' containing peptide bonds. Every polypeptide has an 'amino end' with an amino group present and a 'carboxyl end' with a carboxyl group present. However, the order of R-groups along different chains varies.

There are twenty different amino acids available and polypeptide chains may be formed with any number and any different order of amino acids. It follows that it is possible to form an infinite number of different polypeptides with different properties.

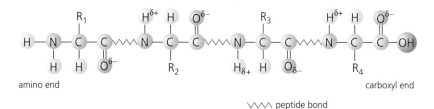

Figure 3.34 *A polypeptide (just four monomers long)*

Note: 1 Only the R-groups vary along the chain. The rest of the chain is always the same and is referred to as the 'backbone'.

    2 The $\overset{|}{C} = O$ and $-\overset{H}{\underset{|}{N}}-$ groups either side of the peptide bonds carry small charges, as shown, because of the distribution of electrons.

> **Remember**
>
> The order of R-groups along the polypeptide depends upon the sequence of amino acids forming monomers in the chain. Every different polypeptide is formed from a different sequence of amino acids. It is this order of R-groups which determines the shape and the properties of the polypeptide

Using a simple mathematical formula:

No. of different orders possible =

$$\text{No. of different amino acids available}^{\text{No. of monomers in chain}}$$

For example: if there were only two different amino acids available to make a tripeptide (3 monomers long), it would be possible to make eight different tripeptides (2^3).

8 How many different polypeptides would it be possible to form if twenty different amino acids were available and if the chain were to be one hundred monomers long? Give your answer in the style of the formula. *(1 mark)*

3.17 Levels of protein structure

1 Primary structure of proteins

This refers to the exact sequence of amino acids in the polypeptide(s) within a protein molecule. Only peptide bonds are involved in forming this sequence. Frederick Sanger was the first scientist to work out the primary structure of a protein. He took ten years (1944–1954) to analyse the structure of the protein, insulin. This relatively simple protein is a hormone which helps to control the amount of glucose present in the blood. The structure of insulin is shown in Figure 3.35.

2 Secondary structure of proteins

Figure 3.34 shows that parts of the backbone of every polypeptide carry small positive or negative charges. Hydrogen bonds form between these charges.

The secondary structure refers to the shape taken up by the polypeptide chain(s) within a protein molecule as the result of the formation of such hydrogen bonds.

As the backbones are the same in all polypeptides, the same shapes can be taken up by different polypeptides (or part of them). Therefore the shape is **not specific** to particular polypeptides. The shape is regular and is repeated along the chain.

The two commonest types of secondary structure are the alpha-helix and the beta-pleated sheet.

In the **alpha-helix**, the hydrogen bonds are formed between the CO of one amino acid with the NH of an amino acid four further along the chain. This twists the chain into a spiral (helical) form where the 'twists' are held in place by the hydrogen bonds. Just a small portion of a short chain may take up this configuration or long chains may become twisted into an alpha-helix along the whole length. Keratin, the insoluble protein of hair, nails and feathers, has molecules which are largely in this shape.

Primary and quaternary structure are shown but the coiling and folding of the secondary and tertiary structures are not demonstrated.

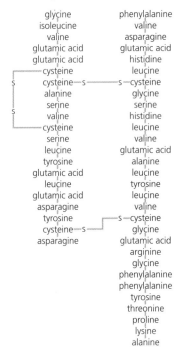

Figure 3.35 The structure of a molecule of insulin

In the **beta-pleated sheet**, adjacent portions of different polypeptide chains, if formed in opposite directions to each other (anti-parallel), may form a beta-pleated sheet. Hydrogen bonds form the –CO groups of one chain and –NH groups of neighbouring chains. This gives a stronger, but less elastic structure than the alpha-helix. An example of a protein with a structure largely based upon the beta-pleated sheet is the protein which makes up silk (fibroin).

Figure 3.36 Common types of secondary structure of polypeptide chains

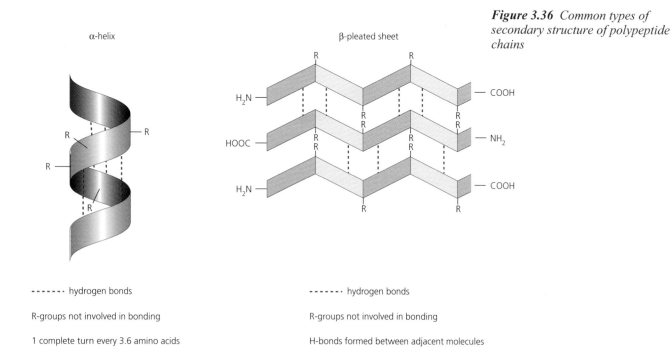

α-helix

β-pleated sheet

- - - - - - hydrogen bonds

R-groups not involved in bonding

1 complete turn every 3.6 amino acids

- - - - - - hydrogen bonds

R-groups not involved in bonding

H-bonds formed between adjacent molecules

3 The tertiary structure of proteins

This refers to the shape taken up by the polypeptide chain(s) of some proteins as a result of various bonds formed between parts of the **R-groups** of the chains. As every different polypeptide has a different order of R-groups, the bonds form in different places in every different polypeptide, leading to different shapes.

There are three types of bond which may be formed between R-groups, and these are mainly responsible for folding a polypeptide into its tertiary structure. They are the hydrogen bond, the ionic bond and the disulphide bond.

The **hydrogen bond** is very common but is the weakest of the three bonds. It is formed when the electropositive H atoms of the –OH or –NH of one R-group attract the electronegative O of a CO group in another R-group.

Ionic bonds form between amino and carboxyl parts present on some R-groups. These are stronger than hydrogen bonds but in water they are much weaker than the disulphide bond.

The **disulphide bond** is a covalent bond which is formed between the R-groups of amino acids such as cysteine which have –SH groups. This is the strongest bond of the three.

 Remember

The tertiary structure of every different polypeptide is different. The shape is said to be **'specific'**. As the function of a protein depends upon its shape, this fact is very significant

Figure 3.37 Bonds involved in formation of tertiary structure

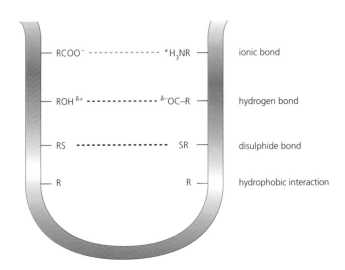

The shape which the chain takes up is also affected by the presence of hydrophobic R-groups which tend to take up a position away from water protected by other parts of the molecule.

All of these bonds and interactions tend to cause the protein to fold into an irregular, compact globular shape with hydrophilic parts on the outside in an aqueous environment. One molecule may become surrounded by a 'shell' of water molecules and become separated from others. Such proteins are said to be soluble forming a 'colloidal' solution. They are referred to as **globular proteins**. Insulin is an example of a globular protein. Parts of a polypeptide which fold in this way may already be in the form of an alpha-helix or beta-pleated sheet.

It is important to note that not all proteins fold into a tertiary structure, especially if they have very long polypeptide chains rich in hydrophobic amino acids. Proteins such as keratin, collagen and fibroin are insoluble and the molecules are unfolded and have a non-specific fibrous structure. They are referred to as **fibrous proteins**.

4 Quaternary structure of proteins
This refers to how many polypeptide chains are present in a protein molecule and how they are linked together.

It can also be used to describe the structure of **conjugated proteins**. Conjugated proteins have molecules in which polypeptide chain(s) are linked to a non-protein part of the molecule. The non-protein part is called the **prosthetic group**. A well-known conjugated protein is haemoglobin. This molecule contains four polypeptide chains and four 'haem' groups.

9 Using information from Figure 3.35, describe the quaternary structure of insulin.
(2 marks)

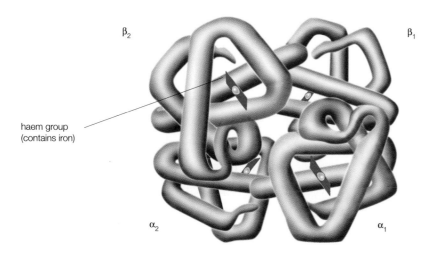

β₂   β₁

haem group
(contains iron)

α₂   α₁

Figure 3.38 Structure of a haemoglobin molecule

The molecule consists of 4 polypeptide chains (α_1, α_2, β_1 and β_2).
Each chain is attached to a 'haem' group.

Table 3.7 Summary of levels of protein structure

Level	Description	Bonds involved	Specificity	Where found
primary structure	order of amino acids cysteine | alanine | lysine | glycine | leucine	peptide bonds	specific	all proteins
secondary structure	repeating pattern formed by bonds between backbone	hydrogen bonds (may be stabilised further)	non-specific	most proteins
tertiary structure	irregular folding formed by bonds between R-groups	hydrogen bonds ionic bonds disulphide bonds (hydrophobic interactions)	specific	globular proteins
quaternary structure	linking of polypeptide chains in molecule	any of bonds above	specific in globular proteins	most proteins

Table 3.8 *Fibrous and globular proteins*

Fibrous proteins	Globular proteins
polypeptide chains parallel with little or no tertiary folding	polypeptide chains have tertiary structure and fold into compact shape
different proteins may have similar shapes and lengths of chains of same protein may vary	each protein has its own specific shape and length of chains
insoluble in water	soluble in water, making colloidal solutions
stable and tough	easily changed chemically, so not stable
have structural functions	have metabolic (chemical) functions

3.18 The 'stability' of proteins

A molecule is regarded as chemically stable if it does not react with other chemicals readily and is not changed easily by changing conditions, such as temperature.

The tertiary shape of globular proteins and, therefore, their vital properties are easily altered. The shape is dependent upon weak hydrogen and ionic bonds. A rise in temperature causes the molecules to vibrate more. This disrupts the hydrogen bonds and, as they break, the shape of the molecule alters.

The hydrogen bonds and ionic bonds are also affected by a change in pH of the solution because the changes in concentration of the positively charged hydrogen ions affect the forces of attraction holding the protein molecule in shape.

So globular proteins in solution are unstable as their shape is easily changed. If this happens, they cannot carry out their functions and they are said to be **denatured**. This is very significant if the globular proteins are enzymes (see Section 4.4, page 104).

The insoluble fibrous proteins, on the other hand, are much more stable.

3.19 Collagen

Collagen is an important fibrous protein. It is a major component of the connective tissues of the bodies of many animals. Connective tissues hold other tissues together and are found, for example, in tendons, blood vessel walls and fibres holding teeth in gums. Collagen is also important in bone where it binds inorganic crystals together, preventing the bones from being brittle and easily broken.

The collagen molecule is very stable and extremely strong. Each molecule consists of three polypeptide chains wound round each other to form a triple helix (rather like the strands of a rope twined around each other). The amino acid sequence in each chain is very regular and is mainly based on repetition of three amino acids. The lengths of the chains and hydrophobic nature of most of the R-groups make the molecule insoluble. Bonding between the three polypeptide chains gives the molecule strength. The molecules are further assembled into fibres which may be several millimetres long. The fibres produced are flexible but cannot be stretched.

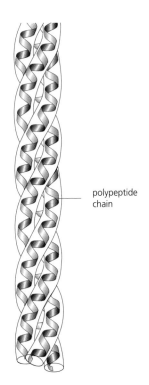

polypeptide chain

Figure 3.39 *The structure of a collagen molecule – the triple helix*

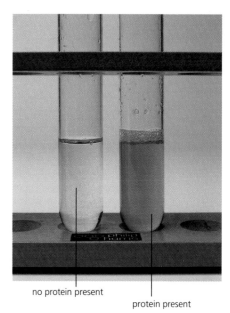

?

10 Vitamin C is involved in the formation of collagen. Explain why symptoms of 'scurvy', a disease associated with a lack of vitamin C, include the loosening of teeth and internal bleeding. *(3 marks)*

3.20 **Biochemical test for the presence of a protein (the biuret test)**

This test depends upon the fact that proteins react with alkaline copper(II) sulphate solution to form a mauve/lilac-coloured compound called 'biuret'.

Procedure A food sample is crushed in water and placed in a test tube. An equal volume of biuret reagent is added to the sample.

Result if protein present A mauve colour develops.

This test may also be carried out using separate solutions.

Procedure A food sample is crushed in water and placed in a test tube. An equal volume of 5% potassium hydroxide solution is added and mixed. Two drops of 1% copper sulphate solution are added and mixed.

Result if protein present A mauve colour develops.

no protein present

protein present

Figure 3.40 The biuret test

3.21 **The role of proteins**

Globular proteins

Globular proteins are found in colloidal solution or in cell membranes. Their functions are metabolic (chemical). A protein's specific shape enables it to 'fit' a particular, specific substance and carry out its function on that substance only. The most common roles of globular proteins are described below.

Globular proteins act as **enzymes**. The specific active site on the enzyme molecule fits its substrate, speeding up a reaction involving that substrate.

They also act as **carriers in membranes**. Some proteins in membranes combine with specific substances and transport them across the membrane, either by facilitated diffusion or by active transport.

Another role for globular proteins is as **receptor sites in membranes**. These proteins, found in membranes, fit a particular substance such as a hormone on the outside of the membrane. This combination triggers a particular reaction inside the cell. (Insulin fits into specific receptor sites in cell membranes, triggering cellular reactions. Insulin itself is also a protein, although this is not true of all hormones.)

Globular proteins are also useful as **antibodies**. The specific shape of antibodies enables them to fit specific antigens when defending the body against disease.

Various other functions are carried out by globular proteins. These include the transport of oxygen in the blood by the conjugated globular protein, haemoglobin, and the 'storage' of oxygen in muscle by myoglobin.

Fibrous proteins

The function of fibrous proteins depends upon their insolubility, strength and flexible, fibrous nature rather than their specific shape. However, different fibrous proteins do have slightly different properties. For example, the fibrous protein 'elastin' is more elastic than collagen and is predominant in tissues such as ligaments, where return to shape is important.

The functions of fibrous proteins are mainly related to support and movement. Some examples are as follows. Collagen gives **flexible strength** to tendons, blood vessel walls and skin. Elastin gives **strength and elasticity** to ligaments. Keratin is the **main substance** of hair, feathers and scales. Actin and myosin are needed for **muscle contraction**.

3.22 A useful biochemical technique – paper chromatography

Sometimes a solution may contain several solutes; for example, a mixture of sugars or a mixture of amino acids. Paper chromatography is a technique that allows you to separate and identify the solutes which are present. (You may have used it already to separate the chlorophyll pigments.)

The technique depends upon the fact that different solutes have different solubilities in the same solvent. In other words, some substances are more soluble than others in the same solvent. These substances are separated as the more soluble ones will stay in solution longer and be carried further along the paper. The simple procedure is summarised in Figure 3.41.

Figure 3.41 Paper chromatography

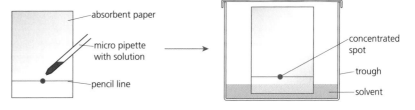

1 A drop of the solution is placed on a pencil line on absorbent paper and dried. This is repeated to concentrate the solute spot.

2 The paper is placed in a solvent.

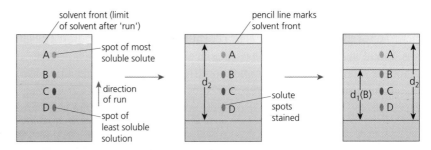

3 As the solvent 'runs' up the paper, it carries the solutes with it. The more soluble solutes are carried further.

4 A pencil line marks the distance moved by the solvent (d_2). If the solutes are colourless the spots are stained with a 'locating agent'.

5 The distance moved by each solute (d_1) is also measured. Calculation of d_1/d_2 gives the R_f value for a solute in that solvent. The R_f value for a solute in a given solvent is always the same and can be looked up in tables.

Two way paper chromatography

Sometimes two solutes in the same mixture have very similar solubilities, and it is difficult to distinguish between their spots. If this occurs, further separation can be achieved, as shown in Figure 3.42.

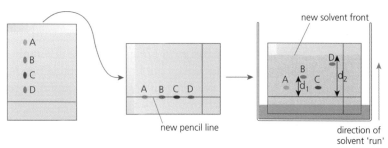

Figure 3.42 *Two way paper chromatography*

1 After completing the procedure above, the paper is turned through 90° and a pencil line is drawn through the line of solute spots.

2 The paper is placed in a different solvent. The further separation caused by the different solubilities in the second solvent makes it easier to measure the solute fronts. The R_f value of the solute in the second solvent is calculated.

Summary – ③ Biological molecules

- Molecules present in living organisms may be inorganic or organic.

Inorganic molecules

- Water – the dipolar nature of the water molecule makes water a good solvent for polar molecules and it is the medium in which metabolic reactions take place. Hydrogen bonds between the molecules give water important properties, such as high specific heat capacity and high latent heat of vaporisation as well as high cohesion and surface tension.

- Inorganic ions – a wide variety of ions are dissolved in the water in cytoplasm and extracellular fluids. They maintain the correct water potential of body solutions and have varied individual functions.

Organic molecules

- Carbohydrates provide energy and have the general formula $C_x(H_2O)_y$. They are divided into monosaccharides, disaccharides and polysaccharides.

- Monosaccharides are soluble reducing sugars with the formula $C_n(H_2O)_n$. These include trioses ($n = 3$), pentoses ($n = 5$) such as ribose, and hexoses ($n = 6$) such as glucose, fructose and galactose.

- Disaccharides are soluble sugars with the formula $C_{12}H_{22}O_{11}$. They are formed by the condensation of two hexose molecules. Examples include maltose and lactose which are reducing sugars and sucrose which is a non-reducing sugar.

- Polysaccharides are insoluble condensation polymers of glucose with the formula $(C_6H_{10}O_5)n$. Starch and glycogen act as energy stores. Cellulose gives structure to plant cell walls.

- Lipid molecules contain carbon, hydrogen and oxygen only. Lipids include triglycerides, waxes, steroids and phospholipids.

- Triglycerides are fats and oils. They have a high energy value. Their molecules are formed when glycerol condenses with three fatty acids forming ester bonds.

- Waxes make waterproof covering layers.

- Steroids are the basis of many hormones and cholesterol is a component of cell membranes.

- Phospholipids (which also contain phosphorus) have similar molecules to triglycerides but one fatty acid 'tail' is replaced by a hydrophilic phosphate 'head'. The molecules have hydrophobic and hydrophilic parts causing them to orientate themselves into bilayers in cell membranes.

- Proteins contain carbon, hydrogen, oxygen and nitrogen. They are polymers of amino acids. There are twenty common amino acids, all of which contain amino groups and carboxyl groups but have different R-groups. These condense together to form polypeptide chains in which they are linked by peptide bonds. A protein molecule consists of one or more polypeptide chains. The sequence of amino acids (and therefore R-groups) along a polypeptide chain determines the nature of the protein.

- Protein structure is considered on four levels: primary, secondary, tertiary and quaternary.

- Primary structure is the order of amino acids condensed in the polypeptides.

- Secondary structure is the repetitive pattern taken up by the chain as a result of hydrogen bonds formed between parts of the backbone. It is non-specific.

- Tertiary structure is the irregular folding into a compact shape as a result of bonds between the R-groups. It is specific and superimposed upon secondary structure.

- Quaternary structure is the arrangement of polypeptide chains in the protein molecule.

- Proteins may be subdivided into globular and fibrous proteins.

- Globular proteins are soluble with specific shapes as the result of tertiary folding; they have metabolic functions.

- Fibrous proteins are insoluble fibres with no tertiary structure; they have structural functions.

- Conjugated proteins are compounds whose molecules contain a protein part and a non-protein part (prosthetic group).

Table 3.9 *Summary of biochemical tests for the presence of biological molecules. (For experimental details, see original descriptions in this chapter)*

Procedure	Result if present
1 Reducing sugar, e.g. glucose or maltose • add Benedict's solution • heat the mixture at 90 °C for four minutes	a brick red precipitate is formed in the original blue solution
2 Non-reducing sugar e.g. sucrose • boil in a water bath with dilute hydrochloric acid for two minutes • cool the mixture • neutralise by adding dilute sodium hydroxide solution (confirm by using Universal Indicator paper) • carry out the Benedict's test, as described above	a brick red precipitate is formed
3 Starch • add yellow iodine solution	a blue-black colour is produced
4 Lipid • add ethanol and shake the mixture vigorously • allow to settle and then pour ethanol into another tube containing cold water	the mixture becomes cloudy as tiny droplets of lipid come out of solution, forming an emulsion
5 Protein • crush food sample in water and pour into a test tube • add an equal volume of biuret reagent	a mauve colour develops

? Answers

1 (a) Alpha-glucose and fructose. *(1)* **(b)** Alpha-glucose and galactose. *(1)*

2 (i) Amylose monomer is alpha-glucose, cellulose monomer is beta-glucose. amylose monomers are not inverted, alternate cellulose monomers are inverted. amylose chain coils, cellulose chain does not coil. *(max 2)*

(ii) Glycogen chains shorter than amylopectin chains. Glycogen chains more branched than amylopectin chains. *(2)*

3 No precipitate forms originally in Benedict's test as no reducing sugar present.*(1)* Boiling in acid hydrolyses sucrose as follows *(1)*: sucrose + water = glucose + fructose. *(1)* Glucose and fructose are reducing sugars and so produce a precipitate in the Benedict's test. *(1)*

4 The blue-black compound is formed with amylose. *(1)* There is no amylose in glycogen or cellulose. *(1)*

5 Amylose is a condensation polymer, a triglyceride is not. Only one type of basic unit (alpha-glucose) in amylose; a triglyceride has glycerol and fatty acids. Amylose has glycosidic bonds; a triglyceride has ester bonds. *(max 2)*

6 (a) A bond formed when glycerol condenses with a fatty acid. *(1)* **(b)** A molecule containing a carboxyl group attached to a hydrocarbon chain which contains, at least, one double bond between the carbon atoms *(1)*.

7 Triglyceride units are not similar. *(1)* Units are not arranged in a long chain. *(1)*

8 20^{100} *(1)*.

9 Insulin consists of two polypeptide chains *(1)* linked by two disulphide bonds. *(1)*

10 Poor development of collagen *(1)* which forms part of the tissue holding teeth in the gums *(1)* and making a major part of blood vessel walls. *(1)*

End of Chapter Questions

1 You are provided with normal laboratory equipment, water and amylase solution (which speeds up the hydrolysis of starch to maltose). Explain how, in three steps, you could produce pure cellulose powder from a dry mixture of powdered starch, sucrose, glucose and cellulose. *(3 marks)*

2 For each of the following compounds: **(a)** phospholipid, **(b)** collagen, **(c)** cellulose, **(d)** a globular protein,

(i) state **one** function of this compound in an organism,

(ii) describe **one** feature of its molecular structure which makes it suitable for its role. *(8 marks)*

3 Figure 3.38 shows a diagrammatic view of a molecule of the conjugated protein, haemoglobin. For this molecule, explain what is meant by its primary, secondary, tertiary and quaternary structures. *(4 marks)*

4 The following are organic compounds: glucose, triglyceride, cellulose, globular protein, sucrose, conjugated protein, glycogen, phospholipid, fibrous protein, starch.

(a) For which of the above compounds are the following statements true?

(i) They contain carbon, hydrogen and oxygen only.

(ii) They contain glycosidic bonds.

(iii) They can be hydrolysed into smaller molecules.

(b) With reference to the above compounds make up a statement which would be true for:

(i) starch and glycogen only,

(ii) starch, glycogen and triglyceride only,

(iii) starch, glycogen, triglyceride, fibrous protein and cellulose only.

(6 marks)

5 The diagram below shows the structure of a lipid molecule.

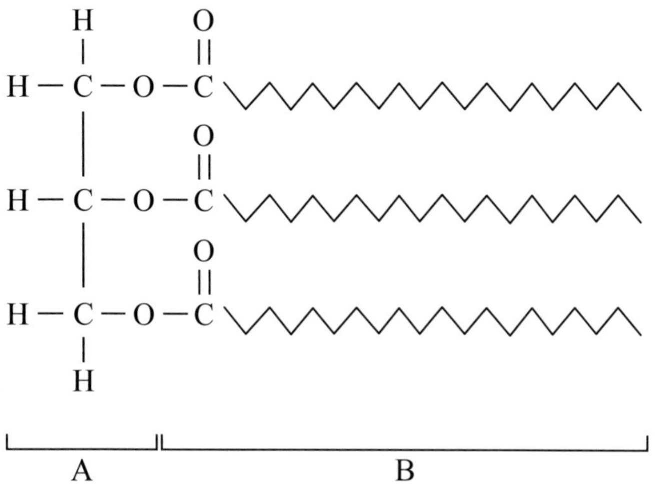

(a) **(i)** Name the parts labelled A and B. *(2 marks)*

(ii) Name this type of lipid. *(1 mark)*

(iii) Name the chemical reaction used to form the bonds between A and B. *(1 mark)*

(b) **(i)** State *one* function of this type of lipid in living organisms. *(1 mark)*

(ii) State *one* feature of the molecules of this type of lipid which makes them suitable for the function you have given. *(1 mark)*

(Total 6 marks)

Edexcel (London) 1997

6 An investigation was carried out to identify the biological compounds present in a seed. Samples from the seed were tested with a number of different reagents.

(a) Complete the table to show the conclusions which could be drawn from the results.

Test	Result of test	Conclusion
iodine in potassium iodide solution added	blue/black colour	
boiled with Benedict's or Fehling's solution	blue colour	
biuret solution added	lilac colour	

(3 marks)

(b) Describe how the investigator could have tested for cellulose and give the result which would confirm its presence. *(2 marks)*

(Total 5 marks)

AQA (NEAB) 1997

7 Observe the diagram of a paper chromatogram below. A, B and C represent three amino acids.

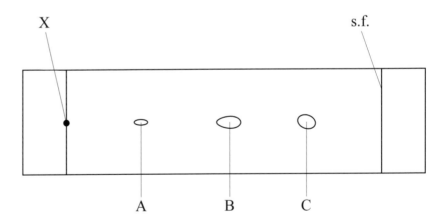

(a) What does s.f. represent? *(1 mark)*

(b) What would originally have been present at point X? *(1 mark)*

N3.2 (c) The R_f value of an amino acid is the distance moved by the amino acid divided by the distance between X and s.f. What is the R_f value of amino acid B? (Show your working.) *(2 marks)*

(d) Suggest why the R_f values of A, B and C are different. *(1 mark)*

(Total 5 marks)

OCR (Oxford) 1998

8 The table below refers to *two* organic molecules.

If the statement is correct for the molecule, place a tick (✓) in the appropriate box. If it is incorrect, place a cross (✗) in the appropriate box.

Statement	Triglyceride	Glycogen
contains only carbon, hydrogen and oxygen		
glycosidic bonds present		
soluble in water		
provides storage of energy		
occurs in flowering plants and animals		

(Total 5 marks)

Edexcel (London) 1998

4 Enzymes

You will probably be most familiar with **extracellular** enzymes, which are secreted by some cells, and catalyse reactions outside the cell. The enzymes of digestion, which break down food into smaller molecules, are good examples of these. However, all cells contain many enzymes which never leave the cell. These are called **intracellular** enzymes. Their role is to catalyse biochemical reactions taking place within the cell.

This chapter includes:
- enzyme structure and function
- factors which affect enzyme activity
- types of enzymes
- commercial uses of enzymes
- immobilised enzymes.

4.1 What are enzymes?

Enzymes are **catalysts**. A catalyst is a substance which increases the rate of a chemical reaction without itself being used up. Industrial processes use catalysts to speed up the production of important chemicals, reducing the need for high temperatures and pressures. The reactions inside living things have to take place at atmospheric pressure and very low temperatures when compared with industrial reactions. For example, the human body temperature is 37°C, and without catalysts the reactions would be too slow to sustain life.

As well as this, an organism's **metabolism** consists of thousands of *different* reactions: each of these needs a different catalyst to enable the reaction to take place. These catalysts are called **enzymes**.

The substance (or substances) upon which the enzyme acts is called its **substrate**.

Metabolism consists of hundreds of reactions linked together, where the product of one reaction is the substrate for the next. This is known as a **metabolic pathway**, and each step is catalysed by a different enzyme, as shown by this simple equation, where the letters A to E represent different compounds in a metabolic pathway:

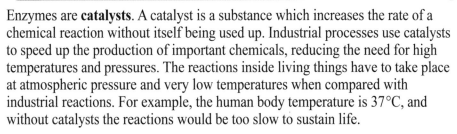

$$A \xrightarrow{\text{enzyme}_1} B \xrightarrow{\text{enzyme}_2} C \xrightarrow{\text{enzyme}_3} D \xrightarrow{\text{enzyme}_4} E$$

?

1 If a cell was unable to make enzyme$_2$, what would happen in the cell to the level of: (a) compound C; (b) compound B? *(2 marks)*

4.2 How enzymes work

Since there are thousands of different reactions happening in cells, and each requires a different, or **specific** enzyme, it follows that enzymes must be made of a type of chemical which can vary enormously in its structure. This is the case. Enzymes are proteins, which in turn are composed of sub-units called amino acids (see Section 3.16, page 83 for a description of protein structure).

There are about twenty different amino acids, and these can be linked together in an almost infinite number of different ways. This means that the primary structure (and also the tertiary structure) of enzymes can show the variability needed to achieve specificity. In particular, this specificity depends upon the shape of a small part of the enzyme molecule where the enzyme actually comes into contact with the substrate molecule, called the **active site**. This is a small 'cleft' in the

Definition

An enzyme is an organic catalyst which speeds up chemical reactions in organisms.

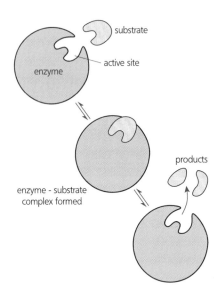

Figure 4.1 *'Lock and key' model of enzyme action*

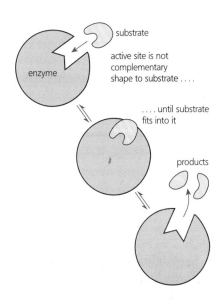

Figure 4.2 *Induced fit model of enzyme action*

surface of the enzyme where certain amino acid residues are exposed. The substrate molecule fits into the active site and interacts with these amino acids by ionic and hydrogen bonding, forming an **enzyme-substrate complex**. A reaction then occurs, and the product leaves the active site.

This mechanism is known as the **lock and key** model of enzyme action, where the substrate is analogous to a key fitting into the enzyme's lock (Figure 4.1). The precise shape of the active site is important: it must be **complementary** to the shape of the substrate.

A more recent version of this mechanism is the **induced fit** model. This suggests that the enzyme's active site does not 'fit' the substrate until the substrate actually enters it. In other words the shape of the enzyme is flexible and moulds to fit the substrate, rather like a hand changing the shape of a glove when the glove is worn (Figure 4.2). Only the new, *induced* configuration of the enzyme is catalytically active.

?

2 Explain the main difference between the lock and key and the induced fit models of enzyme action. *(3 marks)*

Notice that in both Figure 4.1 and Figure 4.2 the reactions are shown as **reversible**. This is true of all enzyme-catalysed reactions. The enzyme will catalyse the reaction equally well in either direction. The direction which the reaction takes depends on the relative concentrations of the substrate(s) and product(s). For example, in the following reaction:

$$A + B \rightleftharpoons C$$

If the concentration of C is high, the reaction will go from right to left, and if the concentrations of the reactants A and B are high, the reaction will go from left to right. An enzyme has no effect on the *point* of equilibrium: it just affects the *time taken* to reach equilibrium. In cells this is not normally important, because the products are removed by being converted into something else, or used up in some other metabolic process. This means that the reaction will go forwards, from left to right.

4.3 **Energy changes during reactions**

When a chemical reaction takes place, bonds in the reacting molecules will first need to be broken and then new bonds formed in the products. Breaking bonds requires energy (it is **endergonic**) whereas forming bonds gives out energy (**exergonic**). There will be a difference in the energy contained within the reactant and product molecules. If the product molecules contain more energy than the reactants, the overall reaction will be endergonic, requiring an external source of energy for it to happen.

Metabolism consists of **anabolism** and **catabolism**. Anabolic reactions are the type where large, complex molecules are built up from smaller ones. These reactions are endergonic. A good example is the synthesis of proteins from amino acids in the cell (see Section 5.7, page 132). **Photosynthesis** is also an anabolic reaction, using light energy to 'drive' the process. Catabolic reactions, where large, complex molecules are broken down into simpler ones, are exergonic. In **respiration**, for example, food is oxidised to liberate the chemical energy it contains. However, *all* reactions begin with the breaking of bonds, and the energy to do this is called the **activation energy**.

All catalysts, including enzymes, work by *lowering the activation energy* for the reaction which they catalyse. They do this by forming an enzyme-substrate complex. This complex (Figure 4.1) has a lower energy level than the first breakdown products of the substrate would have *without* the enzyme. In other words, the enzyme-substrate complex allows the initial breaking of bonds in the substrate to take place more easily. This is easiest to visualise as a graph, where the energy of the chemical system is plotted against the course of the reaction (Figure 4.3).

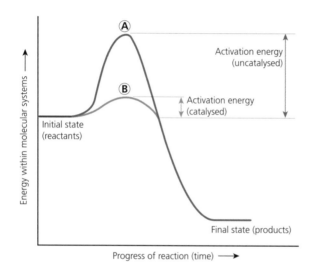

Figure 4.3 Energy contained within chemical systems before, during and after a reaction

Ⓐ = Energy of transition state in uncatalysed reaction.
Ⓑ = Energy of transition state, ie enzyme-substrate complex, during catalysed reaction.

Take the example of starch breakdown, as happens in digestion. If no enzyme is available, the activation energy for starch to be hydrolysed to maltose is very high. At body temperature and with the chemical conditions of the body it would not happen. But when the enzyme amylase is present (as in the mouth or intestine) the activation energy for the hydrolysis reaction is lowered by the starch combining with the amylase. The starch can now be converted into maltose.

3 Explain the difference between an endergonic and an exergonic reaction.

(2 marks)

 Remember

Chemical reactions which give out energy are called **exergonic**. If this energy is in the form of heat (for example, when a fuel is burned) the reaction is called **exothermic**. The opposite case is when a reaction takes in energy. This is called **endergonic**. If the energy for this is in the form of heat, the reaction is called **endothermic**.

4.4 Factors affecting the activity of enzymes

The activity of an enzyme is a measure of how well it catalyses its particular reaction. This can be found from the rate of formation of products, or the rate of disappearance of the substrate. Various factors affect this activity. These include:

● temperature

● pH

● concentration of enzyme

● concentration of substrate

● presence of molecules called inhibitors.

Temperature

An increase in temperature will increase the kinetic energy of molecules. In the case of enzymes, this will mean that the increased movement of both enzyme and substrate molecules will result in more collisions between them, and more successful conversions of the substrate into product. So as the temperature rises, the rate of an enzyme-catalysed reaction increases. However, beyond a certain point, higher temperatures begin to change the shape of the enzyme molecule. Remember that enzymes are globular proteins (see Section 3.17, page 88). Their tertiary structure is maintained by bonds between the amino acid R-groups of a polypeptide chain. High temperatures cause these bonds to break, damaging the tertiary structure of the protein. If the three-dimensional shape of the active site is altered, substrate molecules will be unable to combine with it, and the rate of the reaction will decrease. The rate at any particular temperature therefore depends on the balance between these two factors, producing an **optimum temperature** where the reaction takes place most rapidly (Figure 4.4).

This irreversible change in the structure of the enzyme at high temperatures is called **denaturation**. In the same way, the protein of egg-white is denatured by boiling, and changes from a clear runny liquid to a white solid. Denaturation is a gradual process, and the extent to which it takes place will depend on the time of exposure of the enzyme to high temperatures, as well as the actual temperature. It also depends on the type of enzyme. Organisms have evolved enzymes which are adapted to the temperature of their surroundings. Most enzymes of the human body have an optimum temperature of about 40 °C, but some species of bacteria which live in hot springs have enzymes which are not denatured by temperatures as high as 95 °C.

> ### Remember
>
> Denaturation is a permanent change in the tertiary structure of a protein. It is due to bonds between R-groups of the polypeptide chain being broken. In the case of enzymes, this alters the shape of the active site, so that it is no longer complementary to the shape of the substrate. The enzyme can therefore no longer catalyse the reaction.

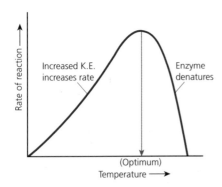

Figure 4.4 The effect of temperature on the activity of an enzyme

pH

Most enzymes also have an **optimum pH** at which they function best (Figure 4.5). A change in pH means a change in the concentration of hydrogen ions (H^+) in the surroundings of the enzyme, which affects the ionisation of R-groups in the amino acid residues of the protein molecule. This also affects the shape of the active site and binding with the substrate. At the optimum pH, the shape of the active site is best suited to the formation of an enzyme-substrate complex.

In the human body most enzymes have an optimum pH of about 7 (neutral) but there are exceptions. Pepsin, the enzyme secreted by the stomach which digests proteins, has an optimum pH of about 2, whereas arginase, which is involved with the synthesis of urea by the liver, has an optimum pH of 10. Either side of the optimum, a change of pH results in a decrease in the rate of the enzyme-catalysed reaction. If the pH is far from the optimum this can result in irreversible denaturing of the enzyme.

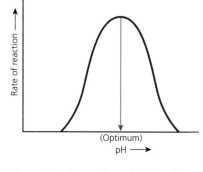

Figure 4.5 The effect of pH on the activity of an enzyme

Enzyme concentration

An enzyme is not used up during the reaction which it catalyses, and the active site can be used again and again for further catalysis. Enzymes therefore work efficiently at very low concentrations. Usually the substrate molecules are in excess, and the rate of reaction is limited by the concentration of the enzyme. Therefore, if the concentration of the enzyme is increased, the number of collisions with the substrate molecules, and hence the rate of reaction, will increase (Figure 4.6).

Substrate concentration

If the concentration of the substrate is low, some of the active sites of the enzyme molecules will be unoccupied, and the rate of reaction will be low. If, under these conditions, the concentration of the substrate is increased, more enzyme-substrate complexes can form and the rate will increase. This happens until the substrate is at a high enough concentration to be in excess. The rate will then approach a maximum called V_{max} (Figure 4.7) when all the active sites at any moment are occupied or **saturated** with substrate.

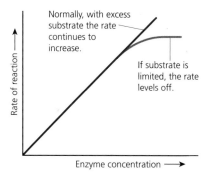

Figure 4.6 The effect of enzyme concentration on the activity of an enzyme

! Did You Know

The maximum number of substrate molecules that can be turned into product by one molecule of enzyme per minute is called the enzyme's **turnover number**. It is a measure of the enzyme's catalytic power. Enzymes vary a good deal in their turnover number, but the record goes to **carbonic anhydrase**. This is an enzyme which catalyses the combination of carbon dioxide with water to form carbonic acid in red blood cells (see Section 11.7, page 321). Carbonic anhydrase has a turnover number of 36×10^6, or 36 million molecules per minute.

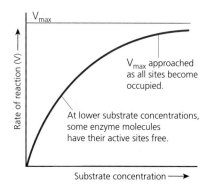

Figure 4.7 The effect of substrate concentration on the activity of an enzyme

4 Assuming all other factors are kept constant, explain why increasing the concentration of substrate does not always increase the rate of reaction.

(1 mark)

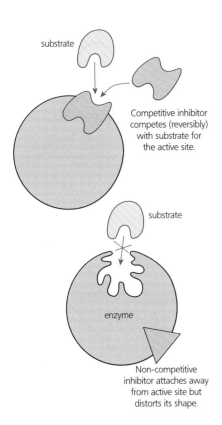

substrate

Competitive inhibitor competes (reversibly) with substrate for the active site.

substrate

enzyme

Non-competitive inhibitor attaches away from active site but distorts its shape.

Figure 4.8 *Competitive and non-competitive enzyme inhibitors*

Inhibitors

Inhibitors are chemicals which reduce the rate of an enzyme-catalysed reaction, and they all do so by altering the shape of the active site, either directly or indirectly. There are various categories of inhibitor. One way that they are classified is into **reversible** and **non-reversible** (or **permanent**) inhibitors. Reversible inhibitors only bind temporarily to the enzyme, so that their effect is not permanent, whereas non-reversible inhibitors bind permanently, leaving the enzyme unable to carry out further catalysis.

Reversible inhibitors may also be **competitive** or **non-competitive**. Competitive inhibitors have a molecular shape which is similar to the substrate. They can fit into the active site of the enzyme, preventing the substrate from occupying it, and reducing the number of enzyme-substrate complexes. They are sometimes referred to as **active-site directed** inhibitors. Competitive inhibitors therefore *compete* for the active site with the substrate, but since this is only temporary, when the inhibitor leaves, the substrate can occupy the active site. With competitive inhibitors the degree of inhibition depends on the relative concentration of substrate and inhibitor. Increasing the concentration of the substrate will reduce the effect of the competitive inhibitor. Non-competitive inhibitors do not become attached to the active site, but bind to other parts of the enzyme, altering the overall shape of the enzyme molecule, including the active site (Figure 4.8). These are also called **non-active site directed** inhibitors.

> **Remember**
>
> The terms 'competitive' and 'reversible' and 'non-competitive' and 'non-reversible' do not mean the same thing. This causes confusion in examinations (and in some text books)!
>
> - competitive inhibitors are always reversible
> - non-competitive inhibitors may be reversible or permanent
> - non-reversible inhibitors are always non-competitive

Non-reversible inhibitors leave the enzyme permanently damaged. For example, ions of heavy metals such as mercury (Hg^+), silver (Ag^+) and arsenic (As^+) irreversibly alter the tertiary molecular structure of a protein by breaking its disulphide bonds.

> **Remember**
>
> Denaturation of an enzyme can take place as a result of:
>
> - high temperatures
> - extremes of pH
> - the presence of non-reversible inhibitors

> **Did You Know**
>
> Another non-reversible enzyme inhibitor is the ion cyanide (CN^-). This extremely toxic substance combines with enzymes involved in cellular respiration, preventing energy production by cells, rapidly resulting in death.

> ❓
>
> 5 What are the definitions of the following terms:
>   *(a)* active site   *(3 marks)*
>   *(b)* enzyme specificity   *(2 marks)*
>   *(c)* denaturing?   *(5 marks)*

Extension

Box 4.1 Classification of enzymes

Early biochemists did not use a systematic approach when naming enzymes, and many are still known by their old names, such as trypsin, pepsin, rennin and catalase. More modern nomenclature simply adds the suffix *-ase* to the name of the substrate. For example, the enzyme which hydrolyses lipids to fatty acids and glycerol is called lipase; the enzyme involved in the replication of DNA is called DNA polymerase. In 1961 the International Union of Biochemistry introduced a system of classification which divided enzymes into six groups according to the general type of reaction they catalysed. The six groups are:

1. Oxidoreductases Catalyse transfer of H or O atoms, or electrons, from one compound to another (i.e. oxidation-reduction reactions), e.g. *dehydrogenases*, *oxidases*.

2. Transferases Catalyse the transfer of a particular group from one compound to another, e.g. the transfer of an amino-group (*transaminases*) or a phosphate (*phosphorylases*).

3. Hydrolases Catalyse hydrolysis reactions, splitting of covalent bonds by the addition of water, e.g. *amylase*, *lipases*, *peptidases*.

4. Lyases Catalyse elimination of a group on the substrate to form a double bond, or addition of a group across a double bond, e.g. *decarboxylases*.

5. Isomerases Catalyse intra-molecular rearrangements – one isomer being converted into another, e.g. *isomerases*, *mutases*.

6. Ligases Catalyse bond formation between two compounds using energy derived from hydrolysis of a molecule such as ATP, e.g. *synthetases*.

4.5 The commercial uses of enzymes

Enzymes synthesised by bacterial and fungal cells have been used for thousands of years in processes like brewing, baking and cheese manufacture. However, the process of catalysis by enzymes within whole cells is inefficient, because the products may be used up by the cells, or contaminated with cell debris and by-products. Enzymes separated from the cells which produce them (cell-free preparations) are more useful, since they retain their catalytic powers while giving greater efficiency of substrate conversion and greater yield of product.

Enzymes have enormous powers of catalysis when compared with inorganic catalysts, and they catalyse their reactions in aqueous solutions at low temperatures and at atmospheric pressure. Because of these properties, and because the reactions which they catalyse are *specific*, the market for commercially produced enzymes is very large, and growing (in 1999 it was estimated to be worth about £1 billion). This growing market is due to the increased use of micro-organisms to produce enzymes in bulk and on demand.

! Did You Know

The word 'enzyme' means 'in yeast', and was first used to describe the active ingredient, made by yeast, which was capable of fermenting sugar to alcohol.

6 Why is it advantageous to carry out industrial processes at low temperatures and pressures? *(2 marks)*

Enzymes are used in a number of processes, including food manufacture, the production of pharmaceuticals and chemicals, analytical methods and medical research. Several hundred enzymes have been identified which have a commercial application. Table 4.1 shows a summary of some commonly used enzymes.

Table 4.1 *Some commercial applications of isolated enzymes*

Enzyme	Reaction	Use
α-amylase	starch hydrolysis	stain remover for clothes, dishwasher additive, conversion of starch to glucose in food industry, thickening sauces, flour improver, paper manufacture, vegetable juice extraction and many other uses
catalase	breakdown of hydrogen peroxide to water and oxygen	preservative in soft drinks, production of oxygen to form bubbles in foam rubber
cellulases	breakdown of cellulose in plant cell walls	washing powder colour brightener, clarification of fruit juices
glucose isomerase	conversion of glucose to fructose (which has sweeter taste)	sweetener in soft drinks, making cakes, jams, fillers and icings
glucose oxidase	oxidation of glucose	preservative in soft drinks, detection of glucose levels in blood of diabetics
lactase (β-galactosidase)	hydrolysis of the milk sugar lactose to glucose and galactose	sweetening milk drinks, preparing milk products for lactose-intolerant people
pectinases	breakdown of pectin in plant cell walls	clarification of wine and fruit juices, release of juice from fruit and citrus peel extracts for soft drinks
proteases	digestion of protein	additive to make 'biological' detergents for washing machines and dishwashers, flour improvers, leather manufacture, making meat extracts and many other uses
rennin (chymosin)	coagulation of milk protein (casein)	cheese production and baby food manufacture. Use of microbially produced rennin avoids need to obtain rennin from stomachs of calves

It is worthwhile considering some examples of the commercial uses of enzymes in more detail.

Enzymes in detergents

You may have thought that 'biological' washing powders and liquids were a relatively new invention. In fact the first patent for the use of pancreatic enzymes to digest proteins was issued as long ago as 1913. However, its use was limited, due to the low stability of the enzyme preparation. In the 1960s an alkaline protease called 'subtilisin' was obtained from the bacterium *Bacillus subtilis*. This enzyme is stable in the conditions needed for a detergent wash, that is high pH, presence of phosphates and other ingredients, and temperatures of up to 60°C.

Modern biological detergents contain a number of enzymes which digest protein-based stains such as blood, gravy and grass as well as starchy stains (Figure 4.9). These can work efficiently at temperatures as low as 40°C, saving energy and preventing damage to delicate fabrics. Addition of a cellulase to the washing powder breaks down microfibrils that form on cotton cloth during wear. This enhances the colour of the washed clothes. There has been less success in the use of lipid-digesting enzymes in washing powders, as the lipases do not function well in water. They digest the fatty dirt better during the spin part of the cycle, when the clothes are not soaking. It may soon be possible to 'tailor' the amino acid sequence of genetically engineered lipases to improve their efficiency during the wash cycle.

Persil Performance Tablets contain amongst other ingredients:	
Less than 5%	Soap, Aliphatic hydrocarbon, Zeolite, Polycarboxylate, Phosphonate, Nonionic surfactants.
5% - 15%	Anionic surfactant, Oxygen based bleaching agent (percarbonate).
More than 30%	Phosphate.
Also contains enzymes and a brightening agent.	

Figure 4.9 *Enzymes in biological detergents*

7 What are the advantages of a biological washing powder? Can you think of any disadvantages?   *(4 marks)*

Pectinases and cellulases in food and drink manufacture

The primary cell wall of plant cells consists mainly of cellulose, but contains smaller amounts of other polysaccharides such as **hemicelluloses** and **pectin**. Hemicelluloses, like cellulose, are composed of β-glucose, but with additional side chains of other sugars. Pectins are made of the sugar galactose and its organic acid, galacturonic acid, which forms a salt with calcium ions, called calcium pectate. This pectate attracts water molecules, forming a **gel** which acts as an interstitial 'cement' between the cellulose microfibrils, bonded to the cellulose by the hemicellulose molecules.

This ability of pectin to form a gel is used in the manufacture of jam, but it is not wanted in the production of fruit juices and other products. A group of enzymes called **pectinases** will break down pectin into its monosaccharide building blocks. If pectinases are added to crushed fruit such as grapes and apples, breakdown of the pectins allows more juice to be extracted, and **clarifies** (clears) the juice. Pectinases are also used to clarify wine and vinegar, and to prevent concentrated fruit juices from forming gels.

Similarly, **cellulases** break down cellulose to shorter chains of sugars and β-glucose. They can be used to clarify orange and lemon juice, as well as beer. They also improve the release of colour from fruit skins. Cellulases are used to break down cellulose in rye grass and straw to produce an animal feed supplement, and they have great potential for use in dealing with other waste plant materials such as sawdust and paper.

Enzymes as analytical reagents

Enzymes, because of their high degree of specificity, can be used to identify one type of molecule from a mixture of different types. They are also very sensitive, so can be used as analytical reagents, measuring the level of substances even when they are present in very low concentrations.

Urea assay

The enzyme **urease** has long been used for analysing body fluids (blood and urine) for the waste product urea. Urease hydrolyses the urea in a blood or urine sample into carbon dioxide and ammonia:

$$\underset{\text{urea}}{CO(NH_2)_2} + H_2O \rightarrow CO_2 + \underset{\text{ammonia}}{2NH_3}$$

The ammonia formed can be measured by the colour change it produces when reacted with an indicator. The degree of colour development is measured in a colorimeter, and is proportional to the concentration of ammonia, which is in turn proportional to the concentration of urea. This method can easily be used to measure the normal levels of urea in blood ($2.5–6.0$ mmol dm^{-3}). More recently, biosensors (see Box 4.2) have been developed which employ the same method.

Glucose assay

Two enzymes are used in another analytical method, for determining the concentration of glucose in blood or urine. **Glucose oxidase** catalyses the oxidation of glucose to gluconic acid and hydrogen peroxide:

$$\text{glucose} + O_2 \rightarrow \text{gluconic acid} + H_2O_2$$

The hydrogen peroxide produced then oxidises a colourless organic **chromogen** XH_2 to its coloured form, X, by removal of hydrogen. A chromogen is a substance which develops (*gen*erates) a colour:

$$\underset{\text{(colourless)}}{XH_2} + H_2O_2 \rightarrow 2H_2O + \underset{\text{(coloured)}}{X}$$

This second reaction is catalysed by another enzyme called **peroxidase**. The amount of the coloured substance X produced is a direct measure of the concentration of glucose present at the start, and can be measured in a colorimeter. The method is very specific for glucose: the reactions will not be affected by other sugars in the biological fluid. The glucose oxidase, peroxidase and XH_2 can be attached to a cellulose pad on a test strip (e.g. 'clinistix' or 'urostix') and used by people with diabetes to test their blood or urine for glucose.

Box 4.2 Biosensors

The ability of enzymes to recognise specific molecules means that they can be used as molecular **probes** or **biosensors**. A biosensor is an instrument for quickly and easily carrying out a diagnostic test, such as the monitoring of a metabolite in the blood. The biosensor contains an immobilised enzyme (see Section 4.6, below), which reacts with the molecule which is to be detected. The reaction causes a change which is converted (transduced) into an electrical signal. The change might be the formation of a product of the reaction, or the movement of electrons during it, or even the emission of light (Figure 4.10a).

One of the first biosensors to be developed uses the enzyme **glucose oxidase** described above. At the tip of the probe, the immobilised enzyme is held in a gel attached to an oxygen electrode. This measures the concentration of oxygen dissolved in a solution. When the tip is placed in a drop of blood, glucose in the blood diffuses into the enzyme gel, and oxygen is used up as the enzyme breaks down the glucose. The electrode monitors the oxygen level and converts it to an electrical signal and a digital display which is calibrated to show the concentration of glucose in the blood. Such a biosensor is invaluable to people with diabetes, who need to quickly and easily monitor their blood glucose levels (Figure 4.10b).

Biosensors are not just used in medicine. They have been developed for monitoring the presence of many chemicals in various areas of industry, agriculture and environmental science. For example, nitrate and pesticide pollutants can be measured in water supplies, or drugs and alcohol in human blood.

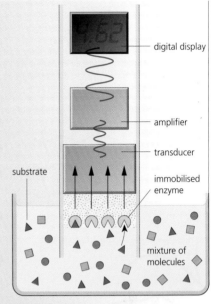

Figure 4.10 (a) Principles of a biosensor

(b) Blood glucose biosensor

4.6 Immobilisation of enzymes

Enzymes which are isolated from cells or tissues are much more useful if they are not in solution, but instead **immobilised** by being attached to, or trapped within, an insoluble material. This has several advantages over the use of dissolved enzymes:

- The enzymes are much more stable at high temperatures.

- They are more resistant to changes in pH.

- They are less likely to be degraded by organic solvents.

- The products are uncontaminated by enzyme and can be collected more easily.

- The enzyme can be retained and re-used.

- Use of columns of immobilised enzyme allows automation of the industrial process.

These advantages are very important for industrial processes. Such processes often need to use high temperatures and extremes of pH, as well as organic solvents, to work efficiently. Elevated temperatures produce an increased rate of yield of product. Costs are also minimised if the enzyme is not lost with the product, but trapped in the immobilised form to be used for further reactions.

A number of different substances have been developed as materials for binding enzymes, including alginate, cellulose, porous glass, agar gel, nylon, collagen and porous alumina. There are five basic methods of immobilisation (Figure 4.11):

● **adsorption** onto a material such as porous glass

● **covalent bonding** to a solid such as cellulose

● **crossing-linking** between enzyme molecules using reagents such as glutaraldehyde

● **entrapment** within the internal structure of a polymer such as collagen or alginate

● **encapsulation** within a selectively permeable membrane, such as nylon.

Each method has advantages and disadvantages. For example, covalent bonding is commonly used, but is expensive. The enzyme forms stable covalent links with the supporting matrix, but it must be ensured that the active site on each molecule is exposed. Entrapment is also widely used. Since the enzyme is trapped, rather than bound, its catalytic properties are not affected. Adsorption was the first method of immobilisation to be developed, but although it is a relatively simple and cheap method, the enzyme can quite easily be washed from the adsorptive material, so more efficient methods are now preferred.

An example of a commercially used immobilised enzyme is lactase. Lactase (also called β-galactosidase) is used to hydrolyse the sugar lactose, present in milk, to glucose and galactose. This process has various applications. Some people are lactose-intolerant (unable to digest lactose). If they drink milk, the lactose it contains is fermented by gut bacteria, causing stomach cramps, nausea and diarrhoea. Immobilised lactase can be used to produce lactose-reduced milk and milk products for consumption by people with this problem.

The liquid 'whey' from cheese manufacture can also be treated with lactase to make 'whey syrup', a sweet-tasting additive used in the confectionery industry. The lactase is immobilised in porous beads and retained in a column, through which the substrate is passed. Lactase is an expensive enzyme, and this method allows it to be retained and re-used, lowering the cost of the product.

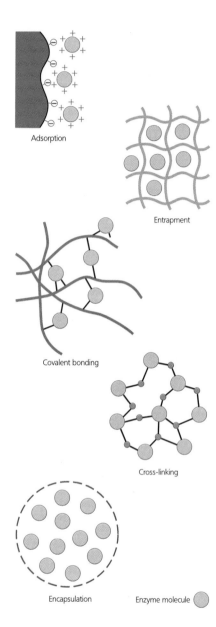

Adsorption

Entrapment

Covalent bonding

Cross-linking

Encapsulation   Enzyme molecule

Figure 4.11 *Methods for the immobilisation of enzymes*

> **! Did You Know**
>
> Despite their liking for milk and cream, many cats are also lactose-intolerant. Dairy products may cause cats to have problems similar to those in lactose-intolerant humans

Summary – (4) Enzymes

- Enzymes are organic catalysts which speed up reactions in organisms by lowering the activation energy of a reaction.

- Enzymes are proteins with an active site where the substrate binds to the enzyme and products are formed. The precise shape of this site confers specificity.

- Enzymes are sensitive to factors in their environment such as temperature, pH, concentration of enzyme and substrate and presence of inhibitors.

- An increase in temperature increases the activity of an enzyme, but above the optimum temperature the enzyme is denatured.

- Changes of pH affect the shape of enzymes: each enzyme has an optimum pH level. Extremes of pH may denature an enzyme.

- Most enzymes work at very low concentrations so that most metabolic reactions are limited by the concentration of the enzyme.

- Chemicals called inhibitors can reduce the activity of an enzyme. Inhibitors may be competitive or non-competitive, and reversible or permanent.

- Cell-free preparations of enzymes have wide-ranging commercial applications in industrial, medical and analytical areas.

- Immobilising enzymes makes them more stable and more useful in many applications.

❓ Answers

1 The level of compound C would decrease *(1)* and the level of compound B would increase *(1)*.

2 The lock and key model suggests that the shape of the substrate is complementary to that of the active site *(1)* before the substrate binds *(1)*, whereas the induced fit model suggests that the shape is only complementary after an enzyme-substrate complex has formed *(1)*.

3 An endergonic reaction uses up energy *(1)*, whilst an exergonic one gives out energy *(1)*.

4 If the concentration of substrate molecules is increased until they are in excess, the active sites of the enzyme will be saturated with substrate *(1)*, and so the rate of reaction will approach a maximum value.

5 (a) Active site: a region on the enzyme's surface which has a shape complementary to the substrate *(1)*. It is the place where the substrate binds *(1)* and the catalysed reaction occurs *(1)*. The products formed then leave the active site.

(b) Enzyme specificity: an enzyme will only catalyse one reaction, or group of closely related reactions *(1)*, because the shape of the active site is specific to one substrate, i.e. only one substrate will fit into it *(1)*.

(c) Denaturing: the process whereby bonds are broken between the amino acid R-groups of the polypeptide chains of the enzyme *(1)*. This causes the tertiary structure of the enzyme to be damaged *(1)*, including the shape of its active site *(1)*. The substrate can no longer attach to the active site *(1)* so the enzyme loses its catalytic ability. Denaturing can be the result of high temperatures, extremes of pH or presence of permanent inhibitors *(1)*.

6 Low temperatures and pressures are easier to achieve *(1)* and require less energy, lowering costs *(1)*.

7 Biological washing powders are good for removing organic stains *(1)* and work at low temperatures, saving energy *(1)*, and protecting delicate fabrics *(1)*. Their main disadvantage is that some people are allergic to the enzymes they contain *(1)*.

End of Chapter Questions

1 Complete the following description of enzymes by adding the most appropriate word *or words* in the gaps:

Enzymes are biological catalysts which increase the rate of a reaction by reducing the _____ energy needed for the reaction to take place. Enzymes are globular _____ which possess a region on their surface where binding to a substrate occurs. This region is called the _____ . The bonds which maintain the tertiary structure of the enzyme can be disrupted by factors such as _____ and _____ , reducing the catalytic action of the enzyme. Ions of heavy metals such as mercury cause _____ inhibition of enzymes. Other inhibitors reduce enzyme activity because they are a similar shape to the enzyme's substrate. These are called _____ inhibitors.

(7 marks)

2 Read this account of an enzyme experiment and answer the questions which follow:

Powdered milk contains the protein casein. When powdered milk is mixed with water, it forms an opaque white suspension. If a proteolytic enzyme such as trypsin is added to this suspension, it will clear, becoming translucent.

In an experiment, the effect of trypsin on a suspension of the milk at different temperatures was investigated. 10 cm^3 of milk suspension and 10 cm^3 of trypsin solution were incubated separately in a water bath at room temperature. After allowing the tubes to equilibrate to the temperature of the water bath, their contents were mixed and the time taken for the mixture to clear was recorded. The rate of the reaction (cm^3 per minute or cm^3 min^{-1}) was calculated by dividing the volume of milk by the time for the reaction to finish. The investigation was repeated at different temperatures. The results are given in Table 4.2.

(a) Plot a graph of the rate of reaction at different temperatures.   *(4 marks)*

(b) Explain the effect of temperature on the rate

  (i) between 10 °C and 40 °C;   *(2 marks)*

  (ii) between 50 °C and 70 °C.   *(3 marks)*

(c) From Table 4.2 and your graph, estimate the optimum temperature for trypsin activity.   *(1 mark)*

(d) Name one other condition which should be kept constant during the experiment.   *(1 mark)*

(e) Trypsin is a digestive enzyme in the human body. Body temperature is 37 °C. Trypsin might be expected to have a maximum rate of reaction at 37 °C. Suggest a reason for the different optimum obtained from the graph.   *(1 mark)*

(f) In the experiment described above, the point when the milk suspension had gone clear was simply estimated by eye. Suggest a more reliable method which could be used.   *(1 mark)*

(Total 13 marks)

Table 4.2

Temp/°C	Rate of reaction /cm^3 min^{-1}
10	0.80
20	1.95
30	4.40
40	7.45
45	8.30
52	8.05
57	7.10
60	6.00
65	2.65
70	1.00

3 The diagrams below illustrate one model of enzyme action.

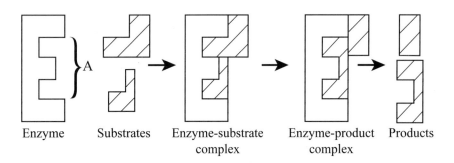

Enzyme Substrates Enzyme-substrate Enzyme-product Products
complex complex

(a) Name the part of the enzyme labelled A.   *(1 mark)*

(b) Explain how this model can account for enzyme specificity.   *(2 marks)*

(c) With reference to this model, explain the effect of a competitive
inhibitor on an enzyme-catalysed reaction.   *(2 marks)*

(Total 5 marks)

Edexcel 1998

4 (a) Explain how the following are related to the protein structure of enzymes:

(i) the effect of high temperature on an enzyme-catalysed reaction;

(ii) substate specificity;

(iii) the effect of inhibitors.   *(10 marks)*

(b) Suggest a simple method by which you could find out whether
an enzyme-catalysed reaction is being inhibited by a competitive
or a non-competitive inhibitor.   *(2 marks)*

(Total 12 marks)

NEAB 1997

5 Read the passage and then answer the questions which follow. ⚿ C2.2

Biosensors

Living organisms need to detect chemical compounds in their environment in
order to survive. Biological sensing of chemical compounds has therefore
been around for a long time. The cell membrane serves as a biological
recognition layer. This is the principle of a biosensor, where a biological
5 recognition layer is linked to a transducing device which converts the
recognition process into an electrical signal.
A wide variety of immobilised biological recognition layers has been tried,
including antibodies, enzymes and cell membrane receptors. Of these,
10 enzymes form the most successful systems from which recognisable signals
can be extracted. To monitor glucose in the blood of a diabetic the glucose
biosensor has been miniaturised into a needle shape that can be inserted under
the skin. Intact mammalian and microbial cells have also been used as
biosensors. Biosensors could play an important role in the monitoring of the
environment for pollutants such as heavy metal ions and organic toxins and
pesticides, which at present depends on complex chemical testing.

(Reproduced from: *Interface, Biological Sciences Review, Vadgama, P., by permission of Philip Allan.*)

(a) Explain how the glucose biosensor detects the amount of glucose in the
blood of diabetics. (line 9) *(5 marks)*

(b) (i) What features of molecules such as enzymes and cell membrane receptors
enable them to be used in biological recognition systems? (lines 4–7)
(3 marks)

(ii) Suggest why enzymes have proved to form the most successful systems
from which a detectable signal can be obtained. (lines 7–8)
(2 marks)

(c) Heavy metal ions inhibit the activity of enzymes. Suggest how biosensors
might be used to monitor heavy metal ion pollution in a river. *(2 marks)*

(Total 12 marks)

NEAB 1998

5 DNA – structure and function

A gene is a section of DNA found in the nucleus and a chromosome contains a strand of genes. Genes determine the activities of cells and the features of organisms. Genes can do this because DNA controls which enzymes and other proteins are synthesised by cells. DNA can also accurately copy itself (replicate) allowing genes to be inherited. Changes to DNA cause mutations which can be harmful.

This chapter includes:
- structure of nucleic acids
  - structure of a nucleotide
  - structure of DNA
  - structure of RNA
- functions of DNA
  - the evidence for DNA being the genetic material
- DNA replication
- the genetic code
- the roles of DNA and RNA in protein synthesis
- mutations
  - examples of gene mutations.

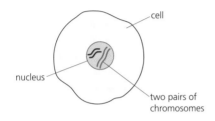

Figure 5.1 *The chromosomes are in the nucleus*

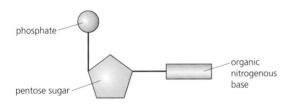

Note: DNA and RNA contain both phosphate and nitrogen (in the base)

Figure 5.2 *Structure of a nucleotide*

5.1 The structure of nucleic acids

DNA (deoxyribonucleic acid) and **RNA** (ribonucleic acid) are **nucleic acids**. These are **polynucleotides**, i.e. polymers built up from basic units or monomers called **nucleotides**. Each nucleotide has three parts; a pentose sugar, a phosphate and an organic nitrogenous base (Figure 5.2). Note that both DNA and RNA contain phosphate and nitrogen.

The nucleotides as monomers can be joined together to form a polymer (**polymerisation**). The phosphate group of one nucleotide is joined with a **phosphodiester bond** to a pentose sugar of another by a **condensation reaction**.

Joining up forms a **polynucleotide** chain with a **sugar-phosphate backbone**. The bases stick out to the side. As there are different types of nucleotides, the bases can be in any order along the chain (Figure 5.3).

Figure 5.3 *The nucleotides join together to form a polynucleotide chain*

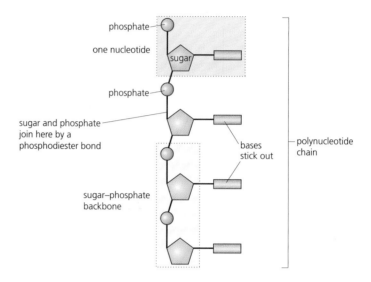

5.2 The structure of DNA

DNA is built up from four types of DNA nucleotide which have different bases.

The bases **adenine** and **guanine** are larger with a double ring structure. They are **purines**. The bases **thymine** and **cytosine** are smaller with a single ring structure. They are **pyrimidines**.

Therefore there are *four* types of DNA nucleotide depending upon which type of base is present: A, G, T and C. The phosphate and the deoxyribose is the same for each type of nucleotide.

Figure 5.4 *DNA nucleotides*

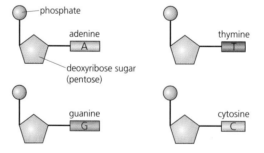

Specific or complementary base pairing
DNA consists of *two* polynucleotide chains or strands linked by **hydrogen bonds** between the bases. (See Section 3.1, page 62.)

The base adenine (A) can only pair with thymine (T) as they both form two hydrogen bonds. Cytosine (C) can only pair with guanine (G) as they form three hydrogen bonds.

$$A = T \qquad\qquad C \equiv G$$

2 hydrogen bonds   3 hydrogen bonds

This **specific** or **complementary base pairing** is essential to the understanding of the function of DNA and RNA, in particular the functions of DNA replication and protein synthesis.

The precise order and sequence of the different bases along a strand varies. It is this sequence of bases which forms the genetic information stored by the DNA.

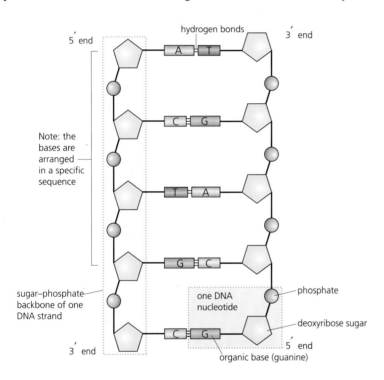

Figure 5.5 *The structure of the DNA molecule as two polynucleotide strands, joined by hydrogen bonds*

The double helix

The two DNA strands are twisted to form a **double helix**. The helical arrangement and the hydrogen bonds between the bases help to make the DNA molecule very *stable*. This is very important for DNA's function as a store of genetic information. The DNA will tend to stay unchanged for the lifetime of the cell.

By being double stranded with the bases attached to each other, the bases and their specific sequence are protected from most damage. Damage (**mutation**) is fairly rare.

Note that the two strands are **antiparallel**. The strands run in opposite directions to each other. Each strand has a 5'end, where the carbon-5 of the pentose sugar is nearest to the end, and a 3'end, where the carbon-3 of the pentose sugar is nearest to the end. The 5'end of one strand lies next to the 3'end of the other strand.

?

1 Each DNA nucleotide has three components – sugar, phosphate and base. Which two components are joined to form:
(a) the backbone of one strand of DNA? *(1 mark)*
(b) the link between two strands of DNA? *(1 mark)*

Extension

Box 5.1 Purines and pyrimidines
In addition, note that a purine must pair with a pyrimidine because of their relative sizes. A smaller base must pair with a larger molecule to keep the two strands the same distance apart. Purines are larger with a two ringed structure. Pyrimidines are smaller with a one ringed structure.

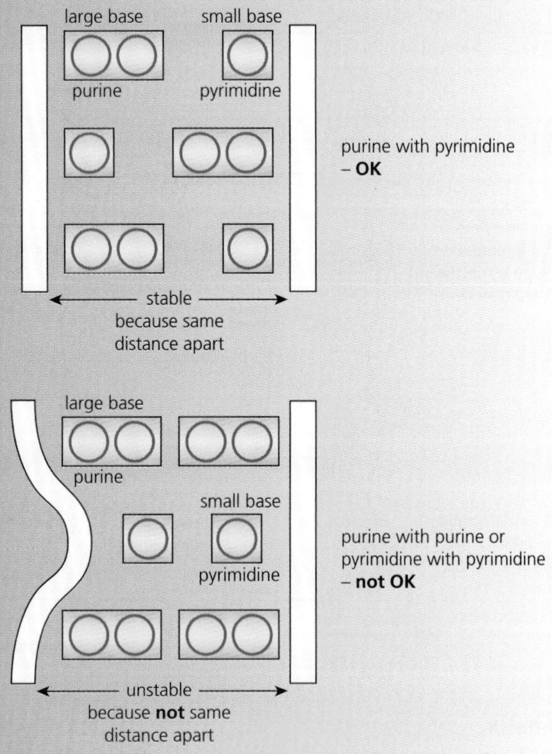

Figure 5.6 The relative size of bases is important in pairing

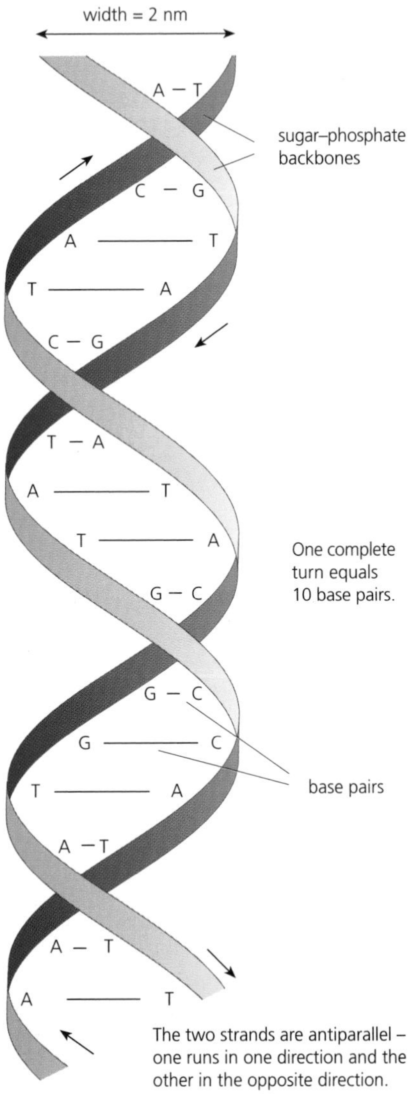

Figure 5.7 The double helix

width = 2 nm

sugar–phosphate backbones

One complete turn equals 10 base pairs.

base pairs

The two strands are antiparallel – one runs in one direction and the other in the opposite direction.

The relative amounts of bases in DNA
Because of specific base pairing the relative amounts of bases A and T will always be the same as will the amounts of C and G. For instance, if a sample of DNA has 10% of base A it must also have 10% of base T. Wherever there is an A it will be attached to a T.

However, because each species is genetically different with a unique sequence of bases, the total amounts of A added to T will always be different to C plus G. This means that species X may have 10% A, 10% T, 40% C, 40% G but species Y has 15% A, 15% T, 35% C, 35% G.

2 If a sample of DNA had 18% of guanine nucleotides, what percentage of its nucleotides would be thymine? *(1 mark)*

3 Which one or more of the following equations accurately reflects DNA base pairing?

(a) $\dfrac{A + G}{C + T} = 1.0$ (b) $\dfrac{A + T}{G + C} = 1.0$ (c) $\dfrac{G\,A}{C} = T$ *(1 mark)*

5.3 The structure of RNA (ribonucleic acid)

RNA (ribonucleic acid) is a nucleic acid built up from four types of RNA nucleotide each with a different base (Figure 5.8). The larger purine bases are adenine and guanine. The smaller pyrimidine bases are **uracil** and cytosine. This is similar to DNA except that the base *uracil* replaces *thymine* and the pentose sugar *ribose* replaces *deoxyribose*.

Figure 5.8 RNA nucleotides

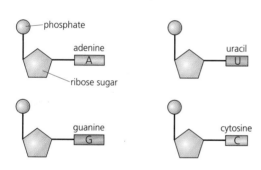

RNA nucleotides are polymerised to produce **single polynucleotide chains**. There are three types of RNA: **messenger RNA**, **transfer RNA** and **ribosomal RNA**.

Messenger RNA (mRNA) is formed in the nucleus. It has a single chain twisted into a helix whose length and base sequence vary. It has a short life and it is involved in protein synthesis.

Transfer RNA (tRNA) has a single chain folded into a clover leaf shape. There are many different types of tRNA. The structure is always similar except for the three bases of the **anticodon** which determine which amino acid attaches. tRNA is also involved in protein synthesis (Figure 5.12).

Ribosomal RNA (rRNA) is made in the nucleolus and forms over half the mass of ribosomes.

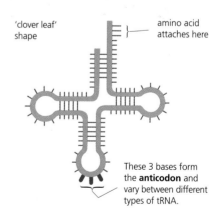

Figure 5.9 Transfer RNA

Extension

Box 5.2 DNA and the double helix – missing out on a Nobel Prize!!

'Suddenly I became aware that an adenine–thymine pair held together by two hydrogen bonds was identical in shape to a guanine–cytosine pair held together by at least two hydrogen bonds. All the hydrogen bonds seemed to form naturally; no fudging was required . . . .'

James D Watson, *The Double Helix*, Penguin 1968.

'What was it like to live with the double helix? I think we realised almost immediately that we had stumbled onto something important. According to Jim, I went into the Eagle, the pub across the road where we lunched every day, and told everyone that we'd discovered the secret of life.'

Francis Crick, *What Mad Pursuit*, Weidenfield and Nicolson 1989.

The double helix structure of DNA was discovered in 1953. It has been called the greatest scientific discovery of the 20th century. It is usually associated only with James Watson and Francis Crick. In fact other scientists also made important contributions. The work of Erwin Chargaff provided evidence of the ratio of bases in DNA, and Maurice Wilkins and Rosalind Franklin provided evidence of a helical structure. Watson, Crick and Wilkins were awarded the Nobel Prize in 1962. Sadly Rosalind Franklin had died from cancer in 1958, preventing her from also sharing the Nobel Prize as it cannot be awarded posthumously.

Figure 5.10 James Watson and Francis Crick with DNA model

Figure 5.11 Maurice Wilkins

Figure 5.12 Rosalind Franklin

Table 5.1 Summary of structural differences between DNA and RNA

DNA	RNA
double polynucleotide chain	single polynucleotide chain
bases are adenine, guanine, cytosine and thymine	bases are adenine, guanine, cytosine and uracil
pentose sugar is deoxyribose	pentose sugar is ribose
only one type	three types (mRNA, tRNA and rRNA)
amount per diploid cell is constant in any one species	amount varies from cell to cell

4 List two similarities between DNA and RNA. *(2 marks)*

A gene is a sequence of DNA bases which codes for the correct sequence of amino acids in a particular polypeptide (protein)

5.4 Functions of DNA

DNA is the genetic material as it is inherited and contains the coded information for protein synthesis.

DNA contains coded information in the form of **genes**. The precise order and sequence of the different bases along a strand of DNA varies. It is this **sequence** which forms the genetic information or **genetic code** stored by the DNA (Figure 5.5). By controlling which **proteins** (particularly enzymes) are made, genes determine the characteristics and development of organisms. The Human Genome Project is working out the complete sequence of bases for human DNA (see Box 16.7, page 501).

Extension

Box 5.3 Evidence that DNA is the genetic material

This research provides experience of deduction from experimental results. (See also Question 1, page 148, on the work of Hershey and Chase.)

1. The experiments of Griffith, Avery, Macleod and McCarthy on the bacterium *Pneumococcus*

In 1928 Griffith worked with *Pneumococcus*, a bacterium that exists in two forms. They found that:

● Injecting live S-type bacteria into mice caused the mice to develop pneumonia and to die.

● Injecting live R-type had no effect on the mice.

● Injecting a mixture of live R-type and dead S-type caused death by pneumonia and live S-type were found in the dead mice.

Deduction from this evidence: material from the dead S-type could pass to the live R-type and alter the characteristics of the R-type to produce the S-type.

Further work on *Pneumococcus* was done in 1943 by Avery, Macleod and McCarthy. They named the material transferred from the S to the R as the 'transforming substance' and they prepared extracts of it which they treated in various ways. The results are shown in Table 5.2.

Extension

Box 5.3 Evidence that DNA is the genetic material (cont'd)

Table 5.2

Treatment of 'transforming substance'	Result after mixing 'transforming substance' with R-type bacteria
add enzymes to remove carbohydrates	S-type bacteria produced – transformation has occurred
add enzymes to remove proteins	S-type bacteria produced – transformation has occurred
add enzymes to remove DNA	S-type bacteria *not* produced – transformation has *not* occurred

Deduction from this evidence: the 'transforming substance' is DNA and not protein or carbohydrate. When DNA is removed, transformation of R- to S-type does *not* occur. This is evidence that DNA is the genetic material able to determine the characteristics of organisms. DNA is able to change R-type to S-type bacteria.

2. Research by Beadle and Tatum (1941) on the bread mould *Neurospora*

This research helped establish that DNA controls cells by controlling the synthesis of proteins, particularly enzymes. They used X-rays to produce mutant moulds which lacked the enzyme necessary to produce one of the amino acids required for growth. The mutant mould could not grow unless this amino acid was provided externally. By allowing these mutants to reproduce they demonstrated that the defect could be inherited in the same way as a single gene. They concluded that the enzyme responsible for the synthesis of the amino acid was controlled by a single gene.

In the mutant, one gene and therefore one enzyme was missing. They named this the '*one gene one enzyme hypothesis*'.

However, because genes code for all proteins and not just enzymes, this has now been modified to the '*one gene one polypeptide hypothesis*'. This states that one gene is the section of DNA which codes for one polypeptide.

5.5 Replication of DNA

DNA has the only set of genetic instructions in a cell. These instructions are different for each species. When new cells are made in cell division each new cell must receive an exact copy of the instructions to function properly. Replication is also essential for inheritance. The DNA has to copy itself accurately to allow offspring to inherit genes from parents.

DNA replication is **semi-conservative**. The two DNA strands unzip and each strand acts as a template for the formation of a new strand. Each new DNA molecule contains one of the old strands and one new strand. The old molecule is **semi-conserved** (half conserved).

Definition

The **replication** of DNA is the process by which a DNA molecule can produce an exact copy of itself

Figure 5.13 Semi-conservative replication of DNA

1.

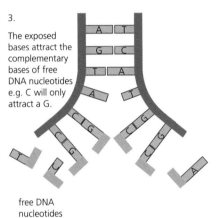

base pairs

sugar phosphate backbone

one original molecule of DNA

2.

The enzyme DNA helicase breaks the hydrogen bonds between the bases causing the strands to separate (to unzip) from one end.

3.

The exposed bases attract the complementary bases of free DNA nucleotides e.g. C will only attract a G.

free DNA nucleotides

4.

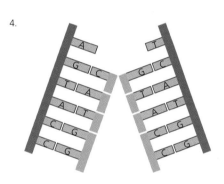

Complementary bases join with hydrogen bonds and free nucleotides link up to form a new strand.

5.

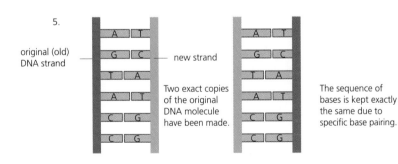

original (old) DNA strand — new strand

Two exact copies of the original DNA molecule have been made.

The sequence of bases is kept exactly the same due to specific base pairing.

Replication is semi-conservative – each new molecule of DNA has one 'old' strand and one 'new' strand.

The important points about DNA replication are as follows:

- The two strands of DNA are separated by the enzyme **helicase**. This breaks the **hydrogen bonds** between the bases, causing the strands to separate from one end.
- Replication is **semi-conservative**.
- Each strand now acts as a template for the formation of a new strand.
- Free DNA nucleotides join up to the exposed bases by s**pecific base pairing**.
- Adenine pairs with thymine and cytosine with guanine due to the number of hydrogen bonds each can form.
- For the new 5' to 3' strand the enzyme **DNA polymerase** then catalyses the joining of the separate nucleotides 'all in one go' to make the completed new strand.
- For the new 3' to 5' strand **DNA polymerase** produces short segments of strand but these sections then have to be joined by the enzyme **DNA ligase** to make the completed new strand.
- Specific base pairing has ensured that two identical copies of the original DNA have been formed.

Remember

DNA replication is **semi-conservative** because each new DNA molecule contains one old and one new strand

Box 5.4 Evidence for the semi-conservative replication of DNA

Extension

The work of Meselson and Stahl on the bacterium *Escherichia coli* (1957)

Cells of the bacterium were grown for many generations on a medium containing the heavy isotope of nitrogen, nitrogen-15. This labelled all the DNA of the bacteria so that it was heavy (sample 1). The medium containing nitrogen-15 was now replaced by a medium containing normal light nitrogen, nitrogen-14, and the bacteria allowed to continue to grow. During each generation of bacteria the DNA replicates once. Samples of bacteria were removed from the culture after one generation (sample 2) and after two generations (sample 3). The samples were then centrifuged and the DNA obtained tested by recording its absorption of ultraviolet light.

Figure 5.14 Meselson and Stahl – evidence for semi-conservative replication of DNA

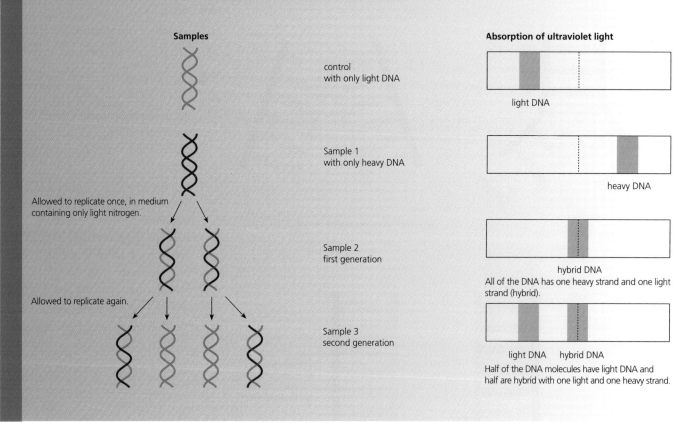

Samples

control with only light DNA

Sample 1 with only heavy DNA

Allowed to replicate once, in medium containing only light nitrogen.

Sample 2 first generation

Allowed to replicate again.

Sample 3 second generation

Absorption of ultraviolet light

light DNA

heavy DNA

hybrid DNA
All of the DNA has one heavy strand and one light strand (hybrid).

light DNA   hybrid DNA
Half of the DNA molecules have light DNA and half are hybrid with one light and one heavy strand.

Box 5.4 Evidence for the semi-conservative replication of DNA cont'd

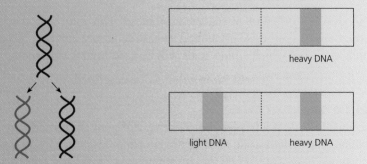

Figure 5.15 Results that would have been obtained if replication was conservative

N.B.

This result is **NOT** found, so replication is **not** conservative.

heavy DNA

light DNA   heavy DNA

Replicates in medium containing only light nitrogen.

Half of the DNA molecules have 2 light strands and half have 2 heavy strands

As can be seen in the figures with only light DNA (the control), the absorption of ultraviolet light gives a 'band' to the left. Sample 1 with only heavy DNA gives a band to the right. The crucial result is sample 2. After replicating once, all of the DNA has one light and one heavy strand, therefore giving a band *midway* between light and heavy strands. This result could only be achieved if replication is semi-conservative. The strands of the 'old' heavy DNA separate and each strand acts as a template to copy a 'new' light strand. Therefore after replication each DNA molecule has one 'old' heavy strand and one 'new' light strand.

?

5 The samples could also be tested in a different way. The following give the results of centrifugation of the extracted DNA:

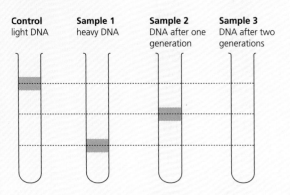

| **Control** | **Sample 1** | **Sample 2** | **Sample 3** |
| light DNA | heavy DNA | DNA after one generation | DNA after two generations |

Figure 5.16

(a) Which part of the DNA molecule would have been labelled with the heavy nitrogen? *(1 mark)*

(b) Copy and complete the diagram for sample 3. *(1 mark)*

(c) Explain the result for sample 2. *(2 marks)*

(d) Copy and draw in the result for sample 2 if replication was conservative instead of semi-conservative. *(1 mark)*

Definition

The triplet code

Each amino acid is coded for by a sequence of three DNA bases. This is known as a triplet code

Did You Know

The first complete genetic 'blueprint' for a multicellular organism was published on the Internet in December 1998.

C. elegans is a tiny, one millimetre long nematode worm. It has only 959 cells but it has 19,099 genes. These genes have 97 million letters (DNA bases) – 25 times longer than the novel *War and Peace*

Table 5.3 *Singlet, doublet and triplet codes*

5.6 The genetic code

DNA stores information as sequences of bases. This information acts as instructions to synthesise proteins. The base sequence acts as a language or code which spells out which amino acids will be used to make a protein.

The features of the **genetic code** will now be described.

A triplet code

The genetic code is a **triplet code**. Twenty different amino acids are used to make proteins. The genetic code must be able to code for all twenty. In a singlet code each single base would code for one amino acid. With only four bases this could only code for four amino acids. As can be seen from Table 5.3 a doublet code with two bases coding for one amino acid allows sixteen amino acids to be coded for. This is still insufficient for all twenty amino acids. A triplet code of three bases per amino acid produces sixty-four possible combinations, more than enough.

Singlet code

A, G, C, T = Codes for 4 amino acids.

Doublet code

AA, AG, AC, AT	
GA, GG, GC, GT	16 possible combinations
CA, CG, CC, CT	Codes for 16 amino acids.
TA, TG, TC, TT	

Triplet code

AAA	AAG	AAC	AAT
AGA	AGG	AGC	AGT
ACA	ACG	ACC	ACT
ATA	ATG	ATC	ATT
GAA	GAG	GAC	GAT
GGA	GGG	GGC	GGT
GCA	GCG	GCC	GCT
GTA	GTG	GTC	GTT
TAA	TAG	TAC	TAT
TGA	TGG	TGC	TGT
TCA	TCG	TCC	TCT
TTA	TTG	TTC	TTT
CAA	CAG	CAC	CAT
CGA	CGG	CGC	CGT
CCA	CCG	CCC	CCT
CTA	CTG	CTC	CTT

64 possible combinations
More than enough to code for the 20 different amino acids.

Each amino acid is coded for by a three-letter 'word' consisting of a sequence of three DNA bases. This is the triplet code, e.g. CGT codes for amino acid alanine. The complete code – the genetic dictionary – is shown in Table 5.7, page 149.

6 Why must the genetic code be triplet and not doublet?　　　*(2 marks)*

A degenerate code
There are 64 different triplets of DNA bases and only 20 different amino acids which means there is excess capacity in the genetic code. The code is referred to as a **degenerate** code because some amino acids are coded for by *more than one triplet* of DNA bases. Also some base triplets act as a full stop to end the series of triplet words, e.g. TAA.

One important implication of degeneracy is that a mutation which substitutes one DNA base for another may not alter the amino acid coded for. The mutation may have no effect on the protein produced.

A non-overlapping code
Each DNA base only contributes to the code for one amino acid and so the code is **non-overlapping**. More information could be stored in the same space using an overlapping code but this would limit flexibility because each word would depend partly upon the bases of the previous word. (see Figure 5.17)

Definition

The genetic code is **degenerate** because some amino acids are coded for by *more than one triplet* of DNA bases. e.g. CGT and CGC both code for the amino acid alanine

Remember

Exam hint

Remember TUND: Triplet, Universal, Non-overlapping, Degenerate code.

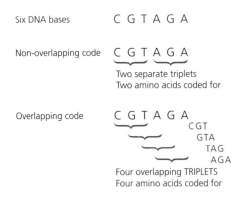

Figure 5.17

7 The gene for one of the polypeptide chains in haemoglobin consists of 438 DNA bases. How many amino acids are in the polypeptide? *(1 mark)*

A universal code

The DNA base triplets code for the same amino acids in all organisms whether bacteria or baboon, human or herring, grass or giraffe, and so are a **universal** code.

This has made the development of gene technology possible as it means that genes from one organism, e.g. human, can be inserted into a totally different organism, e.g. yeast, and are still able to function. (See Chapter 16, page 481.)

8 Mutations can change DNA bases causing a different amino acid to be coded for. If a mutation changes one base, suggest:
(a) why a non-overlapping code is better than an overlapping one. *(2 marks)*
(b) why a degenerate code is better than a non-degenerate code. *(2 marks)*

5.7 Protein synthesis

Protein synthesis occurs in all cells at the **ribosomes** and involves the assembly of amino acids in the correct order into polypeptide chains as directed by the genetic code on the DNA. Polypeptides are then later modified into proteins.

In eukaryotic cells the DNA is found in the nucleus but protein synthesis occurs at ribosomes which are in the cytoplasm. Transporting the DNA instructions to the cytoplasm would risk damage to the vital DNA. Instead the instructions are *copied* from the DNA to **messenger RNA** (mRNA) which takes the 'message' to the ribosomes where the mRNA directs the synthesis of the particular polypeptide.

5.8 Significance of protein synthesis

The fertilised egg (zygote) of a human contains only *one* full set of DNA instructions. These instructions must be able to control:

- the development of the single-celled zygote into the billions of cells of the adult

- the metabolic activities of each cell

- the characteristics of the organism (together with environmental influences).

DNA is able to achieve this by controlling protein synthesis. Different proteins have many different metabolic and structural functions.

In terms of **phenotype** the most important proteins are enzymes. All enzymes are proteins and enzymes control chemical reactions and metabolic pathways in cells. Therefore by controlling which proteins and, in particular, which enzymes are synthesised, DNA is able to determine the characteristics and the development of organisms.

The flow of information:

DNA ⟶ RNA ⟶ PROTEIN

is known as the '*central dogma of molecular biology*'.

> **Definition**
>
> The **phenotype** is a word used to describe both the physical characteristics (appearance) and the functional characteristics (the workings of cells and the body) of an organism. Phenotype depends upon both the DNA of the genes and the effects of the environment

Figure 5.18 *The flow of information in protein synthesis*

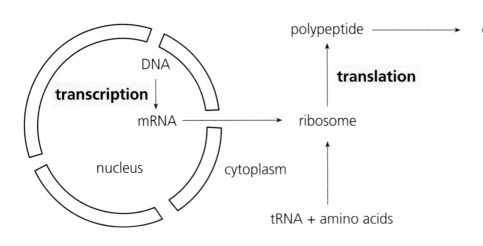

5.9 The stages of protein synthesis

Stage 1: Transcription

At the site of one gene the two strands of DNA unwind and the hydrogen bonds between the bases are broken. This is catalysed by the enzyme **RNA polymerase**.

One of the DNA strands, **the coding strand**, acts as a template for the copying of a complementary strand of **messenger RNA** (mRNA). Free RNA nucleotides attach to the exposed DNA bases on the coding strand by complementary base pairing, e.g. the base cytosine will only join with the base guanine. The RNA nucleotides now join up to make a strand. This is also catalysed by **RNA polymerase**. Each sequence of *three* bases on the **mRNA** is called a **codon** and it codes for *one* amino acid.

The DNA base sequence of the gene has been copied to a complementary sequence of bases on the mRNA.

Stage 2: mRNA carries information to ribosomes

The completed strand of mRNA now leaves the nucleus via a nuclear pore and enters the cytoplasm. Carrying the instructions (the message) from the DNA, the mRNA moves to a **ribosome**.

In the nucleus, the bases on the two strands of DNA now rejoin and the DNA molecule rewinds. This protects the gene as the bases are no longer exposed.

Stage 3: Amino acid activation

There are many different types of **transfer RNA** (tRNA). Each tRNA becomes attached to a particular **amino acid**. This attachment requires energy from ATP. Each tRNA has a different sequence of three bases called the **anticodon**. It is the anticodon which determines which amino acid joins to the tRNA.

Stage 4: Translation

After attachment, the ribosome moves along the mRNA strand 'reading' the information of the codons. At the ribosome the mRNA strand and the tRNAs are brought close together. Each **codon** of **mRNA** bases attracts a **tRNA** with the complementary **anticodon** due to specific base pairing. As each tRNA carries a particular amino acid, this results in the building up of amino acids in a specific sequence.

Peptide bonds form between the amino acids, joining them up into **a polypeptide chain**. The sequence of amino acids in the polypeptide represents the **primary structure** of the protein (see Section 3.17, page 86). The tRNAs now become detached from the amino acids and leave the ribosome to collect another amino acid. Messenger RNA is relatively short lived but it may be used a number of times before it is *broken down*. This avoids synthesising excess protein.

The sequence of bases on the mRNA has been translated into a specific sequence of amino acids. The sequence of amino acids is determined by the sequence of mRNA which in turn was determined originally by the DNA base sequence of the gene.

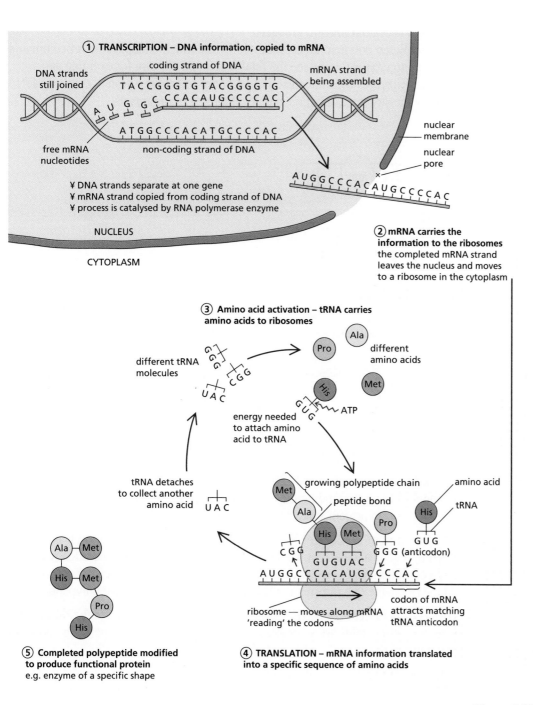

① **TRANSCRIPTION – DNA information, copied to mRNA**

DNA strands still joined

coding strand of DNA

T A C C G G G T G T A C G G G G T G

C C A C A U G C C C C A C

A U G G C

mRNA strand being assembled

A T G G C C C A C A T G C C C C A C

non-coding strand of DNA

free mRNA nucleotides

¥ DNA strands separate at one gene
¥ mRNA strand copied from coding strand of DNA
¥ process is catalysed by RNA polymerase enzyme

nuclear membrane

nuclear pore

A U G G C C C A C A U G C C C C A C

NUCLEUS

CYTOPLASM

② **mRNA carries the information to the ribosomes**
the completed mRNA strand leaves the nucleus and moves to a ribosome in the cytoplasm

③ **Amino acid activation – tRNA carries amino acids to ribosomes**

different tRNA molecules

G G G

C G G

U A C

Pro

Ala

different amino acids

His

Met

G U G

ATP

energy needed to attach amino acid to tRNA

tRNA detaches to collect another amino acid

U A C

Met

Ala

growing polypeptide chain

peptide bond

His   Met

C G G

Pro

G G G (anticodon)

G U G U A C

A U G G C C C A C A U G C C C C A C

ribosome — moves along mRNA 'reading' the codons

amino acid

His   tRNA

G U G

codon of mRNA attracts matching tRNA anticodon

Ala   Met

His   Met

Pro

His

⑤ **Completed polypeptide modified to produce functional protein**
e.g. enzyme of a specific shape

④ **TRANSLATION – mRNA information translated into a specific sequence of amino acids**

Figure 5.19 *Outline of protein synthesis*

Stage 5: Functional protein produced
The completed polypeptide is processed by the rough endoplasmic reticulum and the golgi apparatus to produce the final functional protein, for example an enzyme. Enzymes control cell activities, so by controlling protein synthesis DNA controls the structure, function and development of organisms.

Figure 5.20 *Triplets, codons and anticodons*

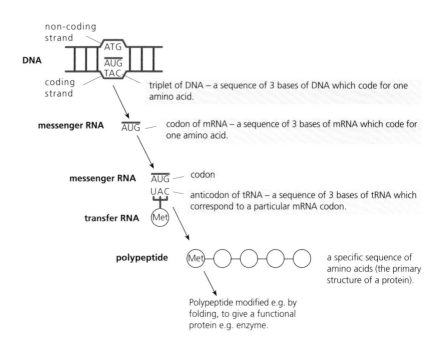

triplet of DNA – a sequence of 3 bases of DNA which code for one amino acid.

codon of mRNA – a sequence of 3 bases of mRNA which code for one amino acid.

codon

anticodon of tRNA – a sequence of 3 bases of tRNA which correspond to a particular mRNA codon.

a specific sequence of amino acids (the primary structure of a protein).

Polypeptide modified e.g. by folding, to give a functional protein e.g. enzyme.

 Remember

Triplets, codons and anticodons
It can be easy to confuse these terms. Figure 5.20 helps to distinguish between them and it provides *definitions* of the three

 Did You Know

Each human cell has approximately 60,000 genes. They do not all actively produce mRNA and synthesise proteins at the same time. Different genes are switched on in different cells and at different times. In white blood cells only 66 genes are active whereas in brain cells 30,000 are active. For more information on switching on genes, see Box 16.1, page 487

Key facts about protein synthesis
In addition to understanding the overall process the particular *functions* of the *key 'players'* in protein synthesis have to be recognised.

The function of messenger RNA is to copy the genetic information from the DNA of a gene and carry it from the nucleus to the ribosome. The mRNA strand has a complementary sequence of bases to the DNA due to specific base pairing. At the ribosome this information is used to synthesise a specific polypeptide.

Different transfer RNAs (tRNAs) carry different amino acids to the ribosome. Here the amino acids are assembled in a particular sequence depending upon the matching of the mRNA codon with the tRNA anticodon.

The ribosome is the site of protein synthesis. The ribosome moves along the mRNA 'reading' the information of the codons. It brings the tRNAs and the mRNA close together so that the anticodons can join with the codons. This also brings the amino acids into position so that they can link by peptide bonds to form the polypeptide.

RNA polymerase is the enzyme involved in transcription – the first stage of protein synthesis. It catalyses the breaking of the hydrogen bonds between the bases of the gene. This separates the DNA strands at the gene. It also catalyses the assembly of the mRNA strand from free RNA nucleotides.

5.10 Comparison between transcription, translation and replication

It is very important to be able to clearly distinguish between the processes of **transcription**, **translation** and **replication** of DNA.

In transcription a specific sequence of bases on DNA acts as a template for the formation of a strand of mRNA by complementary base pairing.

The information of the DNA triplets is **transcribed** into a specific sequence of mRNA codons. It occurs in the nucleus.

In translation tRNAs carrying particular amino acids join with mRNA, determined by a matching of tRNA anticodons with mRNA codons. This causes the amino acids to link up in a particular sequence to form a specific polypeptide. It occurs at ribosomes in the cytoplasm.

Details of **replication** of DNA are given in Section 5.5, on page 126.

Table 5.4 gives you a summary of the features of these three processes.

	Transcription	Translation	Replication
mRNA copied from DNA	✔	✘	✘
occurs at ribosomes	✘	✔	✘
DNA copied from DNA	✘	✘	✔
catalysed by RNA polymerase	✔	✘	✘
catalysed by DNA polymerase	✘	✘	✔
involves joining with tRNA	✘	✔	✘
involves producing codons	✔	✘	✘
assembles amino acids into polypeptide	✘	✔	✘
occurs in nucleus	✔	✘	✔
involves joining of codon with anticodon	✘	✔	✘
occurs in cytoplasm	✘	✔	✘
all of the DNA unzips	✘	✘	✔

Did You Know

In the synthesis of human haemoglobin, amino acids are added to each poly-petide at a rate of 15 per second! Because there are so many ribosomes and so many cells, the human body as a whole synthesises a huge 5×10^{14} molecules of haemoglobin every second!

Table 5.4 Transcription, translation and replication

Remember

Exam hint

The concept of complementary **base pairing** is crucial to your understanding of these topics. It is also very popular in exam questions. You are often asked to work out which base goes with which and to fill in the missing bases. Remember to change the T of DNA to a U in RNA. Almost all of this type of question include a U in mRNA to try to catch you out!

Remind yourself about base pairing (see Section 5.2, page 121) and then try questions 7 and 8 at the end of this chapter

9 *(a)* Give two similarities between transcription and DNA replication.

(2 marks)

(b) Give two differences between transcription and translation. *(2 marks)*

(c) Give two differences between translation and DNA replication. *(2 marks)*

Box 5.5 Non-coding DNA – introns and exons

Only about 10% of our DNA is used directly to code for proteins (i.e. forms genes). The other 90% is non-coding DNA which has a variety of functions:

- operator genes which help control protein-synthesising genes (see Box 16.1, page 487).

- old 'extinct' genes or parts of genes which no longer function

- minisatellites – function not known but used in genetic fingerprinting (see Section 16.1, page 487).

- **introns** – non-coding DNA found within split genes.

Split genes

Some genes have the coding DNA separated (split) by sections of DNA which do not code for protein. The coding sections are called **exons** because they are **ex**pressed. The non-coding sections are called **introns** because they **int**errupt the coding DNA. The introns are transcribed but they are cut out of the mRNA before translation by enzymes.

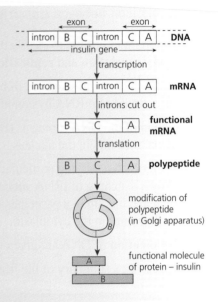

Figure 5.21 *Synthesis of insulin from a split gene – introns and exons*

5.11 Mutation

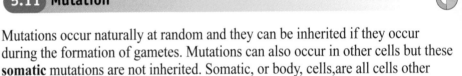

Definition

A **mutation** is a change in the amount or structure of DNA in an organism.

Mutations occur naturally at random and they can be inherited if they occur during the formation of gametes. Mutations can also occur in other cells but these **somatic** mutations are not inherited. Somatic, or body, cells,are all cells other than sex cells. These somatic cells do NOT produce gametes.

Chromosome mutations

These involve changes in the number of chromosomes or changes to large sections of chromosome. Therefore *many* genes are changed. One example in humans is Down's Syndrome which is caused by having one extra copy of chromosome 21.

Gene or point mutations

These occur at a *single* gene (locus) on a chromosome. A *gene* mutation involves a change in the sequence of the DNA bases of the gene and therefore may lead to a change in the *amino acid sequence* in the polypeptide. This change in polypeptide structure may alter the way the protein *functions*. For example, the shape of the active site of an enzyme may be altered so that the enzyme does not function. This may block a metabolic pathway, e.g. respiration. Most gene mutations occur as errors during DNA replication. Most of these errors are proof-read and corrected by the enzyme DNA polymerase. However, some errors 'slip through' and so mutations occur.

Sometimes a distinction is made between **point** and **gene** mutations. Point mutations cause a change to *one* triplet of DNA bases, whereas gene mutations can affect a *number* of triplets and involve several point mutations.

Box 5.6 Ribosomes and polyribosomes

Ribosomes are made of ribosomal RNA and protein. They are made in the nucleus in a structure called the nucleolus. In eukaryotic cells ribosomes may be found attached to rough endoplasmic reticulum or in the cytoplasm. Smaller ribosomes are also found separately in mitochondria, chloroplasts and in prokaryotic cells. The shape of a ribosome is shown in Figure 5.22.

A **polyribosome** is a group of ribosomes attached to the same mRNA molecule. The ribosomes move along the mRNA in sequence. Each produces the same polypeptide, therefore speeding up synthesis. See Figure 5.23.

Extension

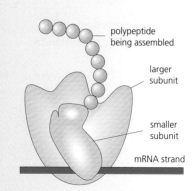

Figure 5.22 Ribosome – actual shape

The same polypeptide is being made but they are at different stages of synthesis.

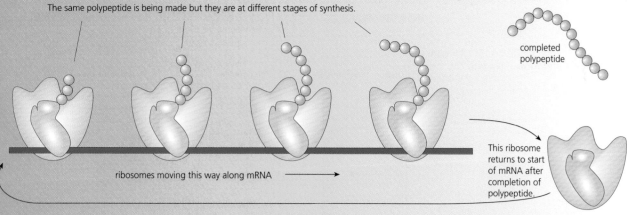

ribosomes moving this way along mRNA

This ribosome returns to start of mRNA after completion of polypeptide.

Figure 5.23 Polyribosome (polysome)

Causes of mutations

The natural mutation frequency is approximately 1 to 30 mutations per million gametes. Mutation is spontaneous and random. Substances known as **mutagens** increase this natural mutation rate. Mutagens include: ionising radiation; ultra-violet light; substances such as tobacco, colchicine, formaldehyde, nitrous acid, mustard gas and some pesticides.

Mutations and variation

Mutations are the *only* source of new alleles (new genes). Therefore mutations are one source of variation in a population.

Many mutations are harmful and are unlikely to persist for more than one generation. However, a few may code for a more advantageous protein. These

Remember

Exam hint

In exam answers you must spell out precisely how mutations may lead to a change in the structure and function of the protein being coded for. The *change in DNA* leads to a *change in mRNA* which leads to *change in the polypeptide* and a *change in the function* of the protein. For examples see Section 5.13, page 143 will give a selective advantage to the individual. The mutation has produced a new allele which will increase in frequency over many generations due to natural selection. The natural frequency of 1 to 30 mutations per million gametes seems a low number. However, given the large number of gametes produced per lifetime (particularly by males), it provides sufficient variation for natural selection to act upon.

5.12 Types of gene mutation

There are various types of gene mutation of which three will be considered here. **Substitution** mutations occur where one or more DNA bases are replaced by another. **Deletion** mutations occur when one or more DNA bases are lost. **Addition** mutations occur when one or more DNA bases are added.

These types of mutation are explained in Figures 5.24–5.27. As stressed earlier, note the sequence: DNA affects mRNA and then mRNA affects protein.

Figure 5.24 No mutation – normal DNA

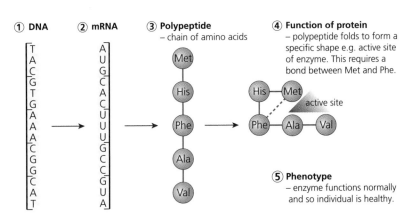

Figure 5.25 Deletion gene mutation (causing a frame shift)

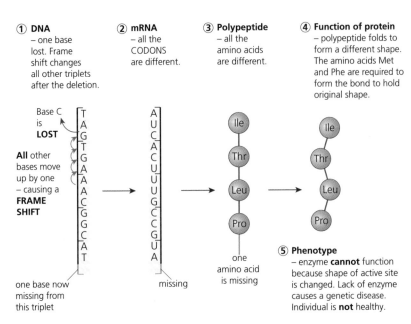

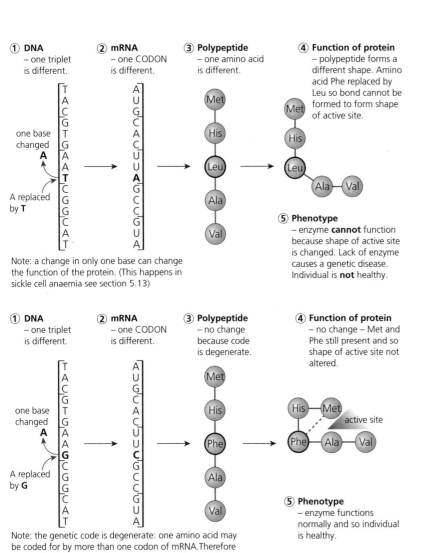

Figure 5.26 *Substitution gene mutation – type 1*

① **DNA**
 – one triplet is different.

② **mRNA**
 – one CODON is different.

③ **Polypeptide**
 – one amino acid is different.

④ **Function of protein**
 – polypeptide forms a different shape. Amino acid Phe replaced by Leu so bond cannot be formed to form shape of active site.

⑤ **Phenotype**
 – enzyme **cannot** function because shape of active site is changed. Lack of enzyme causes a genetic disease. Individual is **not** healthy.

Note: a change in only one base can change the function of the protein. (This happens in sickle cell anaemia see section 5.13)

Figure 5.27 *Substitution gene mutation – type 2*

① **DNA**
 – one triplet is different.

② **mRNA**
 – one CODON is different.

③ **Polypeptide**
 – no change because code is degenerate.

④ **Function of protein**
 – no change – Met and Phe still present and so shape of active site not altered.

⑤ **Phenotype**
 – enzyme functions normally and so individual is healthy.

Note: the genetic code is degenerate: one amino acid may be coded for by more than one codon of mRNA. Therefore some substitution mutations may have no effect on the structure and function of the protein synthesised.

It is very important to understand the different consequences of substitution, addition and deletion gene mutations, which are shown in Table 5.5.

The consequences of mutations can be seen if we represent the DNA language of DNA triplets as three-letter words in English as shown in Figure 5.28.

Table 5.5 *Comparison of substitution, deletion and addition mutations*

Substitution	Deletion and addition
one base replaced by a different base	one base lost or added
usually has less effect because only *one* amino acid changed – *no frame shift*	usually has more effect because causes a *frame shift* and *many* amino acids changed
may have *no* effect because the code *is degenerate* and a different codon may still code for *same* amino acid	

141

Figure 5.28 *The consequences of mutations shown by representing DNA triplets as three-letter words in English*

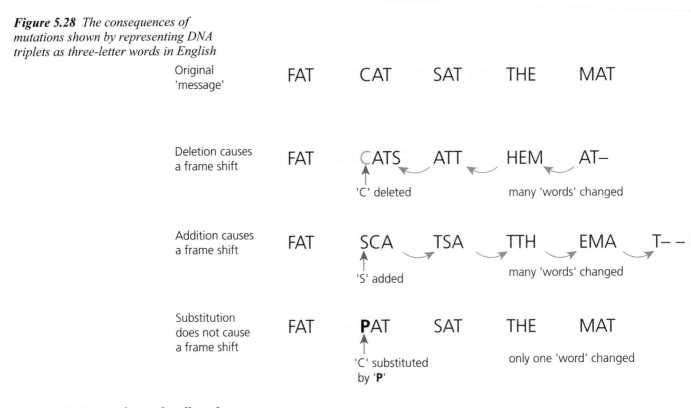

Figure 5.29 *Stop codons – the effect of mutations*

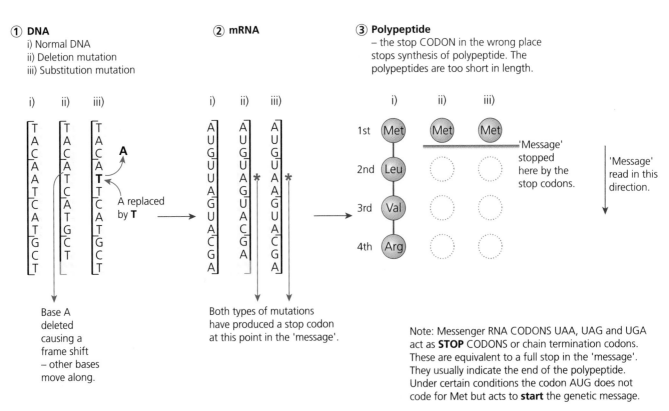

The effects of mutations on stop codons

Another effect of mutations can be to produce a stop codon early in the message.

This can have a major effect on the function of the protein produced because the polypeptide will be too short. See Figure 5.29.

10 For each of the following state whether it would cause a **frame shift** (all of the DNA triplets changed) or not, i.e. yes or no? *(4 marks)*

(a) deletion of 6 bases
(b) deletion of 1 base
(c) substitution of 1 base
(d) addition of 3 bases
(e) deletion of 3 bases
(f) deletion of 4 bases
(g) addition of 1 base
(h) substitution of 3 bases

Did You Know

The cystic fibrosis mutation.
The exact location on chromosome 7 of the cystic fibrosis gene was first discovered in 1985 after a research effort by a number of centres that cost an estimated 150 million US dollars

5.13 Examples of gene mutations

Cystic fibrosis

A person affected by cystic fibrosis has mucus which is too thick. Amongst other problems this causes the lungs to become rather blocked, making breathing difficult.

Cystic fibrosis is caused by a deletion mutation. The polypeptide coded for by the cystic fibrosis gene is very long – 1480 amino acids. The mutation leads to the loss of just *one* amino acid, number 508, but this causes the serious genetic disease of cystic fibrosis. See Figure 5.30. Note, this deletion mutation does *not* cause a frame shift because three bases (one complete triplet) are deleted.

Figure 5.30 Cystic fibrosis – a deletion mutation

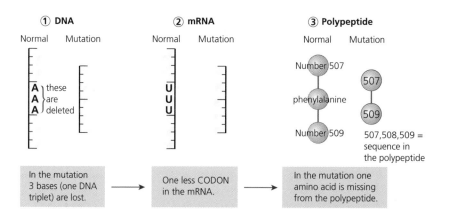

Sickle cell anaemia

The mutation occurs in the gene which codes for one of the polypeptides which make up haemoglobin. Only *one* of the 438 DNA bases in the gene is substituted but this changes the mRNA codon and changes the amino acid which is coded for. Changing the structure of the polypeptide alters the function of the protein. The altered haemoglobin (haemoglobin S) is less soluble. The haemoglobin S molecules tend to stick together, distorting the shape of the red blood cells.

Figure 5.31 Sickle cell anaemia – a substitution mutation

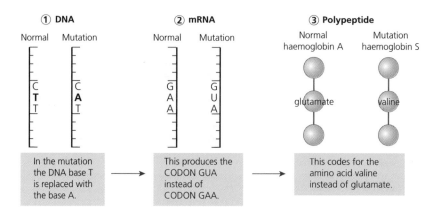

① **DNA**

Normal   Mutation

C   C
T   A
T   T

In the mutation the DNA base T is replaced with the base A.

② **mRNA**

Normal   Mutation

G   G
A   U
A   A

This produces the CODON GUA instead of CODON GAA.

③ **Polypeptide**

Normal   Mutation
haemoglobin A   haemoglobin S

glutamate   valine

This codes for the amino acid valine instead of glutamate.

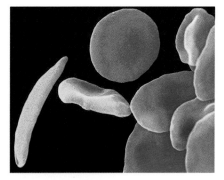

Figure 5.32 Normal and sickled red blood cells (SEM × 2500)

For people with sickle cell anaemia the presence of the sickled red blood cells has many effects on the phenotype including the carriage of much less oxygen by the blood, causing serious tiredness. The cells also tend to clump together, blocking blood vessels and producing a risk of heart failure.

Note how *a mutation of just ONE base can cause a serious genetic disease.*

Remember

Exam hint

Exam questions may require you to use data from a full or part genetic code. Usually this is given as a table of mRNA codons rather than the DNA triplet codes given in Table 5.7 on page 149. However, check the question carefully as the code can be given as DNA, mRNA or even tRNA. Common questions are as follows:

(a) on the base pairing between DNA and RNA (see Section 5.2, page 120)

(b) the features of the genetic code (triplet, degenerate etc. – see Section 5.6, page 130)

(c) the effects of mutations on protein synthesis.

Now try End of Chapter Question 3 which is based upon a mRNA genetic code.

Extension

Box 5.7 Mutations and metabolic pathways – phenylketonuria (PKU)

Phenylketonuria (PKU) is caused by a gene mutation. Sufferers of this disease cannot synthesise the liver enzyme phenylalanine hydroxylase. This can result in severe brain damage. All children in the UK are tested at birth for PKU. Those affected are treated by being given a modified diet which is very low in the amino acid phenylalanine.

The PKU mutation affects part of a larger metabolic pathway. It is one of at least three diseases that are caused by mutations affecting three different enzymes in this metabolic pathway: PKU, albinism and alkaptonuria (see Figure 5.33). Albinism causes a lack of pigment in the body. People with albinism are very light skinned with white hair and pink-coloured eyes. Alkaptonuria can cause a painful form of arthritis when a person is older.

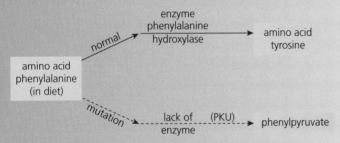

A build up of phenylalanine and phenylpyruvate causes brain damage in PKU sufferers.

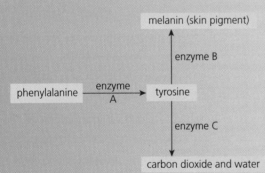

Mutation A blocks synthesis of enzyme A and causes PKU.
Mutation B blocks synthesis of enzyme B and causes albinism.
Mutation C blocks synthesis of enzyme C and causes alkaptonuria.

Figure 5.33 *Mutations affecting the metabolism of phenylalanine*

Summary – ⑤ DNA – structure and function

Structure of DNA and RNA

- DNA and RNA are nucleic acids.

- They are polymers built up from nucleotide monomers.

- Each nucleotide has a pentose sugar, a phosphate and an organic base.

- DNA is built up from four types of nucleotide, each with a different base – A, T, C, G.

- The DNA molecule consists of two polynucleotide chains twisted to form a double helix.

- Specific base pairing means that A can only join with T and C can only join with G.

- This specific or complementary base pairing is essential to the functions of DNA.

- RNA is single stranded and has four types of nucleotides with different bases – A, C, G and U instead of T.

- There are three different types of RNA molecule – mRNA, tRNA and rRNA.

Functions of DNA and RNA

- DNA contains coded information in the form of genes.

- An exact copy of the DNA can be made by DNA replication.

- DNA replication allows new cells and new organisms to receive the genetic instructions.

- The genetic code is a triplet code – a sequence of three DNA bases codes for one amino acid.

- The genetic code is also a degenerate code where one amino acid may be coded for by more than one triplet of DNA bases.

- DNA, mRNA and tRNA are all involved in protein synthesis.

Protein synthesis

- DNA controls the activities of cells and the development of organisms by controlling the synthesis of proteins, particularly enzymes.

- Transcription: the strands of DNA separate at the gene; the coding strand of DNA acts as a template for the copying of a mRNA strand; the mRNA leaves the nucleus and joins with a ribosome in the cytoplasm.

- Amino acid activation: specific tRNA molecules become attached to a particular amino acid determined by the anticodon on the tRNA.

- Translation: at the ribosome the mRNA strand and the tRNAs are brought close together; each codon of three mRNA bases will join with the matching anticodon of three bases on the tRNA. This results in a building up of the amino acids carried by the tRNAs into a particular polypeptide.

Mutations

- Mutations are changes in DNA which can cause a change to the protein synthesised.
- As a result the protein, e.g. an enzyme, may not function and so harm the organism.
- Mutations can be helpful, producing new genes and increasing variation.
- Deletion, addition and substitution are types of gene mutation only affecting one gene.
- Substitution is where one or more bases are replaced by a different base. This may cause one amino acid to be changed.
- Deletion is where one or more bases are lost.
- Addition is where one or more bases are added.
- Deletions and additions usually cause a frame shift which causes many amino acids to change.

Answers

1 (a) sugar with phosphate *(1)*
   (b) base with base *(1)*

2 32% *(1)* (18 + 18 = 36: 100 − 36 = 64: 64 − 2 = 32)

3 A and C *(1)* (B is extremely unlikely, all 4 bases would have to be 25%.)

4 Various choices: both are polymers; both have nucleotide monomers;
   both have the bases C, G and A; both have pentose sugars; both have phosphates. *(2)*

5 (a) The bases (they contain nitrogen). *(1)*

   (b) *(1)*

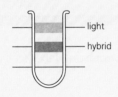

   (c) Replication is semi-conservative. *(1)* Each DNA has one old strand (heavy) and one new strand (light) each strand is hybrid and therefore its position is halfway *(1)*

(d) *(1)*

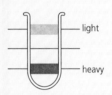

6 The doublet only produces 16 combinations – not enough to code for all twenty amino acids. *(2)*

7 146 (438 ÷ 3) *(1)*

8 (a) With non-overlapping it only changes one DNA triplet and therefore only one amino acid. With overlapping it could change three triplets and three amino acids. *(2)*

   (b) With a degenerate code the new triplet may still code for the same amino acid with no change to the protein function. *(2)*

9 (a) Both involve copying from a specific DNA base sequence
       Both involve breaking hydrogen bonds to separate the DNA strands. *(2)*

   (b) Any two from Table 5.4. *(2)*

   (c) Any two from Table 5.4. *(2)*

10 Yes: **(b), (f), (g)** No: **(a), (c), (d), (e), (h)** *(4)*

End of Chapter Questions

C2.2

1 Read the passage and answer the questions at the end.
Evidence that DNA is the genetic material. The work of Hershey and Chase (1952).

A phage is a virus that is a parasite of bacteria such as *E. coli*. The phage has a simple structure consisting only of DNA with a protein coat. Part of the phage enters the bacterium and causes the bacterium to produce new phages.

This experiment was designed to prove whether it was the protein or the DNA from the phage that entered the bacterium. Whichever substance entered was able to control the activities of the bacterial cell and instruct it to produce new phages, i.e. this substance would be the genetic material. Was it the protein or was it the DNA? The results are shown in Table 5.6.

Table 5.6 Results of Hershey and Chase's experiment

Experiment 1	Experiment 2
Prepare phages with radioactively labelled sulphur.	Prepare phages with radioactively labelled phosphorus.
▼	▼
Phages infect bacteria.	Phages infect bacteria.
▼	▼
Bacteria *do not* become radioactive.	Bacteria *do* become radioactive.
▼	▼
Allow phages to complete life cycle inside bacteria.	Allow phages to complete life cycle inside bacteria.
▼	▼
The new generation of phages released from bacteria contain *no* radioactivity.	The new generation of phages released from bacteria *do* contain radioactivity.

(a) Which molecules in the phage were being labelled by
    (i) radioactive sulphur?
    (ii) radioactive phosphorus? *(2 marks)*

(b) Why was radioactive carbon not used to label the phage? *(1 mark)*

(c) (i) Which part of the phage enters the bacteria? *(1 mark)*
    (ii) What is the evidence? *(2 marks)*
    (iii) In experiment 2, why were some of the new generation of phages radioactive? *(3 marks)*

(Total 9 marks)

2 Table 5.7 shows the full genetic code as DNA triplets. This does not have to be learnt but you may be asked to use the information in questions.

Table 5.7 *The genetic code – the genetic dictionary as DNA triplets*

Base triplet in DNA	Amino acid it codes for	Base triplet in DNA	Amino acid it codes for	Base triplet in DNA	Amino acid it codes for	Base triplet in DNA	Amino acid it codes for
AAA	Phe	GAA	Leu	TAA	Ile	CAA	Val
AAG	Phe	GAG	Leu	TAG	Ile	CAG	Val
AAT	Leu	GAT	Leu	TAT	Ile	CAT	Val
AAC	Leu	GAC	Leu	TAC	Met	CAC	Val
AGA	Ser	GGA	Pro	TGA	Thr	CGA	Ala
AGG	Ser	GGG	Pro	TGG	Thr	CGG	Ala
AGT	Ser	GGT	Pro	TGT	Thr	CGT	Ala
AGC	Ser	GGC	Pro	TGC	Thr	CGC	Ala
ATA	Tyr	GTA	His	TTA	Asn	CTA	Asp
ATG	Tyr	GTG	His	TTG	Asn	CTG	Asp
ATT	stop*	GTT	Gln	TTT	Lys	CTT	Glu
ATC	stop*	GTC	Gln	TTC	Lys	CTC	Glu
ACA	Cys	GCA	Arg	TCA	Ser	CCA	Gly
ACG	Cys	GCG	Arg	TCG	Ser	CCG	Gly
ACT	stop*	GCT	Arg	TCT	Arg	CCT	Gly
ACC	Trp	GCC	Arg	TCC	Arg	CCC	Gly

* = Stop triplets – these act as full stops for the genetic 'message'. They stop more amino acids being added to the polypeptide – they represent the *end* of the polypeptide.

Abbreviations are given for the amino acids, e.g. Leu = leucine (see page 152 for full names).

(a) Give the sequence of amino acids represented by the following DNA bases:

AGT   CCC   GAT   AGA   *(1 mark)*

(b) The DNA message is read from left to right. What is wrong with this sequence which forms part of one gene?

TTC   ACT   TTT   CAT   *(2 marks)*

(c) Used as a non-overlapping code, the DNA bases AGATAG would code for the amino acids Ser and Ile. How many *complete* amino acids could be coded for if the code was overlapping? What are they?   *(2 marks)*

(Total 5 marks)

3 Use the genetic code in Table 5.8 (which is based upon mRNA codons) to answer the following questions:

Second base

		U	C	A	G	
U		UUU ⎱ Phe UUC ⎰ UUA ⎱ Leu UUG ⎰	UCU UCC UCA Ser UCG	UAU ⎱ Tyr UAC ⎰ UAA Stop UAG Stop	UGU ⎱ Cys UGC ⎰ UGA Stop UGG Try	U C A G
C		CUU CUC Leu CUA CUG	CCU CCC Pro CCA CCG	CAU ⎱ His CAC ⎰ CAA ⎱ Gln CAG ⎰	CGU CGC Arg CGA CGG	U C A G
A		AUU ⎱ AUC Ile AUA ⎰ AUG Met	ACU ACC Thr ACA ACG	AAU ⎱ Asn AAC ⎰ AAA ⎱ Lys AAG ⎰	AGU ⎱ Ser AGC ⎰ AGA ⎱ Arg AGG ⎰	U C A G
G		GUU GUC Val GUA GUG	GCU GCC Ala GCA GCG	GAU ⎱ Asp GAC ⎰ GAA ⎱ Glu GAG ⎰	GGU GGC Gly GGA GGG	U C A G

First base / Third base

Table 5.8 *The genetic code – as mRNA codons, e.g. the mRNA codon UUU codes for the amino acid phenylalanine.*

Amino acids key

Ala = alanine	Leu = leucine
Arg = arginine	Lys = lysine
Asn = asparagine	Met = methionine
Asp = aspartic acid	Phe = phenylalanine
Cys = cysteine	Pro = proline
Gln = glutamine	Ser = serine
Glu = glutamic acid	Thr = threonine
Gly = glycine	Try = tryptophan
His = histidine	Tyr = tyrosine
Ile = isoleucine	Val = valine

(a) Use examples to explain what is meant by: a degenerate code; a triplet code; a codon. *(6 marks)*

(b) Give the DNA bases which would code for the amino acid Met. *(1 mark)*

The following are sequences of mRNA bases:

normal: A G C C U G A U G G C A
mutation 1: A C C U G A U G G C A
mutation 2: A G C U U G A U G G C A
mutation 3: A G C G U G A U G G C A

(c) Name the three types of mutation: 1, 2, 3. *(3 marks)*

(d) Which will have the most effect on the protein synthesised? Why? *(2 marks)*

(e) Which will have the least effect and why? *(2 marks)*

(f) Give the amino acids coded for by the normal mRNA (read from left to right). *(1 mark)*

(g) Give the anticodons corresponding to the normal mRNA. *(1 mark)*

(Total 16 marks)

4 Fill in the blanks in the following passage with the most appropriate biological term.

A molecule of DNA is composed of many polymerised units called nucleotides. Each nucleotide consists of a _____ base joined to a _____ sugar with a _____ group. The DNA consists of two strands running parallel to each other and coiled in a double helix. The strands are held together by _____ bonds which must be broken by the enzyme _____ during replication. In RNA, the base _____ is replaced by _____ and the sugar present is _____. Three types of RNA exist in cells. One type, _____ RNA, is found in high concentration in the specialised part of the nucleus called the _____ , where it is probably synthesised. The pores seen in the nuclear envelope are probably important in allowing _____ RNA to pass out to the _____ situated on the endoplasmic reticulum. The third type of RNA is _____ RNA and this combines with _____ in the cytosol in order to locate them correctly during protein synthesis.

(Total 7 marks)

OCR 1999

5 (a) The following is a sequence of nitrogenous bases from the 'sense' strand in a sample of DNA. Indicate, in the appropriate spaces, the *names* of the corresponding complementary bases in: **(i)** the complementary strand; and **(ii)** the mRNA strand formed from the sense strand of this DNA.

	(i) complementary	(ii) mRNA
Thymine	_____	_____
Guanine	_____	_____
Adenine	_____	_____
Guanine	_____	_____
Cytosine	_____	_____
Adenine	_____	_____ (2 marks)

(b) For how many amino acids would this sample of DNA code? *(1 mark)*

(c) To which class of nitrogenous base does guanine belong? *(1 mark)*

(d) What name is given to the formation of mRNA from DNA? *(1 mark)*

(e) Name *two* enzymes involved in the process described in **(d)**. *(2 marks)*

N3.2 **(f)** If a particular sample of DNA contains 28% adenine, how much cytosine does it contain? Show your working. *(2 marks)*

(Total 9 marks)

OCR 1999

6 The diagram shows a molecule of tRNA.

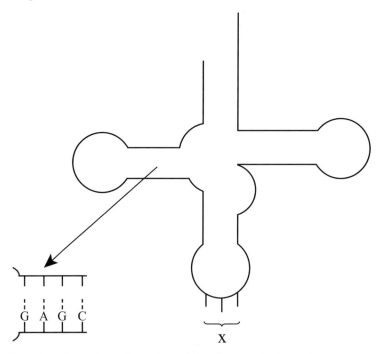

(a) Complete the enlarged section of the diagram by inserting the correct bases. *(1 mark)*

(b) What is the importance in protein synthesis of the part of the molecule labelled X on the diagram? *(2 marks)*

(c) Give *two* ways in which the structure of a molecule of tRNA differs from the structure of a molecule of DNA. *(2 marks)*

(Total 5 marks)

NEAB 1998

7 The diagram shows the information flow in protein synthesis.

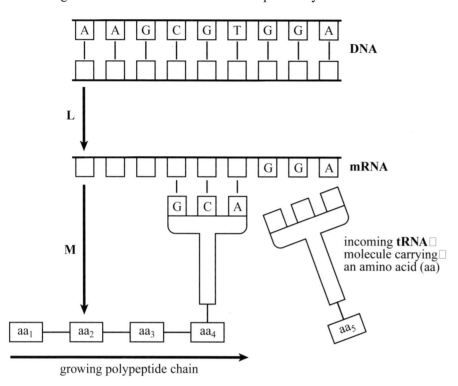

(a) Write in the boxes in the diagram the missing initial letters of the bases on the

  (i) DNA strand

  (ii) mRNA

(b) (i) Write in the boxes in the diagram the missing initial letters of the three bases on the incoming tRNA molecule.

  (ii) What name is given to this triplet of bases on the tRNA molecule?

(c) Name the process shown by

  (i) arrow **L**

  (ii) arrow **M**.

(d) In which organelle does the process shown by arrow **M** take place?

(Total 7 marks)

AEB 1986

8 (a) Name the type of bond that holds together the two strands of nucleotides in a DNA molecule. *(1 mark)*

Genetic drugs are short sequences of nucleotides. They act by binding to selected sites on DNA or mRNA molecules and preventing the synthesis of disease-related proteins. There are two types.

Triplex drugs are made from DNA nucleotides and bind to the DNA forming a three-stranded helix.

Antisense drugs are made from RNA nucleotides and bind to mRNA.

(b) Name the process in protein synthesis that will be inhibited by:

(i) triplex drugs *(1 mark)*

(ii) antisense drugs. *(1 mark)*

(c) The table shows the sequence of bases on part of a molecule of mRNA.

Base sequence on coding strand of DNA								
Base sequence on mRNA	A	C	G	U	U	A	G	C	U
Base sequence on antisense drug								

Complete the table to show:

(i) the base sequence on the corresponding part of the coding strand of a molecule of DNA *(1 mark)*

(ii) the base sequence on the antisense drug that binds to this mRNA. *(1 mark)*

(Total 5 marks)

AEB 1998

6 Cell division

Cells are the basic unit of all living organisms. You have seen in Section 1.20, page 25 that most organisms have cells which are **eukaryotic**. In a eukaryotic cell, the DNA is organised into chromosomes which are contained in a membrane-bound nucleus.

An organism produced by sexual reproduction starts life as a single cell, a **zygote**, which has been formed by the joining of two cells known as **gametes** (see Section 7.2, page 183). Each gamete contains one set of chromosomes in its nucleus (**haploid**) and so the zygote contains two sets (**diploid**).

The zygote divides repeatedly to produce all the cells of the adult organism. In most organisms, all the cells of this body contain the same number of chromosomes, with the same DNA content, as the original zygote. Therefore, the type of division involved is a very precisely organised process. It is known as **mitosis**.

Some body cells divide to produce gametes. Here a special form of division is involved, known as **meiosis** or **reduction division**. During this process a diploid cell divides, producing haploid cells.

This chapter includes:
- **chromosomes and their behaviour before a cell divides**
- **chromosome number**
- **the cell cycle and the process of mitosis**
- **the significance of mitosis**
- **cloning**
- **the process of meiosis**
- **the significance of meiosis.**

6.1 Chromosomes and their behaviour before cell division

It is essential that each body cell of an organism has all the chromosomes (and so all the DNA) found in the cells of that species so that it has all the genes available. Some genes are switched on in all cells while others (e.g. the gene which codes for insulin) may be switched on only in certain specialised cells.

As you have seen in Section 1.7, page 8, the chromosomes are not visible in animal or plant cells which are not undergoing cell division. This is because the DNA of the chromosomes is partly uncoiled and appears, after staining, as thin tangled threads. Other parts of the DNA in the chromosomes remain slightly more coiled and appear as clumps of more densely staining material. All this DNA is referred to as **chromatin**. Some of the DNA is active and must be uncoiled in order for it to take part in protein synthesis. It follows that if such a cell were simply divided by pulling it into two halves, the two cells produced would have only some of the DNA of the original cell and chaos would soon follow!

Such chaos is prevented by the behaviour of chromosomes before the nucleus divides. An outline of this behaviour is shown in Figure 6.1.

Figure 6.1 Behaviour of a chromosome before a nucleus divides

1. A chromosome is a long strand of DNA bound to proteins called histones.

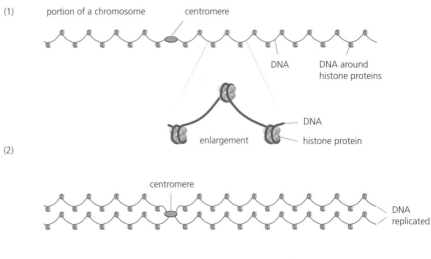

(1) portion of a chromosome   centromere

DNA   DNA around histone proteins

DNA

enlargement   histone protein

*2. Before a cell begins to divide, each DNA strand replicates (see Section 5.5, page 126) and associates with new histone proteins. The two replicated strands of the chromosome remain attached to each other at a structure called a **centromere**.*

(2)

centromere

DNA replicated

*3. Each strand coils and supercoils, as shown, until the chromosome is visible under a light microscope as an easily stainable 'double' structure. Each chromosome, having replicated, shows two sister **chromatids**. Each chromatid is identical to its sister and to the original chromosome. (Eventually, sister chromatids separate, and are pulled into different daughter cells during the process of nuclear division known as **mitosis**.)*

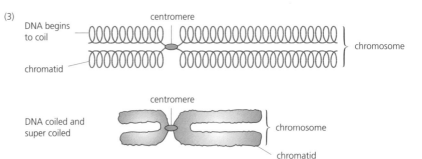

(3) DNA begins to coil   centromere

chromosome

chromatid

DNA coiled and super coiled   centromere

chromosome

chromatid

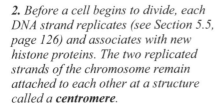
Remember

The replication provides enough DNA for two identical cells. The coiling condenses the DNA into convenient packages to distribute into two cells

Remember

Although not strictly accurate, the following can act as reminders:
- mi**T**osis usually produces **T**wo sets of chromosomes
- **D**iploid – **D**ouble set of chromosomes
- **H**aploid – **H**alf as many chromosomes as normal

6.2 Chromosome number

The number of chromosomes present in each body cell is normally the same for all members of the same species.

In most plants and animals, the cells of the body each contain two sets of chromosomes. More precisely, this means that there are several **pairs** of chromosomes, known as **homologous pairs**. Each member of a pair is usually similar in size and shape to the other. This is because each member of a pair possesses alleles of the same genes in the same order as its partner. In the original zygote, one of each pair is derived from the mother (maternal) and the other from the father (paternal).

An organism, or a cell within it, which contains such homologous pairs of chromosomes is said to be in the **diploid** condition (represented as $2n$).

A cell which contains only one of each type of chromosome (one from each homologous pair) is said to be in the **haploid** condition (represented as n). Some simple organisms contain cells with haploid nuclei but in higher forms it is mainly only the gametes (sperms and eggs) which are haploid. Haploid cells are normally produced by a special kind of cell division. (This is called **meiosis** and will be described later: see Section 6.9, page 168.)

Box 6.1 The human karyotype

In humans, the diploid number is 46 (2*n* = 46). If the chromosomes of a cell are photographed under a microscope, the photograph can be cut and the pictures of chromosomes arranged in pairs. This makes the number and types of chromosomes clear. This is referred to as the **karyotype**. The karyotype of a human female is shown here.

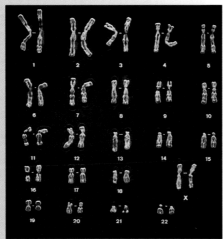

Figure 6.2 *Photograph of human female karyotype*

6.3 The cell cycle

As an organism grows from the original zygote, the cells divide repeatedly by mitosis. During development, some cells specialise and divide less frequently than others and some stop dividing altogether. However, even in the adult organism, some cells continue to divide and replace those cells which die. The sequence of events which takes place in a cell between its formation and the time when it has divided, producing daughter cells, is known as the **cell cycle**.

The time taken to complete the cycle varies enormously according to the type of cell and the conditions. For example, in mammals, depending upon external factors, cells lining the intestine may divide every 8–10 hours, liver cells may divide once a year, skin epidermal cells may divide every 24 hours, but nerve cells do not divide. In onions, root tip cells may divide every 20 hours.

Figure 6.3 *The diagram shows approximate relative durations of each stage of the cell cycle although these do vary considerably*

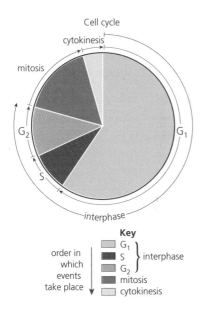

6 Cell division

> ### 💡 Remember
>
> It may help you to remember the stages, if you think of the following:
> **IPMAT** = Interphase, Prophase, Metaphase, Anaphase, Telophase.
> Pro = first, before.
> Metaphase = chromosomes in **M**iddle.
> Anaphase = chromatids move **A**part.
> Telophase = **T**wo nuclei

Stages of the cell cycle

1. **Interphase** (the non-dividing stage). Interphase is subdivided into:

   (a) G_1 (first growth phase). Much protein synthesis occurs and the cell 'grows'. More organelles are produced and the volume of cytoplasm increases. The cell carries out its usual functions. If the cell is not going to divide again, it remains in this phase.

   (b) **S phase** (replication phase). The cell enters this phase only if cell division is to follow. The DNA replicates.

   (c) G_2 (second growth phase). This is a shorter growth phase during which the proteins necessary for cell division are synthesised. (It will be seen, for example, that proteins are needed for the microtubules which form the spindle fibres.)

2. **Mitosis** (the division of the nucleus). Mitosis is the process by which a nucleus divides producing two daughter nuclei, each with the same number of chromosomes as the original nucleus. The cells produced are genetically identical to the parent cell and each other. The process is complex and will be described in the next section.

3. **Cytokinesis** (the division of the cytoplasm). The division of the cytoplasm and formation of two daughter cells is called **cytokinesis**. The mechanics of this process are different in animal cells and plant cells but in each case two separate daughter cells are produced from one parent cell. The processes will be described later (see Section 6.5, page 161).

6.4 The process of mitosis

This is a continuous process which follows immediately after the completion of the G_2 stage of interphase. For convenience, it is considered in four stages, **prophase, metaphase, anaphase and telophase**.

The events of each stage are drawn in Figure 6.4 as they would be seen in an animal cell with two pairs of homologous chromosomes ($2n = 4$), using the high power of a light microscope. In the drawings, only the cell structures relevant to mitosis are labelled. For clarity, one member of each homologous pair is shown in red and the other in yellow. The photographs show mitosis in plant cells where chromosome behaviour is similar but there are no centrioles.

Table 6.1 The time taken to complete each stage of mitosis and the rest of the cell cycle varies with type of tissue, species and conditions. The times represent those taken by mammalian skin cells at 36 °C which are dividing every 24 hours.

Stage of cell cycle	Time
prophase	35 minutes
metaphase	20 minutes
anaphase	10 minutes
telophase	40 minutes
cytokinesis	25 minutes
interphase	21 hours 50 minutes

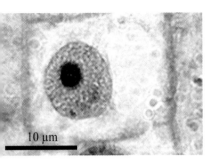

10 μm

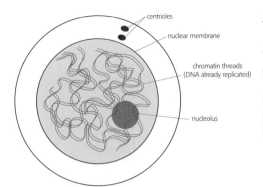

Figure 6.4 *The process of mitosis*

1. Cell at the end of interphase

(i) DNA already replicated, but not coiled, so no chromosomes visible.
(ii) Nuclear membrane present.
(iii) Two centrioles present.
(iv) Nucleolus present.

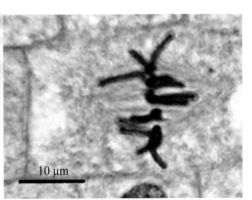

10 μm

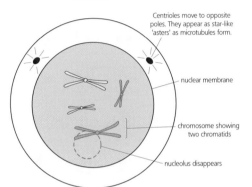

2. **Prophase**

(i) DNA coils and condenses into compact shapes, so that each chromosome becomes stainable and is seen as two chromatids attached at a centromere.
(ii) Nuclear membrane present.
(iii) Centrioles move apart towards opposite poles of the cell. Microtubules assemble around each centriole.
(iv) Nucleolus disappears.

10 μm

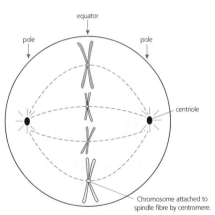

3. **Metaphase**

(i) The nuclear membrane breaks down.

(ii) Centrioles have reached opposite poles and microtubules extend between them, forming the fibres of a nuclear spindle.

(iii) Chromosomes move to the equator of the spindle and each one becomes attached to a spindle fibre by its centromere.
(Plant cells have no centrioles. The spindle fibres form without focusing on a centriole and are therefore parallel to each other.)

Figure 6.4 *(cont.)*

4. Anaphase

(i) *The centromeres divide and the movement and contraction of spindle fibres pull the sister chromatids apart towards opposite poles of the cell.*

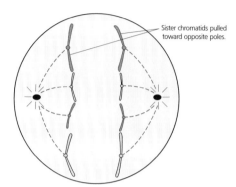

Sister chromatids pulled toward opposite poles.

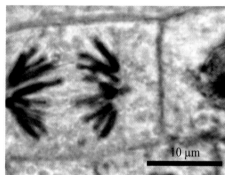

10 μm

5. Telophase

(i) *Each chromatid has become a separate structure and is now called a chromosome. A nuclear membrane forms around each group of chromosomes.*

(ii) *The chromosomes unwind into chromatin.*

(iii) *Nucleoli form in each new nucleus.*

(iv) *Spindle fibres disappear and the centrioles may divide into two.*

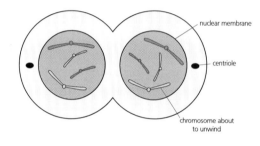

nuclear membrane

centriole

chromosome about to unwind

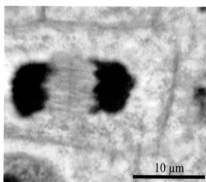

10 μm

?

1 Describe two functions of a centromere during mitosis. *(2 marks)*

2 Look at the photograph in Figure 6.5 which shows onion root tip cells dividing. Identify which stage (interphase, prophase, metaphase, anaphase or telophase) best describes the appearance of each of cells A–E. *(5 marks)*

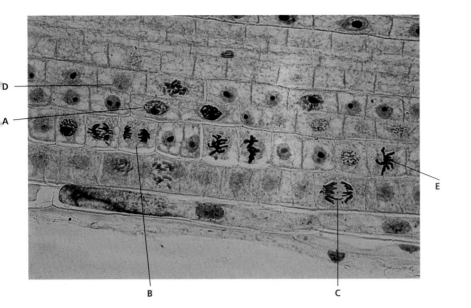

Figure 6.5 Onion root tip cells dividing (× 150)

6.5 Division of cytoplasm (cytokinesis)

This usually follows mitosis. If it does not, a multi-nucleate cell is produced.

Cytokinesis in animal cells

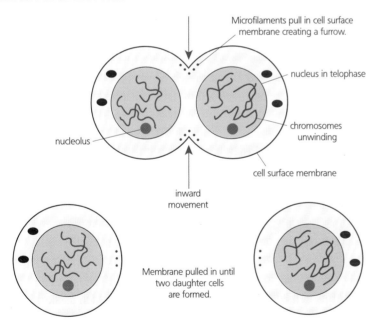

Microfilaments pull in cell surface membrane creating a furrow.

nucleus in telophase

chromosomes unwinding

cell surface membrane

nucleolus

inward movement

Membrane pulled in until two daughter cells are formed.

Figure 6.6
1. Protein filaments, called microfilaments, attach to the inside of the cell surface membrane around the centre. These filaments draw the membrane inwards, creating a furrow.

2. The membrane is pulled in until the cell is divided.

The process may begin before mitosis is complete. It is also called **cleavage** as the cell cleaves into two (Figure 6.6).

Cytokinesis in plant cells

This takes place after mitosis is complete and involves **cell plate** formation (Figure 6.7).

Figure 6.7

1. Some microtubules remain in the central area and guide many Golgi vesicles to the equator of the cell.

2. The vesicles enlarge and fuse together, forming a cell plate.

3. Inside each vesicle, a middle lamella is formed with cellulose either side. This forms the basis of new cell walls separating the cells. The membranes of the vesicles form the new cell surface membranes. Small gaps left between the vesicles form plasmodesmata. (See Section 1.16, page 17.)

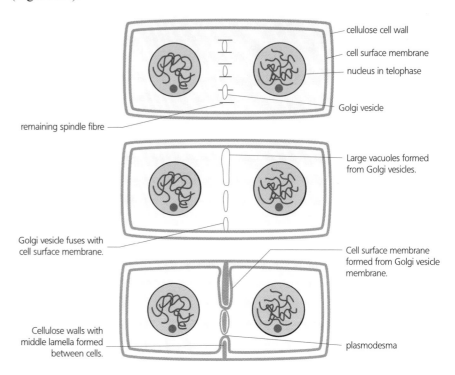

cellulose cell wall
cell surface membrane
nucleus in telophase
Golgi vesicle
remaining spindle fibre
Large vacuoles formed from Golgi vesicles.
Golgi vesicle fuses with cell surface membrane.
Cell surface membrane formed from Golgi vesicle membrane.
Cellulose walls with middle lamella formed between cells.
plasmodesma

 3 Describe **two** differences between cell division in animal cells and plant cells. *(4 marks)*

6.6 The significance of mitosis

Mitosis is the type of division which is involved when it is essential that the daughter cells have the same genes as the parent cell and each other.

Mitosis in growth and cell replacement

When a multicellular organism is formed from a single cell, each cell must have all the genes present in the original cell. Some proteins are produced by all cells and so the genes which code for them must be present in all cells. As an organism develops, some of its cells differentiate into different types such as skin cells or nerve cells. These different cells still produce many of the same proteins as each other. They switch on different genes to make their own special proteins as well.

Mitosis in asexual reproduction

Mitosis forms an essential part of asexual reproduction, as cells of the parent divide by mitosis to produce cells which will form the offspring.

The production of genetically identical individuals (**clones**) can enable a species to reproduce rapidly in an environment which suits the parent and therefore will suit identical offspring. So numbers can increase very rapidly, exploiting favourable conditions.

> **Definition**
>
> Asexual reproduction takes place when a new individual is produced from one parent without the formation and fusion of gametes. The offspring is genetically identical to the parent. If several offspring are produced in this way from the same parent, they are members of a **clone**

Box 6.2 Asexual reproduction in a strawberry plant

Figure 6.8

1. The plant may produce long side-shoots, known as runners.

parent plant

scale leaf and bud

long horizontal stem (runner)

soil level

root

2. A bud on the runner grows into a small plant.

parent plant

young plant grows from bud

soil level

3. The small plant becomes a separate individual as the runner degenerates.

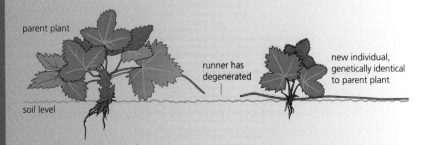

parent plant

runner has degenerated

new individual, genetically identical to parent plant

soil level

Mitosis is involved in the production of all the cells of the new plant. Therefore, it is genetically identical to the parent. All the offspring produced in this way from one parent will be clones of each other.

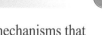

6.7 Cancer

Normally cells divide in a highly controlled way. There are mechanisms that regulate how often and how many times different types of cells in the body divide. (One such mechanism is described in Box 6.3.)

Cancer is a condition which may arise if a cell's control mechanisms break down. The cell may divide repeatedly to produce a mass of undifferentiated cells known as a primary **tumour**. Such tumours may grow at different rates and in different tissues. They may remain as intact growths which can easily be removed by surgery. Such tumours are considered as **benign**.

Sometimes cells are shed from the primary tumour and are carried around the body, often in the lymph or blood systems. These cells carry on dividing, wherever they are deposited, producing secondary tumours (**metastases**) anywhere in the body. Such a cancer is **malignant**. It is very difficult to remove or treat the cancer once it has spread in this way.

The tumours are dangerous because the cancer cells compete with the normal tissues. The growths can physically compress normal tissues, affecting their normal blood and nerve supplies. The invasion often leads to the death of vital tissues, such as brain or lung tissue.

A cell's control mechanisms can break down as a result of gene mutations (see Section 5.11, page 138). Mutations of genes known as **oncogenes**, which are involved in the control of cell division, can lead to cancer. Although these may happen spontaneously, most cancers are produced as a result of exposure to cancer-causing agents (**carcinogens**) in the environment which cause DNA damage.

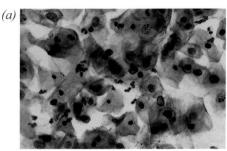

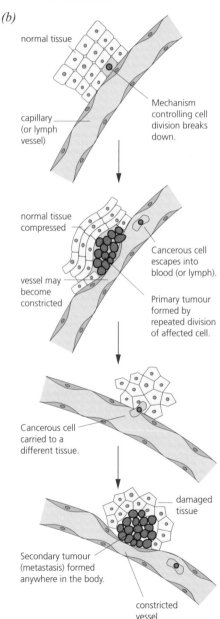

(a)

(b)

normal tissue

capillary (or lymph vessel)

Mechanism controlling cell division breaks down.

normal tissue compressed

vessel may become constricted

Cancerous cell escapes into blood (or lymph).

Primary tumour formed by repeated division of affected cell.

Cancerous cell carried to a different tissue.

damaged tissue

Secondary tumour (metastasis) formed anywhere in the body.

constricted vessel

Figure 6.9
(a) A cervical smear showing cancerous cells. (b) Formation of a secondary tumour (metastasis)

Box 6.3 Telomeres, cancer and ageing

Extension

At the tips of the chromosomes are short lengths of non-coding DNA, called **telomeres**. These are essential for the successful replication of DNA.

Every time a cell divides by mitosis, the chromosomes do not replicate right to the end. Therefore the telomeres become shorter and shorter each time the cell divides. When the telomeres are too short, genes are activated which prevent the cell dividing any more. This limits the number of times that a cell can divide.

This mechanism acts as a protection against the uncontrolled cell division which can produce cancer. There are some cells in the body which need to divide repeatedly, such as those which produce blood cells. These cells produce an enzyme, telomerase, which constantly rebuilds the telomeres. If certain chemicals or viruses cause other cells to produce telomerase, these cells too will divide without limit, leading to the development of cancers.

An unfortunate outcome of the role of telomeres in limiting cell division is that it prevents the tissues and organs from renewing themselves for ever. As we get older, our telomeres get shorter and this is thought to be one of the factors responsible for the ageing of our bodies.

Some cancer-causing agents are:

● chemical carcinogens such as asbestos, hydrocarbons in cigarette smoke and benzene

● some types of radiation such as gamma rays, X-rays and ultraviolet light

● viruses such as EB virus and HIV-1.

 Did You Know

Cancer cells behave differently from normal animal cells. They divide without limit in culture. Cells taken from cancerous tissue in a young American woman, Henrietta Lacks, who died of cancer in 1951, are still alive and dividing in cell cultures around the world.

6.8 Cloning

Asexual reproduction and the production of clones is fairly common in simple forms of life. However, it is relatively rare in complex plants and animals. Some higher plants undergo varied forms of asexual reproduction known as **vegetative propagation**. The strawberry plant's production of one or more offspring by runners is one example of this (see Box 6.2, page 163).

Farmers sometimes make use of this ability of some plants to reproduce vegetatively. For example, they often plant stem cuttings of sugar cane rather than seeds in order to produce a crop. Similarly, potato plants are often grown from 'seed' potatoes which are really the swollen tips of underground stems and not seeds at all. Mammals do not reproduce asexually. Examples of clones amongst mammals can only occur naturally if, after the first mitotic division of a zygote, the two daughter cells separate and develop into separate individuals known as identical twins.

Cloning in the production of plants

If an individual plant happens to have the genes for many desirable characteristics, it would clearly make commercial sense to be able to produce many identical plants quickly for sale. However, not all plants reproduce quickly asexually and a technique known as *micropropagation* is now commonly used by plant producers to overcome this problem.

The technique relies upon the fact that all the living cells of a plant contain all the genes and remain **totipotent** (retain the ability to develop into different types of plant cells). Although much skill is needed, the principles of micropropagation are simple. They involve the stages shown in Figure 6.10.

4 Suggest four advantages of producing plants by micropropagation.

(4 marks)

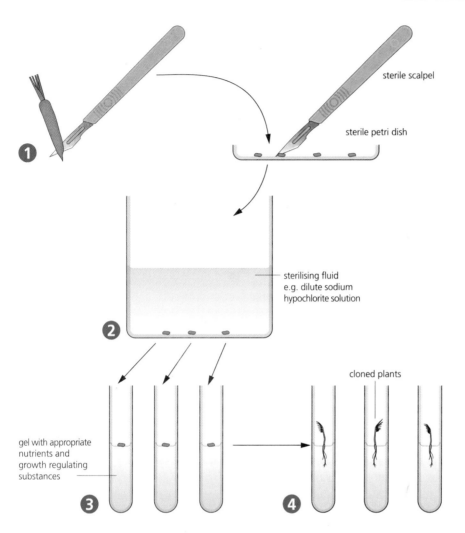

Figure 6.10 *The principles of micropropagation*
1. A piece of tissue is taken from the desired plant, for example a piece of carrot root, stem tissue or cauliflower bud and cut into small pieces

sterile scalpel

sterile petri dish

2. Each tiny piece of tissue must be sterilised to prevent the growth of any pathogens such as bacteria

sterilising fluid e.g. dilute sodium hypochlorite solution

cloned plants

gel with appropriate nutrients and growth regulating substances

3. Each tissue piece is placed in a gel containing nutrients and appropriate growth-regulating substances

4. The tissue cells divide by mitosis and the cells differentiate to produce small plants. These plants may be subdivided to produce even more plants in a similar way

Cloning in the production of animals

Although adult animal body cells contain all the genes, they are difficult to grow in culture without very special treatment. Given correct nutrients, cells of adult tissues normally grow and divide only about fifty to one hundred times before dying.

Also adult cells do not easily produce cells which can differentiate into other tissues (they are **not** totipotent). So micropropagation of animals along similar lines to those used in plants is not yet possible. However, some techniques of cloning animals have been developed.

Cells from a young embryo do divide repeatedly in culture and can produce cells of all the tissues of the animal. If the cells of an embryo at the eight- or sixteen-cell stage are carefully separated and cultured, they are each capable of producing a separate embryo. The procedure can be repeated with the new embryos to produce even more. This technique is now used in cattle production when the embryos are finally implanted into surrogate mother cows to complete their development. (See Figure 6.11.)

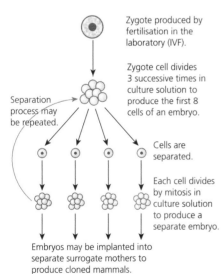

Zygote produced by fertilisation in the laboratory (IVF).

Zygote cell divides 3 successive times in culture solution to produce the first 8 cells of an embryo.

Separation process may be repeated.

Cells are separated.

Each cell divides by mitosis in culture solution to produce a separate embryo.

Embryos may be implanted into separate surrogate mothers to produce cloned mammals.

Figure 6.11 *The principles of producing clones from mammal embryos*

The nucleus of an adult cell may be placed in an egg cell from which the nucleus has already been removed. If this is done, the egg cell can divide and produce all the tissues of a new individual. For this to happen, some factor in the egg cytoplasm must re-programme the adult nucleus's genes to an embryonic state. This was shown to happen in frogs many years ago but it was not until 1996 that the first mammal was cloned in this way and Dolly the sheep was born. (See Figure 6.12.)

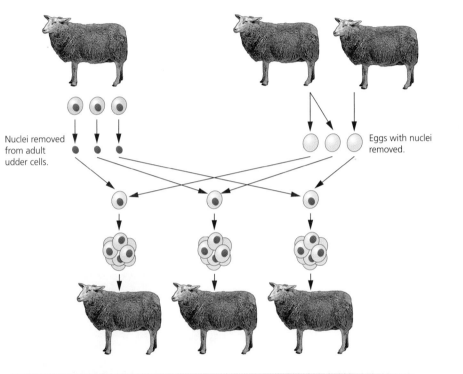

Nuclei removed from adult udder cells.

Eggs with nuclei removed.

Figure 6.12 *Cloning in mammals using an adult cell and an egg cell with the nucleus removed*

1. To produce Dolly the sheep, cells were taken from the udder of a six year-old ewe (female sheep)

2. Eggs were taken from other ewes and the haploid nuclei were removed from these eggs

3. A diploid nucleus from a six year-old udder cell was placed into each egg

4. Each 'egg' was allowed to start developing and the young embryo was placed into the uterus of a sheep, to complete its development

Dolly was the only successful cloned individual to be born out of the first 277 trials

?

5 Which is Dolly's clone (and identical twin)? Is it the sheep who provided the udder cells, the sheep who provided the egg or the sheep in whose uterus Dolly grew?   *(1 mark)*

Is Dolly really a clone or just a 'Dolly mixture'?
You may have the correct answer to question 5, but how correct is it really?

The mitochondria in any cell each possess a DNA loop containing a few genes (see Section 1.11, page 12). In sheep cells there are 37 genes in each mitochondrion. These make up about 0.02% of all the genes in the cell, the rest being in the nucleus.

When Dolly and nine other cloned sheep were examined, it was found that the mitochondria in their cells were all derived from those in the cytoplasm of the egg. (This is a little surprising as some udder cell cytoplasm might have entered the egg with the nucleus.) So Dolly may possess the nuclear genes from the udder cell donor but she has different mitochondrial genes. Animals produced by this '**nuclear transfer**' method are not perfect clones in the way that identical twins are. They can develop significant physical differences from the donor of the nucleus.

Extension

Box 6.4 How old is Dolly?

Dolly grew from an egg with the nucleus from a six year-old sheep. She was born in 1996. Dolly had the body and vigour of a three year-old sheep in 1999. However, her telomeres (see Box 6.3) were seen to be too short for her age. In fact, they were more like those of a nine year-old. Only time will tell the effect of this upon Dolly. Will she age quickly, die 'young' or live a normal life span?

There has been talk of similar methods being used to clone humans. Why not produce a clone of an individual who has proved specially gifted? Consider:

● Who would you like to clone?

● Would such a clone grow old before his or her time?

● Would a different environment alter the development of these gifts in the clone, in spite of almost genetic identity?

● Is such an idea desirable anyway?

Figure 6.13 Dolly

6.9 The principle of division by meiosis

Meiosis follows the G_2 stage of interphase (as mitosis does) so the DNA has replicated before the onset of meiosis.

It is a continuous process consisting of two distinct divisions, **meiosis 1** followed by **meiosis 2**.

Definition

Meiosis is the process by which a diploid nucleus ($2n$) divides to produce four haploid daughter nuclei (n) which are not genetically identical to each other or the parent nucleus

6 In Figure 6.14, the cell numbered '1' is diploid and the cells numbered '4' are haploid. Are the cells numbered '3' haploid or diploid? Explain your answer.   *(3 marks)*

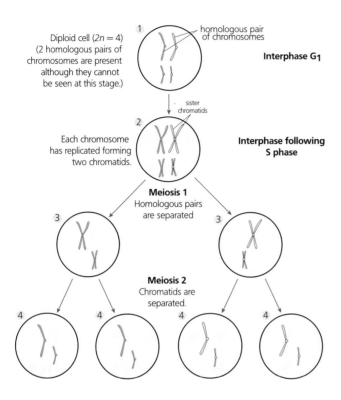

Figure 6.14 *Principles of meiotic division*

6.10 The process of meiosis

The events of meiosis are shown in Figure 6.15 as they would be seen in an animal cell with two pairs of homologous chromosomes ($2n = 4$) using the high power of a light microscope. In the drawings, only cell structures relevant to meiosis are shown. For clarity, one member of each homologous pair is shown in red and the other in yellow.

7 In prophase 1 of meiosis, how many (a) chromatids and (b) chromosomes are there in one bivalent? *(2 marks)*

8 If a cell had a diploid number $2n = 26$, how many bivalents would be visible at prophase 1? *(1 mark)*

6.11 The significance of meiosis

Meiosis is an essential part of sexual reproduction.

Even when, as in some flowering plants, gametes from the same parent fuse (**self-fertilisation**), the offspring differ genetically from the parent. Therefore, as a result of sexual reproduction, there is **genetic variation** among the offspring and they will have different characteristics. This is important for the survival of a species. If all the members of a species were identical, any sudden change in the environment such as the emergence of a new virus would affect all the individuals in the same way and could kill them all. If some individuals were slightly different from the others, they might be resistant to the virus and survive. (Continued on page 174.)

 Definition

Sexual reproduction is the production of a new individual by the fusion of two haploid gametes, usually derived from separate parents. The offspring differ genetically from the parent(s) and each other

Figure 6.15 The process of meiosis

1. Cell at the end of interphase

(i) DNA already replicated, but not coiled, so no chromosomes visible.

(ii) Nuclear membrane present.

(iii) Two centrioles present. (No centrioles in plant cells.)

(iv) Nucleolus present.

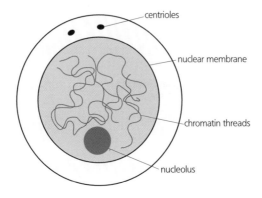
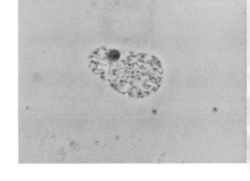

Key
M = maternal chromosome
P = paternal chromosome

Meiosis 1
2. Early prophase 1

(i) DNA condenses, each chromosome becomes stainable and is seen as two chromatids attached at a centromere.

(ii) Nuclear membrane present.

(iii) Centrioles begin to move towards opposite poles of the cell. Microtubules assemble around each centriole.

(iv) Nucleolus disappears.

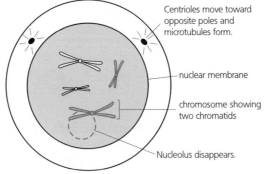
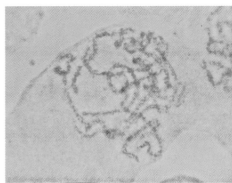

3. Mid prophase 1

(i) Homologous chromosomes pair up and lie alongside each other. (This is called **synapsis**.) Each double structure is called a **bivalent**.

(ii) The centrioles move further towards opposite poles.

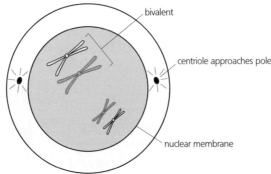
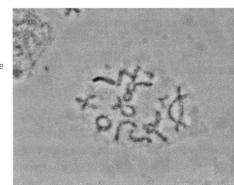

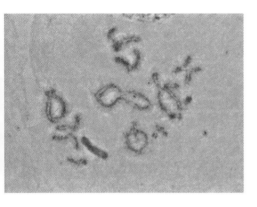

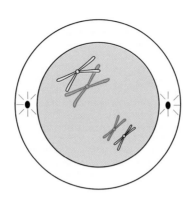

Figure 6.15 *(cont.)*

4. **Late prophase 1**

(i) *The chromatids in a bivalent tangle and pass over each other at points called chiasmata (singular chiasma). The chromatids may break at these points and rejoin with a different chromatid, as shown. If a portion of a chromatid becomes attached to a chromatid of the other chromosome, then a new combination of genes is produced and* **crossing over** *has occurred. The reformed chromosomes are called* **recombinants**.

Crossing over (may occur more than once)

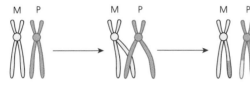

| Homologous chromosome at synapsis. | Chromatids tangle and pass over each other at a chiasma. Chromatids break at chiasma. | After homologous chromosomes separate, parts of chromatoids are exchanged between them. |

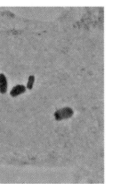

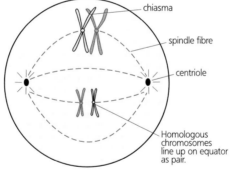

5. **Metaphase 1**

(i) *The nuclear membrane breaks down.*

(ii) *The nuclear spindle forms.*

(iii) *The bivalents move to the equator of the spindle and each chromosome becomes attached to a spindle fibre by its centromere.*

chiasma

spindle fibre

centriole

Homologous chromosomes line up on equator as pair.

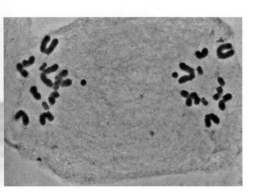

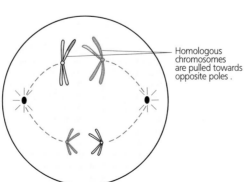

Homologous chromosomes are pulled towards opposite poles .

6. **Anaphase 1**

(i) *Movement and contraction of the spindle fibres causes whole chromosomes to move apart towards opposite poles. So homologous chromosomes separate.*

Figure 6.15 *(cont.)*

7. Telophase 1

(i) A nuclear membrane forms around each group of chromosomes.

(ii) Spindle fibres disappear and centrioles divide into two.

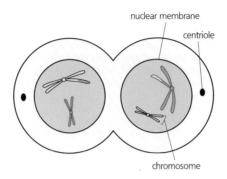

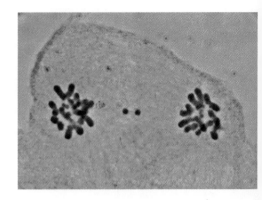

8. Cytokinesis follows and there may or may not be a short pause.

Meiosis 2

9. Prophase 2

(i) Centrioles move towards opposite poles.

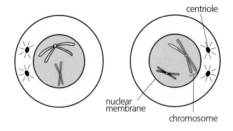

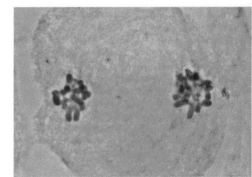

10. Metaphase 2

(i) The nuclear membranes disappear and nuclear spindles form at right angles to the plane of the first spindle.

(ii) The chromosomes move to the equator and attach to spindle fibres by their centromeres.

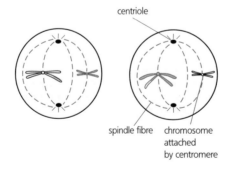

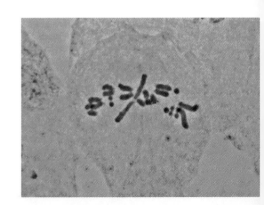

 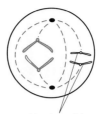

sister chromatids
pulled towards
opposite poles

Figure 6.15 *(cont.)*

11. **Anaphase 2**

(i) *The centromeres divide and sister chromatids move towards opposite poles (i.e. the sister chromatids separate)*

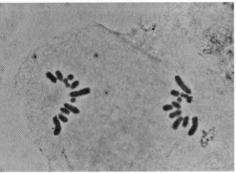

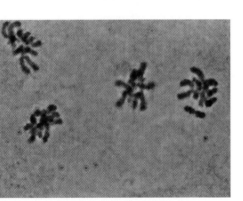

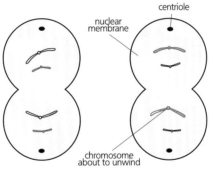

centriole

nuclear
membrane

chromosome
about to unwind

12. **Telophase 2**

(i) *Each chromatid is now called a chromosome. A nuclear membrane forms around each group of chromosomes.*

(ii) *Spindle fibres disappear and the centrioles may divide into two.*

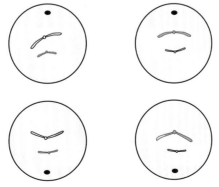

Note from shading pattern that no two
cells have the same assortment of maternal
and paternal genes

13. *Cytokinesis follows and four haploid daughter cells are produced, each of which is genetically different from the others, although only one example of crossing over is shown.*

Meiosis leads to variation among the offspring of sexual reproduction in three ways.

The causes of variation are: crossing over, reduction (followed by fusion of gametes) and independent assortment.

Crossing over

At prophase 1, crossing over usually occurs. This creates a new combination of genes on one chromosome. So offspring inheriting this chromosome are inheriting a totally new gene combination.

Reduction and fusion of gametes

Meiosis produces cells with the haploid number of chromosomes. This allows a gamete, which may develop from one of these cells, to fuse with another cell with a different haploid set, producing a zygote which has the normal diploid number of chromosomes but a new combination of genes. In this way, the chromosome number remains constant from generation to generation although variation occurs.

Independent (random) assortment

At metaphase 1, homologous pairs of chromosomes lie in these pairs at the equator of the spindle. It is purely by chance which 'way round' each pair lies. As seen in Figure 6.16, chromosomes inherited from the mother may pass into the same gamete or different ones. So the gametes differ in the paternal and maternal chromosomes they contain and, as a result, so will the offspring.

***Figure 6.16** Independent assortment*

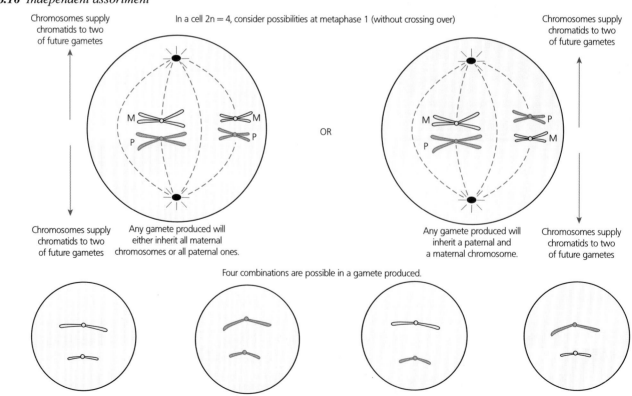

Key: M = maternal chromosome   P = paternal chromosome

Box 6.5 Possible combinations

A mathematical formula shows how many possible assortments of maternal and paternal chromosomes may be found in a gamete produced from a diploid cell by meiosis.

Number of possible combinations in a gamete = 2^n (where n = haploid number of the species).

9 If a diploid cell ($2n = 6$) divides by meiosis, how many different combinations of chromosomes would it be possible to find in a gamete produced from this cell? *(1 mark)*

In humans ($n = 23$) any one of 8,388,608 combinations of maternal and paternal chromosomes may be found in one gamete. If the effects of crossing over are also considered, the amount of variety possible is endless.

Remember

It is important to note that meiosis can only produce *new combinations* of genes, not *new genes*. Only mutations can provide this important source of variation and these may or may not occur during mitosis or meiosis

6.12 Comparison between mitosis and meiosis

Both mitosis and meiosis are involved in cell division and therefore there are many similarities between the processes.

10 List three similarities between mitosis and meiosis. *(3 marks)*

Important differences between mitosis and meiosis are listed in Table 6.2.

Table 6.2 Differences between mitosis and meiosis

Mitosis	Meiosis
one nuclear division, separating chromatids	two nuclear divisions, first separating homologous chromosomes and second separating chromatids
two daughter cells produced	four daughter cells produced
chromosome number remains same	chromosome number halved (haploid cells produced)
no association between homologous chromosomes	homologous chromosomes associate and form bivalents
no crossing over occurs	crossing over may occur at chiasmata
chromosomes only form single row at equator at metaphase	at metaphase 1, chromosomes form double row at equator
daughter cells genetically identical with each other and parent cell	daughter cells differ genetically from each other and parent cell

6.13 The 'root tip squash' – a useful practical technique

When animals grow, mitosis takes place all over the body. However, in plants, mitosis is restricted to areas known as **meristems** where cells are constantly dividing. The tips of roots and shoots contain meristems and so provide a suitable place to observe the stages of mitosis.

The technique described below produces thin layers of whole cells with the chromosomes stained for observation.

Figure 6.17 *Preparing a root tip squash to observe the stages of mitosis*

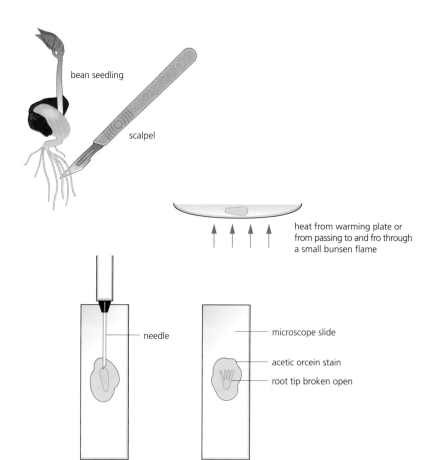

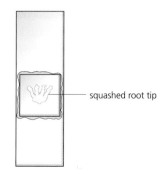

- *The tip of a root, such as the side root of a bean plant, is cut off (about 5 mm long).*

- *The tip is placed in a watch glass in a mixture of 10 parts acetic orcein stain and 1 part hydrochloric acid and warmed gently for 5 minutes to soften the tissues. (Take care to avoid the fumes!)*

- *The tip is then placed on a microscope slide in a few drops of acetic orcein stain and broken open with a needle.*

- *A coverslip is placed over the tip and pressed gently to squash the root tip.*
- *The slide is warmed gently for 10 seconds to intensify the stain.*

Summary – ⑥ Cell division

- Plant and animal bodies consist of millions of **eukaryotic** cells. These cells have their genetic material (DNA) bound with histone proteins in **chromosomes**. These chromosomes are enclosed in a nucleus.

- The body cells are **diploid** as they possess pairs of homologous chromosomes. One of each pair is derived from the mother (maternal) and one is derived from the father (paternal).

- **Gametes** (sperms and eggs) are **haploid** cells, as these contain only one of each pair of chromosomes. Fusion of these gametes at fertilisation produces a diploid cell, the **zygote**. This then divides repeatedly by **mitosis** to produce all the cells of the body.

- As cells divide to produce more body cells, they undergo cycles of events. Each cycle is known as the **cell cycle**.

- Each cycle consists of:
  1. A non-dividing **interphase** which can be subdivided into: a **growth phase (G$_1$)** during which the cell undergoes its normal functions; a **DNA replication phase (S)**; and a **second growth phase (G$_2$)** when proteins are made which are necessary for division.

  2. **Mitosis**, which is a division of the nucleus to produce two daughter nuclei, with the same number of chromosomes as the parent nucleus and each other. The nuclei are genetically identical.

  3. **Cytokinesis** during which the cytoplasm divides to produce two daughter cells.

- Mitosis distributes the replicated DNA equally into two daughter cells which therefore possess the same DNA (and therefore genes) as the parent cell. This is important during **growth and body repair** as all the cells of the body require all the genes.

- Mitosis is also important in **asexual reproduction**. Here cells, produced by cell division, are budded off the parent to produce identical separate individuals. The offspring are produced quickly and, as they are genetically identical to the parent, they are likely to survive in an environment which suited the parent.

- **Clones** of identical individuals can be produced artificially but the type of nuclear division involved is always mitosis.

- **Meiosis** is the type of nuclear division which follows G$_2$ in a diploid cell which is dividing and producing four haploid cells, each of which will vary genetically. These cells usually develop into or produce gametes.

- Meiosis is a complex process involving two nuclear divisions. It distributes the replicated DNA so that each of the four daughter cells has one of each homologous pair of chromosomes. Each daughter cell has a different combination of genes.

- Meiosis contributes to the production of variety among offspring produced by **sexual reproduction**. It allows the gametes produced from a cell to differ genetically through the processes of **crossing over** and **independent assortment**. By **reducing** the number of chromosomes to the haploid number, it allows the fusion of two gametes to take place and restore the diploid number in a new individual. The offspring, therefore, inherits a new combination of chromosomes.

- It is important that individuals of a species differ from one another. The whole species could die if all its members, being identical, were susceptible to a particular change in the environment.

? Answers

1 To hold chromatids together as they move to equator *(1)*.
To attach chromosome to spindle fibre *(1)*.

2 A = prophase; B = telophase;
C = anaphase; D = interphase;
E = metaphase *(5)*

3

Animal cells	Plant cells
Centriole – acts as focus for spindle fibres.	No centriole *(1)* – so spindle fibres parallel. *(1)*
Cytokinesis by cleavage	Cytokinesis by cell plate formation *(1)*
– cell membrane pulled in.	– Golgi secretes new cell walls *(1)*.

4 Large numbers produced quickly.
Genetic certainty – all plants will have required characteristics. Can be produced in any season. Can be produced in a small space. *(4)*

5 Sheep who provided the udder cells. *(1)*

6 Haploid *(1)* as only one of each homologous pair of chromosomes present *(1)* although each chromosome replicated *(1)*.

7 (a) 4 *(1)*
(b) 2 *(1)*

8 13 *(1)*

9 $2^3 = 8$ *(1)*

10 Both follow G_2 stage of interphase (start with replicated DNA) *(1)*. Both involve formation of a spindle *(1)*. Both have similar sequences of events at similar phases *(1)*.

End of Chapter Questions

⌐O N2.2

1 (a) A cell in the G_1 stage of interphase had 10 arbitrary units of DNA contained in six pairs of homologous chromosomes. If it divided by mitosis, how many units of DNA and how many chromosomes would there be,

(i) in the nucleus at the end of G_2?

(ii) during metaphase?

(iii) in each nucleus at the end of telophase?

(b) If the same cell divided by meiosis instead, how many units of DNA and how many chromosomes would there be

(i) in the nucleus at the end of G_2?

(ii) in the cell during anaphase 1?

(iii) in each nucleus at the end of meiosis 1?

(iv) in each nucleus at the end of meiosis 2? *(14 marks)*

2 The graphs in Figure 6.18 show the amounts of DNA and numbers of chromosomes present during various stages of the cell cycle when a cell divides by meiosis. Using some of the terms below, list the most suitable ones to apply to each of the stages A–H.

N2.1

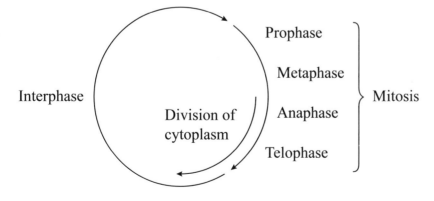

Figure 6.18

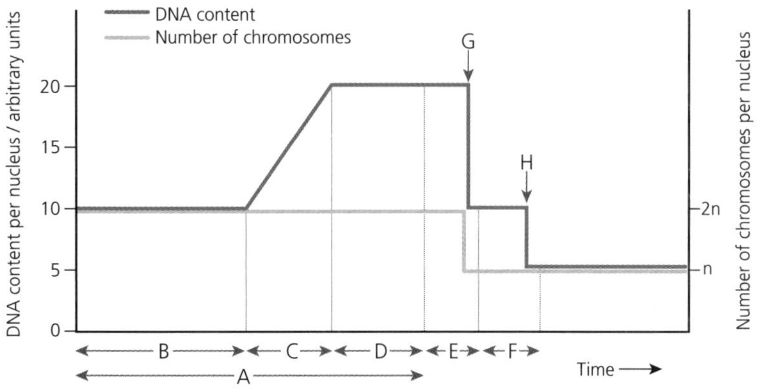

Meiosis 2, telophase 1, G_1, anaphase 2, S, meiosis 1, interphase, metaphase 1, mitosis, G_2, prophase 1, telophase 2, metaphase 2.   *(8 marks)*

3 Compare and contrast the significance of mitosis and meiosis.   *(5 marks)*

4 **(a)** A diploid cell has three pairs of chromosomes X and X', Y and Y', Z and Z'.

This cell undergoes meiosis and crossing over does not occur. List all the possible combinations of chromosomes which could be found in a daughter cell produced.

(b) If crossing over did occur, explain how this would increase the possible genetic variation which could be found among the daughter cells.

(6 marks)

5 The diagram shows the main stages in the cell cycle.

Figure 6.19

Interphase

Prophase

Metaphase

Anaphase

Telophase

Mitosis

Division of cytoplasm

(a) At what stage in the cell cycle do the following events take place:

(i) separation of daughter chromatids?   *(1 mark)*

(ii) replication of DNA?   *(1 mark)*

N2.2

(b) What evidence would you see on a prepared slide of a bean root tip which would show that metaphase takes longer than anaphase? *(1 mark)*

(c) There are 44 chromatids present at the beginning of prophase of mitosis in a rabbit cell.

(i) How many *chromatids* would there be in a cell from a rabbit at the beginning of meiosis? *(1 mark)*

(ii) How many *chromosomes* would there be in a sperm cell from a rabbit? *(1 mark)*

(Total 5 marks)

AQA (AEB) 1998

6 The table below refers to the first and second divisions of meiosis.

If the statement is correct, place a tick (✔) in the appropriate box and if the statement is incorrect, place a cross (✗) in the appropriate box.

Statement	First division of meiosis	Second division of meiosis
pairing of homologous chromosomes occurs		
chromosomes consist of pairs of chromatids during prophase		
chiasmata are formed		
chromatids are separated		
independent assortment of chromosomes occurs		

(Total 5 marks)

London 1998

7 (a) Explain why root tips are particularly suitable material to use for preparing slides to show mitosis. *(1 mark)*

(b) Give a reason for carrying out each of the following steps in preparing a slide showing mitosis in cells from a root tip.

(i) The tissue should be stained. *(1 mark)*

(ii) The stained material should be pulled apart with a needle and gentle pressure applied to the coverslip during mounting. *(1 mark)*

(c) The drawing has been made from a photograph showing a cell undergoing mitosis.

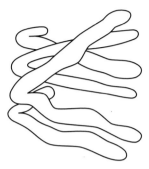 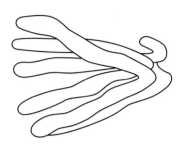

    (i) In which stage of mitosis is the cell shown in this drawing?   *(1 mark)*

    (ii) Describe **one** piece of evidence, visible in the drawing, which could be used to confirm that this cell is *not* in the first division of meiosis.   *(1 mark)*

                                       (Total 5 marks)

NEAB 1998

8 (a) What is:

    (i) a bivalent;   *(1 mark)*

    (ii) a chiasma?;   *(1 mark)*

Diagrams **A**, **B** and **C** show the same stage in mitosis, meiosis I and meiosis II in a plant cell.

     A   B   C

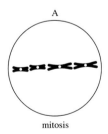 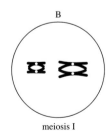 

   mitosis   meiosis I   meiosis II

(b) Identify the stage shown giving your reason. *(1 mark)*

(c) The cell in diagram **A** has 20 units of DNA. How many units of DNA would there be in a cell from this plant at the end of:

(i) mitosis *(1 mark)*

(ii) meiosis? *(1 mark)*

AQA(AEB) 1994

Sexual reproduction is the only type of reproduction that takes place in mammals. It always involves the production of haploid gametes by **meiosis**. The nuclei of a male gamete and a female gamete fuse producing a diploid cell, the zygote, which is the first cell of a new individual.

The general principles of sexual reproduction in mammals are summarised as follows.

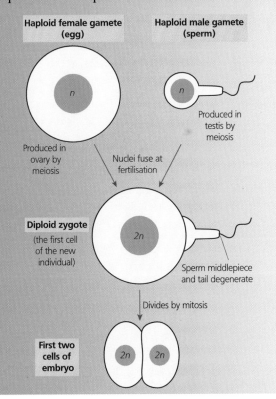

This chapter includes:
- the structure of the human reproductive system
- gametogenesis (the formation of gametes)
- hormones and the events of the menstrual cycle
- fertilisation in humans
- the use of hormones in the artificial control of human reproduction
- pregnancy in humans – implantation and the structure and functions of the placenta
- the role of hormones in birth and in milk production in humans
- reproduction in other mammals – oestrous cycle and the uses of hormones in farming.

Figure 7.1 General principles of sexual reproduction in mammals

7.1 The structure of the human reproductive system

The structure of the male and female reproductive systems is illustrated and described in Figure 7.2.

7.2 Gametogenesis (the formation of gametes)

In mammals, a female gamete is called an **egg** or **ovum** (plural **ova**) and the male gamete is called a **sperm** or **spermatozoon** (plural **spermatozoa**). **Ova are formed in the female's ovaries and spermatozoa are formed** in the male's testes. Organs (ovaries and testes) which produce gametes are called **gonads**. The process of formation of female gametes (ova) is called **oogenesis** and the formation of male gametes (spermatozoa) is called **spermatogenesis** (Figure 7.3).

Figure 7.3 shows an outline of gametogenesis. It may not be necessary to remember the names of all the stages shown in the diagram, but it is important to note the following. During the formation of all gametes, there are three main phases:

- a **multiplication** phase, during which many diploid cells are produced, so that many gametes can be formed eventually

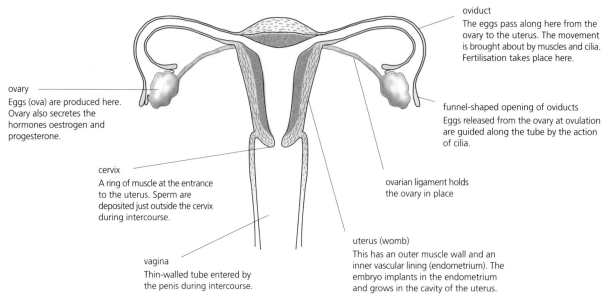

ovary
Eggs (ova) are produced here. Ovary also secretes the hormones oestrogen and progesterone.

oviduct
The eggs pass along here from the ovary to the uterus. The movement is brought about by muscles and cilia. Fertilisation takes place here.

funnel-shaped opening of oviducts
Eggs released from the ovary at ovulation are guided along the tube by the action of cilia.

cervix
A ring of muscle at the entrance to the uterus. Sperm are deposited just outside the cervix during intercourse.

ovarian ligament holds the ovary in place

vagina
Thin-walled tube entered by the penis during intercourse.

uterus (womb)
This has an outer muscle wall and an inner vascular lining (endometrium). The embryo implants in the endometrium and grows in the cavity of the uterus.

Figure 7.2
(a) Structure and function of the human female reproductive system. Longitudinal section – seen from the front

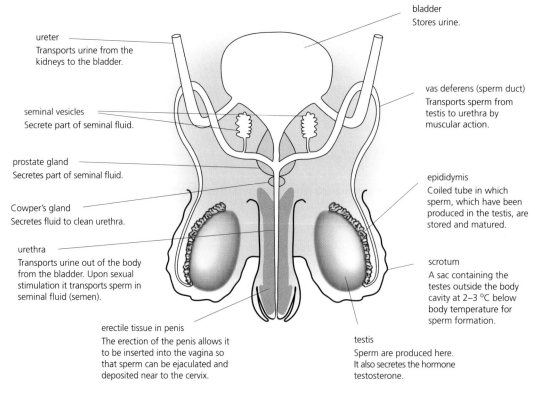

ureter
Transports urine from the kidneys to the bladder.

bladder
Stores urine.

seminal vesicles
Secrete part of seminal fluid.

vas deferens (sperm duct)
Transports sperm from testis to urethra by muscular action.

prostate gland
Secretes part of seminal fluid.

epididymis
Coiled tube in which sperm, which have been produced in the testis, are stored and matured.

Cowper's gland
Secretes fluid to clean urethra.

urethra
Transports urine out of the body from the bladder. Upon sexual stimulation it transports sperm in seminal fluid (semen).

scrotum
A sac containing the testes outside the body cavity at 2–3 °C below body temperature for sperm formation.

erectile tissue in penis
The erection of the penis allows it to be inserted into the vagina so that sperm can be ejaculated and deposited near to the cervix.

testis
Sperm are produced here. It also secretes the hormone testosterone.

Figure 7.2
(b) Structure and function of the human male reproductive system. Longitudinal section – seen from the front

Figure 7.3 Gametogenesis – a comparison between oogenesis and spermatogenesis

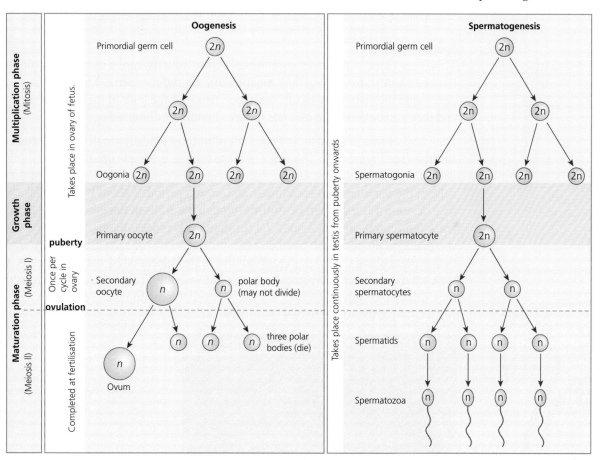

- a **growth** phase, during which more cytoplasm is formed and food reserves may be stored by each cell

- a **maturation** phase, during which the cell divides by meiosis. This produces haploid cells which develop into gametes.

Figure 7.3 also shows that there are some differences between the processes of oogenesis and spermatogenesis. The main differences are:

- In spermatogenesis, the meiotic division of one cell produces four equal haploid cells, each of which develops into a sperm. However during oogenesis, the cytoplasm does not divide equally in meiosis. Although each of the four daughter cells contains a haploid nucleus, one has much more cytoplasm than the others. Only this one develops into an ovum and has enough food reserves to support early embryo development. The other three cells, the polar bodies, die.

- Spermatogenesis takes place continuously in the testes from puberty onwards. Oogenesis begins in the ovary of a fetus and then stops until a girl reaches puberty. It then continues, with one cell maturing each month as described below.

1 Why is it advantageous for an ovum, rather than a sperm, to store some food reserves for early development of the embryo? *(2 marks)*

Spermatogenesis

This takes place in the testes continuously from puberty until a man is very old. It has been known for men in their nineties still to produce sperm. The sperm develop in the seminiferous tubules which make up the bulk of the testis tissue and they can be produced at a rate of three hundred million a day.

Each testis is made up of more than 1 km of microscopically small **seminiferous tubules** (see Figure 7.4). The walls of these tubules are made up of cells undergoing spermatogenesis. The spermatogonia are produced by division of the cells of the outer layer of each tubule and, over a period of about two months, they develop as they progress inwards through the walls of the tubules until they reach the central cavities. Figure 7.4 (c) shows this process diagrammatically. The spermatozoa produced are freed into the lumen (cavity) of each tubule. They are then pushed along the seminiferous tubules in fluid secreted by the Sertoli cells to the epididymis where they mature over about 14 hours. They are stored here until they finally pass out of the body through a vas deferens and the urethra. See Figure 7.5 for the structure of a spermatozoon.

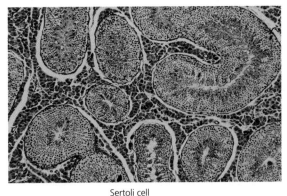

(b)

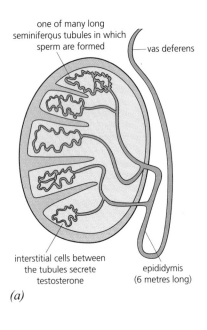

(a)

Figure 7.4 *Spermatogenesis*
(a) Simplified version of structure of a mammalian testis
(b) Light micrograph of section through seminiferous tubule showing interstitial cells between tubules (✕ 50)
(c) Diagrammatic section through a seminiferous tubule showing how developing sperm move inwards in the wall of the tubule

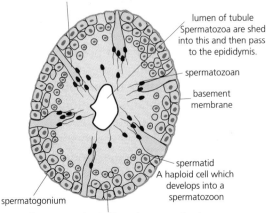

(c)

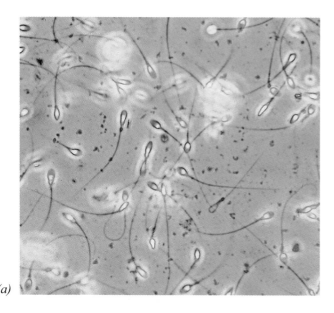

(a)

Figure 7.5
(a) Human spermatozoa
(b) Structure of a spermatozoon

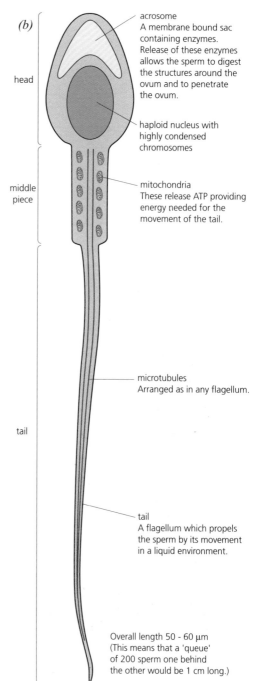

(b)

head
- acrosome
  A membrane bound sac containing enzymes. Release of these enzymes allows the sperm to digest the structures around the ovum and to penetrate the ovum.
- haploid nucleus with highly condensed chromosomes

middle piece
- mitochondria
  These release ATP providing energy needed for the movement of the tail.

tail
- microtubules
  Arranged as in any flagellum.

- tail
  A flagellum which propels the sperm by its movement in a liquid environment.

Overall length 50 - 60 μm
(This means that a 'queue' of 200 sperm one behind the other would be 1 cm long.)

Oogenesis and the development of a Graafian follicle in the human ovary

The formation of the female gametes begins in the ovary of the female while she is still a fetus.

In the fetus cells from the epithelium of the developing ovary divide by mitosis to produce **primary follicles** which sink into the tissues of the ovary. Each primary follicle consists of a sphere of flattened cells surrounding another diploid cell which will eventually form the ovum. This central cell grows and becomes a **primary oocyte**.

When the fetus is born, the baby girl may contain about two million primary follicles, containing primary oocytes, in her ovaries. Many of these follicles die during her childhood and none develop any further until she reaches puberty.

After puberty, each month a few primary follicles develop further but only one usually completes its development, while the others stop and die. The complete development involves the formation of a **Graafian follicle** which contains a **secondary oocyte**. Eventually the mature follicle rises to the surface of the ovary and releases the **secondary oocyte**. This process is called **ovulation**. After ovulation, the outer follicle cells, left in the ovary, heal and form a structure called a **corpus luteum** (yellow body). This sinks back into the ovary. If the egg is not fertilised (and so pregnancy does not occur), the corpus luteum degenerates after a few days. These events are explained in Figures 7.6 and 7.7.

In humans, the cycle of events which involves the formation of a Graafian follicle, ovulation and preparation for a repeat of these events, is referred to as the **menstrual cycle** (from the Latin term *mensis* for month). Each cycle is usually complete in 28 days.

Figure 7.6 *The ovary and development of the ovum*
(a) Micrograph of a Graafian follicle
(b) Diagram to show the developmental stages of an ovum

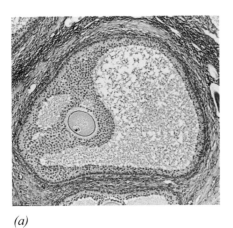

(a)

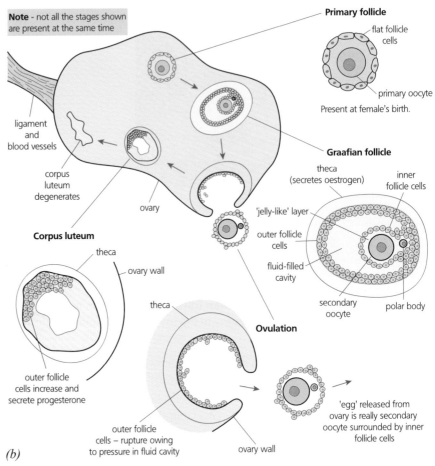

(b)

Figure 7.7
(a) TEM of released secondary oocyte and surrounding structures
(b) Diagram to show structure of the 'egg' at its release from the ovary

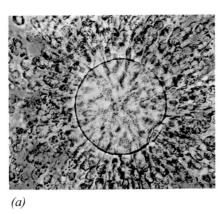

(a)

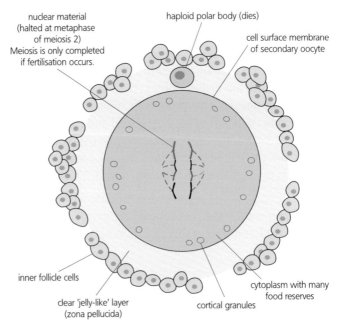

(b)

Most primary follicles die and atrophy (degenerate). During a woman's reproductive life, only about 400–450 follicles mature. However, by about the age of 45–50 years, she has no primary follicles left which have the ability to develop. She has reached the **menopause**.

7.3   The events of the menstrual cycle

The length of the menstrual cycle varies between different women. In the following account, the events of a typical cycle of 28 days are described. During each cycle, a series of changes takes place in the uterus (uterine events) and in the ovaries (ovarian events). These are summarised in Table 7.1 and Figure 7.8.

Table 7.1   *The events of the human menstrual cycle*

	In the ovary	In the uterus
Days 1–5	Graafian follicle begins to develop	the endometrium is shed. (Menstruation occurs)
Days 6–13	Graafian follicle matures	endometrium is repaired
Day 14	ovulation occurs	
Days 15–24	corpus luteum develops	endometrium becomes thicker and many blood vessels develop in it (vascularisation)
Days 25–28	corpus luteum degenerates if fertilisation does not take place	endometrium is fully thickened and begins to break down

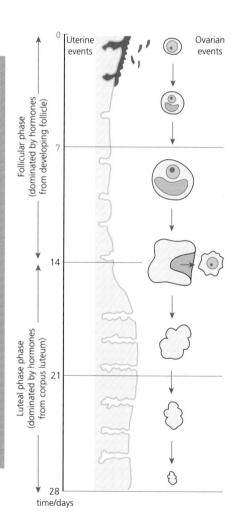

Figure 7.8   *Events of the human menstrual cycle*

Definition

A **hormone** is a chemical substance that is produced in special cells or glands (endocrine glands). It is carried in the blood and has an effect on particular target organs elsewhere in the body

7.4 **How hormones control the menstrual cycle**

There are four hormones which control the events of the menstrual cycle.

Two of these hormones (the **pituitary** or **gonadotrophic** hormones) are produced in a gland just below the brain called the **anterior pituitary gland**. They are **follicle stimulating hormone** (FSH) and **luteinising hormone** (LH).

The other two (the **ovarian** or **gonadal** hormones) are produced in the ovaries. They are: **oestrogen** and **progesterone**. Oestrogen is a mixture of hormones produced by the outer layers (theca) of the Graafian follicle (a little is also produced by the corpus luteum). Progesterone is produced by the corpus luteum.

Figure 7.9 shows the pattern of secretion of these hormones during a typical 28-day cycle. Relate these graphs to the basic account below which shows how these hormones interact with each other and control the cycle.

Figure 7.9 The control of the menstrual cycle by reproductive hormones

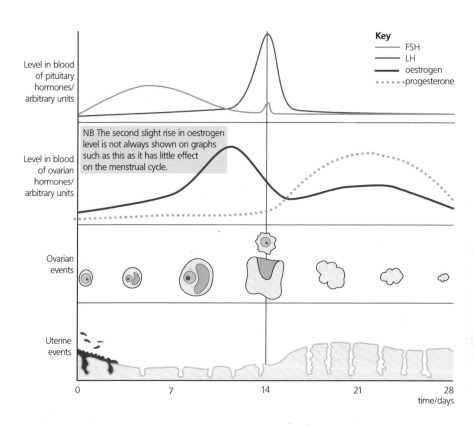

1. Days 1–5 FSH secretion peaks. This

● stimulates the development of a Graafian follicle

● stimulates its theca to produce oestrogen.

2. Days 6–12 Oestrogen secretion increases. This

- promotes the repair of the endometrium
- when it reaches a certain level, stimulates the production of LH
- inhibits the production of FSH. (The lack of FSH leads to less oestrogen being produced.)

3. Days 13 and 14 LH secretion peaks. This

- stimulates ovulation (in the presence of oestrogen)
- stimulates the development of the corpus luteum
- stimulates the corpus luteum to produce progesterone.

4. Days 15–24 Progesterone secretion increases. This

- promotes the thickening and growth of blood vessels in the endometrium
- inhibits the production of FSH and LH.

5. Days 25–28 As LH secretion is inhibited, its level falls, causing the corpus luteum to degenerate and the production of progesterone to decrease.

1. Days 1–5 More FSH is secreted as its production is no longer inhibited, and the cycle begins again. As there is not enough progesterone to maintain the endometrium, this is shed during menstruation.

The role of 'negative feedback' mechanisms in the menstrual cycle
You will see later that the body's physiology is geared to keeping the internal environment balanced and constant. This is done by **negative feedback** mechanisms.

The levels of the reproductive hormones are controlled by negative feedback mechanisms. For example, FSH stimulates the production of oestrogen, causing the oestrogen level to rise. However, oestrogen inhibits the production of FSH, causing FSH level to fall and so, because of lack of stimulation, oestrogen level then falls. So the levels of both hormones are kept cycling in a balanced way.

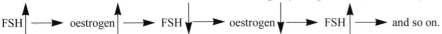

Remember

An easy way to remember the general pattern of the activity of these hormones is by the 'FOLP' diagram

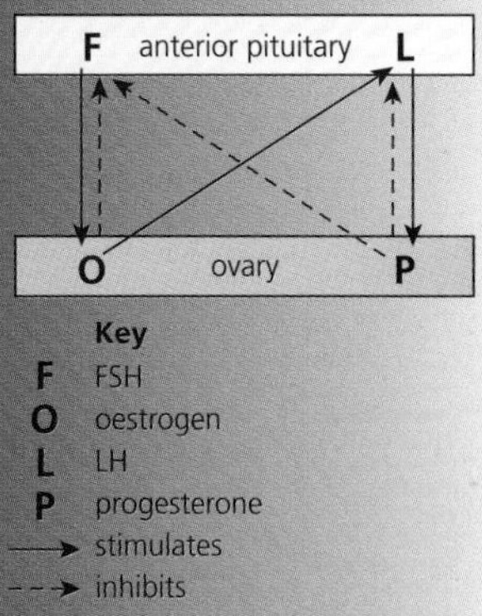

Key
F FSH
O oestrogen
L LH
P progesterone
→ stimulates
⇢ inhibits

Figure 7.10 The 'FOLP' diagram

?

2 Explain how a negative feedback mechanism controls the levels of the other two reproductive hormones. *(3 marks)*

3 Explain why there is a small rise and fall in the level of FSH at about day 14 of the menstrual cycle (see Figure 7.9). *(2 marks)*

Definition

In a negative feedback mechanism, any change from the normal level (of a substance or temperature) triggers a mechanism which restores that normal level

Box 7.1 How hormones control sperm production

From puberty onwards, the anterior pituitary gland in a male secretes similar gonadotrophic hormones to those in a female. However, the effects are different.

● **LH** – stimulates the interstitial cells in the testes (cells of Leydig) to produce the hormone **testosterone**. LH is therefore also known as **interstitial cell stimulating hormone (ICSH)**.

● **FSH** – stimulates sperm production in the testis by promoting spermatogenesis directly and by causing the Sertoli cells to produce substances necessary for sperm production.

The gonadal hormone, **testosterone**, has several roles.

● A little is produced in the fetus, controlling the development of the male reproductive organs.

● At puberty, the increased production controls the enlargement of the reproductive organs and the development of secondary sexual characteristics (characteristics not directly involved in reproduction). These include a spurt in growth and muscle development, the lengthening of vocal cords, which causes the voice to deepen, and the growth of body hair.

● From puberty onwards, it maintains these characteristics and aids sperm production.

7.5 Fertilisation in humans

Movement of sperm through the female reproductive tract
Stimulation of the penis leads to a series of reflexes which include waves of peristaltic contraction. These propel sperm which were stored in the epididymis along the vas deferens. Various secretions are added to the sperm from the prostate gland and seminal vesicles forming seminal fluid (semen). This is ejaculated from the end of the penis.

500 million sperm are deposited in about $5\,cm^3$ of seminal fluid at the cervix by one ejaculation during sexual intercourse.

The seminal fluid contains:

● **alkaline salts** (secreted by the prostate gland). These neutralise acidity of the vagina.

● **fructose** (secreted by the seminal vesicles). This provides energy for the swimming sperm.

● **prostaglandins** (secreted by the seminal vesicles). These promote contractions of the uterus and oviducts which help the sperm reach the egg.

The force of ejaculation propels some sperm through the cervix. Then swimming movements of the sperm and contractions of the uterus help the sperm to move to the oviducts where fertilisation takes place.

It is not thought that the ovum secretes chemicals which attract the sperm. A few hundred sperm may reach the ovum, high in the oviducts, by chance.

Definition

Fertilisation is the fusion of the haploid nuclei of a male and a female gamete to produce the diploid nucleus of a zygote

Fertilisation

The main events that take place during fertilisation are shown in Figure 7.11.

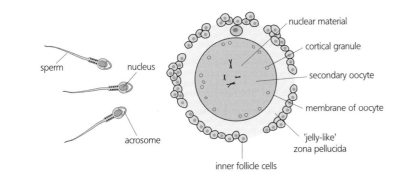

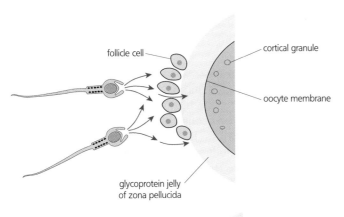

Figure 7.11 Fertilisation
1. Many sperm encounter the secondary oocyte in the oviduct. Their acrosomes have matured since their release, during a process known as **capacitation** *(developing the capacity to fertilise).*

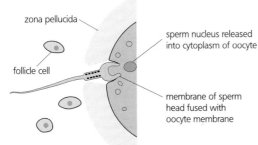

2. The **acrosome reaction** *occurs, during which enzymes are released from the acrosomes of many sperms by exocytosis. These enzymes digest the material between the inner follicle cells and the glycoprotein jelly of the zona pellucida, allowing sperm to pass. One sperm usually reaches the oocyte membrane first.*

3. The membrane of a sperm head fuses with that of the oocyte, the head is engulfed and the sperm's chromosomes are released into the cytoplasm of the oocyte.

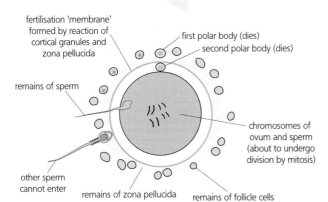

4. This leads to three events.
- *The* **cortical reaction** *occurs. Cortical granules are released quickly from the oocyte by exocytosis. These react with the glycoprotein of the zona pellucida to form a fertilisation membrane which prevents the entry of further sperm.*
- *Meiosis 2 is completed in the oocyte, producing the ovum and a polar body.*
- *The chromosomes from the sperm join those of the ovum and a diploid zygote is formed.*

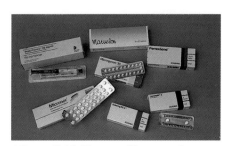

Figure 7.12 *Forms of hormonal contraceptions*

7.6

The use of hormones in the artificial control of human reproduction

Reproductive hormones can be extracted from other mammals or synthesised in the laboratory. They can then be used to treat humans either as contraceptives or, conversely, to promote fertility.

Hormones and contraception

If the secretion of FSH and LH are suppressed, it follows that a Graafian follicle will not develop and ovulation cannot occur. Therefore pregnancy can never take place. Progesterone inhibits the production of both of these hormones and oestrogen inhibits FSH. This is the basic principle behind the use of hormonal contraceptive treatments. Progesterone also thickens the mucus in the cervix, helping to block the entry of sperm. The main methods of treatment are shown in Table 7.2. In these treatments, **progestogen** is used. This is a synthetic form of progesterone derived from testosterone. Unlike progesterone, it is not destroyed in the stomach and can be given by mouth.

Table 7.2 *Hormonal methods of contraception*

combined pill	contains **oestrogen** and **progestogen**. It is taken for 21 days of the cycle and then during the next 7 days a withdrawal bleed occurs, preventing abnormal build-up of the endometrium. It is very effective, although side-effects may include a slightly increased risk of thrombosis (see Box 10.5, page 289) and, occasionally, nausea and water retention. Care should be taken when antibiotics are being taken or during stomach trouble. These may prevent the hormones being absorbed and so ovulation could take place
progestogen-only pill	contains no oestrogen and avoids the increased risk of thrombosis. It is sometimes recommended for older women or smokers
depo-provera injection	injections containing progestogen are made into the muscle about every three months. Slow release of the hormone into the blood inhibits FSH production and thickens mucus in the cervix
implant e.g. Norplant	slowly releases hormones including progestogen into the blood and can remain effective for five years by inhibiting FSH and thickening cervical mucus
morning-after pill	contains a high level of a synthetic oestrogen, diethylstibestrol. It can be taken shortly after intercourse and prevents the embryo becoming implanted. It is effective but can have side-effects. It is not intended for regular use but as an occasional emergency measure

Did You Know

Contraception and the Mexican yam

Various forms of contraception have been used by ancient civilisations. Chinese women have swallowed live tadpoles while, in other parts of Asia, a drink made of the Kallhambha plant mixed with the feet of jungle flies was supposed to make sure that a woman became permanently childless!

Herbal medicines have been used all over the world. Many have been investigated by scientists, who found that while some were dangerous, others contained chemicals likely to induce miscarriages.

The root of the Mexican yam has been found to contain a substance called diosgenin from which progesterone can be produced. It was this discovery in 1941 which led to the large-scale production of progesterone and eventually to the development of the contraceptive pill.

Hormones and human fertility treatment

Couples may not be able to have babies for several reasons. 10% do not conceive within a year of trying and sometimes, even though conception occurs, a woman may not be able to have a successful pregnancy owing to hormone imbalance.

Some factors, in women, which make conception unlikely are:

- Some women have no potential ova in their ovaries. This condition is not treatable although they can have babies using donated eggs and *in vitro* fertilisation (IVF) – see below.

- Some women have potential ova, but growth of Graafian follicles and ovulation do not occur. A common cause of this is that the woman does not produce enough FSH to initiate the menstrual cycle. Treatment is possible with drugs such as clomiphene citrate which stimulates FSH production or by injections of FSH itself. Much care is needed to prevent too much FSH leading to multiple ovulation, and so to multiple births. Multiple births can cause health risks because birth weights can be very low and birth may be premature.

- Some women have blocked or damaged oviducts, caused genetically or by a previous infection. An oocyte may be released normally, but the sperm cannot reach it! This blockage can sometimes be cleared by inflation or surgery. If repair is not possible, then this would be a case where IVF (*in vitro* fertilisation) is very helpful.

Figure 7.13 *The Slater quads with their elder sister Jessica. Multiple births can result in healthy babies.*

The principles of IVF are shown in Figure 7.14. Before undergoing IVF, a woman has her normal menstrual cycle halted by drugs. She is then treated with high doses of FSH or drugs to stimulate high FSH production. This means that a large number of Graafian follicles are stimulated to grow and reach maturity at a predictable time. In this way a surgeon can retrieve many eggs from her ovaries in one operation.

4 Suggest why, although a woman may take some steroid hormones (see Section 3.12, page 79) such as oestrogen by mouth, it is necessary to inject a protein hormone such as FSH. *(2 marks)*

5 A good source of FSH, which is needed for infertility treatments, is the urine of post-menopausal women. Suggest why it is likely that women have high levels of FSH after they have reached the menopause. *(3 marks)*

Figure 7.14 Principles of in vitro fertilisation (IVF) techniques

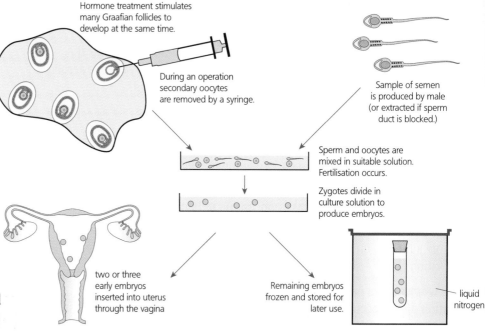

Hormone treatment stimulates many Graafian follicles to develop at the same time.

During an operation secondary oocytes are removed by a syringe.

Sample of semen is produced by male (or extracted if sperm duct is blocked.)

Sperm and oocytes are mixed in suitable solution. Fertilisation occurs.

Zygotes divide in culture solution to produce embryos.

two or three early embryos inserted into uterus through the vagina

Remaining embryos frozen and stored for later use.

liquid nitrogen

⚠ Did You Know

Some research suggests that there has been a general trend for sperm counts to become lower in recent years. There are also significant differences between men in different areas. Several possible environmental causes are being investigated including the plastic wrapping on foods! Oestrogen-like compounds are becoming more commonly used and are even found in milk and soya beans. The environment has become polluted by such chemicals, including detergents and dioxins. Male fish in polluted waters have been found with female characteristics.

Infertility can also be caused by problems in men.

● The sperm count may be low or he may produce a high proportion of abnormal sperm. This faulty spermatogenesis can sometimes be improved by improving general health and reducing smoking and alcohol intake.

● The sperm duct may be blocked so that although semen may be ejaculated, it contains no sperm.

IVF can also help to overcome these problems. Sperm from a sample of semen, or extracted from the testes, can be selected and introduced to the egg in a laboratory. It has even been possible to fertilise eggs with extracted spermatids (immature sperm with no tails). These have been injected directly into eggs artificially.

Box 7.2 Embryos and ethics

IVF treatment helps many people to have much-wanted families, but it can lead to problems. Spare embryos are kept frozen for a fixed time in case they are needed for implantation into the mother. These embryos may consist of just a few cells, but they are genetically unique and can be considered as separate individuals.

Below are some of the ethical questions raised by IVF:

● What should be done with embryos not required by the parents?

   (a) Should they be destroyed?

   (b) Should they be offered to infertile couples?

   (c) Should they be used for useful medical research, such as that described in Box 7.3?

   (d) Should the parents decide what to do?

If the parents divorce before all the embryos are used,

   (a) should an embryo be implanted into the mother against the father's wishes?

   (b) should the father pay maintenance if she does?

   (c) who has custody of the embryos?

● If the parents die, still childless, should the embryos inherit their estate?

● Should embryos from IVF be offered to anyone, for example,

   (a) a post-menopausal woman in her fifties or sixties?

   (b) someone with a terminal illness?

7.7 Pregnancy in humans

Implantation

If fertilisation takes place normally, high in the oviducts, then the zygote begins to divide by mitosis. It produces a hollow ball of cells which reaches the uterus about four days later. The young embryo, now called a blastocyst, becomes embedded in the endometrium about six to seven days after fertilisation. This embedding is called **implantation**. The details of this process are shown in Figure 7.15.

The young embryo is nourished at first by nutrients absorbed directly from the mother's endometrium through the trophoblastic villi, but as further development takes place the **placenta** is formed.

Figure 7.15 *Early development and*
implantation of the embryo

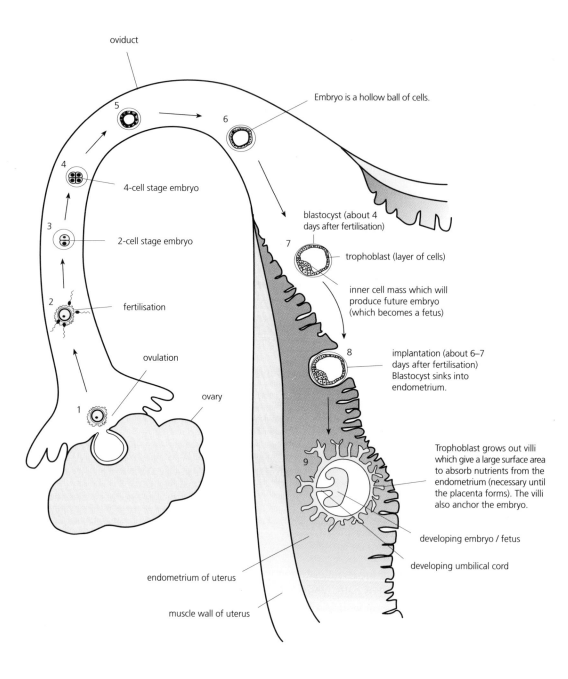

oviduct

Embryo is a hollow ball of cells.

5

6

4

4-cell stage embryo

blastocyst (about 4
days after fertilisation)

7

trophoblast (layer of cells)

3

2-cell stage embryo

inner cell mass which will
produce future embryo
(which becomes a fetus)

2

fertilisation

8

implantation (about 6–7
days after fertilisation)
Blastocyst sinks into
endometrium.

ovulation

1

ovary

Trophoblast grows out villi
which give a large surface area
to absorb nutrients from the
endometrium (necessary until
the placenta forms). The villi
also anchor the embryo.

9

developing embryo / fetus

developing umbilical cord

endometrium of uterus

muscle wall of uterus

Box 7.3 Embryonic stem cells and 'organ banks'

A few days after fertilisation, a mammal embryo has reached a stage called a blastocyst (Figure 7.15, page 198). The group of cells inside the blastocyst, the inner cell mass, consists of **embryonic stem cells (ESCs)**. These cannot be used to form whole cloned embryos as they cannot form a placenta if placed in a surrogate mother. However, they do still have the ability to divide repeatedly and to develop into any kind of tissue. Human ESCs usually keep this ability for about eight days in a developing embryo. After this, different stem cells begin to form different tissues with limits on their powers of division and type of development.

ESCs will divide in cultures. Researchers feel that if they can mimic the complex conditions inside the embryo which cause an ESC to develop into a particular tissue, they could grow chosen tissues and organs in the laboratory.

Before the time comes when organ and tissue banks can be developed to supply the needs of transplant surgery, there are many problems to be overcome. These include:

● In an embryo there are hundreds of chemical growth factors and physical forces which cause an ESC to develop into a particular tissue. These are far from being understood and so cannot yet be applied artificially in a laboratory.

● Although much research is possible on mammals such as mice, the main source of human ESCs is discarded embryos from IVF clinics (see Box 7.2, page 197). These are relatively rare, even if embryonic research on them is allowed.

Techniques such as that indicated in Figure 7.16 could eventually be used to provide tissue to replace diseased tissue in particular patients.

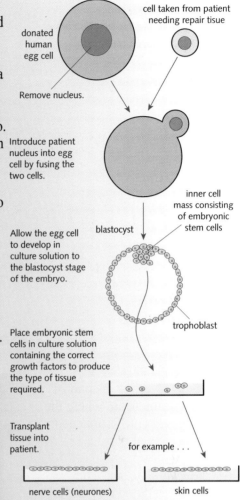

Figure 7.16 The production of 'personalised' repair tissue

Structure of the placenta

The embryo grows and is pushed out of the endometrium into the cavity of the uterus where it is surrounded by a sac of embryonic tissue known as the **amnion**. This sac secretes **amniotic fluid** which fills the space between the amnion and the embryo/fetus. The fluid protects the embryo physically by acting as a shock absorber. The embryo remains attached to the endometrium by the **umbilical cord** which contains blood vessels. The structure of the placenta is illustrated in Figure 7.17.

Functions of the placenta

The placenta forms a selective barrier between the mother's blood and the fetal blood. It allows some substances to pass from one to the other, as follows:

● Nutrition – water, mineral salts, glucose, amino acids, lipids and vitamins pass from mother to fetus by a mixture of diffusion, active transport and pinocytosis (see Section 2.3, page 42).

 Remember

When the embryo develops recognisable human structures such as limbs, it is usually called a **fetus**.

Figure 7.17
(a) Position of the placenta
(b) Photograph of a 'scan' showing a developing fetus

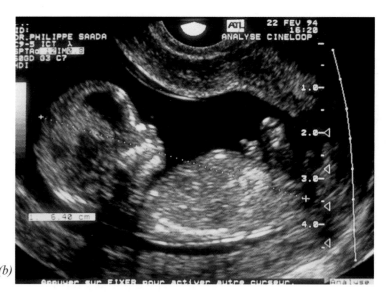

oviduct

fetus

ovary

The placenta is formed from part of the endometrium and from embryonic tissue.

muscle wall of uterus

endometrium

umbilical cord connecting fetus to placenta

amnion (membrane which encloses the fetus in the fluid filled amniotic cavity – protecting against physical shocks)

(a)

💡 **Definition**

The placenta is the part of the endometrium where the umbilical cord is attached. It consists of part endometrium and part embryonic tissue. The mother's blood and the embryo's / fetal blood are brought close to each other to allow substances to be exchanged between them but the bloods never mix. Figure 7.17 shows the details of the position and structure of a placenta.

(b)

- Gas exchange – oxygen diffuses from mother to fetus. Fetal haemoglobin has a higher affinity for oxygen than adult haemoglobin (see Section 11.6, page 319). Carbon dioxide diffuses from the fetus to the mother.

- Excretion – as well as carbon dioxide, nitrogenous waste materials, such as urea, diffuse from the fetus to the mother.

- Protection – antibodies pass from the mother to the fetus, giving the fetus and young baby temporary passive immunity to some diseases (see Section 11.13, page 331).

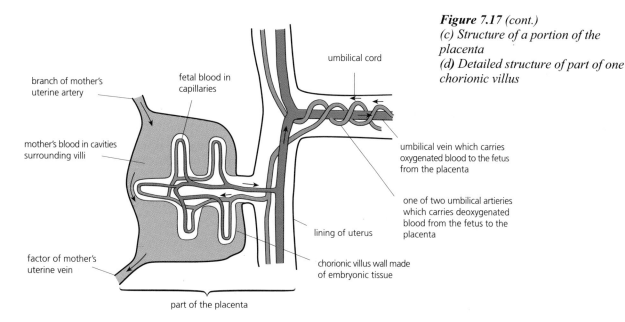

Figure 7.17 (cont.)
(c) Structure of a portion of the placenta
(d) Detailed structure of part of one chorionic villus

branch of mother's uterine artery

fetal blood in capillaries

umbilical cord

mother's blood in cavities surrounding villi

umbilical vein which carries oxygenated blood to the fetus from the placenta

one of two umbilical artieries which carries deoxygenated blood from the fetus to the placenta

lining of uterus

factor of mother's uterine vein

chorionic villus wall made of embryonic tissue

part of the placenta

c)

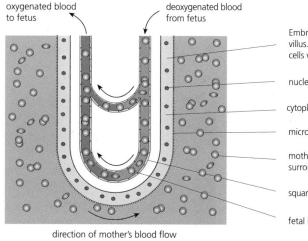

oxygenated blood to fetus

deoxygenated blood from fetus

Embryonic tissue making wall of villus. It consists of a single layer of cells which have merged together.

nucleus in villus wall

cytoplasm with many mitochondria

microvilli

mother's blood cell in cavity surrounding villus

squamous cell of fetal capillary wall

fetal blood cell

direction of mother's blood flow

Note

(1) The blood of the fetus is always separated from the mother's blood but sometimes they are only 7 µm apart.

(2) Mother's blood flow is in the opposite direction to fetal blood flow. This countercurrent system maximises exchange of substances (see Section 9.14, page 263).

Key

fetal oxygenated blood

fetal deoxygenated blood

mother's blood

d)

?

6 Study Figure 7.17 and suggest,
(a) three structural features which facilitate the passage of substances between the maternal and fetal blood by diffusion
(b) one **other** feature which suggests that active transport may also be involved. *(4 marks)*

However, the bloods do *not* mix and it is vital that the exchange of some substances is prevented. For example, if maternal hormones pass into a male fetus, it could affect his development. The passage of pathogens, such as viruses, is prevented as they can cause much harm if they reach the fetus. A few viruses can cross the placenta, such as HIV and the rubella virus. The rubella viruses only cause the mild disease known as 'German measles' in an adult, but they can lead to problems such as deafness or mental impairment if they reach a fetus. To prevent the chance of mothers developing this disease during pregnancy, vaccination against rubella is offered to pre-school children (see Section 11.13, page 331).

If the bloods mixed, the high blood pressure of the mother's blood would damage the delicate fetal blood vessels.

The placenta secretes hormones essential in pregnancy:

● It secretes human chorionic gonadotrophin (HCG) for the first three months. This maintains the corpus luteum and allows it to continue to produce oestrogen and progesterone during this time until the placenta takes over this role.

● It secretes oestrogen and progesterone. After three months, it takes over this function completely from the corpus luteum.

● It secretes placental lactogen which stimulates the growth of the mammary glands (which will eventually produce milk) in the breasts.

> **Extension**
>
> **Box 7.4 HIV and pregnancy**
>
> A pregnant woman who is HIV positive has a 25 to 35 per cent chance of infecting her baby, if she has no medical treatment at all. If she takes the drug AZT during the last three months of pregnancy, the risk of infection can be reduced to less than ten per cent. The viruses can also be transmitted during childbirth and via breast milk. If the mother chooses to give birth by Caesarean delivery and does not breast feed, then the risk of this type of transmission can be cut to two per cent or less.
>
> Some research has suggested that taking a mixture of 'AIDS drugs' during pregnancy can lead to birth defects in a few babies, but this is outweighed by the reduction in the chance of being infected with HIV.

7.8 The roles of hormones in birth (parturition)

In humans the length of pregnancy (gestation period) is about forty weeks.

During this time, the placenta secretes progesterone and oestrogen. The hormones have several functions. For example, both stimulate the growth of the mammary glands and both inhibit FSH secretion, and so further ovulation, during pregnancy.

In addition oestrogen stimulates the increase in size of the muscles of the uterus wall and makes them sensitive to a hormone called **oxytocin**. Progesterone inhibits the release of oxytocin from the posterior pituitary gland.

At about the thirty-eighth week of pregnancy, the fetus itself triggers the events leading to its birth. The details are not fully understood, but an outline of these events is given below.

The fetus reaches a certain stage of maturity or slight stress.

↓

The adrenal cortex gland *in the fetus* is stimulated to secrete a hormone.

↓

This hormone is carried in fetal blood to the placenta.

↓

The placenta responds by
(i) secreting prostaglandins
(ii) producing less progesterone.

↓

As the progesterone level falls, the mother secretes oxytocin
(also oxytocin secretion is increased as the fetus presses against the cervix).

↓

Oxytocin and prostaglandins stimulate the contraction of the uterus
muscles, and birth follows.

7.9 The roles of hormones in milk production (lactation)

Milk production involves three phases:

(1) The mammary glands must grow and be ready to produce milk before birth.

(2) After birth, the mammary glands must secrete milk.

(3) This milk must be ejected into the ducts of the mammary glands (let down) so that the baby can receive it, as it sucks.

Hormones are involved in all of these phases. The placenta secretes oestrogen, progesterone and a hormone called placental lactogen which stimulate the growth of the mammary glands during pregnancy. Oestrogen and progesterone inhibit the secretion of the hormone **prolactin** by the anterior pituitary gland and prevent the effectiveness of any which is secreted. Prolactin stimulates the mammary glands to secrete milk. So, as oestrogen and progesterone levels fall at the time of birth, prolactin is secreted and milk production starts.

The sucking of the baby stimulates a nervous reflex action (the suckling reflex). As the baby sucks the nipples, nervous impulses are transmitted to the part of the brain which, in turn, stimulates the posterior pituitary gland to secrete oxytocin. Oxytocin is carried in the blood and, on reaching the muscles around the mammary glands, it stimulates them to contract. This squeezes the milk into the ducts with force.

Table 7.3 Summary of the roles of hormones in the menstrual cycle, birth and milk production

Hormone	Menstrual cycle	Effects in birth	Milk production
FSH	Growth of follicle Stimulates oestrogen production		
LH	Ovulation Formation of corpus luteum Stimulates progesterone production		
oestrogen	Repair of endometrium Stimulates LH Inhibits FSH	Growth of uterus muscle Sensitises muscle to oxytocin	Growth of mammary glands Inhibits prolactin
progesterone	Vascularisation of endometrium Inhibits LH Inhibits FSH	Inhibits oxytocin Inhibits uterine contractions	Growth of mammary glands Inhibits prolactin
oxytocin		Stimulates uterine contractions	Stimulates milk ejection
prolactin			Stimulates milk production
prostaglandins		Stimulate uterine contractions	
lactogen			Growth of mammary glands

7.10 Oestrous cycle in other mammals

Many mammals do not shed the lining of the endometrium but reabsorb its components into the blood. Therefore they do not menstruate. The length of the cycle varies in different mammals. So the term 'menstrual cycle' is not appropriate and is replaced by the term **oestrous cycle**.

This name is used because, unlike humans, many female mammals are only willing to mate at a definite time in the cycle. This time, just before ovulation, is known as **oestrus** or 'heat'. It is the time in the cycle when mating is most likely to lead to fertilisation and therefore the production of offspring.

Figure 7.18 shows the timing of hormone levels and events in the oestrous cycle of a cow. It can be seen that the general pattern of hormone secretion and events is similar to that in humans but there are some significant differences.

There is a distinct advantage in having a time of oestrus in the cycle. In the wild, herd animals similar to cows live in groups where one male serves all the females in his herd. If the females only allow him to mate with them when fertilisation is likely, then he is prevented from wasting his energy.

Remember

It is necessary to distinguish between the spelling of the words:

Oestr**ous** describes the type of cycle which contains a period of oestr**us** (heat)

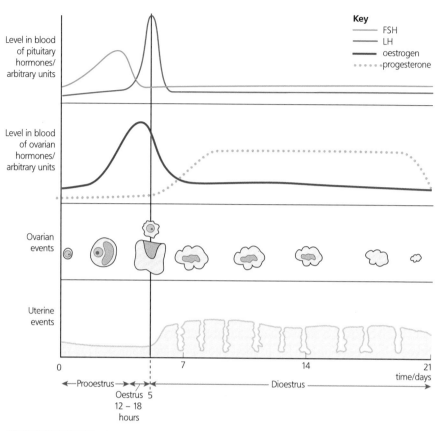

Key
— FSH
— LH
— oestrogen
· · · · progesterone

Figure 7.18 The oestrous cycle of a cow

Figure 7.19 A Friesian cow in heat – standing to be mounted even by other cows!

7 List three differences between the oestrous cycle of a cow and the menstrual cycle of a human. *(3 marks)*

The cow's behaviour changes during oestrus. These changes can be noted by a farmer, who may introduce a bull at the appropriate time or, more likely, carry out artificial insemination using sperm from a donor bull.

These behaviour changes include: restlessness, with more walking about, and nudging and butting other cows; mounting other cows or allowing herself to be mounted; withholding milk.

After ovulation, there is a mucus discharge from the vagina. Oestrus is over and the farmer's chance has been missed!

Did You Know

Breeding like rabbits

Unlike most mammals with fixed times of ovulation, rabbits ovulate as a response to mating, so that the eggs are produced at exactly the best time to favour fertilisation. Five or six eggs from each ovary pass into each oviduct at the same time, giving rise to large litters. The pregnancy only lasts thirty days. The young rabbit is mature enough to breed in four months. It is not surprising that rabbits have earned a reputation as fast breeders!

7.11 The use of hormones in farming

Hormones can also be used to manipulate the reproduction of other mammals. It is not surprising that livestock breeders have discovered this and have found ways to affect the breeding behaviour of farm animals to improve profitability.

Hormones and multiple embryos
Techniques related to those used by doctors in human IVF treatments can be used on other mammals. For example, FSH or drugs to stimulate excess FSH production can be used to promote multiple ovulation in cows.

The ova can be fertilised inside a suitable cow by artificial insemination with semen from a bull also with desirable characteristics. The embryos are flushed out and inserted separately into surrogate mothers.

Alternatively, the ova can be removed directly from the ovaries (sometimes after the cow has been slaughtered). These ova are fertilised in the laboratory and the embryos are cultured for five days. The embryos can then be frozen for later use or immediately inserted into surrogate mothers.

It is also possible for the nucleus to be removed from each ovum and then a nucleus derived from a stem cell of a suitable embryo can be injected into it. The embryos which develop can be inserted into surrogate mothers. This way clones of cattle with desirable characteristics can be produced.

8 The recipient cows must be at the right stage of the oestrous cycle, if successful implantation is to take place. Suggest at which stage in the cycle this should be.   *(1 mark)*

Hormones and the timing of the oestrous cycle
It is very helpful and economical if a whole herd of cows or sheep come into oestrus at the same time chosen by the farmer. This means that the farmer can artificially inseminate cows or hire a particular ram to serve the sheep on one occasion. It also means that the animals will give birth at about the same time, and at a time suitable to the farmer. For example, the lambs will be ready at the same time to take to market.

The progesterone level falls at the end of the reproductive cycle as the corpus luteum degenerates. As progesterone inhibits FSH production, it is this fall in progesterone level which is followed by FSH secretion and Graafian follicle formation.

It is this principle which is used by farmers to make a whole herd ovulate at the same time. A farmer may insert a device into the vagina of a sheep or a cow which releases progesterone into the blood of the animal. This prevents ovulation in any animal until all are past the end of their normal cycle. The farmer removes the device from the herd on the same day and all the animals will ovulate a few days later. Alternatively, a farmer may inject all the animals with prostaglandins on the same day. This causes the corpus luteum in each animal to degenerate and ovulation soon follows.

These techniques are particularly useful for sheep farmers. Unlike cows, sheep do not show behaviour changes at oestrus, making it very difficult for the farmer to know when to introduce the ram or carry out artificial insemination.

The oestrous cycle of sheep is basically the same as that of cows except that it lasts 14–18 days. In many breeds in this country, FSH production is only stimulated as the periods of daylight length shorten and the oestrous cycles only take place in the autumn. The reproduction of these breeds can, therefore, only be manipulated by the farmer during the autumn.

9 The period of gestation (duration of pregnancy) in sheep is about five months. What is the advantage to sheep in this country of only having oestrous cycles in the autumn?   *(2 marks)*

Hormones and milk production

BST (bovine somatotrophin) is a growth hormone, produced naturally by the anterior pituitary gland of cows. Injections of BST (produced by genetically engineered micro-organisms) into the adult cow increase the amount of milk produced as it causes glucose and fatty acids to be diverted to the mammary (milk-forming) glands. Milk production can be increased by 20%. Clearly this is an economic advantage to the farmer, if the price obtained for the milk outweighs the extra cost of the increased food required.

However, there are concerns about the use of BST.

- Treated cows may need drugs to boost the immune system.

- Some BST may enter the milk (although this may not be dangerous).

- Occasionally metabolic disorders may occur in the cows.

- Cows receiving BST are more likely to suffer from mastitis (udder infections) than other cows. This may encourage farmers to use more antibiotics which may remain in the milk. Over-use of antibiotics favours the evolution of antibiotic-resistant bacteria (see Section 17.11, page 532).

BST is used widely in milk production in the USA, but this use of the hormone was banned in the European Community in 1986. This ban has caused much controversy and is under regular review.

Did You Know

In the past, farmers have used simpler but effective methods to help them know when particular sheep had mated and, therefore, were likely to give birth. The belly of the ram (male) was painted, so that he left tell-tale paint marks on the ewes (females) with which he had mated. By changing the colour each week the farmers knew approximately when to expect lambs to be born

Summary – (7) Reproduction in mammals

- Sexual reproduction in mammals involves fusion of a haploid male gamete nucleus and a haploid female gamete nucleus to produce a diploid **zygote**.

- The male gametes (**spermatozoa**) are formed in the testes during **spermatogenesis**, in **seminiferous tubules**. They are stored in the **epididymis** and deposited in the vagina of the female during sexual intercourse.

- The female gametes (**ova**) are formed in the ovaries during **oogenesis**. At birth, the ovaries contain **primary follicles**, each containing potential ova. Ova only develop further at a rate of one per month between puberty and the menopause.

- The menstrual cycle is a 28-day cycle in women during which:

  (i)   **FSH** from the anterior pituitary stimulates a **Graafian follicle** to mature and release oestrogen

  (ii) **oestrogen** inhibits FSH, causes the endometrium to heal and stimulates the anterior pituitary to produce LH

  (iii) **LH** stimulates **ovulation** and then promotes the formation of the **corpus luteum** and its secretion of progesterone

  (iv) **progesterone** inhibits FSH and LH and vascularises the endometrium. If fertilisation does not occur, the corpus luteum degenerates, progesterone level falls and the endometrium is shed again.

- **Fertilisation** in humans takes place in the **oviducts**. The mature sperm shed enzymes from the acrosomes, which digest the path through surrounding cells and jelly to the oocyte. The nucleus from one sperm enters, the oocyte completes its development into an ovum and the nuclei fuse. Cortical granules are released from the ovum and react with surrounding jelly to form a fertilisation membrane which prevents the entry of more sperm.

- The reproductive hormones can be used to manipulate the reproductive process:

  (i) progesterone and oestrogen can be used in **contraceptive** techniques

  (ii) FSH can be used in techniques to enable infertile couples to have babies.

- In humans, a zygote divides as it passes down the oviduct to produce a simple multicellular embryo. The embryo becomes **implanted** in the endometrium and develops **trophoblastic villi** which absorb nutrients from the endometrium.

- The embryo develops and is pushed into the uterus cavity, but it remains connected to the endometrium at the **placenta**.

- In the placenta, embryonic **chorionic villi**, containing capillaries of the fetus, are bathed by maternal blood. Oxygen, nutrients and antibodies pass from mother to fetus while urea and carbon dioxide pass from fetus to the mother. The bloods do not mix and the placenta acts as a barrier to many substances and pathogens which would harm the fetus.

- When the fetus releases a hormone from its adrenal glands, this reaches the placenta, causing it to secrete **prostaglandins** which promote the contraction of the uterus. Pressure from this and the fall in progesterone, produced by the placenta, stimulates the posterior pituitary to release **oxytocin**. Oxytocin also causes contraction of the uterus, and birth follows.

- Oestrogen and progesterone cause the **mammary glands** to grow during pregnancy. **Prolactin**, released after birth, causes these glands to produce milk. Sucking by the baby stimulates oxytocin release and this causes the ejection of the milk from the glands.

- Other mammals have similar cycles but usually the endometrium is reabsorbed and there is only a short time before ovulation when the female is willing to mate. This is **oestrus** and the cycle is called the **oestrous cycle**.

- Hormones are used in farming techniques:

  (i) FSH can be used in various techniques which produce multiple embryos, possessing desirable characteristics, in farm animals

  (ii) progesterone and prostaglandins can be used to time the cycles of farm animals to suit the farmer

  (iii) BST can be used to increase milk production.

Answers

1 The sperm is the gamete which has to move to reach the other gamete *(1)*. More energy would be needed for movement if food reserves were carried *(1)*.

2 LH stimulates progesterone production *(1)*. As progesterone level rises, it inhibits LH production *(1)*. As LH level falls, progesterone level decreases *(1)*.

3 Oestrogen level is falling so FSH not inhibited and rises *(1)*. Then progesterone rises and FSH inhibited so its level falls *(1)*.

4 Some steroid hormones can be absorbed through gut wall *(1)*. Protein hormones digested in the gut *(1)*.

5 No primary follicles left which can be stimulated *(1)*. No oestrogen can be produced *(1)*. FSH not inhibited *(1)*.

6 **(a)** Short distance between maternal and foetal blood/breakdown of mother's capillary walls, thinness of villus wall *(1)*. Numerous chorionic villi, giving large surface area of proximity between maternal and fetal blood *(1)*. Microvilli on the villi increasing surface area for diffusion *(1)*.

(b) Many mitochondria in villus wall *(1)*.

7 Cow has period of oestrus, human does not *(1)*. Cow's cycle lasts 21 days, human's lasts 28 days *(1)*. Cow has short follicular phase and long luteal phase, phases equal in humans *(1)*.

8 During early luteal phase, as progesterone has vascularised the endometrium, preparing it for implantation *(1)*.

9 Lambs will be born in the spring *(1)*. Grass beginning to grow to provide food for growing lamb *(1)*.

7 Reproduction in mammals

End of Chapter Questions

N2.2

1 If the diploid number of chromosomes for a species is 46, how many chromosomes are present in

    (a) a spermatogonium

    (b) a primary oocyte

    (c) a secondary oocyte

    (d) a polar body? *(4 marks)*

2 Describe

    (a) three differences and

    (b) three similarities

    between the formation of male and female gametes in humans. *(6 marks)*

3 Unlike humans, some mammals have large numbers of young at the same time. Rabbits and pigs have such large litters. After ovulation, a corpus luteum remains in the ovary for some time, if pregnancy occurs. It is possible to dissect a pregnant mother and determine how many fetuses are present in the uterus and how many corpora lutea are present in the ovaries.

    (a) Why would you expect the number of corpora lutea to be similar to the number of fetuses? *(2 marks)*

    (b) Give two reasons why there could be more corpora lutea than fetuses. *(2 marks)*

    (c) Give a reason why there could be more fetuses than corpora lutea. *(1 mark)*

    (Total 5 marks)

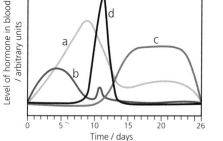

Figure 7.20 *Level of reproductive hormones in the blood of an un-named mammal during its reproductive cycle*

4 Study the graph in Figure 7.20.

    (i) Name the hormones labelled (a)–(d). *(4 marks)*

    (ii) Give the likely day of the cycle on which ovulation takes place and give a reason for your answer. *(2 marks)*

5 What effect do the following hormones have on the size of follicles?

    (a) FSH

    (b) LH *(2 marks)*

    (Total 6 marks)

6 Describe how the structure of the placenta is designed to make it an efficient organ for the exchange of substances between the fetus and the mother. *(5 marks)*

7 The diagram below represents a section through a mammalian ovary.

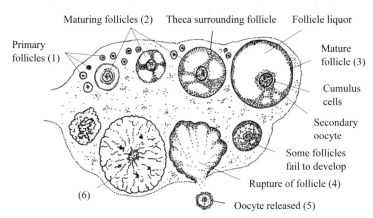

Maturing follicles (2) Theca surrounding follicle Follicle liquor

Primary follicles (1)

Mature follicle (3)

Cumulus cells

Secondary oocyte

Some follicles fail to develop

Rupture of follicle (4)

(6)

Oocyte released (5)

Figure 7.21

(a) (i) Name the structure labelled (6). *(1 mark)*

(ii) What is the origin of this structure? *(1 mark)*

(iii) What is the function of this structure if an ovum has been fertilised? *(1 mark)*

(iv) State what will happen to this structure next if pregnancy has *not* occurred. *(1 mark)*

(b) (i) State which hormone is needed to cause the changes seen in the diagram and indicated by the sequence (1) ⟶ (2) ⟶ (3). *(1 mark)*

(ii) From where does this hormone originate? *(1 mark)*

(c) Briefly explain the distinction between a *gonadal* hormone and a *gonadotrophic* hormone. *(1 mark)*

OCR (Oxford) 1998 *(Total 7 marks)*

8 The table below refers to four hormones associated with the human menstrual cycle.

If the statement is correct, place a tick (✔) in the appropriate box and if the statement is incorrect place a cross (✗) in the appropriate box.

Hormone	Secreted by ovaries	Reaches highest level in blood before ovulation
follicle stimulating hormone (FSH)		
luteinising hormone (LH)		
oestrogen		
progesterone		

Edexcel (London) 1997 *(Total 4 marks)*

9 The diagram shows the process of sperm formation in a mammalian testis.

Figure 7.22

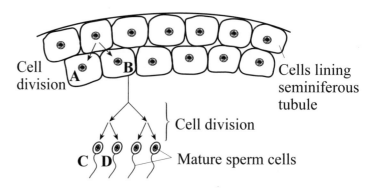

(a) Explain why cells **A** and **B** are genetically identical. *(1 mark)*

(b) Describe **two** ways in which cell division leads to cells **C** and **D** being genetically different. *(2 marks)*

(c) Briefly describe how the process of gamete formation in an ovary leads to a smaller number of larger gametes being produced in a female mammal. *(1 mark)*

(d) Both testis and the ovary contain a large number of blood vessels. Other than cell division, what specific function of these organs is associated with these blood vessels? *(1 mark)*

(Total 5 marks)

AQA (AEB) 1998

10 The dog has 39 pairs of chromosomes in each of its body cells. The diagram shows stages in the development of an ovarian follicle and corpus luteum in the ovary of a female dog (bitch).

Figure 7.23

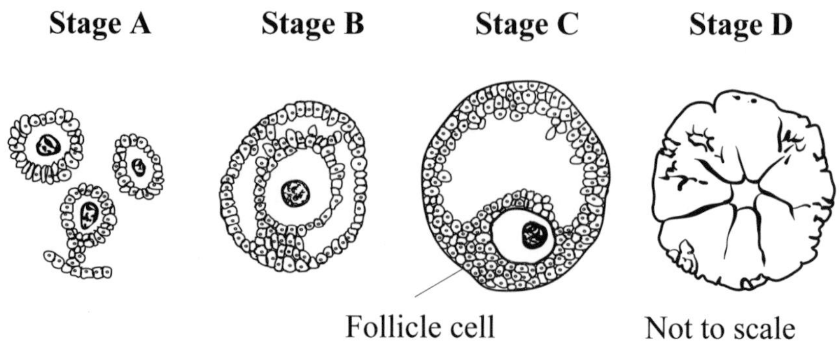

Stage A **Stage B** **Stage C** **Stage D**

Follicle cell   Not to scale

(a) **(i)** How many chromosomes are there in a follicle cell? *(1 mark)*

(ii) Name the main hormone secreted by a follicle cell. *(1 mark)*

(b) Describe the function of the corpus luteum. *(2 marks)*

(c) Which of the stages shown in the diagram would be present in a pregnant bitch? *(1 mark)*

(d) Give **two** similarities between a female gamete from a bitch and a female gamete from a flowering plant. *(2 marks)*

AQA (AEB) 1998 *(Total 7 marks)*

1 The table shows the concentration of some sex hormones in the blood of a cow over a period of time.

Time/days	Concentration of hormone in the blood/arbitrary units		
	progesterone	oestrogen	LH
0	1	14	32
2	2	8	1
4	4	7	1
6	10	7	1
8	14	7	1
10	18	7	1
12	19	7	1
14	19	7	1
16	18	7	1
18	8	18	1
20	1	14	32
22	1	8	32
24	2	8	1

(a) Use the figures in the table to estimate the length of the cow's oestrous cycle. Explain how you arrived at your answer. *(2 marks)* ⚷ N2.1

(b) Explain how the high concentration of LH on day zero caused an increase in progesterone in the days which followed. *(3 marks)*

(c) Progesterone is responsible for growth of the lining of the uterus and the development of its blood supply. Suggest how and explain why the figures for progesterone would differ from those in the table if the cow had become pregnant. *(2 marks)*

(d) The concentration of progesterone in milk can be measured. It gives a very early indication of whether or not a cow is pregnant.

(i) Suggest how progesterone gets into the milk. *(1 mark)*

(ii) Explain why it is an advantage for a farmer to know as early as possible whether or not a cow is pregnant. *(2 marks)*

(e) Describe how hormones may be used as contraceptives and in controlling infertility in humans. *(5 marks)*

(Total 15 marks)

AQA AS-level Specimen Paper 1999

8 Sexual reproduction in flowering plants

Sexual reproduction is the most common form of reproduction in flowering plants. Some may also reproduce asexually by **vegetative propagation** producing clones of offspring (see Figure 6.8, page 163). The principles of sexual reproduction are similar to those in mammals and the offspring show genetic variation. A haploid male gamete, formed in a **pollen grain**, fuses with a haploid female gamete, contained in an **ovule**. The diploid zygote produced develops into an embryo inside a **seed**. The **flowers** are the organs of the plant involved in these processes.

This chapter includes:
- the structure and functions of the parts of flowers
- pollination
- the formation of gametes
- events leading to fertilisation
- summary of events which follow fertilisation.

8.1 Structure of a generalised flower

The structure of flowers varies between different species of plant, depending upon the evolutionary relationships of the plant and the way in which pollen is transferred. However, the parts which make up the flowers are very similar and carry out the same types of functions in most flowers. Figure 8.1 shows the parts of a generalised flower and gives an indication of the usual functions of these parts. Sometimes several flowers grow on the same stem. If this happens, the whole structure is called an **inflorescence**.

Definition

Pollination is the transfer of pollen from the anther of a flower to the stigma of the same or a different flower

8.2 Pollination

Pollen grains are produced in the anthers of the stamens. The pollen grains contain the male gametes. These male gametes must reach the female gametes which are found in the ovules. For this to happen, the pollen grains must first be deposited on the stigma of a flower. This transfer is called **pollination**.

As plants cannot move, some agent such as an insect or the wind is necessary to carry the pollen grains. Some flowers are adapted for **insect pollination** (entomophilous) while others are adapted for **wind pollination** (anemophilous). Other agents, such as birds, bats or water, may also carry pollen.

As many flowers are **hermaphrodite** (possess both male and female organs), it is possible for pollen grains to be deposited on the stigma of the same flower or another flower on the same plant (**self-pollination**). However, it is an advantage to the species if the pollen is transferred to the stigma of a flower on a different plant of the same species (**cross-pollination**). This enables **cross-fertilisation** (outbreeding) to follow and will provide greater genetic variation among the offspring. Therefore flowers often show adaptations which make cross-pollination more likely to take place than self-pollination.

Remember

If male gametes fertilise female gametes on the same plant, following self-pollination, any offspring produced will still vary genetically from each other. This is because gametes vary (see Section 6.11, page 169). The offspring do result from **sexual** reproduction and are **not** clones. However, they will not show as much genetic variation as the offspring of cross-fertilisation

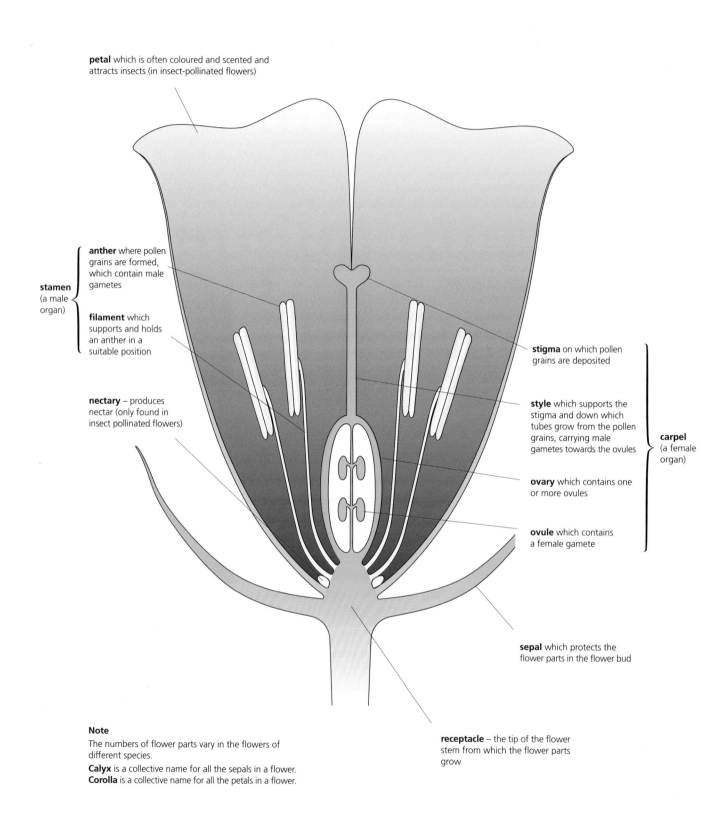

petal which is often coloured and scented and attracts insects (in insect-pollinated flowers)

anther where pollen grains are formed, which contain male gametes

stamen (a male organ)

filament which supports and holds an anther in a suitable position

nectary – produces nectar (only found in insect pollinated flowers)

stigma on which pollen grains are deposited

style which supports the stigma and down which tubes grow from the pollen grains, carrying male gametes towards the ovules

carpel (a female organ)

ovary which contains one or more ovules

ovule which contains a female gamete

sepal which protects the flower parts in the flower bud

receptacle – the tip of the flower stem from which the flower parts grow

Note
The numbers of flower parts vary in the flowers of different species.
Calyx is a collective name for all the sepals in a flower.
Corolla is a collective name for all the petals in a flower.

Figure 8.1 *A vertical half of a generalised flower*

As the structure of flowers varies according to whether they are pollinated by wind or insects and according to the cross-pollination mechanism employed, the range of types of flowers is vast. Figure 8.2 shows a range of flowers.

(a)   (b)   (c)

(d)   (e)   (f)   (g)

Figure 8.2 *A range of flowers*
(a) Lily flowers – insect pollinated flowers
(b) Male hazel flowers (catkins) – Separate male and female wind pollinated flowers are found on the same tree
(c) Cocksfoot grass flowers – wind pollinated flowers with protruding anthers
(d) Bee orchid flowers – complex insect pollinated flowers resembling bees. This tricks bees into trying to mate with them which accidentally pollinates the flowers
(e) A sunflower – Many flowers grow together on one stem, appearing like one large flower that is attractive to insects. Only the outer flowers have petal-like structures
(f) Male holly flowers – insect pollinated flowers. There are separate male and a female flowers on different trees
(g) Wild arum flowers (Lords and Ladies) – The trumpet shaped bracts enclose the real flowers. Insects are imprisoned inside so helping pollination

8 Sexual reproduction in flowering plants

Figure 8.3 *Structure of a rape flower:*

(a) Oil seed rape growing in a field. Newer varieties were derived from artificial crosses between related Brassica *species even before modern genetic modifications*

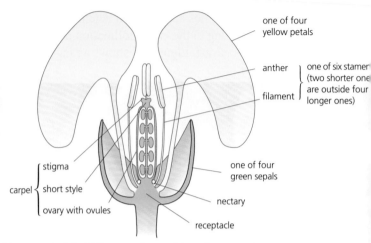

(b) A vertical half flower of rape (Brassica napus)

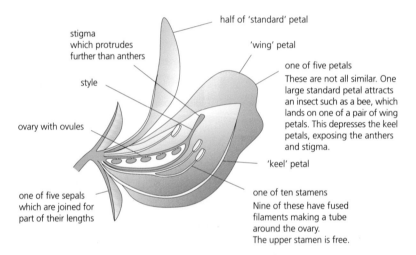

(b) A vertical half flower of a sweet pea (Lathyrus *sp.*)

Figure 8.4
(a) Rhododendron flower, (insect pollinated)

8.3 Insect-pollinated flowers and wind-pollinated flowers

Figure 8.3 shows the structure of a rape flower (a wild, close relative of oil seed rape) and Figure 8.4b shows the more complex structure of a sweet pea flower. Both of these flowers are insect pollinated and, in spite of belonging to different families of plants, they show many similar features which adapt them to be pollinated by insects.

- They have large, coloured and often scented petals which attract insects and provide landing stages for them.
- They have nectaries providing nectar for the insects to drink.
- They have anthers *within* the flowers. Insects brush against them as they reach for nectar. This makes it likely that the insects pick up pollen on their bodies.
- They have small, sticky stigmas within the flowers. Insects touch them, brushing off pollen as they reach for nectar.
- They produce large pollen grains with ridges and grooves. These cling to insects.

(a)

Figure 8.5 *Structure of perennial rye grass flowers (wind pollinated)*
(a) An inflorescence of perennial rye grass
(b) Detailed structure of a flower of perennial rye grass (Lolium perenne)

Part of the inflorescence
(collection of flowers on one stem)

several flowers in one spikelet forming part of the complete inflorescence

One flower

green bract

protruding feathery stigma

one of three protruding anthers

Flower with one bract removed

bract

large, loosely jointed anther

stigma   ovary   style

(b)

(a)

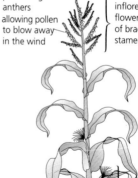

(b)

Figure 8.6 *Maize flowers (wind pollinated)*
(a) Female maize flowers
(b) Male maize flowers
(c) Part of a maize plant (Zea mays) *showing the separation of male and female flowers*

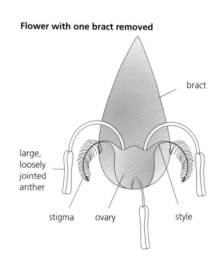

protruding anthers allowing pollen to blow away in the wind

inflorescence of male flowers, each consisting of bracts and protruding stamens only

inflorescence of female flowers
Several bracts surround many carpels growing from a central stem. Each carpel has a long style and feathery stigma which protrudes from the tip of the 'cob'.

(c)

Figure 8.5 shows the structure of a flower of perennial rye grass and Figure 8.6 shows the arrangement of flowers on a maize plant. Both of these are wind pollinated and show features which adapt them for this:

- They have no petals. (Small green leaf-like structures called **bracts** may be present which protect flower parts.)

- They have no nectaries and produce no nectar.

- They have stamens with long filaments. These allow large, loosely jointed anthers to hang out of the flowers. The pollen is easily caught in the wind and blown away.

Did You Know

A strange inflorescence, the wild arum (see Figure 8.2), is a protogynous flower with a difference! It emits a smell of rotting meat which attracts small insects. These slip down into the 'flower' and rub off any pollen they are carrying from other plants onto ripe stigmas at the base. They are trapped there by a ring of bristles overnight, until the stamens above ripen. The bristles then wither, allowing the insects to escape, picking up pollen as they go.

● They have long branched stigmas which hang out of the flower. These feathery structures are suitable for trapping pollen which is blowing through the air.

● The chances that a pollen grain will be deposited on a stigma when carried by wind are low. Large numbers of pollen grains are produced. They are small and light and can be carried for long distances.

?

1 Give a definition of *(a)* a flower, *(b)* a carpel. *(2 marks)*

2 Give three structural differences between a stamen of an insect-pollinated flower and a stamen of a wind-pollinated flower. *(3 marks)*

8.4 Cross-pollination mechanisms

The ways in which flower structure favours cross-pollination vary. In some flowers only cross-pollination is possible. In other flowers cross-pollination is more likely but self-pollination is still possible, if cross-pollination does not take place. (Self-pollination can be useful if cross-pollination has not occurred. It is better than no pollination at all!)

The main types of mechanism are as follows:

● Some plants have male flowers (with no carpels) on one plant, and female flowers (with no stamens) on a different plant. Such plants are **dioecious** (having separate sexes) and self-pollination is impossible. Holly trees are dioecious (Figure 8.2).

● Some plants have anthers which mature and shed their pollen before the stigma of the same flower is ripe enough to receive pollen. This mechanism is called **protandry**. Older flowers nearby may be the correct age to be receptive to this pollen. Dandelions and daisies are protandrous.

● The ripening of stigmas and their loss of the ability to receive pollen before the anthers on the same flower mature, is called **protogyny**. Such flowers can only be pollinated by pollen from older flowers. This is less common than protandry but equally effective. Bluebells and woodrush are protogynous.

● The pollen of some flowers is unable to develop, because of chemical incompatibility, if it lands on a stigma of a flower on the same plant. Even if the pollen is transferred, it cannot go on to bring about fertilisation. This is known as **self-sterility**. It does not prevent self-pollination but it does prevent self-fertilisation. Clover is self-sterile.

● The structure of many flowers favours cross-pollination. For example, Figure 8.4 shows the structure of a sweet pea flower. If a bee lands on one of the wing petals and this forces the keel petals down, this exposes the central parts of the flower. As the bee reaches for nectar by inserting its tongue down the tube made by the filaments, it touches the stigma first and may brush off pollen picked up from other flowers. It cannot touch the lower anthers until *after* it has brushed against the stigma. This is a simple device. Many flowers have much more elaborate mechanisms. One other system is described in Box 8.1.

Table 8.1 Main differences between insect-pollinated and wind-pollinated flowers

Insect pollinated flowers	Wind pollinated flowers
coloured, scented petals	no petals
may produce nectar	never produce nectar
anthers inside flower	anthers outside flower
stigma inside flower	stigma outside flower
stigma small and sticky	stigma large and feathery
pollen sticky	pollen light and dry
fewer pollen grains	more pollen grains

3 Although separate-sexed plants ensure cross-pollination, this is a rare mechanism. Describe two disadvantages of this system when compared with the more usual hermaphrodite (**monoecious**) nature of plants.   *(2 marks)*

Figure 8.7
Hibiscus flower being visited by a humming bird.

Extension

Box 8.1 Cross-pollination mechanism in primroses

There are two types of primrose flower. The pin-eyed types occur on different plants from the thrum-eyed types.

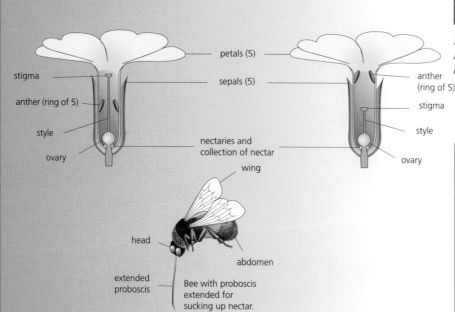

Figure 8.8 The two types of primrose flower

Look at Figure 8.8 and answer the following question.

4 *(a)* A bee lands on the flat upper part of a petal of a thrum-eyed flower and leans over to reach nectar. On which part of its body is it likely to pick up pollen?   *(1 mark)*

(b) It then flies to a plant with pin-eyed flowers and again reaches for nectar. On which part of a flower is it likely to rub off this pollen?   *(1 mark)*

(c) If it visited a pin-eyed flower and then a thrum-eyed flower, how would a bee transfer the pollen?   *(2 marks)*

(d) Explain why it would be unlikely for pollination to be carried out if a bee visited one thrum-eyed flower after another.   *(1 mark)*

(e) Using the answers to the above questions, explain why primroses are more likely to be cross-pollinated than self-pollinated.   *(2 marks)*

(f) Primroses are also self-sterile. When, especially, might this mechanism be important in preventing self-pollination in primroses?   *(1 mark)*

Did You Know

Flowers in warm regions which are pollinated by birds are usually large, red and without scent. This is because birds rarely have a sense of smell and have vision similar to ours, being quickly attracted to reds. Insects are much more sensitive to blue.

Some insects have eyes which are sensitive to ultraviolet light (UV). Insect-pollinated flowers sometimes have petal markings which reflect UV and can be seen by insects (but not by humans). These marks usually guide the insects to the nectaries and are known as 'honey guides'. They can be revealed in photographs

A stamen

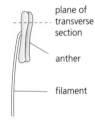

plane of transverse section

anther

filament

Transverse section through an anther

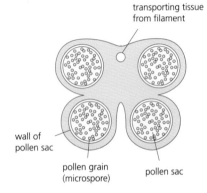

transporting tissue from filament

wall of pollen sac

pollen grain (microspore)

pollen sac

Figure 8.9 *Structure of an anther*

8.5 The formation of gametes

The formation of male gametes

Figure 8.9 shows that an anther contains four **pollen sacs**. Many pollen grains are produced in each pollen sac, which eventually splits to release them.

In an immature anther, many diploid cells, known as **pollen mother cells** (or **microspore mother cells**), are produced by mitosis (see Section 6.4, page 158). Each pollen mother cell divides by meiosis (see Section 6.10, page 169), producing four haploid cells, each of which develops into a pollen grain (which is also known as a **microspore**). Two male gametes are produced within each pollen grain by mitosis. Each male gamete consists of a haploid nucleus only. The details of these processes are shown in Figure 8.10.

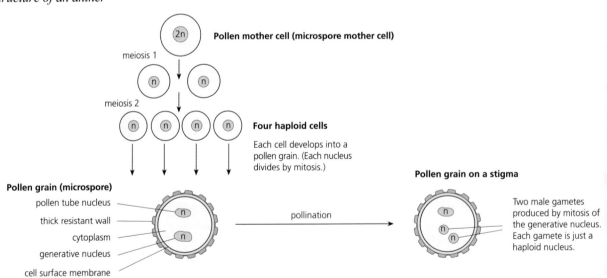

Pollen mother cell (microspore mother cell)

meiosis 1

meiosis 2

Four haploid cells

Each cell develops into a pollen grain. (Each nucleus divides by mitosis.)

Pollen grain (microspore)

pollen tube nucleus
thick resistant wall
cytoplasm
generative nucleus
cell surface membrane

pollination

Pollen grain on a stigma

Two male gametes produced by mitosis of the generative nucleus. Each gamete is just a haploid nucleus.

Figure 8.10 *Formation of male gametes*

The formation of female gametes

One female gamete is produced inside each ovule. The process is rather complex and the basic details are shown in Figure 8.11. Within each immature ovule there is a diploid cell known as a **megaspore mother cell**. This cell divides by meiosis, producing four haploid cells. Three of these degenerate, leaving one large cell, the **megaspore**. The haploid nucleus of the megaspore then divides by three successive mitotic divisions, producing eight haploid nuclei. Some of these nuclei may become surrounded by membranes and so can be regarded as separate cells. One of these is the **female gamete** which is sometimes known as the 'egg cell'. The eight haploid nuclei are enclosed within the enlarged membrane of the original megaspore and this whole structure is called the **embryo sac**.

Figure 8.12 shows the structure of a mature ovule which contains the fully developed embryo sac. All of the tissues around the embryo sac are made of diploid cells.

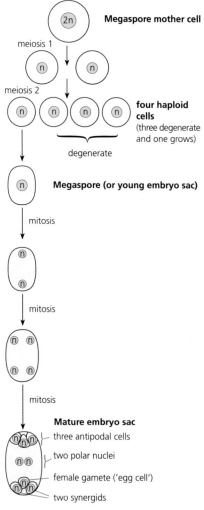

Figure 8.11 *Formation of a female gamete*

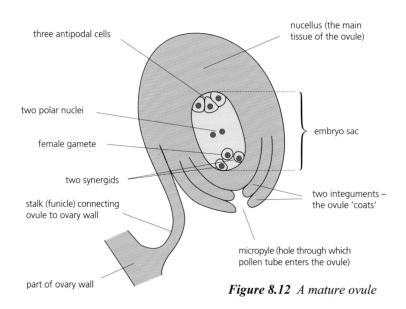

Figure 8.12 *A mature ovule*

5 Give one difference and one similarity between the male gametes of flowering plants and the male gametes of mammals.   *(2 marks)*

8.6 The events leading to fertilisation

Following pollination, further development, involving the growth of a **pollen tube**, usually only takes place if the pollen grains are on the stigma of a plant of the same species. There are three mechanisms which help to ensure this.

● A sugar solution secreted by the stigma must be of the correct concentration range.

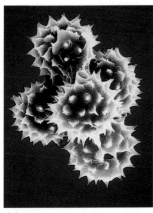

(a)

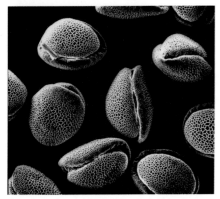

(b)

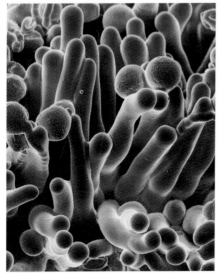

(c)

Figure 8.13 *Scanning electron micrographs*
(a) daisy pollen grains (× 800)
(b) iris pollen grains (× 150)
(c) pollen grains lodged on a stigma (× 600).

- The ridge and groove patterns on pollen grains and stigma are often complementary, encouraging the pollen grains to cling. Figure 8.13 shows such patterning.

- The tissues of the style must be chemically compatible with those of the pollen tube, allowing the tube to grow.

If the pollen is on an appropriate stigma, the following sequence of events occurs. (The events are summarised in Figure 8.14.)

1. The pollen grain absorbs water from the solution on the stigma and the contents swell and burst through a weak point in the pollen grain wall. A pollen tube emerges and grows into the tissues of the stigma and then the style. The pollen tube nucleus is carried near the tip of the tube and governs the growth of the tube, with its genes coding for the necessary proteins. The generative nucleus divides by mitosis producing two haploid nuclei which are carried in the cytoplasm behind. These nuclei *are* the two male gametes.

2. The pollen tube grows down the style using the tissues of the style as nourishment. It is attracted by chemicals released from the micropyle of an ovule and grows towards it through the ovary wall.

3. The pollen tube grows through the micropyle and the tissues of the nucellus of the ovule are digested. The pollen tube nucleus degenerates and the pollen tube tip bursts open, releasing the two male gametes into the embryo sac.

4. The first male nucleus to enter fuses with the egg nucleus, producing a diploid **zygote nucleus**. The second male nucleus fuses with the two polar nuclei, producing a triploid **primary endosperm nucleus**. This is called **double fertilisation** although only the first fusion process represents **true** fertilisation. The synergids and antipodal cells degenerate.

Remember

Fertilisation is **internal** in both mammals and flowering plants. This means that the male gamete reaches the female gamete inside the body. However, in mammals, the male gametes swim to the female gamete. On the other hand, in flowering plants, the male gametes are carried passively in the cytoplasm of the pollen tube to the female gamete. This explains the differences between the two types of male gamete.

?

6 How do the different methods of fertilisation in mammals and flowering plants explain the differences in male gamete structure? *(2 marks)*

Figure 8.14 *The events leading to*
fertilisation:
(a) Emergence of the pollen tube;
(b) Fertilisation;
(c) Detail showing double fertilisation

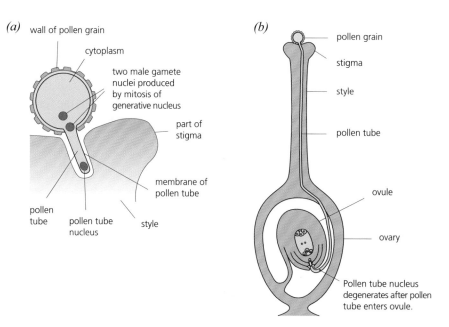

(a)
wall of pollen grain
cytoplasm
two male gamete
nuclei produced
by mitosis of
generative nucleus
part of
stigma
membrane of
pollen tube
pollen
tube
pollen tube
nucleus
style

(b)
pollen grain
stigma
style
pollen tube
ovule
ovary
Pollen tube nucleus
degenerates after pollen
tube enters ovule.

(Note: The ovary is shown to contain one ovule. If many ovules
are present, each ovule receives a separate pollen tube.)

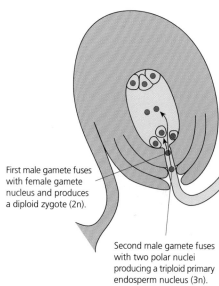

(c)
First male gamete fuses
with female gamete
nucleus and produces
a diploid zygote (2n).

Second male gamete fuses
with two polar nuclei
producing a triploid primary
endosperm nucleus (3n).

8.7 The events which follow fertilisation

The zygote nucleus divides repeatedly by mitosis and eventually develops into an embryo plant. This embryo is contained within the fertilised ovule, which is now referred to as a **seed**.

The primary endosperm nucleus divides repeatedly by mitosis, forming a mass of tissue, the **endosperm**, which nourishes the developing embryo inside the seed. It may or may not disappear as the seed matures. The nucellus disappears as the embryo grows but the integuments toughen and become the protective seed coat, the **testa**. The style and stigma shrivel and the ovary becomes a **fruit**. The protection and eventual dispersal of the seeds inside the fruit are aided by changes in the ovary wall. The modified ovary wall is now called a **pericarp**.

7 If the diploid number of chromosomes in a species of plant is 18, how many chromosomes are there in
(a) a cell of the endosperm
(b) a cell in the embryo
(c) the female gamete
(d) each of the polar nuclei
(e) a cell of the testa? *(5 marks)*

8 Which of the following only contain chromosomes derived from the female parent (and therefore none from the male gamete)?
(a) a synergid
(b) the embryo
(c) the testa (seed coat)
(d) the endosperm. *(2 marks)*

Summary – 8 Sexual reproduction in flowering plants

- Sexual reproduction in flowering plants, as in mammals, involves the fusion of the haploid nuclei of male and female gametes producing a diploid zygote.

- Flowers are the reproductive organs. They usually have **sepals** which protect the bud, **petals** which attract insects, male **stamens** and female **carpels**.

- **Pollen grains**, produced in the anthers of the stamens, are **microspores** in which male gametes are formed. They must be transferred by an agent such as insects or wind to the stigmas on carpels before fusion of gametes is possible. This transfer is called **pollination**.

- Insect-pollinated flowers usually have scented, coloured petals which attract insects. They produce nectar and have anthers and sticky stigmas within the flower where they can come into contact with insects. Wind-pollinated flowers usually do not have petals and do not produce nectar. They have large anthers and feathery stigmas outside the flower which catch the wind. The pollen is abundant and light.

- **Cross-pollination** (the transfer of pollen to the stigma of a flower on a different plant of the same species) is followed by cross fertilisation. This is preferable to **self-pollination** (transfer of pollen to the stigma of a flower on the same plant) as this leads to self-fertilisation. Offspring of cross-fertilisation show more genetic variation than those of self-fertilisation.

- Flowers have mechanisms which favour cross-pollination including **separate-sexed plants**, **protandry**, **protogyny**, **self-sterility** and numerous structural adaptations.

- Formation of a pollen grain involves meiosis. It contains a haploid pollen tube nucleus and a haploid generative nucleus which divides by mitosis, after pollination, producing two male nuclei which are the male gametes. These are carried by a **pollen tube** which grows from the grain down the style and enters the **ovule** via the **micropyle**.

- In the ovule, meiosis produces a **megaspore** with a haploid nucleus which divides mitotically three times, producing eight nuclei, one of which is the female gamete.

- One male gamete fuses with the female gamete nucleus, producing a diploid zygote, and the other male gamete nucleus fuses with two **polar nuclei**, producing a triploid **primary endosperm nucleus**. This is referred to as **double fertilisation**.

- The fertilised ovule becomes the **seed** which contains an **embryo** plant which has developed from the zygote. Triploid **endosperm** tissue nourishes the embryo and often disappears before the seed is mature.

Answers

1 (a) A plant organ which contains the parts involved in sexual reproduction *(1)*.

(b) The part of a flower consisting of an ovary containing ovules, a style and a stigma *(1)*.

2 In wind-pollinated flowers, the filaments are relatively longer and the anthers hang out of the flowers. In insect-pollinated flowers, the shorter stamens hold anthers within the flowers *(1)*. The anthers are more loosely attached to the filaments in wind-pollinated flowers than in insect-pollinated flowers *(1)*. The anthers are relatively larger in wind-pollinated flowers than in insect-pollinated flowers as they hold more pollen *(1)*.

3 Only half the plants are able to produce seeds *(1)*. Self-pollination is never possible and pollination may not take place at all unless male and female plants occur close to each other *(1)*.

4 (a) Its head *(1)*.

(b) The stigma *(1)*.

(c) As the proboscis is extended down the pin-eyed flower to reach nectar, it picks up pollen *(1)*. As the proboscis is extended down the thrum-eyed flower, it pushes past the stigma at the level where the pollen is present on the proboscis and pollen is deposited on the stigma *(1)*.

(d) The pollen picked up on the head would only rub against more anthers in another thrum-eyed flower *(1)*.

(e) Pollen is picked up from stamens on a part of the bee's body which will rub against stigmas of the opposite type of flower *(1)*. The different types of flower are only borne on different plants *(1)*.

(f) Pollen could fall on the stigma from the anthers in a thrum-eyed flower *(1)*.

5 Difference – plant gamete has nucleus only, mammal gamete has head middle piece and tail/acrosome/mitochondria/flagellum *(1)*. Similarity – both have a haploid nucleus *(1)*.

6 The mammal gamete needs a flagellum to swim/mitochondria for energy to swim and transport the nucleus to the female gamete *(1)*. The plant gamete does not need these as it is carried passively to the female gamete *(1)*.

7 (a) 27 *(1)* **(b)** 18 *(1)* **(c)** 9 *(1)* **(d)** 9 *(1)* **(e)** 18 *(1)*

8 (a) a synergid *(1)*; **(b)** the testa *(1)*.

End of Chapter Questions

1 Describe one similarity and one difference between the ways in which male gametes are formed in flowering plants and mammals.   *(2 marks)*

2 Look at Figure 8.15 and answer the following.

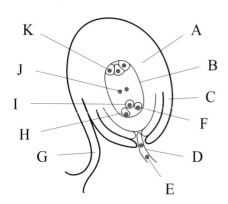

Figure 8.15 An ovule just before fertilisation

Give the letter indicated and name the structure which:

(i) is produced from the whole megaspore.

(ii) will form the seed coat.

(iii) will fuse with a male gamete to produce a zygote.

(iv) will fuse with two nuclei which are genetically different from each other.

(v) will fuse with two nuclei which are genetically identical to each other.

(vi) carries the male gametes to the ovule.

(vii) is made of cells which are genetically identical to those of G and C.

(7 marks)

3   With reference to flowering plants, distinguish between:

   (a) pollination and fertilisation   *(2 marks)*

   (b) pollen grain and male gamete   *(2 marks)*

   (c) ovule and female gamete.   *(2 marks)*

   (Total 6 marks)

4   **(a)** The diagram below shows a germinating pollen grain and a mature ovule from an insect-pollinated flower. Some nuclei have been labelled.

Figure 8.16

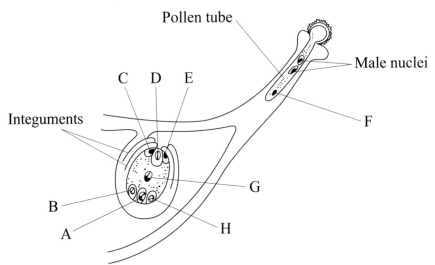

Give the letter of the nucleus which fuses with a male nucleus to form each of the following.

The zygote

The endosperm   *(2 marks)*

   (b) Give TWO ways in which the structure of an insect-pollinated flower differs from that of a wind-pollinated flower or a grass.   *(2 marks)*

   (c) Describe ONE mechanism which prevents self-fertilisation in flowering plants.   *(2 marks)*

Edexcel specimen 2000   *(Total 6 marks)*

5 The diagram represents a flower.

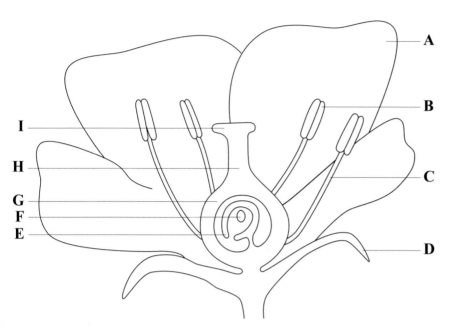

(a) Give the letter of the structure which:

(i) becomes the fruit wall;

(ii) becomes the testa (seed coat);

(iii) produces pollen grains. *(3 marks)*

(b) Explain **two** ways, shown in the diagram, in which this flower is adapted for insect pollination. *(2 marks)*

AQA 1999

(Total 5 marks)

9 Gas exchange

All organisms respire, it is one of the seven characteristics of living things. Respiration releases energy which is needed for all cell activities, for movement, beating of the heart and the breathing movements in mammals. Generally oxygen reacts with food, usually glucose, to release this energy. This is called **aerobic** respiration as oxygen is required. Gas exchange is the process of acquiring gases, like oxygen, from the environment and returning waste gases. In humans a ventilation mechanism, breathing, brings a continuous supply of air into the lungs. Special gas exchange surfaces, the alveoli, are adapted for efficient gas exchange. Their large surface area, moist surface, thin wall and proximity to blood, increase the rate of diffusion of oxygen into the blood and carbon dioxide out of the blood. Plants have holes in the leaf called **stomata**, through which gases can enter and leave.

9.1 Surface area and exchange surfaces

The surface across which materials are exchanged between an organism and its surroundings is called an **exchange surface**. In some single-celled organisms this is the external or outer membrane, used both for gas exchange and the intake of nutrients. In larger organisms the gas exchange surface might be part of a specialised gas exchange organ, such as the lungs in mammals or gills in fish.

Gas exchange surfaces

Gas exchange surfaces are the surface in the organism through which the exchange of gases takes place, between the organism and its environment.

When a gas exchange surface is used for the diffusion of gases for respiration, it can also be called a **respiratory surface**.

The type of gas exchange surface depends on the size and shape of the organism, which affects its **surface area to volume ratio**, and its habitat.

Surface area is the amount of surface an organism has. If we could remove our skin, flatten and measure it, this would be our surface area.

Volume is the space taken up by an organism. Large organisms take up more space and so have larger volumes. The way an organism obtains oxygen and nutrients depends on its surface area to volume ratio.

This chapter includes:
- surface area and exchange surfaces
- surface area to volume ratio
- gas exchange surfaces
- features of gas exchange surfaces
- the human thorax
- gas exchange in the alveoli
- ventilation (breathing)
- control of breathing in humans
- respiration and fitness
- gas exchange in plants
- gas exchange in fish.

Definition

A respiratory surface is the surface across which oxygen and carbon dioxide are exchanged between the organism and the environment for the purpose of respiration

231

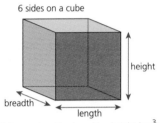

6 sides on a cube

height
breadth
length

Volume = length x breadth x height (cm³)

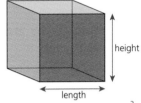

height
length

Surface area = length x height x 6 (cm²)

Figure 9.1 *Measuring volume and surface area in cubes*

Table 9.1 *To show the volume and surface area in different-sized cubes*

Remember

As animal size increases, the surface area to volume ratio decreases

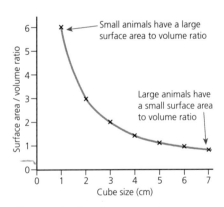

6 — × ← Small animals have a large surface area to volume ratio
5 —
4 —
3 — × Large animals have a small surface area to volume ratio
2 — ×
1 — × × ×
0 —
0 1 2 3 4 5 6 7
Cube size (cm)

Surface area / volume ratio

Figure 9.2 *Graph to show the relationship between cube size and surface area to volume ratio*

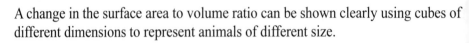

9.2 Surface area to volume ratio

A change in the surface area to volume ratio can be shown clearly using cubes of different dimensions to represent animals of different size.

Measuring volume and surface area in cubes

Volume is the space taken up

Volume = length × breadth × height (in cm^3)

Surface area is the outer surface

Surface area = length × height × 6 (in cm^2)　　　(6 surfaces)

$1\,cm^3$
This represents a **small** animal.
Volume = $1 \times 1 \times 1 = 1\,cm^3$
Surface area = $1 \times 1 \times 6 = 6\,cm^2$
Surface area to volume ratio
6:1

$2\,cm^3$
This animal is a little **larger**.
Volume = $2 \times 2 \times 2 = 8\,cm^3$
Surface area = $2 \times 2 \times 6 = 24\,cm^2$
Surface area to volume ratio
3:1

Cube size (cm)	Volume (cm^3)	Surface area (cm^2)	Surface area / volume ratio
1	1	6	6:1 *
2	8	24	3:1
3	27	54	2:1
4	64	96	1.5:1
5	125	150	1.2:1
6	216	216	1:1
7	343	294	0.8:1
50	125 000	15 000	0.12:1
100	1 000 000	60 000	0.06:1 **

* Small animals have a large surface area to volume ratio.

** Large animals have a smaller surface area to volume ratio.

Figure 9.2 shows that as the cube size increases, the surface area to volume ratio decreases: this is **negative correlation**.

Unlike cubes, the shape of animals is not uniform and some large animals have a large surface area to volume ratio. This is achieved by flattening of the body, or by enlargement of extremities such as ears or tails.

9.3 Gas exchange surfaces

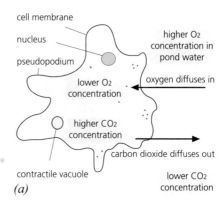

These can be external or internal.

External exchange surfaces

Single celled organisms, like *Amoeba* and *Euglena*, and flat multicellular (many-celled) organisms, like tapeworms, have a lot of surface compared to their small volume. They are described as having a **large surface area to volume ratio**. Their external surface can be used as a gas exchange surface, as the large surface area is able to supply sufficient oxygen to the small volume.

The outer surface area can be used as an exchange surface if it is permeable. Any surface that is permeable to oxygen and carbon dioxide will also be permeable to water, which is a smaller molecule, and therefore gas exchange surfaces will be moist because water diffuses out of the organism.

 Remember

Gas exchange surfaces are moist due to their permeability to water and gases

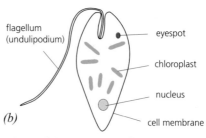

Amoeba and *Euglena* are unicells that live in water surrounded by the materials they need. (See Figure 9.3.)

The water surrounding the organism has a higher concentration of oxygen than is found in the organism. Oxygen **diffuses** through the outer membrane of the organism into the cell where oxygen is at a lower concentration. Oxygen diffuses through the surface of the *Amoeba* and can reach every part of its small volume. In the same way carbon dioxide from the *Amoeba* diffuses out to the lower concentration in the pond.

This is possible as unicells have a lot of surface compared to their small volume.

Similarly, animals in the phylum **Platyhelminthes**, the multicellular **flatworms**, have a large surface area to volume ratio. This enables diffusion to successfully provide every cell with oxygen and to remove carbon dioxide. There are both free-living and parasitic flatworms, but all are the same flat shape. (see Figure 9.4)

Planarians are so thin in cross-section that oxygen can diffuse to reach all their cells.

Tapeworms are parasitic flatworms that may infect humans who have eaten contaminated pork. This is very rare in the developed world. These tapeworms live in the small intestine of sufferers, surrounded by digested food. Tapeworms do not have a transport system like blood, to carry the absorbed food to all their cells.

Figure 9.3 *Diagrams of (a)* Amoeba *and (b)* Euglena *(single-celled organisms or unicells)*

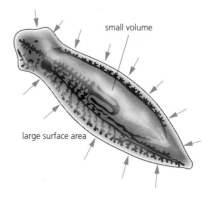

Figure 9.4
Transverse section of a free-living flatworm, a planarian showing the large surface area to volume ratio.

1 Explain why a transport system is not necessary in tapeworms. *(1 mark)*

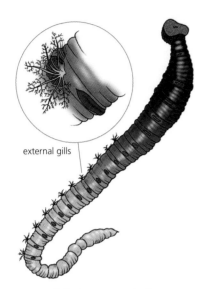

external gills

Figure 9.5 *Drawing of a lugworm and part of one external gill. Lugworms have external gills to increase the surface area for gas exchange*

Diffusion can provide every cell with oxygen and carbon dioxide can similarly be removed, as no cell is far from the exchange surface. Diffusion is only efficient over short distances, about 1 mm, and using the outer surface as an exchange surface is therefore limited to single-celled and flat multicellular organisms.

Larger animals have a small surface area compared to their larger volume, a **small surface area to volume ratio**. The large volume creates a demand for oxygen which the small surface area is unable to supply. The external exchange surface may be increased by folding, in order to enable sufficient oxygen to diffuse through to the increased volume. The **external gills** in young tadpoles and lugworms enable more oxygen to diffuse into the body. This is possible in an aquatic environment where the external gas exchange surface is moist and therefore permeable to gases. (See Figure 9.5.)

External gills are only found in aquatic organisms where the loss of water through the permeable membrane does not cause dehydration.

Although a folded external exchange surface may provide sufficient oxygen for a large volume, some of the cells are too far from the outer surface for diffusion to supply their needs.

Hence, a **transport system** is required to efficiently deliver oxygen to cells and to remove the carbon dioxide produced by the cells.

Animals that have a transport system to supply cells with oxygen and nutrients are not dependent on diffusion, which is only efficient over short distances. This has allowed the evolution of animals of increased size.

?

2 Insects are surrounded by a waterproof, impermeable exoskeleton. Oxygen diffuses through little holes in the exoskeleton and then along little tubes called tracheoles to reach every cell.
Suggest one reason why there are no large insects. *(1 mark)*

Internal exchange surfaces

To increase the surface for gas exchange in large animals with a small surface area to volume ratio, **internal gas exchange surfaces** may be present. This not only achieves a larger exchange surface but also protects the exchange surface from physical damage and drying out, which is essential in land organisms.

Diffusion of oxygen takes place through internal folded membranes such as the **alveoli** in the mammalian lungs and **gills** in fish.

Mammals have moist, internal lungs found deep inside the body which can be used for gas exchange at all times. Some water evaporates from the alveolar surface but this is minimal compared to evaporation from an external surface.

Folding of the alveoli or gills increases the surface through which diffusion takes place and so increases the rate of uptake. (Fick's Law, see Section 2.4, page 45).

These specialised **gas exchange surfaces** increase the efficiency of gas exchange and provide the large volume of oxygen required for animals with a high metabolic rate. In these larger organisms, a transport system is needed to carry oxygen to all the cells.

Gas exchange in land organisms

Terrestrial organisms, those that live on land, have a particular problem with gas exchange.

Gases will only diffuse across membranes which are also permeable to water and thus respiratory surfaces are moist. This presents no difficulty if the organism lives in water, but on land a moist respiratory surface would be exposed to the drying action of the air.

Earthworms use their moist outer covering as a gas exchange surface but have a problem with desiccation and consequently are restricted to damp habitats.

Organisms that have successfully colonised land have reduced the drying effect by having a **dry, waterproof outer layer** through which water loss is minimal, like the skin in humans, the chitinous exoskeleton in arthropods and the waxy cuticle in plants. This evolutionary development has greatly increased the range of habitats available for colonisation. However, the waterproof outer layer means that it is unsuitable for gas exchange and a specialised gas exchange surface is essential.

Frogs and gas exchange

The change of gas exchange surface in the life cycle of a frog demonstrates the link between habitat and gas exchange surface. Initially, fertilised eggs develop into aquatic tadpoles with **external gills** and these are gradually replaced by **internal gills**. As the adult frog emerges, internal **lungs** develop which are more suited to the semi-terrestrial lifestyle. These changes correspond with the move from an aquatic to a more terrestrial habitat and provide moist, permeable gas exchange surfaces without the risk of dehydration. Frogs also use their moist skin as a gas exchange surface.

Plants

Plants are less active than animals and consequently their gaseous requirements are relatively low. The flat shape of the leaves through which most gases enter, tends to increase the surface area in proportion to their volume and no cell is far from the exchange surface. Plants are therefore able to supply all the cells with oxygen and carbon dioxide by diffusion and similarly remove waste gases through the **stomata** of the leaves. (See Chapter 12.)

Plants on land, like animals, are exposed to the drying action of the air and are therefore covered by a waterproof waxy cuticle. The waxy cuticle has enabled them to flourish in a variety of land habitats. On land, more oxygen and carbon dioxide are available than in water, for respiration and photosynthesis. Light is plentiful, unlike the dark ocean deeps where photosynthesis and therefore life for plants is not possible.

Remember

The development of a waterproof outer covering has enabled land to be successfully colonised, as organisms no longer risk the major problem of dehydration

Remember

Gas exchange in plants enables both the exchange of respiratory gases, oxygen diffusing in and carbon dioxide out, and the exchange of gases required for photosynthesis, carbon dioxide in and oxygen out. The spongy mesophyll cells in the leaf are not just a respiratory surface as exchange of gases is for both **respiration** and **photosynthesis**

However, a waterproof covering means the outer surface is impermeable to water and gases and cannot be used for gas exchange. The moist, permeable gas exchange surfaces are therefore situated internally where the drying action of the air is reduced.

The gases enter the leaf through the stomata and pass by diffusion through the moist, permeable surface of the **spongy mesophyll cells**, which are the main gas exchange surface in plants.

These cells provide a large surface area for gas exchange by diffusion of gases, for both respiration and photosynthesis.

However, water vapour is lost through the leaf surface, particularly through the stomata, so the leaf surface area cannot increase beyond a critical point otherwise too much water may be lost. (See Chapter 12.)

The leaf surface area may restrict the habitat range of plants, as they need to be able to replace the water lost through the leaves in order to survive.

The large surface area of **root hair cells** compared to their small volume is sufficient to provide the roots with oxygen by diffusion (Figure 12.14, page 353).

Summary

● Gases can only diffuse across membranes permeable to both water and gases, thus a moist membrane indicates one that is permeable to gases. The respiratory surface may be the outer membrane, in small organisms with a large surface area to volume ratio. Large organisms, with a smaller surface area to volume ratio, and organisms with high oxygen requirements, have specialised surfaces for gas exchange to take in the large volume of oxygen required. Organisms with a high level of activity therefore have special **gas exchange or respiratory surfaces**.

9.4 Features of gas exchange surfaces

Gas exchange surfaces include surfaces providing gases for respiration and photosynthesis. For efficient gas exchange, a gas exchange surface must be **thin**, have a **large surface area** and be **moist**, which indicates it is **permeable** to gases.

The gas exchange surface is more efficient if it is close to a transport system and well ventilated. Breathing movements bring in a fresh supply of well-aerated water or air to maximise the concentration gradient and therefore increase the rate of diffusion.

As gases pass across membranes by diffusion, any factor which speeds up the rate of diffusion will speed up the exchange of gases. (See Section 2.4, page 44, on diffusion and Fick's Law.)

Large surface area

A folded gas exchange surface, for example alveoli or gills, provides more surface for oxygen to pass through by diffusion. This increased surface area allows the diffusion of increased volumes of oxygen, required by larger animals and those with high levels of activity.

Remember

Respiration and gas exchange are two processes which are often confused and must be clearly distinguished. **Respiration** is the release of energy from food, usually by the process of oxidation. This takes place in every cell in an organism and is called cellular respiration. Energy is needed for most biochemical reactions in cells.
Gas exchange is the process in which organisms take in gases from their environment and return gases to it. This process of gas exchange takes place by diffusion

Moist

Oxygen and carbon dioxide can only diffuse across membranes permeable to water. Therefore all gas exchange surfaces are moist.

Thin membrane

Gas exchange surfaces are thin so that diffusion is efficient. The thinner the membrane, the faster the rate of diffusion.

Permeable

Only membranes that are permeable to water and therefore gases can be used; waterproof surfaces are not permeable to gases.

Transport system

Oxygen diffuses through the gas exchange surface from the higher partial pressure in the organism's surroundings, to the lower partial pressure of oxygen in the blood. It is essential that the oxygen is carried away from the exchange surface in order to maintain a lower partial pressure in the blood there. Only then will the diffusion of oxygen continue.

Thus a transport system ensures a partial pressure gradient exists, in mammals, between the air and the blood in the alveoli. The blood carries the oxygen to all parts of the body for respiration.

A **respiratory pigment** in the blood, like **haemoglobin**, increases the uptake of oxygen. This is particularly important for organisms living in areas where the supply of oxygen is limited. (See Section 11.2, page 312.)

Ventilation mechanisms

The change in air or water in contact with a gas exchange surface is caused by ventilation movements. Some species have a ventilation mechanism.

In humans, ventilation is called **breathing**. This ensures a constant supply of air into and out of the lungs. It provides a fresh supply of oxygen and removes carbon dioxide, so maintaining a difference in partial pressure, maximising the rate of diffusion of oxygen into the blood and carbon dioxide out.

In fish water is drawn into the mouth and pushed out through the gills by ventilation movements. This brings in a constant supply of aerated water, maximising the difference in partial pressure and the rate of diffusion. This is necessary for aquatic 'breathers' that gain oxygen from water. Aquatic breathers need to pass a greater volume of water over their gas exchange surface to provide enough oxygen. The flow of water efficiently removes the carbon dioxide.

Ventilation movements due to differences in pressure are caused by changes in volume, and are examples of **mass flow** (see Table 9.3, page 245).

Remember

Water contains less than 1% oxygen, compared to 20% in air

9.5 The human thorax

9.5 The human thorax

The human **thorax** is the part of the body between the head and the abdomen. It contains the lungs and heart and is protected by the rib cage. Figure 9.6 shows the structure of the human thorax.

Figure 9.6 The human thorax

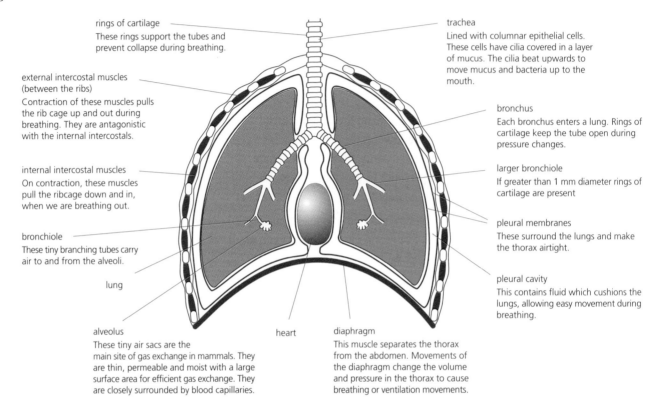

rings of cartilage
These rings support the tubes and prevent collapse during breathing.

external intercostal muscles (between the ribs)
Contraction of these muscles pulls the rib cage up and out during breathing. They are antagonistic with the internal intercostals.

internal intercostal muscles
On contraction, these muscles pull the ribcage down and in, when we are breathing out.

bronchiole
These tiny branching tubes carry air to and from the alveoli.

lung

alveolus
These tiny air sacs are the main site of gas exchange in mammals. They are thin, permeable and moist with a large surface area for efficient gas exchange. They are closely surrounded by blood capillaries.

heart

diaphragm
This muscle separates the thorax from the abdomen. Movements of the diaphragm change the volume and pressure in the thorax to cause breathing or ventilation movements.

trachea
Lined with columnar epithelial cells. These cells have cilia covered in a layer of mucus. The cilia beat upwards to move mucus and bacteria up to the mouth.

bronchus
Each bronchus enters a lung. Rings of cartilage keep the tube open during pressure changes.

larger bronchiole
If greater than 1 mm diameter rings of cartilage are present

pleural membranes
These surround the lungs and make the thorax airtight.

pleural cavity
This contains fluid which cushions the lungs, allowing easy movement during breathing.

Ventilation movements produce a **tidal flow** of air into and out of the lungs. Air passes through the nasal cavity (the nose) and mouth, past the larynx or voice box, down the trachea and along the bronchi which enter the lungs.

As the air passes through the mouth it is moistened. In the **nasal cavity**, the air is *cleaned* by the little hairs which act as a filter. Small particles are trapped by the sticky mucus. The air is *moistened* by mucus and *warmed* by close contact with numerous blood vessels. The ease with which the nose bleeds indicates how close the blood vessels are to the surface of the skin. This may occur when blood vessels widen, called **vasodilation**, due to sudden hot weather or a rush of **adrenaline**.

3 Why is it better to breathe through your nose than through your mouth?

(1 mark)

The **trachea** is a large tube leading from the back of the nose and mouth down towards the lungs. It is lined with ciliated **columnar epithelial cells** which are covered with a sticky layer of mucus. Figure 9.7 shows a simplified longitudinal section through the trachea.

Goblet cells in the trachea produce the sticky mucus which coats the **cilia** to which bacteria and dirt stick. The cilia beat upwards and the mucus is carried up. Bacteria and dirt breathed in become trapped in the sticky mucus lining the trachea. They are swept up in the moving stream of mucus to the mouth and swallowed. As a result many bacteria and dust particles are kept out of the lungs, thus keeping them clean. The swallowed mucus with bacteria and dirt passes down to the stomach, where the high acid levels, pH 2, ensure the destruction of most bacteria.

Thus the air that passes into the lungs has been cleaned, warmed and moistened and is less likely to cause damage.

Smokers and sufferers of **cystic fibrosis** produce excessive amounts of mucus which the cilia are unable to sweep up. Not only are the bacteria and dirt not removed, but the warm, moist mucus acts as a breeding ground for the bacteria leading to infections and damage to the lungs. (See Section 9.7, page 243.)

Coughing results from the attempt to remove the excess mucus. **Chronic**, or long-lasting, coughing can cause the thin delicate membranes of the alveoli to burst, so reducing the surface area for diffusion of oxygen (Figure 9.8).

The trachea is supported by **rings of cartilage**. These incomplete rings support the trachea yet allow movement and flexibility. The rings of cartilage help to keep the trachea open during breathing, when pressure changes could cause the tube to collapse and stick together.

The left and right **bronchi** branch off the trachea, one entering each lung. These tubes, like the trachea, are lined with ciliated columnar epithelial cells covered in mucus, again secreted by goblet cells, which serve the same function. The incomplete rings of cartilage are present in these tubes.

The **lungs** are surrounded by **pleural membranes** containing pleural fluid. The pleural membranes and fluid surrounding the lungs act as a lubricant, cushioning and protecting the lungs from damage by the hard ribs and allowing easy movement of the lungs during breathing. Together, the pleural membranes and the pleural fluid surrounding the lungs make up the airtight **pleural cavity**.

Each bronchus divides into smaller tubes, called **bronchioles**, once they enter the lungs. There are large numbers of these small tubes in each lung. Only the larger bronchioles near to the bronchus are supported by rings of cartilage. These larger bronchioles are lined with ciliated columnar cells also covered with sticky mucus. Inhaled air passes along these airways.

As the breathing tubes get smaller and closer to the alveoli, the epithelium changes to flatter cuboidal cells. Some gas exchange takes place here and, as the cells are flatter, there is less diffusion distance for oxygen, so increasing the rate of gas exchange.

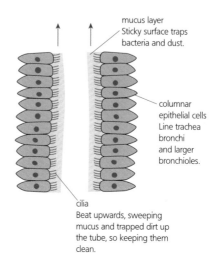

mucus layer
Sticky surface traps bacteria and dust.

columnar epithelial cells Line trachea bronchi and larger bronchioles.

cilia
Beat upwards, sweeping mucus and trapped dirt up the tube, so keeping them clean.

Figure 9.7 Longitudinal section through the trachea

Healthy alveolar sac

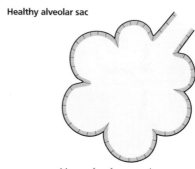

More surface for gas exchange. More oxygen passes into the blood for respiration.

Smoker's alveolar sac

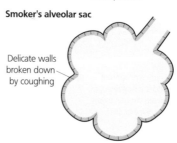

Delicate walls broken down by coughing

Less surface for gas exchange. Less oxygen passes into the blood for respiration.

Figure 9.8 Effect of chronic coughing on alveolar structure (diagrammatic)

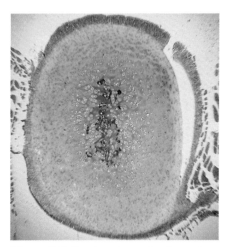

Figure 9.9 Section through a bronchus – the rings of cartilage have collapsed into the centre

Box 9.1 Asthma and breathing

All the air tubes, trachea, bronchi and bronchioles, contain circular smooth muscle which can contract and relax. When the muscle contracts, the air tube is narrowed and the volume of air reaching the alveoli is reduced. This is particularly problematic with the narrow tubes as the diameter is already small. People suffering from asthma have narrowed bronchioles during an asthma attack (see Box 11.6, page 333). They therefore have difficulty breathing. **Bronchodilators** are given to widen or dilate the bronchi and bronchioles, by causing the smooth muscle to relax. An inhaler of Ventolin, for example, can be used as a bronchodilator.

To add to the problem of narrowed breathing tubes, excess mucus is secreted by the goblet cells, further blocking the already narrowed tubes.

The tiny bronchioles end in air sacs called **alveolar sacs**. These tiny sacs are folded into a 'bunch of grapes' shape, so increasing the surface area for diffusion. Each 'grape shaped' cavity is called an **alveolus** (plural: alveoli). There are approximately 300 million alveoli in each human lung. This provides a combined total surface area from both lungs of about 70 square metres, similar to the surface area of a tennis court. This vast surface area allows for efficient gas exchange by diffusion. The alveoli are the main gas exchange surface of the lungs (Figure 9.10).

The moist, permeable alveolar surface situated, deep inside the body, reduces loss of water by evaporation, essential for life on land.

9.6 Gas exchange in the alveoli

The membrane around each alveolus is composed of a thin layer, one cell thick. These thin, flat cells are called **squamous** or **pavement epithelia**. They form an efficient exchange surface and allow a rapid rate of diffusion due to the reduced distance for gases to travel (Figure 9.10).

Gases can diffuse across the moist, permeable membrane of the alveoli. Capillaries closely surround each lobe or 'grape' of the alveolus, and the capillary wall is also only one cell thick. Therefore gases only have to diffuse across two thin cells between the alveolus and the blood. The short diffusion distance speeds up the rate of diffusion.

Alveolus surface is folded to form a large surface area.

Moisture in which oxygen dissolves.

direction of blood flow

alveolar sac

high concentration O_2

O_2 diffuses into the blood

low concentration O_2

blood

blood capillary (thin and permeable)

The *low concentration* of O_2 in the blood is maintained, as blood carries the oxygen *away* from the alveolar sac.

(a)

Figure 9.10
(a) Outline structure of alveolus
(b) Diagram of diffusion surface of alveolus

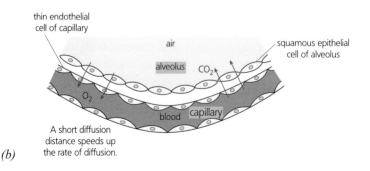

thin endothelial cell of capillary

air

alveolus CO_2

squamous epithelial cell of alveolus

O_2

blood capillary

A short diffusion distance speeds up the rate of diffusion.

(b)

Ventilation brings in a fresh supply of air into our lungs approximately 12 times per minute at rest. This **tidal air** does not enter far into the alveoli, so not all the air in the alveoli is replaced. The remaining air is called **alveolar air** (Figure 9.11).

There is a difference in the concentration of oxygen in the alveolus, with a higher concentration in the tidal air and a lower concentration in the alveolar air. Oxygen diffuses down the concentration gradient from the tidal air, 20.95%, to the alveolar air, 13.8% oxygen. Tidal air is, in effect, air that is breathed in. Alveolar air is the air in the alveolus that is not replaced during breathing. Expired air is the air breathed out.

Gas %	Tidal air	Alveolar air	Expired air
oxygen by volume	20.70	13.2	14.5
carbon dioxide	0.04	5.0	3.9
nitrogen	78.00	75.6	75.4
water vapour	1.26	6.2	6.2

Less oxygen is breathed out than is breathed in, as some diffuses through to the blood.

4 Why does carbon dioxide diffuse from the alveolar air through to the tidal air? *(1 mark)*

The percentage of nitrogen breathed out appears to be lower than the percentage breathed in, although there is actually no difference in the amount entering and leaving the lungs. It appears to decrease due to an increase in the volume of water vapour present.

Oxygen
Oxygen dissolves in the moisture lining the alveoli and then diffuses through the squamous epithelium of the alveolus and capillary into the blood. The blood carries oxygen away from the alveoli, so keeping the partial pressure of oxygen in the blood low.

Gases diffuse from a higher **partial pressure** of the gas to an area with a lower partial pressure. The rate of diffusion depends on the difference in partial pressure between the air and the blood. (See Box 9.2.) In practice, there is little difference between the percentage and partial pressures of gases in the air.

In the blood, oxygen continues to diffuse through the plasma and into the red blood cells, where it combines with **haemoglobin** to form **oxyhaemoglobin** (see Section 11.2, page 312). Haemoglobin is a respiratory pigment with a strong affinity or attraction for oxygen. This increases the uptake of oxygen and is particularly important for animals that live in areas of low oxygen availability, such as at high altitude or in poorly aerated water. Narrow capillaries mean that

Table 9.2 Comparison of tidal, alveolar and expired air

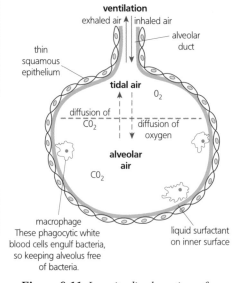

Figure 9.11 Longitudinal section of an alveolus to show the position of tidal and alveolar air

Remember
It is important to understand that the rate of diffusion of a gas within the *same* medium, like water, depends on the difference in concentration (Fick's Law). However, the rate of diffusion of a gas between two *different* media, like air and water, depends instead on the difference in the partial pressure of the gas

Extension

Box 9.2 Partial pressure

The partial pressure of a gas is the pressure contributed by one gas in a mixture of gases. In a fixed volume, the molecules of a particular gas are moving and collide with the sides of the container. This exerts a pressure called a *partial pressure*. The partial pressure is different for each gas in the mixture, depending on the number of molecules of that gas present. In fact, the percentage of a gas and its partial pressure have very similar proportions with respiratory gases in the air. For example, the percentage of oxygen in the air is 20.95%, and the partial pressure is 21.1 kPa. The percentage of carbon dioxide in the air is 0.04% and the partial pressure is also 0.04 kPa.

red blood cells are pressed close to the capillary wall, reducing the diffusion distance for oxygen.

There is low blood pressure in the vessels to the lungs. This is caused by the thinner muscle of the right ventricle contracting with less force. This results in a slower blood flow to the lungs which gives more time for diffusion to take place. The newly oxygenated blood returns to the heart and is then pumped to the rest of the body, thus maintaining a difference in the oxygen partial pressure between the alveoli and the blood. This difference in partial pressure ensures continued diffusion.

Carbon dioxide

The higher partial pressure of carbon dioxide in the blood capillaries causes diffusion of carbon dioxide in solution across to the alveolus where the partial pressure is lower. Carbon dioxide diffuses across the squamous epithelium of the blood capillary and alveolus, into the alveoli. From here diffusion of carbon dioxide continues into the tidal air where the concentration of carbon dioxide is lower, and air with the extra carbon dioxide is breathed out. The expired air therefore contains less oxygen and more carbon dioxide than was breathed in, and more water vapour, produced by evaporation from the moist surfaces lining the respiratory tract.

Rate of diffusion

The rate of diffusion depends on the surface area, the difference in partial pressure and thickness of the exchange surface.

The **surface area** is increased by:

● the large number of alveoli

The **difference in partial pressure** is maintained by:

● the attraction of haemoglobin for oxygen
● the removal of oxygen by the blood, so keeping the partial pressure low near the alveoli
● ventilation providing a constant supply of fresh air.

These factors all maintain a difference in the partial pressure of gases between the alveoli and the blood.

The **thickness of the exchange surface** is minimised by the following:

- the walls of alveoli are made of thin squamous epithelia
- the walls of the capillary are also made of squamous epithelia and are very thin
- the capillary is very narrow and close to the alveoli, so red blood cells are forced close to the alveolar wall.

These factors reduce the thickness of the exchange surface and therefore the diffusion distance, so speeding up the rate of diffusion of gases.

Box 9.3 Advantages of lungs

The development of internal lungs was a major evolutionary step allowing air breathing without risk of dehydration and, combined with a waterproof outer covering, allowed the colonisation of land. Not only did this open up new habitats, but the greater percentage of oxygen in the air could be used to increase energy release in respiration. The extra heat produced enabled the evolution of endothermic animals to take place.

Mammals and birds are called **endotherms** ('inner heat'). They maintain a constant body temperature with heat produced internally in respiration. It is interesting to note that endotherms are air breathers through lungs. Only air contains sufficient oxygen to enable a high **metabolic rate**, or rate of respiration, to be maintained and release sufficient heat. An efficient gas exchange system, the alveoli, provides the oxygen.

Endotherms have a constant body temperature which means that they are more independent of external conditions and can live in a greater variety of habitats. Their enzymes are able to work at their optimum and maintain a high metabolic rate.

Remember

singular	plural
bronchus	bronchi
alveolus	alveoli
cilium	cilia
bronchiole	bronchioles
epithelium	epithelia
bacterium	bacteria

Remember

Alveoli show all the features of a gas exchange surface:
- large surface area
- moist
- thin
- close to a transport system
- permeable

9.7 Smoking and health

Smoking kills. It causes lung cancer, chronic bronchitis, emphysema, coronary heart disease and strokes.

Lung cancer

This is the most common form of cancer in males, making up 21% of all cancers. In females the figure is lower at 12% of all cancers, but it is still the second-highest form of cancer in women (1995 Cancer Research Campaign). Tobacco smoke contains many **carcinogens** or substances that cause cancer. Of these **tar** is the most important. Tars irritate the epithelial cells, stimulating extra cell division and thickening of the epithelium, which may develop into a cancerous tumour. A cancerous or malignant tumour usually develops in the bronchial tubes, and may spread to invade other tissues.

Did You Know

Almost 99.7% of those that die from lung cancer are smokers.
Four out of every ten people will develop cancer at some point in their lives (Cancer Research Campaign 1996).

Chronic bronchitis

Tar coats the lining epithelium of the breathing tubes, causing irritation and the production of excess mucus from the goblet cells. As well as causing cancer, tar paralyses the cilia that sweep mucus and bacteria away from the lungs so pathogens and mucus build up, causing infection. The smoker coughs to try to clear the mucus and this further damages the epithelium which becomes inflamed, resulting in a narrowing of the bronchial tubes. Bacteria may infect the mucus, producing pus which is coughed up in greenish-yellow sputum. Infection of the mucus can lead to other diseases like pneumonia.

Britain has the highest death rate in the world from chronic bronchitis and smokers are six times more likely to develop this disease than non-smokers. Narrower bronchial tubes combine with excess mucus to reduce the air flow to the alveoli. Coughing and breathlessness over many years damage the respiratory system, with the bronchioles narrowing and breathing becoming more difficult. **Carbon monoxide** in tobacco smoke will combine with **haemoglobin** permanently, so preventing the transport of oxygen. Long-term shortage of oxygen can lead to death. This disease may also develop into **emphysema**.

Emphysema

Irritation of the lungs over many years from smoking or inhaling industrial dust causes emphysema. 25% of smokers will develop this disease. Tobacco smoking stimulates the secretion of protein-digesting enzymes. These proteases break down the elastic tissue in the lungs, in particular the elastin in the thin alveolar walls. This enlarges the air space and reduces the surface area for gas exchange (Figure 9.8).

Coughing can burst some of the weakened alveoli and over many years the surface for gas exchange is reduced. Little gas exchange means insufficient oxygen diffuses into the blood to reach the cells for respiration. Lack of energy and increasing breathlessness make it difficult for a sufferer to walk even a few metres.

Coronary heart disease and strokes

Nicotine diffuses into the blood and quickly increases blood pressure, heart rate and narrows blood vessels. It also raises the level of fat in the blood. These effects combine to increase the likelihood of narrowing the arteries and forming a blockage.

Both nicotine and **carbon monoxide** damage the endothelium lining the blood vessels. This makes it easier for fats and cholesterol to enter the blood vessel, so increasing their deposition inside the arteries. This causes hardening of the arteries or **atherosclerosis**, which leads to coronary heart disease and strokes (see Box 10.5, page 290).

Extension

Box 9.4 Pneumoconiosis

A disease common among coalminers caused by breathing in the dust from coal over a long period.

It causes the growth of nodules in the bronchioles which block the flow of air to the alveoli. This eventually leads to emphysema and possibly bronchitis. Persistent coughing, breathlessness and the production of black sputum are symptoms of pneumoconiosis.

The risk of developing the disease can be reduced by sprinkling water to reduce coal dust and by wearing masks which filter the air.

Mass flow

The movement of air into and out of our lungs is due to differences in pressure. This is an example of **mass flow**. Mass flow is the bulk movement of substances due to differences in pressure. Substances are moved from a region of higher pressure to one with lower pressure. This is how substances are transported in large plants and animals where diffusion is too slow to meet requirements.

In mammals, mass flow systems are involved in **ventilation** and in the flow of blood through the heart, known as the **cardiac cycle**. In plants, mass flow systems are involved in the **movement of sucrose** through phloem and the **movement of water** through xylem. In each case differences in pressure cause substances to move from a higher to a lower pressure region (Table 9.3).

Table 9.3 *Mass flow systems*

Process	Higher pressure	Lower pressure	Movement
Ventilation breathing in	outside in air	in lungs, due to increase in volume of thorax	air moves from higher pressure outside to lower pressure in the lungs
breathing out	in lungs due to decrease in volume of thorax	outside in air	air is forced out from the higher pressure in the lungs to the lower pressure outside
Cardiac cycle atrial diastole	in veins	in atria, due to relaxing of atrial muscles, which increases volume	blood moves from higher pressure in veins to lower pressure in atria, i.e. blood enters the heart
ventricle systole	in ventricles, due to contraction of ventricle muscles decreasing the volume	in arteries	blood is pushed out of the heart from higher pressure in ventricles to lower pressure in arteries
movement of solutes through a plant	top of phloem due to influx of sugar drawing in water by osmosis, causing high hydrostatic pressure	roots and growth areas where water and sucrose are used up, causing low hydrostatic pressure	sucrose and amino acids are carried from higher pressure regions to lower pressure regions which are linked by phloem
movement of water through a plant	in roots due to entry of water and root pressure	in leaves due to loss of water in the process of transpiration	water passes up the xylem by cohesion–tension, from the higher pressure in the roots to the lower pressure in the leaves

9.8 Ventilation

Ventilation (breathing) is an example of mass flow.

The tidal flow of air into and out of the lungs is caused by differences in pressure between the thorax and the atmosphere. Air always moves from an area of higher pressure to an area of lower pressure. A ventilation mechanism ensures that a constant supply of fresh air is available to provide adequate oxygen for gas exchange and to remove carbon dioxide.

The **diaphragm** is a sheet of muscle separating the thorax above, from the abdomen below. The ribs and the **intercostal muscles** between them, form the sides of the **thorax** (Figure 9.6). The thorax is an airtight cavity, apart from the trachea, and changes in volume will cause pressure changes. If there is a difference in pressure between the thorax and the outside, then air will move by mass flow. Figure 9.12 shows the change in shape of the thorax during breathing.

Breathing in – inhaling
As air moves from high to low pressure, air will only enter our lungs if the pressure is lower in the lungs than outside. To create lower pressure in the thorax:

- the diaphragm muscle contracts and flattens
- the external intercostal muscles contract and pull the rib-cage up and out
- both these movements increase the volume in the thorax
- when the volume increases, the pressure decreases
- a lower pressure in the thorax causes air to enter from the higher atmospheric pressure outside
- breathing in occurs.

Breathing out – exhaling
Air will only pass out of our lungs if the pressure is higher inside the thorax than outside. To create higher pressure in the thorax:

- the diaphragm muscle relaxes and rises into an arch shape
- the internal intercostal muscles contract and the rib-cage is pulled down and in
- both these movements decrease, the volume in the thorax
- when the volume decreases the pressure increases
- a higher pressure in the thorax forces air out of the lungs to the lower atmospheric pressure outside
- breathing out occurs.

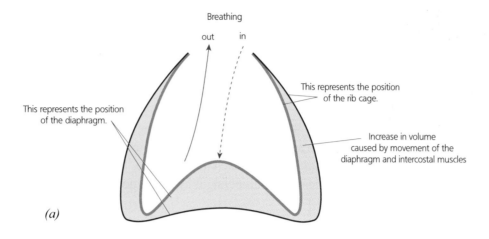

Breathing

out   in

This represents the position
of the diaphragm.

This represents the position
of the rib cage.

Increase in volume
caused by movement of the
diaphragm and intercostal muscles

(a)

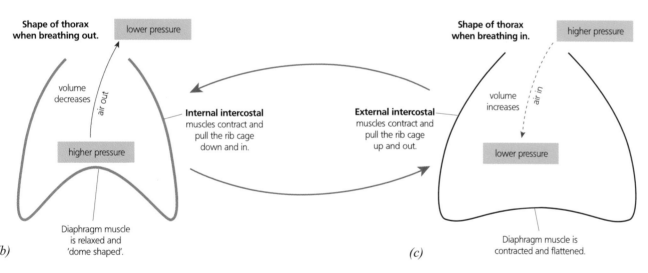

**Shape of thorax
when breathing out.**

lower pressure

volume
decreases

air out

higher pressure

Diaphragm muscle
is relaxed and
'dome shaped'.

Internal intercostal
muscles contract and
pull the rib cage
down and in.

External intercostal
muscles contract and
pull the rib cage
up and out.

**Shape of thorax
when breathing in.**

higher pressure

volume
increases

air in

lower pressure

Diaphragm muscle is
contracted and flattened.

(b)

(c)

Figure 9.12 *Diagram to show the
change in shape of the thorax during
breathing*
(a) difference in volume
(b) breathing out
(c) breathing in

5 What makes air flow into our lungs?   *(2 marks)*

6 What effect would a puncture through to the lungs have on breathing?
                                                                            (1 mark)

The elasticity of the lungs and chest wall cause an elastic recoil which also pushes
air out.

When the pressure changes in the thorax, it affects the whole cavity, including the
space between the pleural membranes. This is due to the pleural membranes
sticking to the rib-cage, diaphragm and lungs.

Figure 9.13 A spirometer

9.9 Lung capacity

During normal, relaxed breathing, we breathe in and out about 12 times in a minute. The volume of air exchanged can be measured using a **spirometer** (Figure 9.13). This instrument measures the volume of gases breathed in and out of the lungs.

The volume of air exchanged during quiet breathing is called the **tidal volume** and is approximately $500 \, cm^3$ in an average man. The **ventilation rate** is the volume of air breathed in per minute. This is worked out by calculating the tidal volume and multiplying it by the number of breaths in one minute. (See Figure 9.14.)

Figure 9.14 Lung volumes

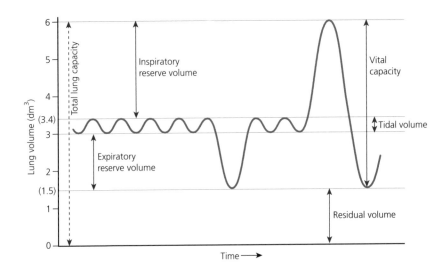

Our lungs can contain far more air, which enables us to adapt to changing needs. During exercise, our tidal volume increases to provide more oxygen for respiration.

If we take a deep breath, about $3000 \, cm^3$ extra air can enter the lungs: this is called the **inspiratory reserve volume**. This brings in more air containing oxygen and delivers more oxygen to the alveoli during periods of activity.

If we breathe out normally and then continue to expel as much air as possible by forced breathing, an extra $1000 \, cm^3$ of air is expelled. This is the **expiratory reserve volume**, caused by increased contraction of the internal intercostal muscles.

If we take a large breath in and then breathe out as much air as possible, this is the maximum volume of air that we can expel, our **vital capacity**. This indicates the maximum volume of air that can be exchanged. It combines the tidal volume, and the inspiratory and expiratory reserve volumes.

The vital capacity, or maximum amount of air moved in and out of the lungs, varies between 3000 and 5000 cm^3 in healthy adults. Obviously large, fit men have a larger vital capacity or volume than small, unfit women. Smokers and those suffering from asthma will have reduced vital capacities.

The **total lung capacity** is all the air present in the lungs. This includes the vital capacity which can be measured, and the air that remains in the lungs, the **residual air**. Even after the maximum expiration, 25% of our total lung volume will still contain air. Approximately 1500 cm^3 of air remains in our lungs. This prevents our lungs collapsing even when we force air out of our lungs. Residual air cannot be measured with a spirometer. The total capacity of the lungs varies between 3500 and 8000 cm^3, the volume depending on the age, height, build, sex and health of the person.

When breathing quietly, about 500 cm^3 of air enters and leaves the lungs, but only about 350 cm^3 of this air reaches the alveoli. Therefore only 70% of the air breathed in is available for gas exchange. Only one-fifth of this air is oxygen, so the volume of oxygen taken in is really quite small, but this can be increased during deep and rapid breathing. Air remains in the trachea, bronchi and bronchioles and this can be called **dead space**, as no gas exchange takes place here.

Definition

Tidal volume is the volume of air exchanged during quiet breathing.
Ventilation rate is the volume of air breathed in per minute (tidal volume × number of breaths).
Inspiratory reserve volume is the extra air that enters during deep breathing.
Expiratory reserve volume is the extra air that can be expelled by forced breathing out.
Vital capacity is the maximum volume of air that can be expelled from the lungs.
Residual air is the air that remains in the lungs after breathing out.
Total lung capacity is all the air in the lungs, combining the vital capacity with the residual air

Extension

Box 9.5 Minute volume (V$_E$)

This is the total volume of gases breathed in one minute. The volume varies depending on the individual's level of activity.

Minute volume = tidal volume × breathing rate
    (V$_E$)

At rest – values found in an average woman:

V$_E$ = tidal volume × No. of breaths
     (cm^3)   (min)

   = 350 cm^3 × 13 breaths per minute

   = 4 550 cm^3 per minute

When exercising, the rate and depth of breathing increase.

V$_E$ = 700 cm^3 × 24 breaths per minute

   = 16 800 cm^3 per minute

The total volume of gases breathed in has increased over 3 times, so providing more oxygen for respiration. Exercise requires more energy. This is provided by increased cellular respiration, possible due to higher oxygen intake.

Remember

During quiet breathing, only a small amount of oxygen diffuses through to the blood

Extension

Box 9.6 Surfactant

Moisture can cause problems due to surface tension, as water molecules tend to stick together forming a 'skin' when water is in contact with air. (This surface tension is made use of by insects like pond-skaters that can run over the 'skin' of water at the pond surface.)

In the lungs, the lobes of the alveoli are coated by a layer of moisture, typical of gas exchange surfaces. Surface tension tends to pull water molecules together and this could be a problem for the concave alveoli, especially during breathing out, when the alveoli deflate. It could cause the sides of the alveoli to collapse and stick together, so reducing the surface area for gas exchange.

A surfactant is a chemical which, like detergent, reduces the surface tension of a fluid. Surfactant is produced constantly from special alveolar cells. This reduces the surface tension of the moisture lining the alveoli, so stopping the alveolar walls from collapsing and sticking together.

Surfactant starts to be produced in the developing fetus from 20 weeks and is not properly functioning until 30 weeks of pregnancy. A baby born prematurely before this age will suffer from **respiratory distress**, due to lack of surfactant. The breathing difficulties are caused by the high surface tension of the liquid in the alveoli which causes alveolar collapse following each expiration.

Smokers have less surfactant than non-smokers.

Box 9.7 Respirometers

A respirometer is used to find out the volume of oxygen taken in by an organism and the volume of carbon dioxide produced in a given time. The level of activity or metabolic rate of an organism can then be determined. The ratio of carbon dioxide produced, divided by the oxygen used, is called the **respiratory quotient** or **RQ**, and indicates the respiratory substrate.

$$\text{Respiratory quotient (RQ)} = \frac{\text{carbon dioxide produced}}{\text{oxygen taken in}}$$

For example, the RQ of glucose is 1.0, when the volume of carbon dioxide produced equals the volume of oxygen taken in.

$$6O_2 + C_6H_{12}O_6 \longrightarrow \text{Energy} + 6CO_2 + 6H_2O$$

i.e. $\dfrac{6CO_2}{6O_2} = 1.0$

The RQ of lipids is 0.7, that of protein 0.9.

A simple respirometer can be used to find out the volume of oxygen taken in by woodlice (Figure 9.15). Woodlice are placed in a gauze basket positioned above sodium hydroxide solution in a boiling tube. Sodium hydroxide solution absorbs carbon dioxide. The boiling tube is airtight and connected via a short glass tube to the capillary tube, which has a scale attached. The

Box 9.7 Respirometers cont'd

apparatus contains air, sealed by the oil droplet inserted at the right-hand side of the capillary tube, near the start of the scale, as shown in Figure 9.15.

Oxygen taken in

As the woodlice take in oxygen during respiration, the volume of air in the boiling tube decreases. Carbon dioxide produced by the woodlice does not replace the oxygen used up, as it is absorbed by the sodium hydroxide. Therefore the volume of air in the boiling tube decreases in proportion to the oxygen taken in, and the pressure falls.

Air moves from the higher pressure in the capillary and side tube to the lower pressure in the boiling tube, drawing the oil droplet along towards the woodlice.

The distance moved by the oil droplet indicates the volume of oxygen taken in by the woodlice. Knowing the distance moved and the diameter of the capillary tube allows the volume to be calculated, using the formula:

Volume of cylinder $= \Pi r^2 l$

(where l = the distance moved by the oil droplet)

Knowing the mass of the woodlice enables the oxygen uptake per gram to be calculated.

For example

$$\frac{\text{Total volume of oxygen taken in (mm}^3)}{\text{Total mass of woodlice (g)}} = \frac{50}{10} = 5\,\text{mm}^3 \text{ oxygen per gram of woodlice.}$$

The information can usefully be recorded over a fixed time period, e.g. one hour, at a specific temperature, and for a particular mass of woodlice, repeated and averaged to give a more accurate answer.

This gives a measure of the **metabolic rate** in terms of rate of oxygen taken in per unit mass of an organism.

Carbon dioxide produced

To calculate the volume of carbon dioxide produced, the same apparatus can be used without the sodium hydroxide. *The difference between the position of the oil droplet with and without sodium hydroxide indicates the volume of carbon dioxide produced.* The distance between the two oil droplets can be measured in a fixed time period and the same calculations carried out.

With sodium hydroxide, carbon dioxide is removed and the oil droplet moves to the left due to the decrease in pressure caused by the decrease in carbon dioxide. Without sodium hydroxide, carbon dioxide is not removed and the oil droplet may not move at all. If the same volume of oxygen is taken in as carbon dioxide produced, then there will be no change in the volume of gas and the oil droplet will not move. If less carbon dioxide is produced than oxygen is taken in, then the fall in pressure will move the oil droplet a little to the left.

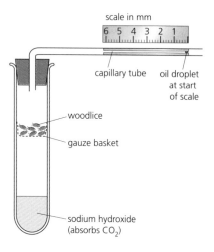

Figure 9.15 *A simple respirometer*

Extension

Box 9.7 Respirometers cont'd

Using respirometers with plants

Plants respire all the time, taking in oxygen and producing carbon dioxide. During the day plants also photosynthesise, taking in carbon dioxide and producing oxygen.

Therefore to find out the respiration rate with plants, it is necessary to stop photosynthesis because it confuses the results. Seeds are simple to use as they do not photosynthesise and the same apparatus can be used as with the woodlice. If a plant with leaves is to be used, then the apparatus must be covered with foil to stop light reaching the plant.

9.10 Control of breathing in humans

Breathing in and out, or ventilating, brings oxygen into the lungs for gas exchange and removes carbon dioxide. The amount of oxygen we need varies, depending on the level of activity, so there must be control of the breathing process. The respiratory centre that controls the breathing rate is found in the part of the brain called the **medulla**, located at the top of the spinal cord. This alters the breathing rate as required.

During breathing **at rest**, regular nerve impulses are sent to the diaphragm and intercostal muscles, causing rhythmic contraction and relaxation of these muscles. This causes the volume and pressure changes in the thorax that cause breathing.

Breathing in is caused by the diaphragm and external intercostal muscles contracting and increasing the volume in the thorax. As a result air passes into the lungs. The lungs are stretched by the air, so stimulating **stretch receptors** in the bronchi (Figure 9.16). These stimulated stretch receptors send nerve impulses to the respiratory centre which stop the process of breathing in, by stopping contraction of the diaphragm and external intercostal muscles. The volume in the thorax starts to decrease and breathing out begins.

Breathing out is caused by the relaxation and rising of the diaphragm and contraction of the internal intercostal muscles, which decrease the volume in the thorax. Air passes out of the lungs and the lungs deflate. The stretch receptors are no longer stimulated and inhaling is no longer inhibited, the muscles contract again and breathing in resumes. The nerve connecting the stretch receptors to the brain is the *vagus* or 'wandering' nerve. The vagus nerve is an example of a *cranial* nerve. Cranial nerves are normally restricted to the head and neck region, so the vagus is described as 'wandering' as it extends to more distant organs of the body, such as the lungs, heart, kidneys and stomach.

If body activity increases, then the rate of respiration goes up and the level of carbon dioxide in the blood rises.

Breathing in

(1) External intercostal muscles contract and pull rib cage up and out. Diaphragm muscle contracts and flattens.

(2) Volume increases pressure decreases.

(4) Stretch receptors in bronchi are stimulated by air rushing in. Nerve impulses sent to brain.

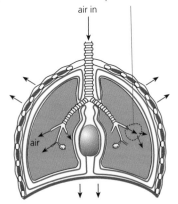

air in

(3) Air flows in and expands lungs.

(5) Impulses from brain stop the contraction of diaphragm and halt the process of breathing in.

Breathing out

(2) Internal intercostal muscles contract and pull rib cage down and in. Diaphragm muscle relaxes and rises.

(1) Stretch receptors in bronchi are no longer stimulated. Nerve impulses are not sent to the brain.

air out

(3) Volume decreases pressure increases.

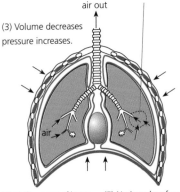

(4) Air flows out of lungs.

(5) No impulses from brain to stop contraction of diaphragm and external intercostal muscles. (Inhibition of breathing removed.)

Breathing in resumes.

Figure 9.16 *Control of breathing and stretch receptors*

Did You Know

Hyperventilation is forced deep breathing.
Breathing in and out deeply reduces the carbon dioxide level in the blood.
As it is the increase in carbon dioxide in the blood that triggers breathing,
low levels suppress the stimulus to breathe. Divers and snorkellers
hyperventilate before going underwater, to decrease the urge to breathe,
therefore allowing them to stay underwater longer. Young children and
others may hyperventilate during a panic attack. The loss of the urge to
breathe may deprive the brain of oxygen and cause fainting. Breathing
resumes once conscious control is lost

Chemoreceptors, sensitive to changes in the carbon dioxide level, are found in
the medulla, aorta and in the carotid artery. If the level of carbon dioxide rises, the
chemoreceptors are stimulated and transmit impulses along nerve fibres to the
respiratory centre in the medulla. The control centre in the medulla is stimulated
and impulses are sent along phrenic nerves to the diaphragm and along intercostal
nerves to the intercostal muscles. The impulses are sent more frequently, so
speeding up the rate and depth of breathing. The increased breathing rate reduces
the level of carbon dioxide in the blood and brings in more oxygen. As the level
of carbon dioxide falls, the chemoreceptors are no longer stimulated and the
breathing rate returns to normal.

Control of ventilation – a summary

Ventilation is controlled by impulses from:–

- **Chemoreceptors** – in medulla, aorta and carotid arteries. These detect the
  CO_2 concentration of the blood.

- **Stretch receptors** – in wall of bronchi. These detect the extent of lung
  inflation, how much air is in the lungs.

This is an example of a **negative feedback mechanism**, controlling the level of
carbon dioxide in the blood. Any change in the carbon dioxide level in the blood
is detected, corrected and returned to the normal level (Figure 9.17).

 Definition

Negative feedback occurs
when any change in the
normal level is detected,
corrected and returned to
the normal level

Figure 9.17 Graph to show the effect of carbon dioxide on the rate and depth of breathing

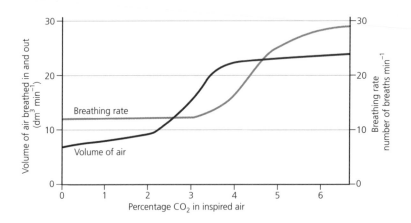

This graph shows the following information:

● Increasing the percentage of carbon dioxide in inspired air causes an increase in the volume of air breathed in and the breathing rate.

● There is no change in the breathing rate until the percentage of carbon dioxide rises above 3%.

● The fastest rise in volume of air breathed in and breathing rate occurs when the carbon dioxide inspired rises above 3% to 4%.

● Although the rates continue to rise as the percentage of carbon dioxide rises, above 5% the rate of rise slows down particularly in the volume of air breathed in.

It is interesting that the stimulus for breathing is not a fall in oxygen, but an increase in carbon dioxide. This may be because levels of oxygen in the blood do not fall much. Haemoglobin remains at a high level of saturation until atmospheric levels fall very low, for example at high altitudes.

Remember

A rise in the carbon dioxide level in the blood causes an increase in the rate and depth of breathing

Extension

Box 9.8 Resuscitators

The fact that increased carbon dioxide concentration in the blood stimulates breathing is made use of in mouth-to-mouth resuscitation (the kiss of life). The high level of carbon dioxide breathed into the patient, 4%, compared to 0.04% in the air, increases the concentration in their lungs. Some carbon dioxide diffuses into the patient's blood and stimulates their chemoreceptors, hopefully leading to breathing and recovery. Exhaled air contains about 16% oxygen and some will diffuse into the patient's blood and reach the brain cells to provide oxygen until the patient resumes breathing. It is essential to restart ventilation before permanent brain damage occurs due to lack of oxygen. Hospitals and ambulances have **resuscitators** which achieve the same purpose.

Breathing into someone who has stopped breathing will provide them with oxygen and raise the level of carbon dioxide in their blood to stimulate their medulla to start the breathing process.

Box 9.9 Respiration and fitness

Respiration is the process in which energy is released from organic molecules. Respiration takes place in every cell; more active cells will respire at a faster rate and produce more energy in the form of ATP molecules.

Aerobic respiration requires oxygen for respiration and this process takes place in the mitochondria (see Section 1.11, page 12). More energy is released during aerobic respiration as the organic materials are completely broken down. For example, when glucose is respired aerobically, 38 ATP molecules are produced from each glucose molecule.

Anaerobic respiration is respiration that occurs when oxygen is in short supply. Without oxygen, less energy is released as the organic material is incompletely broken down. When glucose is respired anaerobically, only 2 ATP molecules are produced from each glucose molecule. The remaining energy is trapped as **ethanol** in plants, or **lactate** in animals. Either way, it is not all available for the respiring organism. During anaerobic respiration, glucose is not completely broken down and lactate starts to build up in animals. Muscle fatigue is caused by an increase in blood lactate and the consequent decrease in blood pH.

Aerobic exercise can take place if sufficent oxygen is available throughout a period of exercise. Glucose is completely broken down to carbon dioxide and water, and lots of energy is produced. The deep and rapid rate of breathing during **aerobics** should provide enough oxygen for **sustained aerobic respiration**.

A build-up of lactate can cause **cramp** and the sufferer then has to breathe deeply. We say that an **oxygen deficit** has built up. Deep breathing enables enough oxygen to reach the cells to break down the lactate to carbon dioxide and water. The amount of oxygen required to remove the lactate is called the **oxygen debt**.

Once the lactate has been oxidised and removed, the athlete can resume vigorous exercise. Footballers can frequently be seen sitting on the pitch in agony with cramp, breathing deeply to provide oxygen to remove the lactate. Trainers rub the footballers' legs to increase the rate of blood flow to the muscle cells where the oxygen is needed, to remove the lactate, stop the pain and get them moving again.

Fit, active athletes have a large vital capacity and are therefore able to provide more oxygen to their cells to maintain aerobic respiration, to release the large amounts of energy required. Sustained exercise increases the size of blood vessels to the muscles. The wider blood vessels are able to supply the extra materials required for increased respiration, and growth, and consequently these muscles increase in size. Have you ever noticed the differing sizes of a tennis player's arms? **Physical fitness** is the ability to cope with the physical demands we might encounter. A 'couch potato' existence is not the way to keep us fit. Exercise allows us to maintain and

Box 9.9 Respiration and fitness cont'd

improve our fitness and it also has been proved to reduce stress.

When we exercise, more energy is needed, which is best provided by aerobic respiration in the cells. This requires oxygen and glucose to reach the cells as fast as possible. To bring more oxygen into the body, we breathe faster and deeper.

The larger our lung capacity, the greater the intake of air. Normal breathing, at 12 times per minute, provides about $60\,000\,cm^3$ of air. Fit athletes can increase their intake to about $70\,000\,cm^3$ in females and up to $100\,000\,cm^3$ in males. Increased fitness enables a person to adapt quickly to changing needs by increasing their lung volume and the blood supply to the lungs.

Our breathing rate will increase in response to exercise, but this is faster and more efficient in athletes. Increased exercise makes the heart muscle stronger and more efficient as well as widening the **coronary arteries** as a result of the increased blood flow to the heart. Wider coronary arteries are less likely to be blocked, so reducing the chances of a **coronary thrombosis** (see Box 10.5, page 289). A stronger heart can pump blood with oxygen more efficiently to respiring cells, so maintaining aerobic respiration. Therefore exercise and keeping healthy benefit the person in many ways.

9.11 Gas exchange in plants

Plants live in habitats with differing amounts of water. Their mode of gas exchange therefore depends on the availability of water. There are three main groups of plants.

Mesophytes are plants that live on land where water is not in short supply. Most plants native to the UK are called mesophytes. They have no problems replacing the water lost in transpiration and no special adaptations are required to reduce water loss.

Xerophytes are plants that live in areas where water is in short supply such as deserts, where the water potential of both the air and soil is low and plants risk losing water by osmosis. There is little water in the soil and therefore water loss in transpiration must be minimised. Exposing a moist gas exchange surface would risk dehydration and special adaptations exist to both retain water and reduce water loss (see Figure 12.8, page 347).

Hydrophytes are plants that live in fresh water, either floating on the surface like water lilies or with most of their structure submerged, as with water crowfoot and rushes. Rice is a swamp plant with its roots permanently waterlogged. (See Section 15.2, page 440.) Obviously hydrophytes have no problem with water availability.

Gas exchange in mesophytes

Gases enter and leave plants mainly through the stomata in the leaves and the lenticels in stems. Lenticels exist in the woody parts of plants such as tree trunks. They are small patches of loose permeable cells that allow oxygen to reach cells for respiration (Figure 9.18).

The main gas exchange surface is the **spongy mesophyll** layer found inside the leaves. The spongy mesophyll cells are loosely packed, thus increasing the surface area for gas exchange. Gases are needed for both respiration and photosynthesis. (See Figure 12.3, page 344 for leaf structure.)

The spongy mesophyll layer is specially adapted for gas exchange. The cells are coated in a layer of water in which gases can dissolve. The cell walls are thin, so reducing the distance for diffusion of gases into the cell. The many widely spaced cells present a large surface area for gas exchange, easily reached by air entering through the stomata. A concentration gradient is maintained due to the rapid diffusion of gases in air.

Air enters through the stomata by diffusion; there is no ventilation process.

As leaves are thin, and up to 40% of the volume is air, gases can diffuse quickly through to the spongy mesophyll from the stomata. Gases can diffuse 10 000 times more quickly in air than in water.

At night, when only respiration is taking place, oxygen readily dissolves and diffuses through the walls of the spongy mesophyll cells and is transported along to other cells by diffusion. This maintains a lower concentration of oxygen in the spongy mesophyll cells than is present in the air in the leaf. This difference in concentration ensures continued diffusion of oxygen into the spongy mesophyll cells. The numerous small holes of the stomata allow the entry and exit of a sufficient quantity of air to keep the concentration of oxygen high in the air spaces. Carbon dioxide produced during respiration diffuses from the spongy mesophyll leaf cells, where it is present at a higher concentration, to the air spaces in the leaf where carbon dioxide is at a lower concentration. Carbon dioxide diffuses and passes out through the stomata by diffusion to the even lower concentration of carbon dioxide in the environment.

During the day, both respiration and photosynthesis are taking place. The plant needs oxygen for respiration and carbon dioxide for photosynthesis.

In bright light, the rate of photosynthesis is greater than the rate of respiration. Therefore carbon dioxide is needed in larger quantities than is produced in respiration. A difference in concentration exists with a higher concentration of carbon dioxide in the leaf air spaces and a lower concentration in the spongy mesophyll cells. Therefore carbon dioxide dissolves and diffuses through the walls of the spongy mesophyll from the leaf air space and into the **palisade** cells, in particular, for use in photosynthesis. This keeps the concentration of carbon dioxide low in the palisade and spongy mesophyll cells.

Thus, a difference in concentration exists with a higher concentration of carbon dioxide in the leaf air spaces and a lower concentration in the spongy mesophyll

Remember

The cell walls of the spongy mesophyll are the main gas exchange surface in mesophytic plants

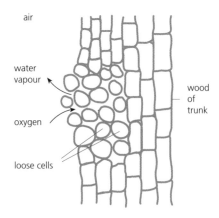

air

water vapour

oxygen

loose cells

wood of trunk

Figure 9.18 *Structure of a lenticel*

257

cells. Constant usage of the carbon dioxide will maintain this difference in concentration and diffusion of carbon dioxide into the cells will continue.

Oxygen will be produced in photosynthesis in larger quantities than is required for respiration. The excess oxygen will diffuse through to the spongy mesophyll cells. As a result, the concentration of oxygen in these cells will be higher than the concentration in the leaf air space. Oxygen will therefore diffuse out to the lower concentration in the leaf air space, and across the narrow leaf to the stomata and out, as the outside concentration of oxygen will be even lower. The removal of oxygen maintains a difference in concentration and ensures the process of diffusion continues.

Some of the moisture on the gas exchange surface evaporates and diffuses out of the leaf through the stomata in the process of **transpiration** (see Section 12.1, page 343). The spacing and size of the stomata allow sufficient gas exchange yet minimise water loss. This water loss is an inevitable consequence of gas exchange surfaces being moist. Land plants site their moist gas exchange surface inside the leaf to reduce the water lost and xerophytes have perfected the reduction of water loss in dry conditions. Plants are able to close their stomata if water loss becomes excessive, which also reduces the entry and exit of air for gas exchange. However, the large volume of air in the air spaces in the leaf provides a sufficient reservoir, and gas exchange is rarely affected.

The spongy mesophyll is well adapted as a gas exchange surface. It is permeable to gases and it presents a large surface area for gas exchange. The diffusion of air into and out of the stomata maintains a difference in concentration or **diffusion gradient**, so allowing continued diffusion.

Gas exchange in xerophytes

Marram grass, *Ammophila*, shows many xerophytic adaptations associated with the dry conditions in which it lives (see Figure 12.10, page 349). Growing along the seashore with strong winds and salt from the sea, fresh water is in short supply. Transpiration must be reduced and marram grass has many adaptations to achieve this. The leaf can roll up to reduce water loss but this reduces the entry of gases and the surface area exposed to light for photosynthesis.

The moist surface for gas exchange is found deep inside the leaf due to the **sunken stomata**, and air movement is restricted by **hairs**. All of these combine to minimise air movement and therefore to reduce transpiration. However, the rapid diffusion of gases in air, and the air spaces in the leaf, ensure that plenty of respiratory gases will be available. Photosynthesis will be reduced when marram is in a rolled condition as less surface will be facing the light.

Sorghum (see Section 15.2, page 440) grows in hot, dry conditions and displays all the adaptations of a typical xerophyte. Its extensive root system reaches widely for any available water and the **thick cuticle** and **sunken stomata**, as with marram grass, reduce the water lost in transpiration. In addition, sorghum is able to withstand very high temperatures which increase the rate of transpiration.

Gas exchange in hydrophytes

Hydrophytes run no risk of dehydration and their structure has adapted accordingly. As water provides support and allows full turgidity at all times, hydrophytes have little lignified material and xylem is poorly developed, as water transport is not a problem. Little waxy cuticle, if any, is present on the leaves and stem as there is no need to reduce water loss.

Water lilies and **duckweed** are hydrophytes with floating leaves. Most of the stomata are found on the upper surface of their leaves, so providing an entry to gases from the air, a much richer source of gases than water. Oxygen can easily diffuse in and carbon dioxide out. The inner gas exchange surface is kept moist with no risk of dehydration.

Plants with their roots anchored in the soil at the bottom of ponds and streams, such as water lilies, rushes and water crowfoot, have their roots submerged at all times. Their roots need oxygen for aerobic respiration and little is present dissolved in the water. Rushes and other hydrophytes with submerged roots have large continuous air spaces in their stems, called **aerenchyma**, to allow the movement of gases down to the roots (Figure 9.19). These 'hollow' stems are like straws sticking up out of the water gaining access to air, so providing the roots with oxygen for respiration. Air spaces in the stem and leaves also provide buoyancy.

Some aquatic plants have leaves that extend up into the air and therefore have access to gases for both respiration and photosynthesis (Figure 9.20).

Rice plants, with roots submerged in water, despite aerenchyma, are unable to provide enough oxygen to their roots for aerobic respiration at all times. Anaerobic respiration therefore takes place, producing ethanol. These plants are able to tolerate the build-up of ethanol and can therefore survive with roots in anaerobic conditions.

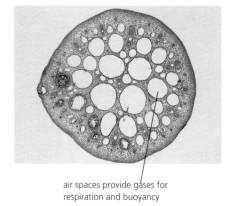
air spaces provide gases for
respiration and buoyancy

Figure 9.19 Transverse section of a water lily leaf stalk to show **aerenchyma** *tissue (large continuous air spaces in the stem)*

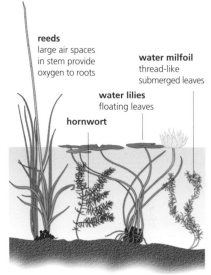
reeds
large air spaces
in stem provide
oxygen to roots

water milfoil
thread-like
submerged leaves

water lilies
floating leaves

hornwort

Figure 9.20 Hydrophytes in a pond

Extension

Box 9.10 The water crowfoot

The water crowfoot is interesting in that it has two types of leaves (Figure 9.21).

The **aerial leaves** have a large flat surface, typical of land plants with access to both air and light for respiration and photosynthesis. Aerenchyma in the stem acts as a reservoir of air along which diffusion of gases between the leaves and the roots takes place, allowing aerobic respiration in the waterlogged roots.

The **submerged leaves** are stringy and offer little resistance to moving water. This prevents tearing and damage to the leaves here and reduces the risk of dislodging the plant. This structure is typical of hydrophytes.

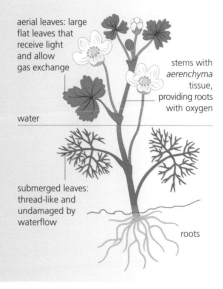
aerial leaves: large
flat leaves that
receive light
and allow
gas exchange

stems with
aerenchyma
tissue,
providing roots
with oxygen

water

submerged leaves:
thread-like and
undamaged by
waterflow

roots

Figure 9.21 The water crowfoot, Ranunculus aquatilis, *an example of a hydrophyte*

9.12 Ventilation in fish

Fish are aquatic breathers, using oxygen in solution from water and passing carbon dioxide out in solution to water. Water contains low levels of oxygen compared to air, 1% compared to 21%. Therefore to obtain enough oxygen, fish need to pass large quantities of water over their gas exchange surface, the gills. This is achieved by a good ventilation system. Living in water means there is no risk of dehydration and respiratory surfaces can be exposed more freely to the water, assuming they are adequately protected from damage.

Keeping the respiratory surface moist does not require a layer of mucus in aquatic animals, and so the diffusion distance is reduced. A good ventilation system and a short diffusion distance increase the efficiency of gas exchange in fish.

Gas exchange in bony fish

Bony fish are large animals with a small surface area to volume ratio. Diffusion of respiratory gases through their outer surface would not provide sufficient oxygen for their large volume, so they need specialised gas exchange surfaces. These are the **gills**.

A ventilation mechanism causes the pressure differences needed to provide a

Extension

Box 9.11 Cartilaginous and bony fish

There are two main groups of fish.

Cartilaginous fish have a skeleton made of cartilage, e.g. sharks and skates. Their mouth is normally found on the ventral or under surface of the body. An operculum or flap covering the gill slits is not present and the gills are exposed.

Bony fish, e.g. trout, goldfish and herring, as their name suggests, have a skeleton made of bone. Their mouth is normally at the front or anterior end and their body is covered with scales. An operculum covers their gills, so the slits are not visible.

(a)

(b)

Figure 9.22
(a) A bony trout and
(b) a cartilaginous shark

constant stream of water over the gills. Water is drawn in through the mouth, passes over the gills and leaves through the operculum, which is the flap covering the gills. Thus a fresh supply of aerated water flows constantly over the gills (Figure 9.23).

Ventilation in fish, as with humans, is an example of **mass flow** (see Table 9.3, page 245). Here the bulk movement of water depends on pressure differences. Therefore if water is to enter the mouth, it is necessary to lower the pressure there, so water enters from the higher pressure outside.

Lower pressure is created by increasing the volume (Figure 9.24). The volume is increased by lowering the floor of the mouth (the buccal cavity) and the expansion or widening of the mouth cavity. The increase in volume causes a decrease in pressure. It is now lower than the pressure in the water outside. With the opercular valve shut, water can enter only through the open mouth, moving from the higher pressure outside to the lower pressure inside. The mouth now closes and the pressure is increased.

Higher pressure is created by decreasing the volume (Figure 9.24). The volume is decreased by raising the floor of the mouth cavity and narrowing of the mouth cavity. This decrease in volume causes an increase in pressure. It is now higher than the pressure in the water outside. With the mouth closed and the opercular valve open, water is forced out over the gills to the lower pressure outside.

This process of expanding and reducing the volume of the mouth cavity causes pressure differences, so maintaining a regular supply of fresh water over the gills. This is essential in an aquatic environment, if the gills are to have access to sufficient oxygen. Watching goldfish, the regular opening and closing of the mouth and movements of the operculum are visible evidence of ventilation in fish. As the water flows over the gills, gas exchange takes place (Figure 9.25).

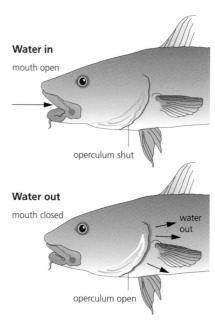

Water in
mouth open

operculum shut

Water out
mouth closed

water out

operculum open

Figure 9.23 *Passage of water through a fish*

Remember

Water, like air, always moves from a higher pressure to a lower pressure region

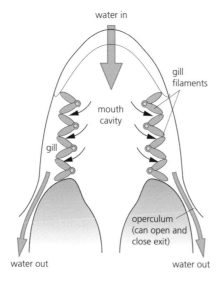

water in

gill filaments

mouth cavity

gill

operculum (can open and close exit)

water out   water out

Figure 9.25 *Section through mouth cavity and gill region of a bony fish*

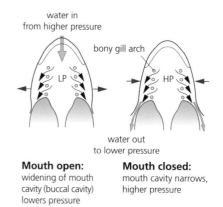

water in from higher pressure

bony gill arch

LP   HP

water out to lower pressure

Mouth open:
widening of mouth cavity (buccal cavity) lowers pressure

Mouth closed:
mouth cavity narrows, higher pressure

Figure 9.24 *Effect of expansion and narrowing of mouth cavity on ventilation in fish (LP = Low Pressure HP = High Pressure)*

9.13 Structure of gills and gas exchange

Figure 9.26 Gill from bony fish

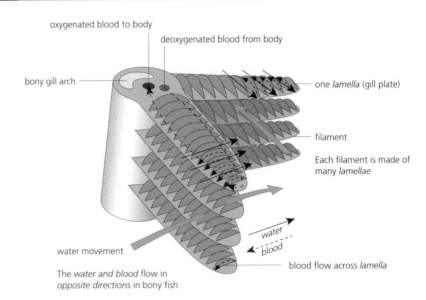

oxygenated blood to body

deoxygenated blood from body

bony gill arch

one *lamella* (gill plate)

filament

Each filament is made of many *lamellae*

water

blood

water movement

blood flow across *lamella*

The *water and blood* flow in *opposite directions* in bony fish

A gill is made up of two piles of filaments attached to a bony gill arch. The fragile filaments occur in large piles. Water allows them to separate to expose the surface for gas exchange. (Out of water the stacks of filaments stick together and less surface area is available to supply oxygen.)

Bony fish have four pairs of bony **gill arches** arranged in a semi-circle shape. These are supports to which the **gill filaments** are attached. There are about 70 pairs of filaments attached to each gill arch and this makes up a **gill** (Figure 9.26). A gill is made up of a gill arch with its attached gill filaments. Two rows of gill filaments are attached to each gill arch, forming a V-shape. Between the gill arches are five slits through which water passes out of the fish.

Each filament is made up of many **lamellae** or **gill plates** and these provide a large surface area for the exchange of gases. These lamellae are richly supplied with blood capillaries for this purpose. The tips of the gill filaments overlap and this slows down the flow of water over the gills, therefore allowing more time for the diffusion of gases across the lamellae. *The gill lamellae are the gas exchange surfaces in fish.* The rich blood supply in the lamellae ensures that the exchange of gases is maximised and gases can be quickly transported round the body.

The lamellae or gill plates are very thin, with walls only one cell thick. Each lamella is well supplied with blood capillaries, which also have a wall only one cell thick. These capillaries are very near the surface of the lamella. Thus the water containing the oxygen is close to the blood, so reducing the diffusion distance and increasing the rate of diffusion. Oxygen only has to diffuse across two thin cells to pass from the water into the blood.

The blood transports the oxygen away from the gills, so maintaining a low concentration of oxygen in the lamellae. The many blood capillaries present ensure that gas exchange takes place over most of the lamella.

Lamellae are well adapted as a gas exchange surface, having the following features:

- large surface area
- thin
- moist
- close to blood
- a ventilation mechanism.

Water, drawn in by ventilation movements, flows from the mouth cavity, across the lamellae and out through the operculum.

9.14 Parallel and countercurrent flow in fish

Oxygen diffuses from the water into the blood and two different mechanisms exist for this transfer. A **parallel flow arrangement** is found in cartilaginous fish. Here the water and blood flow in the same direction, parallel to each other across the lamellae. A **countercurrent mechanism** in bony fish means that the water and blood are flowing in opposite directions across the lamellae. (See Figure 9.27.)

Parallel flow

The difference in oxygen concentration at the start will be great, with more in the water and less in the blood, and diffusion will occur. But as the blood and water continue to flow together, the difference in concentration decreases, which slows down the rate of diffusion. Eventually the concentration of oxygen will be the same in both water and blood and diffusion will cease.

We call this point **equilibrium**, and there is no further net movement of oxygen. This may occur about half-way along the lamella and will result in only half the oxygen entering the blood, about 50%, the same quantity remaining in the water. This is inefficient, as less oxygen enters the blood and diffusion only takes place over some of the lamella, effectively reducing the surface area for gas exchange. (See Figure 9.27.)

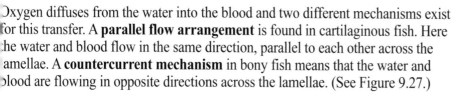

7 Why does gas exchange only take place over part of the gill plate in the parallel flow mechanism? *(2 marks)*

Countercurrent mechanism

A difference in the concentration of oxygen between the water and the blood is maintained across the whole lamella. The blood comes into contact with water which always has a higher concentration of oxygen. This maintains a difference in the oxygen concentration between the water and the blood, so maximising the rate of diffusion. It also means that diffusion of gases takes place over the whole lamella, so increasing the surface area for gas exchange.

As a result more oxygen diffuses into the blood than in the parallel flow system. At the end of the lamella, the blood will contain a higher concentration of oxygen, approximately 80%, and the water a lower concentration of oxygen. Bony fish are

Parallel flow
(in cartilaginous fish e.g. sharks)

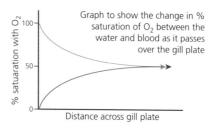

A gill plate (lamella)

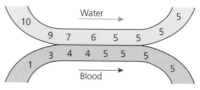

Graph to show the change in % saturation of O_2 between the water and blood as it passes over the gill plate

Water and blood flow in parallel, in the **same** direction

Counter current (counterflow)
(in bony fish e.g. trout)

A gill plate (lamella)

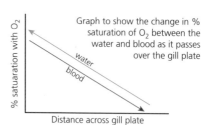

Graph to show the change in % saturation of O_2 between the water and blood as it passes over the gill plate

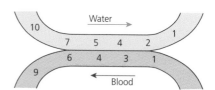

Water and blood flow in **opposite** directions

Figure 9.27 *A comparison of countercurrent and parallel flow exchange systems. The numbers given represent the relative concentration of oxygen (in arbitrary figures)*

able to achieve 80% absorption of oxygen through the countercurrent system, compared to 50% in the parallel flow system.

Bony fish are very well adapted for gas exchange. This is achieved by having a large surface area for gas exchange, a thin surface to reduce the diffusion distance and by maintaining a concentration gradient to maximise diffusion.

The **large surface area** for gas exchange is achieved by:

● each gill having many filaments

● each filament having many lamellae

● a countercurrent mechanism enabling all the lamellae to be used for gas exchange as equilibrium is not reached

● many blood capillaries maximising the surface for gas exchange.

All these features increase the surface area for gas exchange.

The **thickness of the exchange surface** is minimised by:

● the lamellae having walls only one cell thick (squamous epithelium)

● the capillary wall being only one cell thick (squamous epithelium)

● blood being close to the surface of the plate

● gill plates being very thin so water is close to the blood.

All these features reduce the diffusion distance, so increasing the rate of diffusion.

A **difference in concentration** is maintained by:

● the constant flow of aerated water over the lamella; this is caused by the ventilation mechanism

● the constant movement of blood removing oxygen from and bringing carbon dioxide to the gills

● the countercurrent mechanism maintaining a difference in concentration between the water and blood, by preventing equilibrium being reached.

These features ensure that a difference in concentration is maintained over the whole lamella, increasing the rate of diffusion (Fick's Law).

9.15 Gas exchange in insects

In common with all arthropods, insects have an outer skeleton called an **exoskeleton**. The mammalian skeleton, found on the inside, is called an **endoskeleton**. The exoskeleton made of **chitin** is tough, light and allows movement. It is covered with a waxy, waterproof cuticle, in order to reduce water loss. The waxy cuticle found in leaves serves the same function. The waterproof outer skeleton provides support, and enables insects to live on land without risk of dehydration.

Gas exchange surfaces are moist, so an internal respiratory surface is essential to prevent excessive water loss.

Insects are **air breathers**, gaining oxygen from the air. Air enters through holes in the exoskeleton, called **spiracles**, located on both sides of the thorax and abdomen. Figure 9.28 shows the **tracheal** system of an insect.

Spiracles lead to a system of tubes extending into the insect. The larger tubes, 1 mm in diameter, are kept open by rings of chitin (similar to the rings of cartilage in mammals). Chitin is impermeable, so gas exchange cannot take place in the larger tubes. These tubes branch extensively and form narrow tubes called **tracheoles** which run close to all the cells in the insect. The tracheoles branch into tiny tubes 0.7 μm in diameter, some of which actually penetrate cells. No chitin is present in these tiny tubes and they are freely permeable to gases. The tracheoles extend from the outside deep into the insect, so supplying oxygen directly to the tissues. Blood is not used to transport respiratory gases. Similarly, carbon dioxide is removed through the tracheoles.

The walls of the tracheoles are the gas exchange surface in insects.

Oxygen normally enters by diffusion as there is a lower concentration in respiring cells. The higher concentration of carbon dioxide produced by respiring cells can similarly be removed by diffusion.

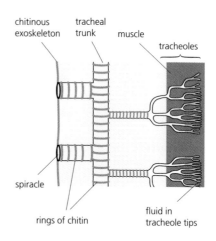

Figure 9.28 *The tracheal system of an insect*

Ventilation in insects

In some insects, rhythmical flattening and expanding of the thorax and abdomen take place, creating differences in volume and therefore pressure. These cause air to enter and leave the insect; in other words, ventilation takes place.

In locusts and grasshoppers air enters through the thoracic spiracles and leaves through the abdominal ones. This achieves a better system of gas exchange, as only fresh air enters the tracheoles for the delivery of oxygen, it is not mixed with expired air. Figure 9.29 shows an experiment which demonstrates this ventilation mechanism.

Figure 9.29 *Experiment to demonstrate the ventilation mechanism in grasshoppers*

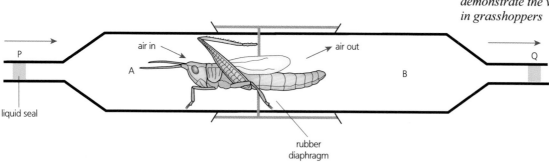

The rubber diaphragm fits around the grasshopper snugly, making an airtight fit. The only way that air can pass from A to B is through the grasshopper. After 30 minutes the liquid seals in P and Q move to the right. This indicates that pressure has fallen in A and increased in B. This can only be caused by air passing from A to B through the insect. Air must enter the thoracic spiracles in A and leave via the abdominal spiracles in B.

A ventilation mechanism helps to speed up the movement of respiratory gases, thus increasing the efficiency of oxygen delivery. However, the overall process still relies on diffusion of gases which is a slow process, only efficient over a

At rest

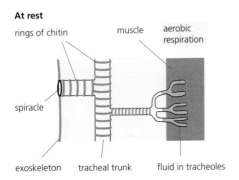

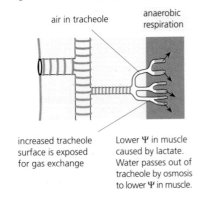

During strenuous activity e.g. flying

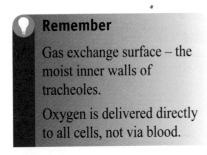

Figure 9.30 Effect of exercise on fluid in tracheoles

> **Remember**
>
> Gas exchange surface – the moist inner walls of tracheoles.
>
> Oxygen is delivered directly to all cells, not via blood.

short distance. Every cell relies on diffusion along tracheoles for gas exchange as respiratory gases are not transported in the blood of insects. This restricts the size insects can reach and although large insects may be 16 cm long, they are never more than 2 cm broad.

Insects and muscular activity

The tracheoles contain a watery fluid at their tips which keeps the tracheole walls moist but reduces the surface area through which gases can diffuse to cells. Figure 9.30 shows the effect of strenuous exercise on the fluid in the tracheoles.

During flying and other strenuous activity, the muscles of an insect run out of oxygen and start respiring anaerobically. This produces lactate in the tissues. Lactate produces a lower water potential than the watery fluid in the tracheole and consequently water passes by osmosis from the tracheole and into the tissues. The volume of liquid in the tracheoles is reduced, so exposing more surface for gas exchange. The increased diffusion of oxygen into the tissues provides the extra oxygen required for exercise. The amount of watery fluid in the tracheoles can be altered depending upon the oxygen requirements of the insect.

Coping with dry conditions

Some of the moisture in the tracheoles will inevitably evaporate and diffuse out through the spiracles. In hot, dry and windy conditions insects can reduce water loss through spiracles by closing them using a muscular valve. Hairs around the spiracle can trap moist air, also reducing water loss. Control of water loss has enabled insects to extend their range into dry habitats, making them a highly successful group of animals.

How insects achieve efficient gas exchange – a summary

Large surface area

- extensive system of branching tracheoles
- withdrawal of fluid in tracheoles during exercise, further increasing surface area for gas exchange.

Maintaining a diffusion gradient

- use of oxygen by cells in respiration keeps the concentration low in cells
- production of carbon dioxide by cells increases the concentration assisting its diffusion out of the insect
- some insects have a ventilation system which increases the concentration gradient.

Thickness of membrane (diffusion distance)

A short diffusion is achieved by:

- thin tracheole walls
- a lack of chitin, increasing permeability
- withdrawal of fluid enabling air to reach closer to more cells, so reducing diffusion distance.

Summary – 9 Gas exchange

- In both plants and animals, a large surface area to volume ratio allows exchange of gases by diffusion. This can take place through either external or internal membranes.

- Moist exchange surfaces are permeable to gases.

- Aquatic unicells are able to gain enough oxygen by diffusion through moist external membranes, as they have a large surface area to volume ratio. Oxygen can then reach all other cells by diffusion; no transport system is necessary.

- Large organisms, with a smaller surface area to volume ratio, have specialised gas exchange surfaces which supply the increased oxygen required for their larger volume. This is achieved by a folded external or internal exchange surface.

- A transport system is required in larger animals, to distribute the oxygen efficiently to every cell and to remove carbon dioxide.

- With land animals and plants, the outer surface area must be **waterproof** and dry to prevent desiccation, and therefore cannot function as a gas exchange surface.

- The damp exchange surfaces are normally found inside land organisms, which reduces water loss.

- **Humans** have a high oxygen requirement and have adaptations to maximise the uptake of oxygen to the cells.

- A ventilation mechanism, breathing, maximises the volume of air reaching the gas exchange surface and consequently increases the amount of oxygen entering the blood and the carbon dioxide removed.

- The alveoli in the lungs are the specialised gas exchange surface through which oxygen diffuses into the blood and carbon dioxide diffuses out.

- A respiratory pigment, haemoglobin, increases the efficiency of the transport of oxygen in mammals to the cells.

- In **plants**, the spongy mesophyll is the main gas exchange surface. It has a thin, moist surface which is permeable to gases and a large surface area.

- A constant supply of air through the stomata maintains a difference in concentration.

- In **fish**, the lamellae or gill plates are the gas exchange surface.

- The lamellae or gill plates provide a large surface area for gas exchange. The membrane is very thin and close to blood, so the diffusion distance is short. The gill plates are moist and permeable to gases.

- A ventilation mechanism brings in a constant supply of fresh water, bringing in oxygen and removing carbon dioxide.

- A countercurrent mechanism maximises the concentration gradient and the surface area for diffusion, in bony fish.

Answers

1 Tapeworms are flat and thin, with a very large surface area to volume ratio. Food can therefore be successfully transported by diffusion to all cells *(1)*.

2 Insects, with a large surface area to volume ratio, can carry oxygen to every cell by diffusion. If they were larger, this would not be possible. This restricts the size that insects can reach as they can only transport oxygen by diffusion; a transport system is not used for this purpose in insects *(1)*.

3 In the nose, air is cleaned, warmed and moistened before entering the lungs. In the mouth, the air is not cleaned as hairs are not present to filter the air *(1)*.

4 Carbon dioxide is at a higher concentration in the alveolar air, 5.5%, than in the tidal air, 0.04%. Therefore carbon dioxide diffuses through from the alveolar air to the tidal air and is breathed out *(1)*.

5 Air moves from a high pressure to a lower pressure. A lower pressure is achieved in the lungs by an increase in volume. Flattening of the diaphragm and lifting of the rib-cage increase the volume, so lowering the pressure and air enters *(2)*.

6 A punctured lung allows air into the previously airtight thorax. This prevents a pressure difference existing between the thorax and the air. Breathing, which relies on differences in pressure, will be affected *(1)*.

7 Oxygen diffuses from the water into the blood as the water passes over the gills. Eventually, equilibrium is reached, when oxygen levels are the same in both the water and the blood. Diffusion then ceases as there is no longer a difference in concentration. This occurs about half-way along the gill plate or lamella, and there is then no further net gas exchange *(2)*.

End of Chapter Questions

1 Name the gas exchange surface in: **(a)** humans **(b)** plants **(c)** fish.   *(3 marks)*

2 State four features of any gas exchange surface.   *(4 marks)*

3 Explain why, in terrestrial organisms, water is always lost from the gas exchange surface.   *(2 marks)*

4 Why do large organisms require gas exchange surfaces in addition to the outer membrane?   *(2 marks)*

5 Explain how efficient gas exchange is achieved in plants.   *(3 marks)*

6 Briefly describe three features of the alveolar epithelium that allows efficient gas exchange between the alveolus and the blood in the alveolar capillaries.

     (3 marks)

7 The graph shows the changes in pressure inside the lungs of a person breathing normally.

Figure 9.31

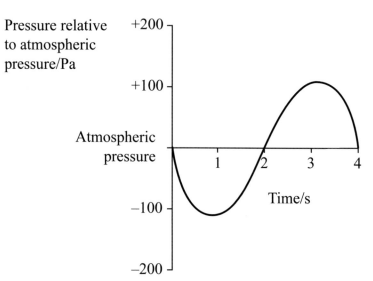

Pressure relative to atmospheric pressure/Pa

(a) Use the graph to calculate the rate of breathing in breaths per minute.

(1 mark) N2.1 N2.2

(b) (i) Between what times is this person breathing out? *(1 mark)* N2.1

   (ii) What is the evidence from the graph to support your answer to (b) (i)?

(1 mark)

(c) Explain how the pressure inside the lung may be decreased. *(2 marks)*

NEAB 1997

(Total 5 marks)

C2.2 **8** **(a)** (i) Give **one** similarity between the way in which oxygen from the atmosphere reaches a muscle in an insect and the way it reaches a mesophyll cell in a leaf *(1 mark)*

(ii) Give **one** difference in the way in which carbon dioxide is removed from a muscle in an insect and the way in which it is removed from a muscle in a fish. *(1 mark)*

The diagram shows the way in which water flows over the gills of a fish. The graph shows the changes in pressure in the buccal cavity and in the opercular cavity during a ventilation cycle.

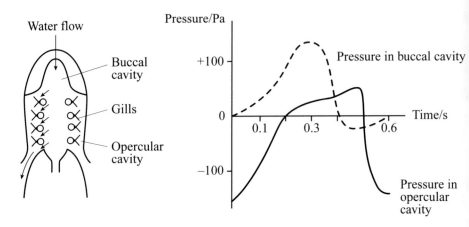

(b) Use the graph to calculate the rate of ventilation in cycles per minute. *(2 marks)*

(c) For most of this ventilation cycle, water will be flowing in one direction over the gills. Explain the evidence from the graph that supports this. *(1 mark)*

(d) Explain how the fish increases pressure in the buccal cavity. *(2 marks)*

NEAB 1997 *(Total 7 marks)*

The heart is a muscular organ which pumps blood round the body. **Arteries** carry blood away from the heart and **veins** carry blood to the heart. Blood is pumped to the lungs to pick up oxygen and release carbon dioxide, and nutrients are added to the blood from the small intestine. Oxygen and nutrients like glucose are carried to all the cells of the body in the blood, and waste like urea is taken away by the blood. Arteries divide into smaller vessels called **arterioles** and further division forms **capillaries** which are so small that their wall is only one cell thick. These tiny vessels are permeable and enable food and oxygen to pass from the blood to the cells and waste to pass back. Capillaries join to form **venules** or small veins, which link together to form veins. When we exercise, our heart rate increases to supply oxygen and glucose more quickly to the cells to provide the energy needed. Our heart rate also increases when we are frightened or excited due to the hormone **adrenaline**.

This chapter includes:
- double circulation
- heart structure
- cardiac cycle
- control of heart rate
- exercise and the heart
- blood vessels
- tissue fluid and lymph.

10.1 Double circulation

In mammals blood flows through the heart **twice** during one complete pathway round the body. One circuit from the heart to the lungs and back is the **pulmonary circulation**. The other circuit from the heart to the rest of the body is the **systemic circulation** (Figure 10.1).

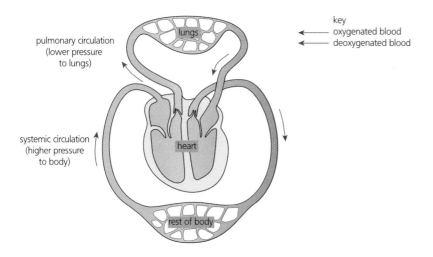

> **Remember**
>
> Mammals have a **double, closed**, circulatory system.
> *Double* – blood is pumped twice by the heart in each complete circuit.
> *Closed* – blood is contained in blood vessels

Figure 10.1 Pulmonary and systemic circulation

As there are two circuits, this is called a *double circulatory system*. Blood is pumped twice by the heart, from the right ventricle to the lungs and from the left ventricle to the body. These two chambers have thick walls made of cardiac muscle, but the muscle of the left ventricle is thicker than the muscle of the right ventricle. Therefore the blood pumped by the left ventricle will be pushed harder and under greater pressure than blood from the right ventricle. In other words, it is a two-pressure system with higher pressure to the body from the left ventricle and lower pressure to the lungs from the right ventricle.

The advantage of a double circulatory system is that it is possible to have a two-pressure system.

> **Remember**
>
> Heart diagrams are normally drawn as if you are looking at the body from the front. Thus what appears to the observer to be on the right is actually on the left side of the body

Ventricle	Muscle	Pressure	Effect
right	thinner	lower	blood pushed slowly to lungs giving more time for gas exchange
left	thicker	higher	blood pushed quickly to body cells carrying oxygen

Table 10.1 Comparison of the left and right ventricles of the heart

Pulmonary circulation

In humans, blood is pumped from the right ventricle along the **pulmonary artery** to the lungs (Figure 10.2). The pressure is fairly low due to the thinner muscle of the right ventricle contracting with less force. In the lungs, the pulmonary artery divides into smaller and smaller vessels to form the tiny blood vessels called **capillaries** which have walls only one cell thick.

Diffusion always takes place through capillaries, as only these blood vessels are thin enough to be permeable. Dividing into tiny vessels slows the blood, due to the increased **friction** caused by blood touching the walls of the many narrow vessels. The lower pressure to the lungs means that blood is flowing slowly next to the alveoli so giving more time for the diffusion of gases in gas exchange. Also the pressure is low enough to prevent plasma being pushed through the thin capillary wall and damaging the alveoli. The oxygenated blood then slowly returns to the heart in the **pulmonary vein** to be pumped out by the left ventricle into the **aorta**.

Systemic circulation

The thicker muscle of the left ventricle is able to contract with greater force to produce a higher pressure, so blood with oxygen is efficiently carried to the rest of the body. The pressure to the body is so high that some of the liquid part of the blood, plasma, is pushed through the thin capillary wall to form **tissue fluid**, which is essential for exchange of material between the blood and the cells (see Section 10.12, page 302).

If the blood did not return to the heart after picking up oxygen in the lungs, then the blood would continue to travel very slowly and oxygen delivery to the cells would be less efficient.

Figure 10.2 Simplified diagram to show blood flow through the heart

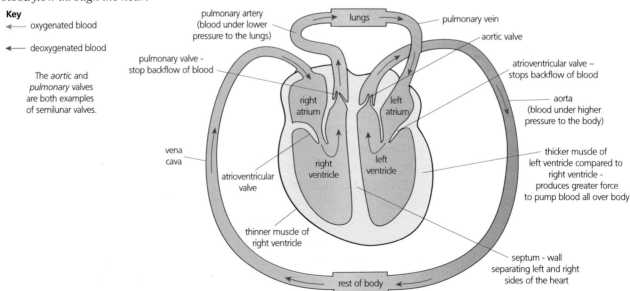

Key
← oxygenated blood
← deoxygenated blood

The *aortic* and *pulmonary* valves are both examples of semilunar valves.

pulmonary artery (blood under lower pressure to the lungs)

lungs

pulmonary vein

aortic valve

pulmonary valve - stop backflow of blood

atrioventricular valve – stops backflow of blood

right atrium

left atrium

aorta (blood under higher pressure to the body)

vena cava

right ventricle

left ventricle

thicker muscle of left ventricle compared to right ventricle - produces greater force to pump blood all over body

atrioventricular valve

thinner muscle of right ventricle

septum - wall separating left and right sides of the heart

rest of body

In the tissues the blood vessels divide into capillaries to allow diffusion and the blood is slowed once again. The blood returns to the heart in the **vena cava** and is then pumped to the lungs to be oxygenated.

Passing through **capillary beds** in the lungs or the body slows the blood, but is necessary for **diffusion**. With a double circulation, blood returns to the heart after each capillary bed so boosting the pressure. The blood is therefore kept moving both to the lungs and to the body cells, thus providing an efficient transport system.

A double circulatory system means that pressure is maintained and oxygen pick-up is maximised in the lungs.

Fish have a *single circulation*, which means that blood only travels through the heart once (Figure 10.3). Blood is pumped to the gills from the heart under pressure. The vessels divide into tiny capillaries so increasing the amount of friction and slowing the blood. The oxygenated blood is carried directly to the rest of the body from the gills. It does not return to the heart before going to the rest of the body. This slows the blood and lowers the pressure, which results in a slower delivery of oxygen to the tissues than with a double circulatory system.

However, fish do not appear to be disadvantaged by this system and actively swim through water. This system provides enough oxygen for respiration to produce energy for activity, but a different system has evolved to meet the higher metabolic needs of mammals.

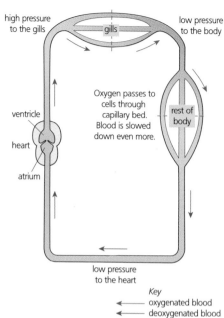

Figure 10.3 *Single circulation in fish*

Remember

A two-pressure system in mammals is caused by the *difference in thickness* of the *ventricle muscle*. The thicker left ventricle muscle creates the higher pressure to the body cells, and the thinner right ventricle muscle produces the lower pressure to the lungs

1 What are the advantages of a double circulation over a single circulation?

(2 marks)

10.2 Structure of the heart

The heart is a bag of muscle containing four chambers. The smaller upper chambers are called **atria** and the larger lower chambers are called **ventricles**. The heart is totally divided into a left and a right side, separated by a wall called a **septum**, which stops blood flow between the two sides. Therefore the right side of the heart has an atrium connected to a ventricle, and the left side has an atrium connected to a ventricle. (See Figure 10.2.)

The heart is made of a special type of muscle called **cardiac muscle**. This muscle can contract and relax rhythmically over many years without tiring. Cardiac muscle needs lots of energy which is provided by respiration of the muscle cells. The heart is well supplied with blood to provide the raw materials for respiration.

The **coronary artery**, which branches off the aorta, carries oxygen and glucose. It divides into a left and a right coronary artery. Each coronary artery branches into tiny vessels running all over the heart, so providing all the cardiac muscle cells with oxygen and glucose for respiration (Figure 10.4).

In some people, smokers in particular, a branch of the coronary artery may become narrowed and a blockage may occur. This can lead to a heart attack, if some of the muscle cells do not receive oxygen quickly. (See Box 10.5, page 289.)

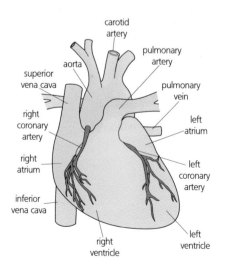

Figure 10.4 *Structure of the human heart, external features*

The atria and ventricle walls are composed of cardiac muscle which can contract and relax. The atria have thinner cardiac muscle and produce less force when they contract than the ventricles, with thicker cardiac muscle. Blood enters the atria and is then pushed into the ventricles below. This does not require much force and the thin muscle of the atria can provide the little force required.

Once in the ventricles, blood is pushed out with greater force due to the thicker muscle of the ventricle walls. A higher pressure is required as the blood needs to be pushed further. The right ventricle pumps the blood to the lungs and the left ventricle pumps blood to the rest of the body, both requiring greater force or pressure than that needed by the atria. This extra force is possible due to the thicker muscle of the ventricle walls.

Between the atria and ventricles are valves called **atrioventricular** or cuspid valves. These valves, made of tough flaps, close to prevent backflow of blood into the atria when the ventricles contract. The atrioventricular valve between the right atrium and the right ventricle is called the **tricuspid valve**, and on the left side of the heart, the **bicuspid valve** separates the left atrium and ventricle. These valves are now generally referred to as atrioventricular valves.

When the ventricles contract, the thick cardiac muscle produces a high pressure which forces blood up and out of the heart in the arteries. At the same time the atrioventricular valves are forced shut by the high pressure, which prevents the backflow of blood into the atria. There is now enormous pressure on the closed atrioventricular valves to burst open upwards.

Connected to the atrioventricular valves are strong threads called **chordae tendinae** or heart tendons (Figure 10.5). These heart tendons are attached at their lower end to **papillary muscle**. When muscles contract, they shorten and thicken. If the papillary muscles contract and shorten, the heart tendons are pulled down, which pulls the atrioventricular valves down. This prevents them bursting up and open under the pressure caused by contraction of the ventricles. Therefore the papillary muscles contract at the same time as the ventricle muscle. Papillary muscle is clearly visible as a light, shiny pink muscle in the heart.

In the arteries carrying blood out of the heart, the aorta and the pulmonary artery, small pocket valves called **semilunar** valves are found. These are also present in veins, which are returning blood to the heart. The semilunar valves, like the valves in the heart, prevent backflow and therefore keep the blood flowing in one direction. If blood is flowing in the required direction, the valves stay open, but if the blood drops back, the pockets fill with blood and the valves close. The semilunar valve in the pulmonary artery is called the **pulmonary valve**. The semilunar valve in the aorta is called the **aortic valve**.

Figure 10.5 shows open atrioventricular valves, which indicates that blood is passing from the contracted atria to the ventricles. The ventricles are relaxed and filling with blood. Blood is therefore not being pushed up into the aorta and pulmonary artery and the blood in the arteries drops back, so closing the semilunar valves. The closed semilunar valves are clearly visible in Figure 10.5.

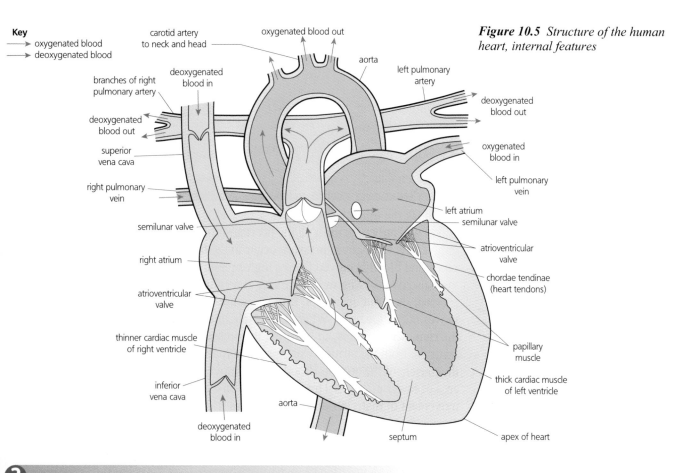

Key
→ oxygenated blood
→ deoxygenated blood

Figure 10.5 *Structure of the human heart, internal features*

carotid artery to neck and head

oxygenated blood out

aorta

left pulmonary artery

deoxygenated blood in

branches of right pulmonary artery

deoxygenated blood out

deoxygenated blood out

superior vena cava

oxygenated blood in

left pulmonary vein

right pulmonary vein

semilunar valve

left atrium
semilunar valve

atrioventricular valve

right atrium

chordae tendinae (heart tendons)

atrioventricular valve

thinner cardiac muscle of right ventricle

papillary muscle

thick cardiac muscle of left ventricle

inferior vena cava

aorta

deoxygenated blood in

septum

apex of heart

---

2 Why do you think there are two pulmonary veins entering the heart?

(1 mark)

The pathway through the heart can be summarised as follows (Figures 10.2 and 10.6). Blood enters the right atrium from the **vena cava** and is pushed through the open atrioventricular valve into the right ventricle when the atrium muscle contracts. The muscle of the right ventricle now contracts, forcing the atrioventricular valve shut and pushing blood up into the **pulmonary artery** which carries blood to the lungs to be oxygenated. The force of blood in the artery pushes open the pulmonary valve. The oxygenated blood returns to the heart in the **pulmonary vein** and enters the left atrium. The muscle of the left atrium contracts and blood is pushed through the open atrioventricular valve into the left ventricle. When the muscle of the left ventricle contracts, forcing the atrioventricular valve shut, blood is pushed out of the heart under high pressure to the rest of the body in the **aorta**. The aortic valve is pushed open. The oxygenated blood carries oxygen and nutrients to the body cells and the deoxygenated blood returns to the heart in the **vena cava**. When the ventricles are not contracting, blood is not pushed up the arteries and drops back, which closes the semilunar valves.

Remember

Arteries carry blood away from the heart and **veins** carry blood to the heart

Table 10.2 Relationship between ventricle muscle and associated structures in the heart

	Ventricle muscle	
Structure	**contracted**	**relaxed**
semilunar valve	open	shut
atrioventricular valve	shut	open
papillary muscle	contracted	relaxed
heart tendons	taut	loose

Ventricle muscle contracted
Blood is pushed out of the heart.

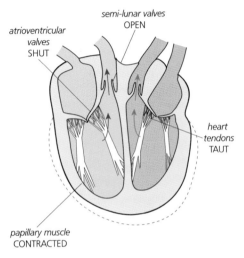

Ventricle muscle relaxed
Blood passes from atria to ventricles.

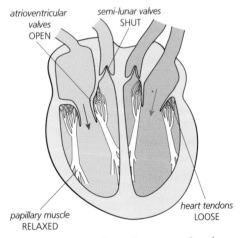

Figure 10.6 *Effect of contracted and relaxed ventricle muscle on atrioventricular and semilunar valves (aortic and pulmonary valves)*

Why does the blood move?

Blood will only pass through the heart and round the body if there are differences in pressure. Changes in pressure occur in the heart when muscles contract and relax, and blood is moved from a high-pressure to a lower-pressure region. When the muscle of the ventricle contracts, the volume of the chamber is reduced. The pressure therefore increases. If the pressure is higher than in the arteries, blood moves out of the heart. When the muscle of the ventricle relaxes, the volume of the chamber increases, so lowering the pressure. Blood will move into the ventricle from the atrium where pressure may be higher due to the contraction of the muscle of the atrium. Blood always moves from an area of high pressure to an area of lower pressure. This is therefore an example of **mass flow**, the bulk movement of materials due to differences in pressure. (See Table. 9.3, page 245.)

10.3 Cardiac cycle

This is the sequence of contraction and relaxation of the heart chambers during one heartbeat. **Systole** is the term used when the heart muscle is **contracted**. **Diastole** is the term used when the heart muscle is **relaxed**.

There are three stages in the cardiac cycle (Figure 10.7):

1 atrial and ventricular diastole

2 atrial systole

3 ventricular systole.

Atrial and ventricular diastole – *Blood flows from the veins into the atria.* Both the atria and ventricle muscles are relaxed during this stage.
Blood will only move from the veins into the atria if the pressure is higher in the veins and lower in the atria. A low pressure is achieved in the atria when the muscles there relax. This increases the volume of each atrium and lowers the pressure. Blood therefore moves from the veins which have higher pressure to the atria where the pressure is lower, on both sides of the heart.

The pressure starts to rise in the atria as blood enters from the veins and this reduces the volume. There is therefore a higher pressure in the atria and a lower pressure in the ventricles. Blood moves from the atrium where the pressure is higher to the ventricle where pressure is lower, pushing open the atrioventricular valves.

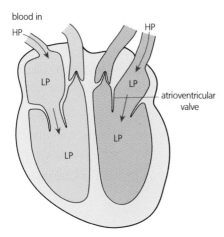

Key
HP High pressure
LP Low pressure

1 Diastole • Atrial muscles relaxed.
• Ventricle muscles relaxed.
• Volume increases so pressure decreases.
• Blood enters atria from veins with higher pressure.
• Semilunar valves shut.
• As pressure rises in atria due to entry of blood, blood starts to move into the ventricles where the pressure is lower.
• Atrioventricular valve pushed open.

blood always moves from high pressure to low pressure

2 Atrial systole • Atria muscle contracted, volume decreases so pressure rises.
• Ventricle muscle relaxed, so lower pressure.
• Blood pushed from atria to ventricle.
• Atrioventricular valve open.
• Semilunar valve shut

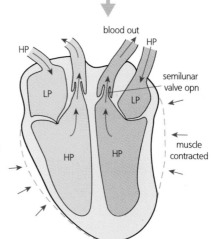

3 Ventricle systole • Ventricle muscle contracted, volume decreases, so pressure high.
• Atrial muscle relaxed, so lower pressure.
• Blood pushed out of heart to arteries.
• Semilunar valves (aortic and pulmonary) open.
• Blood enters atria from veins.
• Atrioventricular valve shut.

Figure 10.7 *The cardiac cycle*
1 Diastole
2 Atrial systole
3 Ventricular systole

In this way blood enters the heart (and some blood passes from the atria to the ventricles as the pressure rises in the atria).

Atrial systole – *Blood flows from the atria into the ventricles.* During this stage the atria muscles contract and the ventricle muscles stay relaxed. Blood will only move from the atrium to the ventricle if the pressure is higher in the atrium and lower in the ventricle.

A further increase in pressure occurs when the muscle in the wall of the atrium contracts. This causes a decrease in the volume of the chamber, so increasing the pressure and forcing any remaining blood down to the ventricles, where the pressure is lower as the muscle is relaxed. Valves prevent blood squirting back into the veins.

Thus blood is pushed from the atria to the ventricles.

Ventricular systole – *Blood flows from the ventricles to the arteries.* In this stage, the ventricle muscles are contracted and the atrial muscles are relaxed. Blood will only move out from the ventricles to the arteries if the pressure is higher in the ventricles and lower in the arteries. The pressure starts to rise in the ventricles as blood enters from the atria, and the atria muscles start to relax. A further increase in pressure occurs when the thick ventricle muscles contract. This causes a decrease in the volume of the lower heart chambers and therefore an increase in pressure, forcing the atrioventricular valves shut.

Remember

The cardiac cycle is the sequence of events during one heartbeat, made up of three stages.

1 *Diastole* – all the heart muscle is relaxed and blood enters the atria from the veins.

2 *Atrial systole* – the atria muscles contract pushing blood down to the ventricles.

3 *Ventricular systole* – the ventricle muscles contract and blood is pushed out of the heart

Remember

Blood always moves from an area of high pressure to an area of lower pressure. Changes in pressure are caused by the contraction and relaxation of the muscles around the chambers in the heart

Remember

The high pressure produced by the left ventricle effectively transports blood and therefore oxygen to the body's cells and causes the production of tissue fluid

The papillary muscles also contract to prevent the valves from bursting open under the pressure. The pressure is now higher in the ventricles and lower in the arteries, so blood moves out of the heart and into the arteries. As blood flows into the arteries, the aortic and pulmonary valves are pushed open. These are examples of semilunar valves which ensure that blood flows in only one direction.

In this way blood is pushed out of the heart.

The next stage is the relaxation of both atria and ventricles, in other words a return to atrial and ventricular diastole, and the cycle starts again.

The changes in volume of the heart chambers and corresponding changes in pressure are due to liquids being incompressible.

3 During which stage(s) in the cardiac cycle are the semilunar valves shut? Explain your answer. *(2 marks)*

Extension

Box 10.1 Measuring blood pressure

The force of blood pushing against the wall of a blood vessel is called **blood pressure**. It is measured using a **sphygmomanometer**. A cuff or strap is placed around the arm above the elbow. A rubber bag inside the cuff is expanded with air until the blood supply along the artery is stopped. Then enough air is released from the cuff to allow some blood to squeeze through the artery, but only when the ventricle contracts. A **stethoscope** placed over the artery in the arm will now detect some tapping sounds. This is the highest blood pressure, or **systolic blood pressure**, produced during ventricular systole, and is measured at about 120 mm of mercury, or 16 kPa. This is the average systolic blood pressure for a young, fit individual.

Air is slowly released from the cuff allowing blood through more freely, even blood at low pressure. There are no blood sounds now and this is the lower blood pressure, or **diastolic blood pressure**, produced by elastic recoil of arteries when the ventricles are relaxed. This is measured at about 80 mm Hg or 10 kPa.

Therefore a blood pressure reading of 120 over 80 is expected in a healthy person at rest. If the reading is much higher, this is called **high blood pressure**.

10.4 Pressure changes through the heart during the cardiac cycle

Length of heart beat

The pressure changes in the heart during a cardiac cycle are shown in Figure 10.9. Where the pattern starts to repeat, is the start of a new heartbeat.

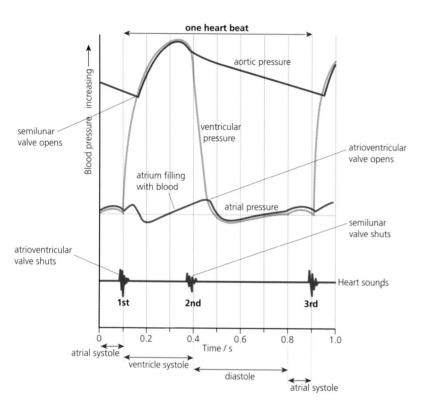

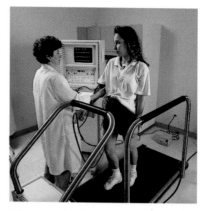

Figure 10.8 *Blood pressure being measured using a sphygmomanometer*

Figure 10.9 *Graph to show changes in pressure in the left side of the heart during a cardiac cycle*

The ventricle pressure line rises steeply at 0.1 s and this is repeated at 0.9 s, showing that the length of a heartbeat here is 0.8 s. As there are 60 s in one minute, it follows that there are:

$$\frac{60}{0.8} = 75 \text{ beats in one minute, in this example.}$$

Looking at the differences in pressure between the atrium and the ventricle, it can be seen that from 0 s to 0.1 s, the pressure is higher in the atrium, so blood is pushed into the ventricle where the pressure is lower. The high pressure in the atrium is due to contraction of the atrium, at atrial systole, but notice how low the pressure is compared to levels reached during ventricular systole.

Did You Know

The human systolic blood pressure of 120 mm Hg creeps up to about 140 mm Hg by the age of 60 and to 160 mm Hg by the age of 80. Life insurance companies are interested to know people's blood pressure as generally the higher the blood pressure, the greater the risk of death from heart disease.

4 Why is the highest pressure reached in the atrium much lower than the pressure reached in the ventricle? *(1 mark)*

At 0.1 s, the pressure suddenly rises in the ventricle due to contraction of the muscle during ventricular systole. This forces the atrioventricular valve shut which produces the **first heart sound**. At 0.17 s, the pressure in the ventricle has risen higher than that in the aorta and blood is therefore pushed out of the heart and into the aorta, pushing open the aortic valve. This continues until the pressure in the ventricle falls below that in the aorta at 0.4 s. Blood then drops back from the aorta forcing the valve shut, which produces the **second heart sound** at 0.4 s. When a stethoscope is used to listen to the heart, it is these heart sounds that can be heard, first the atrioventricular valve shutting and then the semilunar valve.

The pressure remains lower in the atrium than the ventricle from 0.1 s until 0.47 s due to atrial diastole, when the muscle relaxes. The reason the pressure rises from 0.2 s until 0.47 s is due to blood entering the atrium from the veins. At 0.47 s, the pressure is higher in the atrium than in the ventricle and blood moves down to the ventricle, forcing the atrioventricular valve open.

No sound is made when the valves open, only when they close. As blood passes down into the ventricle the pressure falls slightly in the atrium and rises in the ventricle so the pressure lines get closer. This takes place during atrial and ventricular diastole.

At 0.8 s, the atrium muscle contracts at atrial systole and forces any remaining blood into the ventricles. This is followed by ventricular systole and the cycle starts again.

Figure 10.10 shows the pressure and volume changes of the cardiac cycle in more detail. It can be seen that when the ventricle contracts, its volume decreases and pressure increases. The blood is incompressible and unable to escape until the pressure rises higher in the ventricle than in the arteries.

The events shown in Figure 10.10 can be summarised as follows:

- Up to B, with atrial systole, blood is pushed down into the ventricle where the pressure is lower.

- At B, pressure rises due to ventricular systole and the atrioventricular valve shuts.

- From C, with pressure higher in the ventricle than the aorta, blood is pushed out to the aorta.

- At D, pressure in the ventricle falls below that in the aorta and the semilunar valve shuts as blood falls back.

- Meanwhile, from C to D, with atrial diastole, the pressure in the heart is low and blood enters from the veins.

- From E, the pressure is higher in the atrium than in the ventricle, although both are in diastole, and therefore blood passes to the ventricle. This continues through atrial systole until B, when ventricular systole resumes.

The heart sounds are shown by the phonocardiogram.

Did You Know

Generally, the bigger the animal, the slower the heart rate. An elephant's heart beats only 25 times per minute compared to between 600 and 700 times per minute in a mouse

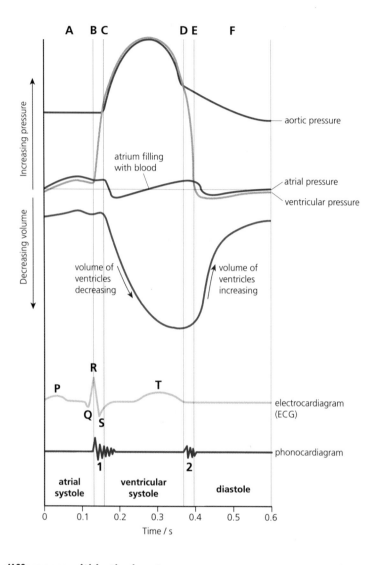

A B C   D E   F

Increasing pressure

Decreasing volume

— aortic pressure

atrium filling
with blood

— atrial pressure

ventricular pressure

volume of
ventricles
decreasing

volume of
ventricles
increasing

R

P   T

Q S

— electrocardiagram
(ECG)

— phonocardiagram

1   2

atrial
systole

ventricular
systole

diastole

0   0.1   0.2   0.3   0.4   0.5   0.6
Time / s

Figure 10.10 *Graph to show the pressure and volume changes in the left side of the heart in the cardiac cycle of a human*

Pressure differences within the heart

Different pressures are found in the different parts of the heart. The atria, which have the thinnest muscle in the heart, can only achieve a low pressure compared to other parts. Both the left and right atria produce a similar pressure due to a similarity in their muscle thickness. Ventricles, with much thicker muscle, are able to produce much higher pressures when they contract.

The left ventricle, with the thicker muscle, will on contraction generate a higher pressure than the thinner muscle of the right ventricle. As a consequence of the differing pressures produced in the ventricles, the pressure in the pulmonary artery will be lower than the pressure in the aorta. Figure 10.11 shows the maximum pressures reached in the heart chambers and arteries coming out of the heart.

5 Why is the maximum pressure similar in both atria? *(1 mark)*

6 Explain why higher blood pressure is produced in the aorta than in the pulmonary artery. *(1 mark)*

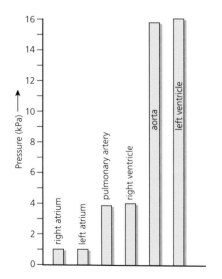

Figure 10.11 *Graph to show the maximum pressure reached in the heart chambers, and arteries coming out of the heart*

Pressure is always higher in arteries than in veins, as arteries carry blood away from the heart under pressure when the ventricles contract. Veins carry blood from capillary beds in the tissues back to the heart slowly, with no push from the heart, while increased friction further reduces the pressure. Therefore, the blood in veins is carried back to the heart at very low pressure.

10.5 Coordination of the cardiac cycle

Cardiac muscle is unique in that the heartbeat is initiated at regular intervals without nervous or hormonal stimulation. It is therefore called **myogenic muscle**, as it can generate its own beat without outside stimulation. All other muscles are **neurogenic** as they require nervous stimulation before they will contract.

The human heart beats about 70 times per minute in adults; the rate is much higher in young children. This rate varies depending on the requirements of the body. For example, during exercise, when our body cells need more energy, oxygen and glucose are carried more quickly due to a faster heart rate speeding up the blood flow and waste is quickly removed. Therefore the heart rate needs to be controlled, so in addition to being myogenic or self-generating, the heart rate can be altered by nerves or hormones in response to changing needs.

 Did You Know

It is possible to remove a heart from a mammal and disconnect it from all nerves and blood vessels and it will continue to beat, provided it is in an oxygenated salt solution at 37°C

Did You Know

A human's heart, beating 70 times a minute, will beat 2 500 000 000 times in an average life

Figure 10.12 Myogenic control of the heart

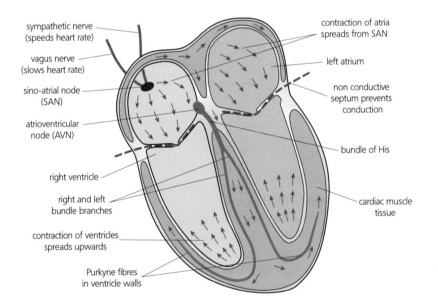

Myogenic control of the heart
The sequence in which the heart chambers contract is critical to the efficient functioning of the heart. Clearly blood cannot be pushed out of the ventricles until they contain blood to push, so atrial systole must take place before ventricular systole.

This coordination is achieved by the activity of the **sino-atrial node** or **SAN**, better known as the **pacemaker** which is found in the wall of the right atrium (Figure 10.12). The heart muscle contracts when it receives a signal from this patch of specialised tissue. The SAN is a patch of cardiac muscle connected to nerve endings which form part of the autonomic or involuntary nervous system. It is these nerves that are able to alter the basic rhythm of the heart in line with the requirements of the body.

An action potential or electrical signal originates in the SAN, and spreads over the heart to coordinate the sequence known as the cardiac cycle. The SAN produces a wave of electrical activity which spreads across the heart muscle at about 1 metre per second. These waves of excitation are sent spontaneously at regular intervals and initiate the events of the cardiac cycle or heartbeat.

Once generated, the wave of excitation spreads across both atria causing muscle fibres there to contract, in other words causing atrial systole. The atria contract at more or less the same time. Between the atria and the ventricles is a layer of **non-conductive tissue**, which prevents the spread of the wave of excitation passing directly from the atria to the ventricles (Figure 10.12). The only conducting route for the wave of excitation to the ventricles is via the **atrio-ventricular node** or **AVN**. Waves of excitation from the SAN reach the AVN and then there is a short time delay before the waves of excitation pass down to the base of the ventricles.

The AVN is connected to specialised muscle fibres called the **bundle of His**, which transmits a wave of excitation down both sides of the septum to the base of the ventricles. Special fibres called **Purkyne fibres**, which branch upwards, conduct the waves of excitation to all parts of the ventricles, causing them to contract from the bottom up. This ensures that blood is pushed up from the ventricles into the arteries. The time delay in the AVN gives time for blood to fill the ventricles from the atria before being pushed up and out of the heart.

The two ventricles contract at exactly the same time during ventricular systole. The times at which excitation reaches the various parts of the heart can be seen in Figure 10.13.

It is interesting that ventricles contract about 0.16–0.20s after the atria contract, so giving sufficient time for blood to be fully squeezed into the ventricles from the atria, before they start to contract.

Cardiac muscle is myogenic or self-generating and therefore does not require external stimulation. It is composed of branching fibres, so allowing the rapid spread of impulses across the muscle. This ensures that all parts of an atrium or ventricle contract at the same time. The cross connections give strength and help to resist tearing when the muscle contracts. Cardiac muscle has a rich blood supply to provide the raw materials for respiration and to remove the waste. It can continue to contract without fatigue, as it has a long **refractory period**, which is the time for recovery between contractions.

Terms connected with coordination of the heartbeat include the following:

- myogenic – able to initiate its own contraction
- sino-atrial node – the pacemaker, sends out waves of electrical activity at regular intervals
- atrioventricular node – the only route through the non-conductive septum to the ventricles. (It causes a time delay in the excitation reaching the ventricles.)
- bundle of His – conducts the wave of excitation from the AVN down to the base of the ventricles so that they contract from the bottom up

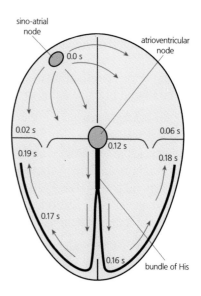

Figure 10.13 *Diagram to show the spread of impulses through the heart and the time taken (in seconds) to reach the various parts*

Box 10.2 Artificial pacemakers

The natural conducting systems of the heart (the SAN, AVN and bundle of His) can become damaged by disease or ageing. As a result the coordination of the heartbeat can be disrupted – a condition often called *heart block*.

An *artificial pacemaker* can overcome heart block by generating electrical impulses artificially and conducting them to the muscles of the heart. This stimulates contraction of the heart chambers. In Britain about 10 000 people a year receive an artificial pacemaker. Pacemakers consist of a pulse generator and one or two electrodes. The generator is small – about the size of a thin matchbox – and it is powered by a lithium battery.

It is implanted under the skin, usually in the upper chest. Two wires lead down veins to the heart ending in electrodes which touch the muscle of the right atrium and right ventricle. Newer pacemakers can sense changes in the body, e.g. exercise, and adjust the heart rate accordingly.

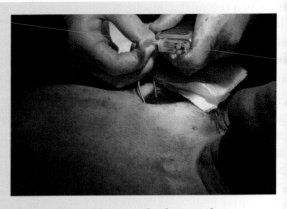

Figure 10.14 Photograph of pacemaker

Did You Know

The human infant has a heart rate of 130 beats per minute and this slows to 70 in the adult.

- non-conductive septum – prevents the wave of excitation passing directly from the atria to the ventricles, so preventing the two chambers contracting at almost the same time. (The delay caused gives time for the ventricles to fill with blood.)

- cardiac cycle – the regular sequence of contraction and relaxation of the four heart chambers. (One complete cycle (one heartbeat) involves diastole, atrial systole and ventricular systole.)

- diastole – relaxation of the heart muscle

- atrial systole – contraction of the two atria

- ventricular systole – contraction of the two ventricles.

10.6 Control of the heart rate

Both **adrenaline** and nerves can increase heart rate. Nerves can also slow heart rate.

Nervous control

The cardiac control centre is located in the **cardiovascular centre** in the **medulla** of the brain. There are two types of nerves connecting the cardiac centre in the brain to the heart, the sympathetic nerves which speed up heart rate and the parasympathetic nerves which slow down heart rate.

If impulses are carried down the **sympathetic** nerves to the heart, they increase the heart rate. Sympathetic nerves stimulate the SAN to increase the frequency of the waves of excitation over the heart. This speeds up the cardiac cycle and blood is pumped more quickly round the body.

If impulses are carried down the **parasympathetic** nervous system to the heart, they slow the heart rate. Parasympathetic nerves decrease the frequency of waves of excitation from the SAN, which slows the cardiac cycle and the rate of blood flow.

Hormonal control

The hormone adrenaline is secreted by the adrenal medulla glands during times of stress. Like all hormones, it diffuses into the blood and is carried in the blood to its target organs, which include the heart.

When we are excited, nervous or scared, we need more energy to either fight or run, to escape danger. Adrenaline achieves this by increasing the supply of glucose and oxygen reaching the cells for respiration and thereby increasing the production of energy. The effect of adrenaline on the heart is to speed up the heart rate, by stimulating the SAN to increase the frequency of waves of excitation. In effect, it produces the same response as stimulation by the sympathetic nervous system.

Role of chemoreceptors

There are receptors sensitive to chemicals in the blood. They are called **chemoreceptors** and are found in the walls of the aorta and in the carotid arteries. These include receptors sensitive to the levels of carbon dioxide and oxygen in the blood. (Figure 10.15)

During exercise, the rate of respiration increases and so does the production of carbon dioxide. Carbon dioxide dissolves in plasma to form carbonic acid which leads to an increase in hydrogen ions and acidity. This increase in hydrogen ions is detected by the chemoreceptors in the carotid arteries and the aorta. Once stimulated, these chemoreceptors cause impulses to be sent to the cardiovascular centre in the medulla. This triggers impulse along the sympathetic nervous system to the heart, so increasing the heart rate. An increase in the heart rate speeds up the transport of blood to the lungs, where carbon dioxide is removed and oxygen taken in. Thus the level of carbon dioxide is lowered back to a normal level.

This is an example of a negative feedback mechanism, where any increase in the level of carbon dioxide is detected and changes are brought about to lower the level of carbon dioxide back to its normal level.

Role of pressure receptors (baroreceptors)

These are receptors sensitive to changes in pressure. The **baroreceptors** in the carotid arteries and the aorta respond to changes in blood pressure. (Figure 10.15)

High blood pressure stretches and stimulates the baroreceptors and impulses are sent to the medulla. The medulla responds by firing off impulses along the vagus nerve, which is part of the parasympathetic nervous system, to the heart.

This causes a decrease in heart rate, by slowing down the frequency of impulses from the SAN, so reducing the blood pressure. Once again, this is an example of a negative feedback mechanism, as an increase in blood pressure brings about changes that reduce it.

Low blood pressure means that the baroreceptors are not stretched and stimulated and fewer impulses are sent to the brain. As a result, the medulla sends impulses along sympathetic nerves to the heart leading to an increase in the heart rate. Impulses from the medulla also cause vasoconstriction of arterioles. This narrowing of the blood vessels also increases the blood pressure, so bringing it back to normal.

Extension

Box 10.3 Baroreceptors and blood pressure

There are three specific mechanisms concerned with baroreceptors and blood pressure. These mechanisms are all nervous reflexes – automatic responses to a stimulus (Figure 10.15).

(1) The carotid sinus reflex helps to maintain the correct blood supply to the brain. The baroreceptors for this reflex are located in the carotid sinus – swellings at the base of the carotid arteries.

(2) The aortic reflex helps to maintain the general body (systemic) blood pressure. This reflex is initiated by baroreceptors in the aortic arch.

(3) The Bainbridge reflex regulates pressure in the veins, and is initiated by baroreceptors in the vena cava, and right atrium.

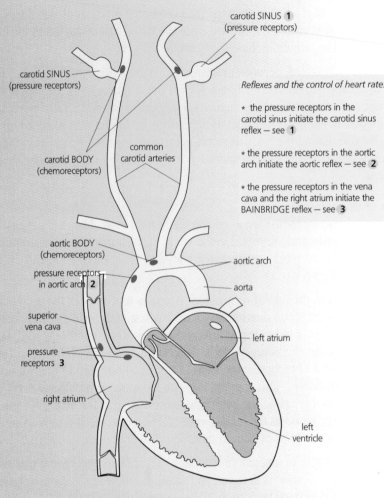

Reflexes and the control of heart rate:

* the pressure receptors in the carotid sinus initiate the carotid sinus reflex — see **1**

* the pressure receptors in the aortic arch initiate the aortic reflex — see **2**

* the pressure receptors in the vena cava and the right atrium initiate the BAINBRIDGE reflex — see **3**

Figure 10.15 Diagram to show the position of the chemoreceptors and baroreceptors

10.7 Exercise and the heart

When exercising, more energy is needed for active muscles. An increased rate of cellular respiration in the muscles provides this energy. The greater demand for oxygen and glucose can be met by increasing the blood supply to the muscles. This is only possible if blood flow to other areas is decreased as the total blood volume is the same.

Consequently during vigorous exercise, the blood flow to unnecessary organs is reduced and the blood flow to essential structures is increased. Dilation or widening of the veins leading from the muscles to the heart, will increase the blood entering the heart and cause the ventricle muscles to contract more, so increasing the volume of blood pumped at each beat. The volume of blood pumped at each heartbeat is called the **stroke volume**.

Remember

Increased contraction of the ventricles follows an increase in the blood entering

To provide more blood to the ventricles it is necessary to reduce the blood flow elsewhere. Narrowing of the blood vessels (vasoconstriction), leading to the gut, kidneys and liver reduces the blood flow there. It means that more blood is available elsewhere, for example in the skeletal muscles and in the ventricles. Vasoconstriction occurs when the circular smooth muscles in the arterioles contract and narrow the vessel. The percentage of blood passing to particular organs and tissues can be altered during exercise to meet body requirements.

Table 10.3 *Redistribution of blood flow in response to exercise*

Structure	At rest		Vigorous exercise	
	cm³ min⁻¹	% of total	cm³ min⁻¹	% of total
heart	190	3.3	740	3.9
liver	1340	23.5	590	3.1
adrenal glands	24	0.4	24	0.1
brain	690	12.1	740	3.9
lung tissue	100	1.8	200	1.0
kidneys	1050	18.4	590	3.1
skeletal muscles	740	13.0	12450	65.9
skin	310	5.4	1850	9.8
other parts	1256	22.0	1716	9.1
total blood flow	5700		18900	

7 How is the percentage of blood calculated in this table?　　　*(1 mark)*

The table shows a large reduction in both the actual volume and percentage of blood flowing through the liver and kidneys during exercise despite an enormous rise in the total blood flow. The actual volume and percentage to the skeletal muscles rise considerably.

8 Can you explain the figures for skeletal muscle at rest and during exercise?　　　*(1 mark)*

The blood supply to the brain is relatively stable, the volume showing little change at rest and during exercise.

Finally, vigorous exercise raises body temperature, and vasodilation of the arterioles in the skin occurs, leading to increased heat loss by radiation. This is clearly seen by the data showing a huge increase in the volume of blood flowing to the skin during exercise, as well as as an increase in the percentage flow.

Extension

Box 10.4 Changes in cardiac output with exercise

The volume of blood pumped at each heartbeat is called the **stroke volume**. This can be *increased* by the ventricles contracting more vigorously.

If, as a result of vasoconstriction to the liver and gut, a greater volume of blood returns to the heart, the cardiac muscle is stretched more and this results in a greater contraction of the muscles during systole. This will increase the volume of blood expelled by the ventricles, in other words the stroke volume will increase.

The amount of blood expelled from the left ventricle into the aorta each minute depends on (a) the **stroke volume** (volume of blood expelled from a ventricle each heartbeat) and (b) the **heart rate** (the number of heartbeats in one minute). The *cardiac output* is the total amount of blood expelled from the heart in one minute, measured in dm^3 min^{-1}. (1 dm^3 equals 1000 cm^3.)

cardiac output = stroke volume $\times$ heart rate

At rest

If the heart pumps out 76 cm^3 of blood at each beat, this is the *stroke volume*.

If the heart beats 75 times in one minute, then this is the *heart rate*.

The cardiac output = $76 \times 75 = 5700$ cm^3 min^{-1} (or 5.7 dm^3 min^{-1}) at rest.

Thus the amount of blood passing through the heart in one minute at rest is 5.7 dm^3.

During exercise

There is a need to increase the cardiac output in order to provide the cells with enough oxygen and glucose for respiration. Similarly, the increased waste produced can be removed efficiently by the increased blood flow. During vigorous exercise, the cardiac output can increase significantly.

If the heart now pumps out 105 cm^3 of blood at each beat (stroke volume) and beats 180 times in one minute (heart rate):

cardiac output = $105 \times 180 = 18\,900$ cm^3 (or 18.9 $dm^3 min^{-1}$, during exercise.

This increases the cardiac output from about 5.7 dm^3 of blood in a minute when resting to 18.9 dm^3 of blood per minute when exercising, a rise of over 300%.

Fit athletes can increase their cardiac output as their heart muscle is stronger and the volume of each chamber can be increased. This enables them to increase their stroke volume, as thicker muscle can contract with greater force to expel more blood. As they can pump more blood out in each heartbeat, they can expel the same volume of blood in fewer beats than an unfit person with a smaller cardiac output.

Therefore a fit athlete may have a lower heart rate of 55 beats per minute compared to the usual 70 and still have the same cardiac output as a less fit individual.

Increased exercise makes the **heart** muscle stronger and more efficient as well as widening the **coronary arteries** as a result of the increased blood flow to the heart. Wider coronary arteries are less likely to be blocked, so reducing the chances of a **coronary thrombosis** (see Box 10.5, below). A stronger heart can pump blood with oxygen more efficiently to respiring cells, so maintaining aerobic respiration.

Remember

Summary of changes in the heart during exercise:
- the heart rate increases
- the size of the heart muscle increases over time
- the stroke volume (the volume of blood pumped at each heart-beat) increases
- therefore the cardiac output (the volume of blood pumped in one minute) increases.

Box 10.5 Coronary heart disease and strokes

Coronary heart disease (CHD) is a disease of the arteries supplying blood to the muscle forming the walls of the heart. The blockage of a coronary artery is called a *coronary thrombosis* or heart attack, causing extreme gripping chest pains. If a coronary artery is blocked, part of the heart muscle does not receive any blood. The muscle cells receive no oxygen, they cannot respire and therefore they die. The size of the heart attack depends upon the size and position of the coronary artery blocked. If a small branch of an artery is blocked, only a small amount of muscle dies causing a small heart attack. If a large artery is blocked, the whole heart may stop beating – a **cardiac arrest**.

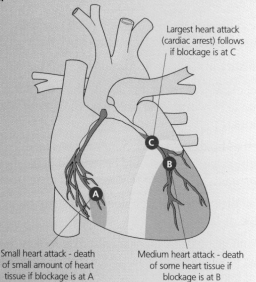

Largest heart attack (cardiac arrest) follows if blockage is at C

Small heart attack - death of small amount of heart tissue if blockage is at A

Medium heart attack - death of some heart tissue if blockage is at B

Figure 10.16 Different-sized heart attacks

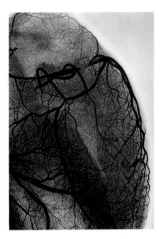

Figure 10.17 The human heart showing a blockage of a coronary artery

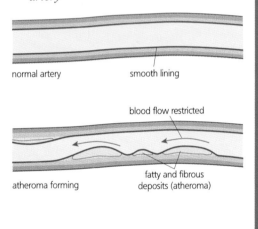

normal artery   smooth lining

blood flow restricted

atheroma forming   fatty and fibrous deposits (atheroma)

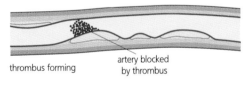

thrombus forming   artery blocked by thrombus

if clot breaks free it may cause a blockage (embolism) elsewhere in the circulation – for example a blockage in a blood vessel in the brain causes a stroke

Figure 10.18 The development of atherosclerosis

 Did You Know

Inhaling other people's cigarette smoke can increase your chances of a stroke by up to 82% in non-smoking men and 66% in women (*Guardian* 17.8.99)

Extension

Box 10.5 Coronary heart disease and strokes cont'd

Atherosclerosis is the main cause of CHD. It is commonly known as *hardening of the arteries*. This is the progressive blockage or 'furring up' of arteries with atheroma (Figure 10.17). *Atheromas* are deposits (*plaques*) of cholesterol and fibrous tissue which narrow the arteries, reducing blood flow, making the artery walls less elastic and roughening their inner surface. See Figure 10.18

The reduction of blood flow to the heart muscle can cause *angina* whose symptoms include: gripping pains in the chest, pains in the left arm and breathlessness. Angina is an 'early warning' that a complete blockage of a coronary artery, a thrombosis, is becoming more likely.

The final blockage of the artery is usually caused by a blood clot or *thrombus*.

The atheroma deposits make the lining of the artery rougher and this roughness triggers the formation of blood clots. These clots are often formed in arteries elsewhere in the body from where they can travel in the blood to the heart. If the coronary arteries have been narrowed by atheroma then these clots are likely to get 'stuck' at these points, completely blocking the artery (Figure 10.18). A blockage in a blood vessel in the brain causes a *stroke*.

Strokes

If a blood clot forms a blockage in an artery, it can weaken part of the artery wall and cause it to swell up to form an **aneurysm**. These swellings can burst and if this bursting takes place in the brain it leads to a **stroke**. This may cause some brain damage depending on the degree of tissue affected. Strokes vary in their effects but commonly the middle cerebral artery is affected causing some **paralysis** down one side of the body, which may disappear or be permanent to some extent. If speech is affected, then the stroke occurred on the right side of the brain. Strokes can kill and are the single main cause of serious disability in the UK.

The influence of diet

Many factors influence the risk of getting CHD and these can be hard to separate. They include genetic factors, smoking, the level of exercise and diet.

The main dietary influences are as follows:

● The level of *cholesterol* in the diet, as cholesterol is a main component of atheroma. However, note that some cholesterol is essential e.g. for membranes.

● The types of lipids in the diet. *Saturated* fats tend to increase blood cholesterol levels. These should be reduced in the diet and replaced by *unsaturated* fats which help to lower blood cholesterol.

● High *fibre* diets tend to lower blood cholesterol by influencing the absorption of fat.

● *Obesity* and being overweight are also risk factors for CHD, probably by raising blood pressure. Clearly the overall energy intake of the diet is important here.

● There is some evidence that a high salt intake is linked with raised blood pressure.

High blood pressure and CHD

High blood pressure or *hypertension* is also a major risk factor for CHD because the heart has to work harder and because atheroma and clots are more likely. Hypertension also has many causes including a high *salt* intake and obesity which are related to diet. Hypertension and CHD are interrelated. For example, the narrowing of arteries caused by CHD tends to raise blood pressure.

The influence of smoking

Coronary heart disease and **strokes** are far more common in smokers than in non-smokers.

Nicotine diffuses into the blood and quickly increases blood pressure, heart rate and narrows blood vessels. It also raises the level of fat in the blood. These effects combine to increase the likelihood of narrowing the arteries and forming a blockage. Both nicotine and **carbon monoxide** damage the endothelium lining the blood vessels. This makes it easier for fats and cholesterol to enter the blood vessel, so increasing their deposition inside the arteries.

Thus smokers have narrow arteries due to the increased cholesterol and fatty deposits on the inner surface of the artery wall causing *atherosclerosis*.

Tobacco smoke induces platelets to stick to the wall of the endothelium, so speeding up the formation of a blood clot.

Treatment of coronary heart disease

Coronary by-pass surgery: coronary arteries damaged by atherosclerosis can be successfully by-passed using parts of a vein or artery taken from elsewhere in the body. See Figure 10.19.

> **Remember**
>
> Nicotine and carbon monoxide in tobacco smoke increase the tendency for a blood clot to form and block the arteries. Smokers are therefore more likely to suffer from coronary heart disease and strokes

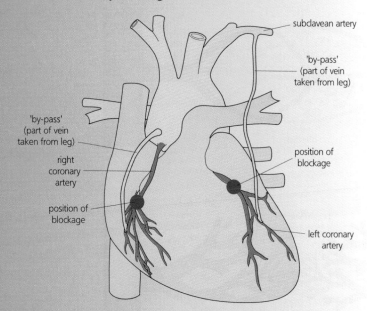

Figure 10.19 A coronary by-pass

Extension

Box 10.5 Coronary heart disease and strokes cont'd

Heart transplant surgery: with severe heart damage or complete heart failure a heart transplant may be possible using a heart from somebody who has died. Heart transplants are not very common for a variety of reasons including the shortage of donors, the risk of the heart being rejected by the patient's immune system (see Section 11.9, page 324) and the high cost. Scientists are investigating the possibility of using animal hearts for human transplant to overcome the shortage of donated human hearts. Also it may be possible using gene technology to develop animal organs which are less likely to be rejected by the human patient (see Section 16.9, page 492).

CHD is a major killer in *developed* countries and illustrates the issue of prevention or cure. There are genetic factors which means that not all CHD can be prevented in every individual. Curative treatments will still be required. However, the evidence is now very clear that many of the factors likely to cause CHD are *preventable* including unhealthy diets, lack of exercise and smoking. So a healthy lifestyle could prevent a lot of ill health and early death from CHD.

Blood vessels

These are hollow tubes that carry blood around the body. There are three main types of blood vessel:

● arteries – these carry blood away from the heart

● capillaries – these tiny vessels link arteries to veins

● veins – these carry blood to the heart.

heart ⟶ **artery** ⟶ arteriole ⟶ **capillaries** ⟶ venule ⟶ **veins** ⟶ heart

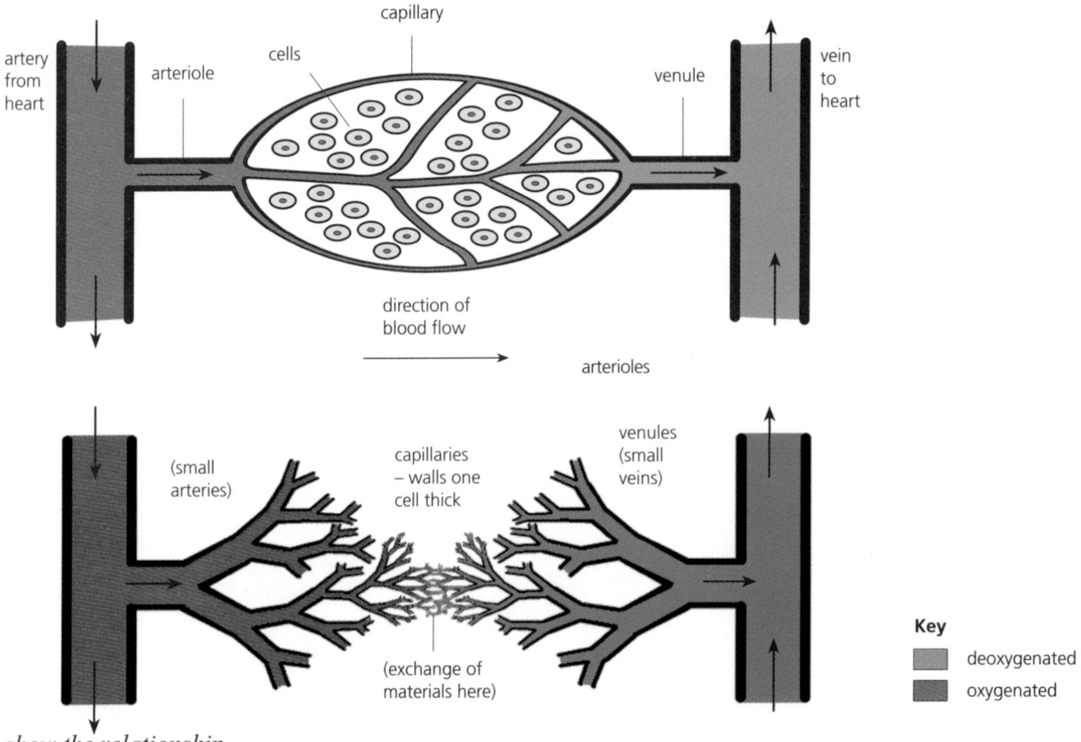

Figure 10.20 Diagram to show the relationship between the three types of blood vessels

10.8   Arteries

Arteries carry blood away from the heart under pressure, due to the pumping action of the heart. Blood moves in pulses, i.e. in a regular rhythm in time with the contraction of the ventricles. The pulse is a pressure wave passing through the liquid blood. The pulse is easily felt in the neck. As the blood surges into the artery there, it expands the vessel and this is the pulse or swelling we can feel. Each time the ventricle contracts, blood is pushed along and a pulse is felt. Counting the number of pulses enables us to count the number of heartbeats in a minute.

The pressure is higher in spurts, requiring a strong wall to withstand the high pressure without bursting and **elastic tissue** to allow stretching when blood surges in. Arteries have a small **lumen**, or space for blood, and a thick wall made of elastic tissue, collagen and smooth muscle which provide strength (Figure 10.21).

The closer arteries are to the heart, the higher the pressure, so arteries here have more elastic tissue to allow expansion without causing damage, and more **collagen** to prevent bursting (see Section 3.19, page 90).

When the ventricle contracts during systole, blood is pushed into the aorta, the lumen enlarges and the elastic tissue is stretched back. When the ventricle relaxes, blood is not pushed into the aorta and the stretched elastic wall now springs back and squeezes the blood forwards. Therefore the high pressure is maintained in the aorta, even at diastole, due to the **elastic recoil mechanism**. The blood is not able to drop back into the heart due to the presence of the semilunar valves which prevent backflow.

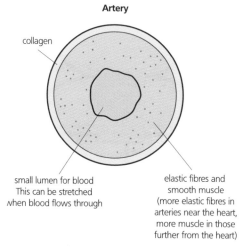

Figure 10.21 *Transverse sections of blood vessels*

Artery

collagen

small lumen for blood
This can be stretched
when blood flows through

elastic fibres and
smooth muscle
(more elastic fibres in
arteries near the heart,
more muscle in those
further from the heart)

High pressure

Capillary

waste material
e.g. carbon dioxide

oxygen and
food molecules

squamous epithelium
This thin wall is adapted
for diffusion. It is
permeable, moist and
provides a short distance for
exchange of material.

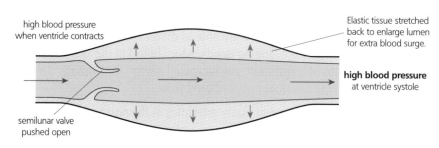

(a) Ventricle systole – blood enters artery

high blood pressure
when ventricle contracts

Elastic tissue stretched
back to enlarge lumen
for extra blood surge.

high blood pressure
at ventricle systole

semilunar valve
pushed open

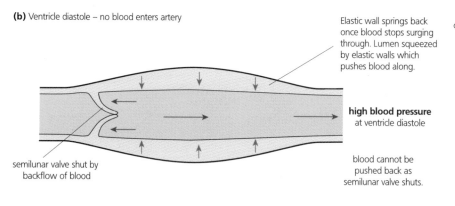

(b) Ventricle diastole – no blood enters artery

Elastic wall springs back
once blood stops surging
through. Lumen squeezed
by elastic walls which
pushes blood along.

high blood pressure
at ventricle diastole

semilunar valve shut by
backflow of blood

blood cannot be
pushed back as
semilunar valve shuts.

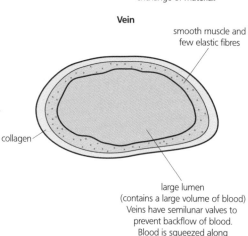

Vein

smooth muscle and
few elastic fibres

collagen

large lumen
(contains a large volume of blood)
Veins have semilunar valves to
prevent backflow of blood.
Blood is squeezed along
when skeletal muscles contract

Low pressure

Figure 10.22 *The elastic recoil mechanism (in the aorta)*

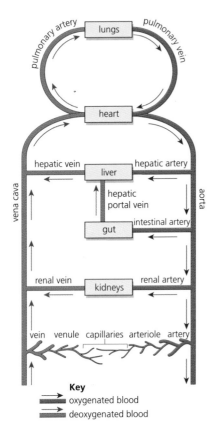

Figure 10.23 *Major blood vessels in the mammalian body*

The effect of this elastic tissue is to smooth out the blood flow and maintain the pressure.

The **aorta**, which carries oxygenated blood away from the heart to the body, is a large artery with a very thick wall. Branches lead off this vessel to enter the different body organs. Figure 10.23 shows the major blood vessels in the mammalian body.

The hepatic artery enters the liver from the aorta and the renal artery enters the kidneys. The pressure drops throughout the system due to increased distance from the pumping action of the heart, and increased friction. In small arteries, a larger proportion of the blood is in contact with the wall, as the tubes are much narrower, so increasing friction and slowing blood flow.

The arteries continue to branch into smaller arteries called **arterioles** (Figure 10.20). Increasing distance from the heart, and greater friction, lower the pressure even more and there may be no indication of the heart contracting and relaxing, i.e. no pulse. With pressure low there is less need for elastic tissue, and arterioles, with a very small lumen, have a greater proportion of smooth muscle in their comparatively thick wall.

If this circular muscle contracts and narrows the lumen, less blood can flow through. This narrowing is called **vasoconstriction**. When the circular muscle in the arterioles relaxes, the lumen widens or dilates, allowing more blood to flow through. This is **vasodilation**. By altering the size of the lumen, blood flow can be controlled and redistributed. (See Section 10.7, page 287.)

When we are too hot, the circular smooth muscle in the arterioles in our skin relaxes, widening the lumen and therefore increasing blood flow to the skin surface. This allows more heat loss by radiation and enables us to cool down.

During vigorous exercise, blood flow can be reduced in some areas, for example the gut, by vasoconstriction of the arterioles, and increased to the skeletal muscles by vasodilation. By this means we are able to divert resources and maximise performance to cope with changing needs. More blood to the skeletal muscles allows a higher rate of respiration and increased energy for running. Thus, the smooth muscle in the arteries controls blood flow.

Sphincter muscles are found in many arterioles at the point where they divide into capillaries. These circular muscles are able to contract and prevent blood entering the capillaries from the arterioles. This enables blood to pass directly from the arterioles to the small veins in 'shunt' vessels. Thus muscles are able to control the amount of blood flowing through the capillaries.

Components of artery wall	Function	Largest arteries e.g. aorta	Small arterioles
elastic tissue	allows expansion of the lumen without causing damage. It keeps the pressure high by the elastic recoil mechanism and smooths out the flow of blood	lots of elastic tissue to cope with erratic, high pressure	little elastic tissue as pressure lower
smooth muscle	this muscle can contract and narrow arterioles by vasoconstriction, so reducing blood flow. This muscle can relax and widen arterioles by vasodilation, so increasing blood flow and controlling the distribution of blood	little smooth muscle as lumen too large to close	lots of smooth muscle to control blood flow by vasoconstriction
collagen	this fibrous protein provides strength to stop arteries bursting when the pressure is high	lots of collagen to give strength to prevent bursting	little collagen as pressure is low and so less strength needed

Table 10.4 Structure of arteries

Most arteries carry oxygenated blood and branch off the aorta. This includes the hepatic artery, the renal artery and the carotid artery (Figure 10.23 and 10.4). The exception is the pulmonary artery which carries deoxygenated blood from the heart to the lungs to be oxygenated. However, as the arteries carry blood away from the heart, they all carry blood under pressure from the ventricles and have the thick wall described to allow expansion without damage. Having a thick wall means that arteries and arterioles are not permeable and materials cannot enter or leave the blood through the thick wall.

9 Would you expect more elastic tissue in the wall of the aorta or the pulmonary artery? Explain your answer.   *(2 marks)*

Remember

Main points about blood flow in arteries:
- thick wall made of elastic tissue, smooth muscle and collagen
- small lumen which can expand when blood enters
- arterioles can constrict or narrow if muscle contracts, to control blood flow
- impermeable as wall is too thick to allow diffusion through it
- semilunar valves in arteries near the heart to stop backflow
- carry blood away from the heart
- blood is oxygenated except in the pulmonary artery
- blood is under high pressure in spurts
- blood flows quickly
- pressure and speed decrease with increasing distance from the heart

Arterioles eventually divide into tiny blood vessels with walls only one cell thick called **capillaries**.

10.9 Capillaries

These tiny blood vessels form a branching network called a capillary bed, which extends through organs of the body, so linking arteries to veins. The capillary bed branches between cells, so no cell is far from blood (see Figure 10.26).

Capillaries have a wall, or endothelium, only one cell thick made of **squamous** or **pavement epithelium**, which always indicates an exchange surface (Figure 10.21). The thin squamous epithelium is permeable to water and solutes, therefore allowing exchange of material between the blood and the cells. There is no muscle, elastin or collagen in the wall which keeps the wall as thin as possible, to reduce the diffusion distance and so speed up the rate of diffusion. Lacking muscle, capillaries are not capable of constriction, but the blood flow through them can be altered by changes in the muscle of the arterioles leading to them.

The network of capillaries is so vast that it presents an enormous surface area for exchange of materials. As the vessels are so narrow, red blood cells, which have a similar diameter, can only just squeeze through. This slows the blood flow to less than 1 mm per second, thus allowing more time for diffusion.

The thin endothelium of the capillary lets water and solutes through, but the larger blood cells and proteins are too large to pass through the membrane. Substances like glucose, amino acids and oxygen diffuse to the cells from the blood, while waste from the cells, like carbon dioxide and urea, diffuse into the blood.

As blood flows along the capillary bed, exchange of material takes place and the blood becomes increasingly deoxygenated. Oxygenated blood enters the capillaries at the arteriole end, and deoxygenated blood emerges at the venule end. Capillaries are therefore the only blood vessels to carry both oxygenated and deoxygenated blood. At the venule end of the capillary bed, capillaries join together to form small veins or venules. These vessels combine to form even larger vessels called veins.

10.10 Veins

Veins return the blood that has passed through organs to the heart. The distant pumping action of the heart has no effect on blood flow in the veins and the narrow capillary bed acts as a 'brake', slowing the blood and reducing the pressure. Therefore the blood in veins flows slowly and the pressure is low.

A large lumen is present and the wall is thinner than in arteries, with only a little muscle, some collagen and few elastic fibres (Figure 10.21). The large lumen means that veins can hold a large volume of blood at a time; almost half the total volume of blood is found in the veins which therefore act as a reservoir.

Veins have semilunar valves throughout the system to ensure blood flows in one direction only. This is particularly necessary where blood is flowing against gravity and the heart has no effect on pushing the blood along. Blood is moved along veins due to their proximity to skeletal muscles, like those of the arms and legs. Some veins are found running between powerful muscles like the leg

Remember

How capillaries are adapted for their role in exchange materials:
- thin wall made of squamous epithelium, permeable to water and solutes
- large surface area for diffusion
- capillaries are close to body cells
- blood flows slowly, giving time for diffusion
- capillaries are more extensive in organs where the metabolic rate is high

muscles, and when these muscles contract, the veins are squeezed (Figure 10.24). When the vein is squeezed, blood can only be pushed in one direction due to the semilunar valves which close if backflow occurs. When the leg muscles relax, blood can only drop back as far as the valves.

It is therefore important that we continually use our muscles to keep the circulation going. Blood flow in veins depends on movement of the skeletal muscles, hence the importance of getting people moving quickly after operations. This is more of a problem in old people and those with a sedentary lifestyle. The slow movement of blood in veins can be seen when we cut ourselves and blood just dribbles out.

Apart from the pulmonary vein, all veins carry deoxygenated blood.

?

10 How would you expect blood to emerge if you cut an artery and why?
(1 mark)

> **Remember**
>
> How veins are adapted for their role of returning blood to the heart:
> - a large lumen reduces friction and helps to increase the speed of blood flow
> - the semilunar valves help to stop backflow
> - veins are found between arm and leg muscles which give them a push

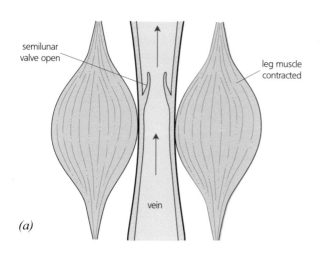

(a)

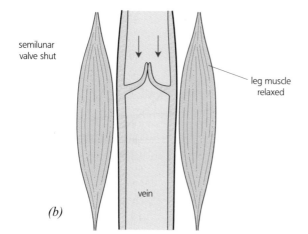

(b)

Figure 10.24 *Movement of blood in veins*

(a) When leg muscles contract the vein is squeezed and blood is pushed along.

(b) When leg muscles relax, the veins running between them are not squeezed. The blood is not pushed and therefore falls back by gravity, closing the semi lunar valves. Blood is kept moving along veins by the contraction of skeletal muscles.

10.11 Comparing blood vessels

Generally, the smaller the diameter of the lumen, the greater the friction and resistance to flow, as a higher proportion of the blood is in contact with the wall.

Table 10.5 Relationship between the diameter of the lumen in blood vessels and rate of blood flow

Vessel	Diameter of lumen	Rate of blood flow in cm s^{-1}
artery	0.4 cm	40–10
arteriole	30.0 μm	10–0.1
capillary	8.0 μm	Less than 0.1
venule	20.0 μm	Less than 0.3
vein	0.5 cm	0.3–5.0

Source: AEB 1994

Blood pressure

The pressure in blood vessels decreases as the distance from the heart increases. The pressure starts high in the arteries leaving the heart, as they are most affected by contraction of the ventricles. The left ventricle with thicker muscle can contract with greater force than the thinner muscle of the right ventricle. Consequently, the pressure is higher in the aorta than in the pulmonary artery.

Figure 10.25 Blood pressure in the blood vessels from the left and right sides of the heart

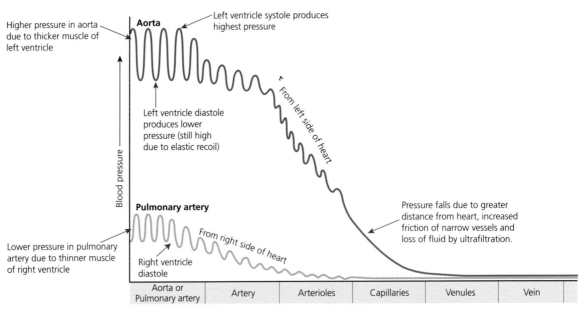

The effects of the ventricle contracting and relaxing, can be clearly seen producing peaks and troughs in the pressure in the arteries. (Figure 10.25). The pressure remains high during diastole, due to the springing back of the elastic wall of the arteries, in the elastic recoil mechanism. Moving away from the heart, the pressure falls due to increasing distance from the heart and increased friction. The pressure falls dramatically in the capillaries due both to the above and to loss of fluid through the capillaries.

The main features of blood vessels are as follows:

- In arteries, blood flows in spurts or pulses because the contraction of the ventricles is not continuous.

- A high-pressure pulse is caused by the contraction of the ventricles and blood is forced into the arteries.

- Lower pressure between pulses is due to the ventricles relaxing. The fall in pressure is reduced by the elastic recoil mechanism.

- The greatest drop in blood pressure takes place in the arterioles because of increased friction combined with increasing distance from the heart.

- Elastic tissue allows expansion of the arteries without bursting, maintains high pressure and smooths out the flow.

- Smooth muscle allows vasoconstriction and vasodilation which can be used to regulate the distribution of blood in temperature regulation and to divert more blood to the muscles during exercise (by reducing blood to the gut, for example).

- Capillaries are thin and permeable, allowing exchange of materials between the cells and the blood.

- Veins contain a lot of blood in their large lumens and there is very low pressure.

- Blood is pushed along in veins by contraction of the large muscles they pass through, and semilunar valves keep the blood flowing in one direction.

Table 10.6 *Comparison between arteries, veins and capillaries*

Artery	Capillary	Vein
carry blood away from the heart	join arteries to veins	carry blood to the heart
high blood pressure	pressure falling	low blood pressure
blood moves in pulses	no pulse	no pulse
blood flows rapidly	blood flow slowing	slow blood flow
thick wall with lots of elastic tissue, smooth muscle and collagen	thin wall made of squamous epithelium	wall thinner than artery, less muscle and elastin
impermeable to water and solutes	permeable to water and solutes	impermeable to water and solutes
few semilunar valves in arteries	no semilunar valves	semilunar valves common
carry oxygenated blood (apart from pulmonary artery)	blood starts oxygenated and becomes deoxygenated	carry deoxygenated blood (apart from pulmonary vein)

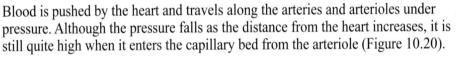

10.12 Formation of tissue fluid and lymph

Blood is pushed by the heart and travels along the arteries and arterioles under pressure. Although the pressure falls as the distance from the heart increases, it is still quite high when it enters the capillary bed from the arteriole (Figure 10.20).

Figure 10.26 shows what happens when blood under pressure from the heart enters the narrow capillaries in the capillary bed.

The blood pressure can be referred to as **hydrostatic pressure** as it is due to a liquid ('hydro' means 'water'). When the blood under high hydrostatic pressure reaches the capillary bed, some of the watery part of the blood, **plasma**, is pushed through the thin permeable wall and out of the blood capillary. This watery liquid now bathes the cells and is called **tissue fluid**.

Only small molecules pass out of the blood as they have to pass through the squamous epithelium, which acts like a filter, or through the tiny gaps in the capillary walls. This process can be referred to as **ultrafiltration** or filtration under pressure. Larger molecules, like proteins and blood cells, are too large to filter through and therefore remain in the blood. As a result of some plasma-like fluid leaving the blood, the amount of liquid in the capillaries falls, which lowers the blood pressure even more. The tissue fluid has the same composition as the plasma, apart from the absence of plasma proteins which are too large to be filtered through.

The loss of watery liquid from the blood at the arteriole end of the capillary bed, lowers the **water potential** in the blood and increases the water potential in the tissue fluid. Osmosis should result in water passing from the higher water

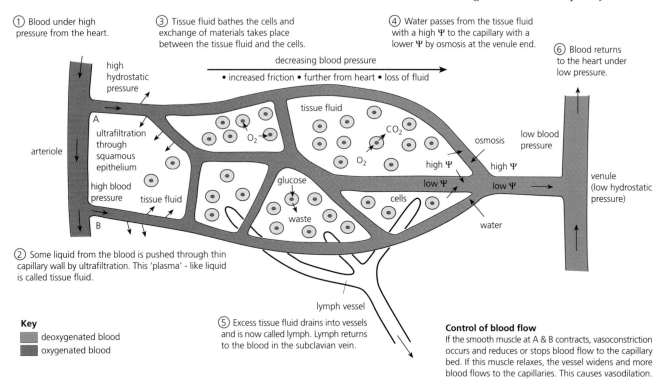

Figure 10.26 The capillary bed

① Blood under high pressure from the heart.

③ Tissue fluid bathes the cells and exchange of materials takes place between the tissue fluid and the cells.

④ Water passes from the tissue fluid with a high Ψ to the capillary with a lower Ψ by osmosis at the venule end.

⑥ Blood returns to the heart under low pressure.

decreasing blood pressure

• increased friction • further from heart • loss of fluid

high hydrostatic pressure

tissue fluid

A

ultrafiltration through squamous epithelium

O_2

CO_2

osmosis

low blood pressure

arteriole

O_2

high Ψ

high Ψ

high blood pressure

glucose

low Ψ

low Ψ

venule (low hydrostatic pressure)

tissue fluid

cells

B

waste

water

② Some liquid from the blood is pushed through thin capillary wall by ultrafiltration. This 'plasma' - like liquid is called tissue fluid.

lymph vessel

Key

▮ deoxygenated blood

▮ oxygenated blood

⑤ Excess tissue fluid drains into vessels and is now called lymph. Lymph returns to the blood in the subclavian vein.

Control of blood flow

If the smooth muscle at A & B contracts, vasoconstriction occurs and reduces or stops blood flow to the capillary bed. If this muscle relaxes, the vessel widens and more blood flows to the capillaries. This causes vasodilation.

potential in the tissue fluid to the lower water potential in the blood (see Section 2.7, page 47). However, this does not occur at the arteriole end, as the force of the hydrostatic pressure is greater than the osmotic force at this point.

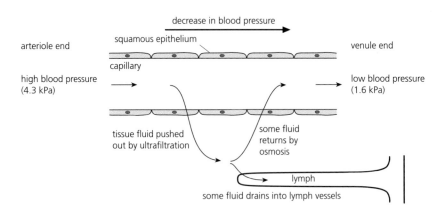

Figure 10.27 Formation of tissue fluid – simplified

decrease in blood pressure

arteriole end

squamous epithelium

venule end

capillary

high blood pressure (4.3 kPa)

low blood pressure (1.6 kPa)

tissue fluid pushed out by ultrafiltration

some fluid returns by osmosis

lymph

some fluid drains into lymph vessels

Tissue fluid containing water, glucose, amino acids, oxygen and other soluble products of digestion surrounds the cells. Diffusion takes place between the cells and the tissue fluid, so providing every cell with substances carried by the blood. Tissue fluid carries soluble materials from the blood to every cell, their proximity reducing the diffusion distance. In this way cells acquire materials from the blood. Waste materials, like carbon dioxide and urea, diffuse from the cells into the tissue fluid surrounding them and from the tissue fluid, they diffuse back into the blood. Therefore tissue fluid can be described as a 'go-between', transporting materials from the blood to the cells and vice versa.

Remember

Formation of tissue fluid depends on high hydrostatic pressure at the arteriole end of the capillaries combined with a permeable wall

11 What effect would thinner muscle in the left ventricle have on tissue fluid?

(2 marks)

Exchange of materials results in changes in the contents of the tissue fluid and the blood. Oxygen diffuses out of the blood, through tissue fluid and into the cells and carbon dioxide moves in the opposite direction back into the blood. Therefore the blood at the venous end of the capillary bed is deoxygenated and high in waste products.

The pressure along the capillary bed falls in three ways: loss of fluid at the arteriole end, increased friction due to the narrow vessels, and increased distance from the heart reducing the 'push' effect from the ventricles. Therefore by the time the blood reaches the venule end, the hydrostatic pressure is very low.

The water potential is higher in the tissue fluid due to the addition of 'plasma' without plasma proteins by ultrafiltration. It is lower in the blood due to the plasma proteins present and the loss of plasma. This difference in water potential allows **osmosis** to take place, and hydrostatic pressure is too low to prevent it at the venule end of the capillaries. Water therefore passes from the tissue fluid with a higher water potential, into the blood which has a lower water potential, through the thin epithelium. As a result of osmosis at the venule end, more liquid returns to the blood and the pressure rises a little.

Approximately 90% of the plasma which left the capillary returns to the blood at the venule end. The remaining tissue fluid drains into tubes called lymphatic vessels. This tissue fluid that has 'escaped' is called **lymph**, and it has almost the same composition as tissue fluid. Lymph does, however, contain fat droplets.

Tissue fluid therefore provides the cells with necessary materials and removes waste. It also keeps the composition and temperature around the cells fairly constant, so allowing them to function more efficiently. The moisture it provides around the cells allows gas exchange into and out of the cells.

Lymph is carried around the body in lymph vessels, which at intervals swell into nodes or glands. Tonsils and adenoids are examples of lymph nodes. Lymph nodes contain phagocytic white blood cells, called macrophages, that ingest bacteria by phagocytosis (see Section 11.8, page 324). Therefore, bacteria in our lymph will be destroyed, and 'cleaned' lymph returns to the blood in the subclavian vein. This is in effect a 'cleaning' system keeping the blood free of bacteria. When we are ill, the lymph nodes swell up due to the increase in the number of macrophages to help destroy the bacteria.

Figures 10.28 and 10.29 show the lymphatic system and its relationship with the blood system.

During digestion, lipids are hydrolysed or broken down to fatty acids and glycerol. These products of digestion are absorbed through the villi in the small intestine and enter the lymph as lipid droplets. Lymph transports these fats to the subclavian vein where they are added to the blood.

Tissue fluid cannot be continually lost from capillary beds and this system of lymph vessels returns the escaped tissue fluid or lymph to the blood.

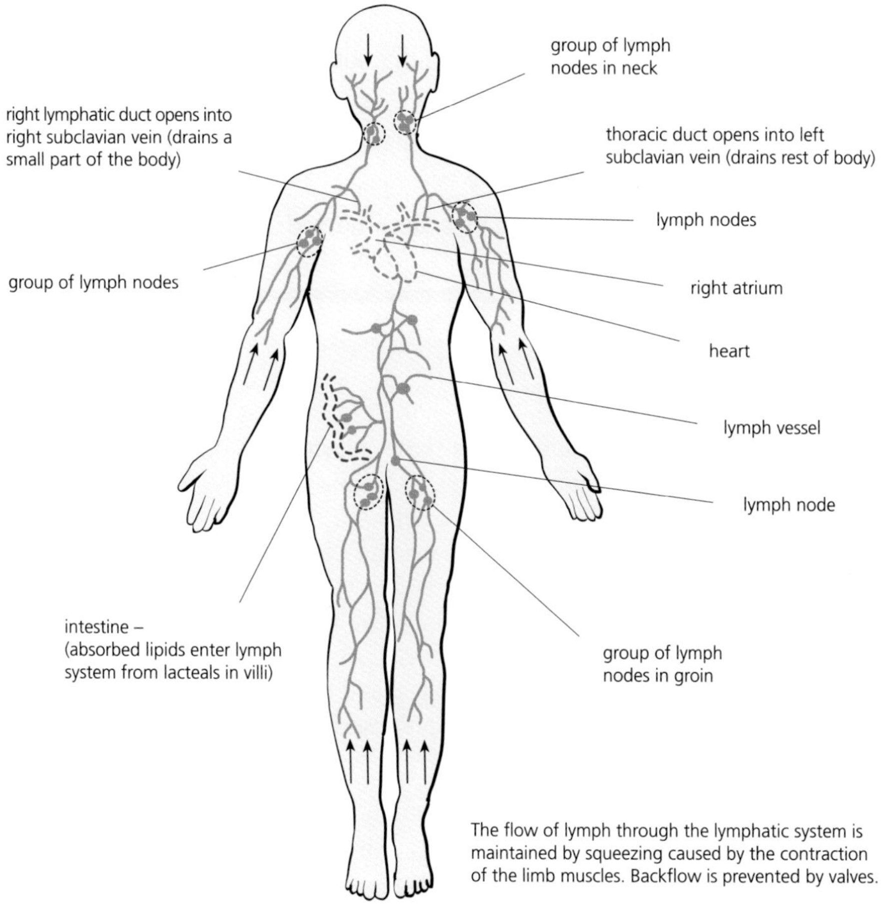

Figure 10.28 The human lymphatic system

group of lymph nodes in neck

right lymphatic duct opens into right subclavian vein (drains a small part of the body)

thoracic duct opens into left subclavian vein (drains rest of body)

lymph nodes

group of lymph nodes

right atrium

heart

lymph vessel

lymph node

intestine – (absorbed lipids enter lymph system from lacteals in villi)

group of lymph nodes in groin

The flow of lymph through the lymphatic system is maintained by squeezing caused by the contraction of the limb muscles. Backflow is prevented by valves.

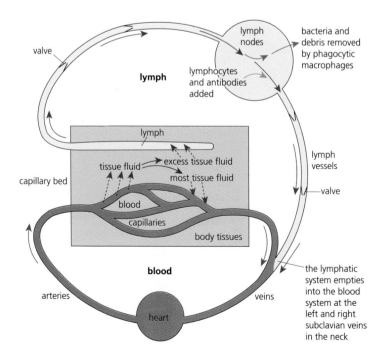

Figure 10.29 Relationship between the blood and lymphatic systems

valve

lymph nodes

bacteria and debris removed by phagocytic macrophages

lymph

lymphocytes and antibodies added

lymph

tissue fluid → excess tissue fluid

most tissue fluid

lymph vessels

capillary bed

valve

blood

capillaries

body tissues

blood

the lymphatic system empties into the blood system at the left and right subclavian veins in the neck

arteries

veins

heart

Table 10.7 *The difference between plasma, tissue fluid and lymph*

Liquid	Composition	Location
plasma	water, soluble products of digestion, hormones, plasma proteins	in blood vessels
tissue fluid	water, soluble products of digestion, hormones, no proteins	bathes cells
lymph	same as tissue fluid plus fats absorbed through the villi	lymph vessels

Remember

Events at the capillary bed:
- high hydrostatic pressure pushes some 'plasma' out of the blood by ultrafiltration at the arteriole end
- the tissue fluid formed, bathes the cells
- diffusion takes place between the tissue fluid and the cells, i.e. exchange of materials
- glucose and oxygen pass to the cells, waste like carbon dioxide and urea pass to the tissue fluid
- at the venule end, osmosis takes place and water returns to the blood
- excess tissue fluid drains into lymph vessels to form lymph

Summary – **10** Heart and blood vessels

- As blood flows through the heart twice in mammals, it is called a double circulation. This achieves a high-pressure system to the body cells, efficiently providing them with oxygen and nutrients and removing waste material.

- The heart is made of cardiac muscle which contracts and relaxes in a rhythmical way, initiated by waves of excitation from the sino-atrial node (SAN). As it is self-generating, it is called myogenic.

- Blood moves through the heart due to changes in pressure caused by the contraction and relaxation of the heart muscle in a regular sequence set by the pacemaker.

- Blood is pushed out of the heart into the arteries when the pressure is higher in the ventricles than in the arteries leading out of the heart.

- Arteries have a thick wall with lots of elastic, smooth muscle and collagen to enable them to stretch when blood enters without bursting.

- The elastic fibres in arteries keep the pressure fairly constant.

- The muscle in arterioles, in particular, can cause vasoconstriction and vasodilation to control blood flow.

- The heart rate can be increased by impulses from the sympathetic nervous system, and adrenaline, and slowed by impulses from the parasympathetic nervous system.

- Chemoreceptors and baroreceptors control the heart rate by a negative feedback mechanism, keeping the level of carbon dioxide and pressure fairly constant.

- The volume of blood pumped at each heartbeat, the stroke volume, can be increased during exercise to supply the increasing needs of cells at this time.

- Blood can be redistributed by vasoconstriction and vasodilation of arterioles to provide more blood to cells with a greater need and less to others.

- Capillaries are permeable. High hydrostatic pressure forces some plasma out through the capillaries to form tissue fluid which bathes the cells.

- Exchange of materials takes place between the cells and the tissue fluid.

- Veins return the blood to the heart, squeezed along by contraction of the big muscles through which they pass.

- Tissue fluid that does not return to the capillaries at the venule end drains away to form lymph.

Answers

1 A double circulation allows a two-pressure system with higher pressure to the body cells and lower to the lungs, so preventing damage there. A double circulation therefore allows oxygenated blood to be pumped efficiently to the body cells under pressure, a single circulation does not. High pressure to the tissues allows the formation of tissue fluid which is essential for exchange of materials between the body cells and the blood *(2)*.

2 One comes from the right lung and the other from the left lung *(1)*.

3 The semilunar valves are closed during diastole and atrial systole. At these times, the ventricle muscle is relaxed, the volume increases and the pressure decreases. Therefore blood in the arteries is at a higher pressure and blood moves from the higher pressure in the arteries to the lower pressure in the ventricles, the backflow closing the semilunar valves *(2)*.

4 The atria have thinner muscle than ventricles. Therefore when the atrial muscle contracts, the force or pressure generated is much lower than the force produced by the ventricles which have thicker muscle *(1)*.

5 The maximum pressure in the atria is similar as they have a similar thickness of cardiac muscle, which can contract with equal force *(1)*.

6 A higher pressure can be reached in the aorta as it contains blood pushed by the thicker muscle of the left ventricle. The thinner muscle of the right ventricle cannot generate the same pressure in the pulmonary artery *(1)*.

7 In the heart at rest, for example,

$$\text{percentage} = \frac{\text{volume of blood}}{\text{total volume}} \times 100$$

$$= \frac{190}{5700} \times 100 = 3.3\,\%$$
(1)

8 The volume of blood reaching the skeletal muscles rises from 740 to $12\,450\ cm^3\ min^{-1}$ when exercising. This increase in blood volume means that oxygen and glucose can be carried more quickly to the muscle cells for respiration and therefore energy can be released more quickly to allow continued exercise *(1)*.

9 The aorta should have more elastic tissue in its wall to cope with the higher pressure generated by contraction of the left ventricle. This has thicker muscle and will contract with more force than the right ventricle, which pumps blood into the pulmonary artery *(2)*.

10 If you cut an artery, the blood will come out in spurts in time with the contraction of the ventricles. The blood will be under high pressure *(1)*.

11 If the left ventricle had thinner muscle, then it would contract with less force and blood would be travelling at a lower pressure *(1)*. Lower hydrostatic pressure at the capillaries would result in less tissue fluid being formed as there is less 'push' through the squamous epithelium *(2)*.

End of Chapter Questions

1   Give two reasons why the pressure decreases as blood flows along the capillary bed.   *(2 marks)*

2   There are two heart sounds during each heartbeat. Explain what events in the cardiac cycle produce these sounds.   *(2 marks)*

3   What are the advantages of having a thicker muscle in the left ventricle?   *(2 marks)*

4   What is the function of the smooth muscle in the wall of the arterioles?   *(2 marks)*

5   State two ways in which capillaries are adapted for their function.   *(2 marks)*

6   The diagram shows a vertical section through a human heart. The arrows represent the direction of movement of the electrical activity which starts muscle contraction.

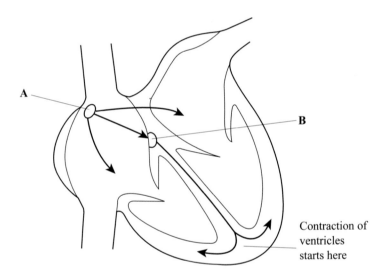

Contraction of
ventricles
starts here

(a) Name structure **A**.   *(1 mark)*

(b) Explain why each of the following is important in the pumping of blood through the heart.

(i) There is a slight delay in the passage of electrical activity that takes place at point **B**.   *(1 mark)*

(ii) The contraction of the ventricles starts at the base.   *(1 mark)*

(c) Describe how stimulation of the cardiovascular centre in the medulla may result in an increase in heart rate.   *(2 marks)*

(d) Arteries may become blocked by the formation of fatty material on the walls. An operation called balloon angioplasty may be used to correct this. The procedure is shown in the diagram.

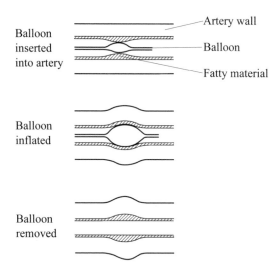

(i) Suggest why the artery wall 'bounces back' when the balloon is removed. *(1 mark)*

(ii) Explain why the ability of the artery wall to bounce back is important in a normal, healthy artery. *(2 marks)*

NEAB 1997 *(Total 8 marks)*

7 The graphs show how the pressure of blood in two arteries in a healthy person varies with time. The brachial artery supplies blood to the muscles of the arm.

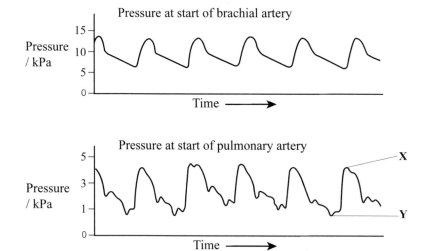

(a) Which chamber of the heart pumps blood into the pulmonary artery?

(1 mark)

N2.1 **(b)** Describe what is happening in the heart

    (i) at the time labelled **X** on the graph;

    (ii) at the time labelled **Y** on the graph. *(4 marks)*

(c) (i) Explain what causes the difference in the maximum pressure recorded in the two arteries. *(1 mark)*

    (ii) Suggest **one** advantage of this difference in maximum pressure.

(1 mark)

NEAB 1998 *(Total 7 marks)*

8 A small tube called a catheter can be inserted into the blood system through a vein. It can be threaded through the vein and into the through the heart until its tip is in the pulmonary artery. A tiny balloon at the tip can then be used to measure the pressure changes in the pulmonary artery. The diagram shows a section through the heart with the catheter in place. The graph shows the pressue changes recorded in the pulmonary artery.

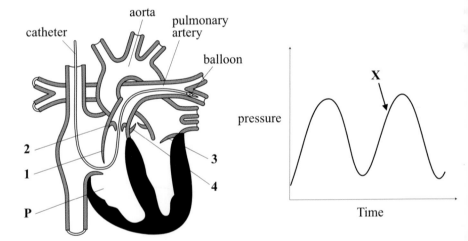

(a) Name the chamber of the heart labelled **P**. *(1 mark)*

(b) Complete the table by placing ticks in the appropiate boxes to show which of valves **1** to **4** will be open and which closed at time **X** on the graph.

Valve	Open	Closed
1		
2		
3		
4		

(1 mark)

(c) (i) Sketch a curve on the graph to show the pressure changes which you would expect if the pressure in the aorta were measured at the same time. *(2 marks)*

(AEB 1999) *(Total 4 marks)*

11 Blood – structure and function

Blood is made up of red cells, white cells and cell fragments called platelets together with a watery liquid called plasma. Blood has two main functions – transport and defence against disease. The red blood cells contain haemoglobin which carries oxygen around the body, picking it up in the lungs and releasing it to the respiring cells. The white blood cells can destroy harmful bacteria and viruses, either by phagocytosis, where the invader is surrounded and destroyed or by the production of antibodies which attack specific bacteria or viruses. Platelets are involved in forming blood clots when the skin is cut, both to reduce blood loss and to prevent the entry of germs. Plasma carries soluble materials around the body, including carbon dioxide (as hydrogencarbonate ions), glucose, amino acids, hormones, urea and antibodies.

> **This chapter includes:**
> - the structure of blood – red cells, white cells and plasma
> - the transport of oxygen by haemoglobin
> - the transport of carbon dioxide
> - defence against disease
> - the ABO system of blood groups.

11.1 The structure of blood

Blood consists of a variety of **cells**, cell fragments (**platelets**) and **plasma** – the liquid that they are present in (Figure 11.1). Blood makes up about 8% of human body weight, with human blood volume varying between 4 to $6\,dm^3$ for adults depending upon body size. Blood is a specialised fluid **tissue**. Because it contains a number of different cell types, it is classified as a **compound tissue** unlike, for example, squamous epithelium which is a **simple tissue** with only one cell type.

Figure 11.1 The structure of blood – features for identification

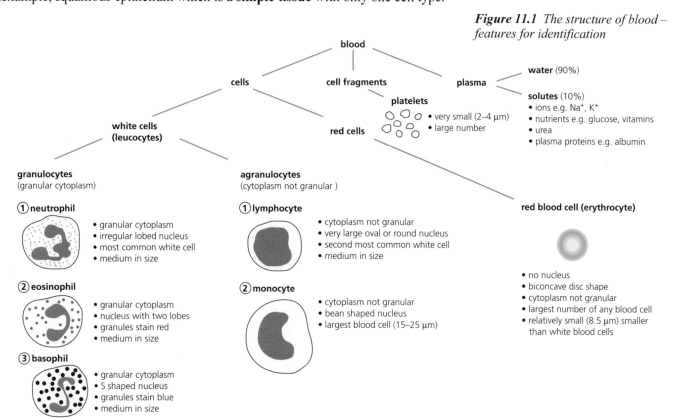

⑪ Blood – structure and function

Plasma

This is the liquid part of the blood. It consists of about 90% water and about 10% of a wide variety of dissolved substances. A list of some of these substances is given in Table 11.1, page 313. The levels of some of these substances, e.g. hormones and antibodies, vary according to the circumstances of the body at any one time. The levels of other dissolved substances, e.g. glucose, are controlled in a very exact manner by homeostatic mechanisms and stay almost constant. This rather complex composition of plasma, and the **tissue fluid** derived from plasma which surrounds all cells, forms the major part of the body's internal environment (see Section 10.12, page 300). **Homeostasis**, the maintenance of this internal environment at constant levels, is vital to health and survival.

The plasma contains a number of **plasma proteins** including **fibrinogen** which is involved in blood clotting and **albumin** which helps transport nutrients. Taken together the plasma proteins also have an important role in maintaining the **solute potential** of the blood. (See Section 10.12, page 300.)

Cell fragments or platelets

These are formed as a result of the breaking up of large cells found in the bone marrow. Platelets are involved in the **blood clotting** process, helping to stop loss of blood from a wound. Clotting is also part of the body's defence against disease (see Section 11.8, page 324).

Blood cells

Blood cells can be divided into two groups – red blood cells or **erythrocytes** and white blood cells or **leucocytes**. All blood cells are produced in the bone marrow.

It is important to be able to identify the different types of blood cell from photographs or drawings of blood smears (Figure 11.2).

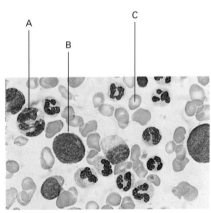

Figure 11.2 *Light micrograph of a blood smear*
A – neutrophil
B – lymphocyte
C – red blood cells

1 Give two structural differences between neutrophils and lymphocytes.
Give one structural similarity between lymphocytes and monocytes. *(3 marks)*

Red blood cells or erythrocytes

There is only a single type of red blood cell and its main function is the *transport of the respiratory gas oxygen*. Red blood cells are also involved in the transport of carbon dioxide. They are small, circular, biconcave discs, 8.5 µm (micrometres) in diameter. They are the most common type of blood cell with very large numbers present – about 5 million in each mm³ of blood (about the size of a pin-head). They are produced in the bone marrow. Because they do not contain a nucleus, they are unable to make new proteins and therefore have a short life-span of about four months.

Replacement red blood cells have to be made throughout life. Each one contains about 250 million molecules of the protein **haemoglobin**, requiring a huge rate of protein synthesis. It is the haemoglobin which gives them their red colour.

Red blood cells contain haemoglobin for the transport of oxygen and they also help in the transport of carbon dioxide (see Section 11.7, page 321). The structure of a red blood cell is well adapted to this transport function in many ways (Figure 11.3).

(a)

It has **no nucleus**, therefore more space for more haemoglobin and more oxygen can be carried.

Figure 11.3
(a) How the structure of red blood cells is adapted to their function of the transport of oxygen and carbon dioxide
(b) Scanning electron micrograph of red blood cells – (× 1750)

contains haemoglobin (a respiratory pigment – 250 million molecules per cell). This collects oxygen easily at the lungs and releases it easily at the respiring tissues.

Round, disc-like shape, allows cell to be squeezed through narrow capillaries.

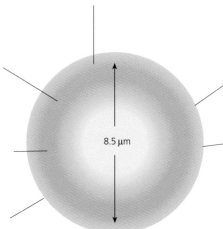

8.5 μm

contains the enzyme carbonic anhydrase – needed for transport of CO_2.

It acts as a **container.** By enclosing haemoglobin it prevents haemoglobin being filtered out and lost from body in kidneys. Also as a container it keeps the various 'reagents' close together so they can react more efficiently e.g. carbonic anhydrase kept close to haemoglobin.

Flexible cell surface **membrane** – helps allow cell to be squeezed through narrow capillaries. Also helps resist bursting due to changes in volume (to a limited extent).

transverse section

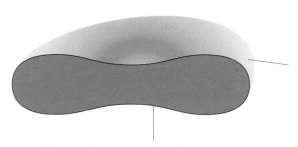

Thin cell surface membrane giving a short diffusion distance into and out of cell.

Biconcave shape increases the surface area to volume ratio. This provides a proportionally larger surface for the diffusion of gases into and out of the cell. This speeds up diffusion. Also shape helps resist bursting due to changes in volume to a limited extent.

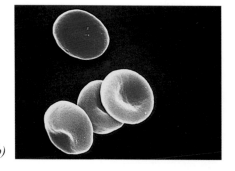

(b)

White blood cells or leucocytes

There is a variety of types which are usually divided into **granulocytes**, which have granules in their cytoplasm, and **agranulocytes**, which do not. They are all concerned with defence against disease and are all made in the bone marrow. They can be identified using the features given in Figure 11.1.

There are three types of **granulocytes: neutrophils, eosinophils** and **basophils**. Neutrophils are phagocytic, engulfing and removing bacteria, and they are the commonest white blood cell, making up about 70% of the total white cells. Eosinophils are far fewer in number and are involved in allergic reactions. Basophils are also fewer in number and help cause inflammation to stimulate the repair of damaged tissue.

Extension

Box 11.1 Red blood cells and high altitudes

At high altitudes less oxygen is available and it is difficult to supply enough to the respiring tissues. The body of a mammal cannot adapt immediately if it moves to a high altitude but with time a number of changes occur. These include an increase in the number of red blood cells present as the body responds to the altitude and produces more. This allows more oxygen to be carried by the blood (by the red cells) at any one time. This is one of the reasons why some athletes will move to higher altitudes for training as it will increase their ability to supply oxygen to their respiring muscles and therefore increase their performance.

Athletes who were born and have grown up at high altitudes can have an advantage. The Mexico City Olympic Games were held at high altitude. Six of the first eight finishers in the 10 000 metres race had lived most of their lives at high altitudes. In the Tokyo Olympics held at low level only two of the first eight were from high altitudes.

There are two main types of **agranulocytes**: **monocytes** and **lymphocytes**.

Monocytes are formed in the bone marrow and spend only about 40 hours in the blood before they enter the tissues, e.g. inside the alveoli, where they become **macrophages**. Like neutrophils, **macrophages** are phagocytic, engulfing bacteria and other large particles such as dirt. **Lymphocytes** are of two types which both develop from stem cells produced originally in the bone marrow. They are present in relatively large numbers (24% of white blood cells). **B lymphocytes** are involved in antibody production as part of immune responses. **T lymphocytes** develop in the thymus gland and are involved in other aspects of the immune response. (See Figure 11.15, page 325 for the origin of lymphocytes.)

11.2 The transport of oxygen

A major function of the blood is the transport of a wide range of substances from place to place within the body (Table 11.1). Some substances, e.g. oxygen, are added to the blood at one site, usually an exchange surface, and then removed at a different site. Other substances stay more or less permanently in the blood, e.g. plasma proteins.

Haemoglobin and respiratory pigments

A major adaptation of red blood cells for the transport of oxygen is that they contain **haemoglobin – a respiratory pigment**. There are various respiratory pigments found in different species. Haemoglobin is one of the commonest, found in all mammals and in some other animals. There are different types of haemoglobin which are adapted for the different environments of the species concerned.

A respiratory pigment has two features. Firstly, it allows the blood to carry more oxygen than would be possible just dissolved in solution in the plasma. 98% of the oxygen is transported by haemoglobin, with the rest carried dissolved in solution in the plasma. Secondly, it combines with oxygen easily where the oxygen concentration is high but releases the oxygen easily where the oxygen concentration is low.

Materials transported	Examples	Transported from	Transported to	Transported in
respiratory gases	oxygen	lungs	respiring tissues	haemoglobin in red blood cells
	carbon dioxide	respiring tissues	lungs	hydrogencarbonate ions in plasma
nutrients	glucose	intestines	respiring tissues/liver	plasma
	amino acids	intestines	liver/body tissues	plasma
	vitamins	intestines	liver/body tissues	plasma
	calcium	intestines	bones/teeth	plasma
	iron	intestines/liver	bone marrow	plasma
excretory products	urea	liver	kidney	plasma
hormones	insulin	pancreas	liver	plasma
plasma protein	albumin	liver	stays in blood plasma	
heat	heat from respiration	liver and muscles	all parts of body	all parts of body

As the concentration of available oxygen increases at the lungs, haemoglobin starts to combine with oxygen. Each haemoglobin can carry four oxygen molecules. The first molecule of oxygen to attach does so with difficulty and as it attaches it distorts the shape of the haemoglobin molecule. This distortion makes it easier for other oxygens to attach. The subsequent three molecules of oxygen attach progressively more quickly. This process is called **co-operative binding**.

The reverse process occurs where the concentration of oxygen is low, e.g. at respiring tissues. The release of one of the oxygens from oxyhaemoglobin changes the shape of the haemoglobin molecule to make release of the other oxygens increasingly easy.

These processes explain why the **oxygen dissociation curve** is **sigmoid** (S-shaped) with haemoglobin having a **high** *affinity* for oxygen where oxygen concentration is *high* and having a **low** *affinity* where oxygen concentration is *low*. (See Section 11.3, page 315.)

2 If one red blood cell contains 250 million molecules of haemoglobin, how many molecules of oxygen can it carry? *(1 mark)*

This is very important. To be an efficient carrier of oxygen haemoglobin needs to be able firstly to *collect as much oxygen as possible* where oxygen is being provided, i.e. at the lungs, but secondly to *release it easily* to the parts of the body where oxygen is needed, i.e. at the respiring tissues. The affinity of haemoglobin for oxygen is *not fixed* – it changes as it travels to different parts of the body. At the lungs a high affinity is required but if it was still high when the haemoglobin reached the respiring tissues it would tend to hold on to the oxygen and not release enough to the cells. *To be efficient the affinity needs to change.*

Table 11.1 *The transport functions of blood*

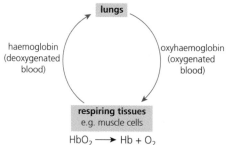

Hb + O_2 ⟶ HbO_2 oxyhaemoglobin
- high partial pressure of oxygen
- high affinity of Hb for O_2
- maximum take up of oxygen from air

lungs

haemoglobin (deoxygenated blood)   oxyhaemoglobin (oxygenated blood)

respiring tissues e.g. muscle cells

HbO_2 ⟶ Hb + O_2
- low partial pressure of oxygen
- low affinity of Hb for O_2
- maximum release of O_2 to tissues

Figure 11.4 *Oxygen concentration and the changing affinity of haemoglobin for oxygen*

 Remember

Haemoglobin has a high affinity for oxygen, i.e. it combines with it easily, where oxygen concentration is high and it has a low affinity where oxygen concentration is low

Box 11.2 Haemoglobin

Haemoglobin is a reddish-purple respiratory pigment which gives blood its red colour. It combines with oxygen to form **oxyhaemoglobin** which is a brighter red in colour. It is a globular protein and one haemoglobin molecule consists of four polypeptide chains. Each chain is associated with a **haem** group which contains iron (Figure 11.5). One of the main reasons for needing an adequate supply of iron in the diet is that it is needed as a component of haemoglobin.

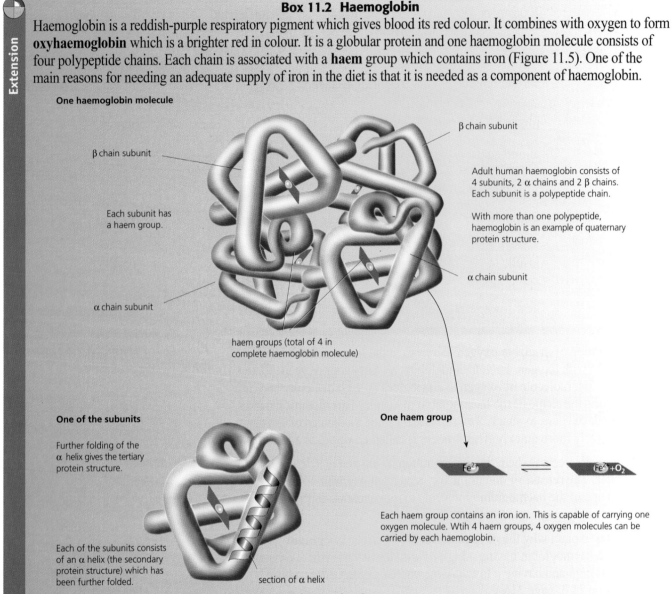

One haemoglobin molecule

β chain subunit

Each subunit has a haem group.

α chain subunit

β chain subunit

Adult human haemoglobin consists of 4 subunits, 2 α chains and 2 β chains. Each subunit is a polypeptide chain.

With more than one polypeptide, haemoglobin is an example of quaternary protein structure.

α chain subunit

haem groups (total of 4 in complete haemoglobin molecule)

One of the subunits

Further folding of the α helix gives the tertiary protein structure.

Each of the subunits consists of an α helix (the secondary protein structure) which has been further folded.

section of α helix

One haem group

Each haem group contains an iron ion. This is capable of carrying one oxygen molecule. Wtih 4 haem groups, 4 oxygen molecules can be carried by each haemoglobin.

Figure 11.5 The structure of haemoglobin – a good example of protein structure

Haemoglobin provides a good example of the different levels of protein structure (see Section 3.17, page 86). With four polypeptide chains it has a quaternary structure and the haem group is an example of a (non-protein) prosthetic group-making haemoglobin also an example of a conjugated protein.

One oxygen molecule attaches to each haem group and therefore with four haem groups, one haemoglobin molecule can transport four molecules of oxygen.

This is shown correctly as:

$$Hb + 4O_2 \rightleftharpoons HbO_8$$

haemoglobin   oxygen   oxyhaemoglobin

However, this is usually shown (incorrectly) as:

$$Hb + O_2 \rightleftharpoons HbO_2$$

11.3 Oxygen dissociation curves

Partial pressure is used as a measure of the oxygen concentration, e.g. there is a low partial pressure of oxygen (low concentration) at the respiring tissues because the oxygen is being constantly used up in respiration. **Oxygen tension** and the symbol **pO₂** have the same meaning as **oxygen partial pressure** and all three terms are used. For exam answers the term partial pressure is advisable. Partial pressure is measured in units of pressure – kilopascals (kPa).

Oxygen dissociation curves

The affinity of haemoglobin for oxygen can be measured experimentally by exposing samples of blood to mixtures of air containing different partial pressures of oxygen. The results are plotted to give a graph called an **oxygen** (or oxyhaemoglobin) **dissociation curve** (Figure 11.6).

> **Definition**
>
> The **partial pressure** of a gas is the pressure contributed by one gas to the total pressure of a mixture of gases

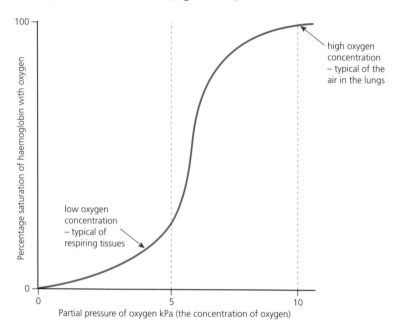

Figure 11.6 The oxygen dissociation curve for haemoglobin (adult human)

The *x* axis gives the oxygen concentration measured as partial pressure, i.e. how much oxygen is available. The *y* axis gives the % saturation of haemoglobin with oxygen, i.e. how much oxygen the haemoglobin is carrying.

As the oxygen partial pressure increases the haemoglobin collects more oxygen and its percentage saturation increases. However, instead of the expected (predicted) **straight** line the oxygen dissociation curve is **sigmoid** (S shaped) and this is significant.

Remember that the haemoglobin is constantly being transported around the body in the red blood cells between areas with lots of oxygen (the lungs) and areas with little oxygen (respiring tissues). At the right side of the graph the oxygen partial pressure is *high* and therefore the percentage saturation of haemoglobin is *high*. This situation is typical of the *lungs* where fresh oxygen is constantly provided by breathing in and out. At partial pressures of 8 kPa and above, most haemoglobin molecules are fully saturated with oxygen and increasing the partial pressure above this has little effect. The curve stays relatively flat. Although the partial pressure in the lungs is about 12 kPa, the haemoglobin does not usually get more than 95% saturated. This is maximum saturation. The sigmoid shape of the curve shows that the haemoglobin has a higher affinity for oxygen than would be predicted at high partial pressures and therefore collects oxygen more easily (Figure 11.7).

Figure 11.7 The oxygen dissociation curve for haemoglobin – the significance of the sigmoid shape

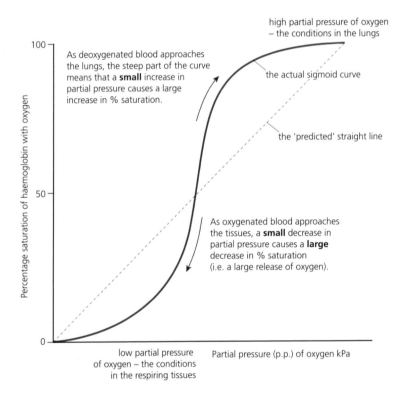

The blood carrying the oxyhaemoglobin leaves the lungs and travels to the heart and then out into the aorta and arteries. Away from the lungs the oxygen partial pressure begins to fall. However, the flatness of the sigmoid curve means that the saturation of the haemoglobin falls very little, i.e. very little oxygen is released. As the blood approaches the capillaries supplying respiring tissues the partial pressure is much lower because the oxygen is being used up in respiration. The curve gets much steeper corresponding to a sudden decrease in saturation as oxyhaemoglobin dissociates and oxygen is released (Figure 11.7).

The partial pressure in the respiring tissues is *low*, typically 5 kPa, and this reduces the affinity of haemoglobin for oxygen, causing a lot of the oxygen to be *released*. Note that haemoglobin never releases *all* the oxygen under normal conditions. This situation is shown on the left side of the dissociation curve where the sigmoid shape means that the affinity is less than predicted and oxygen is released more rapidly.

Upon the return of the deoxygenated blood to the lungs, as partial pressure increases and reaches the steep part of the curve a small rise in partial pressure causes a large rise in the percentage saturation of haemoglobin. The reasons for the sigmoid shape are given in Section 11.2, page 312. The overall effect is that haemoglobin is very well adapted for the transport of oxygen.

To summarise, haemoglobin has a high affinity for oxygen where the oxygen partial pressure is high. This means that it takes up oxygen easily where it needs to, in the lungs. However, in the respiring tissues where the partial pressure is low it has a low affinity and it releases the oxygen rapidly to the cells which require the oxygen for respiration.

11.4 Dissociation curve positions

Taking the adult human haemoglobin curve as the standard, an important feature should be noted. An *increased* affinity of the haemoglobin for oxygen will produce a curve moved to the *left* when the curve is plotted. (Figure 11.9)

A *decrease* in affinity will move the curve to the *right*.

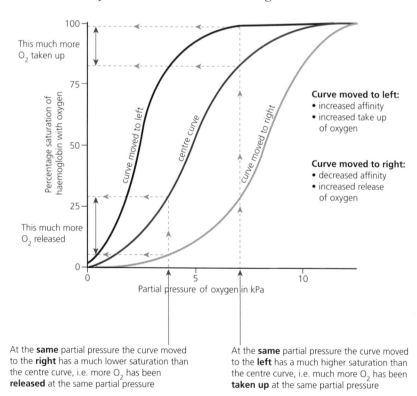

Curve moved to left:
• increased affinity
• increased take up of oxygen

Curve moved to right:
• decreased affinity
• increased release of oxygen

At the **same** partial pressure the curve moved to the **right** has a much lower saturation than the centre curve, i.e. more O₂ has been **released** at the same partial pressure

At the **same** partial pressure the curve moved to the **left** has a much higher saturation than the centre curve, i.e. much more O₂ has been **taken up** at the same partial pressure

Remember

Exam hint

As with some other topics in biology, different terms may be used to mean the same thing. This is certainly true of the topic of oxygen transport and it can cause confusion!

The two crucial ideas to understand are firstly the collection of oxygen by haemoglobin and secondly its release to the tissues. Which of the terms in Figure 11.8 you use is less important than having a clear understanding of what is happening

At the lungs
(where partial pressure of oxygen is high):

haemoglobin + oxygen ⟶ oxyhaemoglobin

| haemoglobin is | collecting combining with loading with associating with taking up | oxygen |

At the respiring tissues
(low partial pressure of oxygen):

oxyhaemoglobin ⟶ haemoglobin + oxygen

| (oxy)haemoglobin is | releasing unloading dissociating giving up | oxygen |

Figure 11.8 Choice of terms concerning oxygen transport

Figure 11.9 The oxygen dissociation curve – moving it to the left or right

A curve to the left shows a higher affinity for oxygen and therefore will mean a higher percentage saturation at a particular partial pressure of oxygen. This will make the haemoglobin better at collecting oxygen and becoming saturated even when there is little oxygen available.

A curve to the right shows a lower affinity for oxygen and a lower percentage saturation at a particular partial pressure. This is an adaptation to speed up the release of oxygen. The haemoglobin gives up its oxygen easily even at relatively high partial pressures.

'Moving' the curve occurs for one type of haemoglobin (e.g. the Bohr effect – see Section 11.5, below). In addition there are different types of haemoglobin with different properties (e.g. fetal haemoglobin – see Section 11.6, page 317) and the curves for these may be positioned either to the left or the right compared to adult human haemoglobin.

?

3 The prairie dog spends much of its time resting in underground burrows where the oxygen partial pressure is low. Predict whether its haemoglobin dissociation curve will be positioned to the left or to the right, compared to adult human haemoglobin. Why? *(2 marks)*

11.5 **The effect of carbon dioxide – the Bohr effect**

The properties of haemoglobin are affected by the concentration of carbon dioxide present, as well as by the oxygen concentration. Increasing the carbon dioxide concentration decreases the affinity of the haemoglobin for oxygen. When plotted as a dissociation curve this moves the curve to the right. A lower than usual carbon dioxide concentration will increase the affinity and shift the curve to the left. This feature is known as the **Bohr effect**. (Figure 11.10)

Figure 11.10 Oxygen dissociation and changes in carbon dioxide concentration – the Bohr effect

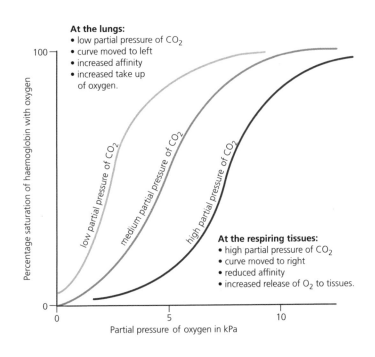

The Bohr effect increases the efficiency of haemoglobin for oxygen transport. Carbon dioxide concentration is high in tissues, e.g. muscle, which are actively respiring. The greater the rate of respiration, the higher the levels of carbon dioxide produced in respiration. The *higher* the levels of carbon dioxide, the *lower* the affinity of haemoglobin for oxygen and the *more* the curve is moved to the *right*. The haemoglobin will release more of its oxygen to the tissues. This is exactly what is required, as tissues with a high rate of respiration require increased amounts of oxygen.

At the lungs, because it is regularly breathed out, the carbon dioxide concentration is relatively *low*. This *increases* the affinity, moving the curve to the *left*. As it has a stronger affinity the haemoglobin can load itself with *more* oxygen – it can become fully saturated more easily. Again this is exactly what is required so that the blood can have the maximum amount of oxygen to take to the tissues.

The transport of oxygen is in fact connected with the transport of carbon dioxide. The mechanism of carbon dioxide transport helps explain the cause of the Bohr effect. This is discussed later (see Section 11.7, page 321).

It is important to remember how the concentration of oxygen and the concentration of carbon dioxide *both* help to make haemoglobin efficient. At respiring tissues *oxygen* concentrations are *low* but *carbon dioxide* concentrations are *high*. Both factors have the *same* effect, *decreasing* the affinity of haemoglobin for oxygen and causing it to *release* more of its oxygen to the tissues. The reverse situation occurs at the lungs. Remember to discuss the effects of *both* concentrations in exam answers.

Dissociation curves and pH

Secondly, the mechanism of carbon dioxide transport explains the connection between carbon dioxide concentration and pH. *Increasing* carbon dioxide makes conditions *more* acidic (lower pH) and vice versa. As a result, changing the pH will also change affinity and move the curve. *Increasing* acidity will *decrease* affinity and move the curve to the *right*. A higher pH (*more alkaline*) will *increase* affinity and move the curve to the *left*.

11.6 Fetal haemoglobin

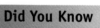

The fetus of mammals, including humans, has haemoglobin with a different structure and different properties compared to adult haemoglobin. The dissociation curve is positioned to the *left* compared to adult haemoglobin, as the fetal haemoglobin has a *higher* affinity for oxygen than that of the adult (Figure 11.11). This is an essential adaptation for the fetus. The fetus is living inside the uterus of the mother, it cannot breathe for itself and can only obtain oxygen and get rid of carbon dioxide via the mother's blood and the mother's lungs. Exchange between mother and fetus occurs through the placenta. At the oxygen partial pressures found in the placenta the mother's blood (mother's haemoglobin) *must release* oxygen and the fetal haemoglobin *must collect* oxygen. Therefore the *fetal* haemoglobin must have a *higher* affinity at the same partial pressure. It must "pull" the oxygen from the mother's haemoglobin. With equal affinities the mother would hang on to the oxygen, releasing very little to the fetus. Without oxygen the fetus would die.

Did You Know

Fetal and adult haemoglobin

Fetal haemoglobin is different from adult haemoglobin. After birth large numbers of the fetal red blood cells are destroyed and gradually replaced with new red cells containing adult haemoglobin. The structure of fetal haemoglobin consists of two alpha polypeptide chains and two gamma chains whereas adult haemoglobin has two alpha and two beta chains (see Box 11.2, page 314). This difference explains the difference in the dissociation curves

Extension

Box 11.3 Other haemoglobins

Haemoglobin is found in many different types of animals including worms, fish and reptiles, as well as mammals. There are many different types of haemoglobin which each have differences in their protein structure. Each type of haemoglobin has different oxygen-carrying properties with different dissociation curves. These differences are related to the environment in which the animal lives and to their way of life.

The main difference is having the dissociation curve positioned either to the left or to the right compared to adult human haemoglobin. This is not the temporary move to the left or right caused by the Bohr effect but is because the haemoglobin has a different structure and when plotted the curve is permanently positioned to the left or to the right (Figure 11.11).

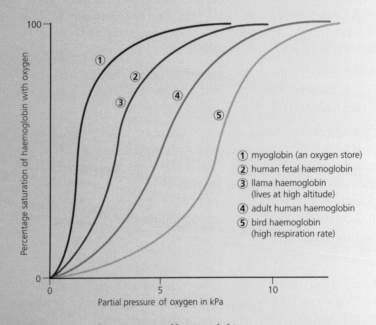

① myoglobin (an oxygen store)
② human fetal haemoglobin
③ llama haemoglobin (lives at high altitude)
④ adult human haemoglobin
⑤ bird haemoglobin (high respiration rate)

Percentage saturation of haemoglobin with oxygen

Partial pressure of oxygen in kPa

Figure 11.11 *Oxygen dissociation curves for a variety of haemoglobins*

Curves to the *right* are typical of species with a very *high respiration rate*, such as birds. The reduced affinity means that oxygen is released more easily to meet the high respiration rate of the tissues. The species lives in an environment with plenty of oxygen available and the priority is fast *release of oxygen* rather than improving the take-up of oxygen from the air. More of the oxygen is released at relatively high partial pressures.

Curves to the *left* are typical of species where the priority is the reverse, i.e. for the *loading* of oxygen rather than the unloading to the tissues. These are mainly animals which live in environments with *low levels* of available oxygen and it may be difficult to collect enough. One example is the llama which lives at a high altitude where the partial pressure of oxygen is low.

A curve to the left is due to increased affinity, allowing the haemoglobin to become saturated at the relatively low partial pressures which may be the maximum available.

An important example of a curve positioned to the left is the haemoglobin of the mammalian fetus.

Other curves to the left are where the haemoglobin or other respiratory pigment acts as an *oxygen store*. Examples include air-breathing animals which spend time swimming underwater where they cannot breathe, e.g. crocodiles. The pigment only releases oxygen when the partial pressure in the tissues becomes very low, conserving the supplies whilst underwater. **Myoglobin** is a *different* respiratory pigment which acts as an oxygen store of this type. It is found in various species including in the muscles of humans. It stays permanently in the muscles and does not travel in the blood like haemoglobin.

4 Why is it more important for a woman than a man, that fetal haemoglobin is replaced by adult haemoglobin?   *(1 mark)*

11.7 The transport of carbon dioxide

Carbon dioxide is transported by the blood in three ways: **85%** as **hydrogencarbonate ions** mostly dissolved in the plasma, **10%** attached to haemoglobin (as **carbamino-haemoglobin**) in the red blood cells, and **5%** dissolved in **solution** in the plasma.

Transport as hydrogencarbonate ions

Carbon dioxide is carried by the blood from the respiring tissues to the lungs. It leaves the blood at the lungs to be removed from the body by breathing out. The processes involved are shown in Figure 11.12.

1 At the respiring tissues carbon dioxide is constantly being produced by respiration, maintaining a high concentration in the tissues. Carbon dioxide diffuses down a concentration gradient out of the tissues and into the blood where most enters the **red blood cells**. The enzyme **carbonic anhydrase** is present in red blood cells and this catalyses the combining of carbon dioxide and water to produce **carbonic acid**. This removal of carbon dioxide maintains a low concentration in the red blood cells and ensures that carbon dioxide continues to diffuse out of the respiring tissues down a concentration gradient.

2 Carbonic acid tends to dissociate to give **hydrogencarbonate ions** and **hydrogen ions**. The hydrogencarbonate ions diffuse out into the **plasma** and are carried in solution in the blood plasma to the lungs. It is as hydrogencarbonate ions that *most* carbon dioxide is transported by the blood. Note that although carbon dioxide is not transported by the red blood cells, the red cells play an *essential* role because they contain **carbonic anhydrase** and therefore the formation of hydrogencarbonate ions occurs in the red cells.

3 At low oxygen partial pressures haemoglobin has a higher affinity for hydrogen ions than for oxygen. The oxyhaemoglobin readily combines with the hydrogen ions to form **haemoglobinic acid** and this displaces the oxygen which is then released from the haemoglobin. This oxygen diffuses from the blood into the respiring tissues. This provides the explanation for the **Bohr effect** (see Section 11.5, page 318) and shows how the transport of oxygen and carbon dioxide are interrelated. The faster the rate of respiration in the respiring tissues, the greater the concentration of carbon dioxide produced. This leads to a high level of hydrogen ions, which in turn causes an increase in the release of oxygen to the tissues. Cells which are respiring more, produce more carbon dioxide, triggering a greater supply of the oxygen the cells require for respiration – a very logical adaptation. In effect increasing the partial pressure of carbon dioxide decreases the affinity of the haemoglobin for oxygen, and moves the dissociation curve to the right – the Bohr effect. At the lungs these processes are reversed.

> **Remember**
>
> Note that it is this production of hydrogen ions which explains why increasing the carbon dioxide concentration also increases the acidity. Also it explains why changing the pH affects the affinity of haemoglobin and the position of the curve – see Section 11.5, page 318

> **Remember**
>
> **The Bohr effect**
> Cells with a high rate of respiration produce lots of CO_2 and need a lot of O_2. As more CO_2 is released, more H^+ ions are produced. Haemoglobin has a higher affinity for H^+ ions than O_2 and it takes up the H^+ and releases O_2.
> Therefore as the partial pressure of CO_2 increases, the affinity of haemoglobin for oxygen decreases and more oxygen is released to the cells.
> This is exactly what is required

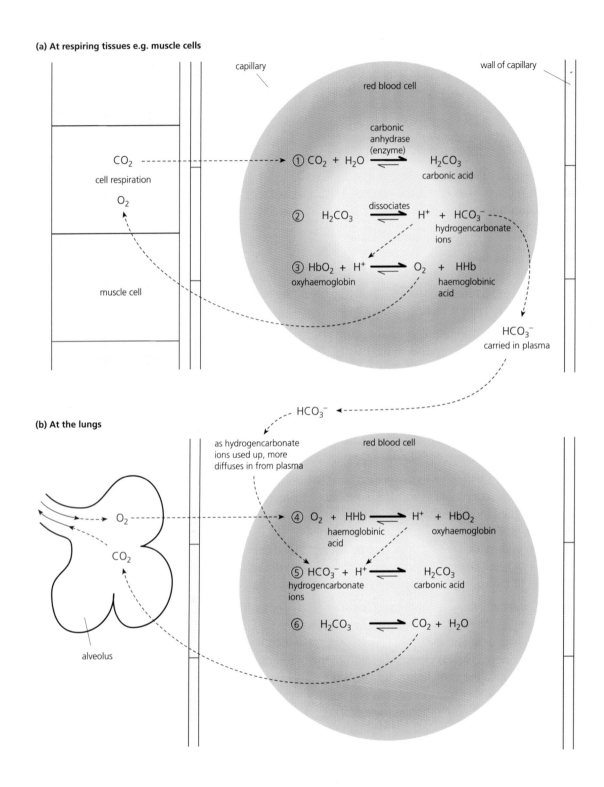

Figure 11.12 *The transport of carbon dioxide*

4 The concentration of oxygen in the lungs is high due to ventilation and oxygen diffuses from the lungs into the red blood cells. Because of the high partial pressure of oxygen, the haemoglobin has a higher affinity for oxygen, so it readily combines with oxygen to give oxyhaemoglobin and this displaces the hydrogen ions.

5 These displaced **hydrogen ions** combine with **hydrogencarbonate ions** to give **carbonic acid**.

6 Catalysed by **carbonic anhydrase**, the carbonic acid dissociates to produce water and **carbon dioxide**. The carbon dioxide diffuses from the red blood cells to the lungs and is removed from the body.

7 As the hydrogencarbonate ions are used up in the red cells, more diffuse in from the plasma.

The buffering of the blood – control of blood pH

It is important to keep the pH of the blood constant so that chemical reactions in the blood are not upset. pH is kept constant by buffers. The blood is buffered in three ways:

a) In the red cells haemoglobin acts as a buffer by accepting hydrogen ions to produce haemoglobinic acid.

b) In the plasma, hydrogencarbonate ions join with hydrogen ions to give carbonic acid.

c) In the plasma, plasma proteins join with hydrogen ions to give proteinic acid.

5 Most CO_2 is transported as HCO_3^- ions. Some HCO_3^- ions are formed in the plasma but why is much more made in the red blood cells? *(2 marks)*

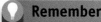

> **Remember**
>
> **Carbamino-haemoglobin and carboxyhaemoglobin**
> It is important to distinguish between these two terms.
> Some CO_2 is transported combined with haemoglobin as carbaminohaemoglobin. This is useful to the body.
> $Hb + CO_2 \rightleftharpoons$ carbamino-haemoglobin.
> This is a reversible reaction.
> **Carboxyhaemoglobin is definitely not useful!** It is formed when carbon monoxide combines with haemoglobin and the reaction is irreversible. The affinity of haemoglobin for carbon monoxide is 250 times greater than for oxygen. Smoking releases carbon monoxide into the blood and about 10% of the haemoglobin of smokers is in the form of carboxyhaemoglobin. In this form it cannot carry oxygen and therefore smokers have a reduced capacity to transport oxygen. More serious carbon monoxide poisoning can occur, e.g. in accidents with faulty gas fires or car exhausts. If most of the haemoglobin is in the form of carboxyhaemoglobin then not enough oxygen can be carried by the blood to keep someone alive.

① Neutrophil is attracted to the bacterium by chemicals released by the bacterium.

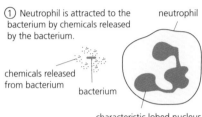

neutrophil

chemicals released from bacterium

bacterium

characteristic lobed nucleus

② Neutrophil binds to the bacterium.

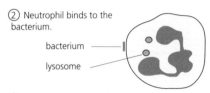

bacterium

lysosome

③ Pseudopodia form and engulf the bacterium to form a vacuole; the lysosomes move to the vacuole.

pseudopodium – arm like projections

④ Lysosomes fuse with vacuole releasing enzymes to digest the bacterium.

vacuole (phagosome)

⑤ Bacterium is fully broken down and the products are absorbed.

Figure 11.13 Phagocytosis of a bacterium by a neutrophil (phagocytic white blood cell)

Definition

Phagocytosis is the engulfing of pathogens and cell debris by the formation of a vacuole, which allows the material to be taken into the cell, where it is digested by enzymes and broken down

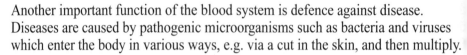

11.8 **Defence against disease**

Another important function of the blood system is defence against disease. Diseases are caused by pathogenic microorganisms such as bacteria and viruses which enter the body in various ways, e.g. via a cut in the skin, and then multiply.

There are two main types of response by the body to disease – general and specific responses. General responses are non-specific, they are a general defence against all pathogens. There is also the specific immune response triggered by a particular pathogen. The body responds to pathogens at the same time in both ways. Pathogens are microorganisms which cause disease.

General responses include blood clotting and phagocytosis.

Blood clotting

This seals cuts and wounds, preventing the entry of pathogens and stopping the loss of blood. Loss of blood lowers blood pressure which can reduce the efficiency of processes such as tissue fluid formation (see Section 10.12, page 300). The process of clotting is complex but it involves the platelets and eventually the conversion of the soluble plasma protein **fibrinogen** into strands of the insoluble protein **fibrin**. If clotting occurs at the wrong time or in the wrong place, it can be dangerous. For example, a clot occurring in a coronary artery can cause a coronary thrombosis (see Box 10.5, page 289).

Phagocytosis

Phagocytosis means cell eating and refers to the engulfing of substances by endocytosis (see Section 2.8, page 53). Two types of white blood cell, **neutrophils** and **macrophages**, are phagocytic. They get rid of invading pathogens and cell debris such as damaged cells.

Neutrophils circulate in the blood but can squeeze out of blood capillaries and into the tissues when required. Macrophages develop from **monocytes** and are not found in the blood but in **lymph nodes** (see Box 11.4, page 329) and in certain tissues such as the inside of alveoli. Neither neutrophils nor macrophages have a fixed shape, their cell surface membranes can be extended into projections called **pseudopodia** (false feet) and they can move by altering their shape (**amoeboid movement**). The process of phagocytosis is shown in Figure 11.13.

11.9 **The specific immune response and immunity**

The **immune response** is another aspect of our body's defence against pathogens – this time involving different types of white blood cell, the **B** and **T lymphocytes**. The immune response depends upon the concept of **self** and **non-self** and upon the recognition of **antigens**.

Antigens act as labels or markers. They provide a way in which the body can recognise something that should not be present and that therefore may be harmful, e.g. an invading bacterium. Antigens are usually chemicals, particularly proteins or carbohydrates, on the surface of the cell. When they enter the body the antigen is recognised by the immune system and triggers an immune response from the lymphocytes.

Self and non-self

All organisms are genetically different (except clones or identical twins) and have different molecules on the surface of their cells. Each different molecule is a different specific shape. Which molecules are present is determined genetically. Because these molecules are different and specific to an individual, the body can distinguish between its own molecules ('*self*') and different molecules ('*non-self*'). Normally the body does not respond to its own 'self' molecules and does not attack its own cells. However, 'non-self' molecules can act as antigens. They are recognised as 'non-self' and they trigger an immune response which will usually destroy the cells carrying the antigens. 'Self' therefore refers to cells that are part of the body, they belong, whereas 'non-self' cells do not belong, they are invaders, potentially harmful and need to be destroyed. (See Figure 11.14)

This reaction to 'non-self' is one of the main problems to overcome when transplanting an organ or tissue from one individual to another. The recipient is likely to 'reject' the donated organ.

Lymphocytes and the immune response

There are two types of lymphocyte which look the same but which have developed in different ways and have different functions. As with other white blood cells they are formed from stem cells in the bone marrow but then **B lymphocytes** develop in the bone marrow whereas **T lymphocytes** develop in the **thymus gland**. (See Figure 11.15)

The body contains thousands of different varieties of B and T lymphocytes. Each has specific protein receptor sites on its cell surface membrane whose molecular *shape* matches the *shape* of one particular antigen. The shapes match by a 'lock and key' mechanism, similar to enzymes. This allows the recognition of, and response to, a huge range of different antigens.

B lymphocytes respond to antigens by producing **antibodies**. The antibodies then attack the antigens. This is sometimes known as the **humoral immune response** because 'humour' is an old name for body fluid and the antibodies circulate in the blood plasma – a body fluid.

T lymphocytes do not produce antibodies but respond in a variety of rather complex ways. One of these involves producing **T killer cells** which directly destroy infected body cells. Because of the direct involvement of the T killer *cell*, the response of the T lymphocytes is known as the *cell*-mediated immune response.

B and T lymphocytes do not work in isolation. They interact and work together in quite complex ways which are not yet fully understood.

11.10 B lymphocytes and the production of antibodies

Antibodies form a crucial part of the body's defence against disease. Antibodies are specific – different antibodies are produced to deal with different pathogens. The structure of an antibody is given in Figure 11.16.

There are probably over a million different types of B lymphocyte. Each has surface receptors of a specific shape which match the shape of one particular antigen. The B lymphocyte receptors are, in fact, the same molecules as the antibodies which are eventually produced. These B lymphocytes are present in the

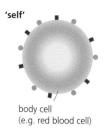

'self'

body cell
(e.g. red blood cell)

molecules of specific shapes (● and ◆) found on cell surface membrane. These shapes are recognised as 'self' – they do <u>not</u> trigger an immune response, they are <u>not</u> attacked.

'non-self'

bacterium
(an invading
pathogen)

molecules of a specific shape (▼) found on surface of bacterium. The shape is recognised as 'non-self' – it does <u>not</u> belong – the surface molecule acts as an antigen, triggering an attack from the body's defences.

Figure 11.14 *Antigens and the concept of self and non-self*

Definition

Antigens are specific molecules, e.g. proteins, which trigger an immune response from the lymphocytes. Antigens occur on cell surface membranes or cell walls or they may be the excretory products of pathogens

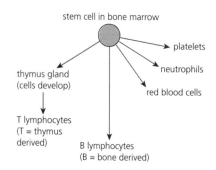

stem cell in bone marrow

platelets

neutrophils

red blood cells

thymus gland
(cells develop)

T lymphocytes
(T = thymus
derived)

B lymphocytes
(B = bone derived)

All blood cells originate by cell division from stem cells in the bone marrow.

Figure 11.15 *The origin of lymphocytes and other blood cells*

Figure 11.16 *The structure of antibodies*

Definition

Antibodies are specific globular proteins (immunoglobulins) secreted by B lymphocytes in response to stimulation by the appropriate antigen. They are capable of reacting with the antigen to neutralise a pathogen

antigen – antibody reaction

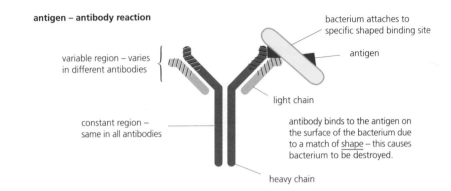

variable region – varies in different antibodies

constant region – same in all antibodies

bacterium attaches to specific shaped binding site

antigen

light chain

antibody binds to the antigen on the surface of the bacterium due to a match of <u>shape</u> – this causes bacterium to be destroyed.

heavy chain

blood and in the lymph nodes in an inactive state but acting as a defensive screen 'on the look-out' for invading pathogens. Some B lymphocytes will spend their entire lives without being activated. Others will be triggered into action by coming into contact with their particular 'target' pathogen.

B lymphocytes respond mainly to pathogens such as bacteria and viruses. The stages of this process are shown in Figure 11.17.

Figure 11.17 *The response of B lymphocytes to an antigen (the humoral response)*

• Invading bacteria enter the body.
There are specific antigens on the surface of the bacteria.

surface antigen

bacterium

• The bacteria are detected by the specific B lymphocytes which have surface protein receptors which match the shape of bacterial antigens. This B lymphocyte binds to the antigen.

B lymphocyte

other B lymphocytes with different receptor sites

• The B lymphocyte is triggered to divide by mitosis to produce plasma cells + memory cells.

plasma cells

memory cell – remains in the body for a long time providing immunity

• The plasma cells secrete large quantities of one type of antibody (up to 2000 molecules per second) which circulates in the blood.

antibody

• These antibodies are specific to the bacterial antigen. They attach to the antigen due to a match in shape.
• This causes the destruction of the bacterium in two ways
a) precipitation and agglutination where lots of bacteria are clumped together and are therefore more easily destroyed by phagocytic white blood cells.
b) the antibodies directly cause lysis – the rupturing of the cell walls of the bacteria.
• The function of memory cells is discussed later in Section 11.12, page 329
• The plasma cells die after a few days; the antibodies remain in the blood for varying lengths of time and the memory cells may stay in the blood for years or even for life.

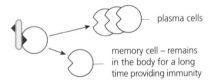

antibody

bacterium

antibody

11.11 The response of T lymphocytes

T lymphocytes respond and cause the destruction of body cells which have been altered so as to have non-self antigens on their cell surface membranes. Cancer or infection by viruses can cause non-self antigens to occur on the surface of body cells. By destroying these cells the immune system helps prevent the spread of the virus or the cancer. Note that this is different to B lymphocytes which mainly respond to the *actual* pathogen, e.g. bacteria, rather than to altered *body cells*.

T lymphocytes will also be activated by transplants, e.g. a kidney transplant or skin graft. Because the donated tissue comes from a genetically different individual it will have proteins on its cell surface which the recipient will recognise as non-self and may attack. The T lymphocyte response is summarised in Figure 11.18.

Taking the example of a body cell which has been infected by a virus, the stages of the response are as follows. The virus lives inside the body cell where it cannot be detected directly. However, the activity of the virus causes non-self antigens to occur on the cell surface membrane of the infected cell. Many different T lymphocytes are present in the body, each with different receptor proteins on the surface. The antigens on the virus-infected cell are detected by the T lymphocyte with receptors which match the shape of the antigen. When the receptors bind to the antigen, this triggers the T lymphocyte to divide by mitosis to produce various types of T cell, including helper cells, memory cells and killer cells. T helper cells help other parts of the immune system to kill the infected cells. Memory cells retain a memory of the specific antigen, providing immunity (see Section 11.12, page 329). T killer cells destroy infected cells directly by attaching to the antigens on the surface of the infected cell and punching holes in the cell surface membrane.

① Infection of body cells with a virus causes surface antigens to be present.

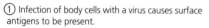

② The 'correct' T lymphocyte recognises the antigen on the infected cell due to match in shape. The T lymphocyte binds to the antigen.

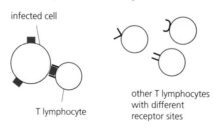

③ The T lymphocyte is triggered to divide by mitosis to produce different types of T cell.

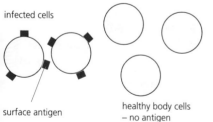

④ The T killer cells are specific to the infected cell antigen due to a match in shape. They circulate in the body, attach to the antigens of infected cells and then kill the cells.

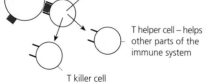

Figure 11.18 *The response of T lymphocytes to an antigen (the cell-mediated response)*

The action of B and T lymphocytes is summarised in Table 11.2.

Table 11.2 Summary of the function of B and T lymphocytes

	B lymphocyte Humoral response	T lymphocyte Cell-mediated response
site of production	stem cells made in bone marrow	stems cells made in bone marrow then mature in thymus gland
respond mainly to	pathogenic micro organisms, e.g. bacteria	cells transplanted from another individual or own cells changed by cancer or viruses
response triggered by	able to attach to bacteria because of match between specific antigen on bacteria and specific surface proteins on B lymphocyte	able to attach to foreign cell because of match between specific antigen on cell and specific surface protein on T lymphocyte
nature of response	B lymphocytes divide to produce plasma cells which produce specific antibodies which attach to matching antigens causing destruction of the bacteria	T lymphocytes produce specific killer T cells which attach to matching antigens and kill the foreign cells, e.g. transplanted cells
memory cells produced	yes	yes
primary and secondary response	yes	yes

?

6 Monoclonal antibodies are mass-produced antibodies used commercially, e.g. to detect particular molecules in test kits. What property of antibodies is being used? *(1 mark)*

7 For B and T lymphocytes, give two differences and two similarities in how they function. *(4 marks)*

Box 11.4 Structure and functions of a lymph node

Lymph is collected from all parts of the body so the lymph nodes are able to provide a defence against sources of infection from any part of the body.

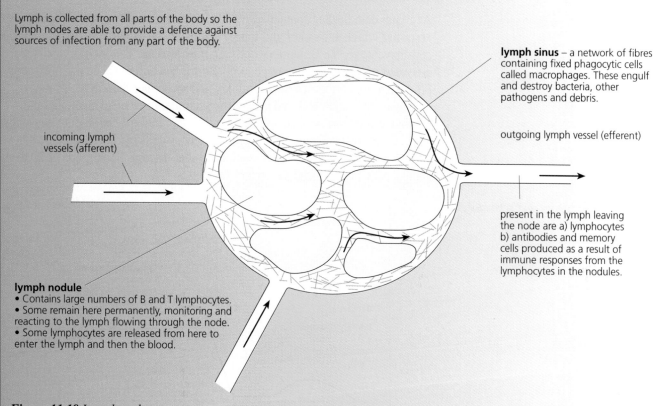

lymph sinus – a network of fibres containing fixed phagocytic cells called macrophages. These engulf and destroy bacteria, other pathogens and debris.

outgoing lymph vessel (efferent)

present in the lymph leaving the node are a) lymphocytes b) antibodies and memory cells produced as a result of immune responses from the lymphocytes in the nodules.

incoming lymph vessels (afferent)

lymph nodule
• Contains large numbers of B and T lymphocytes.
• Some remain here permanently, monitoring and reacting to the lymph flowing through the node.
• Some lymphocytes are released from here to enter the lymph and then the blood.

Figure 11.19 Lymph node

Summary of the role of lymph nodes in defence against disease

1 Phagocytic macrophages to engulf and destroy bacteria in the lymph

2 Presence of B lymphocytes to react to antigens by the production of antibodies

3 Presence of T lymphocytes to react to antigens by production of killer T cells

11.12 Primary and secondary immune responses

These occur with both B and T lymphocytes but are usually discussed in relation to B lymphocytes and the production of antibodies.

The **primary response** is the immune response triggered by the body's first-ever contact with a particular antigen. As there has been no previous contact, there are no **memory cells** for that particular antigen present and the response is relatively slow. This is because the matching B lymphocyte must first divide to produce many plasma cells and this takes time. The slowness of the response means that the pathogen has time to multiply and to cause disease before being destroyed by the antibodies.

However, part of this primary response involves producing B memory cells specific to that particular antigen. These retain a '*memory*' of the antigen and they remain in the blood much longer than the plasma cells. There are also many more of them than the original particular B lymphocytes.

At a later date further contact with the *same* antigen will trigger a **secondary response** which is quicker and longer lasting. Even though the original plasma cells have gone, the B memory cells are now present. The memory cells are activated very rapidly by contact with their target antigen. The memory cells produce more antibodies, more quickly and for longer than in the primary response. The quickness and size of the secondary response mean that the pathogens are usually destroyed before they can multiply enough to cause disease. This is **immunity**. The presence of the memory cells means that the person will not catch the disease – they are *immune* to that disease. See Figure 11.20 to compare the primary and secondary responses.

Figure 11.20 *Primary and secondary immune responses*

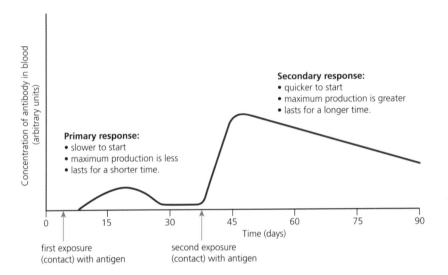

Secondary response:
• quicker to start
• maximum production is greater
• lasts for a longer time.

Primary response:
• slower to start
• maximum production is less
• lasts for a shorter time.

Concentration of antibody in blood (arbitrary units)

Time (days)

first exposure (contact) with antigen

second exposure (contact) with antigen

Definitions

The primary response is the immune response triggered by the body's first contact with a particular antigen. Firstly the B lymphocyte has to divide to form plasma cells which then produce antibodies. Production of antibodies is relatively slow and short lived, and disease may occur.

The secondary response is the immune response triggered by the second or subsequent contact with the same antigen which had previously caused a primary immune response. B memory cells specific to the antigen are present and these are activated by the antigen. They produce more antibodies, more quickly and for longer than the original primary response and disease does not usually occur.

Memory cells are lymphocytes produced by the body's first contact with an antigen. They are long lived, staying in the blood for a long time and retaining a memory of the specific antigen. If there is further contact with the antigen the memory cells are activated and they respond very quickly to prevent disease. Memory cells provide **immunity** to disease

8 How would the blood of someone who was immune to a disease be different to the blood of someone who was not immune to that disease? *(1 mark)*

11.13 Immunity

There are two basic types of immunity, **active** and **passive**. In addition, both types may be acquired naturally or artificially.

Active immunity

Active immunity occurs when the body produces its own antibodies to a particular antigen. It is *natural* when it occurs as a result of having an infection which causes the primary immune response and the production of memory cells. Further contact with the antigen does not cause disease because the memory cells respond quickly enough and produce antibodies. This type of immunity is very effective and may last for life (because the memory cells may last for life). However, it does involve suffering from the disease the first time. This may not matter too much for some relatively harmless infections but is to be avoided, if possible, with more serious diseases such as typhoid and cholera. As a result, a lot of effort has gone into the development of **immunisation** – *artificial* active immunity.

Immunisation began two hundred years ago with the work of Jenner on smallpox (see Box 11.5, page 332). Small amounts of the antigen (the **vaccine**) are injected into the person in a way that largely avoids the person becoming ill. The antigen stimulates the primary immune response and the production of memory cells. The memory cells provide immunity. The immune system has been tricked into responding as if it was a real infection. This procedure is called **vaccination** or immunisation (the two terms are used interchangeably).

More than one injection of the vaccine may be required to provide the initial immunity and also the immunity may not be life long, requiring further vaccination after a certain number of years.

Different types of vaccine are used and in each case care must be taken that the antigen in the vaccine does not cause the disease. Types of vaccine include:

a) living pathogens (with the antigens on their surface) that have been treated so they are safe, e.g. measles vaccine;

b) dead pathogens, e.g. typhoid;

c) toxoids – the toxins produced by the pathogen, e.g. tetanus;

d) extracted or artificial antigens – just the molecules which act as antigens are extracted from the pathogen or produced by gene technology, e.g. hepatitis B. This last type is ideal because with only the antigen and not the complete pathogens present in the vaccine, there is no risk at all of pathogens being introduced which might then multiply in the body.

> **Definition**
>
> **Immunity** is the ability of the body to respond quickly enough to an infection so as to destroy the pathogens and prevent disease. Immunity is specific to each different infection because the body can recognise the particular antigens of each type of pathogen, i.e. immunity to one disease does not usually give immunity to a different disease.

Box 11.5 Edward Jenner and the discovery of immunisation

Edward Jenner was a doctor in Gloucestershire in the 18th century. He observed that people who caught the mild disease cowpox seemed to be less likely to catch the more serious disease, smallpox. He decided to carry out an experiment. He took some pus from a cowpox boil from a dairy maid with the disease and using a thorn he scratched the skin of an eight-year-old boy to get some of the pus into the boy's bloodstream. Because the diseases are similar, this stimulated the boy's body to produce the same antibodies as would happen with smallpox. The boy was now immune to smallpox.

Today this type of experiment would be considered unethical but this was a historic discovery and has led to the development of immunisation against a wide range of diseases. Fittingly for Jenner's memory, one of the greatest modern-day victories against disease has been the complete worldwide eradication of smallpox using immunisation. (See Box 17.2, page 530.)

Figure 11.21 *Edward Jenner*

Passive immunity

In **passive immunity** the body does not make its own antibodies, it receives antibodies from someone else. This gives immediate protection, unlike active immunity which takes time to build up. However, the protection does not last very long because antibodies soon break down and they are not being replaced by the body making its own.

Passive immunity may be gained *naturally* when antibodies made by the mother cross the placenta to the fetus and also the baby receives some in breast milk. Both of these methods give the young baby protection until its own immune system is fully functional.

In *artificial* passive immunity, antibodies obtained from another person are injected to give immediate protection or to give rapid help in treating a condition. For example after some wounds, an injection of tetanus antibodies may be given to help prevent the disease tetanus developing.

The different types of immunity are summarised in Table 11.3.

Table 11.3 Summary of different types of immunity

	Active – **body receives antigens**	**Passive –** **body receives antibodies**
natural	natural active – e.g. fighting infection	natural passive – from mother via milk or placenta
artificial	artificial active – vaccination (injection of antigens.	artificial passive – injection of antibodies

Box 11.6 Allergies

Allergies are an example of the immune system responding incorrectly. The immune system overreacts to molecules that are usually harmless and treats them as antigens, so that an immune response is triggered. Molecules which produce this kind of response are called **allergens**. A typical and very common allergic response is **hay fever** where the allergens are usually plant pollens. The pollen acts as an antigen causing the production of lots of an antibody called IgE. In turn this causes the release of a chemical called **histamine** which has a variety of effects on the body including: swollen eyes; runny nose; the dilation of blood vessels and the constriction of the air passages. A common treatment for allergies is **antihistamines** which block the effects of the histamine. (In a 'normal' response, histamine helps us fight infection by making it easier for white blood cells to leave the capillaries to fight bacteria and other pathogens.)

Asthma can be a more serious and potentially lethal allergic reaction. The allergens which trigger asthma are extremely varied and include food substances such as nuts, pollens and air pollution. The main parts of the body affected are the air passages leading to the lungs. These passages get narrower, making breathing difficult and giving the characteristic 'wheeze' of the asthmatic (see Box 9.1, page 240).

11.14 The ABO blood groups - a special case of antigens

A specialised example of the immune response is seen in human blood groups. There is a variety of blood group systems which depend upon differences in the antigens found on the cell surface membranes of the red blood cells. The most well known is the **ABO system**. This is based upon two different antigens – A and B. These are also known as **agglutinogens**. There are also two different antibodies (or **agglutins**) called a and b which may be found in the blood plasma. If antibody **a** comes into contact with antigen **A** then it causes the red blood cells carrying antigen A to stick together or **agglutinate** (clump). This also happens if antibody **b** comes into contact with antigen **B**. Agglutination is very dangerous as blood vessels can become blocked and heart attacks or strokes may occur. (Note: agglutination is not the same as blood **clotting**.)

The ABO group of a person is determined genetically – it is inherited from the parents and depends upon which of the antigens A or B is present on the cell surface membranes of the red blood cells. In addition, unlike other antibodies, the antibodies a and b are not produced in response to an antigen. They are present in the plasma at all times.

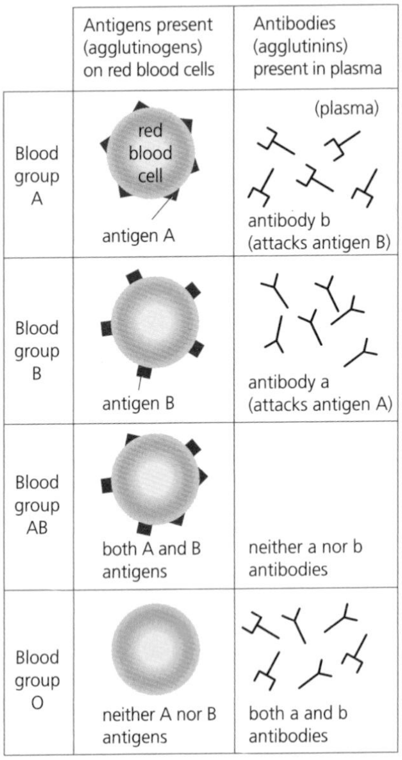

	Antigens present (agglutinogens) on red blood cells	Antibodies (agglutinins) present in plasma
Blood group A	antigen A	(plasma) antibody b (attacks antigen B)
Blood group B	antigen B	antibody a (attacks antigen A)
Blood group AB	both A and B antigens	neither a nor b antibodies
Blood group O	neither A nor B antigens	both a and b antibodies

Figure 11.22 *The ABO blood groups*

Table 11.4 *Safe and unsafe blood transfusions*

Key

✔ blood transfusion **safe**

✘ blood transfusion **not safe** – agglutination occurs

There are four groups in the ABO system. Figure 11.22 shows the distribution of antigens and antibodies between the groups.

For most of the population, most of the time, blood groups have little importance as blood is not mixed between individuals. But blood group information becomes vital when blood needs to be donated (**transfused**) from one person to another, e.g. after loss of blood following an accident. The wrong combination of donor's and recipient's blood could kill the recipient.

The recipient's blood group is carefully checked before the transfusion. When a blood transfusion is given, it is the type of red blood cells, with their particular antigens, that is crucial. If these are attacked by the matching antibodies in the plasma of the recipient's blood, this will cause clumping of the donated blood cells which could block blood vessels and kill the recipient.

The donated blood is recognised as non-self so it is treated like an invading pathogen and attacked. The relatively small amounts of antibody in the small volume of donated plasma are diluted by the much larger volume of the recipient's plasma and do not cause problems to the recipient's red cells. To be a safe transfusion the recipient must not have antibodies to the donated antigens.

Table 11.4 shows the safe and unsafe combinations of blood groups.

Blood group	Can donate blood to	Can receive blood from
A	A and AB	A and O
B	B and AB	B and O
AB	AB	all groups (universal recipient)
O	all groups (universal donor)	O

Recipient		b	a	None	a + b	Antibodies of recipient
Donor		A	B	AB	O	Blood group of recipient
A	A	✔	✘	✔	✘	
B	B	✘	✔	✔	✘	
A and B	AB	✘	✘	✔	✘	
None	O	✔	✔	✔	✔	
Antigens on red blood cells of donor	Blood group of donor					

Universal donors and universal recipients

Blood group O is known as the **universal donor** because it has *no antigens* on its red blood cells and can therefore be safely given to any blood group. Blood group AB is known as the **universal recipient** because it has *no antibodies* in its plasma and so can safely receive blood from any other blood group. This is summarised in Figure 11.23.

Figure 11.23 Summary diagram to show safe blood donations

Rhesus positive and Rhesus negative

Other ways of grouping or classifying blood exist. One of the best known is the **Rhesus** system with only two types, positive or negative. This is particularly of significance for pregnant women as there can be complications if there is the wrong match between the blood of the mother and the blood of her fetus.

Summary – (11) Blood

- Blood is a fluid tissue consisting of a number of different types of cell together with the liquid plasma.

- Red blood cells are adapted for the transport of oxygen and carbon dioxide.

- Red blood cells contain haemoglobin which can combine with oxygen. They have no nucleus so more haemoglobin can be carried. They are a biconcave shape, increasing surface area for the diffusion of gases in and out. They also contain the enzyme carbonic anhydrase which is involved in carbon dioxide transport.

- Haemoglobin is a respiratory pigment which combines easily with oxygen in the lungs where the oxygen concentration is high but releases the oxygen easily to the respiring cells where the oxygen concentration is low and where the oxygen is needed.

- This property of haemoglobin can be plotted as a sigmoid-shaped oxygen dissociation curve.

- In the respiring tissues the concentration of carbon dioxide is high and this reduces the affinity of haemoglobin for oxygen. This causes the dissociation curve to move to the right (the Bohr effect). As a result of the lower affinity more oxygen is released to the respiring cells.

- The fetus has a different type of haemoglobin which has a dissociation curve to the left of the adults. This is because the fetal haemoglobin has a higher affinity, allowing the fetus to obtain oxygen from the mother's haemoglobin.

- Carbon dioxide is transported mainly as hydrogencarbonate ions in the plasma.

- Carbon dioxide diffuses out of respiring cells into the red blood cells. These contain the enzyme carbonic anhydrase which catalyses one of the reactions leading to the production of hydrogencarbonate ions.

- These ions diffuse into the plasma and are transported to the lungs where carbon dioxide reforms and is breathed out of the body.

- The second main function of the blood is defence against pathogens, that is disease-causing organisms such as bacteria and viruses.

- Neutrophil white blood cells engulf and destroy pathogens by phagocytosis.

- B and T lymphocyte white blood cells are involved in the body's immune response to particular antigens.

- Antigens are specific molecules, e.g. on the surface of bacteria, which trigger an immune response.

- The antigens on a particular bacterium will be detected by the matching B lymphocyte. This triggers the production of specific antibodies to destroy the bacterium.

Summary – ⑪ Blood cont'd

● An invading virus will change the antigens on infected body cells and these will then be recognised as 'non-self' by the matching T lymphocyte. This triggers the production of T killer cells to destroy the virus-infected body cells.

● The first (primary) response to a particular antigen is relatively slow but it also produces memory cells. These provide immunity to the pathogen, enabling a much quicker secondary response to the next infection by the same antigen.

● Immunity can also be stimulated artificially via immunisation.

● Human blood can be classified according to an ABO system based upon which antigens are present on the red blood cells. If the wrong type of blood is used for a blood transfusion this can trigger a dangerous immune response.

? Answers

1 Differences: neutrophil has granular cytoplasm and an irregularly lobed nucleus; lymphocyte has non-granular cytoplasm and an oval nucleus. Similarity: neither have granular cytoplasm. *(3 marks)*

2 Each Hb can carry 4 oxygens. 250 million × 4 = 1000 million. Answer = 1000 million molecules of oxygen. *(1 mark)*

3 Positioned to the left compared to adult human Hb. It will have a higher affinity for oxygen enabling it to obtain enough oxygen even though the partial pressure in the burrow is very low. *(2 marks)*

4 Only women can get pregnant. If a pregnant woman still had fetal Hb her fetus would have difficulty obtaining enough oxygen as the affinity of the fetal Hb would not be higher than the mother's. *(1 mark)*

5 Much higher concentration of the enzyme carbonic anhydrase is present in the red blood cells. This enzyme is needed to produce hydrogencarbonate ions. *(2 marks)*

6 Each type of antibody has binding sites of a different specific shape. *(1 mark)*

7 See Table 11.2. *(4 marks)*

8 Memory lymphocytes for the disease would be present in the immune person and not in the non-immune. *(1 mark)*

End of Chapter Questions

1 Use Figure 11.1, page 309 and the following key, to identify cells A, B, C and D. *(4 marks)*

(i) Cell with nucleus	(ii)
Cell without nucleus	Cell A
(ii) Nucleus lobed; granules in cytoplasm	Cell B
Nucleus not lobed; no granules in cytoplasm	(iii)
(iii) Nucleus oval	Cell C
Nucleus bean shaped	Cell D

2 For adult human haemoglobin, state the effect on the oxygen dissociation curve of each of the following, saying whether the curve moved to the left or the right: *(4 marks)*

(a) a decrease in acidity

(b) an increase in carbon dioxide partial pressure

(c) replacing the haemoglobin with fetal haemoglobin

(d) an increase in the concentration of hydrogen ions.

3 The following equations summarise three reversible reactions that occur in mammalian blood.

Equation 1

$$H_2O + CO_2 \rightleftharpoons H_2CO_3$$

Equation 2

$$H_2CO_3 \rightleftharpoons HCO_3^- + H^+$$

Equation 3

$$H^+ + HbO_2 \rightleftharpoons HHb + O_2$$

(a) Which of these reactions involves the enzyme carbonic anhydrase? *(1 mark)*

(b) What is the function of the hydrogencarbonate ions produced in Equation 2? *(2 marks)*

(c) What effect do the reactions from left to right in Equations 1 and 2 have on the oxygen dissociation curve for haemoglobin? *(1 mark)*

(d) In which component of the blood do all of these reactions occur? *(1 mark)*

(Total 5 marks)

4 Jack donated a kidney to his twin sister Jill. Unfortunately she rejected the kidney transplant. As they were twins why did this happen? *(2 marks)*

5 A person ate restaurant food contaminated with bacteria and was ill with food poisoning. One year later they decided to risk the same restaurant and again the food was contaminated but this time they did not get ill. Explain fully what happened. *(4 marks)*

6 (a) If a person is blood group O what can be deduced about which agglutins (antibodies), if any, are present in the plasma? *(1 mark)*

(b) Explain why blood from a donor with blood group B cannot be transfused successfully into someone with blood group A. *(3 marks)*

(c) Why is blood group AB called the universal recipient? *(1 mark)*

(Total 5 marks)

7 The drawing is made from an electronmicrograph of part of a healthy human lung.

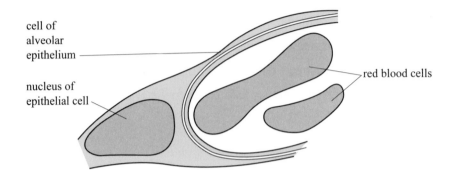

cell of alveolar epithelium

nucleus of epithelial cell

red blood cells

(a) Suggest an explanation for the different shapes of the red blood cells in this drawing. *(1 mark)*

N3.2

(b) (i) By marking a line on the drawing, show the shortest path that a molecule of oxygen would follow in diffusing from an alveolus to a haemoglobin molecule in a red blood cell.

(ii) Given that the diameter of a human red blood cell is approximately 7.5 µm, calculate the length of this path. *(2 marks)*

(c) Suggest how each of the following adaptations of a red blood cell is related to its ability to transport large amounts of oxygen:

(i) the shape of the cell

(ii) the absence of a nucleus. *(2 marks)*

(d) Suggest a possible advantage to a mammal in having haemoglobin confined to red blood cells rather than free in the plasma. *(1 mark)*

AEB 1989

(Total 6 marks)

8 The graph below shows the oxygen dissociation curve for the pigment haemoglobin in a human. The loading tension is the partial pressure of oxygen at which 95% of the pigment is saturated with oxygen. The unloading tension is the partial pressure at which 50% of the pigment is saturated with oxygen.

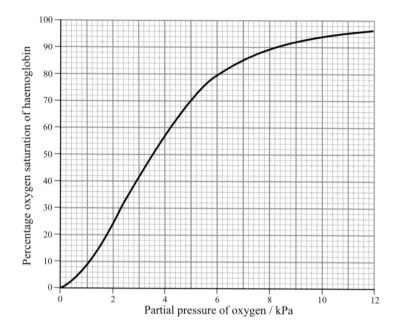

(a) Explain why haemoglobin is an efficient respiratory pigment.   *(2 marks)*   N2.1

(b) (i) From the graph determine the difference between the loading and unloading tensions of the haemoglobin. Show your working. *(2 marks)*   N2.1 N2.2

    (ii) Give *one* location in the human body where partial pressures lower than the unloading tension may be reached. Give a reason for your answer.   *(2 marks)*

(c) Suggest what effects increasing concentrations of carbon dioxide in the blood would have on the loading and unloading tensions of human haemoglobin. Give reasons for your answers.   *(4 marks)*

(d) The oxygen dissociation curve for fetal haemoglobin lies to the left of the curve for adult haemoglobin. Suggest an explanation for this difference.

    (2 marks)

(e) State *three* ways in which carbon dioxide is transported in the blood.

    (3 marks)

London 1996   *(Total 15 marks)*

9 Three genetically identical mice, **A**, **B** and **C** from strain **X**, were given skin grafts from a mouse of strain **Y** in the following experiments.

Treatment		Time for rejection of skin grafts
experiment I	mouse **A** was given two skin grafts, 3 weeks apart	first graft – 9 days second graft – 5 days
experiment II	after it had rejected the first graft, some blood serum was removed from mouse **A** and injected into mouse **B** mouse **B** was then given a skin graft	9 days
experiment III	after it had rejected the first graft, some lymphocytes were removed from mouse **A** and injected into mouse **C** mouse **C** was then given a skin graft	5 days

(a) Explain the results of:

   (i) Experiment I *(2 marks)*

   (ii) Experiment II *(1 mark)*

   (iii) Experiment III *(2 marks)*

(b) Suggest an explanation for the fact that grafts of the cornea are not normally rejected by the recipient, no matter who the donor may be.

(1 mark)

AEB 1989 *(Total 6 marks)*

C2.2 **10** Read the passage

Substitute for blood to be tested

Trials are about to begin in England of a blood substitute that might replace 10 to 20% of transfusions, while making use of blood donations that have passed their 'use-by' date.

The artificial blood is a haemoglobin solution made from the oxygen-carrying part of the red cells in human blood and is being tested in trauma cases. Because the red cell surfaces are missing, patients do not have to be typed and the blood cross-matched before transfusion.

The product has been developed by the US-based Baxter Healthcare which has overcome the problem that pure haemoglobin naturally tends to break into two molecules and be rapidly lost from the body. Baxter has found a way of locking the two sub-units together that makes the haemoglobin an efficient oxygen deliverer and allows it to be heat treated to destroy viruses. The company is taking the haemoglobin from blood donations that have passed their 35-day shelf life – a fate that on average happens to about 5% of donations in England.

Apart from being used in accident, injury and shock cases where oxygen delivery and fluid bulk is needed, one of the artificial blood's most exciting possibilities is that it may offer treatment for strokes. In animal studies, the haemoglobin solution has been able to go round blood clots and reach the parts of the brain being oxygen-starved by the clot. Infusion of the solution soon after a stroke appears to reduce the damage done to brain tissue and thus the effects of the stroke, which in humans can leave the victim paralysed, or their speech affected.

The blood substitute will not reduce the need for donors because it is derived from human haemoglobin. But it will cut out the waste of out-dated blood, allow blood to be used more flexibly and the resulting artificial blood to be stored for long periods.

Adapted from an article in the Independent *(7/5/94)*

(a) The reason blood has a 'use-by' date is that red blood cells have a much shorter life-span than the other cells in the body. Suggest **one** reason, connected with their structure, why red blood cells have a short life-span.

(1 mark)

(b) Explain why artificial blood 'can reach the parts of the brain being oxygen-starved by the clot'.

(2 marks)

(c) Apart from its use in stroke victims, give **two** other advantages of using artificial blood rather than natural whole blood.

(2 marks)

(d) Explain the role of haemoglobin in the loading, transport and unloading of oxygen.

(7 marks)

NEAB 1995

(Total 12 marks)

1 The table below refers to features of three types of cells present in mammalian blood. If a feature is correct place a tick (✔) in the appropriate box, and if the feature is not correct place a cross (✗) in the appropriate box.

Feature	Erythrocyte	Lymphocyte	Neutrophil
Has a lobed nucleus			
Contains haemoglobin			
Produces antibodies			
Shows amoeboid movement			
Can destroy bacteria by phagocytosis			

Edexcel (London) 1999

(Total 5 marks)

Transport in flowering plants

Water and minerals from the soil enter the plant through the **root hair cells**. They are carried up the plant in the **xylem** vessels. Some of the sugar made in photosynthesis passes into the **phloem** tubes, which transport the sugar to the rest of the plant. In the stem, the xylem and phloem tubes are found in **vascular bundles** located around the outer edge of the young stem.

Water is lost through the leaves in the process of **transpiration**. Water vapour passes out to the air through holes in the leaf called **stomata**. Stomata are mainly found on the lower surface of the leaf which does not face the sun. (When leaves are smeared with vaseline, water loss is reduced as the stomata are blocked.)

Transpiration results in the uptake of both water and mineral ions through the roots. The water is needed for photosynthesis, to provide support and to cool plants in hot conditions.

> **This chapter includes:**
> - **transpiration**
> - **xerophytes**
> - **absorption of water and minerals**
> - **xylem, structure and function**
> - **cohesion-tension theory**
> - **phloem, structure and function**
> - **mass flow hypothesis.**

12.1 Transpiration

Water is lost by a plant in the process of **transpiration**. This is the evaporation of water from plants. Water is lost from three main areas of a plant:

- **Stomata** – these holes, mainly on the lower surface of leaves, lose about 90% of the total water as water vapour.

- **Cuticle** – a small amount of water is lost through this waxy layer by diffusion. The thicker the cuticle, the less water lost.

- **Lenticels** – woody stems have loosely packed cork cells on the outer surface through which gas exchange occurs; a little water vapour may be lost here.

As a result of transpiration, water moves through the plant from roots to leaves and is lost into the air as water vapour. This is known as the **transpiration stream** (Figure 12.2). 98% of the water entering leaves is lost to the air in transpiration. It contributes enormously to the **water cycle** as this water vapour forms clouds leading to rain. The remaining 2% is used in photosynthesis, to maintain turgidity and in other metabolic processes.

Deforestation decreases the rate of transpiration due to the large-scale, permanent removal of forests which would normally add water vapour to the air.

Spongy mesophyll is the gas exchange surface in plants. Oxygen is needed for respiration, carbon dioxide for photosynthesis and waste gases need to be excreted. Like all gas exchange surfaces, the spongy mesophyll is thin, moist and offers a large surface area for diffusion of gases (Figure 12.3). The spongy mesophyll cells are moist, indicating that they are permeable to gases, which are therefore able to diffuse across the membrane. (As nitrogen is less soluble it does not readily dissolve and diffuse into cells.)

A moist gas exchange surface inevitably means that some evaporation of water takes place. Water vapour lost from the spongy mesophyll surface increases the concentration of water vapour in the air spaces in the leaf. Outside the leaf the amount of water vapour, the **humidity**, varies depending on weather conditions,

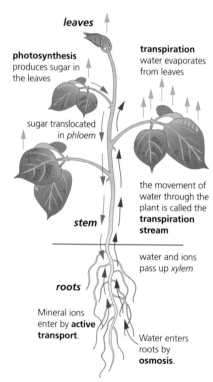

Figure 12.1 A summary of transport in plants

> 💡 **Definition**
>
> Transpiration is the evaporation of water from plants, mainly through the leaves

but generally it will be drier outside. Water vapour therefore diffuses from the higher water vapour concentration inside the leaf to the lower concentration outside. This loss of water vapour by diffusion is called transpiration. It takes place mainly through the stomata (Figure 12.4).

Figure 12.3 Leaf structure (transverse section)

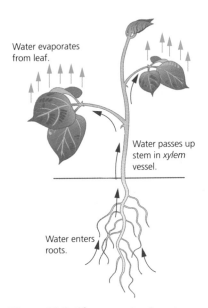

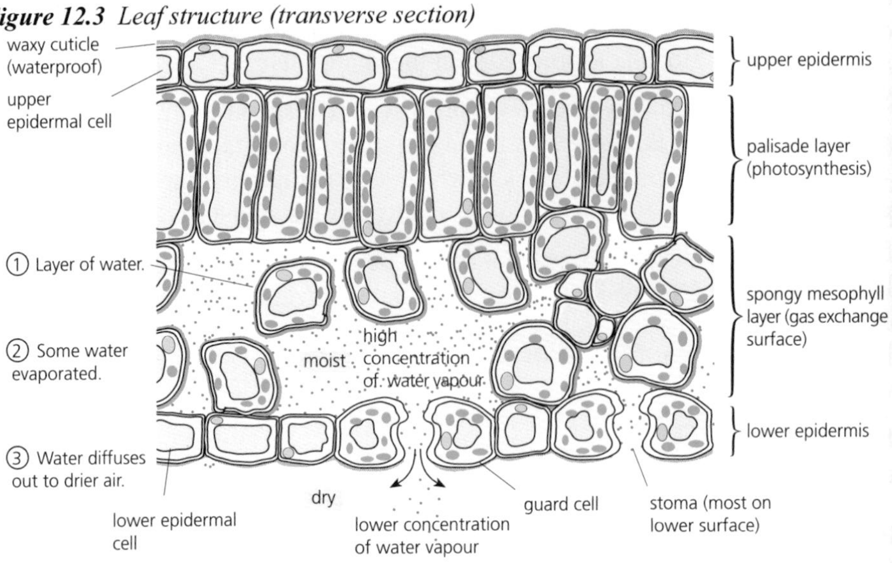

waxy cuticle
(waterproof)

upper
epidermal cell

① Layer of water.

② Some water
evaporated.

③ Water diffuses
out to drier air.

lower epidermal
cell

high
moist concentration
of water vapour

dry

lower concentration
of water vapour

upper epidermis

palisade layer
(photosynthesis)

spongy mesophyll
layer (gas exchange
surface)

lower epidermis

guard cell

stoma (most on
lower surface)

Water vapour diffuses down a water vapour concentration gradient.

High water vapour concentration ⟶ Low water vapour
        (in leaves)   concentration (in outside air)

As it is the diffusion of water, transpiration can also be explained in terms of **water potential**.

Water vapour moves from a higher water potential in the leaf to a lower water potential outside.

Remember

Exam hint

In examination questions the following terms are used but all have the same meaning:
• rate of transpiration
• rate of evaporation from a leaf
• rate of water loss from a leaf

Factors affecting transpiration can be external (environmental) or internal (leaf structure).

Water evaporates
from leaf.

Water passes up
stem in *xylem*
vessel.

Water enters
roots.

Figure 12.2 The transpiration stream

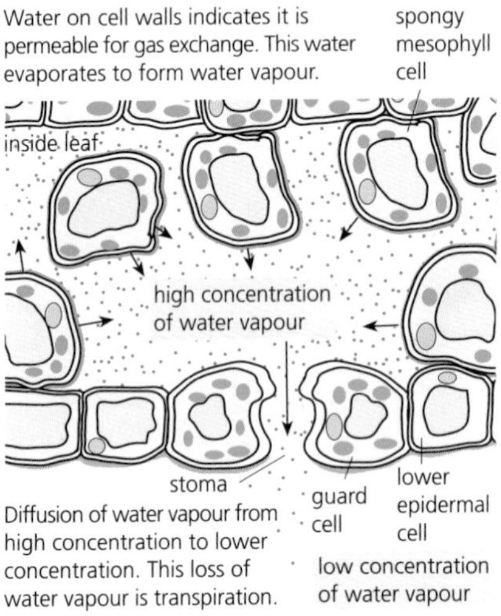

Water on cell walls indicates it is
permeable for gas exchange. This water
evaporates to form water vapour.

spongy
mesophyll
cell

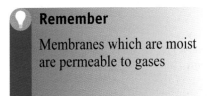

inside leaf

high concentration
of water vapour

stoma   guard   lower
           cell   epidermal
Diffusion of water vapour from   cell
high concentration to lower
concentration. This loss of   low concentration
water vapour is transpiration. of water vapour

Figure 12.4 Detailed look at a stoma

Remember

Membranes which are moist
are permeable to gases

12.2 External factors affecting transpiration

Air movement

On dry, windy days, the water vapour lost from the leaf is quickly blown away. This means that dry air outside is next to the moist air in the leaf, so there is a big difference between the water vapour concentration in the leaf compared to the outside air (Figure 12.5). This increases the loss of water vapour, as the greater the difference in concentration, the greater the rate of diffusion (**Fick's law**, Section 2.4, page 46).

On still days, with little air movement, the water vapour lost to the air lingers around the stomata. This reduces the difference in the water vapour concentration between the leaf and the air outside. The rate of diffusion therefore decreases. **Diffusion shells** can build up on still days, thus reducing the rate of transpiration. Diffusion shells are the layers of decreasing amounts of water vapour found extending from the stomata, caused by transpiration and the process of diffusion. Figure 12.5 shows how diffusion shells build up. The water vapour accumulates when there is no wind to blow it away, so reducing further water loss.

Hairs on the surface of a leaf reduce air movement near the stomata, and so reduce water loss.

Humidity

On days of **high** humidity, with a high concentration of water vapour in the air, the difference in moisture inside and outside the leaf is reduced. This reduces the rate of diffusion as the diffusion rate depends on the difference in concentration.

Low humidity, or little moisture in the air, leads to an increase in transpiration as the diffusion gradient is at a maximum. There is a big difference in the water vapour concentration inside and outside the leaf.

Temperature

High temperatures increase the rate of transpiration. This is because higher temperatures increase the kinetic energy and movement of water molecules, so they move out of the leaf more quickly. High temperatures also reduce the humidity of the air, which leads to a faster rate of diffusion of water vapour from the leaf.

Low temperatures reduce the rate of water loss as the above processes are reversed.

Dry soil

If water is in short supply, plants are unable to replace the water lost in transpiration with water from the soil. Stomatal closure occurs due to lack of water. This reduces water loss by transpiration and increases the chance of survival in dry conditions.

Light

During the day when light is available, stomata open and more water vapour can be lost. In the dark, stomata close, so less transpiration occurs.

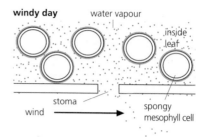

windy day water vapour / inside leaf / stoma / wind / spongy mesophyll cell

Wind blows water vapour away.
Increases transpiration.
There is a big difference in moisture inside and outside the leaf i.e. steep concentration gradient.

still day

diffusion shells

Moist air not blown away – forms diffusion shells.
Reduces transpiration.
There is little difference in concentration of water vapour inside and outside the leaf.

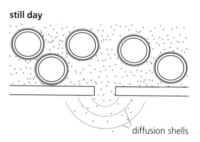

leaf with hairs wind / hair

Hairs trap moist air near to stomata.
Reduces transpiration.
There is little difference in concentration of water vapour inside and outside the leaf.

Figure 12.5 *Effect of air movement on transpiration*

Remember

External factors affecting transpiration:
- air movement
- humidity
- temperature
- light
- soil moisture

Remember

Internal factors affecting transpiration:
- leaf surface area
- distribution of stomata
- waxy cuticle

12.3 Internal factors affecting transpiration

Leaf surface area

Increased surface area increases the rate of transpiration, as more surface with stomata is exposed to the air. A plant with few, thin, narrow leaves, like grass, loses less water in transpiration than dandelion, which has large, flat leaves and therefore a larger surface area (Figure 12.6).

Distribution of stomata

Most stomata are found on the lower leaf surface of land plants (Figure 12.7). The lower surface does not face the sun or the wind. It is therefore cooler with less air movements. By contrast the upper surface is hotter and more exposed to the drying action of the wind. Having most of the stomata on the lower surface reduces transpiration, yet still allows efficient gas exchange.

Figure 12.7 *Diagrammatic structure of a leaf*

Did You Know

The name "Dandelion" comes from the French 'dents de lion' as the leaves look like lion's teeth.

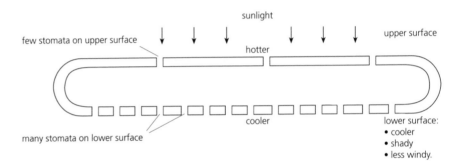

Waxy cuticle

The waxy cuticle is a waterproof layer covering the upper surface of the leaf which faces the sun. It reduces water loss from the waxed surface. In dry places, plants usually have a thicker waxy cuticle to further reduce evaporation and this may be present on both the upper and the lower leaf surface.

Thin narrow leaves
Small surface area means less water is lost in transpiration

grass

1 Land plants have most stomata on the lower leaf surface. Floating aquatic plants have many stomata on the upper surface of their leaves. Why is this not a problem for them? Suggest some advantages of this arrangement.

(2 marks)

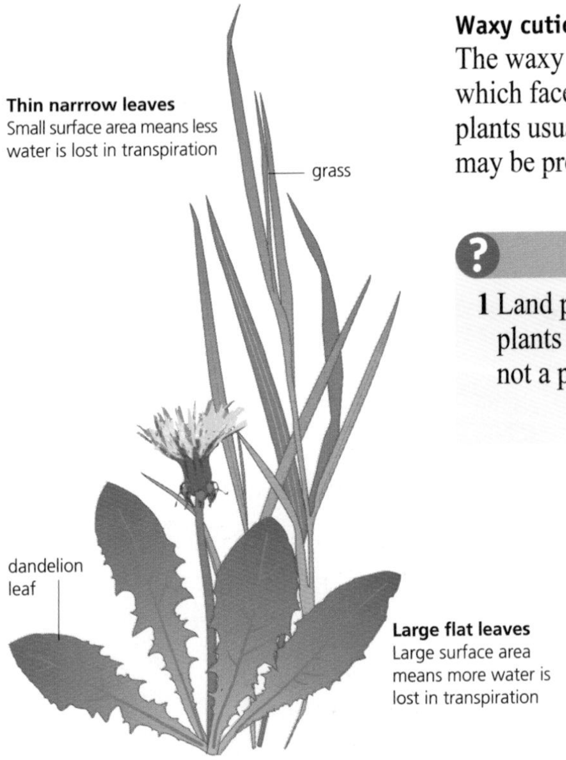

dandelion leaf

Large flat leaves
Large surface area means more water is lost in transpiration

Figure 12.6 *Leaf surface area*

Leaf structure

Leaf structure varies depending on the availability of water (Figure 12.8).

Leaf structure   **Effect on transpiration**

Figure 12.8 The effect of leaf structure on transpiration

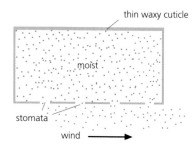

Water vapour diffuses out of the leaf and is blown away by the wind. A big difference in the concentration of water vapour in the leaf and outside ensures a rapid rate of transpiration.

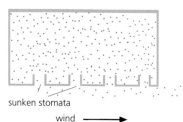

Sunken stomata form little pockets in which water vapour collects. Wind cannot easily blow the water vapour away. There is therefore little difference in the amount of water vapour inside and outside the stomata, so diffusion slows down (Fick's Law).

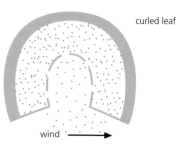

Water vapour builds up in the centre of a curled leaf as wind cannot reach here, so reducing transpiration.

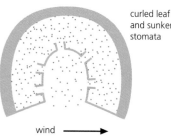

Water vapour accumulates in pockets caused by sunken stomata and in the centre of the curled leaf. This reduces the difference in water vapour concentration between the stomata and the external air. Again this reduces water loss from the leaf as the wind is unable to blow the trapped water vapour away.

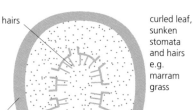

Marram grass and other xerophytes have curled leaves, sunken stomata and hairs to prevent water loss in dry conditions. Not only is the water vapour trapped in pockets and in the centre, but the hairs further restrict the movement of water vapour. The leaves also have a thick waxy cuticle. Wind has very little effect on this well-adapted leaf and transpiration is minimised.

Figure 12.9 The condition of guard cells in relation to stomatal opening

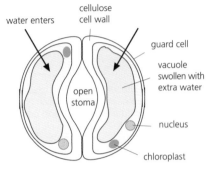

Day – stoma open

Water vapour lost in transpiration.

cellulose cell wall

water enters

guard cell

vacuole swollen with extra water

open stoma

nucleus

chloroplast

Guard cells turgid:
• Water enters guard cell vacuole.
• Vacuole swells with extra water.
• Turgid guard cells bend and pull apart.
Stoma opens.

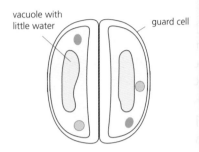

Night – stoma closed

Less water vapour lost in transpiration.

vacuole with little water

guard cell

Guard cells flaccid:
• Little water in guard cell vacuoles.
• Small vacuoles do not push outwards.
• Flaccid guard cells do not bend and pull apart.
Stoma closes.

Control of transpiration

Most water vapour is lost through the stomata when they are open. In order to reduce water loss, plants are able to control the opening and closing of stomata by altering the amount of water in the guard cells (Figure 12.9). Closing the stomata reduces water loss by approximately half. Plants close their stomata at night and on hot, dry and windy days. This reduces the water lost in transpiration.

Importance of transpiration

Water is lost through the leaves but replaced by water from the soil. So water loss at the top of a plant brings in a continuous supply of fresh water. Water is needed for **turgor**, to hold leaves out firmly in order to be exposed to light for **photosynthesis** and to bring in a continuous supply of mineral ions. Herbaceous plants rely on water to provide support for stems. Water evaporating from the leaves **cools** plants, which is important in hot climates. Water vapour from leaves forms part of the **water cycle**, producing clouds and rain. This is particularly important in providing water for plants in continental areas far from the sea.

12.4 Xerophytes – plants adapted to dry conditions

Xeromorphs are organisms adapted for life in dry conditions. They are described as having xeromorphic features. Plants adapted for dry conditions are called **xerophytes**. Dry conditions are usually caused by low rainfall and/or excessive wind. To cope with dry conditions xerophytes often have some of the following features:

● specialised leaves – to reduce water loss

● extensive root systems – to increase water uptake

● swollen stems – to store water

● thick waxy cuticle.

?

2 As you climb up a hill, trees generally get shorter and fewer in number than in the valley below. Suggest reasons why this is so.　　*(2 marks)*

Marram grass is found growing on sand dunes in exposed coastal positions. Here the strong winds, high salt levels and lack of fresh water combine, producing an extreme drying effect. Only specialised plants can tolerate these hostile conditions.

The leaves of marram grass have several **xerophytic features** which reduce water loss by transpiration. These features include curled leaves, sunken stomata, thick waxy cuticles and leaf hairs (Figure 12.10).

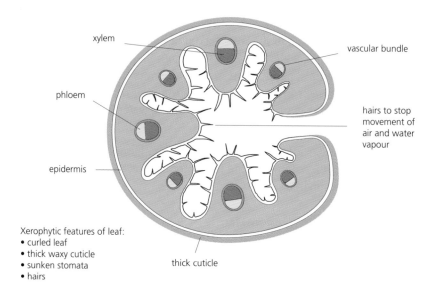

Figure 12.10 Transverse section of a leaf of marram grass (Psamma *sp.*) to show xerophytic features

Xerophytic features of leaf:
• curled leaf
• thick waxy cuticle
• sunken stomata
• hairs

Marram grass is able to store solutes in its roots which lowers the water potential there. This keeps the water potential lower in the plant than in the salty soil. Water will therefore pass from the higher water potential in the soil to the lower water potential in the plant by osmosis. (See Section 2.7, page 49.) If marram did not store solutes in the roots, its water potential might be higher than in the salty soil and the plant would then lose water to the soil by osmosis.

When conditions are dry and windy, marram grass is mainly found in a curled shape, as shown in Figure 12.10. This means that the water vapour is trapped, out of the drying action of the wind. This cuts down water loss but reduces the surface area exposed to the sun. Less light is trapped and therefore less photosynthesis takes place, but the plant is more likely to survive dry conditions.

When water is available, marram grass can uncurl and flatten to expose more surface area to the sun for photosynthesis. However, this also increases water loss in transpiration, which is not a problem when water is available.

This ability to alter leaf shape to cope with changing water availability is one of the features that has enabled marram to be successful in hostile coastal conditions.

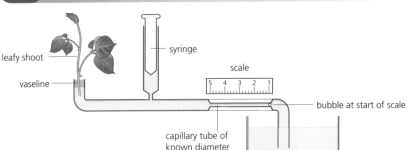

Figure 12.11 A potometer – used to measure the rate of transpiration

Remember

A potometer measures the rate of water uptake, in effect the rate of transpiration

A potometer measures the rate of the water taken in by a plant, the water uptake (Figure 12.11). Most of this water will be lost through the stomata and pass into the air during transpiration. Therefore the amount of water taken in by a plant is almost the same as the water transpired and measuring the water uptake is a good indication of the water lost in transpiration: 98% of the water taken in by a plant is lost in transpiration.

The factors affecting water loss, e.g. wind, temperature, humidity and light, can all be investigated using a potometer, and the water uptake, in effect the rate of transpiration, can be compared.

Extension

Box 12.1 How to set up a potometer

A potometer can be set up as follows (Figure 12.11):

● Cut a leafy shoot under water to stop entry of air.

● Fill a capillary tube with water.

● Fit the leafy shoot to the end of the potometer, sealing it with vaseline to make it airtight.

● Submerge the whole apparatus to ensure that it is airtight.

● Introduce an air bubble into the capillary tube.

● Use a syringe to move the air bubble to the required position at the start of the scale.

● As water evaporates from the leaves, more water will be drawn into the plant, pulling the air bubble along the tube. The distance the bubble moves indicates the volume of water taken in by the plant. This can be measured in a fixed period of time.

● The volume of water taken in can be calculated if the diameter of the tube is known.

● The experiment must be repeated to increase the reliability and accuracy for each condition. The mean can then be calculated.

● All other factors must be kept constant to ensure the accuracy of the findings.

● The same shoot can be tested in different environmental conditions and the rate of transpiration compared.

12.6 Root hair cells and mineral uptake

Root hair cells provide a large surface area for **absorption** and **anchorage**.

Water enters roots by **osmosis**, moving from the higher water potential in the soil water to the lower water potential in the root hair cell. It is therefore essential that plant roots maintain a lower water potential than the soil at all times, or water may be lost from the roots.

Oxygen diffuses from the air in the soil into the root hair cells, where a lower concentration of oxygen is found. In waterlogged conditions, when little air may be present in the soil, roots will be deprived of oxygen and be unable to respire aerobically. Consequently less energy will be available for active transport.

The shape of root hair cells increases the surface area extending into the soil, so allowing firmer anchorage.

Mineral ions mainly enter root hair cells by **active transport**. They are soluble in water and enter root hair cells from the soil, dissolved in water. Mineral ions enter roots mainly by **active transport** but also by **diffusion**.

Active transport
Active transport (see Section 2.6, page 48) takes place when mineral ions pass from a lower concentration of the ion in the soil to a higher concentration of the ion in the root hair cells.

(This is the opposite of diffusion.)

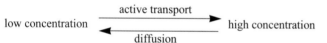

An input of energy is required in active transport, as ions are moving against the concentration gradient, moving **from low to high concentration**. Energy, in the form of ATP, is released in the mitochondria during the process of respiration. The many mitochondria in the root hair cells provide the energy, as ATP, for active transport.

Evidence for active transport is shown in Table 12.1. The concentration of mineral ions is very different in the root hair cells and the soil, e.g. potassium ions at 0.1 in the soil and 94 in the cytoplasm. A far higher concentration of potassium ions in the cell indicates that potassium ions must enter by active transport, because the potassium ions move from a *lower concentration* in the soil to a *higher concentration* in the cell.

Table 12.1 The concentration of ions in the soil and in the root hair cells

	Potassium ions /mmol dm^{-3}	Sodium ions /mmol dm^{-3}	Chloride ions /mmol dm^{-3}
soil	0.1	1.0	1.2
cytoplasm of root hair cell	94	52	59

Remember

Root hair cells:
- absorb water by osmosis and mineral ions by active transport
- contain many mitochondria to provide energy for active uptake of mineral ions
- have a large surface area for both absorption and anchorage
- absorb oxygen by diffusion for aerobic respiration

3 In waterlogged conditions, what would happen to the uptake of mineral ions by root hair cells? Explain your answer. *(3 marks)*

Selectivity is the ability of plants to absorb differing amounts of various ions, independent of their concentration in the environment. This occurs in the alga *Nitella* which lives in pond water. See Figure 12.12.

Figure 12.12 *Graph to show the concentration of ions in pond water and in the cell sap of the green alga* Nitella clavata *which lives in the pond*

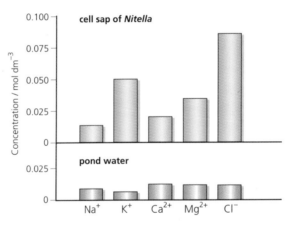

Remember

Many mitochondria in a cell indicate a high level of metabolic activity. This provides lots of energy for active transport

4 Figure 12.12 demonstrates active transport and selectivity. Explain this statement. *(2 marks)*

Diffusion

Passive absorption by diffusion (see Section 2.4, page 44) takes place through root hair cells, when the concentration of a mineral ion in the soil is *higher* than its concentration in the root hair cell. Then the mineral ion can enter the plant by diffusion, moving from where it is in *high* concentration in the soil to where it is in *low* concentration in the roots. No input of energy is required so this is described as **passive**.

?

5 State two differences between diffusion and active transport. *(2 marks)*

Metabolic poisons, e.g. potassium cyanide, stop the process of respiration and therefore the production of energy. Active transport which requires energy will therefore *cease*, but diffusion will continue as no energy is required.

?

6 Figure 12.13 shows an experiment with pieces of beech root in moist air or nitrogen. Over 25 hours the roots absorb 8 units of phosphate when moist air is used but only 0.5 units when nitrogen is used. Explain these findings.

(3 marks)

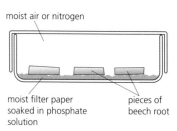

Figure 12.13 Investigation with beech root pieces and absorption of phosphate ions in different conditions (moist air or nitrogen)

12.7 Water uptake by roots

Plants need to replace the water lost in *transpiration* and to provide water for photosynthesis, turgidity and other metabolic processes.

Water passes from the soil water which has a higher *water potential*, into the root hair cells which have a *lower water potential* (Figure 12.14).

Once in the root hair cells, water passes across **parenchyma** cells making up the **cortex**, to the **xylem** (Figure 12.15). Water can then be transported to all parts of a plant in the xylem vessel. As water moves through the root, more water is drawn in, to form a continuous stream.

Water can pass through the root in three ways (Figures 12.14 and 12.15):

- through the cell wall – the **apoplast pathway**
- through the cytoplasm – the **symplast pathway**
- through the vacuole – the **vacuolar pathway**.

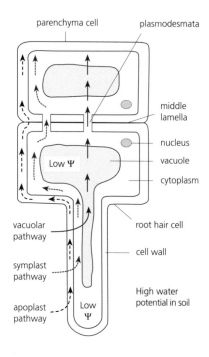

Water passes by osmosis from the high Ψ in the soil to the lower Ψ in the root hair cell.

Figure 12.14 A root hair cell

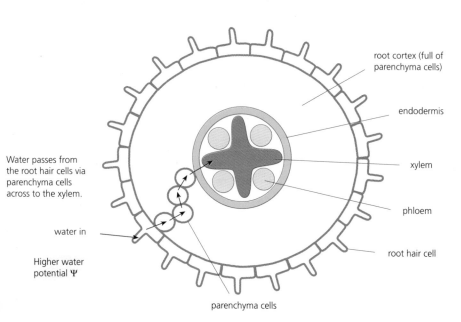

Water passes from the root hair cells via parenchyma cells across to the xylem.

water in

Higher water potential Ψ

root cortex (full of parenchyma cells)

endodermis

xylem

phloem

root hair cell

parenchyma cells

Figure 12.15 Passage of water across a root (transverse section)

The apoplast pathway – through the cellulose cell wall

Water passes along the cellulose cell wall with ease, as its permeable, mesh-like structure offers no resistance to water. Water continues to pass through cell walls until it reaches the **endodermis**. The cell wall of the endodermis contains a **casparian strip**, which is a waterproof barrier made of **suberin**. Water cannot cross this barrier and is diverted into the cytoplasm. This is therefore called an **apoplast block**, as it blocks the apoplast pathway. All the water now travels through the cytoplasm or vacuole and is therefore under the control of the cell. (See Figure 12.17.)

The symplast pathway – through the cytoplasm

Water enters the symplast pathway by **osmosis**, moving from a higher water potential (ψ) in the soil to a lower water potential in the cell through a partially permeable membrane, the cell surface membrane. Water passes into the cytoplasm and continues from one cell to the next via **plasmodesmata** which connect cells across the cellulose cell wall. Water continues to pass along the cytoplasm of the parenchyma cells by osmosis, until the xylem vessel is reached. (See Figure 12.17.)

The vacuolar pathway – through the vacuole

Water also enters the vacuolar pathway by osmosis, passing through the cell surface membrane and into the vacuole, from the higher water potential in the soil. Water continues to pass from *vacuole to vacuole* via the plasmodesmata. Once the endodermis is reached, all the water travels through the cytoplasm or vacuole due to the apoplast block. (See Figure 12.16 and 12.17.)

Salts are actively *pumped* into the **xylem vessels** from the endodermis. This lowers the water potential in the xylem vessel. This draws in water from the higher water potential in the **endodermis** and pericycle, creating a *high pressure* of water in the xylem. This causes **root pressure** and water is pushed a few centimetres up the xylem (see Section 12.8, page 358). More water is then attracted into the endodermis and pericycle from the parenchyma cells by osmosis, as the water potential is now lower in the endodermis (Figure 12.16). Water molecules stick together. The attraction between water molecules is called **cohesion**, and this force maintains a steady stream of water through the root hair cells. (See Section 12.8, page 357.)

Figure 12.16 *How water enters xylem at the roots*

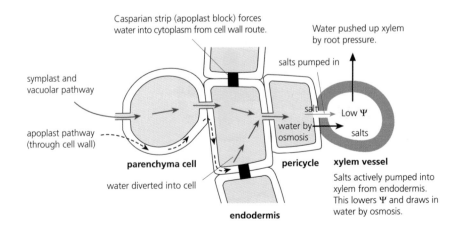

Figure 12.17 *Passage of water across a root*

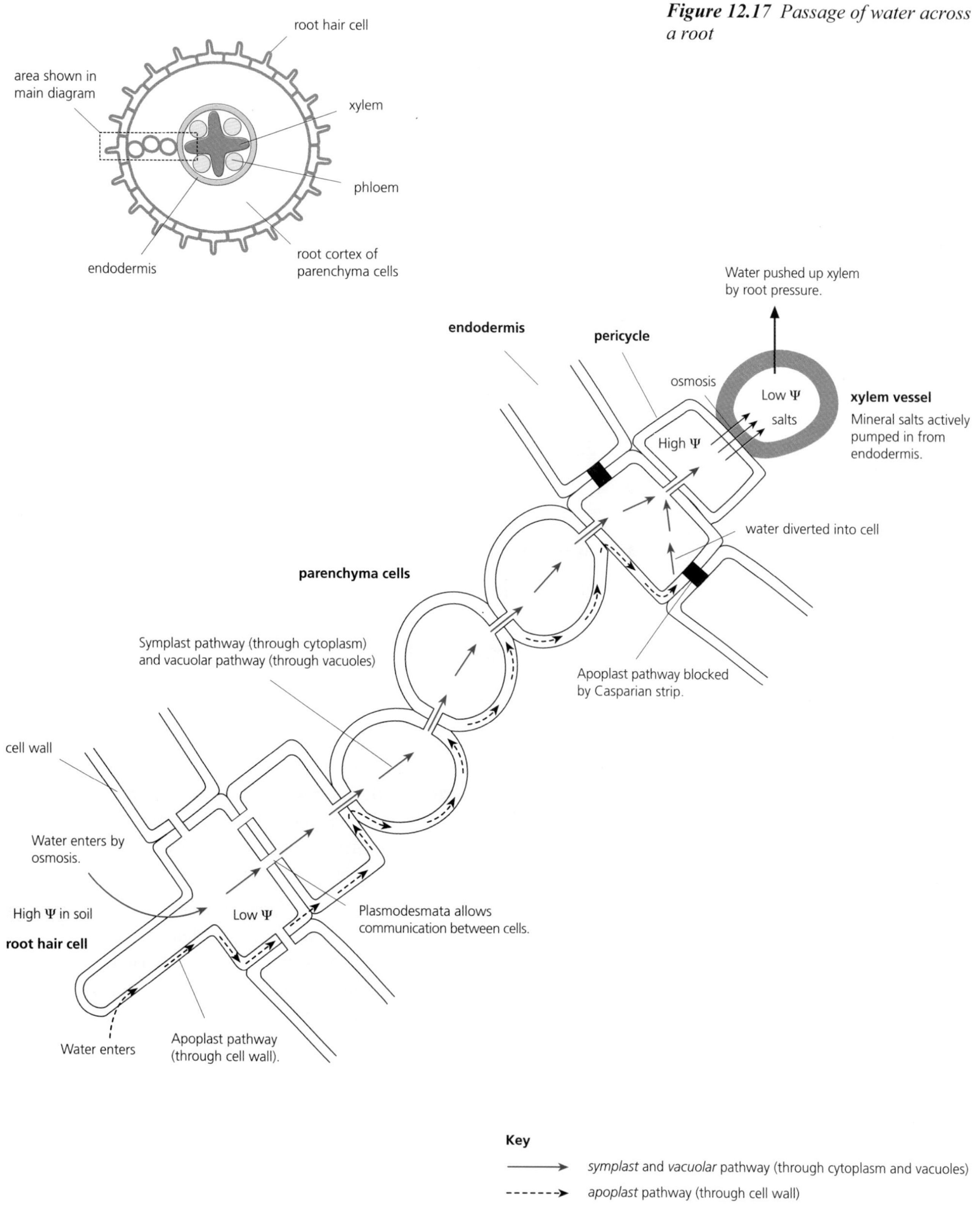

Water movement from the soil into the xylem of the root – a summary

- There is a higher water potential in the soil.

- A lower water potential exists in the root hair cells due to the solutes present.

- Water passes from the soil to the root cells by osmosis.

- Root hairs increase the surface area so more water can enter.

- Water passes along the cytoplasmic route to adjacent cells by the symplast pathway.

- Water passes from vacuole to vacuole by the vacuolar pathway.

- Water passes along cellulose cell walls by the apoplast pathway.

- The casparian strip stops water passing along the apoplast route and diverts all water into the cell and therefore under plant control. The strip also prevents the back diffusion of mineral ions from the xylem, through the cell wall, and the uncontrolled entry of ions into the xylem.

- Salts are actively pumped into the xylem, lowering the water potential.

- Water from the symplast and vacuolar pathways passes by osmosis into the xylem.

- This pressure of water causes root pressure.

- Water is pushed up the xylem.

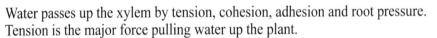

12.8 Water movement up the xylem vessel

Water passes up the xylem by tension, cohesion, adhesion and root pressure. Tension is the major force pulling water up the plant.

Tension

Water lost in **transpiration** pulls more water up the xylem: it is 'sucked' up, like sucking water up a straw. Water is also pulled down by gravity. Thus the column of water is being pulled up by transpiration and down by gravity, causing **tension**, (like stretching a piece of elastic).

About 90% of the force causing mass transport of water up the xylem is caused by water evaporating from the leaves. Water is pulled up. This can be described as a **negative pressure** as the water is passing from atmospheric pressure in the roots, to lower than atmospheric pressure in the leaves, caused by the loss of water in transpiration. Water moves along a pressure gradient from a higher pressure in the roots to a lower pressure in the leaves by **mass flow**.

7 If a tiny hole was made in the xylem, would you expect water to come out or air to go in? Explain your answer. *(2 marks)*

The pull is great enough to move an unbroken column of water from the roots to the top of the tree. The water stays in a continuous stream due to the cohesive forces of the water molecules.

> **Remember**
>
> Water passes up the xylem vessel by:
> - **tension** – water is 'pulled' up
> - **cohesion** – water sticks to water
> - **adhesion** – water sticks to xylem wall
> - **root pressure** – water is 'pushed' up

The greater the water loss in transpiration, the faster water is 'pulled' up the xylem, as transpiration is the main force causing water movement up the plant. This force can cause a decrease in stem diameter and even trunk diameter. The overall effect of tension is to cause minute *shrinkage* in each xylem vessel. This is more pronounced on hot, dry and windy days when water loss by transpiration is at a maximum and the pulling force is strongest.

8 Look at the graph in Figure 12.18, showing the relationship between the rate of transpiration and diameter of a branch. Explain the graph.   *(2 marks)*

On humid days, when transpiration is reduced, movement of water through the xylem is slow. When hot, dry and windy conditions occur, transpiration is rapid and water can move at up to 40 metres per hour.

Cohesion

As water sticks to water by cohesion, a continuous stream of water passes up the xylem, pulled up by tension. The force of attraction between water molecules is caused by the formation of **hydrogen bonds** between them (see Section 3.1, page 62).

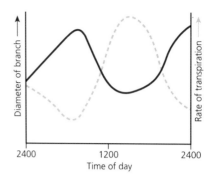

Figure 12.18 Graph to show the relationship between the rate of transpiration and diameter of a branch

> **Remember**
>
> Transpiration is the major force drawing water up the stem

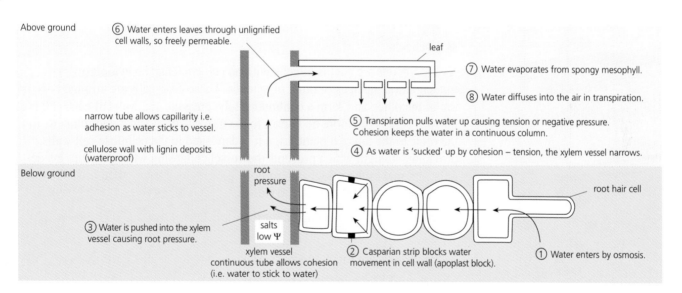

The force caused by transpiration combined with cohesion is considered to be the principal mechanism responsible for water moving up the stem from roots to tip. This is referred to as the **cohesion–tension** theory of transpiration (Figure 12.19). All the other mechanisms play a minor role.

Adhesion

The narrowness of the xylem vessel means that there is a large surface area to volume ratio and lots of water is in contact with the xylem wall. This attraction of water to another material is called **adhesion**, the attraction of unlike materials. The narrower the tube, the more water that can stick to the wall; this principle is called **capillarity**. Clearly adhesion is only possible in plants due to cohesion. Cohesion draws water up the xylem, enabling the water to stick to the xylem wall.

Figure 12.19 Cohesion–tension theory of transpiration

> **Did You Know**
>
> Water can reach heights of over 100 metres in the tallest redwoods in California

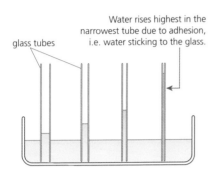

Water rises highest in the narrowest tube due to adhesion, i.e. water sticking to the glass.

glass tubes

Figure 12.20 *Effect of capillarity on water uptake*

An experiment to show the effect of capillarity on water uptake is shown in Figure 12.20.

Water rises highest in the narrowest tube due to adhesion, as a greater proportion of the water sticks to the glass.

Root pressure

The salts actively pumped into the xylem vessel lower the water potential there, which draws in water by osmosis. This pressure pushes water up the xylem, causing **root pressure**. If some actively transpiring plants are cut near the base, water dribbles out of the cut stem as a result of this pressure.

The combination of all these forces, causes water to pass up the xylem from roots to leaves.

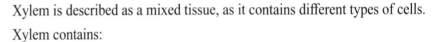
12.9 The structure of xylem

Xylem is described as a mixed tissue, as it contains different types of cells.

Xylem contains:

- xylem vessels
- fibres
- parenchyma cells
- tracheids.

Xylem vessels are chains of cells with no cell contents, no cytoplasm, mitochondria, nucleus or other organelles. These dead cells are arranged one on top of the other, and form a continuous tube once the end walls of each cell break down. There is therefore no barrier to the movement of water and minerals from the roots to the top of a plant. Lignin is deposited in the cellulose cell walls, providing strength which prevents the vessel collapsing when pressure inside falls, and makes the vessel waterproof. Gaps in the lignin, called **pits**, allow for the lateral movement of water to side branches.

Xylem vessels are well adapted for their function of *transporting water* up the stem.

Xylem vessels are found in leaves, stems and roots (Figure 12.21).

They have the following structural features:

- Continuous – an unbroken column of water is possible due to cohesion.
- Narrow – capillarity increases adhesion.
- Lignified – lignin provides strength and makes xylem waterproof, so water does not seep out.
- Pits – these are holes in the lignin through which water can pass laterally.
- Dead – no living contents means flow is not restricted, the lumen is empty.

T.S. Leaf

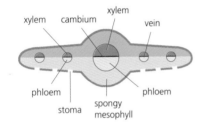

T.S. Stem

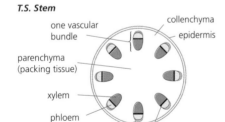

T.S. Root

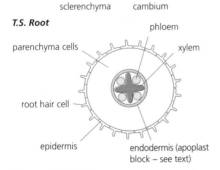

Figure 12.21 *Transverse section of a leaf, stem and root of a dicotyledonous, herbaceous plant*

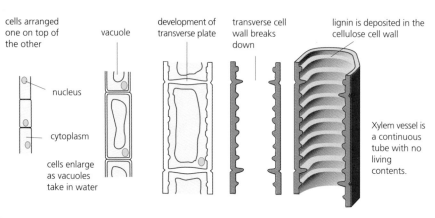

cells arranged one on top of the other

vacuole

nucleus

cytoplasm

cells enlarge as vacuoles take in water

development of transverse plate

transverse cell wall breaks down

lignin is deposited in the cellulose cell wall

Xylem vessel is a continuous tube with no living contents.

Figure 12.22 *Formation of a xylem vessel*

Figure 12.22 shows how xylem vessels are formed.

The lignin can be deposited in a variety of patterns, all giving structural support and waterproofing the tube. In young stems, lignin is deposited in rings and spirals so that flexibility and further elongation of the stem are possible. In xylem vessels formed in older parts of a stem, the lignin forms an almost complete layer and is therefore more rigid, so preventing further growth.

Fibres are elongated cells, smaller than xylem vessels, with thick walls. They do not conduct water and their role is to provide mechanical strength to the xylem tissue. When mature they are dead.

Xylem parenchyma cells have thin cellulose walls and living cell contents, unlike xylem vessels and tracheids. In xylem tissue, the xylem parenchyma cells are loosely packed. Like all parenchyma cells, they provide turgidity and may store starch. Minerals that have transferred from the xylem vessel are stored here, as a means of controlling the amount reaching the leaves. The air spaces between the parenchyma cells allow gaseous exchange.

The experiment in Figure 12.24 shows evidence that xylem carries water. A celery stick is placed in water with blue dye. The coloured water passes up the xylem and colours it blue. This shows that xylem transports water up the plant, not phloem.

Tracheids are elongated single cells, with tapering end walls overlapping other tracheids. Like xylem vessels, these cells are dead and lignified. In mature tracheids, the empty lumen conduct water up the stem of the plant. Once at the end of a tracheid, water passes through pits to the next tracheid.

Tracheids are mainly found in the cone – bearing plants such as conifers. They are efficient enough to transport water from the roots to the top of tall coniferous trees. Flowering plants have fewer tracheids than xylem vessels. Their broad leaves mean they have a greater transpiration rate than conifers, and are better served by xylem vessels.

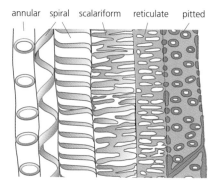

annular spiral scalariform reticulate pitted

Figure 12.23 *Different types of lignin deposition in xylem vessels*

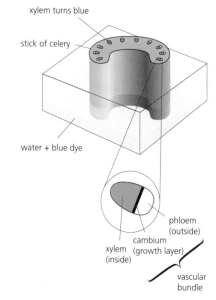

xylem turns blue

stick of celery

water + blue dye

phloem (outside)

cambium (growth layer)

xylem (inside)

vascular bundle

Figure 12.24 *Evidence that xylem carries water*

359

Figure 12.25 *Structure of phloem*

12.10 The structure of phloem

phloem L.S. (simplified and diagrammatic)

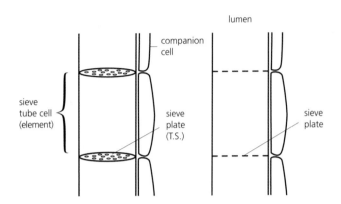

phloem T.S.

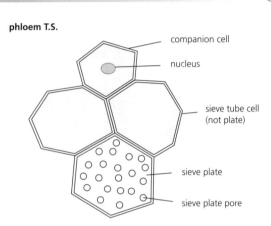

Phloem is a mixed tissue containing many types of cell. Unlike xylem it is mainly a living tissue. Phloem tissue contains:

- sieve tube elements
- companion cells
- fibres
- parenchyma cells.

Phloem sieve tube elements are elongated, with pores at each end in the cross walls, allowing for longitudinal flow of material. These pores and the polysaccharide **callose** make up the **sieve plate**. The sieve tube cells have cytoplasm with a few organelles pushed to the side. These include plastids, smooth endoplasmic reticulum, a few mitochondria but *no nucleus*. Most of the cell does not contain cytoplasmic organelles and is called the *lumen*. The lumen contains slimy sap, with strands of plasma protein running through both the lumen and the pores of the sieve plate. The callose quickly seals and blocks the sieve plates if they are damaged, to prevent loss of valuable solutes.

Companion cells are found next to the sieve tube cells. Cytoplasm is dense in the companion cells and contains a *large nucleus*, numerous mitochondria and rough endoplasmic reticulum. The many mitochondria indicate that lots of respiration takes place, releasing energy. These cells are described as **metabolically active**. The purpose of this energy is not known. Similarly, the extensive rough endoplasmic reticulum indicates that a lot of protein is synthesised and transported. The many plasmodesmata allow communication between the companion cells and the phloem sieve tube cells.

Phloem fibres are dead cells with lignified cell walls. They provide mechanical support to phloem tissue.

Phloem parenchyma cells are thin-walled, unspecialised cells which provide turgidity. Their cell walls contain cellulose which allows the transfer of water between cells. In phloem, the parenchyma cells are elongated and situated next to sieve tube elements. The loosely packed arrangement of parenchyma results in intercellular spaces which allow gas exchange.

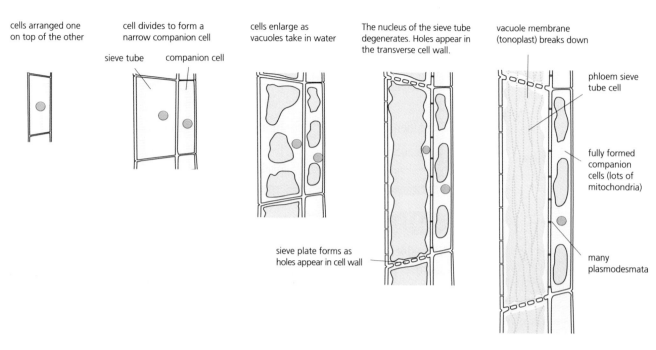

cells arranged one
on top of the other

cell divides to form a
narrow companion cell

sieve tube   companion cell

cells enlarge as
vacuoles take in water

sieve plate forms as
holes appear in cell wall

The nucleus of the sieve tube
degenerates. Holes appear in
the transverse cell wall.

vacuole membrane
(tonoplast) breaks down

phloem sieve
tube cell

fully formed
companion
cells (lots of
mitochondria)

many
plasmodesmata

Figure 12.26 *Formation of phloem tissue*

sieve plate   cellulose wall   nuclear pore

sieve tube
elements

nucleolus

nuclear membrane

nucleus

plastid

smooth
endoplasmic
reticulum

companion cell

Golgi body

mitochondrion

cytoplasm
pushed to
side of cell

rough endoplasmic
reticulum

small vacuole

callose

ribosomes

sieve pore

lumen with slimy sap
and protein strands

plasmodesmata

Figure 12.27 *Longitudinal section of a phloem sieve tube and companion cell as seen under the electron microscope*

Some of the sugar produced in photosynthesis in the leaves, is transported as **sucrose** to growth and storage centres in the rest of the plant. Growth areas include the roots, shoots and cambium. Examples of storage centres are seeds and swollen roots.

9 Why are carbohydrates transported as sugar and not starch?   *(1 mark)*

Table 12.2 *Structure of phloem tissue*

Cell type	Structure
sieve tube element	no nucleus, few organelles, less dense cytoplasm, living, cellulose cell wall
companion cell	nucleus, many organelles, dense cytoplasm, living, cellulose cell wall
phloem fibre	lignified cell walls, dead
parenchyma cells	living, thin cellulose walls, elongated, loosely packed

12.11 Translocation in the phloem – the mass flow hypothesis

Definition

Mass flow is the bulk movement of substances due to differences in pressure

Translocation is the movement of solutes from place to place. For example, sucrose, produced during photosynthesis, is translocated from the leaves to other parts of the plant in the phloem. Phloem is involved in the translocation of **organic solutes** within a plant. The solutes carried include sucrose and amino acids, which, being soluble, are carried in solution through the **phloem sieve tubes**.

The mass flow hypothesis (Figure 12.28) explains the movement of sugars and amino acids in solution from a **high-pressure** region to a **low-pressure** region, through the phloem sieve tubes. (See Table 9.3, page 245.)

High-pressure region

The leaves make sugar in photosynthesis, they are the **source** of sugar.

The sugar is actively pumped into the phloem sieve tubes, so lowering the water potential there. Water therefore enters the sieve tubes by osmosis, making them swollen and turgid. This causes *high hydrostatic pressure* in the phloem near the leaves.

Low-pressure region

Sucrose solution passes from the phloem into the root cells where the sugar is either respired or converted into starch; in other words sugar is removed. Roots can be described as **sinks** as sugar is removed. Growth regions of a plant also use up sugar and can also be described as sinks.

Sucrose passes from the phloem into these sink areas followed by water from the sieve tubes, due to osmosis. As there is less water in the sieve tube cells, this produces a *lower hydrostatic pressure* there.

As the sugar present in the roots and growth areas decreases, the water potential increases. Water leaves sink areas, like the roots, passing to cells with a lower water potential, including the xylem vessel, by osmosis. With less water present, the hydrostatic pressure falls.

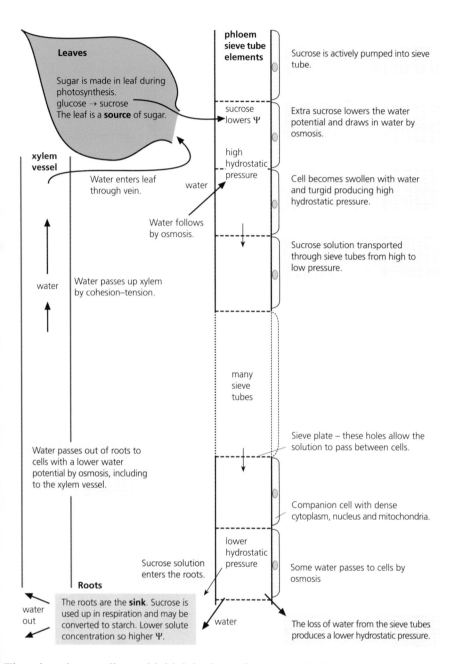

Figure 12.28 *Diagram showing the mass flow hypothesis*

Thus there is a gradient with high hydrostatic pressure in the sieve tubes close to leaves, the source of sugar, and a lower hydrostatic pressure in sieve tubes close to sinks. As the two areas are linked by phloem, liquid flows from high to low pressure, transporting solutes in solution. The liquid is under pressure and if a hole is punctured through to the phloem, the cell sap oozes out. This indicates a **positive pressure**, as it is above atmospheric pressure.

Figure 12.29 A summary of the transport system in plants

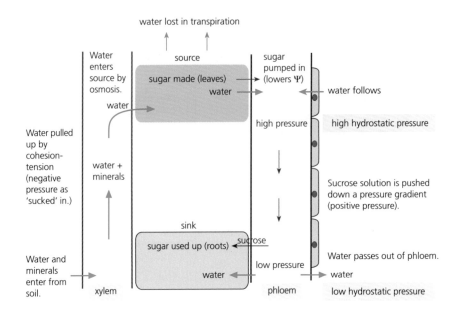

Translocation and transfer cells

Some of the parenchyma cells in the leaf have a very large surface area, due to infolding of the cell wall and cell surface membrane. These specialised cells are the **transfer cells**. Transfer cells are thought to be responsible for moving sucrose from mesophyll cells in the leaf, where sugar is made, into phloem sieve tubes. The process is active and transfer cells provide the energy required.

Figure 12.30 shows the transfer and associated cells from a small vein in the leaf.

Figure 12.30 Diagram to show the position and function of transfer cells in the vein of a leaf

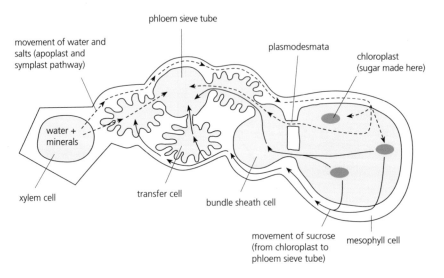

The movement of materials is shown by arrows and involves the apoplast (cell wall) and symplast (cytoplasm) pathways.

In addition, transfer cells carry water and salts from the xylem vessels to both mesophyll cells and phloem sieve tube cells. Wherever active transport occurs in plants, transfer cells may be present to provide the necessary energy. Plants without transfer cells acquire the energy for active transport from other cells.

12.12 Investigating translocation

Translocation can be investigated using **aphids** and **radioactivity**.

Aphids (greenfly) can feed on phloem contents using specialised mouthparts called **stylets**, which are long thin tubes used for feeding. The aphids puncture the phloem wall and penetrate into the sieve tube element where they gain access to the **phloem sap**. The aphid's body can then be removed, leaving the stylet penetrating the phloem (Figure 12.31).

If the aphid's body is removed, leaving the stylets in position, the sap oozes out under **pressure**. This demonstrates that the phloem contents are carried under pressure, so supporting the mass flow hypothesis.

Analysis of the phloem contents shows the presence of sucrose and amino acids in solution, and confirms that these are transported through the phloem sieve tubes.

Radioactive carbon in $^{14}CO_2$ can be supplied to a leaf. When radioctive carbon dioxide is supplied to a leaf, radioactive sucrose appears in the phloem. This shows that the radioactive carbon dioxide taken up by the leaf is used in photosynthesis to make sugar that is radioactive, as it contains the radioactive carbon. Radioactive substances can be detected using a **Geiger counter** and by autoradiography.

Using aphid stylets it is possible to find out when radioactive carbon appears in the phloem and in what form. It is therefore possible to trace the movement of radioactive materials through the phloem (Figure 12.32).

Investigating the speed of movement
When radioactive sucrose first appears in the sap from a stylet at X in Figure 12.32, the time taken for radioactive sucrose to appear in the sap at Y can be recorded, and the distance between them measured.

$$\text{speed} = \frac{\text{distance}}{\text{time}}$$

Thus the speed at which sucrose is translocated can be calculated.

This method can be used to find out the speed at which many solutes are carried in the phloem. It has been found that different solutes are not all carried at the same speed, which is hard to explain using the mass flow hypothesis.

Investigating the direction of movement
The distribution of radioactivity within a plant can be used to investigate the direction radioactive sucrose moves in the phloem.

Figure 12.33 shows the result of **autoradiography** of a plant where one leaf was provided with radioactive carbon dioxide. Autoradiography can be used to demonstrate which parts of a plant are radioactive. This procedure detects and displays radioactivity by the 'fogging' of X-ray film, so radioactive sections appear darker.

When radioactive carbon in $^{14}CO_2$ was supplied to one leaf, radioactive sucrose appeared both *above* and *below* the leaf supplied. This means that sucrose must be carried both up and down the phloem; in other words, it is a two-way system.

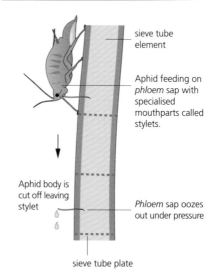

sieve tube element

Aphid feeding on *phloem* sap with specialised mouthparts called stylets.

Aphid body is cut off leaving stylet

Phloem sap oozes out under pressure

sieve tube plate

Figure 12.31 *Use of feeding aphids to investigate the mass flow hypothesis*

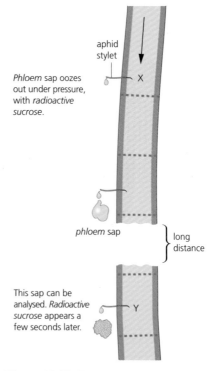

aphid stylet

Phloem sap oozes out under pressure, with *radioactive sucrose.*

X

phloem sap

long distance

This sap can be analysed. *Radioactive sucrose* appears a few seconds later.

Y

Figure 12.32 *Experiment to investigate translocation using aphids and radioactivity*

Mass flow describes the movement of sucrose solution from high to low pressure. High pressure will be found in the leaves, the source of sugar, and the leaves are mainly found near the top of the plant. Roots, at the bottom of the plant, will have lower pressure, resulting generally in the movement of solutes from the top to the bottom of a plant.

However, growth areas are also **sinks**. These areas are found right at the top of the plant, above the leaves. These sink areas will also have a lower hydrostatic pressure, resulting in solutes being carried up the phloem from the higher pressure in the leaves. This means that solutes are carried both up and down the phloem and this can be explained by the mass flow hypothesis.

A transverse section of the stem (Figure 12.33) shows radioactivity only in the phloem, which indicates that the radioactive sucrose is translocated only in the phloem, not in the xylem.

Further evidence that translocation takes place in the phloem
This can be investigated using a **ringing** method. Ringed plants have the outer part of their stems removed. As the phloem is on the outer part of the stem, the phloem is removed but not the xylem (Figure 12.33).

In the experiment shown in Figure 12.33, two privet plants were used. One plant had been ringed above the leaf supplied with $^{14}CO_2$, the other stem was uncut and therefore the phloem was complete. The results of autoradiography showed that the unringed shoot had become radioactive throughout the plant. Transverse sections at A–B and C–D both contained radioactive phloem under

Figure 12.33 *Ringed and unringed shoots of privet*

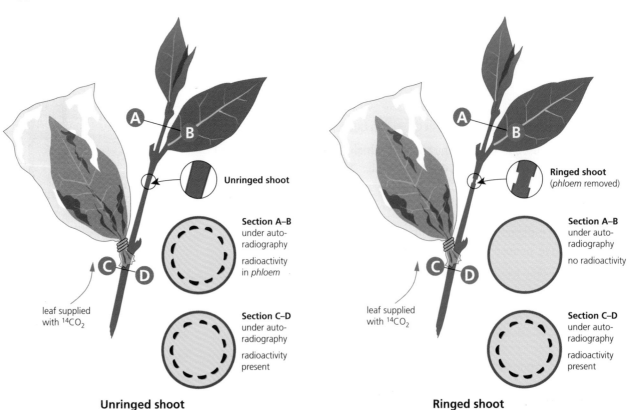

Unringed shoot

Ringed shoot

autoradiography. This demonstrates that phloem contents are carried both up and down the stem. Transverse sections of the ringed shoot were only radioactive in section C–D below the ringed area, not in section A–B. Ringing and removing the phloem blocked the movement of radioactive sucrose. Sucrose was able to move freely all over the plant with complete phloem, making the whole plant radioactive.

This experiment demonstrates that sucrose is carried in the phloem. It also shows that sucrose is translocated both up and down the phloem. If sucrose were carried in the xylem then the sucrose would have travelled to all parts of the ringed and unringed plant, as the xylem was complete in both.

10 When carrying out an experiment like the one in Figure 12.33, what factors must be controlled to make the results reliable?   *(2 marks)*

The sugar concentration in the plant varies according to the time of day. Increased sucrose levels lower the water potential and cause the build-up of hydrostatic pressure. As sugar is only produced during daylight hours, pressure differences and therefore mass flow should only take place during the day and this appears to be confirmed by experiments.

The graph in Figure 12.34 shows the following:

● Phloem has the highest levels of sugar, then the leaf, with xylem having the lowest levels.

● Xylem has a fairly constant, low level of sugar.

● The amount of sugar in the leaf varies during the 24 hours, rising during daylight hours (due to photosynthesis).

● The amount of sugar in the phloem follows a similar pattern to the leaf.

● The similar patterns in the leaf and the phloem suggest that sugar passes from the leaf to the phloem, as the sugar rises in the leaf first. As the phloem has a higher concentration of sugar than the leaf, it suggets that the sugar has been transferred to the phloem by active transport.

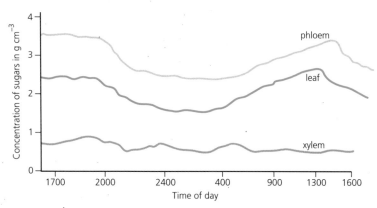

Figure 12.34 Changes in sugar concentration in sugarbeet over 24 hours

Evidence for the mass flow hypothesis

- There is a higher concentration of sucrose in the leaves and a lower concentration in the roots.
- Sucrose solution is flowing under pressure, shown by phloem oozing from aphid stylets which penetrate the phloem.
- Some chemicals applied to the leaves are only translocated when light is present. Light allows photosynthesis and the build-up of sugar which attracts water, causing high hydrostatic pressure, only during daylight hours.
- When leaves are shaded, no translocation takes place in the phloem, as no pressure differences occur at night since no sugar is made.
- When sucrose increases in the leaf, this is followed by an increase of sucrose in the phloem, suggesting it is transferred from leaf to phloem (Figure 12.34).
- A rise in sucrose concentration in the phloem occurs with increasing light intensity, suggesting a direct link between light intensity, leaf and phloem.

Evidence against the mass flow hypothesis

- Mass flow is passive and so does not need ATP, except where sugar is pumped into the sieve tube.
- Companion cells have lots of mitochondria producing ATP with no obvious function.
- Use of potassium cyanide, a metabolic poison which stops respiration, also stops translocation, which suggests that it is an active process.
- If solutes are carried along a pressure gradient, they should all be carried at the same speed, but they are not.
- Role of sieve plates is unclear; mass flow would improve without them.

Box 12.2 Features of phloem and xylem

	Xylem vessel	Phloem sieve tube cell	Phloem companion cell
nucleus	no	no	yes
living cytoplasm	no	yes	yes
empty lumen	yes	no	no
lignin in walls	yes	no	no
cellulose in walls	yes	yes	yes
sieve plate	no	yes	no
transports organic solutes	no	yes	no
role in support	yes	no	no
transports water & inorganic salts	yes	no	no
mitochondria present	no	yes	yes

Remember

Movement in both xylem and phloem is an example of mass flow, when substances move due to differences in pressure

Summary – ⑫ Transport in flowering plants

- Stomata are essential for the entry and exit of gases for gas exchange.
- The gas exchange surface is permeable for the diffusion of gases (and water) across a membrane.
- Some moisture evaporates from the moist spongy mesophyll cells into the air spaces in the leaf.
- It is moist inside leaves and generally drier outside.
- Water vapour diffuses out from the moist leaf to the drier air – this is transpiration.
- Transpiration is a consequence of open stomata and the need for gas exchange.
- Stomata can be closed to reduce water loss but this affects gas exchange.
- Leaf structure and the distribution of stomata are a compromise between efficient gas exchange and the need to reduce water loss.
- Xylem carries water and inorganic salts from the roots to the shoot tips. It is a one-way flow caused mainly by the loss of water in transpiration.
- Water evaporates from leaves.
- There is a strong cohesion or attraction between water molecules.
- This means that a column of water is difficult to break.
- Evaporation of water from leaves (transpiration) pulls a column of water through the xylem vessels.
- The water column is under tension or negative pressure.
- Tension is caused by water being pulled up by the force of transpiration and being dragged down by gravity.
- The combined forces of cohesion and tension pull water up through the xylem vessels.
- Phloem carries organic molecules such as sucrose and amino acids from the source of sugar, the leaves, to roots or growth areas, the sinks.
- Leaves are the source of sugar.
- Sugar is actively pumped into phloem.
- This lowers the water potential in the phloem, making it lower than adjacent cells.
- Water moves by osmosis into the phloem due to the lowered water potential.
- The phloem sieve tubes swell, producing a high hydrostatic pressure.
- Sinks are areas of a plant where sugar is removed, e.g. roots and growth regions.
- Water and sugar leave the sieve tube to pass into the roots.
- This produces a lower hydrostatic pressure in the phloem far from the leaves.
- There is therefore a difference in hydrostatic pressure in the phloem tube.
- Sucrose solution is carried in phloem sieve tube cells from high to low hydrostatic pressure.
- This is a two-way flow as movement takes place both up and down the phloem, from the leaves.
- Both the transport of water in the xylem and organic solutes in the phloem are examples of mass flow as they are movements caused by differences in pressure.

❓ Answers

1 Having stomata on the upper surface allows gases from the air to enter the leaf. There is more oxygen and carbon dioxide in the air than in water, so stomata on the upper surface can provide more of these gases for respiration and photosynthesis. Losing water in transpiration is not a problem for aquatic plants *(2)*.

2 Wind speed increases as you move up a hill which will increase the rate of transpiration. Shorter plants are less affected by wind and therefore will be more successful than taller plants at reducing water loss. Also the soil gets thinner near the top of a hill which makes it harder for roots to penetrate. Only shallow roots can gain firm anchorage and these can only support a smaller tree *(2)*.

3 In waterlogged conditions, roots are unable to absorb much oxygen and respiration will be anaerobic. This produces little ATP, which is necessary for active transport. Consequently active transport will cease and mineral ions will only enter by diffusion, which does not require energy. The concentration of mineral ions in the plant will therefore not be higher than the concentration in the soil *(3)*.

4 Where the concentration of ions is higher in the alga than in the pond water, the ions must enter by active transport, moving from a lower concentration in the pond to a higher concentration in the alga. This requires energy in the form of ATP. Some ions are found in the alga at much higher concentrations than others and this is not related to the concentration in the pond. For example, the concentration of chloride ions in the alga reaches a much higher concentration in the alga than the other ions, but is not present in greater concentration in the pond. The level of potassium ions reaches $0.05\,mol\,dm^3$ in the alga, the second-highest concentration, but is present in the pond at the lowest level, showing the plant is being selective in its uptake *(2)*.

5 Diffusion is when molecules move from where they are in high concentration to where they are in lower concentration and this process is passive, not requiring an input of energy. With active transport, molecules move from low to high concentration and this active process does require an input of energy *(2)*.

6 In moist air, beech roots are able to take in oxygen for aerobic respiration, resulting in the production of lots of energy in the form of ATP. In these conditions active transport can take place and phosphate can pass from a low concentration to a higher concentration in the roots, reaching 8 units of phosphate in the root. In pure nitrogen, oxygen is absent and aerobic respiration cannot take place. Little ATP is produced and active transport which requires energy cannot take place. As a result phosphate can only enter by diffusion and levels in the root are low, 0.5 units *(3)*.

7 If a hole was made in the xylem, air would enter due to the low pressure in the vessel. Air would pass from the higher pressure in the air to the lower pressure in the xylem caused by the suction of the transpiration pull *(2)*.

8 When the transpiration rate is high, the diameter of the branch is small. This is due to the loss of water at the top, sucking up more water by cohesion–tension. The negative pressure caused by transpiration narrows the xylem vessels, causing a reduction in the diameter of the branch. Conversely, when the transpiration rate is low, the diameter of the branch is bigger as less suction and less negative pressure are produced *(2)*.

9 Starch is insoluble and cannot be transported, it would block the narrow tubes. Sugar is soluble and can be transported in solution *(1)*.

10 The privet must be the same species and age and provided with the same amount of radioactive carbon dioxide, to a leaf in a similar position. The leaves must be left for the same length of time in the same conditions of light, water and minerals *(2)*.

End of Chapter Questions

1 What is transpiration? Name three environmental factors which will increase the rate of transpiration. *(2 marks)*

2 What evidence is there that root hairs take in ions by active transport? *(2 marks)*

3 Refer to Table 12.3 and Figure 12.35.

Table 12.3 *Concentration of potassium ions in arbitrary units*

Cell	Stoma closed	Stoma open
guard cell	94	450
A	158	295
B	201	99
C	451	72

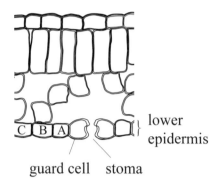

Figure 12.35 *How plants open and close their stomata (t.s. leaf)*

(a) By what process do potassium ions move from cell A into the guard cell during the day? Explain your answer. *(2 marks)*

(b) How does a high concentration of ions affect the water potential of a cell? *(1 mark)*

(c) Use the information in the table to explain the mechanism used by plants to open their stomata. *(3 marks)*

(Total 6 marks)

4 In summer, the diameter of a branch is smaller at midday than at midnight. Explain this observation. *(4 marks)*

5 A mutation caused a tree to have equal numbers of stomata on both upper and lower surfaces of its leaves. It died before reaching maturity. Why? *(2 marks)*

6 If a plant is ringed at ground level, the roots wither and die. Can you explain why? *(2 marks)*

7 The drawing shows a 24-hour cycle for the opening and closing of stomata from the same plant.

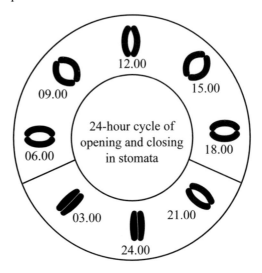

(a) Explain how this cycle of opening and closing of stomata is advantageous to the plant.
(2 marks)

(b) The diagram shows the potassium (K⁺) ion concentrations in the cells around an open and closed stoma in *Commelina*. The concentrations are in arbitrary units.

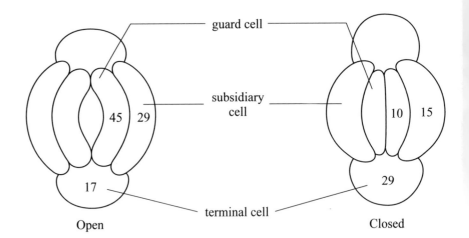

(i) Explain how the movement of K⁺ ions accounts for the opening of the stoma.
(3 marks)

(ii) Explain how K⁺ ions are moved against a concentration gradient.
(2 marks)

NEAB 1998
(Total 7 marks)

The diagram below shows a longitudinal section of two cells of phloem tissue in a plant stem.

cell A 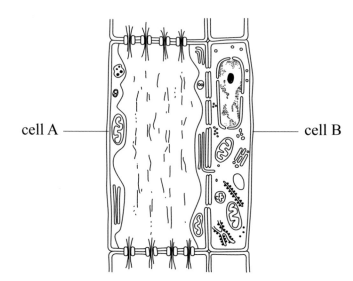 cell B

(a) Name the cells labelled A and B in the diagram.   *(2 marks)*

(b) (i) State the function of phloem in a plant.   *(1 mark)*

(ii) Describe how aphids can be used to investigate the function of phloem
    (3 marks)

London 1998   *(Total 6 marks)*

9 The diagram represents the mass flow hypothesis which explains the movement of substances in the phloem.

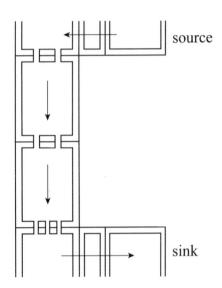

(a) Suggest a plant organ which is a sink. *(1 mark)*

(b) There are companion cells alongside the phloem sieve tubes in a stem. Explain why this does **not** support the mass flow hypothesis. *(2 marks)*

(c) Radioactively labelled molecules applied to illuminated leaves were rapidly transported out of the leaves by the phloem. Radioactively labelled molecules applied to shaded leaves were not transported. Explain how the mass flow hypothesis accounts for these observations. *(2 marks)*

AEB 1997

(Total 5 marks)

13 Heterotrophic nutrition

Nutrition is one of the seven features found in all living things. Animals and plants need food to provide energy, for growth and other life processes. Green plants synthesise their own food by photosynthesis – autotrophic nutrition. Other organisms, including humans, have heterotrophic nutrition. There are different types of heterotrophic nutrition but in each case large complex molecules are broken down (digested) to simpler substances which are then used to build up the molecules the organism requires.

Humans either eat plants, other animals or both. The food that is ingested or taken in, is broken down to smaller, soluble molecules during the process of digestion which takes place in the gut. These smaller molecules are then absorbed through the villi in the small intestine and enter the blood. Digestive enzymes, like amylase, speed up the process of digestion. Heterotrophic organisms depend directly or indirectly upon autotrophs such as photosynthesising green plants as the source of organic molecules. In the food chain heterotrophs are the consumers and decomposers depending ultimately upon the autotrophic producers.

This chapter includes:
- types of heterotrophic nutrition
- components of the human diet
- the structure of the human gut in relation to its function
- digestion in humans
- saprobiontic nutrition in *Rhizopus stolonifera*
- parasitic nutrition in *Taenia solium*
- mutualistic nutrition in *Rhizobium*

Definition

Heterotrophic nutrition involves the breaking down of complex organic molecules into smaller, soluble molecules which can be absorbed to provide the energy and nutrients required for survival and growth

13.1 Types of heterotrophic nutrition

There are four types of heterotrophic nutrition as follows.

Holozoic nutrition is mainly characteristic of more complex animals including mammals, e.g. humans. It involves digesting food inside the body in an alimentary canal or gut.

Saprobiontic (saprophytic) nutrition: the organism feeds on dead organic matter and digestion occurs externally – outside of the organism. Decomposers such as bacteria and fungi are saprobiontic, e.g. *Rhizopus* (see Section 13.7, page 400).

Parasitic nutrition: the parasite obtains food from another living organism, the host, e.g., *Taenia* (see Section 13.8, page 403).

Mutualistic nutrition involves a relationship between organisms from two different species where both gain a nutritional benefit, e.g. *Rhizobium* and legumes (see Section 13.9, page 405).

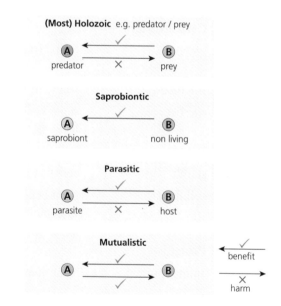

Figure 13.1 *Summary of heterotrophic nutritional relationships*

1 Identify the types of nutrition described for species X and Y, i.e. whether holozoic, saprobiontic, parasitic or mutualistic.
Fungi do not have a gut. One species, X, can be seen as white patches on the sides of living goldfish. X feeds on the goldfish tissue and can eventually kill the fish. Y is a different species of fungus which only feeds on the bodies of dead fish.

(2 marks)

13.2 The balanced diet in humans

 Definition

A **balanced diet** provides adequate amounts of all nutrients to maintain good health – not too much and not too little

To maintain good health, the human diet should have the correct balance of the following nutrients:

- carbohydrates and lipids to provide energy
- proteins for growth and repair
- vitamins, mineral ions and water.

Fibre is also required but it is not classified as a nutrient because it is not digested and absorbed.

The sources and functions of these components are given in Tables 13.1 and 13.2. Details of their biochemistry are given in Chapter 3.

Table 13.1 *Some components of the human diet*

Component	Source in the diet	Function in the body
Carbohydrates		
glucose	fruits, fruit juices, honey	main source of energy – main substrate for respiration
fructose	fruits, fruit juices, honey	source of energy
sucrose	sugar cane, sugarbeet, refined (table) sugar, fruits	source of energy
lactose	milk	source of energy
starch	cereals (e.g. wheat, rice), bread, potatoes	source of energy
cellulose	plant cell walls, particularly from fruits and vegetables	component of fibre – adds bulk to food and helps passage through gut; also helps lower cholesterol level
Proteins		
animal protein	meat, liver, fish, milk, cheese, eggs	source of amino acids to make body protein for growth and repair
plant protein	cereals, beans, peas, bread	
Lipids		
unsaturated fats	most fats and oils from plants, e.g. olive oil, nut oil, nuts	energy source; energy store; thermal insulation under skin; protective cushioning around organs; needed for cell membranes; source of fat-soluble vitamins
saturated fats	most fats and oils from animals, e.g. meat, eggs, cheese	
Water	drinks and in food such as salads and fruits	needed for blood, lymph and tissue fluid. Cell reactions take place in aqueous solution

Name	Source in the diet	Function in the body	Problems caused by deficiency
Vitamins			
A (retinol)	milk and cheese; liver; fish oil; green vegetables and carrots contain carotene which is converted to retinol	needed for vision – component of rhodopsin – and for healthy epithelial tissues	night blindness
B3 nicotinic acid (niacin)	meat; wholemeal bread; potatoes; yeast extract	component of the coenzyme NAD which is essential for respiration	pellagra; skin disease; diarrhoea
C (ascorbic acid)	potatoes; green vegetables	needed for healthy connective tissue, e.g. collagen	scurvy; wounds do not heal; anaemia
D (calciferol)	liver, fish oils, milk and cheese, action of sunlight upon skin	growth of bones and teeth because needed for absorption of calcium and phosphorus	rickets – defective bones
Mineral ions			
calcium (Ca^{2+})	cheese, bread, milk, eggs	bones and teeth; muscle contraction; nerve function; blood clotting	badly formed bones; rickets; muscle spasms
phosphorus (phosphate) (PO_4^{3-})	milk, cheese	bones and teeth; component of ATP, DNA and RNA	not usually deficient
iron (Fe^{2+}, Fe^{3+})	red meat, beans, eggs	component of haemoglobin	anaemia

Table 13.2 *Selected vitamins and mineral ions*

! Did You Know

In August 2000 a huge cod (44 kg) was caught in the seas off Australia. When the fish was cut open the complete head of a man was found in its stomach! So far his identity has not been discovered.

Box 13.1 Dietary reference values

Dietary reference values (DRVs) are tables of values compiled by the government. They list the daily quantities for food energy and selected other nutrients required by different population groups to maintain health. (Table 13.3).

Age	Energy MJ/d	Protein g/d	Vitamin A µg/d	Nicotinic acid mg/d	Vitamin C mg/d	Vitamin D µg/d	Calcium mg/d	Iron mg/d
Males								
0–3 months	2.28	12.5	350	3	25	8.5	525	1.7
4–6 years	7.16	19.7	500	11	30	–	450	6.1
15–18 years	11.51	55.2	700	18	40	–	1000	11.3
19–50 years	10.60	55.5	700	17	40	–	700	8.7
over 75 years	8.77	53.3	700	16	40	10	700	8.7
Females								
0–3 months	2.16	12.5	350	3	25	8.5	525	1.7
4–6 years	6.46	19.7	500	11	30	–	450	6.1
15–18 years	8.83	45.0	600	14	40	–	800	14.8
19–50 years	8.10	45.0	600	13	40	–	700	14.8
Over 75 years	7.61	46.5	600	12	40	10	700	8.7
Pregnancy	+0.80	+6.0	+100	Same	+10.0	10	Same	Same
Lactation	+2.4	+9.5	+350	2.0	+30.0	10	+550	Same

(Adapted from the Department of Health 1991: *Dietary Reference Values for Food Energy and Nutrients for the UK*)

Table 13.3 *Dietary reference values (DRVs) for food energy and selected nutrients for population groups in the UK*

For any particular individual the required quantities of nutrients will vary depending upon factors such as age, sex, level of activity and pregnancy and lactation. These factors have been taken into account to compile **dietary reference values** (DRVs). Tables of the values provide recommended nutrient levels for different categories of people. DRVs are defined in Box 13.1.

Some of the main features of the requirements for different groups are given in Table 13.4. It should be noted that DRVs are recommendations for groups of people. Any particular individual should only use them as a guideline. For example, the energy requirements are set at the mean level for the group. For some individuals in the group this level will be too high and could lead to obesity.

Individuals at risk of health problems caused by nutrition should seek specialist help related to their own particular circumstances.

Population group	Nutritional requirements
pregnant female	increased need for energy and protein for growth of fetus
	increased need for calcium and vitamin D for growth of bones for fetus
	increased need for iron by fetus for blood formation
lactating female (breastfeeding)	as for pregnancy but higher levels
infants	energy requirements increase with increased activity
	increased protein required for growth
	increases in calcium and vitamin D for growth of bones
puberty	energy and protein requirements peak in the late teens
	peak requirements also for calcium for bone growth
	for females the onset of menstruation increases the requirements for iron to make blood
old age	the need for vitamins and minerals remains constant
	protein and energy requirements fall
	a reduction in energy foods, particularly lipids, can cause a reduction in intake of essential vitamins and minerals. For example, there is a risk of osteoporosis (brittle bones) due to a lack of vitamin D – a fat-soluble vitamin

Table 13.4 *Nutritional requirements for different population groups*

Box 13.2 Exercise and diet – the nutritional requirements of a training programme

The precise requirements will vary depending upon the type of sport or exercise. Certain general features include the following.

All exercise requires energy for muscle contraction and so energy intake will usually need to be higher without causing any unnecessary weight gain. Additional carbohydrate is usually preferable to increasing the intake of lipids, particularly saturated fats with their possible effect on heart disease. Carbohydrates can also be respired more efficiently than lipid.

Some sports, e.g. weight lifting, involve increasing muscle bulk and additional protein intake will be required for muscle growth.

All training programmes require careful maintenance of a balanced diet including fresh fruit and vegetables. Any changes of intake should not lead to a lack of essential nutrients such as vitamins. For example, a lack of Vitamin B$_3$ – nicotinic acid – can affect the efficiency of cell respiration and therefore the provision of energy for muscle contraction.

One result of regular training can be to increase the capacity of the muscles to store the polysaccharide glycogen. During longer periods of exercise glycogen is the main source of energy for respiration. Some long-distance runners and other endurance athletes undergo a process called glycogen (or carbohydrate) loading before a race. A few days of relatively low carbohydrate intake are followed by a few days of high intake. This can increase the glycogen stored in muscle from 15 g to 25 g per kg of muscle.

Box 13.3 Frederick Hopkins and the vitamin hypothesis

Hopkins (1861–1947) worked at Cambridge University and carried out the first-ever general scientific study of vitamins. In a famous experiment in 1912 Hopkins investigated the effects of giving small supplements of milk to young rats in addition to their basic food.

Milk provides an almost complete diet of carbohydrates, fats, proteins, minerals and a variety of vitamins. By providing the supplement of milk Hopkins was providing vitamins missing from the rats' diet and demonstrating the importance of vitamins for health and growth.

Now try the End of Chapter Question **3**, page 409.

13.3 Components of the human diet

Food and energy

Energy is needed for the following:

- growth and maintenance of body tissues
- maintenance of body temperature
- voluntary muscle action, e.g. walking, exercise
- involuntary muscle action, e.g. heartbeat.

Energy balance involves comparing energy intake from food with energy output – growth, muscle action etc. If intake exceeds output the person is likely to gain weight as excess energy from food is stored as fat. If output exceeds intake, weight *loss* is likely to occur. By adjusting intake and output it should be possible for most individuals to maintain a *constant* body weight.

Carbohydrates

These include sugars and starchy foods such as potatoes and rice. Carbohydrates are the main source of energy in the diet. Starch and disaccharide sugars are broken down to monosaccharides, particularly the hexose sugar glucose. Glucose is the main respiratory substrate. Although not digested, the polysaccharide cellulose is also an important component of the diet. It provides the main type of **fibre**, certain levels of which are necessary for health. Apart from fibre no specific types of carbohydrate are essential in the diet as long as overall energy requirements are met.

Lipids

These include oils and fats. They are a source of energy but they also have other important functions. Excess lipid is stored under the skin and around internal organs as fat. Here it acts as an energy store but also provides thermal insulation and mechanical cushioning. Lipids are also an essential component of cell membranes (see Section 2.2, page 38). Dietary lipid helps us obtain vital fat-soluble vitamins, e.g. vitamin A.

Most fatty acids can be synthesised in the body but a few, known as **essential fatty acids**, cannot and must be obtained in the diet. A lack of essential fatty acids will cause ill health.

The types of lipid we eat are important for another reason. Reducing the level of **saturated fatty acids** and replacing them with **unsaturated fatty acids** can help reduce the risk of heart disease.

Proteins

These are essential for growth and repair. They are digested to amino acids which are then used by the body to build up new tissues and to repair damage. Important metabolic proteins such as enzymes and hormones also need to be constantly replaced. Approximately 4% of the total body protein needs to be replaced each day, so a certain quantity of protein in the diet is essential for health.

The body requires a supply of twenty different amino acids. Eleven of these are **non-essential** as they can be produced in the body by transamination from other amino acids. The other nine are **essential amino acids** and need to be obtained from the diet.

Generally animal protein provides more of these essential amino acids than plant protein. However, by eating a wide range of plant proteins vegetarians can obtain all of the necessary essential amino acids. The terms *first-class* and *second-class* protein are often used to indicate the range of amino acids, particularly essential amino acids, which are present in a particular source of protein. Meat and eggs would be examples of first-class proteins and cereals such as rice or wheat examples of second-class. If essential amino acids are missing from the diet, proteins such as certain enzymes cannot be synthesised properly, causing ill health.

Water

Water is essential as a component of body fluids such as blood but also because all chemical reactions in cells occur in aqueous solution. Daily water gain and loss is shown in Table 13.5. Note that some water is produced in metabolic reactions, particularly cell respiration. This can be an important source of water for desert animals. Also note the relatively high loss from breathing out.

Vitamins

Humans require a number of vitamins. The details of four of these are given as examples in Table 13.2 on page 377.

Mineral ions

Many different mineral ions are required for the healthy functioning of the body. They are usually divided into two groups: macronutrients, e.g. calcium and phosphate, required in larger quantities and micronutrients (or trace elements) required in smaller quantities, e.g. iron. Three of the mineral ions are given as examples in Table 13.2, page 377.

Definition

Essential amino acids cannot be made in the body and must be obtained in the diet

Table 13.5 Water gain and loss over 24 hours for an adult human

% gain		% loss	
drinking	47	urine	59
in food	39	faeces	4
metabolic reactions	14	evaporation from lungs (breathing out)	35
		sweating	2
total gain	100	total loss	100

N.B. the percentage loss for sweating is very variable depending upon air temperature and the level of activity. As this varies it will affect the other percentages for loss.

Definition

Vitamins are essential nutrients that are needed in small quantities for the healthy functioning of the body. Most of them cannot be made by the body and so must be included in the diet. A shortage of a vitamin causes a deficiency disease.

Definition

Specific **mineral ions** are required in small quantities in the diet for a wide range of functions to maintain the healthy functioning of the body. Examples include calcium, phosphate and iron

Box 13.4 Malnutrition

Malnutrition is nutrition which deviates from normal. It involves an unbalanced diet, that is a diet which does not provide the correct balance of nutrients. Malnutrition can be divided into undernutrition and overnutrition.

Undernutrition

Energy and protein deficiency

Kwashiorkor and marasmus are diseases involving a shortage of both protein and energy. Both are often found in developing countries associated with poverty and/or famine. Kwashiorkor is mainly due to a severe lack of protein in the diet and its symptoms include swelling (oedema) of the belly and legs, flaky skin and a loss of muscle bulk. Marasmus is mainly caused by a very low energy intake. Sufferers are very underweight, have thin arms and legs and a shrunken facial appearance. Treatment for both involves gradually increasing the intake of energy and protein foods.

Anorexia nervosa

This is an eating disorder whose causes are mainly psychological. Mass-media stereotypes, thin supermodels for example, may be a contributory cause, providing social pressure to conform to an ideal of slimness. It usually occurs in relatively well-off families in developed countries and mainly affects teenage girls and women in their early twenties. Sufferers have an obsession with weight loss, which becomes excessive. They have a distorted self-image, seeing themselves as very overweight even when in reality they are very thin.

Very little food is eaten, leading to severe weight loss with loss of muscle bulk and very thin arms and legs. In females menstrual periods may also stop. Treatment is usually a slow and complex process involving the whole family. Some form of counselling may be required to deal with the underlying psychological and emotional problems.

Overnutrition – obesity

Diets can also be unbalanced if food intake is in excess of requirements. We gain weight when energy intake in food exceeds the energy output required for growth, for keeping warm and for exercise. The excess energy is stored as fat. If we are between 110% and 120% of ideal weight (obtainable from published tables), this is categorised as being overweight. Obesity is defined as being over 120% of ideal weight. A more accurate measure involves estimating body fat by using calipers to record skinfold thickness.

People who are overweight or obese have an increased risk of many health problems including: coronary heart disease (see Box 10.5, page 289); high blood pressure; diabetes; cancer; gall bladder disease; strain and damage to the skeleton and joints. Reducing weight needs to involve both increasing energy output by increasing exercise and decreasing energy intake by eating less food.

Dieting should be done carefully as very restricted (crash) diets may be lacking vital nutrients, e.g vitamins or essential fatty acids.

The influence of diet on coronary heart disease, high blood pressure and strokes are considered in Box 10.5, page 289.

The structure of the human alimentary canal (the gut)

The gut is a tube, approximately 10 metres long in adults, which runs from mouth to anus and which is divided into different sections. The tube encloses a space called a **lumen** through which the food passes. The layout of the gut is shown in Figure 13.2. Together with the liver and the pancreas it makes up the digestive system.

Figure 13.2 *The human alimentary canal (gut)*

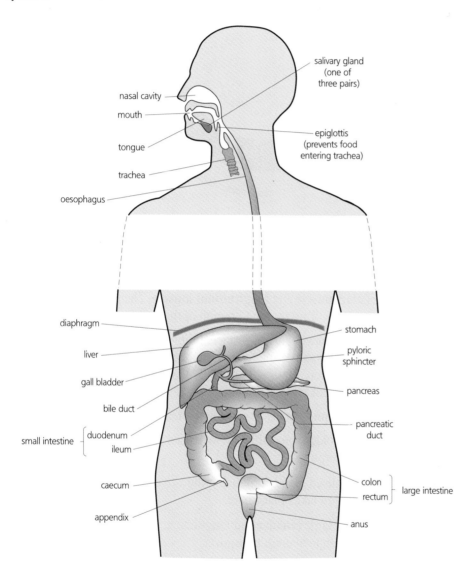

salivary gland (one of three pairs)

nasal cavity

mouth

tongue

epiglottis (prevents food entering trachea)

trachea

oesophagus

diaphragm

liver

gall bladder

bile duct

small intestine { duodenum, ileum }

caecum

appendix

stomach

pyloric sphincter

pancreas

pancreatic duct

colon

rectum

large intestine

anus

***Figure 13.3** The generalised structure of the human gut wall showing features found in different regions of the gut, particularly some of the different types of gland*

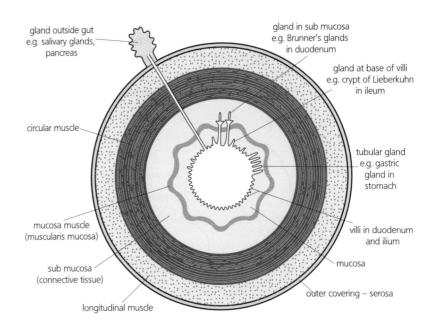

gland outside gut e.g. salivary glands, pancreas

gland in sub mucosa e.g. Brunner's glands in duodenum

gland at base of villi e.g. crypt of Lieberkuhn in ileum

circular muscle

tubular gland e.g. gastric gland in stomach

villi in duodenum and ilium

mucosa

outer covering – serosa

mucosa muscle (muscularis mucosa)

sub mucosa (connective tissue)

longitudinal muscle

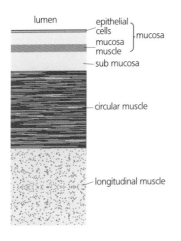

lumen

epithelial cells
mucosa muscle
} mucosa

sub mucosa

circular muscle

longitudinal muscle

***Figure 13.4** Structure of the gut wall of the oesophagus*

The different sections of the gut are specialised for different functions but the basic structure of the gut wall is similar throughout. It is composed of four main layers which can be seen in Figure 13.3. These four layers are the **mucosa**, the **sub mucosa**, **circular muscle** and **longitudinal muscle**. The relative sizes and shapes of each layer vary from region to region of the gut.

The mucosa is the inside layer and its surface, lining the lumen, is the **mucosa epithelium**. The structure and adaptations of these epithelial cells are important for digestion and absorption. Figures 13.4, 13.5, 13.6 and 13.7 show the structure of the gut wall for different regions of the gut.

The gut wall of the **oesophagus** has the following features:

● The mucosa is *not* folded into **villi** – an increased surface area is not required for digestion or absorption.

● There are *no* specialised glands producing digestive secretions (only mucus glands) – no digestion takes place here.

● There are relatively large circular and longitudinal muscles – the food is still bulky, increasing demands upon peristalsis.

● The epithelial cells do *not* have **microvilli** – an increased surface area is not required for absorption.

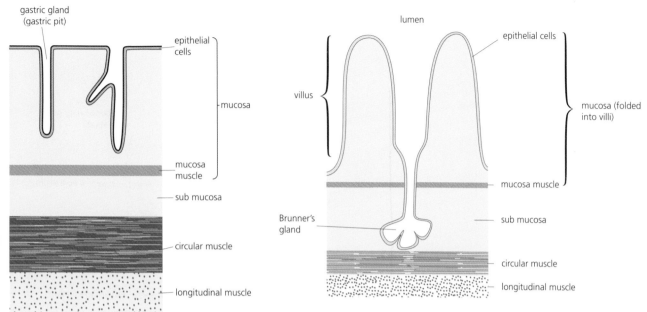

Figure 13.5 *Structure of the gut wall of the stomach*

Figure 13.6 *Structure of the gut wall of the duodenum*

The gut wall of the **stomach** is adapted in the following way:

- The mucosa is *not* folded into villi – an increased surface area is not required for absorption.

- There *are* specialised gastric glands producing digestive secretions (protease enzyme and hydrochloric acid).

- The epithelial cells do *not* have microvilli – an increased surface area is not required for absorption.

The features of the gut wall of the **duodenum** include:

- The mucosa, which *is* folded into villi to increase the surface area for absorption.

- Specialised glands producing alkaline secretions, e.g. Brunner's glands.

- Epithelial cells, which have microvilli to increase the surface area for absorption.

Secretions

One feature of the gut is the many **secretions** (e.g. enzymes) produced in the different sections. Along the whole length of the gut **goblet cells** secrete **mucus** which eases the movement of food by reducing friction.

The mucus also helps to protect the lining of the gut from being damaged by the digestive enzymes. In addition various **glands** also produce secretions. Some of these are outside the gut wall, e.g. the **salivary glands**, **liver** and **pancreas**. Other glands are within the gut wall, e.g. **Brunner's glands** in the **duodenum**. The secretions concerned with carbohydrate digestion are summarised in Tables 13.6, 13.7 and 13.8 on pages 391 and 394.

> **Remember**
>
> The layers of the gut wall provide an example of the **tissue** level of organisation. Each different layer, e.g. the circular muscles, contains *one type of cell* with the *same* function. These work together as *a tissue* doing the *same job*. In turn all of the different tissues in the gut wall of different sections of the gut work together as an **organ**, e.g. the stomach. Many different organs are grouped into a **system** – the digestive system. These organs include the stomach, the liver and the small intestine.

The structure of the gut wall of the **ileum** is the *same* as that of the duodenum except that there are no Brunner's glands in the ileum.

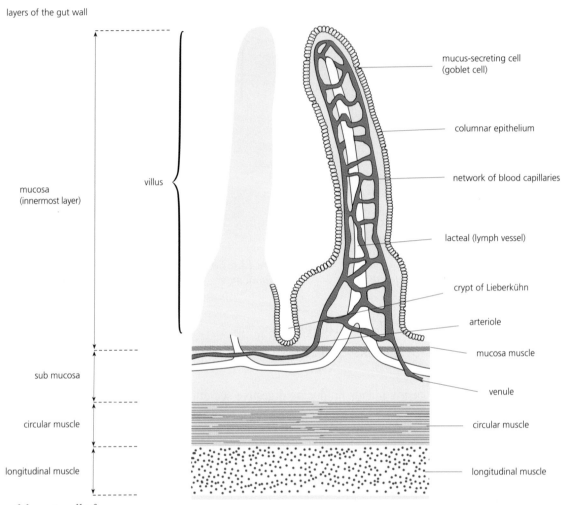

layers of the gut wall

mucosa (innermost layer)

villus

sub mucosa

circular muscle

longitudinal muscle

mucus-secreting cell (goblet cell)

columnar epithelium

network of blood capillaries

lacteal (lymph vessel)

crypt of Lieberkühn

arteriole

mucosa muscle

venule

circular muscle

longitudinal muscle

Figure 13.7 Structure of the gut wall of the ileum, showing structure of villus

Figure 13.8 Scanning electron micrograph showing many villi on surface of small intestine (× 152)

? 2 Why is mucus needed to protect the cells lining the gut from protein-digesting enzymes?
(1 mark)

Structural adaptations of the ileum for digestion and absorption
The **small intestine** is divided into a short **duodenum** followed by a longer **ileum**. Most food substances are absorbed in the ileum. In addition the final stages of protein and carbohydrate digestion also occur in the ileum. Enzymes are present in the membranes of the epithelial microvilli which catalyse this final breakdown. The structure of the ileum is shown in Figures 13.7 to 13.11.

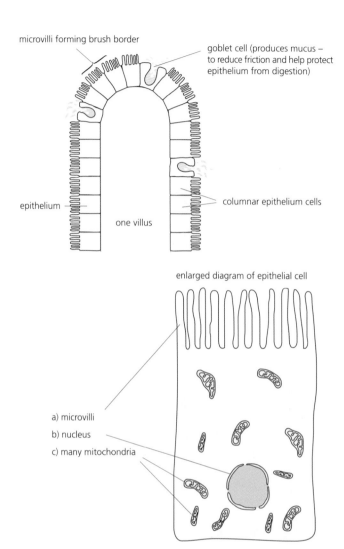

microvilli forming brush border

goblet cell (produces mucus – to reduce friction and help protect epithelium from digestion)

epithelium

one villus

columnar epithelium cells

enlarged diagram of epithelial cell

a) microvilli
b) nucleus
c) many mitochondria

Figure 13.9 *The structure of the epithelium of the ileum*

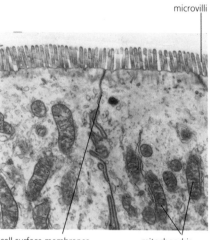

microvilli

cell surface membranes between two epithelial cells

mitochondria

Figure 13.10 *The ultrastructure of the columnar epithelial cells of the ileum (×15 000)*

The inner layer of the ileum wall (the mucosa) forms finger-like projections called **villi**. The layer of cells covering the villi and in contact with the food is called the epithelium. This epithelium consists of two types of cells, **goblet cells** secreting mucus and **columnar epithelial cells**. The cell surface membranes of the columnar epithelial cells are folded into **microvilli**. Collectively the microvilli of all of the cells form a **brush border**.

Structural adaptations of the ileum for *digestion* include:

● The microvilli membranes of the columnar epithelial cells have digestive enzymes bound to them.

● The very large overall surface area of the ileum means a very large surface area of enzymes available to digest the food.

● Each villus contains muscle fibres. Contraction of these moves the villi and mixes up the gut contents. This increases the contact between the food and the enzymes on the microvilli membranes.

Structural adaptations of the ileum for *absorption* include:

● A very large surface area for absorption is achieved by the ileum being very long; the presence of villi; and the presence of microvilli (Figure 13.11).

Remember

Exam hint

Students often confuse villi and microvilli. A villus is a projection containing thousands of cells. Microvilli are foldings of the cell surface membrane of one cell

Figure 13.11 Features of the small intestine which increase surface area

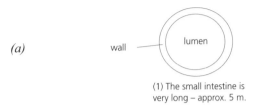

(a)

wall — lumen

(1) The small intestine is very long – approx. 5 m.

one villus

(2) .... and the mucosa forms finger like projections called villi.

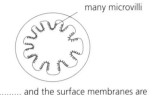

many microvilli

(3) .... and the surface membranes are folded into microvilli, thus increasing the surface area by 600 times.

(b) **Section of small intestine**

(c)

(b) and (c) The effects of the villi in increasing surface area can be seen clearly when shown in three dimensions.

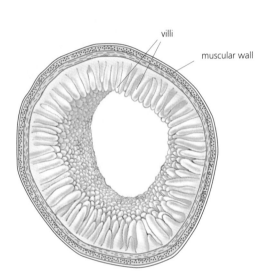

villi

muscular wall

villus

epithelium

capillary network

blood vessels supplying villus

circular muscle

longitudinal muscle

- The columnar epithelial cells have many mitochondria to provide lots of energy for active transport.
- Villi contain many capillaries to transport absorbed molecules away quickly, therefore maintaining the concentration gradient for diffusion.
- Each villus contains a lymph vessel to remove absorbed lipids.
- The epithelial layer is thin, providing a short diffusion distance.
- The villi are moved by the contraction of muscle fibres increasing the contact between the gut epithelium and the food molecules.

> ### Definition
>
> **Peristalsis** is the process by which food is pushed along the gut. It consists of a wave of muscular contraction and relaxation of the circular and longitudinal muscles of the gut wall

Movement of food along the gut by peristalsis

Food is moved in a pellet called a **bolus** which is pushed along by a muscular process called peristalsis (Figure 13.12).

The muscles involved are the circular and longitudinal muscles of the gut wall. These are made of a type of muscle called smooth muscle which can continue to contract and relax for long periods without fatigue. Smooth muscle is also known as involuntary because it works without the need for conscious instruction from the brain. A wave of muscular contraction and relaxation of the circular and longitudinal muscles pushes the food along the gut.

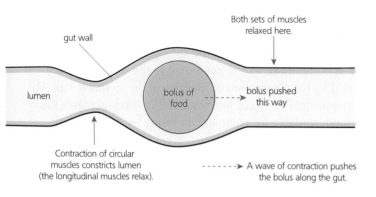

gut wall

Both sets of muscles relaxed here.

lumen

bolus of food

bolus pushed this way

Contraction of circular muscles constricts lumen (the longitudinal muscles relax).

- - - - - - ▶ A wave of contraction pushes the bolus along the gut.

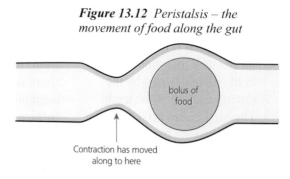

Figure 13.12 Peristalsis – the movement of food along the gut

bolus of food

Contraction has moved along to here

?

3 Why can't humans just rely on gravity to move food down the gut? *(1 mark)*

13.5 Digestion

To be of use to the body food molecules must pass out of the gut and reach the blood. To make this possible large insoluble molecules must be made smaller and soluble. This process is called **digestion**. The main stages of holozoic nutrition in humans are shown in Figure 13.13.

Definition

Digestion is the process by which large insoluble molecules are broken down into smaller soluble molecules which can then be absorbed.

In humans and other mammals digestion involves both chemical and mechanical processes

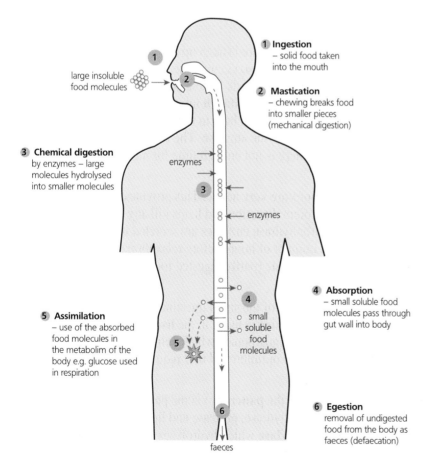

1 Ingestion
– solid food taken into the mouth

large insoluble food molecules

2 Mastication
– chewing breaks food into smaller pieces (mechanical digestion)

3 Chemical digestion
by enzymes – large molecules hydrolysed into smaller molecules

enzymes

enzymes

4 Absorption
– small soluble food molecules pass through gut wall into body

5 Assimilation
– use of the absorbed food molecules in the metabolim of the body e.g. glucose used in respiration

small soluble food molecules

6 Egestion
removal of undigested food from the body as faeces (defaecation)

faeces

Figure 13.13 Summary of stages of holozoic nutrition in humans

Definition

Mastication is the mechanical digestion of food in the mouth caused by the chewing action of the teeth. The food is also mixed with saliva, making movement through the gut easier by reducing friction

Did You Know

In 1822, a Canadian fur-trapper called Alexis St Martin was accidentally shot. He recovered but a hole remained in his side giving direct access to his stomach. He had to have the side of his body bandaged to prevent food from escaping from his stomach through the hole.

He agreed to cooperate with a US army doctor in a series of experiments to investigate the process of digestion. In one experiment the doctor tied string around a piece of meat and poked it through the hole into Alexis' stomach. At intervals he removed the meat using the string to find out how long it would take for the meat to be digested.

Figure 13.14 *Alexis St Martin*

Mechanical (physical) digestion

This involves the purely physical breaking up of large pieces of food into smaller pieces. This process starts in the mouth with the slicing and chewing action of the teeth (**mastication**). It is continued to a lesser extent in the stomach by the churning action caused by the contraction of muscles in the stomach wall. By breaking the food up into smaller pieces mechanical digestion increases the *surface area* of the food available for chemical digestion by enzymes.

Chemical digestion

This is the chemical breakdown by enzymes of the individual food molecules into smaller, soluble molecules. This usually occurs in a number of stages.

All digestive enzymes are hydrolases – they break chemical bonds by the addition of water (see Box 4.1, page 107).

There are three main groups of digestive enzymes:

- **carbohydrases** hydrolyse carbohydrates eventually to monosaccharides
- **proteases** hydrolyse proteins eventually to amino acids
- **lipases** hydrolyse lipids to fatty acids and glycerol.

The digestion of carbohydrates

Our diet contains a variety of carbohydrates. Sugars require little or no digestion but starch and glycogen are broken down in stages to give glucose which can be absorbed. The stages of carbohydrate digestion are considered in Table 13.6 and Figure 13.15.

In the **mouth**, large pieces of starch are broken up by the mechanical digestion of chewing. Some chemical digestion also occurs. The food is mixed with saliva produced by three pairs of salivary glands. Saliva contains the enzyme **salivary amylase** which hydrolyses some of the **starch** into the disaccharide **maltose**. Saliva also contains mineral ions which help to maintain a pH of 7, which is the optimum for the action of the enzyme amylase. The food is soon swallowed and leaves the mouth, therefore there is not enough time for much starch digestion to occur.

In the **stomach**, the conditions are very acidic. This provides the correct pH for the enzymes involved in protein digestion and helps kill any harmful bacteria present on the food. No carbohydrase enzymes are secreted in the stomach. Food stays in the stomach for a number of hours before relaxation of the pyloric sphincter muscle allows the **chyme** (partly digested food) to enter the **small intestine**.

The **duodenum** is the first 20 cm of the small intestine. Many secretions are added to the chyme here. **Bile** which is made in the **liver** enters here via the bile duct. It contains sodium hydrogencarbonate which helps to reduce the acidity from the stomach, providing the optimum pH of 7 required for the enzymes in the duodenum.

Pancreatic juice is secreted by the **pancreas** via the pancreatic duct into the duodenum. This contains carbohydrase, protease and lipase enzymes. The carbohydrase is **pancreatic amylase** which hydrolyses *starch* to *maltose*. Pancreatic juice also contains alkaline salts to help neutralise the acidity from the stomach.

Name of enzyme	Effects of enzyme	Site of production	Site of action	Optimum pH
salivary amylase	starch ⟶ maltose	salivary glands	mouth	7.0
pancreatic amylase	starch ⟶ maltose	pancreas	small intestine	7.0
maltase	maltose ⟶ glucose	membranes of microvilli of ileum epithelial cells		8.0
lactase	lactase ⟶ glucose + galactose			
sucrase	sucrose ⟶ glucose + fructose			

Table 13.6 Summary of carbohydrate digestion in humans

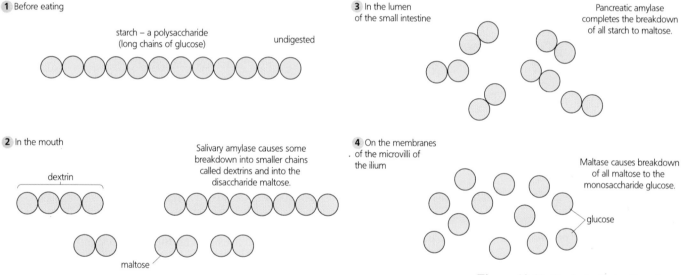

1 Before eating

starch – a polysaccharide
(long chains of glucose)

undigested

2 In the mouth

dextrin

Salivary amylase causes some breakdown into smaller chains called dextrins and into the disaccharide maltose.

maltose

3 In the lumen of the small intestine

Pancreatic amylase completes the breakdown of all starch to maltose.

4 On the membranes of the microvilli of the ilium

Maltase causes breakdown of all maltose to the monosaccharide glucose.

glucose

*Figure 13.15 Carbohydrate digestion: the stages of digestion for **starch***

?

4 The pH in the stomach is very acidic – about pH 2. Why would it be a problem if the pH in the small intestine was 2?　　　*(1 mark)*

The **ileum** is the second and longest part of the small intestine (approximately 5 m long). All chemical digestion is completed here followed by absorption of most of the products of digestion.

The final stage of carbohydrate digestion occurs on the membranes of the microvilli of the epithelium cells in the ileum. Bound to the membranes are **disaccharidases** – enzymes which hydrolyse **disaccharide sugars** to **monosaccharides**, particularly glucose. These enzymes include the enzymes **maltase**, **lactase** and **sucrase**. Proteases are also present (Figure 13.16).

After hydrolysis the monosaccharides produced are small and soluble enough to be absorbed. The absorption of glucose is shown in (Figure 13.19, page 395). Disaccharides, e.g. sucrose, eaten in the diet are only digested when they reach the ileum.

> ! **Did You Know**
>
> A typical human may produce over 10 dm³ of digestive secretions a day including 1.5 dm³ of saliva! Most of this consists of water which is reabsorbed in the large intestine

Cellulose and fibre

Cellulose is also a carbohydrate. Humans do not produce **cellulase** – the enzyme which hydrolyses cellulose. Cellulose in the diet passes through the gut undigested and forms part of the fibre which helps the gut to work properly.

The digestion of proteins

The sites of production and the action of the various proteases are summarised in Table 13.7.

However, three features of protein-digesting enzymes need to be highlighted.

Name of enzyme	Effects of enzyme	Site of production	Site of action	Optimum pH
pepsin secreted as the inactive pepsinogen (activated by HCl)	proteins (polypeptides) ⟶ peptides	inactive pepsinogen secreted by gastric glands in stomach wall	pepsin active in stomach	2.0
trypsin secreted as the inactive trypsinogen (activated by enterokinase)	proteins (polypeptides) ⟶ peptides	inactive trypsinogen secreted by pancreas	trypsin active in small intestine	7.0
enterokinase	inactive trypsinogen ⟶ active trypsin	walls of duodenum	small intestine	7.0
dipeptidase	peptides and dipeptides ⟶ amino acids	membranes of microvilli of ileum epithelial cells		8.0
lipase	lipids ⟶ fatty acids and glycerol	pancreas	small intestine	7.0

Table 13.7 Summary of protein and lipid digestion in humans

Firstly there is the division of the proteases into **endopeptidases** and **exopeptidases** (Figure 13.17).

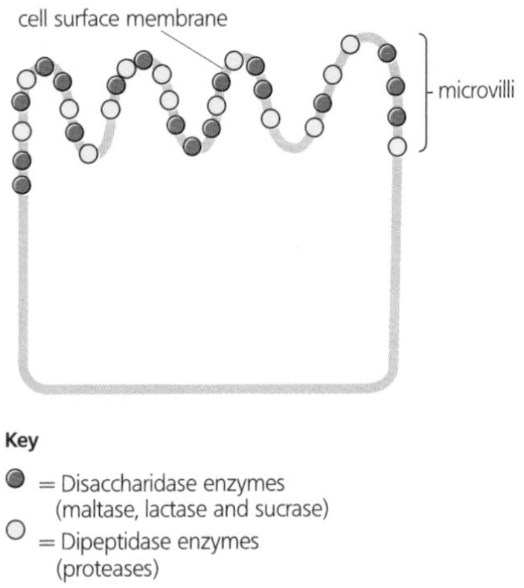

> ! **Definitions**
>
> **Endopeptidases** are protein-digesting enzymes which break peptide bonds in the middle of a polypeptide chain, producing a number of smaller chains called peptides.
>
> **Exopeptidases** are protein-digesting enzymes which break peptide bonds at the end of a peptide chain, releasing either single amino acids or dipeptides (two amino acids).
>
> Note: **endo** – within/inside and **exo** – on the outside

Pepsin and **trypsin** are examples of endopeptidases. They are used in the *earlier* stages of protein digestion, breaking long polypeptides into smaller chains. This gives many more ends (a larger surface area) for the action of the exopeptidases which are used in the *later* stages of protein digestion. In other words it is more efficient for endopeptidases to be used *before* exopeptidases.

Key

- = Disaccharidase enzymes (maltase, lactase and sucrase)
- = Dipeptidase enzymes (proteases)

Figure 13.16 One columnar epithelial cell from the ileum

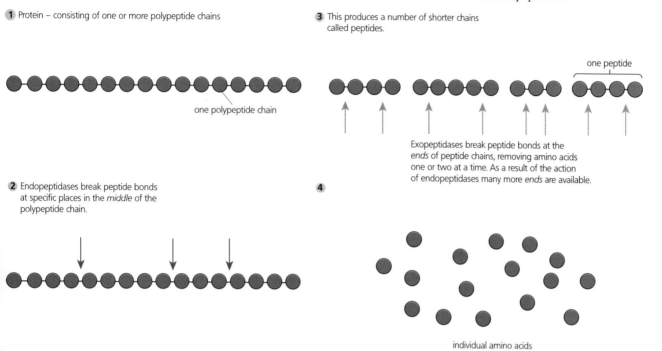

Figure 13.17 *Action of endopeptidases and exopeptidases*

① Protein – consisting of one or more polypeptide chains

one polypeptide chain

② Endopeptidases break peptide bonds at specific places in the *middle* of the polypeptide chain.

③ This produces a number of shorter chains called peptides.

one peptide

Exopeptidases break peptide bonds at the *ends* of peptide chains, removing amino acids one or two at a time. As a result of the action of endopeptidases many more *ends* are available.

④

individual amino acids

Most exopeptidases are found on the microvilli membranes of the epithelium of the small intestine.

The *second* feature involves the secretion of proteases in an *inactive* form. Cells are partly made of protein. Cells which secrete protein-digesting enzymes risk digesting themselves! This is avoided by secreting an *inactive* form of the enzyme which is only *activated* once it is safely in the gut lumen. The mixing with another secretion in the lumen changes the inactive form into the active protease which then starts to function. Pepsin and trypsin are both examples of this (Figure 13.18).

The *third* feature of proteases is that the final stages of protein digestion do not occur in solution. As with carbohydrates the enzymes are *bound* to the cell surface membranes of the epithelial cells of the small intestine (Figure 13.16, page 392). One example is dipeptidases which break down dipeptides into amino acids.

?

5 What would be the disadvantage of using exopeptidases before endopeptidases in the various stages of digestion? *(2 marks)*

The digestion of lipids

Lipid digestion begins in the duodenum where the lipids are mixed with **bile**, which has come from the **liver** via the bile duct. In addition to sodium hydrogencarbonate (see Section 13.5, page 390), bile also contains emulsifying salts, e.g. sodium glycocholate. These **emulsify** the lipids, changing larger droplets into many smaller droplets. Note that this is not chemical digestion – bile

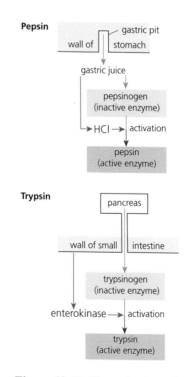

Figure 13.18 *The activation of protease enzymes*

Pepsin

gastric pit

wall of | stomach

gastric juice

pepsinogen (inactive enzyme)

HCl → activation

pepsin (active enzyme)

Trypsin

pancreas

wall of small | intestine

trypsinogen (inactive enzyme)

enterokinase → activation

trypsin (active enzyme)

contains *no* enzymes. The smaller droplets provide a *larger surface area* for the action of the enzyme **lipase** which is produced in the **pancreas** and is present in pancreatic juice. Pancreatic juice enters the gut in the duodenum and the lipase hydrolyses **lipids** into **fatty acids** and **glycerol**. Only one enzyme is involved in lipid digestion (see Table 13.7, page 392 and Table 13.8).

Table 13.8 *Digestive secretions other than enzymes*

Name of secretion	Effects of secretion	Site of production	Site of action
mucus	moistens food in mouth and provides lubrication, reducing friction between food and wall of gut	salivary glands in mouth and goblet cells throughout gut	throughout gut
hydrochloric acid	1. provides correct pH for stomach enzymes 2. converts inactive pepsinogen ⟶ active pepsin 3. kills bacteria	gastric glands in stomach wall	stomach
bile – alkaline salts, e.g. sodium hydrogencarbonate	neutralise the acidity from the stomach to give correct pH for enzymes	liver	small intestine
bile – emulsifying salts, e.g. sodium glycocholate	emulsify lipids – making them into smaller droplets		
alkaline salts in pancreatic juice	neutralise the acidity from the stomach	pancreas	small intestine

> **!** **Did You Know**
>
> The gut is adapted to absorb most substances in the small intestine. However, a few substances are absorbed in the stomach. These include **alcohol** and **aspirin**, so both enter the bloodstream rapidly and their effects will be felt quickly

6 An experiment was done to investigate the effects of bile on lipid digestion. Lipase enzyme and bile were added to a lipid in tube A. Tube B only had the lipid and the lipase. There was a change of pH in both tubes. Explain why:
(a) the pH became acidic; *(2 marks)*
(b) in tube A the pH decreases more quickly than in tube B; *(2 marks)*
(c) the final pH is the same in both tubes. *(2 marks)*

13.6 **The absorption of digested food in the ileum**

By the end of digestion in the ileum:

● all of the **carbohydrates** are present as **monosaccharides** (mainly glucose)

● all of the **proteins** are present as **amino acids**

● all of the **lipids** are present as **fatty acids** and **glycerol**.

To be of use to the body these molecules need to be absorbed from the gut, through the gut wall and into the blood.

Glucose and amino acids are absorbed into the blood capillaries of the villi by a combination of diffusion and active transport. The mechanism for the active uptake of glucose is shown in Figure 13.19.

Fatty acids and glycerol do not pass into the capillaries but instead are absorbed into the lacteals of the villi. These are part of the lymphatic system. Once in the lacteal lipids reform and are carried by the lymph until eventually the lymphatic system empties into the blood system. (See Section 10.12, page 300)

This is an active process requiring the use of ATP as it depends upon the use of a Na⁺/K⁺ pump.

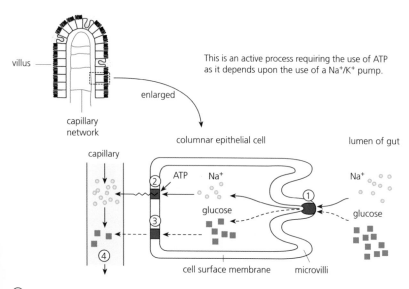

① Carrier protein transports Na⁺ into the cell by facilitated diffusion from a higher concentration to a lower concentration. Glucose is carried into the cell by the Na⁺ as the carrier is a co-transporter requiring both Na⁺ and glucose to function.

② Na⁺/K⁺ pump actively transports Na⁺ out of the cell maintaining a low concentration of Na⁺ in the cell. The pump requires ATP.

③ Carrier protein transports glucose out of the cell by facilitated diffusion from a higher concentration to a lower.

④ Blood flow in the capillary constantly removes the glucose maintaining the glucose concentration gradient with the cell.

Remember

Exam Hint

A common error is to confuse **egestion** with **excretion**. Excretion, e.g. urination, involves removing waste products of the body's metabolism – substances produced by reactions in cells.

Undigested food, e.g. cellulose, has never entered the cells of the body and so its removal is egestion and not excretion.

To further confuse the issue, faeces do contain small amounts of excretory substances (e.g. bile pigments) but, overall, egestion is the correct term to use for the removal of faeces

Figure 13.19 Mechanism for the absorption of glucose

Large intestine
Large amounts of water are absorbed here, making the gut contents less fluid. Huge numbers of bacteria live in the large intestine. These synthesise a number of vitamins, including vitamin K, which are absorbed and used.

Egestion
Eventually the remaining gut contents are removed from the body as semi-solid faeces. Faeces contains approximately 8% bacteria (living and dead) and approximately 15% undigested food – mainly cellulose and lignin. Water makes up most of the rest.

Herbivores and carnivores

Although they all have holozoic nutrition, different mammals do show different adaptations to their diet. Some of the adaptations of herbivorous and carnivorous mammals are shown in Boxes 13.5 and 13.6.

Box 13.5 Holozoic nutrition – the adaptations of herbivores and carnivores to their diet

Herbivores, e.g. sheep	Carnivores, e.g. dogs
plant material consists largely of cellulose. This is low in nutritional value and therefore large volumes have to be eaten. It is also difficult to break down, requiring thorough chewing and grinding and the presence of microorganisms to produce the enzyme cellulase to digest cellulose	meat is high in nutritional value and therefore less has to be eaten. It is also relatively easy to digest. However, prey usually has to be caught and killed which takes time and energy
teeth never stop growing to replace the wear from extensive grinding	teeth stop growing when adult
broad incisors for cropping grass	pointed incisors for nipping and biting
canines absent	canines large and pointed for piercing and holding
diastema (gap) present to allow efficient action of tongue	no diastema
molars and premolars flattened with ridges of enamel for efficient grinding	molars and premolars adapted as carnassial teeth. These are sharp and pointed for cutting and shearing
lower jaw can move sideways for grinding	lower jaw is much 'tighter'; it can only move up and down
relatively long gut as plant material is hard to digest	relatively short gut as meat easy to digest
stomach has four chambers including the rumen. This contains mutualistic microorganisms which digest cellulose	only one stomach – no rumen

Extension

Box 13.5 cont'd

skull of sheep – a herbivore

skull of dog – a carnivore

herbivore molars – the formation of enamel ridges

carnivore carnassial teeth

length of guts

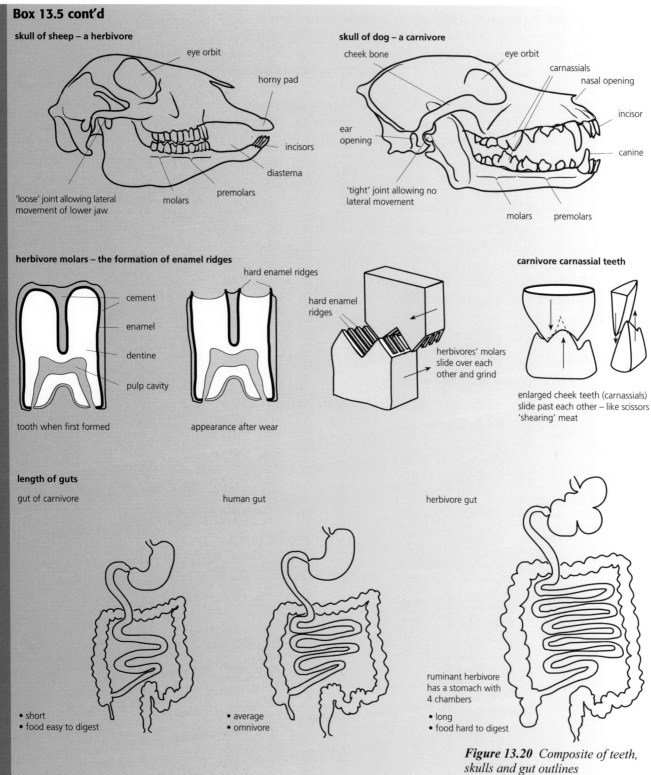

eye orbit

horny pad

incisors

diastema

premolars

molars

'loose' joint allowing lateral movement of lower jaw

cheek bone

eye orbit

carnassials

nasal opening

incisor

canine

ear opening

'tight' joint allowing no lateral movement

molars   premolars

hard enamel ridges

cement

enamel

dentine

pulp cavity

tooth when first formed

appearance after wear

hard enamel ridges

herbivores' molars slide over each other and grind

enlarged cheek teeth (carnassials) slide past each other – like scissors 'shearing' meat

gut of carnivore

human gut

herbivore gut

ruminant herbivore has a stomach with 4 chambers

• short
• food easy to digest

• average
• omnivore

• long
• food hard to digest

Figure 13.20 *Composite of teeth, skulls and gut outlines*

Extension

Box 13.6 Digestion and mutualism in ruminant herbivores

Herbivores such as sheep and cows are **ruminants**. Instead of **one** stomach they have a stomach with **four** chambers. See Figure 13.21. One of these chambers is called the **rumen** – hence ruminant. The rumen acts as a storage area where large numbers of bacteria and other micro organisms can live and multiply safely, kept away from the digestive enzymes in the rest of the ruminant's gut. The bacteria and the ruminant have a **mutualistic** relationship where both benefit.

The processes involved in ruminant digestion are complex – an outline is given below in Figure 13.22.

Three aspects are particularly important:

1. The ruminant relies on the bacteria to **digest the cellulose** in the grass. The cellulose in the cell walls of grass is the main food eaten by ruminants such as cows and sheep. However, cows and sheep, along with other mammals, cannot produce the **cellulase enzyme** needed to digest cellulose so they get the energy they need from their food as follows:

● The grass is eaten by the ruminant and thoroughly ground up by chewing to break up the cell walls into smaller pieces.

● The chewed grass now passes to the *rumen*.

● Here the cellulose is chemically digested to glucose by cellulase enzymes secreted by the bacteria living in the rumen.

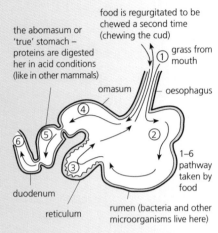

four 'chambers': rumen, reticulum, omasum and abomasum – The abomasum is the true stomach. The other three chambers are extensions of the oesophagus.

Figure 13.21 *The ruminant stomach*

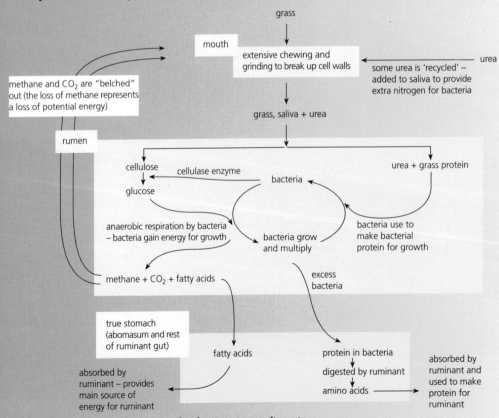

Figure 13.22 *The processes involved in ruminant digestion*

Box 13.6 cont'd

- The glucose is used by the bacteria for their anaerobic respiration (fermentation).

- This provides energy for the bacteria to grow and reproduce.

- *Fatty acids* are also produced as a by-product of respiration and these are absorbed by the ruminant, providing it with its main source of energy.

2. These processes enable ruminants to **survive on diets low in protein**.

- The typical ruminant diet is mainly grass and contains very little protein.

- The ruminant recycles some of its **urea**, keeping it in its body.

- This urea is added to the saliva and passes with the saliva and grass to the rumen.

- The bacteria in the rumen can use the urea as a source of *nitrogen* to make *protein*.

- This protein is used for the growth and reproduction of the bacteria.

- Some 'excess' bacteria are regularly lost from the rumen, passing on to the rest of the gut of the ruminant. (These are quickly replaced as the bacteria reproduce.)

- The excess bacteria are digested by the ruminant so that bacterial protein is broken down to amino acids which the ruminant absorbs and uses to make its protein.

- In effect, the bacteria convert waste urea into usable protein which the ruminant can use to supplement its low-protein diet.

- The bacteria also release plant protein from the grass cells so it becomes available to the ruminant.

3. This relationship provides an example of **mutualistic nutrition** (see Section 13.9, page 405).

- Mutualism is a relationship between two species where both gain nutritionally.

- The ruminant gains a supply of *fatty acids* from the bacteria, following bacterial digestion and respiration of cellulose.

- The ruminant gains a supply of *protein* by digesting excess bacteria.

- The bacteria gain a supply of *cellulose* from the ruminant.

- The bacteria gain a supply of *urea* from the ruminant which is used by the bacteria to make protein.

Remember

Exam Hint

saprobiontic = saprophytic = saprotrophic = saprobiotic Unfortunately you may come across many different terms being used – check which term your own exam syllabus uses. At advanced level all of these terms have the same meaning – they can be used interchangeably

Definition

Saprobiontic (saprophytic) nutrition involves obtaining nutrients and energy from dead organic matter. Enzymes are secreted onto the food and digestion is **extracellular** – occurring outside of the organism. The soluble products of digestion are then absorbed into the organism

Figure 13.23 Rhizopus, *the pin mould, an example of a saprobiont (saprophyte)*

13.7 Saprobiontic nutrition

Saprobiontic nutrition is a type of heterotrophic nutrition. Saprobionts obtain nutrients and energy from dead organic matter and organic waste such as faeces. Enzymes are secreted from the organism onto the food and digestion occurs outside of the organism, that is digestion is **extracellular**. The soluble products of digestion are then absorbed back into the organism where they are used for survival and growth.

Many bacteria and fungi are saprobionts and play a crucial role as decomposers in food chains and nutrient cycles. (See Section 14.5, page 421 and Section 14.9, page 427.)

Saprobiontic nutrition in *Rhizopus*, the pin mould

Rhizopus stolonifera is a fungus which grows on stored foods such as bread, cakes and rice. Like other moulds its body consists of a branching mass of threads or **hyphae** growing on the food material (substrate). Collectively all of these hyphae together are known as the **mycelium**. At intervals upright hyphae are produced with small round sporangia which look like pin heads (hence pin mould). The sporangia are reproductive structures producing spores (Figure 13.23).

The hyphae are not subdivided by cell surface membranes or cell walls. The cytoplasm is continuous throughout the hyphae with nucleii located at intervals. This arrangement is known as **coenocytic**. The outside of the hypha has a cell wall made of chitin and not cellulose as in plants.

Rhizopus secretes hydrolytic enzymes including carbohydrases, proteases and lipases onto the food substrate. Complex insoluble molecules are broken down

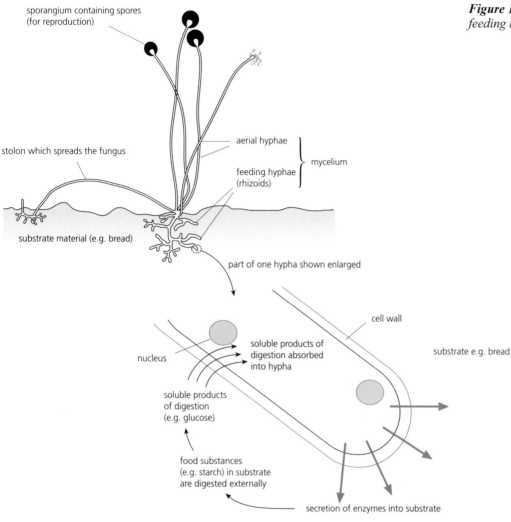

Figure 13.24 Rhizopus – *part of one feeding hypha (rhizoid) enlarged*

sporangium containing spores (for reproduction)

stolon which spreads the fungus

aerial hyphae ⎫
feeding hyphae ⎬ mycelium
(rhizoids) ⎭

substrate material (e.g. bread)

part of one hypha shown enlarged

cell wall

nucleus

soluble products of digestion absorbed into hypha

substrate e.g. bread

soluble products of digestion (e.g. glucose)

food substances (e.g. starch) in substrate are digested externally

secretion of enzymes into substrate

into smaller, soluble molecules by extracellular digestion, e.g. starch is digested to glucose and proteins to amino acids. The soluble products of digestion are then absorbed into the hyphae to provide the nutrients and energy needed for life and growth (Figure 13.24).

Remember

Exam Hint

Some fungal moulds may look greenish in colour and appear rather plant-like. It is important to remember that fungi are *not* plants – none of them photosynthesise and they have chitin rather than cellulose cell walls

Extension

Box 13.7 The use of starch-agar plates for estimating enzyme activity

Agar is a jelly-like substance which is used as a substrate to grow organisms such as bacteria and fungi. Agar can be prepared which has been mixed with starch. Different species of fungi feed naturally upon different substrates using different enzymes. The pin mould *Rhizopus* often feeds upon starchy substrates such as bread and therefore produces a high proportion of the enzyme amylase for its extracellular digestion. The secretion and activity of amylase can be demonstrated using plates (petri dishes) of starch-agar (Figure 13.25). Other fungi feed upon different substrates and produce different enzymes and much less amylase, e.g. the fungal species *Peziza coccinea* feeds mainly upon wood. The level of amylase production and the level of amylase activity can be estimated by growing the different fungi upon starch-agar (Figure 13.25).

Figure 13.25 *Growing* Rhizopus *on starch-agar*

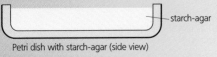

Petri dish with starch-agar (side view)

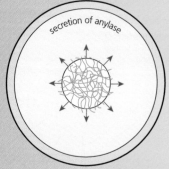

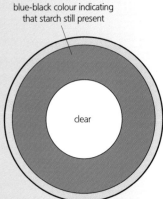

1 Some pin mould (*Rhizopus*) is placed on a starch–agar dish.

2 The mould grows by feeding saprobiontically upon the starch. The enzyme anylase is secreted from the mould into the starch–agar. The amylase digests the starch to soluble sugars.

3 The mould is removed and iodine solution is poured over the dish. (iodine stains starch blue-black) The clear area indicates that the starch has been digested by the amylase, i.e. starch is not present.

Figure 13.26 *Comparison with a different species of fungus, e.g.* Peziza coccinea

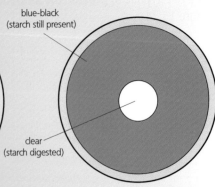

1 Some *Peziza coccinea* fungus is placed on the dish. This feeds mainly on lignin (wood) and not on starch – it produces very little anylase.

2 The fungus grows very slowly because it cannot fully use the available food – the starch.

3 The fungus is removed and iodine solution is poured over the dish. The size of the clear area gives an indication of the extent of enzyme (amylase) activity. In this case there is only a small clear area, showing a low level of amylase activity.

13.8 Parasitic nutrition

A **parasite** obtains its food from a *living* organism of a different species, known as the **host**. The parasite depends upon the host and causes it a certain amount of harm.

Parasites are very varied: some live on the outside of the host (ectoparasites) whereas others live inside (endoparasites); some spend their entire life on or in the host whereas others only attach to the host during feeding.

Most parasites are highly adapted to this way of life with many highly specialised features.

Parasitic nutrition in *Taenia solium*, the pork tapeworm

Taenia solium, the pork tapeworm, is an endoparasite with humans as the primary host and pigs as the secondary host. The adult tapeworm lives in a human and consists of a flattened, ribbon-like body, made up of a large number of segments called **proglottids**. The tapeworm can be from 3 m to 8 m in length with up to one thousand segments. It is approximately 6 mm wide and 1.5 mm thick, i.e. it is *thin and flat*. At one end is a head or **scolex** which is embedded in the wall of the intestine, securely attaching the worm. Behind the head new segments continually form which mature and get larger. Each segment has both male and female reproductive structures (it is **hermaphroditic**) and the older segments are full of fertilised eggs. As the segments get older they move towards the end of the worm where they eventually break off and pass out of the body in the faeces (Figure 13.27).

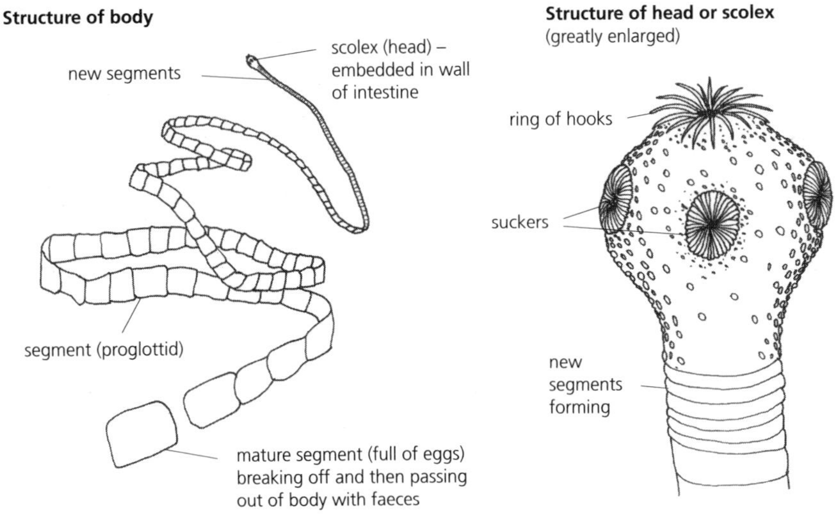

Figure 13.27 Structure of Taenia solium – *the pork tapeworm – an example of parasitic nutrition*

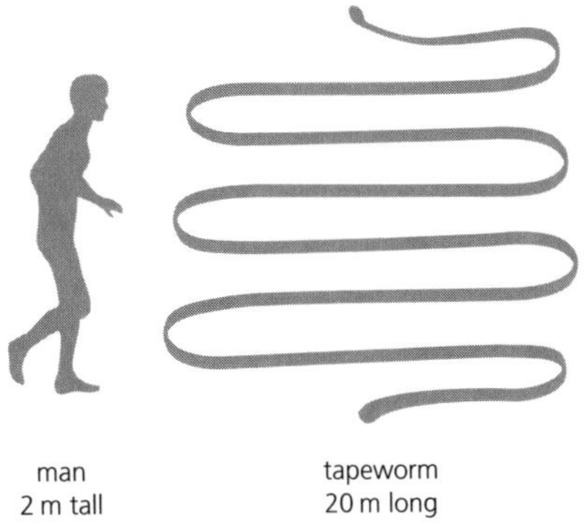

Structure of body

new segments

segment (proglottid)

scolex (head) – embedded in wall of intestine

mature segment (full of eggs) breaking off and then passing out of body with faeces

Structure of head or scolex
(greatly enlarged)

ring of hooks

suckers

new segments forming

man
2 m tall

tapeworm
20 m long

Figure 13.28 The broad fish tapeworm is so long it can block the intestine

Did You Know

Although it may be up to 8 m long, *Taenia solium* does not usually block the intestine because it is thin and flat. Probably the largest human tapeworm is the broad fish tapeworm (*Diphyllobothrium latum*) which can be 2 cm wide and over 20 m long! Being so large it can block the intestine, causing serious health problems (Figure 13.28). Remember that the total length of the adult human gut is approximately 10 metres

The life cycle continues if the eggs which are now in the human faeces are eaten by a pig – the secondary host. The eggs hatch out inside the pig and eventually the larval stage is found in the muscles of the pig. Because pig muscle is the pork meat eaten by humans, it is possible for the life cycle to be completed. If infected pork is not cooked properly, the larvae are not killed by the cooking and living larvae enter the human in the pork. The larvae attach to the intestine wall and change into the adult stage.

The long thin shape of the tapeworm means that the intestine is not blocked and a healthy host suffers little damage apart from the loss of some food.

However, in children or in adults weakened from an existing disease, tapeworms can cause more major problems such as vomiting and loss of appetite.

7 Parasites cause some harm to their host but do not usually kill it.
Why would it be a disadvantage for *Taenia* to kill its host? *(1 mark)*

Adaptations of *Taenia* for a parasitic mode of life include:

- It has attachment structures to keep it securely in the intestine and prevent it being dislodged by the peristalsis of the gut. These structures include the hooks and suckers on the **scolex**.

- By staying in the intestine it has a constant supply of food from the host which has already been digested. *Taenia* has no mouth or gut. It does not need them as soluble molecules produced by the host's digestion are available. It can absorb the food directly through the wall of each segment and it saves the resources which would have been used to produce its own digestive enzymes.

- By being in the intestine *Taenia* could itself be damaged by the host's digestive enzymes. To prevent this it has a protective outer covering called a **cuticle**.

- *Taenia* is also adapted to cope with the anaerobic conditions (low oxygen levels) in the gut.

- There is a reduction in the sense organs (e.g. no eyes as it is dark in the gut).

- *Taenia* is hermaphroditic (has both male and female sex organs) and can fertilise itself without needing to find a mate.

- Each of the many segments produces eggs so that a huge number are released from the body, increasing the chances of completing the life cycle by infecting a pig and hence another human.

13.9 Mutualistic nutrition

Mutualism may also be referred to as **symbiosis** and at advanced level the terms can be used interchangeably.

Some well-known examples of mutualism include:

- bacteria that live in the human large intestine which gain food from us and provide us with vitamins
- microorganisms which live in the stomachs of cows and sheep and digest the cellulose in the grass that is eaten (see Box 13.6, page 398)
- lichens which consist of algae and fungi closely combined.

Mutualistic nutrition in *Rhizobium*

There is a mutualistic relationship between *Rhizobium*, a type of bacteria, and a species of the plant family *Leguminosae*, known as **legumes** for short. Legumes may also be known as the *Papilionaceae*. Types of legume include peas, beans and clover.

Rhizobium bacteria are present in the soil and are attracted towards the roots of legumes by a hormone secreted by the plant roots. Special swellings or **nodules** develop on the roots made of plant cells but with the cells containing huge numbers of *Rhizobium* bacteria (Figures 13.29 and 13.30).

> **Definition**
>
> Mutualism is a close relationship between organisms from two different species where both gain a nutritional advantage.

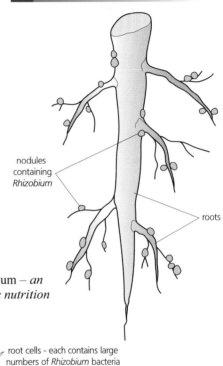

nodules containing *Rhizobium*

roots

Figure 13.29 Rhizobium – *an example of mutualistic nutrition*

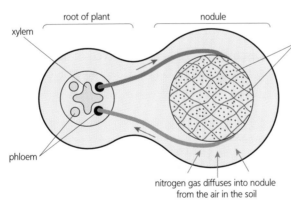

mutualism: both species gain nutritionally

sugars (made in photosynthesis) pass from the plant to the bacteria

ammonia produced by bacteria passes from bacteria to plant

root of plant

xylem

nodule

phloem

root cells - each contains large numbers of *Rhizobium* bacteria

nitrogen gas diffuses into nodule from the air in the soil

Figure 13.30 *Section through a root nodule (enlarged)*

Rhizobium bacteria have a very important ability: they can **fix** nitrogen gas from the air and convert it into ammonia using the enzyme nitrogenase. This ammonia can then be used by the bacteria to make amino acids for its own protein synthesis and growth but at the same time some of the ammonia passes to the plant to be used for the plant's protein synthesis.

This nitrogen fixation reaction requires a lot of energy and the leguminous plant provides the bacteria with large quantities of sugars for respiration to supply this energy. The plant makes this sugar by photosynthesis.

Therefore the overall nutritional advantages are that the *Rhizobium* gains a supply of carbohydrate (sugars) from the leguminous plant and the plant gains a supply of usable nitrogen (as ammonia) from the *Rhizobium*.

8 Suggest one other advantage of mutualism for *Rhizobium* other than nutritional advantages. *(1 mark)*

The wider significance of this mutualistic relationship includes the following aspects:

● *Rhizobium* and other nitrogen-fixing bacteria are very important in the nitrogen cycle (see Section 14.12, page 431).

● All plants need a supply of nitrogen to make proteins for growth. Most plants can only absorb nitrogen as nitrates from the soil. This results in heavy competition for soil nitrate, levels of which often become low.

● This heavy uptake of soil nitrate can encourage overuse of fertiliser by farmers to replace the nitrate (see Section 15.6, page 444).

● In contrast, there is an almost limitless supply of nitrogen as nitrogen gas in the air. Nitrogen fixation uses this gaseous nitrogen rather than nitrates. Legumes are getting their nitrogen from the nitrogen fixed by *Rhizobium* and do not have to compete for soil nitrate.

● Leguminous plants can therefore grow well in soil lacking in soil nitrogen (e.g. nitrates), outcompeting non-leguminous plants.

● However, in soils rich in nitrate and other sources of nitrogen, legumes compete less well with other plants. A lot of the sugars the legume produces by photosynthesis are passed to the bacteria and cannot be used by the plant for its own growth.

● Discovering the genes involved in nitrogen fixation is of major interest for gene technologists (see Box 14.4, page 434).

Summary – (13) Heterotrophic nutrition

- Heterotrophic nutrition involves breaking down complex organic molecules into smaller, soluble molecules, to provide the energy and nutrients for survival and growth.

- There are four different types of heterotrophic nutrition: holozoic, saprobiontic, parasitic and mutualistic.

- Humans have holozoic nutrition where food is digested inside the body in a gut.

- To maintain good health humans require adequate amounts of all nutrients – a balanced diet.

- The quantities of nutrients required vary depending upon factors such as age and level of activity.

- Humans require: carbohydrates and lipids for energy; proteins for growth and repair; vitamins and minerals for healthy functioning; water for blood and as a solvent.

- The risk of coronary heart disease can be influenced by diet.

- The human gut is a tube divided into different sections specialised for different functions. These sections are: mouth; oesophagus; stomach; duodenum; ileum; large intestine.

- The structure of the ileum is adapted in various ways for absorption including: by having a very large surface area due to the presence of villi and microvilli; by each villus having many capillaries and thin walls.

- During digestion in humans, larger molecules are chemically broken down by hydrolase enzymes to smaller, soluble molecules which can be absorbed.

- This chemical breakdown usually takes place in a number of stages involving different enzymes.

- By the end of digestion all the carbohydrates are present as monosaccharides, all the proteins as amino acids, and all the lipids as fatty acids and glycerol. These substances are now absorbed.

- Saprobionts feed on dead organic matter by extracellular digestion.

- *Rhizopus*, the pin mould, is a saprobiontic fungus with a body consisting of a mass of threads called hyphae.

- *Rhizopus* secretes enzymes onto organic material and then absorbs the products of digestion back into the hyphae.

- Parasites feed on living hosts, e.g. the adult *Taenia solium* (the pork tapeworm) lives inside the small intestine of humans, feeding on food the host has digested.

- Tapeworms have many adaptations to their parasitic way of life including: secure means of attachment to the gut; a cuticle resistant to the digestive enzymes of the host; being hermaphroditic so that one worm can reproduce without a mate.

- Mutualistic nutrition is where organisms from two different species gain a nutritional advantage from one another.

- *Rhizobium* is a species of bacteria which lives in swellings in the roots of legume plants.

- Both species gain nutritionally; the bacteria gain sugars produced by the plant and the plant gains ammonia (as a source of nitrogen) from the bacteria.

- *Rhizobium* is a nitrogen-fixing bacterium; it can convert gaseous nitrogen from the air into ammonia.

Answers

1 Species X is a parasite and species Y is a saprobiont *(2)*.

2 Because cells are partly made of protein and would be broken down *(1)*.

3 We do not stand up all the time. The food still needs to be moved along the gut when we are lying down, e.g. when we are asleep *(1)*.

4 This is the wrong pH for the enzymes in the gut, they would be denatured by the acidity and would not work *(1)*.

5 Exopeptidases only remove amino acids one at a time from the ends of polypeptides. Unless the polypeptides are broken up first by endopeptidases there are very few ends for exopeptidases to work on and complete breakdown of the polypeptide will be very slow *(2)*.

6 (a) Lipase breaks down lipids to fatty acids and glycerol; fatty acids are acidic and lower the pH *(2)*.

(b) Bile contains emulsifying salts, changing the lipid into smaller droplets; smaller droplets mean a larger surface area available for the action of lipase and a faster rate of lipid breakdown *(2)*.

(c) Both tubes have the same quantity of lipid to start with, therefore when breakdown is complete the same amount of fatty acids will be present *(2)*.

7 If the host dies there will be no food for *Taenia* and it will die *(1)*.

8 *Rhizobium* gains an environment relatively safe from predators (inside the nodules) *(1)*.

End of Chapter Questions

1 A human becomes infected with *Taenia* by eating infected pork. The *Taenia* larvae therefore start off in the mouth with the food.

(a) Which region of the gut do they need to reach? *(1 mark)*

(b) Why? *(2 marks)*

(c) In their journey from the mouth, suggest two dangers they face. *(2 marks)*

(Total 5 marks)

2 The diagram below shows a part of the beef tapeworm *Taenia saginata*.

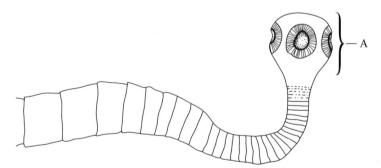

(a) Explain the importance of the part labelled A in the life of the tapeworm. *(2 marks)*

(b) (i) Describe how the tapeworm obtains its nutrition. *(2 marks)*

(ii) How does the nutrition of *Rhizopus* differ from that of the tapeworm? *(2 marks)*

London 1997

(Total 6 marks)

3 An experiment was carried out to investigate the effect on the growth of rats of including milk in the diet.

Two groups (A and B), each consisting of eight young rats, were fed on a synthetic diet consisting of purified casein (a milk protein), sucrose, fat, inorganic salts and water. Group A received a supplement of $3\,cm^3$ of milk per day for the first 18 days then received no further milk. Group B was given no milk for the first 18 days, then received a supplement of $3\,cm^3$ of milk per day. The results are shown in the graph below.

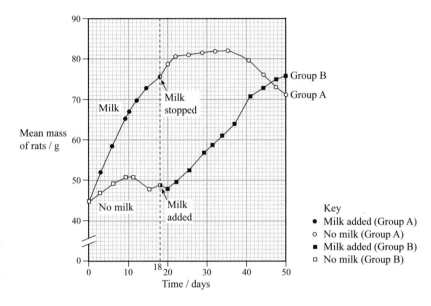

(a) (i) From the graph, find the mean mass of each group of rats at day 10.
Rats which received a milk supplement (Group A)
Rats which received no milk (Group B)   *(2 marks)*

(ii) Describe the changes in mean mass up to day 18, for the rats which received no milk (Group B).   *(2 marks)*

(iii) Compare the changes in mean mass of both groups of rats during the whole experiment.   *(3 marks)*

(b) Suggest why the growth of the rats was faster when they received the milk than when they received no milk.   *(2 marks)*

(c) The inorganic salts provided in the diet included calcium. Describe the importance of calcium to growing rats.   *(3 marks)*

(Total 12 marks)

London 1996

4 Read through the following account of carbohydrate digestion then write on the dotted lines the most appropriate word or words to complete the account.

Digestion of starch starts in the .... where it is hydrolysed to .... by the enzyme .... This process is halted in the stomach but continues in the duodenum, catalysed by an enzyme secreted by the .... Also in the duodenum, sucrose is hydrolysed to .... and .... by enzymes produced by secretory cells in the duodenum wall. *(6 marks)*

London 1996

5 **(a)** The diseases pellagra and beriberi are caused by vitamin deficiencies.

　(i) What is a *vitamin*? *(1 mark)*

　(ii) Which vitamin deficiencies are responsible for pellagra and beriberi? *(2 marks)*

(b) Protein-energy malnutrition may affect individuals who do not eat a balanced diet. Explain the meaning of the terms *balanced diet* and *protein-energy malnutrition*. *(4 marks)*

The table below shows the essential amino acid content of several dietary components.

| amino acid | amino acids in g per 100 g protein | | | | | | | |
	recommended 'ideal' protein for human	cow's milk	beef muscle	broad bean	soya bean	wheat	maize	rice
cysteine and methionine	3.5	3.4	3.8	1.5	1.6	3.9	5.1	4.4
lysine	5.5	7.9	8.7	6.5	6.4	2.0	3.5	4.0
isoleucine	4.0	6.5	5.3	4.0	4.5	3.6	3.6	4.7
leucine	7.0	10.0	8.2	7.1	7.8	6.7	11.6	8.5
phenylalanine and tyrosine	6.0	10.2	7.5	7.5	8.0	7.7	7.2	10.3
threonine	4.0	4.7	4.3	3.4	3.9	2.7	3.9	3.8
tryptophan	1.0	1.4	1.2	0.9	1.3	1.1	0.9	1.2
valine	5.0	7.0	5.5	4.4	4.8	3.7	4.9	7.0

(c) (i) What is meant by the term *essential amino acid*? *(1 mark)*

N3.1

　(ii) A vegan consumes no animal products. From the table above identify a combination of **two** dietary components which would provide a vegan with an adequate intake of **all** essential amino acids. *(1 mark)*

　(iii) Kwashiorkor is a disease of very young infants displaced from their mother's breast and weaned onto a cereal diet. Explain why such infants, if fed solely on an unsupplemented cereal diet, are likely to suffer from kwashiorkor. *(2 marks)*

(d) Certain dietary imbalances are more common in affluent societies. State **two** such imbalances and explain the health risks each poses. *(4 marks)*

Oxford & Cambridge 1998 　　　　　　　　　　　　　*(Total 15 marks)*

6 Read the following procedure for setting up an investigation concerning digestion in the mammalian alimentary canal then answer the questions that follow.

Procedure:
1. From a boiled egg take about ¼ of the egg white and chop up thoroughly.
2. Divide the egg white into five equal amounts and place in boiling tubes labelled A, B, C, D and E.
3. Add the following solutions (as shown in the table below) to each tube.

Tube	Distilled water /cm^3	Dilute HCl /cm^3	Dilute Na$_2$CO$_3$ /cm^3	Pepsin (protease) /cm^3
A	20	0	0	0
B	10	5	0	5
C	10	0	5	5
D	15	5	0	0
E	15	0	5	0

4. Cover the tubes with 'parafilm' (or 'clingfilm') and place in the incubator at 37 °C for about 5 hours. After incubation, examine the contents of the tubes.

(a) Why is egg white used rather than the egg yolk? *(1 mark)*

(b) Suggest why the egg white is chopped thoroughly. *(1 mark)*

(c) What is the purpose of tube A? *(1 mark)*

(d) Explain why 20 cm^3 of distilled water is added to tube A, but different volumes of water to the other tubes. *(1 mark)*

(e) State, with a reason in each case, what result you would expect in:

   (i) Tube B; *(1 mark)*

   (ii) Tube C. *(1 mark)*

(f) Why is tube D set up? *(1 mark)*

(g) Where in the mammal would the protease pepsin be produced? *(1 mark)*

(Total 8 marks)

Oxford 1998

7 The diagram below shows a part of a transverse section through the ileum as seen using a low magnification with a light microscope.

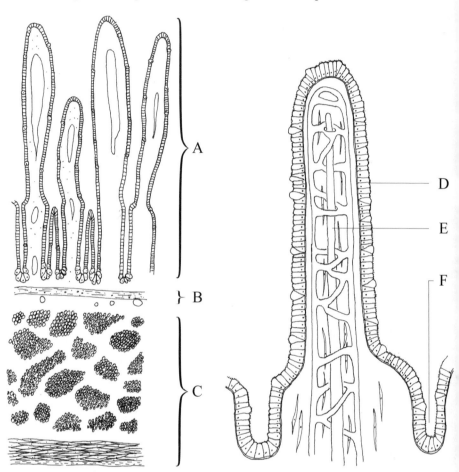

(a) Name the *layers* of the gut wall marked A, B and C. *(3 marks)*

(b) Name the *parts* D, E and F. *(3 marks)*

(c) What are the functions of structures C and E? *(2 marks)*

(d) Briefly describe how *two* features of structure D enable the ileum to carry out its function of absorption. *(4 marks)*

(Total 12 marks)

14 Ecosystems

Living organisms depend upon each other for their survival. Plants absorb light energy from the sun and use it to make large organic molecules, by the process of photosynthesis. In turn, animals feed upon plants and other animals, passing the energy on through food chains. When organisms die, the elements of which they are made are recycled, providing inorganic raw materials for the plants to use again.

As well as being dependent upon other organisms, living things are dependent upon their physical and chemical surroundings. These two components, organisms and their environment, make up an **ecosystem**. Some familiar ecosystems are shown in Figure 14.1.

> **This chapter includes:**
> - the meaning of 'ecology' and some ecological terms
> - energy transfer through an ecosystem
> - trophic levels, food chains and food webs
> - pyramids of number, biomass and energy
> - recycling of nutrients: the water, carbon and nitrogen cycles.

(a) *(b)* *(c)*

Figure 14.1 Different ecosystems:
(a) Tropical rainforest
(b) Rocky shore
(c) Deciduous woodland

14.1 Ecology and ecosystems

Ecology is the scientific study of the relationships between organisms and their environment. It is a relatively recent branch of biology, because although the word 'ecology' was first used in the 1860s, a scientific approach to the study of ecosystems only really began in the 1930s. In the last 30 years, ecology has gained an increasing importance in the minds of the public, as a consequence of the ever-growing concern over the harmful effects of human activities on the environment.

The term 'ecosystem' was invented by the Cambridge biologist Sir Arthur Tansley in 1935. It recognises that any organism does not live in isolation, but forms relationships with other individuals of the same species and with different species. The most obvious of these relationships is through feeding. An organism may feed on others, or be prey to another animal. However, there are many other possible relationships. For instance, the presence of pollinating insects may be necessary to a flowering plant, or a hollow tree may act as a nest site for a bird. These are examples of **biotic** components of an ecosystem, biotic meaning 'living'. The **abiotic**, or non-living, components of the ecosystem are physical and chemical factors.

> **Definition**
>
> **Ecology** is the scientific study of the relationship between organisms and their environment. An **ecosystem** consists of a group of interrelated organisms (the **biotic** component) and their physical and chemical environment (the **abiotic** component)

Abiotic factors include:

● differences in climate, such as light intensity, water availability and temperature

● edaphic (soil) conditions such as clay content, water content and pH

● other factors specific to a particular ecosystem, such as the salinity of water in an estuary or water velocity in a stream.

Clearly there are a very large number of abiotic factors which can influence the types and distribution of organisms, and the importance of these will depend upon the type of ecosystem. Take the example of a freshwater stream. The main abiotic factors in this ecosystem will be water velocity, type of substrate (stones, sand, mud etc. on the bottom of the stream), oxygen concentration, depth of water, pH, concentration of dissolved minerals, turbidity (cloudiness), and presence of any pollutants.

Although the ecosystem is the fundamental 'unit' of ecology and is easily defined in words, the *extent* of a particular ecosystem is not so easy to define. Each is not self-contained, with a barrier surrounding it, but has links with other ecosystems. For instance, a stream running through a wood will provide water and food for animals in the wood, and most of the organic matter entering the stream will be dead plant material from the trees and other plants nearby. It is more a matter of convenience that we refer to a 'deciduous woodland' ecosystem, or a 'rocky shore' ecosystem. In fact, we often talk about the **global ecosystem**, considering all ecosystems on Earth as being interrelated, which they undoubtedly are. The global ecosystem occupies the thin surface layer of the Earth, extending from the deep oceans to the lower regions of the atmosphere. This zone which supports life is called the **biosphere**, and is a thin layer no more than 40 kilometres deep, compared with the Earth's diameter, which is about 12 700 km (Figure 14.2).

Figure 14.2 *The biosphere*

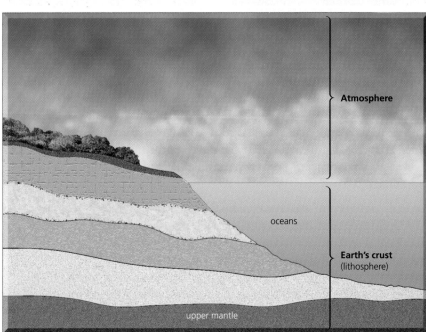

The environment in which a particular organism lives is called its **habitat**. The habitat of a limpet (a type of mollusc) is a rocky seashore, that of an earthworm is the soil. We can talk of a rocky shore *habitat* and a rocky shore *ecosystem*, but they mean different things.

1 Using the example of a freshwater pond, explain the difference between a habitat and an ecosystem. *(2 marks)*

Within an ecosystem there will be several habitats. A wood may have a stream running through it, and the stream may feed into a small lake, each providing a distinctly different habitat. Even within the wood itself, different parts of the trees may be the homes of quite different organisms. For example, the tree trunks may be the habitat of green algae and small snails, whilst the leaves of the tree canopy harbour other small invertebrates such as caterpillars and aphids. These smaller divisions of a habitat are referred to as **microhabitats**. Some examples of microhabitats in a freshwater stream are described in Figure 14.3.

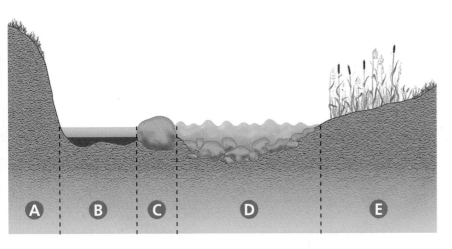

A
Steep bank of stone with little soil. Covered with mosses, liverworts and lichens.

B
Area with little current ('pool'). Mud and detritus sinks to form layer on bottom of stream. Water poorly aerated.

C
Exposed boulder. Surface encrusted with algae and mosses. covered by water when stream floods.

D
Region of fast-moving water ('riffle'). Substrate of algae-covered stones and boulders, little detritus. Stones may be moved when stream floods. Water well aerated.

E
Gentle sloping bank. Deep wet soil with rooted grasses and other flowering plants.

(a)

(b)

Figure 14.3
(a) Section of a small freshwater stream, showing microhabitats found in it
(b) A freshwater stream

2 The organisms in the stream will show adaptations enabling them to live in a particular microhabitat. Referring to Figure 14.3, suggest one adaptation which might be needed by invertebrates living in (a) microhabitat B, (b) microhabitat D. *(2 marks)*

Figure 14.4 shows a number of organisms living in a freshwater pond. In the pond, the plants will include large herbaceous species, sometimes fully submerged, such as Canadian pondweed, floating plants such as duckweed, or those rooted in the marshy areas around the margins of the pond, such as common reed. Apart from the more obvious fish and water birds, the majority of animals present will be invertebrates, particularly insect larvae such as damselfly nymphs, along with adult insects, such as water-boatmen. The muddy bottom of the pond will contain countless bacteria and fungi as well as larger burrowing organisms such as worms and midge larvae. The open water will contain millions of microscopic algae (**phytoplankton**) and animals (**zooplankton**). All these organisms are together known as the pond **community**. They provide the biotic factors operating in the pond, such as competition for food, shelter and predation.

Figure 14.4 Some members of a pond community

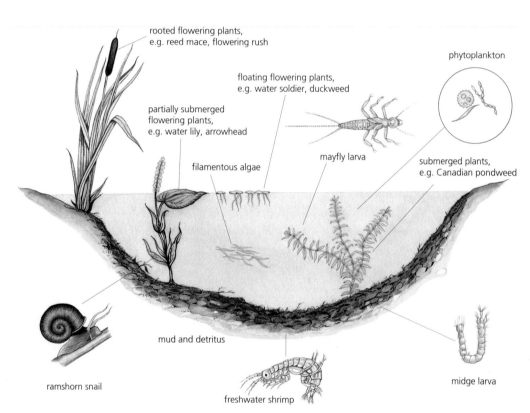

rooted flowering plants, e.g. reed mace, flowering rush

phytoplankton

floating flowering plants, e.g. water soldier, duckweed

partially submerged flowering plants, e.g. water lily, arrowhead

mayfly larva

filamentous algae

submerged plants, e.g. Canadian pondweed

mud and detritus

ramshorn snail

freshwater shrimp

midge larva

Although the term 'community' is used for the entire collection of organisms in an ecosystem, it can also be used to refer to a particular *group* of organisms, such as the phytoplankton community of the pond, or the herbaceous plant community of a meadow. In either case, the word means a collection of organisms of *different species* in a particular area. When we are referring to all the individuals of *one* species found in a habitat, we use the term **population**. For example, we might talk of a population of sticklebacks (small fish) in a pond.

14.3 The energy source of an ecosystem

You will probably already know about one of the fundamental laws of physics: the principle of conservation of energy. This states that energy cannot be created or destroyed: it can only be changed from one form into another. This law applies just as much to ecological as to physical systems. An ecosystem needs an external source of energy which it can 'harness' and convert into other forms.

In the biosphere, this external source of energy is in the form of sunlight. Light energy from the sun falls on green plants and other photosynthetic organisms, such as algae and some bacteria. They use the energy of this light, absorbed by pigments such as chlorophyll, to convert inorganic carbon dioxide and water into organic compounds such as glucose:

$$6CO_2 + 6H_2O \xrightarrow{\text{light}} C_6H_{12}O_6 + 6O_2$$
$$\text{glucose}$$

The glucose can then be converted into other carbohydrates, such as starch and cellulose, or into lipids, or combined with mineral ions to make other organic molecules, such as proteins and nucleic acids. The products of photosynthesis have more energy in them than the reactants, this extra energy having come from the light absorbed by the chlorophyll. In other words, photosynthesis **converts light energy into chemical energy**.

3 What are the two main uses of glucose to a plant?   *(2 marks)*

Organisms which are able to make their own food in this way are known as **autotrophs** ('troph' comes from the Greek word meaning 'food'). Green plants, photosynthetic bacteria and algae are all **photoautotrophs**, since they use light as the energy source for the process.

Some bacteria are called **chemoautotrophs**, since they can fix inorganic molecules into organic ones using chemical energy instead (chemosynthesis). Chemosynthetic bacteria make carbohydrates by using energy not from sunlight, but from the oxidation of simple inorganic materials, such as iron(II), sulphur and hydrogen sulphide. Some of the bacteria involved in the nitrogen cycle (see Section 14.12, page 431) carry out chemosynthesis, for example the nitrifying bacteria *Nitrosomonas* and *Nitrobacter*. These organisms oxidise ammonia and nitrite ions respectively.

Animals, fungi and most bacteria are **heterotrophs** (see Chapter 13, page 375). They depend upon organic materials made by autotrophs as their source of food.

> **Remember**
>
> When inorganic chemicals such as carbon dioxide are converted into organic molecules such as glucose, we say that they are **fixed**, i.e. carbon dioxide is fixed by photosynthesis

Box 14.1 Vent fauna

At the bottom of the deep oceans, where no light can penetrate, there are strange ecosystems relying entirely on the activities of chemosynthetic bacteria. These ecosystems surround zones of superheated, mineral-rich water which is discharged out through vents in the ocean floor. The vents occur along the mid-oceanic ridges at an average depth of 2200 metres and a pressure hundreds of times greater than atmospheric. They discharge water at temperatures up to 400°C. Despite these emergent temperatures, just 15 cm laterally away from a vent, the seawater is cold.

The organisms living there are called 'vent fauna'. They are highly specialised animals, and include tube worms, bivalve and gastropod molluscs and crustaceans. The primary producers for their ecosystem are mainly chemosynthetic sulphur bacteria. These bacteria oxidise inorganic substances such as hydrogen sulphide contained in the superheated water, to provide energy for the synthesis of organic molecules. Some of the bacteria are consumed directly by the animals, while others form symbiotic relationships with the vent fauna. For example, one species of giant tube worm contains bacteria inside its cells. The worm contains a unique form of haemoglobin, which it uses to transport hydrogen sulphide to the bacteria. The bacteria oxidise the hydrogen sulphide and convert carbon dioxide into carbohydrates, which are used by the worm. The adult worm has no mouth or digestive system, but it has a mouth and gut as a juvenile, so that the bacteria can enter its body. Once the two organisms have established the symbiotic relationship, these structures are no longer needed, and disappear.

The ultimate energy source for this community is heat from the Earth's interior, causing the formation of the minerals and enabling them to dissolve. The organisms of the vent fauna have been observed by undersea cameras, but they are adapted for life under enormous pressures and high temperatures, and few survive removal to the surface for study.

The vents probably pre-date life on Earth, having been in existence for some 3.5 to 4 billion years, and some scientists think that the bacterial life in the vents began soon after they formed. The vent fauna were first seen by humans in 1977.

14.4 Primary producers: gross and net primary production

Since autotrophs such as green plants *produce* their own food, they are also called **producers**, or sometimes **primary producers**. This production provides all the energy for all the other organisms in the global ecosystem, and billions of tonnes of carbon dioxide are fixed annually. However, it is a very inefficient process.

At the equator during the day, every second about 1.4 kJ of energy reaches the upper atmosphere from the sun over every square metre. This is equivalent to about 1 or 2 bars of an electric fire, so it is reassuring to know that most of this solar energy never reaches the ground! Over 99% is reflected back into space by clouds and dust, or absorbed by the atmosphere and re-radiated.

Of the solar energy which reaches the ground, most will miss leaves altogether: less than 0.1% actually reaches the surface of leaves and other photosynthetic structures.

When light from the sun *does* hit leaves, a mere 0.5 to 1% of the incident energy is actually used by a plant in photosynthesis (Figure 14.5). Some of the energy is reflected off the leaf, or is transmitted through the leaf and misses the chlorophyll molecules. Over half of the energy consists of light wavelengths which cannot be used in photosynthesis, such as green light or ultraviolet. Finally the reactions of photosynthesis themselves are inefficient, losing much energy as heat.

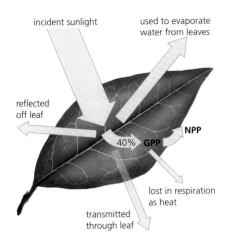

incident sunlight

used to evaporate water from leaves

reflected off leaf

NPP

40% GPP

lost in respiration as heat

transmitted through leaf

Figure 14.5 *The fate of sunlight falling on a leaf.*
GPP = gross primary production
NPP = net primary production

?

4 Explain why a leaf viewed in reflected or transmitted light looks green.

(2 marks)

The 0.5 to 1% of the incident energy which is converted into chemical energy by photosynthesis is called the **gross primary production** or **GPP**. It is usually given in units of energy per metre squared per year ($kJ\,m^{-2}\,yr^{-1}$) or sometimes as the dry mass of organic matter (**biomass**) formed per metre squared per year ($kg\,m^{-2}\,yr^{-1}$). Some of the GPP will be used up by the plant in **respiration (R)**, leaving a fraction called the **net primary production**, or **NPP**. The NPP is the actual rate of production of new biomass or energy by the autotrophs of an ecosystem, and is important because it represents the only biomass that is available for consumption by heterotrophs.

The productivity of different ecosystems can be compared by determination of their NPP values. Table 14.1 shows the NPP of some major ecosystems. They vary widely, as a result of:

- the type of plants growing and their density
- the environmental temperature
- the daylength
- the light intensity
- the availability of soil minerals and water.

Remember

If we subtract the energy of plant respiration from the gross primary production, we get the net primary production, so:

$NPP = GPP - R$

or: $GPP = NPP + R$

Table 14.1 Mean values of NPP in different ecosystems

Ecosystem	NPP/kJ m^{-2} yr^{-1}
extreme desert	260
desert scrub	2600
subsistence agriculture	3000
open ocean	4700
areas of ocean over continental shelf	13500
temperate grasslands	15000
temperate deciduous forest	26000
intensive agriculture	30000
tropical rainforest	40000

After E.P. Odum, *Fundamentals of Ecology*, Third Edition, W. B. Saunders, 1997.

Notice the very high NPP achieved by intensive agriculture, where conditions are managed by humans to maximise productivity, such as by the addition of nitrate and other inorganic fertilisers (see Section 15.6, page 444).

Box 14.2 Maximising primary production in commercial glasshouses

Extension

For a plant to photosynthesise, it needs light, carbon dioxide and a suitable temperature. If any one of these factors is in 'short supply' it is called the **limiting factor**, because it will limit the rate of the photosynthesis reactions. For example, in dim light the limiting factor is the light intensity. If this is increased, it will result in an increase in the rate of photosynthesis (Figure 14.6).

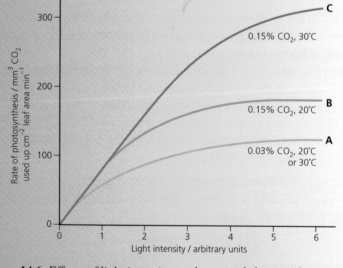

Figure 14.6 Effects of light intensity on the rate of photosynthesis at different concentrations of CO$_2$ and temperature. In experiment A the factor which limits the rate of photosynthesis is carbon dioxide concentration. In B an increase in carbon dioxide concentration results in a higher maximum rate of photosynthesis. In C the maximum rate has been further increased by raising the temperature, even though the carbon dioxide remains at the concentration of experiment B

Extension

However, as the light intensity is increased, there comes a point when it will no longer produce an increased rate of photosynthesis. Above this level of light intensity another factor becomes limiting, for instance the concentration of carbon dioxide in the air, or the temperature. Only if this new limiting factor is increased will the rate be affected. In Britain in summer at midday, the limiting factor for photosynthesis is the level of carbon dioxide in the air.

The principle of limiting factors has been used commercially in glasshouse cultivation of crop plants and flowers, where the factors can be manipulated to produce the maximum primary production. Tomatoes, for example, can be grown in glasshouses with raised concentrations of atmospheric carbon dioxide, produced by burning gas or other fossil fuels. The gas burners increase the temperature, so that this is not a limiting factor. An increased temperature will ensure that enzyme-controlled reactions of photosynthesis proceed at a high rate, but the temperature must not exceed the optimum for the enzyme activity (see Section 4.4, page 104).

Artificial lighting can also be used to prolong the periods when photosynthesis can occur.

Although these measures will theoretically increase GPP, it must be remembered that with a commercial application, the high cost of heating and lighting must be balanced against the profit made by the increased yield: the measures must be economically viable.

14.5   Consumers, food chains and trophic levels

The net primary production of an ecosystem can either remain within the matter of the plants, increasing the plant biomass, or it may be eaten by herbivores. In turn, the herbivores may be eaten by other animals (carnivores). Both herbivores and carnivores have to *consume* food in the form of organic matter, and so are called **consumers**.

There is a third thing that can happen to the NPP of the ecosystem. The producers may die or shed dead leaves, flowers and other parts. This dead material forms **detritus**, which is fed upon by another type of consumer, called a **detritivore**. Detritivores are mainly small invertebrate animals, such as earthworms and insect larvae. They are the first stage in the breakdown of the dead material, both animal and plant in origin, which eventually leads to its recycling (see Section 14.9, page 427). Other organisms which break down the dead plant material are fungi and bacteria, which are known as **decomposers**. These micro-organisms are the ultimate consumers of all dead organic material. Of course, all organisms eventually die, including the decomposers themselves, so they in turn will be eaten by other detritivores and decomposers.

So we can see that the chemical energy contained within the bodies of organisms is passed from one to another along what is called a **food chain**. In turn, this energy is passed to detritivores and decomposers (Figure 14.7)

> ### Remember
>
> A **producer**, or **primary producer**, is an organism which can synthesise its own food from inorganic materials, using an external energy source. Green plants are primary producers, making food by photosynthesis. Their type of nutrition is called **autotrophic**.
>
> A **consumer** is an animal which feeds on organic materials. The nutrition of consumers is called **heterotrophic**

A food chain is described in words as a sequence beginning with the producer, showing the direction of energy flow, for example:

cabbage ⟶ caterpillar ⟶ thrush ⟶ fox

The organisms in the food chain occupy a particular feeding level or **trophic level**. In the food chain shown above, there are four trophic levels:

producer → primary consumer → secondary consumer → tertiary consumer
(herbivore)　　　(first carnivore)　　　(second carnivore)

Food chains rarely contain more than about five trophic levels. In the example above there is no 'super-carnivore' which feeds on the fox. The reason for this will be discussed in more detail in Section 14.8, page 426, but briefly, it is because there is not enough energy entering any chain to support more than a few trophic levels. As we have seen, plants harness less than 1% of the sunlight falling on their leaves. Herbivores only assimilate about 10% of the plant material they eat into their biomass, and carnivores assimilate similar proportions of the animal material they consume. There is a great loss in energy at each trophic level, so that after a few steps in the chain, there is not enough energy left to support a viable population of 'super-carnivores', and the chain ends.

Figure 14.7
(a) Terrestrial food chain
(b) Marine food chain

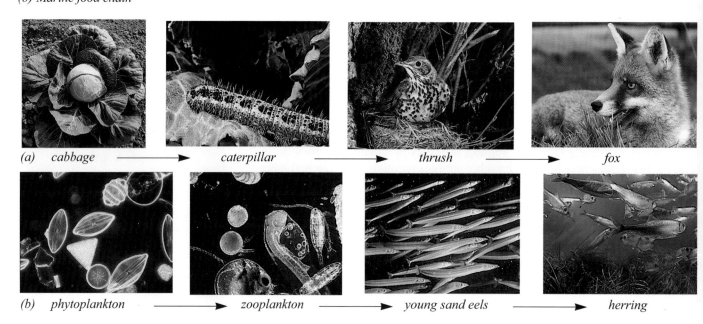

(a)　cabbage ⟶ caterpillar ⟶ thrush ⟶ fox

(b)　phytoplankton ⟶ zooplankton ⟶ young sand eels ⟶ herring

14.6 Food webs

Food chains in an ecosystem do not exist in isolation. In the cabbage ⟶ fox
example shown above, other animals may feed on the cabbage, such as slugs,
aphids or humans, and the fox will feed on many other animals, such as
earthworms or rabbits. An animal may also feed from more than one trophic level,
as with an **omnivore**, which eats both animals and plants. The feeding
relationships are therefore much more complicated than is shown by a simple
chain, and are better described by a diagram linking all the chains together, called
a **food web** (Figure 14.8).

5 To which trophic levels do the following belong: (a) pond snail; (b) dragonfly
larva; (c) perch; (d) midge larva? *(4 marks)*

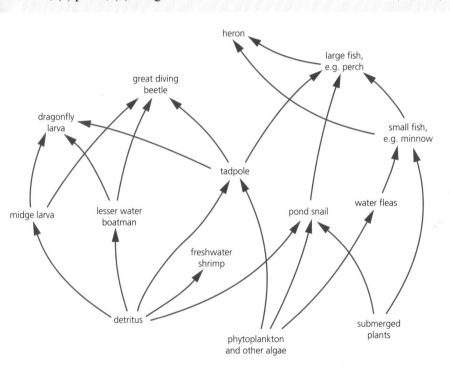

Figure 14.8 A small part of a food web of a freshwater pond

The food web shown in Figure 14.8 is still greatly simplified. A complete web
would be very difficult to draw, having so many food chains both within the
ecosystem and linking to other ecosystems. Ecologists have carried out an
enormous amount of work in establishing the details of food webs and the amount
of energy flowing through the different chains within the web. The approach used
to investigate a food web involves both field and laboratory studies. The first
stage is to observe the predator/prey relationships in the field. In the laboratory,
animals are then dissected to analyse their gut contents and composition of the
faeces, and observations of their food preferences are made. One of the most
useful ways of investigating the size of the energy flow through different chains is
to label plants with harmless radioactive isotopes, such as ^{32}P (radioactive
phosphorus). The amounts of the isotope present can then be measured in the

herbivores which feed on the plants, and in the carnivores feeding on the herbivores.

One use of a food web is to predict the result of disturbances to the community. For example, in the pond community shown in Figure 14.8, suppose that a disease had killed a large number of great diving beetles in the pond. We might predict from the food web that the numbers of herbivores, such as tadpoles and lesser water-boatmen, might increase. However, the very *complexity* of food webs in most ecosystems makes them very stable. In this case, the number of other carnivores such as dragonfly larvae may increase, and the numbers of herbivores remain constant.

Box 14.3 The ecological niche

Any species of organism will have a particular set of biotic and abiotic environmental conditions in which it can survive and reproduce. This set of conditions defines the species' **ecological niche** or role in the habitat. For example, a particular plant species might only grow in alkaline soil of pH 7–8.5, a temperature range of 10–20 °C, and low soil water content. These factors would define its ecological niche, and reflect the plant's specialism in the community. Similarly an animal's ecological niche will be in part determined by its trophic level and feeding method, such as herbivore, grazer, browser or filter-feeder. Other factors may decide an animal's niche, such as the time when it is active (day or night), method of locomotion, and body shape and size.

In different habitats a niche may be filled by a different species. For example, the role of large terrestrial grazing herbivore is filled by deer in Europe, antelope in Africa and kangaroo in Australia. However, two different species cannot occupy the *same* niche in *one* habitat. One will always out-compete the less well-adapted species. This is known as the **competitive exclusion principle**.

14.7 Pyramids of number, biomass and energy

Pyramids of number, biomass and energy are collectively known as **ecological pyramids**. They are different ways of diagrammatically representing the size of the trophic levels in a certain ecosystem, and have different uses, depending on the type of data collected.

Usually, the numbers of organisms at the lower trophic levels are much greater than the numbers at the higher levels. We can show this as a **pyramid of numbers**, where the width of the bars of the pyramid are in proportion to the number of organisms at each trophic level (Figure 14.9). It is basically a bar chart turned on its side.

However, there are several problems with this type of diagram. Firstly, the numbers of organisms at each level may vary enormously, making the pyramid very difficult to draw. For example, a marine ecosystem may have billions of phytoplankton at the base of the pyramid. Secondly, although the size of organism often increases with higher trophic levels, this is not always the case.

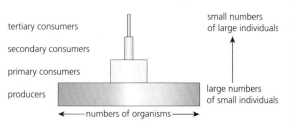

Figure 14.9 *A pyramid of numbers*

A woodland ecosystem might be based on a single oak tree, or a large number of parasites may feed on one organism, producing inverted pyramids (Figure 14.10).

Finally, with many species it is impossible to define what it is that constitutes a 'single' organism. Does a field of grass consist of thousands of separate plants, or one large individual plant connected by its root system? The answer lies somewhere between the two extremes.

These difficulties can be overcome by using a **pyramid of biomass**. This is a diagram showing the total biomass of organisms at each trophic level. The biomass of each species is calculated by multiplying the average mass of an organism by the numbers of organisms. The diagram which results is then usually a pyramid shape. The inverted pyramid shown in Figure 14.10 will now look like Figure 14.11.

If the weight of living organisms is used, this is known as the **fresh** (or **wet**) biomass. However, it is more usual to employ the **dry** biomass. This is the weight of plant or animal material after water has been removed, by drying to a constant weight in an oven. Dry biomass is a more reliable measure, since the water content of organisms, especially plants, can vary a great deal with environmental conditions. Obviously the organisms must be dead for this to be carried out, so it has the disadvantage of being a destructive process.

It is important to note that both pyramids of number and biomass only show the numbers of organisms present *at any one time*. In the case of biomass, this is called the **standing crop**, and does not take into account the changes in biomass over a period of time. This can produce an inverted pyramid. The classic example is that of marine ecosystems, where at certain times of year (early spring around the British Isles) the biomass of zooplankton exceeds that of the phytoplankton (Figure 14.12). This happens because the *primary production* of the phytoplankton is so high and they are *reproducing so fast* that they can support, temporarily, a larger biomass of zooplankton feeding upon them. We say that the phytoplankton have a high **turnover rate**. However, over the whole year, the biomass of the phytoplankton will far exceed that of the zooplankton.

A **pyramid of energy** is probably the most useful type of ecological pyramid, since it shows the productivity for each level in the ecosystem, *during a fixed time period*. If this time period is one year, it will take into account seasonal changes, so the most common units used are $kJ\,m^{-2}\,yr^{-1}$ (kilojoules per square metre per year). Energy also gives more useful information than biomass, since the energy content of different tissues varies a good deal. For example, the energy content of 1 g of fat is higher than 1 g of carbohydrate. So if two animals each weighed one kilogram but one had more fat in its body, it would have the same biomass but a higher energy content. Energy pyramids are never inverted (Figure 14.13).

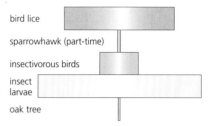

Insectivorous birds include species such as blue tits and great tits. The hawk will feed on birds from more than one tree. Bird lice are blood-sucking parasites of birds (in this case the hawk).

Figure 14.10 *An inverted pyramid of numbers*

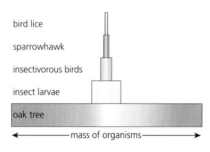

Figure 14.11 *Pyramid of biomass for the same organisms shown in Figure 14.10*

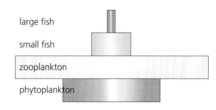

Figure 14.12 *An inverted pyramid of biomass for a marine ecosystem*

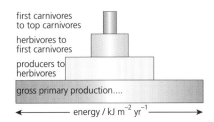

first carnivores
to top carnivores
herbivores to
first carnivores
producers to
herbivores
gross primary production....

⟵ energy / kJ m^{-2} yr^{-1} ⟶

Figure 14.13 *A pyramid of energy*

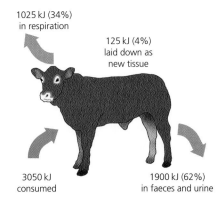

1025 kJ (34%)
in respiration

125 kJ (4%)
laid down as
new tissue

3050 kJ
consumed

1900 kJ (62%)
in faeces and urine

Figure 14.14 *The fate of the energy in the food eaten by a bullock from 1 m^2 of grassland in one year*

! Did You Know

If all humans were to become vegetarians, it would remove a stage in the food chain (the bullock or other source of meat). This would make more efficient use of the energy trapped by plants, by 'cutting out the middle man', and solve any food shortage problems that the world might have.

Alternatively, if vegetarianism does not appeal, we could eat other forms of 'animal protein'. For instance, rabbits can convert grass into meat four times as fast as a bullock!

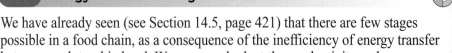

14.8 Energy transfer through food chains

We have already seen (see Section 14.5, page 421) that there are few stages possible in a food chain, as a consequence of the inefficiency of energy transfer between each trophic level. We can now look at the productivity and energy losses of each level in more detail.

Remember that less than 1% of the incident sunlight energy is used by plants in photosynthesis (the gross primary production). Of this GPP, the percentage converted into net primary production (after the plant's respiratory losses have been accounted for) varies widely, depending on the photosynthetic efficiency of the producers. The NPP of a pond ecosystem may be only 40% of its GPP, whereas a more efficient producer, such as a field of corn (maize), has an NPP about 76% of its GPP.

There are three things that can happen to this NPP:

● it can produce an increase in plant biomass

● it can be consumed by detritivores and decomposers

● it can be eaten by herbivores.

Only a small proportion of the NPP passes to herbivores. Consider the example of a bullock (a young bull raised for beef) grazing on a field of grass. The bullock only consumes about 14% of the NPP of the grass. This is less than the amount eaten by other herbivores such as slugs and grasshoppers (about 16%) and much less than the NPP consumed by decomposers (70%).

We can use the bullock as an example of the next stage in the food chain. How much energy does it pass to the carnivores (humans)? The grass will be digested by the bullock, some of the material will be assimilated into its tissues, and some undigested remains pass out of its body in the faeces. So, four things can happen to the energy contained in the grass eaten by the animal (Figure 14.14).

● Some of the energy is lost in the faeces.

● The assimilated energy may be used in respiration and lost as heat.

● The assimilated energy may be used to increase the bullock's biomass, i.e. growth.

● The assimilated energy may be lost as breakdown products in the bullock's urine.

Less than 5% of the energy finishes up as growth of the bullock (and even less forms 'useful' tissues, i.e. meat which can be consumed by humans).

?

6 Young animals convert far more of their food into growth than older ones (in cattle ten times as much). Explain why chickens are killed for meat at three to four months old.

(2 marks)

If we consider ecosystems containing higher trophic levels, the same sort of energy losses take place at each level (Figure 14.15).

We can now see exactly why the energy available to each trophic level (E_1 to E_4) decreases as it is passed along the food chains. By the tertiary consumer stage there is no energy left to support a viable population of carnivores above this level. This is the reason why food chains are rarely more than five stages in length.

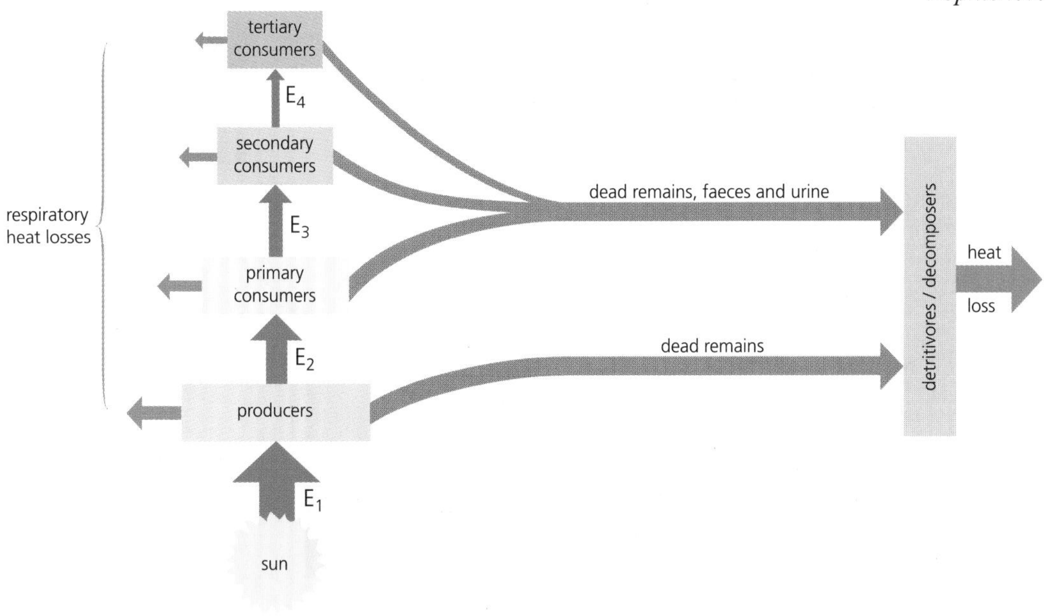

Figure 14.15 Energy flow through trophic levels

14.9 Biogeochemical cycles

Although energy is continually lost from an ecosystem as heat, so that a source of new energy is needed (the sun), there is a finite amount of matter available on the Earth to build the bodies of organisms. The elements which make up living tissues have to be used and re-used over and over again. A molecule of oxygen that you inhale may have been made by a plant during its photosynthesis hundreds of years ago. This is a fundamental difference between matter and energy: energy flow is **linear** while flow of matter is **cyclical**.

All the elements which make up the bodies of organisms take part in cycles, where they alternate between organic and inorganic forms. The biological component of these cycles involves the movement of materials between producers, consumers and decomposers (Figure 14.16), but there is also a geochemical component of the cycles, where the elements pass through rocks, water and the air. This is why they are called **biogeochemical cycles**.

Remember

Energy in an ecosystem is not recycled. There must be an external energy source (usually sunlight) since energy is lost as heat as it passes along food chains. On the other hand there is a finite amount of matter available, and so elements which make up organisms must be recycled when they die

Three important biogeochemical cycles are the carbon, nitrogen and water cycles. They share a common feature in that each involves movement of molecules into and out of the air (as carbon dioxide, nitrogen and water vapour) so that the atmosphere acts as a **global reservoir**. This is of particular importance when we consider the disruption caused to the cycles by human activity (Chapter 15) which can have consequences affecting the global ecosystem.

Figure 14.16 The biological *component of biogeochemical cycles*

The saprobiontic activities of decomposers (fungi and some bacteria) releases inorganic compounds from the dead bodies and waste materials of organisms, producing a supply of raw materials for producers.

14.10 The carbon cycle

Remember that all organic molecules, by definition, contain the element carbon (see Chapter 3, page 61). This carbon is exchanged with the air during two main biochemical processes: photosynthesis and respiration. The air only contains about 0.03 to 0.04% carbon dioxide, and although this seems to be a very small amount, the total mass in the atmosphere is about 7.6×10^{14} kg, which is a little more than that present in all the living organisms on the Earth (Table 14.2).

Table 14.2 Mass of carbon contained *in different parts of the Earth*

Part of the Earth	Mass of carbon/kg $\times 10^{14}$
organisms	5.6
atmosphere	7.6
surface ocean	10
soil	15
ocean sediments	30
deep ocean	370
rocks	500,000

Carbon dioxide also dissolves in water and forms hydrogencarbonate ions (HCO$_3^-$) or carbonate ions (CO$_3^{2-}$). Most of this is present in the oceans: the surface ocean alone contains more carbon than the atmosphere. Not surprisingly, over 99.9% of carbon on Earth is 'locked up' in rocks such as limestone and chalk (calcium carbonate).

Plants and other autotrophs take up carbon dioxide from the air (or from water, if they are aquatic) during photosynthesis. The carbon dioxide is then fixed to form carbohydrates and other organic molecules. Subsequently, the plants are eaten by herbivores, or they die and form food for decomposers. Each of these organisms, plants, herbivores and decomposers, returns carbon dioxide to the air or water as they respire (Figure 14.17).

The amount of carbon fixed by photosynthesis *almost* equals the amount produced by respiration. In certain ecosystems, dead organic material is not fully broken down by decomposers. Millions of years ago, in acid, waterlogged, anaerobic conditions, vegetation which accumulated in peat beds formed layer upon layer of plant debris. This material was compacted and compressed by the weight of sediments above it, eventually forming the hard rock we know as coal (Figure 14.18).

Other types of sedimentary rock contain organic matter from the bodies of marine plankton. These form oil or natural gas deposits in a similar way to the formation of coal.

Coal, oil and natural gas, along with more recently formed peat, are examples of **fossil fuels**. We are adding to the atmospheric levels of carbon dioxide by our burning (**combustion**) of these fuels (the problems that this brings are discussed in Sections 15.23, page 465, and 15.24, page 468). Today the Earth does not have the same extensive swamps and marshy areas to form coal deposits, and the total vegetation is less, so much less carbon is entering the long-term carbon reservoir of fossil fuels.

Despite the greatest proportion of carbon being present in the Earth's rocks and sediments (Table 14.2), very small transfers of carbon occur between this reservoir and the rest of the cycle. Rock containing carbonates, such as limestone, was formed from the calcareous skeletons of plankton or corals millions of years ago. Weathering of these rocks, by the action of acidic rain, along with volcanic activity, returns the carbon to the atmosphere as carbon dioxide again. The full events of the carbon cycle are shown in Figure 14.19.

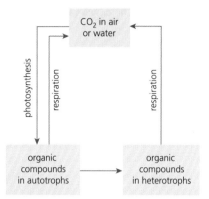

Figure 14.17 *The biological part of the carbon cycle*

Figure 14.18 *The fossilised remains of tree ferns, 300 million years old, show the origin of this coal deposit*

7 In parts of South America, the rainforests are being burned and the soils ploughed for agriculture. How would you expect this to affect the carbon content of (a) the air; (b) the soil? Explain your answers.   *(5 marks)*

Figure 14.19 *The carbon cycle*

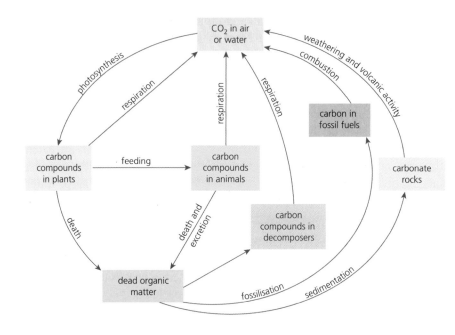

14.11 The water cycle

About two-thirds of the Earth is covered by water, and the oceans make up by far the largest weight of the Earth's water (96%). This water constantly cycles through the biosphere, evaporating from the ocean surface and falling as rain or snow (precipitation) over the sea again, or onto the land (Figure 14.20).

Figure 14.20 *The water cycle*

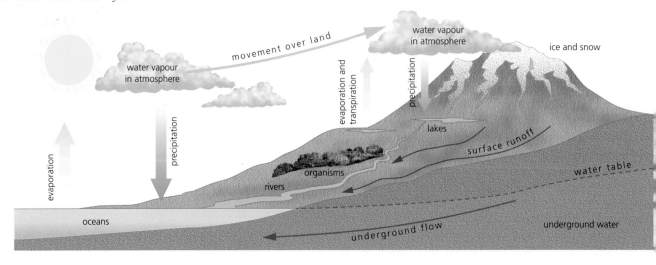

Most of the rest of the water on Earth (3%) is 'locked up' in ice and snow, and a very small percentage (0.03%) enters soil, streams, rivers and lakes. A surprisingly large amount of water (1%) seeps through the soil to the rocks, where it enters the **water table**. This is the highest point below the surface where the rocks are saturated with water, and can vary from a depth of a few centimetres to hundreds of metres. Water flows back to the ocean through this underground source, or through surface runoff.

Some of the water that falls upon the land is taken up by organisms, through drinking by animals or through the roots of plants. The water is returned to the atmosphere by evaporation from gas exchange surfaces such as leaves and lungs, or to the soil by the excretion of urine.

14.12 The nitrogen cycle

Nitrogen is a component of all amino acids and therefore of proteins (see Section 3.16, page 83). It is also a constituent of many other organic molecules, including nucleic acids. The availability of nitrogen to plants is often a limiting factor in the production of new plant biomass, which is why so much nitrogen-containing fertiliser is used in arable farming, in order to increase crop yield.

Although the air contains 79% nitrogen, it is a very stable gas which cannot be used by plants until it is combined with other elements. The source of nitrogen for green plants and other autotrophs is in the form of nitrate ions (NO_3^-) or sometimes ammonium ions (NH_4^+) from the soil or water. Heterotrophs obtain nitrogen from digestion of organic materials.

The nitrogen cycle (Figure 14.21) consists of five main processes:

- **assimilation**, the building up of nitrogen into proteins and other organic molecules by plants
- **ammonification**, where organic matter in the soil (from dead organisms and excreta) is converted to ammonia
- **nitrification**, the oxidation of ammonia to nitrate by other micro-organisms
- **denitrification**, where certain types of bacteria reduce nitrate to nitrogen gas again
- **nitrogen fixation**, where soil bacteria reduce atmospheric nitrogen to ammonia.

Figure 14.21 The nitrogen cycle

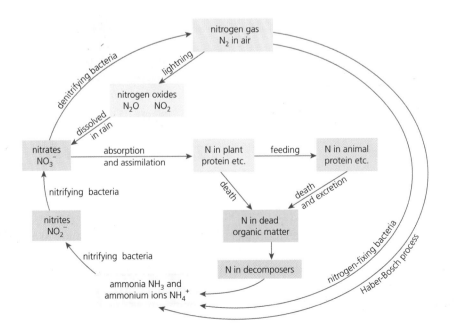

?

8 Explain why (a) nitrification is an oxidation reaction and (b) nitrogen fixation is a reduction reaction. *(2 marks)*

Assimilation

Plants absorb nitrate ions from the soil and carry out the essential step of converting this inorganic form of nitrogen into organic nitrogenous compounds, the process of **assimilation**. In the plant roots, nitrate is reduced to nitrite (NO_2^-) by the action of an enzyme. The nitrite is transported through the xylem to the leaves, where a second enzyme reduces the nitrite to ammonium ions (NH_4^+). The ammonium ions are then combined with carbohydrates to form amino acids. Some plants are able to absorb ammonium ions directly from the soil for this purpose.

Plant protein and other nitrogenous organic compounds form the source of nitrogen for herbivorous animals. In the animal's gut, proteolytic (protein-digesting) enzymes break down proteins into amino acids. These are transported to the cells and assimilated into the proteins of the animal's body (see Section 13.5, page 393). By a similar process of digestion and assimilation, protein in the bodies of herbivores is passed to carnivores.

Animals cannot store protein in their bodies, so excess amino acids are broken down into waste products such as urea (in mammals), uric acid (birds and some reptiles), and ammonia (freshwater fish). These are excreted from the body and all eventually end up as ammonia through the action of soil bacteria.

Ammonification

Dead plant and animal remains, as well as faeces, are also converted to ammonia by the action of soil decomposers (bacteria and fungi). These **saprobionts** feed on the dead organic material and excrete ammonia as a waste product, in the process known as **ammonification**. Ammonia forms ammonium ions (NH_4^+) in solution in the soil water.

Nitrification

In well-aerated soils, ammonium ions are oxidised by other soil bacteria, such as members of the genera *Nitrosomonas* and *Nitrococcus*, to nitrites. Nitrites are oxidised to nitrates by a second group of bacteria, such as *Nitrobacter*:

$$\underset{\text{ammonium}}{NH_4^+} \xrightarrow{\textit{Nitrosomonas}} \underset{\text{nitrite}}{NO_2^-} \xrightarrow{\textit{Nitrobacter}} \underset{\text{nitrate}}{NO_3^-}$$

This process, forming nitrate available for plants to use, is called **nitrification**. The bacteria involved obtain their metabolic energy from these oxidation reactions, which need oxygen to proceed.

If the soil is waterlogged and anaerobic, bacterial oxidation of ammonia to nitrate is prevented, and only ammonia is available in the soil for plants to use. Other conditions, such as acid soil or low temperature, also prevent nitrification. Most nitrate is formed during the spring and summer months when a supply of nitrate builds up in the soil, especially if no crops are being grown on the land.

However, nitrate is very soluble, and will be washed out of the soil by heavy rain, a process called **leaching**. It passes down through the sub-soil, where it is unavailable to plant roots, and into streams, rivers, lakes and the sea. The enrichment of these water bodies with nitrate and other ions is called **eutrophication**, and is dealt with in Section 15.8, page 445.

Other processes add nitrogen to the soil. Lightning oxidises nitrogen gas in the atmosphere, the oxides then combining with rainwater to form nitrate. Nitrate and ammonia is also added to arable land in the form of inorganic fertiliser, made industrially by the Haber-Bosch process.

Denitrification

Denitrification takes place in soil which has a high nitrogen content but becomes anaerobic, through, for example, waterlogging. This process *removes* nitrate from the soil, by reducing it to nitrogen gas by a series of reactions:

$$NO_3^- \longrightarrow NO_2^- \longrightarrow \underbrace{NO \longrightarrow N_2O}_{\text{nitrogen oxides}} \longrightarrow N_2$$

It is carried out by a number of species of bacteria, including *Pseudomonas denitrificans*, *Thiobacillus denitrificans* and some members of the genus *Bacillus*. Reduction of the nitrate to nitrogen gas produces oxygen, which the bacteria can use for aerobic respiration. Waterlogged soils become depleted in nitrate as a result of the activity of these bacteria. To prevent this, farmers reduce waterlogging by implementing soil drainage systems and ploughing to aerate the soil.

Nitrogen fixation

A number of bacteria living in the soil, such as species of *Azotobacter* and *Clostridium*, can reduce nitrogen gas in the air into ammonia, a process called **nitrogen fixation**:

$$N_2 + 6H^+ + 6e^- \longrightarrow 2NH_3$$

This is the equivalent of the industrial Haber-Bosch process, which needs high temperatures and pressures (450°C and 200 Atmospheres) and an iron catalyst. The biological process can work efficiently at 20°C and 1 Atmosphere of pressure because it is catalysed by an enzyme called **nitrogenase**.

One genus of nitrogen-fixing bacteria, *Rhizobium*, forms a **symbiotic** or **mutualistic** relationship with plants known as legumes (such as peas, beans and clover). The bacterium lives in the roots of the legumes, where it causes the growth of swellings called **root nodules** (Figure 14.22).

The bacterium gains carbohydrate and energy from the plant, and the plant uses the ammonia produced by the bacterium, to make amino acids. This relationship is dealt with in more detail in Section 13.9, page 405.

Figure 14.22 *Nitrogen-fixing root nodules on a bean plant*

9 Which of the following groups of organisms are not *essential* for the cycling of nitrogen, and why? Choose from: herbivores, nitrogen-fixing bacteria, denitrifying bacteria, plants, decomposers. *(4 marks)*

Extension

Box 14.4 Nitrogen-fixing genes

An ongoing area of research in gene technology is investigating the possibility of taking genes for nitrogen fixation from *Rhizobium* and incorporating them into non-leguminous plants, particularly cereals. This would have very great economic and environmental benefits. It would increase the yield of the cereal plants, whilst reducing the need for nitrogenous fertilisers and the pollution they cause (Section 15.8, page 445).

One of the difficulties with this idea is that the genes governing nitrogen fixation in *Rhizobium* are part of a very complex system, involving groups of genes controlling:

● infection of legume roots by specific *Rhizobium* species

● synthesis of nitrogenase enzyme

● regulation of the nitrogen fixation reactions.

Nitrogenase itself is a complex enzyme coded for by a number of genes scattered throughout the bacterial genome. This complexity has so far made it difficult to isolate and transfer the necessary genes to cereal plants.

 Did You Know

Before the Second World War, farmers in Britain commonly carried out a practice called **crop rotation**. Their land was divided into four areas and each area was sown with a different crop in a rotating sequence. The crops were root crops, such as turnips and mangolds, barley, a mix of clover and grass, and wheat. The root crops were fed to cattle, sheep or pigs. The clover/grass mixture was either ploughed into the ground or made into hay for winter feed. Barley was used to feed stock, and wheat was used for human consumption. This system was very effective in conserving the mineral content of the soil. Cereals and root crops use up different minerals from the soil. Wheat requires large amounts of nitrate, and clover is a leguminous plant which has root nodules containing *Rhizobium*. When this crop was ploughed into the soil it enriched it with nitrogen, allowing the growth of wheat. Manure from the animals was used to replace the minerals in the soil.

During the war and afterwards, there was great pressure on farmers to produce food faster and more efficiently. One way this was achieved was to grow crops as **monocultures**, where only one species is grown, such as wheat, and no animals are kept. Although this does have advantages, such as ease of harvesting, the single species which is grown tends to exhaust the soil of certain minerals. This can then only be remedied by adding large amounts of artificial fertiliser.

Nowadays, there is a trend amongst 'organic' farmers to go back to crop rotation to remove the need for using chemical fertilisers.

Summary – (14) Ecosystems

- Ecology is the scientific study of ecosystems. An ecosystem consists of a community of organisms (the biotic component) and their physical and chemical environment (the abiotic component).

- An ecosystem contains many habitats. A habitat is the place where an organism lives. Habitats may be further divided into microhabitats. An organism will show adaptations which suit it to its habitat.

- The external energy source for most ecosystems is sunlight, absorbed by chlorophyll of green plants and other photosynthesising organisms. These are called producers, since they produce food for animals and other heterotrophic organisms. Energy is passed on through food chains, which are linked with other chains as food webs.

- The number of organisms, their biomass and energy content at each trophic level can each be represented by diagrams called ecological pyramids, although pyramids of energy are the most useful.

- Energy is lost between each feeding or trophic level of a food chain, through respiratory losses and in waste products, which limits the energy content of higher trophic levels and the length of food chains.

- Although energy transfer through the ecosystem is linear, matter is recycled by processes called biogeochemical cycles.

- The carbon cycle is essentially a balance between photosynthesis, which uses up carbon dioxide, and respiration, which forms it. When organisms die, their carbon-containing compounds are recycled back to carbon dioxide by the respiration of detritivores and decomposers. On top of this, there is the combustion of fossil fuels, which adds to the atmospheric reservoir of carbon dioxide.

- The water cycle describes how water passes from its reservoir in the oceans, precipitates over the land and returns to the oceans through rivers and ground water. The passage of water through organisms forms a relatively small part of this cycle.

- Nitrogen is absorbed by plants as nitrate ions and assimilated into organic compounds such as proteins. The nitrogen in these compounds is passed to animals, and when plants and animals die, to decomposers. Ammonia from decomposition of organisms is recycled back to nitrate ions by the action of nitrifying bacteria. Nitrogen gas in the air is also 'fixed' to ammonia by other micro-organisms and through industrial processes.

❓ Answers

1 The pond as a habitat means just the surroundings, or place where the organisms live *(1)* whereas the pond as an ecosystem means the surroundings and the organisms together *(1)*.

2 **(a)** There are several possibilities, but the low oxygen content of the water might require special adaptations for extracting oxygen, such as the presence of haemoglobin. Another possibility is specialised mouthparts for feeding on detritus *(1)*.

  (b) Likely adaptations are attachment mechanisms, such as hooks or suckers, to stop the animals being washed away. Filter feeding methods are also common, using the flow of water *(1)*.

3 To build up carbohydrate-containing compounds, i.e. growth *(1)* and as a source of energy *(1)*.

4 Green light wavelengths are reflected off leaves and also transmitted through them *(1)*, so they look green when the light enters our eyes. Other wavelengths such as red and blue are absorbed by leaves *(1)*.

5 **(a)** Primary consumer *and* detritivore *(1)*

  (b) Secondary consumer *(1)*

  (c) Secondary *and* tertiary consumer *(1)*

  (d) Detritivore *(1)*

  Alternative names are acceptable, such as herbivore/first/second carnivore.

6 It is more profitable *(1)* to kill a chicken for meat when it is quite young, before its growth rate has slowed. An older bird will still need feeding (which costs money) but will not be turning this food into much meat *(1)*.

7 **(a)** Burning the forests will increase *(1)* the carbon dioxide in the air due to less photosynthesis *(1)* and as a direct result of combustion *(1)*.

  (b) Ploughing reduces *(1)* the carbon stored in the soil, since increased aeration of the soil increases activity of decomposers, converting organic carbon to carbon dioxide *(1)*.

8 **(a)** Conversion of ammonium ions to nitrite, and nitrite to nitrate are oxidation reactions, because they involve the addition of oxygen *(1)*.

  (b) Nitrogen fixation to ammonia is a reduction reaction because it involves the addition of hydrogen *(1)*.

9 The cycle would still be possible without:

  (a) Herbivores *(1)* because nitrogen could still pass from plants to decomposers when the plants die *(1)*.

  (b) Denitrifying bacteria *(1)* because they actually *remove* nitrate from the supply needed by plants *(1)*.

  All the other organisms are essential to maintain a continuous cycle.

End of Chapter Questions

1 Explain the meaning of each of the following ecological terms:

  (a) pyramid of biomass *(2 marks)*

  (b) net primary production (NPP) *(2 marks)*

  (c) community. *(2 marks)*

  (Total 6 marks)

2 A student tried to construct a pyramid of fresh biomass for a pond. She cut the bottom out of a plastic bin and sank the bin in the pond, trapping the pond organisms inside, so that they could be removed and identified. All the plant material in the bin was collected and weighed. The animals were collected in a net and identified. They were then sorted into herbivores or carnivores and weighed. All organisms were then returned to the pond.

Here are her results:

Organisms	Fresh biomass/g
Plants	1790
Herbivores	225
Carnivores	28

(a) Use this data to draw a pyramid of fresh biomass on a piece of graph paper. *(3 marks)* N2.3

(b) Calculate the percentage loss of fresh biomass between the plants and the herbivores. Show your working. *(2 marks)* N2.2

(c) Give two reasons why there is a decrease in mass between the plants and the herbivores. *(2 marks)*

(d) Suggest two errors involved in using this method for constructing a pyramid of fresh biomass for the pond. *(2 marks)*

(Total 9 marks)

3 The diagram below shows part of the nitrogen cycle.

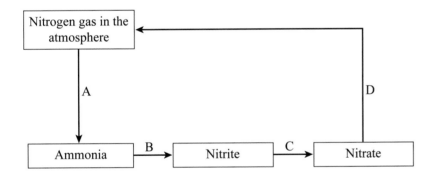

(a) Name a genus of bacteria which is responsible for each of the reactions A, B, C and D. *(4 marks)*

(b) Describe the conditions in which the bacteria responsible for reaction D will thrive. *(2 marks)*

Edexcel 1998 *(Total 6 marks)*

4 An experiment was carried out to compare the uptake of nitrogen in soyabean seedlings grown in an atmosphere enriched with carbon dioxide with that of seedlings grown in a normal atmosphere (control plants). Soyabeans belong to *Papilionaceae* (legumes) and all the experimental plants had root nodules containing *Rhizobium*.

At the beginning of the experiment, the seedlings were 25 days old. The total amount of nitrogen incorporated into compounds in the plants was then measured at intervals until the plants were 100 days old.

The results of the experiment are shown in the graph below.

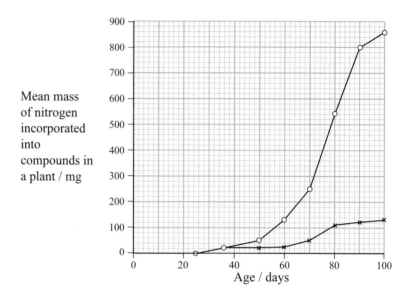

(a) (i) Of the nitrogen incorporated into compounds in the control plants, 75% was taken up from the soil. State the form in which this nitrogen was taken up by the plants. *(1 mark)*

(ii) Explain how the control plants obtained the remaining 25% of their nitrogen. *(2 marks)*

(b) (i) Compare the effect of the atmosphere enriched with carbon dioxide with that of the normal atmosphere on the mass of nitrogen incorporated into the seedlings. *(3 marks)*

(ii) Suggest *one* reason for any differences you observe. *(1 mark)*

(c) A possible application of gene technology would be to incorporate genes for nitrogen fixation into cereal plants.

Suggest possible benefits of such an application. *(2 marks)*

Edexcel 1997

(Total 9 marks)

C3.3 **5** Give an account of the flow of energy through a food web. *(Total 10 marks)*

Edexcel 1999

15 Effects of humans on ecosystems

Historians have estimated that the world human population in AD 500 was about 100 million. By the year 1650 it had steadily risen to 500 million, but over the next 350 years the numbers of humans on the Earth increased dramatically, displaying a **J-shaped growth curve** (Figure 15.1).

In October 1999 the world population officially reached six billion (6 000 000 000), and about 80 million people are added to this total each year – equivalent to adding the population of a country the size of the United States every three years. By 2050, the projected figure is about 9 billion.

The population has been growing this fast largely because of a decline in death rates. This has happened as a result of better nutrition, improved medicine and improved sanitation. Birth rates have also fallen, especially in developed countries, but not as fast as the reduction in death rates.

The human species is different from all others in that it can live in most of the Earth's habitats. We have developed the means to control the biotic and abiotic environment, rather than having to adapt to it. The problem with this is that the enormous human population growth is over-exploiting the Earth's natural resources and crowding out non-domesticated animal and plant species. All people, whether in developed or less developed countries, would like to be fed, clothed, housed and have access to transport and other amenities. As the population increases, more environmental resources must be exploited to achieve these needs. More fuel is needed for industry and transport, more land must be cleared for agriculture and development.

As well as consuming resources, humans are producing waste and pollutants which adversely affect the environment. These products derive from all aspects of human activity, including agriculture, mining and industry. They affect local ecosystems, but frequently have a global effect too.

This chapter includes:
- **human population growth and changes to agriculture**
- **crop plants for different environments**
- **fertilisers and pesticides**
- **environmental problems caused by agriculture**
- **biological control of pests**
- **deforestation and desertification**
- **water pollution by sewage**
- **pollution indicator species**
- **energy resources, fossil fuels and acid rain**
- **the greenhouse effect**
- **biofuels as renewable sources of energy**
- **legislation to control pollution.**

15.1 Agriculture

The human activity which has had the most profound effect on the environment is agriculture. The agricultural revolution 10 000 years ago replaced a nomadic, hunter-gatherer lifestyle with a settled existence, made possible by domestication of animals and planting of food crops. In the last few hundred years, a second agricultural revolution has brought improved methods of cultivation, new crop plants from other countries, and more efficient methods of transportation and storage of food. These changes were a major factor in allowing the exponential rise in human population.

This century, technological innovations such as the use of artificial fertiliser, pesticides and selective breeding of crop and livestock species have further increased food production to such an extent that until the early 1980s, the increase kept pace with the rise in global population. (However, it must be stressed that malnutrition and starvation were, and still are, common in many poorer areas of the world.) Since this time, food production has risen more slowly than population growth.

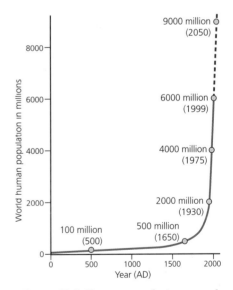

Figure 15.1 Human population growth

(a)

(b)

(c)

Figure 15.2
(a) Maize
(b) Sorghum
(c) Rice

One of the main reasons for this is that many agricultural practices, though effective in the short term, have a detrimental effect on the environment in the long run, reducing the yields that can be sustained. For example, soil erosion and desertification can result from mis-management of land (see Section 15.19, page 458). The slowdown in production has been felt most in poorer countries which are often forced to buy food from countries which produce an excess, such as the United States and Europe. This increases the 'third world debt', leading to poverty and malnutrition.

Problems such as these have led environmentalists to propose the idea of **sustainable agriculture**, which aims to maintain the ability of the land to produce food. Before we can consider this, we must look in more detail at farming methods and the problems they bring for the environment.

15.2 Selection of suitable crop plants

Plants have evolved adaptations which allow them to grow in a particular environment. These adaptations are important in determining suitable crop plants which can be grown in different parts of the world. This can be illustrated by looking at different species of cereal. Cereals are grasses which have been domesticated and artificially selected to improve their yield of edible material, stored in the seed heads. They often form the staple part of the diet of people throughout the world, and include such species as wheat, oats, rice, maize and sorghum. Each species has both structural and physiological adaptations which enable it to grow in a particular habitat. We can illustrate this by considering three examples (see Figure 15.2).

Maize (*Zea mays*) is a tropical plant with a specialised method of photosynthesis. It is an example of what is called a C4 plant. Without going into details of the complex biochemical pathways involved, this name refers to the first product of photosynthesis produced in these plants, which is an organic acid containing 4 carbon atoms. Most temperate plants produce a 3-carbon compound and are known as C3 plants. The relevance of this is that C4 plants like maize can photosynthesise efficiently at very low concentrations of atmospheric carbon dioxide. They can fix carbon dioxide from an atmosphere containing as little as 0.1 ppm (parts per million) carbon dioxide, compared with 50–100 ppm for C3 plants. At atmospheric concentrations of carbon dioxide (0.03–0.04%) they have a higher rate of photosynthesis than C3 plants.

For a C3 plant in temperate climates, the **limiting factor** for photosynthesis in summer, during daylight, is the level of carbon dioxide in the air (for an explanation of limiting factors see Box 14.2, page 420). At the high light intensities and high temperatures of the tropics this is also the case, and here, C4 plants, with their higher rate of fixation of carbon dioxide, are at an advantage.

Although maize was originally a tropical crop, originating in Central America, it was taken north by native Americans. It was adopted by European settlers to the United States (who called it corn) and brought back to Europe. Various strains of maize have been bred, with the result that it now has a wide geographic distribution, throughout North America (where it is mainly used as animal feed) and Europe. It is the third most important cereal crop in the world, after wheat and rice, and there is increasing interest in maize in Africa and Asia as a food crop.

Sorghum (*Sorghum bicolor*) is also a C4 plant, and grows well in hot, dry conditions. Whereas maize comes from the humid tropics, sorghum originates from the semi-arid tropics of Africa. Both the plant and its embryo (in the seed) can tolerate extremely high ambient temperatures, and sorghum will continue to respire and photosynthesise at 35 °C. It shows a number of xerophytic adaptations (see Section 9.11, page 256). These include an extensive root system, which takes advantage of any available water, leaves with a thick waxy cuticle, and reduced numbers of stomata in sunken pits on the leaves, to reduce water loss. The leaves also fold around the midrib (like a butterfly's wings) to reduce exposed surface area.

1 Explain how the location of stomata in sunken pits reduces water loss from the leaf. *(2 marks)*

In terms of area under cultivation sorghum is the world's fifth cereal after wheat, rice, maize and barley. It is grown in several of the drier African countries, as well as Asia, and North and South America. The world's leading producers are the United States, India, Nigeria, Argentina, Mexico and Sudan, and it is used for food, as an animal feed and even for building materials. Only in the cool and wet north-west Europe is the plant not grown.

Rice on the other hand is unique among the cereals in being able to grow in flooded conditions. Soil which is waterlogged lacks oxygen (it is **anaerobic**) and the tissues of most plants cannot survive anaerobic conditions for very long. The rice plant is adapted to do so by having tissues composed of cells separated by prominent gas-filled spaces called **aerenchyma**. As the root grows down into the oxygen-deficient soil, continuous formation of aerenchyma behind the growing tip allows oxygen to diffuse downwards through the air spaces. The leaves produce oxygen from photosynthesis, which is transported to the roots by this pathway.

Rice seeds are also able to tolerate flooded soil, but in a different way. The seed embryo and **coleoptile** (a sheath covering the first leaves to emerge) can respire **anaerobically** (without using oxygen), producing ethanol, which the cells can tolerate. In this way, the seed can survive weeks of immersion in water, until the coleoptile breaks through the water surface and becomes a 'snorkel' for the submerged parts of the plant. The developed roots are just as intolerant to lack of oxygen as those of other species.

Rice is produced in the tropical and sub-tropical regions of all continents, and is second only to wheat in total production. Despite its tropical origins, it is a C3 plant. In the Far Eastern countries, such as China, India, Indonesia and Japan, rice is grown in the familiar 'paddy fields' on 'heavy' soils which retain water, and close to a water supply. The United States is the largest exporter of the cereal, not as a consequence of high production, but because poorer countries consume all they produce. In the USA, rice seeds are soaked in water to make them heavy and then seeded from aeroplanes over the prepared soil. As the seeds grow, they are watered until covered to a depth of several centimetres. Gigantic combine harvesters with huge tyres collect the grain after the water has been drained from the mature crops.

Rice illustrates well a basic feature of all domesticated animal and plant species: it has been greatly modified by artificial selection to produce varieties with improved characteristics. The International Rice Institute in the Philippines has developed strains with features such as:

● rapid growth of the seedlings

● short, stiff stems

● toleration of low temperatures

● resistance to salt in irrigation water

● resistance to disease and pests

● maximum yield of grain.

Rice is an enormously important plant: its growth is critical for feeding the world's increasing population.

15.3 Agriculture controls the biotic and abiotic environment

Many plant and animal species have been domesticated and improved by selective breeding. However, their value as a food source can only be fully realised if they are kept in optimum conditions for growth. To this end, humans have exercised a control over the biotic and abiotic environment, 'improving' conditions to maximise productivity. Examples of these measures include:

● the use of fertilisers to replace nutrients removed from the soil

● the use of herbicides to decrease competition with weeds

● the use of fungicides and insecticides to kill fungal and insect pests

● 'improvement' of poor-quality land to make it suitable for farming.

As we shall see, although these measures have been very successful in achieving the desired results, they have brought with them a number of environmental problems, often of global proportions.

15.4 Fertilisers

In a 'natural' ecosystem, such as a tropical rainforest, the fertility of the soil is maintained by the recycling of minerals. Plants extract these from the soil and combine them with the products of photosynthesis to form all the organic compounds of the plant's tissues. When the plants die, the minerals are returned to the soil through the action of decomposers (see Section 14.9, page 427).

Compare this with an agricultural ecosystem. When crop plants are harvested, the mineral nutrients they have absorbed from the soil are removed from the habitat and not recycled. If this process were to be repeated for even a few harvests, the soil would become deficient in minerals and the crop yield would fall dramatically. As well as this, lack of minerals would make the plants susceptible to disease. The answer is to replace the lost minerals by applying **fertilisers** after the harvest.

There are two types of fertiliser. **Organic fertilisers** consist of decomposing plant or animal remains, whereas **inorganic fertilisers** are mixtures of mineral salts made by industrial chemical companies. They have different effects on soil.

15.5 Organic fertilisers

Organic fertilisers alter both the physical and chemical characteristics of the soil. The most widely used forms are **manures**, such as composted waste plant material, farmyard manure, poultry waste and sewage sludge. Farmyard manure consists of the urine and faeces of animals together with bedding material such as straw (Figure 15.3).

The organic material of manures breaks down only slowly under the action of decomposing micro-organisms, gradually releasing minerals back into the soil. They have a number of other advantages:

- As the organic material breaks down it forms a black sticky substance called **humus** which is essential for maintaining the soil crumb structure. This improves the physical structure of the soil, giving it good water-holding capacity, drainage and aeration, and reducing the possibility of erosion.

- The improvement to the mechanical properties of the soil allows it to be ploughed or worked more easily.

- The organic matter is food for detritivores such as earthworms. These improve soil structure and fertility by mixing the soil, aerating it and reducing particle size as it passes through their intestines.

- Decomposition of the manure releases a complete range of minerals required by plants.

However, organic fertilisers have a number of disadvantages:

- The slow release of minerals may be *too* slow to be sufficient during the growing season of the crop.

- They have a much lower nutrient content than inorganic fertilisers, which means that a much larger mass of organic fertiliser needs to be used.

- They are bulky and difficult to transport. This was not a problem many years ago when farms were small and mixed (farmers kept livestock and grew a variety of crops). Nowadays mixed farming is rare and **monocultures** (growing a single crop species) common, so that manure might need to be transported long distances to the crops.

- The mineral content is variable. It depends on factors such as the source, diet of the animals and so on. This means that the farmer has less control over the quantities of different minerals added to the soil, and mineral imbalance may occur.

- Manures contain much carbon but relatively little nitrogen, so that they may need to be supplemented with inorganic fertiliser containing nitrate or ammonia.

- Farmyard manures may contain plant pathogens such as fungi, and weed seeds.

Figure 15.3 Farmyard manure

Figure 15.4
Combination fertiliser in the proportion N20:P10:K10

Green manure involves growing a crop such as grass, rye or leguminous plants and then ploughing it into the soil to add organic matter. Legumes have the advantage that they enrich the soil with nitrogen as a result of the activity of nitrogen-fixing bacteria in their root nodules (see Section 14.12, page 431).

Sewage sludge is a solid by-product from sewage treatment works. It is very cheap and plentiful, but apart from having the general disadvantages of organic fertiliser, it can contain heavy metals such as lead and cadmium, as well as copper and zinc in high concentrations. These may be toxic to plants and could be passed to humans.

15.6 Inorganic fertilisers

Farmers have been using organic fertiliser for thousands of years. Only in the last hundred years have inorganic fertilisers been available, as a result of industrial production of compounds such as ammonia (by the **Haber-Bosch process**). The main inorganic ions supplied by these fertilisers are nitrate (NO_3^-), ammonium (NH_4^+), phosphate (as $H_2PO_4^-$) and potassium (K^+). Most plants remove ions containing nitrogen, phosphorus and potassium from the soil, and these elements are returned as a mixture of salts known as **combination** or **NPK** fertiliser (Figure 15.4). If the soil is lacking in only one mineral, a 'straight' fertiliser is used.

?

2 Potassium is the main inorganic anion in the intracellular fluid of cells. The elements nitrogen and phosphorus are needed for making various organic compounds. Name two compounds in plants which contain nitrogen and two which contain phosphorus. *(4 marks)*

During and after the Second World War, farmers in the UK were encouraged to increase their crop yields by applying more and more inorganic fertiliser to the land. The result was that by the early 1980s, fertiliser usage had increased some five to six times its level in 1939. This pattern was repeated in countries around the world, where use of fertilisers was necessary to compete in world markets.

Inorganic fertilisers lack many of the disadvantages of organic ones. They are straightforward to apply as granules or pellets, which are easily transported and stored. Although they are expensive, relatively small amounts of the inorganic fertiliser need to be applied: they are a concentrated source of nutrient compared with manure, and they immediately dissolve in the soil water to stimulate plant growth, giving greatly increased yields. Furthermore, the farmer knows exactly how much of each mineral is being applied to the soil, so that the needs of the particular crop can be met.

The excessive use of inorganic fertilisers has, however, resulted in a number of problems:

- Unlike organic manures, they do not form humus to improve the physical properties of the soil by soil crumb formation. The soil may lack water-holding capacity or develop poor drainage.

- Oxidation of fertilisers containing ammonium compounds results in soil acidification.

● Nitrates are very soluble, and can damage plant roots by osmotic effects if their concentration near the roots is high.

● Much of the fertiliser applied to the soil is not taken up by the plants. Cereals extract less than a third of the nitrate applied, although root crops and grass are more efficient. The rest is either denitrified and lost as nitrogen gas (see Section 14.12, page 431) or washed out of the soil by the process of **leaching**.

● Minerals such as nitrates entering rivers, ponds and lakes may result in **eutrophication** and **algal blooms**. These problems are dealt with in more detail in Section 15.8, below.

15.7 The relationship between yield and quantity of fertiliser used

The use of inorganic fertiliser such as nitrate will increase the rate of protein synthesis of the crop plants, so increasing the growth rate and yield of crops. However, if the quantity of fertiliser applied per unit area of land is increased, the yield will not rise proportionately. Eventually a maximum yield is reached, as shown in Figure 15.6.

Above about $150\,kg\,ha^{-1}$ of applied nitrogen fertiliser there is very little increase in yield. The farmer will gain no advantage by using more than this amount. In fact he will lose money, because of the cost of the extra fertiliser. This may be so at lower concentrations too: the balance between the cost of the fertiliser and the extra income from increased yield must always be taken into account.

?

3 If nitrate fertiliser costs £1 per kg (including the costs of application) and the cereal crop is worth £120 per tonne, use the graph to calculate whether it is more economical for the farmer to apply fertiliser at 100 or $150\,kg\,ha^{-1}$.

(5 marks)

The yield reaches a maximum for several reasons. There is a maximum rate of uptake by the plant's roots. Also, if more fertiliser is added, more will be lost by leaching and runoff. As mentioned above, very high concentrations may even damage the roots, reducing uptake.

15.8 Eutrophication and algal blooms

Eutrophication comes from the Greek word *eutrophos* which means 'well-fed'. It refers to the condition of bodies of fresh water which are over-rich in mineral nutrients. Streams, rivers or lakes may be naturally eutrophic, for example lakes may become enriched by phosphates or nitrates from rock erosion. Conversely, a body of water that is naturally low in nutrients and cannot support much life is called **oligotrophic**. However, the *process* of eutrophication has come to mean the artificial enrichment of water through the activities of humans.

The commonest source of excess nutrients is pollution from phosphate and nitrate fertiliser. An unpolluted upland stream is often crystal clear, with a rich diversity of organisms (Figure 15.7).

The levels of nutrients in the water are low. Normally phosphate is the mineral which limits plant growth, due to its low concentration. By comparison, streams

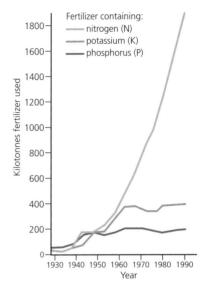

Figure 15.5 Changes in fertiliser use since 1930

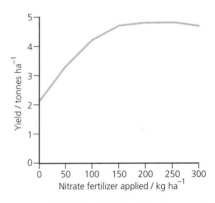

Figure 15.6 Graph of yield of a cereal crop with different applications of nitrate fertiliser

Figure 15.7 An unpolluted upland stream – Glen Etive, Scotland

and rivers which pass through agricultural land can contain high concentrations of nitrate and phosphate. Nitrate is very soluble, dissolving in soil water. Unlike other ions, it does not attach tightly to soil clay particles, and is easily washed out of the soil by rain, a process known as **leaching**. The nitrate enters the ground water and is carried to streams and rivers. This is less of a problem with phosphate fertiliser, but phosphate is washed into waterways by **surface runoff** during heavy rainfall.

The excess phosphates or nitrates stimulate the growth of all plants in the rivers and lakes, but this is usually seen first as a rapid growth of algae and blue-green bacteria. The resulting population explosion is called an **algal bloom**. The algae can increase in numbers to such an extent that they form a thick scum on the surface of the water (Figure 15.8).

❓

4 Suggest why algae or blue-green bacteria are the first photosynthetic organisms to 'bloom' after eutrophication takes place. *(1 mark)*

The algae soon begin to die, and are decomposed by saprobiontic bacteria and fungi. These organisms are aerobic, and if they are present in large numbers can deplete the water of oxygen. In addition, the algae reduce the light reaching other rooted plants, further decreasing the oxygen produced by photosynthesis. The result is that fish and other species which need oxygen die. Sudden 'fish kills' of this kind are common in warm weather, when high temperatures mean that the water can hold less dissolved oxygen, adding to the problem.

Severe cases of eutrophication result in the water becoming **anoxic** (containing very little oxygen) and smelly as a consequence of bacterial production of gases such as hydrogen sulphide and methane. The only living organisms the water contains will be algae on the very surface, and anaerobic bacteria.

Some blue-green algae also produce toxins which can poison fish or even mammals swimming in the water (Figure 15.9).

Although there is usually a decrease in both the number and diversity of organisms in water with low oxygen levels, there are some species which are well adapted to tolerate such conditions. These 'indicator species' are discussed in more detail in Section 15.21, page 461.

Figure 15.8 Algal bloom

Figure 15.9 A poisoned fish from the River Volga, Russia

Nitrates (NO_3^-) can be reduced by anaerobic bacteria in water to nitrites (NO_2^-). In addition to their eutrophication effects, both nitrates and nitrites in drinking water have been linked with possible health risks. Bottle-fed babies who receive milk made from water high in nitrate can develop a disease called methaemoglobinaemia, where the haemoglobin of their blood reacts with the iron, reducing the ability of the blood to carry oxygen. High nitrate levels have also been linked to the development of some cancers, but the evidence is not conclusive. European Union legislation has set the health standard for nitrates in drinking water at less than $45\,g\,m^{-3}$. This level is exceeded in high-nitrate areas of the UK, such as East Anglia, where drinking water has to be mixed with sources low in nitrate before consumption. In 1991, it was estimated that 800 000 people in the UK were drinking water containing nitrate concentrations above the permitted EU limit.

15.9 Herbicides

Herbicides make up the bulk of all the pesticides used in developed countries. For example, in the UK, three-quarters of all pesticides made are herbicides. They are used to kill weeds, which are native plants growing in cultivated soils. Weeds reduce the yield or value of crops by:

- competing with the crop plants for light, water and minerals
- harbouring pests such as aphids and other herbivorous insects
- releasing chemicals into the soil which act as growth retardants on other species
- contaminating grain with weed seeds.

Weeds on grazing land can also be a problem if they are inedible or toxic to animals, for example thistles or nettles.

Effective herbicides reduce **interspecific competition** between weeds and crop plants. There is a range of herbicides available, with different actions on the weeds.

Pre-emergence herbicides are applied to the soil before the crop grows. A good example is Paraquat which is a **contact herbicide**, destroying plant tissues that it touches, and killing any parts of a plant that are above ground. It is very toxic (a teaspoonful will kill a human) and rapidly kills weed seedlings as they emerge from the soil, but it soon breaks down, so that the crop plants can then grow.

Post-emergence herbicides are sprayed over the crops and weeds, but are **selective** in their action, killing the weeds but not the crop plants. The best-known examples are **the phenoxy compounds** such as 2,4-D (2,4-dichlorophenoxyethanoic acid), 2,4,5-T (2,4,5-trichlorophenoxyethanoic acid) and MCPA (2-methyl-4-chlorophenoxyethanoic acid). These all kill broad-leaved plants (dicotyledons) but not monocotyledons such as grasses or cereals. They are synthetic **auxins** (natural plant growth regulators) and cause death of the weeds by promoting abnormal growth. The stems of the weeds elongate and collapse, their leaf buds fail to open and mature leaves are killed. Tissues within the plant divide repeatedly, forming growths which interfere with transport in the phloem and xylem.

Remember

Interspecific competition means competition between members of *different* species, whereas **intraspecific** competition means between members of the *same* species

Systemic herbicides such as Glyphosate are applied either to the leaves of the plant or to the soil. They are transported through the phloem to the growing points of the plant. They are sprayed onto the fields after the crop has been harvested, in order to kill any weeds before new seed is sown.

15.10 Fungicides

Fungicides kill species of fungi (yeasts and moulds) which are parasitic on plants. They are either sprayed onto the leaves of the plants, the soil, or applied to seeds before germination as a seed dressing. As with herbicides, there are a number of available fungicides. Some contain compounds of heavy metals, such as mercury, and are toxic to animals and humans. They are coated onto cereal seeds to prevent diseases such as smuts. Others are systemic fungicides, such as benomyl, which are transported within the vascular tissue of the plant, and are much less toxic to animals.

15.11 Insecticides

Herbivorous insects reduce crop yield either

- directly, by eating or spoiling the parts of the plant that are harvested, or

- indirectly, by feeding on photosynthetic tissues.

Insects also act as vectors of plant diseases, carrying bacteria, viruses and fungal spores from infected plants to uninfected ones. Insecticides are chemicals which kill insect pests. They are either **broad spectrum** insecticides, which kill a wide range of insects, or **narrow spectrum** ones, which target particular species of pest. Insecticides act in various ways:

- **Stomach poisons** have to be eaten by the insect. They are sprayed onto leaves, for example to kill caterpillars on cabbages.

- **Contact poisons** are absorbed through the insect's exoskeleton, for example pyrethrins or DDT.

- **Systemic poisons** are sprayed onto a plant's leaves or the soil, for example malathion. They are absorbed and transported through the phloem, and are particularly effective against insects which feed on sap, such as aphids.

- **Fumigants** are toxic gases or smoke which enter the insects' tracheal breathing system. They are only effective in enclosed areas such as greenhouses.

Naturally occurring insecticides have been used for many years. These include pyrethrins, extracted from the flowers of the African daisy *Pyrethrum cinereafolium*, and nicotine from the tobacco plant *Nicotiana tabacum*. In addition, many artificial chemicals have been synthesised which are used as insecticides. These fall into four main categories: **pyrethroids**, **organochlorines**, **organophosphates** and **carbamates** (Table 15.1).

Group	Examples	Action on insects	Advantages and disadvantages
synthetic pyrethroids	allethrin, cypermethrin, deltamethrin, resmethrin	• lnon-systemic, contact or stomach insecticides • kill by interfering with nerve impulse transmission (exact mechanism not known)	• low toxicity to mammals broad spectrum, kill non-target insects • very toxic to fish relatively fast to break down
organochlorines	aldrin, DDT, chlordane, dieldrin, endosulfan, lindane, methoxychlor, toxaphene	• contact insecticides • kill by binding to membranes around nerve cells, interfering with nerve impulse transmission	• low toxicity to mammals broad spectrum, kill non-target insects • persistent in the environment accumulate in fatty tissues, leading to bioaccumulation (see Section 15.12, page 451)
organophosphates	diazinon, dimethoate, malathion, metasystox, parathion, schradan	• soluble, act as systemic insecticides • inhibit the enzyme acetylcholinesterase, essential for transmission of impulses across synapses	• easily broken down (not persistent in the environment) • *very* toxic to insects very toxic to mammals, including humans
carbamates	aldicarb, carbaryl, carbofuran, methomyl, primicarb	• some systemic, some contact insecticides • also act upon acetylcholinesterase, inhibiting acetylcholine breakdown at synapses	• much less toxic to mammals than organophosphates • most are toxic to 'useful' insects, like bees • some narrow spectrum carbamates have been produced (e.g. primicarb will kill aphids but not ladybirds) • more easily broken down than organochlorines, but less easily than organophosphates

Table 15.1 *The main types of chemical insecticides*

15.12 Problems with pesticides

The over-use of pesticides during the last fifty years has produced a number of ecological problems. These include:

- appearance of strains which are resistant to pesticide

- toxicity to non-target species

- pest resurgence

- persistency and mobility in the environment

- bioaccumulation.

Genetic resistance

When new strains of pests appear which are **resistant** to a pesticide, these **mutants** will have a great advantage over non-resistant forms, so long as the particular pesticide is in use. We say that they have a **selective advantage** over their predecessors. While the non-resistant organisms are killed, the resistant organisms will increase in numbers with each generation, since they will survive the pesticide and breed. There have been thousands of recorded incidences of pesticide-resistant organisms.

For example, the organochlorine insecticide DDT (dichlorodiphenyltrichloroethane) was first used extensively in the 1940s. During the Second World War it was very successful in controlling lice and fleas and reducing diseases carried by these insects. Later it was used in the fight against other insect-borne diseases, such as malaria (carried by some species of mosquito). By the late 1950s many types of insect, including several species of malaria mosquito, had evolved strains resistant to DDT. By 1987, over 500 species of insect had been identified which were resistant to one or more insecticides.

Effects on non-target species

Insects such as bees, or natural predators of a pest insect, may be killed by an insecticide. A fungicide may kill beneficial soil fungi, and a herbicide sprayed onto crops may drift over non-cultivated vegetation. All of these can disrupt food webs (see Section 14.6, page 423) in natural ecosystems. Many pesticides are toxic to humans, and their indiscriminate use, particularly in developing countries, is still responsible for illness and deaths.

Even within the agricultural ecosystem the balance can be disturbed by a pesticide, leading to unexpected results, such as **pest resurgence** (Figure 15.10).

When pesticide is not used, the numbers of pest insect and its natural predators fluctuate around an equilibrium level, showing a classic **predator–prey curve**. Increase in the numbers of prey leads to increase in numbers of predators, which then reduces the population of prey again. Application of a broad spectrum insecticide reduces the population of the pest temporarily, but it has a similar effect on the natural predators. These then take longer to breed and recover to their former numbers than the pest, so the pest population can increase dramatically. This population explosion is called resurgence.

Figure 15.10 Pest resurgence after use of a non-specific insecticide

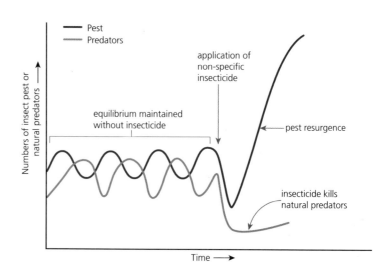

Persistency and mobility in the environment

DDT illustrates another problem with many pesticides: they can persist in the environment, remaining active for many years. When DDT and other organochlorine insecticides were first produced, this was thought to be a good thing, since they would continue to kill pests, but it has turned out to be a major environmental problem. The actual life-span of a substance like DDT is still not clear. If DDT is sprayed onto a previously untreated field, half might still be present ten years later. However, this doesn't mean that 50% has been broken down to harmless products. Most will probably have spread to other habitats, and some breakdown products, such as the similar compound DDE, are still biologically active. The 'half-life' of DDT is probably tens of years, and DDE is even more stable: it may last virtually for ever!

> ### Remember
>
> The **half-life** of a compound is the time it takes for half of any mass of the substance to break down. This measurement is commonly used with radioactive elements, but can be applied to other substances, such as pesticides. For instance, if we have 1 kg of a compound with a half-life of 2 years, after 2 years there will be 500 g left, after 4 years 250 g, after 6 years 125 g and so on.

As well as this, compounds like DDT are very mobile. DDT sticks to dust particles and is blown all round the world in air currents. It has been measured in habitats as different as polar ice-caps and mountain deserts, thousands of miles away from areas where it has been used.

Bioaccumulation

More worrying than the global distribution of compounds like DDT is their affinity for organisms. DDT and other chlorinated hydrocarbons are very soluble in lipid material, and less soluble in water. When herbivores feed on plants which are contaminated with these compounds, they tend to become concentrated in the fatty tissues of the animal. They are not broken down in the bodies of the animals and are not excreted in the urine (in other words they are **non-biodegradable**). When the herbivore is eaten by a carnivore, the process is repeated, leading to a gradual build-up of the pesticide along the food chain. This is called **bioaccumulation**. Persistent pesticides such as DDT have been measured in tertiary consumers at concentrations millions of times higher than in the environment. Bioaccumulation has been particularly evident in some aquatic ecosystems, where the tertiary consumers are fish-eating birds (Figure 15.11).

 ### Did You Know

An ideal insecticide should be narrow spectrum. The carbamate 'Carbaryl' is a contact insecticide particularly effective against chewing insects such as caterpillars, but it is a broad spectrum insecticide. It will also kill bees, hoverflies and other useful insects such as parasitic wasps, which destroy caterpillars. Carbamates work by interfering with transmission of nerve impulses across synapses, by inhibiting the enzyme acetylcholinesterase. Luckily, different species of insect have acetylcholinesterases with slightly different structures. This has enabled biochemists to 'design' carbamates that are much more specific in their action. For example, the carbamate Primicarb is a systemic insecticide that will kill aphids and whiteflies, but not ladybirds which feed on them

5 The concentration of DDT in the fish-eating birds, such as the osprey, is 25 ppm, whereas the level in the phytoplankton is 0.000003 ppm. By what factor has the concentration increased between primary producer and tertiary consumer? *(1 mark)*

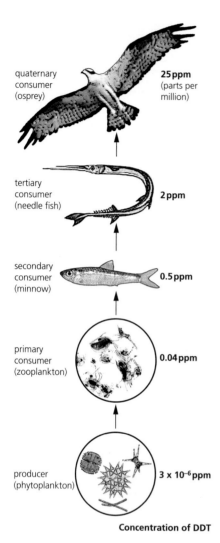

quaternary consumer (osprey) — 25 ppm (parts per million)

tertiary consumer (needle fish) — 2 ppm

secondary consumer (minnow) — 0.5 ppm

primary consumer (zooplankton) — 0.04 ppm

producer (phytoplankton) — 3×10^{-6} ppm

Concentration of DDT

Figure 15.11 Bioaccumulation in an aquatic food chain

Remember

Bioaccumulation means the increase in concentration of toxic compounds (often pesticides, but can be other substances such as heavy metals) in the upper trophic levels of a food chain. It is also called **bio-amplification** or **biomagnification**

Organochlorine insecticides were first used in Britain during the 1940s. In the 1960s it was noticed that the populations of some predatory birds had decreased, starting from the time that these insecticides were introduced. Analysis of fat, muscle and liver tissues of the birds revealed high levels of DDT, DDE and dieldrin present. Although the concentrations were not in themselves lethal, they led to an inability of the birds to deposit calcium in their eggshells. The eggs had thin shells, which tended to crack when the adults incubated them, so that hatching was unsuccessful.

In 1973, DDT and dieldrin were banned in the United States, and in Europe soon afterwards. Their use continues in many developing countries though, as an effective and cheap method of killing pests such as malaria-transmitting mosquitoes. In developed countries they have been replaced by non-persistent pesticides, such as organophosphates, carbamates and pyrethroids. These have their own problems, however. For example, although organophosphates decompose very quickly, they are very toxic to humans – much more so than organochlorines. They have been linked with diseases, such as nerve disorders among farmers employing organophosphates in sheep dips.

15.13 Biological control of pests

Biological control of a pest involves the introduction of an organism which is a predator or parasite of the pest species, in order to reduce the pest population. It avoids the use of pesticides, with their environmentally harmful effects. It is usually **species-specific**, so that other similar organisms which are not pests are unharmed. Various groups of organisms are used as biological control agents, including insects, viruses, bacteria and fungi.

The first biological control agent was used in 1889 to control the cottony cushion scale insect (*Icerya purchasi*), a pest of citrus trees. The Californian citrus fruit industry had started in the 1850s, using trees imported from Australia. Unfortunately, the trees were imported along with the scale insect, but without its natural predators. The scale insect spread rapidly until it threatened the whole industry. A natural predator of *Icerya*, the ladybird beetle (*Rodalia cardinalis*) was introduced from Australia, which rapidly spread and reduced the population of scale insects to very low levels.

Interestingly, when DDT was used in the 1940s to kill pest insects on fruit trees, it was found that *Rodalia* was much more susceptible to the insecticide than *Icerya*, which resulted in a population explosion of the scale insect pest.

Another pest which can be biologically controlled is the whitefly (*Trialeurodes vaporariorum*). This small insect attacks greenhouse crops such as tomatoes and cucumbers. It is parasitised by a minute wasp (*Encarsia formosa*), which lays its eggs in the fly larvae. The larvae of the whitefly are eaten alive by the wasp larvae, leaving black 'husks' (Figure 15.12). The adult wasps also feed directly from the larval whitefly. This method of biological control has been commercially available since the 1920s. More recently, whitefly have been controlled by the introduction of a carnivorous beetle (*Delphastus pusillus*), and whitefly and aphids in greenhouses are also killed using a fungus called *Verticillium lecani*.

An example of a bacterial control agent is the species *Bacillus thuringiensis*. This organism is used to kill caterpillars of butterflies and moths which attack crops, such as the cabbage white butterfly. It has also been used to clear large areas of West Africa of *Simulium* flies (Figure 15.13), which carry the organism responsible for causing African river blindness. The bacterium is supplied as a powder and mixed with water before it is sprayed onto crops. Insects such as caterpillars eat the leaves covered with the bacteria, which kill them within a few days.

> ### ! Did You Know
>
> The larva of the blackfly (*Simulium* sp.) is common in streams in the UK, but the adult British fly isn't a vector for African river blindness, and is normally harmless. However, in the River Stour in Dorset there is a species of the fly which is known locally as the 'Blandford Fly' (*Simulium posticatum*). It is a minute black fly with a bite out of proportion to its size. People who are bitten swell up around the bite, and some suffer swollen lymph glands, dizziness and fever. *Bacillus thuringiensis* has been tried as a biological control agent for this insect in the River Stour, with some success.

Insects are not the only type of organism which have been biologically controlled. Weeds have been successfully controlled by the introduction of herbivorous insects. One of the best-known examples happened in Australia in the 1920s. The prickly pear cactus (*Opuntia* sp.) was threatening to take over much of the countryside. A moth called *Cactoblastis cactorum* was introduced to deal with this weed. The larva of the moth feeds on the tissues of the cactus, and was soon responsible for clearing the plant from tens of millions of hectares of land (Figure 15.14).

Biological control methods don't always rely on increasing the mortality of the pest. Numbers of a pest species can be controlled by reducing its rate of reproduction. A good example of this is the action taken against the screw-worm, an insect which lays its eggs in the skin of cattle. The larvae are common in the southern states of the USA, and often kill the host animal. A biological control method was developed which relied upon knowledge of the screw-worm's life cycle. The female mates only once with a male, and then stores a supply of sperm within her body, which is used throughout her life to fertilise any eggs she lays. At the start of the breeding season, millions of pupae that had been bred in captivity were sterilised by radiation, then released into the wild. When the sterile males hatched, they mated with wild females, which then produced infertile eggs throughout their lives. This severely reduced the population of screw-worm insects to manageable levels.

Biological pest control has been successful in many instances. However, it does have its own problems. Firstly, a good deal of background research has to be carried out into the suitability of different control agents, and this takes much time and money. There is no guarantee of success: there are hundreds of documented attempts at biological control, and only about 20% of them have achieved complete success. Some even caused further problems when the introduced species chose to attack another organism instead of the pest! Nowadays the users

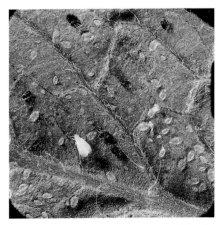

Figure 15.12 *Whitefly adult and black pupal scales parasitised by* Encarsia

Figure 15.13 *Black fly,* Simulium *sp.*

Figure 15.14 Cactoblastis *larvae devouring a prickly pear cactus*

of new biological control agents have to adhere to strict international safety guidelines.

Biological control does not normally aim to wipe out a pest completely, but merely to reduce the numbers in the pest population to a new, acceptable, equilibrium position which is lower than without the control agent (Figure 15.15).

Figure 15.15 *Biological control*

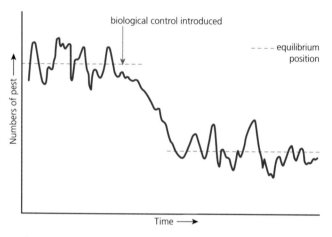

The introduction of a biological control agent does not eliminate the pest but reduces the numbers of the pest to a lower equilibrium position. The new equilibrium position is (hopefully) economically viable.

15.14 Sustainable agriculture

The use of biological control agents is one method in the battle for sustainable agriculture, that is the maintenance of the ability of the land to produce food in the face of an increasing human population. We are always going to rely on pesticides and inorganic fertilisers to a certain extent, and without them, as we have seen, the enormous increases in food production this century would not have happened. However, we must recognise the environmental dangers, and try to introduce an **integrated** approach. This might include measures such as:

- the use of new crop plants, for example from rainforest species (see Section 15.16, page 456)

- the use of genetically modified plants (this is a contentious issue, but GM crops can give higher yields, pest resistance and other useful characteristics)

- encouraging farmers in poor countries, for example by cash subsidies, to grow crops that the people there need, rather than 'cash' crops such as tobacco, sugar or coffee

- encouraging agricultural methods that maintain the structure and quality of the soil, and don't lead to problems such as soil mineral depletion or erosion.

15.15 Deforestation

We often think of the countryside of southern England as being 'natural' or 'unspoilt'. In fact, very little of the land, even that which is not agricultural or built-upon, is unaffected by human activity. If the human population of Britain were to be suddenly removed, in a few hundred years' time most of the country would revert to its natural state of mixed deciduous woodland. The present appearance of the land is a result of the process of **deforestation** that humans have practised here, and throughout the world, for hundreds of years. About 80% of the world's ancient forests have been destroyed, in order to meet two main needs. Firstly, there is the need for wood, as a fuel and building material. Secondly, there is a need for agricultural land to plant crops. With the exponential growth of the human population (see the introduction to this chapter), these needs have been magnified, until the last great natural forests of the world (the tropical rainforests) have become the latest to be under threat.

It is estimated that about a half of the original tropical rainforest has already been destroyed, and every year a further area about the size of England is cut down or cleared by 'slash-and-burn' methods. Yet the remaining rainforests, forming a 'girdle' around the Earth, and making up only 2% of the surface of the biosphere, are home to an estimated 50 to 70% of the species on the planet. The conservation of these areas, and the maintenance of their **biodiversity** (see Section 15.16, page 456), has become a matter of increasing importance in the last few years.

Most of the destruction, about 60%, is due to the activities of small farmers converting the forest to agriculture. From our comfortable perspective, it is easy to be critical of this. However, these farmers are mostly poor, and they carry out deforestation in order to survive. They farm the margins of the forest in order to grow enough food for the next day, week or month. For people engaged in this **subsistence** agriculture, conservation is not a high priority!

The other 40% of the destruction is of a more organised kind, either for logging, or clearing land for cattle ranching. Logging removes about 35 000 hectares of forest every day, the wood being used for products from timber and plywood to pulp and paper. The practices employed in logging are very wasteful and damaging to the environment. Because of the way that the trees of tropical rainforests are intertwined and festooned with thick, woody vines, each tree felled destroys several other younger trees, so that for each mature hardwood tree logged, about 30 other trees are cut down. As well as this, the heavy machinery used to transport the logs severely damages the environment (Figure 15.16).

Figure 15.16 *Rainforest deforestation in Papua New Guinea*

In South-East Asia, the demand for wood is so great that the current rate of logging is expected to destroy all the rainforest by 2010.

Logging is not the only other cause of deforestation. In Central American countries, two-thirds of the rainforests have been cleared mainly for raising cattle. This cheap source of meat is exported principally to the United States, where it is used mainly in beefburgers or other processed beef products.

15.16 The effect on biodiversity

Millions of species of organism live in the tropical rainforests of the Earth. One estimate puts the number of plant and animal species alone at 5 million. Many of these, especially invertebrates, and in particular insects, have not been named, or even discovered yet. Deforestation causes great loss of habitats, and when habitats disappear, species become extinct. Although extinction is a natural process, the activities of humans have been estimated to have increased the rate of extinction by thousands of times the normal 'background' level. A recent estimate has calculated that over a hundred species are now being made extinct every day.

When a species becomes extinct, the loss may have an effect on other organisms, through disruption of food chains, or loss of microhabitats. In addition to this, we are losing a great reserve of genetic diversity. Domesticated species of plants and animals are drawn from very small gene pools. These could be widened using species from the rainforests. Crop plants, for example, could be crossed with non-domesticated species, giving strains with greater yields, improved disease resistance, higher nutritional value, natural insecticides or many other desirable characteristics. Alternatively new 'wild' species could be domesticated. Many of our common food plants originated in tropical forests, such as potatoes, rice, maize, bananas and coffee.

The forests yield medicines as well as food. Forty percent of all prescription drugs used today are based on, or synthesised from, compounds found originally in animals and plants, yet less than 10% of known plant species have been tested for their medicinal properties, and only 1% have been intensively studied.

As the rainforests disappear, we risk losing countless species with untapped potential for agricultural and medical use.

15.17 Other problems caused by deforestation

The soil of tropical rainforests is low in minerals. This is because the trees and other plants extract the minerals from the soil at a high rate. If deforestation takes place, the minerals stored in the biomass of the plants are not returned to the soil through decomposition. As a result, the quality of the soil becomes reduced. In the first year after deforestation, there may be enough nutrients to support annual crops, needed by poor farmers for immediate food supplies. These crops use up nutrients from the soil very quickly, so that in the next year only perennials can be grown, which deplete the soil further, but at slower rates. Finally, the land is only suitable for pasture for animals, or to be left fallow. This steady decrease in the land's productivity is very predictable in deforested areas, and happens very quickly, over a few growing seasons, often leading to crop failure.

The soil that is exposed after deforestation may heat up and dry out. The ground, lacking a protective canopy, is exposed to torrential rainfall and lacks the stabilising effect of tree roots. This can lead to soil erosion on a grand scale (Figure 15.17).

Soil eroded from upland areas can be washed into rivers, leading to an increase in their water levels and the risk of flooding of lowland plains. This happened in China in 1988, where deforestation caused silt deposits to be carried downstream

Remember

The gene pool is the sum total of all the genes in a population of organisms. The idea of conserving forest ecosystems to maintain a large gene pool is sometimes called genetic conservation

Remember

Annuals are plants that complete their life cycle, from seed germination to seed production, within one season, after which they die. **Perennials** are plants that continue their growth from year to year. **Pasture** is land sown with plants (usually grass) for cattle to eat. Land left **fallow** is uncultivated

by the Yangtze River. The floods that resulted destroyed millions of homes and millions of hectares of crops, and killed thousands of people.

Much forest is cleared by the burning of large tracts of vegetation. This has affected the composition of the Earth's atmosphere. The forests are enormous stores of fixed carbon (see Section 14.10, page 428) which burning converts into carbon dioxide. This adds heat-trapping carbon dioxide to the atmosphere, perhaps contributing to the 'greenhouse effect' (see Section 15.24, page 468). In addition to this, the removal of the vegetation is destroying a resource which would normally be *absorbing* carbon dioxide from the air, during photosynthesis (although plants also respire, producing carbon dioxide, their net uptake of carbon dioxide as a result of photosynthesis is much greater).

Another way that deforestation may be affecting the atmosphere is through the lack of transpiration. The forests are a source of atmospheric water vapour, recycled during the water cycle (see Section 14.11, page 430). The vapour later falls as rain over areas nearer the coast. Reduction in the forest areas may disrupt precipitation patterns and result in widespread droughts.

Figure 15.17 *Soil erosion – New Plymouth, New Zealand*

> ## ! Did You Know
>
> Rainforest facts
> - tropical rainforests which 'girdle' the Earth once covered 8 million square miles. They now cover less than 3.2 million square miles
> - each second, an area of forest the size of a football pitch is destroyed
> - rainforest vines can grow 200 metres in length and as thick as a man's body
> - 90% of the world's ferns grow in rainforests
> - Many plants have been found which contain chemicals with cancer-fighting properties. Over 70% of these were discovered in rainforests
> - 17% of all the world's birds, and 33% of all the bird species live in rainforests
> - in a small rainforest reserve in Peru, scientists counted 545 species of bird, 100 species of dragonfly and 800 species of butterfly
> - the rainforests of South-East Asia have 660 mammal species and over 850 amphibian species (Europe has only 130 native mammal species)

Unfortunately, the tropical rainforests are not the only ones that are under threat. Ancient coniferous forests of Canada, northern Europe and Russia are being cut down, so that these areas can be replanted with other, more 'profitable' species. These are mainly pine and spruce trees used to produce pulp for paper. These vast monocultures also result in destruction of habitats and reduced biodiversity.

15.18 Sustainable management of rainforests

Rainforest which provides hardwood timber can be successfully managed. Instead of wholesale destruction of large areas of forest, smaller areas can be cut down and replanted with seedlings after harvesting. This controlled **reafforestation** maintains the stability of the ecosystem by ensuring that different areas have a mixture of tree species as well as trees of different ages. It also reduces the likelihood of soil depletion, erosion or the other catastrophic events we have discussed. Of course, controlled exploitation yields much smaller profits in the short term, but the long-term benefits to the planet are very great.

It is more difficult to suggest solutions to the problem caused by small-scale farming, which encroaches gradually upon areas of rainforest, as in the Amazon basin. The problem is that the farmers are poor, and can only afford to carry out the types of farming methods which inevitably lead to lowered productivity of the land. When the area they cultivate is exhausted, they have to move on to fresh areas of forest. What is really needed is investment in areas which have already been deforested, to improve the land's productivity. This would enable the farmers to stay in these areas and not destroy further areas of the forest. This approach would need money to provide improved agricultural machinery, fertilisers, pesticides, irrigation and transport infrastructure, as well as access to reliable markets. Instead of being concerned only with providing food for themselves and their families, the farmers could start to produce a profit, which would integrate the forest margin areas into the economy of the country, at a lower cost to the environment. The difficulty with this is that the countries involved, such as in South America, are poor, and unable to finance such schemes without the help of richer nations.

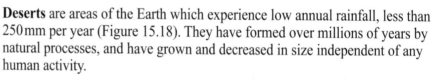

15.19 Desertification

Deserts are areas of the Earth which experience low annual rainfall, less than 250 mm per year (Figure 15.18). They have formed over millions of years by natural processes, and have grown and decreased in size independent of any human activity.

In some extremely arid areas, droughts can continue for longer than a year, so that little vegetation and no crops can grow. On its periphery a desert may be surrounded by a natural barrier, such as a mountain range, or it may gradually change from a dry to a more moist environment. These transition zones are particularly fragile ecosystems, and are prone to conversion into desert proper, a process called **desertification**. The result is a loss of agricultural land, often leading to poverty and famine, affecting millions of people in every continent.

A major cause of desertification is **overgrazing**. Too many sheep, cattle or camels grazing upon insufficient pasture, as well as removal of brushwood for fuel, means that the soil is left unprotected against wind or water erosion. This is made worse by livestock compacting the soil by their hooves and reducing its permeability to water. The exposed topsoil may be blown or washed away, leaving infertile sand or rock. Cultivation on steep slopes, and downhill ploughing, can also increase soil erosion. When rains follow a season of drought, the topsoil is washed away. As is often the case, the root cause of these problems is an increasing human population, and pressure on the land to produce more food.

Desertification and lack of plant cover leads to high rates of evaporation from the soil surface, which draws up moisture from the ground water (see Section 14.11, page 430). This brings with it salts, which are left behind on the surface of the soil – a process called **salinisation**. This problem is made worse by poorly constructed irrigation systems, with inadequate drainage. For example, a supply from a river used to irrigate the land may evaporate, leaving more salts behind.

Definition

Desertification is the process of the conversion of fertile arid or semi-arid land into desert, as a result of human activities and climate change

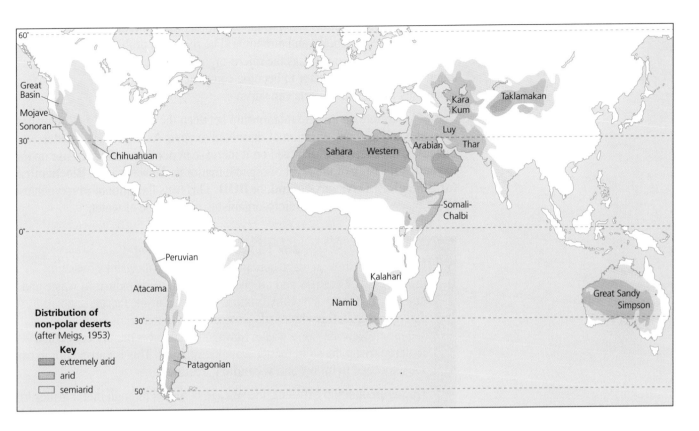

Further irrigation adds to these salt deposits, until a thick encrusting layer is formed, preventing plant growth. Salinisation is a major problem of irrigated agriculture in semi-arid areas of the world (Figure 15.19).

Although human activities undoubtedly increase the rate of desertification, it is unlikely that it is a permanent condition. The available evidence suggests that during periods of favourable climate change and increased rainfall, areas which have become deserts can recover. However, this is no comfort to the people suffering short-term hardships, famine or starvation that desertification brings.

Figure 15.18 *Areas of the world subject to desertification*

15.20 Water pollution by sewage

We have already seen how water pollution by nitrate and phosphate fertilisers can cause the problem of eutrophication and algal blooms (see Section 15.8, page 445). Treated sewage entering rivers and lakes can produce the same problems, since it is rich in minerals, particularly phosphates. The detergents used in washing powders, washing-up liquids and dishwashers all contain added phosphates. Treated sewage also contains high levels of nitrates from decomposed organic matter. Although these minerals can be removed from the sewage effluent before they are discharged, this is not often done, so they add to the eutrophication of water courses.

A more serious problem happens when raw sewage is released into a river by accident. The sewage contains many pathogenic micro-organisms, and is hazardous to human health. As well as this, large volumes of raw sewage feed aerobic bacteria. These decompose the organic material, using up the oxygen in

Figure 15.19 *Salinisation – New South Wales, Australia*

the water. Bacterial action also produces noxious gases, including hydrogen sulphide (bad eggs smell), and ammonia. The river will probably recover from small discharges of sewage, as the micro-organisms break it down, but large amounts can cause the water to become completely anoxic (lacking oxygen), when only anaerobic bacteria can survive.

There is therefore an inverse relationship between the amount of organic matter in the water and the concentration of dissolved oxygen. As the organic matter increases, the bacteria which feed on it increase in numbers, and they use up more oxygen. A measure of the level of organic matter in the water is its **Biochemical (or Biological) Oxygen Demand**, or **BOD**. This tests the amount of oxygen used up by the bacteria and other micro-organisms in a sample of water.

Box 15.1 Sewage treatment

Untreated or 'raw' sewage contains waste from baths, sinks, washing machines, dishwashers and toilets, mixed with some industrial waste and rain water. It is an unhealthy mixture of human urine, faeces, soap, detergents and other chemicals, as well as solid materials such as paper, sanitary towels and food waste. Sewage treatment is mainly concerned with removing the solid matter from the mixture. This is carried out in two stages, called **primary** and **secondary** treatment.

During **primary treatment**, the sewage is sieved through metal grilles to remove large objects such as rags and plastic. It is then allowed to stand in primary sedimentation tanks, where heavier particulate materials settle out, forming primary sludge (the solid fraction) and a liquid fraction.

In **secondary treatment**, the primary sludge is broken down by bacteria in a sludge digesting tank. This anaerobic process reduces the sludge to a smaller volume, when it can be disposed of in land-fill sites or used as an organic fertiliser. The liquid fraction is treated in one of two ways:

● The **trickling filter system**, which sprays the liquid over filter beds, by a rotating arm (Figure 15.20). Micro-organisms in the filter beds oxidise the organic matter to carbon dioxide and water, removing over 90%.

● The **activated sludge process**, where the liquid is aerated by streams of compressed air bubbled through it. This encourages the activities of aerobic bacteria, breaking down 98% of the organic matter.

Figure 15.20 *Sewage filter beds*

The BOD test measures the number of milligrams of oxygen used per dm^3 of water during a standard period of 5 days, at a constant temperature of 20°C, and in darkness. 'Clean' water has a low BOD of 1 or 2 mg/dm^3/5 days, rising to over 20 mg/dm^3/5 days for highly polluted water.

6 Suggest two reasons why it is important to measure the BOD at a standard temperature of 20°C, and explain why the sample must be kept in darkness.

(3 marks)

15.21 Indicator species

Some freshwater animals can only survive in very clean water with a low BOD. Other animals have structural and physiological adaptations which allow them to survive in more polluted water. If we sample from a river or stream, the types of animals we catch can tell us how polluted the water is. The selected species which are used are called **indicator species**.

(a)

Take, for example, the **bloodworm**. This isn't really a worm at all, but a type of midge larva (an insect). It is called a bloodworm because it contains the pigment haemoglobin, similar to that in our red blood cells. As with our haemoglobin, this binds to oxygen, and allows the bloodworm to survive in quite heavily polluted waters, where the oxygen concentration is low (Figure 15.21a). The animal absorbs oxygen all over its body surface, to be taken up by the haemoglobin.

An organism with the delightful name of the **rat-tailed maggot** has a different method of obtaining oxygen. This insect, the larva of a drone fly, has a telescopic breathing tube at one end of its body. It extends this tube to the water's surface, where it has direct access to air. In this way, it too can survive in oxygen-deficient waters (Figure 15.21b).

(b)

Many aquatic invertebrates exchange gases via external gills, such as mayfly and alderfly larvae (Figure 15.21 c and d). These species only survive in relatively clean water, with low levels of organic matter.

Some common indicator species of freshwater pollution are shown in Figure 15.22.

Figure 15.21
(a) Bloodworm (midge larva)
(b) Rat-tailed maggot
(c) Mayfly larva
(d) Alderfly larva

(c)

(d)

Figure 15.22 *Freshwater pollution indicator species (not drawn to scale)*

(a) *Clean water fauna*

A stonefly nymph

B mayfly nymph

C caddis-fly larva

D gammarus (water shrimp)

E dragonfly nymph

F freshwater limpet

(b) *Water with some organic pollutants*

G water hoglouse

H pond snail

I leech

J planarian (flatworm)

K alder fly larva

(c) *Water with heavy organic pollution*

L rat-tailed maggot

M bloodworm

N tubificid worm (sludgeworm)

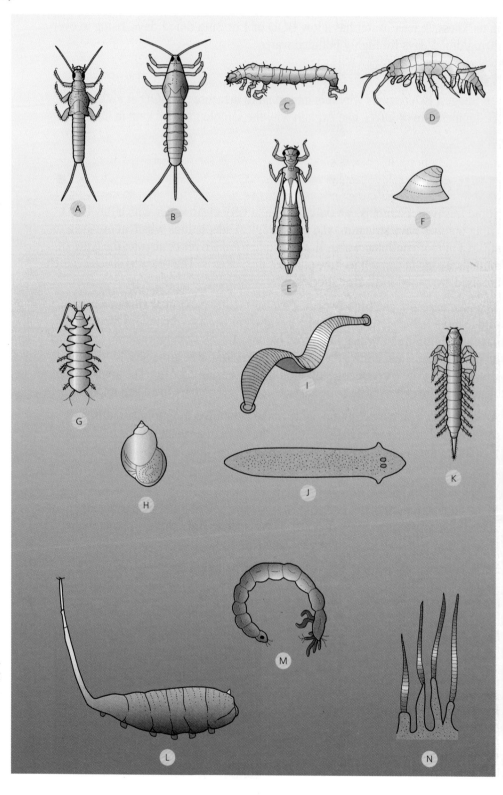

Box 15.2 The Trent Biotic Index

In 1964, the Trent River Authority developed an index of water quality based on the presence of indicator species. It uses a scale of 0 to 15, where 0 is highly polluted water and 15 is very clean water. Nowadays there are more sophisticated biotic indices, but this one illustrates how indicator species can be used to measure pollution, and it is easy to apply, since it uses large, or 'macro', invertebrates. If an ecologist wants to calculate the index for a certain stream, she collects a representative sample of these invertebrates from the stream. Next they are identified and allocated to groups. The nature of a 'group' depends on the type of organism. Sometimes it refers to a single species, sometimes a family, an order or even a class. The abundance of organisms in the group is not important: only the diversity (the number of groups) is taken into account. The groups are shown in Table 15.2.

Table 15.2 Groups used in the Trent Biotic Index

Group	Score
flatworms	score 1 for each species
segmented worms	score 1 if any member of this class is present, excluding genus *Nais*
genus *Nais*	score 1 if present
leeches	score 1 for each species
molluscs (snails)	score 1 for each species
crustacea (shrimps, water hoglouse)	score 1 for each species
stonefly nymphs	score 1 for each species
mayfly nymphs	score 1 for each genus, except *Baetis rhodanii*
mayfly *Baetis rhodanii*	score 1 if present
caddis fly nymphs	score 1 for each family present
alderfly nymphs	score 1 for each species
chironomid midge larvae	score 1 for each family, except bloodworms
bloodworms	score 1 if present
blackfly larvae	score 1 for each family
other fly larvae	score 1 for each species
beetles (adults and larvae)	score 1 for each species
water mites	score 1 for each species

The total score is added up, and Table 15.3 used to calculate the biotic index. This is done by working down the left-hand column, until you reach the first criterion which fits your sample. You then read across the row until you reach the column with the relevant total group score at the top. The index is given where this column and row intersect.

Extension

Box 15.2 The Trent Biotic Index cont'd

Table 15.3 Trent Biotic Indices. The indices are given in the main body of the table. They range from 0 (very polluted) to 15 (very clean)

	Total number of groups present									
	0–1	2–5	6–10	11–15	16–20	21–25	26–30	31–35	36–40	41–45
stonefly nymphs (>1 species)	–	7	8	9	10	11	12	13	14	15
stonefly nymphs (1 species)	–	6	7	8	9	10	11	12	13	14
mayfly nymphs (>1 species)	–	6	7	8	9	10	11	12	13	14
mayfly nymphs (1 species)	–	5	6	7	8	9	10	11	12	13
caddis fly nymphs (>1 species)	–	5	6	7	8	9	10	11	12	13
caddis fly nymphs (1 species)	4	4	5	6	7	8	9	10	11	12
water shrimp *Gammarus* but all above species absent	3	4	5	6	7	8	9	10	11	12
water hoglouse *Asellus* but all above species absent	2	3	4	5	6	7	8	9	10	11
tubifex worms and/or bloodworms present, but all above species absent	1	2	3	4	5	6	7	8	9	10
all above types absent	0	1	2	–	–	–	–	–	–	–

For instance, if 32 groups were present, and more than one mayfly nymph species was found, but no stonefly nymphs, the biotic index would be 12 (very clean water). On the other hand, if only 7 groups were present in the sample, and *Gammarus* shrimps were present, but not stonefly, mayfly or caddis fly nymphs, the index would be 5, indicating much more polluted water.

15.22 The Earth's energy resources

Another consequence of the ever-increasing human population, along with industrialisation and the development of the internal combustion engine, has been the increased need for sources of energy for human activities. Some energy resources, such as fossil fuels, are effectively **non-renewable**, since they take millions of years to form. Once they are 'used up', they are gone for ever. Other sources of energy, such as solar power, hydro-electric power and wind and wave power, will always be available, and are called **renewable** resources. Most of these sources of energy are outside the scope of a biology textbook, but one form will be considered: the use of **renewable biomass** (see Section 15.25, page 472). This is a source of energy which can be managed in a sustainable way.

Fossil fuels are coal, oil and natural gas. The processes which form these fuels, and their involvement in the carbon cycle, have already been discussed in Section 14.10, page 428. Fossil fuels supply most of the energy needs of humans. Their total consumption per year has more than doubled over the second half of this century, and is still rising. There is a commonly held belief that fossil fuels will soon become exhausted. However, the known reserves of oil and natural gas should last for 50 to 60 years at the present rate of extraction, and coal deposits are immense: enough for about 300 years. The main problems with fossil fuels are the adverse effects on the environment that they produce when they undergo combustion.

Fossil fuels are complex mixtures of hydrocarbons (compounds of hydrogen and carbon). When they are burned, the main products are the oxides of hydrogen (water) and carbon (carbon dioxide). Natural gas, which consists mainly of methane, ethane and propane, is a relatively 'clean' fuel, producing little else other than water and carbon dioxide. Oil, and particularly coal, are 'dirtier' fuels, which contain various other elements. Sulphur oxidises to form sulphur dioxide (SO_2). The high temperatures in burning cause atmospheric nitrogen to form oxides of nitrogen, such as NO_2 and NO. Both sulphur dioxide and nitrogen oxides, as well as excess carbon dioxide, are atmospheric pollutants which contribute to a phenomenon called **acid rain**.

15.23 Acid rain

Even without pollutants rain is naturally acidic, with a pH between 5.5 and 6.5. This is because the atmosphere contains carbon dioxide, which dissolves in water to form carbonic acid, a weak acid. Analysis of air bubbles trapped in Arctic ice gives us information about the composition of the atmosphere before the Industrial Revolution. It suggests that the pH of rain for thousands of years before that time was high, with a pH value of 6 or above. During and after the Industrial Revolution, the pH fell, so that by the mid-twentieth century, pollution commonly led to precipitation with a pH as low as 4 to 4.5. Nowadays, the term **acid rain** is used to describe any precipitation (rain, snow, hail etc.) with a pH of less than 5, as well as the deposition of acidic gases and particles such as soot (dry deposition).

The main causes of acid rain are emissions of sulphur dioxide (SO_2), nitric oxide (NO) and nitrogen dioxide (NO_2) from power stations, factories, motor vehicles and homes, as a result of the combustion of fossil fuels, which also adds to atmospheric carbon dioxide (CO_2). These gases are converted into acidic compounds in the atmosphere and carried long distances by the wind, often affecting countries hundreds or thousands of kilometres away from their source of production.

More than half of the sulphur dioxide in the Earth's atmosphere is thought to derive from natural sources, such as volcanoes, forest fires and biological decay processes. However, it is estimated that about 80 million tonnes of SO_2 is produced every year from the burning of fossil fuels, and most of this originates in North America and Europe. For example, 85% of Europe's SO_2 is 'home produced'. This means that much of North America and Europe is suffering from excessive levels of SO_2, causing environmental problems.

Similarly, oxides of nitrogen (NO_X) are released, in the main from decomposition of dead plant material and volcanic sources, but an additional 22 million tonnes are a result of human activity, mainly from vehicle emissions. Table 15.4 shows the main sources of SO_2 and NO_X for the United Kingdom.

Table 15.4 *Sources of SO_2 and NO_X in the UK (1995)*

Sulphur dioxide (SO_2) (Total = 2.37 million tonnes)	Nitrogen oxides (NO_X) (Total = 2.30 million tonnes)
power stations 67%	road vehicle emissions 46%
other industries 11%	power stations 22%
oil refineries 8%	other industries 6%
domestic fuel burning 3%	shipping 5%
commercial fuel burning 2%	domestic fuel burning 3%
road vehicle emissions 2%	commercial fuel burning 2%
iron and steel manufacture 2%	oil refineries 2%
shipping 2%	iron and steel manufacture 2%
unidentified 3%	unidentified 12%

In the atmosphere, sulphur dioxide is oxidised to sulphur trioxide (SO_3). This very soluble gas dissolves in water to form sulphuric acid (H_2SO_4). Similarly, in the atmosphere, nitric oxide oxidises to nitrogen dioxide, which reacts with water to form nitric acid (HNO_3).

The large distance that acid pollutants can travel is a good illustration of the international nature of atmospheric pollution. This is shown particularly well by a study of the sources and effects of acid rain in Norway, although the same situation is true in the rest of Scandinavia, other northern European countries such as Germany, and parts of the north-eastern United States.

Whereas only one fifth of the UK's depositions of sulphur come from other countries, Norway receives over 90% of its sulphur and NO_X pollution from abroad. Much of this has been traced back to its countries of origin (Figure 15.23).

There are two main environmental consequences of acid rain in Norway. One is damage to the coniferous forests of the country, and the other is acidification of freshwater rivers and lakes, leading to destruction of these ecosystems.

Decline of forests

In the 1960s, large numbers of dead and dying conifers were found in the Black Forest region of southern Germany. By the 1980s more than half the forests of the country were affected, and the problem had spread to deciduous trees, such as oak and beech, as well. Investigations revealed the same problems in other countries, including Norway. The health of Norwegian forests has deteriorated since then. Scientists have recorded decrease of leaf densities, yellowing of leaves (needles) and death of trees on a large scale (Figure 15.24).

Figure 15.23 *Maps showing sources of SO$_2$ and NO$_X$ pollution affecting Norway*

(a) SO$_2$

(b) NO$_x$

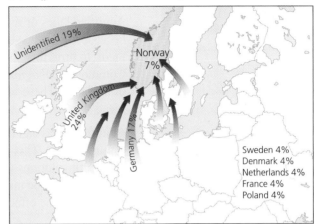

great debate ensued about the cause of the damage. Although there are still no definite answers, it is generally agreed that the most likely cause is acid rain.

Experiments have shown that acid rain can directly damage leaves and pine needles. However, the destruction of Norway's trees seems to be mainly due to the acidity resulting in an imbalance of soil nutrients. Firstly, acidification of the soil kills many of the micro-organisms involved in recycling dead organic material. As well as this, the acid rain leaches out up to 70% of minerals such as calcium and magnesium from the soil. Also, aluminium is normally in an insoluble form in the soil. In very acid conditions, it becomes soluble and is released into the soil water. Here it is toxic to the roots, blocking their uptake of calcium ions. Finally, any NO$_X$ in the acid rain provides nitrogen which actually *fertilises* plant growth, but lacking the balance of other nutrients. Poor nutrient balance leads to the trees being prey to pathogenic organisms, such as fungi, or extreme weather conditions, such as drought or frost, which results in death.

Harvesting the trees for timber increases the acidification, since it removes basic cations from the soil. Normally these would return to the soil when the tree dies and decomposes.

Acidification of rivers and lakes

Acid rain has also been blamed for the death of fish, particularly trout and salmon, in Norwegian lakes and rivers. Acid rain may fall directly upon these bodies of water or, in areas where the soil is acid, runoff or ground water transports the acid into the lakes, along with leached aluminium ions. The combination of low pH and high levels of aluminium kills fish by interfering with their gill function. The gills become covered in a thick mucus, preventing the uptake of oxygen from the water. Young fish (fry) are particularly susceptible. Fish spawn is also affected. Below a pH of 4.5, trout eggs do not hatch, due to their inability to produce an enzyme concerned with breaking down the outer coat of the egg: the young fish become trapped inside the eggs.

Figure 15.24 *Coniferous trees killed by acid rain – Bavaria*

Figure 15.25 Liming to counteract the effects of acid rain – Dyfed, Wales

Since the 1970s about 4000 to 5000 Norwegian lakes are estimated to have lost their stocks of fish. The total area now thought to be seriously affected by acidification is some 120 000 km².

Acidified lakes or rivers have an unexpectedly 'crystal clear' appearance. This is because the acid waters reduce the numbers of phytoplankton that can survive in them. In turn, this disrupts various food chains, decreasing species diversity. Commonly *Sphagnum* moss is the only species which grows, covering the bottom of the lakes. These waters are often incorrectly, but with reason, described as 'dead'.

Acidified lakes can be treated by adding tonnes of powdered lime to the water (Figure 15.25). This raises the pH, and precipitates aluminium. However, more long-term solutions which tackle the cause of the problem are being sought. These measures must be taken by all of the countries responsible for the pollution, or they will not be effective. The measures include:

- purification of fuel. Up to 35% of the sulphur content of coal and oil can be removed by chemical 'washing' before combustion.

- converting power stations from coal to oil, or oil to natural gas, which reduces emissions.

- employing improved energy conservation measures such as better home insulation, so that less fuel is needed.

- removing SO_2 from the waste gases produced by burning coal in power stations, using 'scrubbers' or filters. NO_X can also be removed from the products of combustion, although this is more difficult. A desulphurisation method using sea water has been developed in Norway which removes 95% of the sulphur.

- using 'low NO_X' burners, which work at lower temperatures but reduce NO_X emissions by up to 40%.

- using catalytic converters in car engines, oil burners etc. to remove NO_X.

15.24 The greenhouse effect and global warming

Radiation of various wavelengths reaches the Earth from the Sun. Those wavelengths that are particularly important to organisms are ultraviolet (under 400 nm) through visible light (400 to 700 nm) to infra-red (over 700 nm). Some of the incident light (about 30%) is reflected back into space, and much of the UV is absorbed by the ozone layer of the upper atmosphere.

However, a large proportion of the visible light and infra-red reaches the Earth. Infra-red is radiated heat, and this results in warming of the Earth's surface, which in turn causes infra-red radiation of a longer wavelength to be emitted into the atmosphere (Figure 15.26).

This longer-wavelength infra-red is absorbed by various gases in the atmosphere, and re-radiated back towards the Earth's surface. By analogy with the glass of a greenhouse, these gases are called '**greenhouse gases**' and the warming that this produces is called the **greenhouse effect**. Without the greenhouse effect, the surface of the Earth would be over 30 °C lower than it is. The greenhouse effect is

Remember

The unit nm stands for a nanometre, which is one billionth of a metre or one millionth of a millimetre (10^{-9} metres)

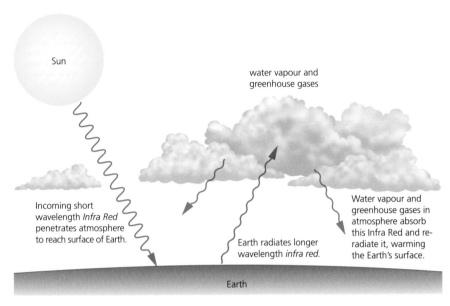

Figure 15.26 The greenhouse effect

water vapour and
greenhouse gases

Sun

Incoming short
wavelength *Infra Red*
penetrates atmosphere
to reach surface of Earth.

Earth radiates longer
wavelength *infra red.*

Water vapour and
greenhouse gases in
atmosphere absorb
this Infra Red and re-
radiate it, warming
the Earth's surface.

Earth

therefore a perfectly natural phenomenon. Without it, a reduction in temperature of 30 °C would not allow life on Earth to exist as it does. The trouble is that the levels of certain greenhouse gases in the atmosphere are *rising*, as a result of human activities. This is thought to be *increasing* the greenhouse effect, producing steadily increasing temperatures on the Earth's surface, a condition called **global warming**. Many scientists feel that global warming is the most serious threat to life on Earth as we know it.

Apart from water vapour, several gases absorb and re-radiate the long-wavelength infra-red. These include carbon dioxide, methane, nitrous oxide, chlorofluorocarbons (CFCs) and ozone. Some of these are produced naturally, such as carbon dioxide by respiration. Others, such as CFCs, are entirely made by human activities. They are known as **greenhouse gases** (Table 15.5).

Carbon dioxide levels in the atmosphere are mainly the result of the balance between the processes of respiration and photosynthesis (see Section 14.10, page 428, on the carbon cycle). We have already seen how destruction of tropical rain-forests may be increasing the carbon dioxide concentration of the atmosphere, by reducing photosynthesis (see Section 15.17, page 456). In addition to this, we are burning billions of tonnes of fossil fuels every year, adding more carbon dioxide to the air. There is no doubt that the concentration of carbon dioxide in the air is rising. Levels of carbon dioxide estimated from air bubbles trapped in ice from Greenland and Antarctica show a steady increase over the last 300 years. Direct atmospheric monitoring this century shows an increase in the *rate of increase* too, as we use more and more fossil fuels (Figure 15.27).

Analysis of carbon dioxide in ice has enabled scientists to estimate how levels have changed for tens of thousands of years before the present time. There have been many fluctuations in the concentration, but there has always been a correlation of low carbon dioxide with cold periods of the Earth's pre-history (ice ages) and high carbon dioxide with warm periods.

Remember

The 'greenhouse effect' is actually mis-named. A greenhouse (or glasshouse) does trap heat, but only a little is trapped by a mechanism similar to that of the Earth's atmosphere. The main reasons why the inside of a greenhouse stays warmer than its surroundings are:
- it reduces evaporation, trapping moist air inside the greenhouse. Evaporation would cool the contents of the greenhouse, just as sweating cools the skin
- it reduces convection currents which would allow heat to be lost

Table 15.5 Common greenhouse gases

Name of gas	Main sources
carbon dioxide (CO_2)	• respiration of organisms combustion of fossil fuels
methane (CH_4)	• bacteria living in marsh land and rice paddy fields • bacteria in the guts of cows and other ruminant animals • decomposition of organic material in landfill sites
nitrous oxide (N_2O)	• denitrifying bacteria acting on nitrates and nitrites • combustion of fossil fuels
chlorofluorocarbons or CFCs	• coolants in refrigerators • expanded foam and other plastic products (CFCs released on incineration) • aerosol propellants
ozone (O_3)	• made by action of sunlight on gases from vehicle exhausts

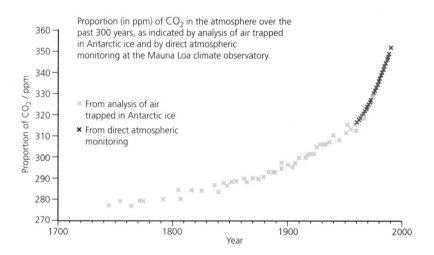

Proportion (in ppm) of CO_2 in the atmosphere over the past 300 years, as indicated by analysis of air trapped in Antarctic ice and by direct atmospheric monitoring at the Mauna Loa climate observatory.

× From analysis of air trapped in Antarctic ice

× From direct atmospheric monitoring

Figure 15.26 Changes in atmospheric CO_2 level over the last 300 years

Methane is formed by the metabolic activities of anaerobic bacteria living in marshes, paddy fields and the guts of animals such as cows and sheep. A cow produces about 200 dm³ of methane every day! Methane is also released from decomposition of vegetation and from decomposing organic matter in waste landfill sites. Methane is a 'stronger' greenhouse gas than carbon dioxide, but it is present in smaller quantities, so its overall effect is less. However, levels of methane in the air have doubled over the last 150 years, and are probably contributing to the greenhouse effect.

Nitrous oxide is mainly produced in the soil as a result of the activity of denitrifying bacteria (Section 14.12, page 431). The increased use of artificial nitrate fertilisers has undoubtedly led to more nitrous oxide (N_2O) in the atmosphere. This is added to by increased combustion of fossil fuels.

Chlorofluorocarbons are entirely a product of human activities. They have only been used for the last 50 years. The two commonest CFCs are $CFCl_3$ and CF_2Cl_2. $CFCl_3$ has been used as an aerosol propellant, and CF_2Cl_2 as a coolant in refrigeration units. Although there have been international efforts to reduce the use of these compounds, they are still commonly employed, and are also used as solvents, in foam packaging and other plastic products. In this form they are released into the air when the disposed-of plastic is destroyed by burning. CFCs are particularly efficient greenhouse gases, more than 12 000 times more effective than carbon dioxide in trapping heat.

The **ozone** contributing to the greenhouse effect is present in the lower atmosphere (known as the troposphere). It is important to realise that this is not the same as the 'ozone layer' which protects the Earth from the harmful effects of ultraviolet light. This natural ozone layer is much higher in the atmosphere, in a region called the stratosphere (see Box 15.3). The tropospheric ozone is mainly made by the effect of sunlight on pollutant gases from vehicle exhausts.

7 The dense atmosphere of the planet Venus is approximately 97% carbon dioxide. Would you expect to find a greenhouse effect on Venus? Explain your answer.   *(1 mark)*

The possible effects of global warming

Many scientists prefer to use the term 'global climate change' rather than 'global warming', since the increase in temperature would not be expected to occur everywhere. Some areas would be likely to increase in temperature, while other areas would experience a temperature fall. Overall, the mean global surface temperature is predicted to rise by between 1.5 °C and 4.5 °C over the next 30 years, if carbon dioxide levels continue to rise. The main consequences of this would be:

- a **rise in sea levels**, as a result of melting of polar ice and glaciers and thermal expansion of water. This would cause flooding of low-lying areas of the world, and habitat destruction. For example, coral reefs grow just under the sea's surface and would be killed by deep water above them. Low areas such as much of south-east England would be under water, and many small islands submerged.

- **disruption of climate and weather patterns**. It is thought that there will be greater warming at the poles than at the equator. This would affect patterns of air circulation in the atmosphere, greatly affecting weather patterns. Regional rainfall could also be affected, leading to drastically altered environmental conditions in all ecosystems.

Some climatologists have predicted more specific effects of global warming. In reality, the global ecosystem is so complex that making definite and specific predictions is very difficult.

Box 15.3 The 'ozone layer'

Ozone in the upper atmosphere (stratosphere) is formed naturally by the action of UV radiation from the sun acting on oxygen molecules:

$O_2 \longrightarrow 2O$ (oxygen molecule split into two atoms of oxygen)

$O + O_2 \longrightarrow O_3$ (atom of oxygen combines with oxygen molecule to form ozone molecule)

The ozone absorbs much UV radiation from the sun, which would otherwise reach the surface of the Earth, damaging the DNA of organisms and causing mutations. It is this outer, stratospheric layer of ozone which is being destroyed by CFCs and other gases such as oxides of nitrogen. This is resulting in the 'thinning' or 'hole' in the ozone layer (Figure 15.27).

Figure 15.28
(a) Ozone hole over the Antarctic 1979
(b) Ozone hole over the Antarctic 1989
(c) Ozone hole over the Antarctic 1999

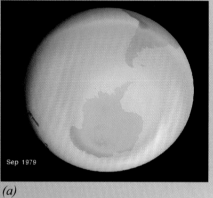
Sep 1979

(a)

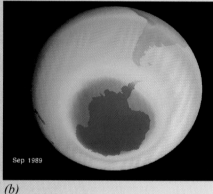
Sep 1989

(b)

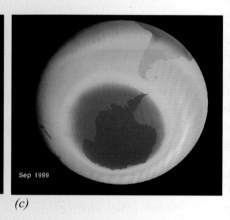
Sep 1999

(c)

The only way to alleviate the problem is to reduce the emissions of greenhouse gases produced by human activities. This can only be achieved by legislation and international co-operation. Even then the benefits may not all be immediate. For example, CFCs are persistent chemicals, which will remain in the atmosphere for tens to hundreds of years.

15.25 Renewable energy sources and reduction of CO_2 emissions

Biofuels are renewable sources of energy based on **biomass**. This is essentially plant material made by photosynthesis. Unlike fossil fuels, the use of biomass as a fuel does not, in the long term, lead to increased carbon dioxide levels. This is because the carbon dioxide released when the fuel is burned is fixed again when new plants are grown.

Fast-growing trees

Fast-growing trees can be used to produce wood for fuel. In Britain, the commonest species used are willow and poplar trees. These are grown in plantations (Figure 15.29) and after one year of growth are cut off near the ground, in a process called **coppicing**.

Figure 15.28 Coppicer working on hornbeams

Coppiced trees grow many new shoots, which are allowed to grow for another three to five years before being harvested for their wood. The wood can be burned to produce heat or to drive steam turbines. The cut shoots will re-sprout and grow new shoots to continue the process. In Britain, wood biofuel produces less than half a percent of our energy needs. However, in some countries such as Sweden, taxes on fossil fuels and subsidised biofuel production have increased the consumption of solid biofuel, which is now providing a respectable 15% of the energy requirements of the country.

Liquid biofuel: bioethanol

Yeasts can convert sugars into ethanol by the process of **fermentation**. Plant biomass can be used as a source of sugars for this process. In Brazil, sugar is extracted from the crushed stems of the sugar cane plant. This sugar, as well as other sugar-containing products of the industry, is fermented to produce a dilute solution of ethanol. This is then distilled to produce **bioethanol**.

This can be used 'neat' as a fuel, or as a mix with conventional petrol (about 20% ethanol and 80% petrol) in the form of **gasohol**. Bioethanol is a 'cleaner' fuel than petrol, producing less carbon monoxide and nitrogen oxides and no sulphur dioxide. The main problems which limit its production are economic ones. Bioethanol is more expensive to produce than petrol. It was first produced in bulk in the 1980s, when Brazil had foreign exchange difficulties which made buying oil from overseas difficult. Nowadays production is only continued through government subsidies to the industry.

Biogas

Organic material can also be fermented by certain species of anaerobic bacteria to produce **biogas**, a fuel which consists mainly of methane, with some carbon dioxide and traces of other gases such as hydrogen sulphide and ammonia. Methane makes an excellent fuel, burning cleanly, to produce carbon dioxide and water. The solid residue from the process can be used as a fertiliser.

The organic material is fermented in a tank called a **digester**. Small domestic digesters have been used in China and India for many years (Figure 15.30). In

Figure 15.30 A digester for producing biogas

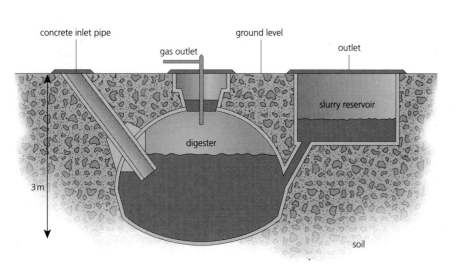

India the digesters use mainly cattle and buffalo dung, which produces biogas with a high methane content but little residual fertiliser. Chinese digesters tend to use a mixture of various types of animal dung, human excrement and vegetable waste. This produces gas of poorer quality, but high-quality fertiliser.

The digester tank is often made of concrete, and is usually built underground, for support and insulation. It has to be gas-tight and able to resist pressure build-up. There needs to be an inlet point for adding more waste organic material, an outlet for the gas, and a way of entering the digester to extract the residues after digestion is finished.

The dung or other waste is first broken down by aerobic bacteria into simpler molecules, but the final stages must take place under anaerobic conditions. This is because they are carried out by **methanobacteria**, which are **obligate anaerobes** (they only ferment the products to methane when no oxygen is present). The process works best at temperatures somewhat higher than ambient (about 30 to 40 °C).

Biogas generation has been mainly carried out in less developed countries, but in recent years larger-scale versions have been built in developed countries to produce gas from a range of waste materials, including animal dung, chicken litter, sewage and domestic organic rubbish. They are particularly successful in disposing of the large quantities of waste produced by intensive farming, such as slurry from pig farms. The gas from the digesters can be burned to heat the pens, or used to generate electricity.

?

8 Explain the difference between biomass, biogas and gasohol. *(5 marks)*

15.26 Legislation to control air and water quality

Improvements in the quality of air and water ultimately rely on international co-operation and agreement. It is necessary to implement policies to reduce the damaging effects of human activities on the environment, and for these to be backed up by law (**legislation**). For example, the **European Community** (now the **European Union**) has been devising laws to protect the environment since 1972, so that over 500 items of Community legislation had been devised by 1999, supported by a number of action programmes to address the problems.

The Treaty of Amsterdam developed the European Union's environment policy, strengthening the principle of 'sustainable development', which is now one of the EU's main objectives. The policy rests on the principles of **precaution, prevention, rectifying pollution at source and 'the polluter pays'**. Some examples of measures which have been adopted to tackle the problems affecting air and water quality include:

● Directives to reduce traffic pollution, setting maximum exhaust emission limits for motor vehicles and introducing tax incentives to encourage consumers to act in a more 'environmentally friendly' manner.

- Control of petrol and diesel fuel components. For example, the sulphur content of all fuels was limited at 0.2% from October 1994, and 0.05% for diesel from October 1996. In 1997 a new limit for both of 0.005% was proposed.

- A pledge to limit carbon dioxide production to 1990 levels by the year 2000, and a reduction in levels by 2005 or 2010, by the introduction of a tax on carbon dioxide emissions by industry. The aim is to promote the more efficient use of energy. Measures have also been proposed to limit the emissions of five other greenhouse gases.

- Directives controlling emissions of sulphur dioxide from large combustion plants, aiming to reduce the production from 14.4 million tonnes per year (1980 figure) to 6.2 million tonnes by 2005.

- Waste water (sewage) treatment plants to be provided for all towns with more than 15 000 inhabitants by 2000 and all other localities by 2005.

- A proposal (1996) for a wide-ranging action programme for integrated groundwater protection and management. This aims to develop integrated planning and management of freshwater resources and a regulatory framework for freshwater abstraction. It also proposes actions in agriculture to curb pollution by nitrates and other fertilisers.

The Earth's biosphere is a global ecosystem (Section 14.1, page 413). Only when we realise this fact, and start to co-operate at an international level with environmental programmes, will we be able to tackle the environmental problems we have caused.

Summary – (15) Effects of humans on ecosystems

- The human population of the Earth has increased exponentially over the last few hundred years. This has been possible because of exploitation of environmental resources and developments in agriculture, but has resulted in disruption and damage to ecosystems.

- Plants have adaptations which enable them to grow in particular environments. Certain species have been selected by humans to exploit as crop plants because of these adaptations.

- Agriculture works by controlling the abiotic and biotic environment of crop plants and domesticated animals to maximise productivity. Measures include the use of fertilisers and pesticides.

- Fertilisers may be organic, such as manures, or inorganic, such as nitrates. Both have their advantages and disadvantages. Organic fertilisers maintain soil structure but are slow to act. Inorganic fertilisers are faster acting and more efficient, but produce a number of environmental problems. In particular, they result in leaching of minerals into water courses, eutrophication and algal blooms.

- Pesticides include herbicides, fungicides and insecticides. They are very efficient at controlling weeds and pests of crops and domestic animals. However, they too produce a number of environmental problems. These include persistence in the environment, toxicity to non-target organisms, bioaccumulation in food chains and emergence of resistant strains of pest.

- An alternative to the use of chemical pesticides is to employ biological control methods, using a predator or parasite of the pest. Biological control methods tend to be less harmful to the environment but are often less effective.

Summary cont'd

- Deforestation of tropical rainforests, for timber or to provide agricultural land, is a major environmental problem. It greatly reduces biodiversity, and results in soil depletion and erosion, as well as climate change. Reafforestation and sustainable management of rainforests are needed.

- Desertification is the process of turning fertile semi-arid land into desert as a result of human activities, such as over-grazing. It may be accompanied by salinisation, where salts are brought to the soil surface, preventing plant growth.

- Release of untreated sewage into rivers increases the Biological Oxygen Demand of the water, and reduces the number of species which can inhabit the river. The degree of pollution can be measured by the presence of certain indicator species.

- Fossil fuels include coal, oil and natural gas. They are non-renewable resources. Their combustion contributes to pollution, including the formation of acid rain. Acid rain is damaging forests of northern Europe and killing organisms in the rivers and lakes of Scandinavia.

- The temperature of the surface of the Earth is maintained by a natural phenomenon called the greenhouse effect. This effect is strengthened by human production of greenhouse gases such as carbon dioxide, which may be producing global warming and long-term climate change. The consequences of global warming could be disastrous for the Earth's ecosystems.

- Whereas fossil fuels are non-renewable, biofuels are renewable sources of energy based on plant biomass. They include fast-growing trees, bioethanol and biogas.

- International laws (legislation) are needed to reduce environmental damage and allow sustainable development.

? Answers

1 Water vapour lost from the stomata tends to remain in the pits and is not removed by air currents *(1)*, while the humid air reduces further evaporation *(1)*.

2 Nitrogen: any two of amino acids/proteins/nucleic acids/DNA/RNA/ATP/chlorophyll *(2)*. Phosphorus: any two of nucleic acids/DNA/RNA/ATP/ phospholipids *(2)*.

3 At $100 \, kg \, ha^{-1}$, yield = 4.2 tonnes (from graph) which is worth $4.2 \times £120 = £504$ *(1)*. But fertiliser costs $£1 \times 100 = £100$. Therefore profit = $£504 - £100 = £404$ *(1)*. At $150 \, kg \, ha^{-1}$, yield = 4.7 tonnes (from graph) which is worth $4.7 \times £120 = £564$ *(1)*. But fertiliser costs $£1 \times 150 = £150$. Therefore profit = $£564 - £150 = £414$ *(1)*. So it is slightly more economical to apply $150 \, kg \, ha^{-1}$.

4 They have the fastest rate of reproduction *(1)*.

5 $25 \div 0.000003 = 8\,333\,333$ (or about 8.3 million times) *(1)*.

6 BOD must be measured at a standard temperature because temperature affects the rate of metabolism/enzyme activity which would affect oxygen uptake *(1)* and the solubility of oxygen in water varies with temperature *(1)*. Darkness is needed to prevent photosynthesis by any algae present, which would produce oxygen *(1)*.

7 Since CO_2 is a greenhouse gas, you would expect to find a strong greenhouse effect on Venus *(1)*. (In fact it increases the planet's surface temperature by several hundred °C!)

8 Biomass is a weight or mass of living material (in this context plant material) *(1)*. Biogas is a fuel, mainly made of methane *(1)*, formed by the action of bacteria on waste organic matter *(1)*. Gasohol is a fuel, a mixture of petrol and alcohol *(1)*, the alcohol made by fermentation of plant material such as sugar *(1)*.

End of Chapter Questions

1 Explain the following terms:

   (a) eutrophication   *(3 marks)*

   (b) bioaccumulation   *(3 marks)*

   (c) desertification   *(2 marks)*

   (d) the greenhouse effect.   *(3 marks)*

                                                       (Total 11 marks)

C3.3

2 Give an account of the causes and effects of pollution of water by
sewage.   *(10 marks)*

Edexcel 1998

3 An insecticide (methyl parathion) was used in Texas in an attempt to control
the tobacco budworm, *Heliothis virescens*. The effectiveness of the insecticide
was monitored over a four-year period, from 1967 to 1970. The insecticide
was applied at three different concentrations ($0.09\,kg\,ha^{-1}$, $0.27\,kg\,ha^{-1}$ and
$0.54\,kg\,ha^{-1}$). The percentage of tobacco budworms killed each year at each
concentration was recorded. The results are shown in the table below. No data
are available for 1969.

Concentration of insecticide /kg ha^{-1}	Percentage of budworms killed each year		
	1967	1968	1970
0.09	99.9	70	20
0.27	Not used	90	40
0.54	Not used	90	50

   (a) **(i)** Describe how the effectiveness of the insecticide changed during the
four-year period.   *(2 marks)*

       (ii) Suggest an explanation for this change in the effectiveness of the
insecticide.   *(4 marks)*

   (b) Bioaccumulation of the toxin is an environmental problem which can
occur as a result of the use of some insecticides.

       (i) Describe how bioaccumulation occurs.   *(3 marks)*

       (ii) Suggest *two* ways in which insecticides may be designed to avoid the
problems resulting from bioaccumulation.   *(2 marks)*

                                                      (Total 11 marks)

Edexcel 1998

4 (a) Many varieities of rice are planted in soil which is flooded with water.

  (i) Suggest why plants of most other species would die if they were planted in these conditions. *(3 marks)*

  (ii) Ethanol is poisonous. Rice is extremely tolerant and can survive with amounts of ethanol in its tissue which would kill other plants. Explain how this tolerance is an adaptation to growing in swampy conditions. *(2 marks)*

(b) The diagram shows a section through the stem of a rice plant.

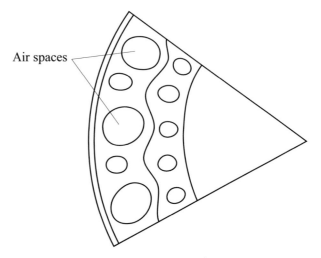

Air spaces

Give **two** ways in which the air spaces in the stem help the rice plant to survive in swampy conditons.

OCR 1999   *(Total 7 marks)*

5 Read through the following account about acid rain and renewable energy sources, then write on the dotted lines the most appropriate word or words to complete the account.

Acid rain has been linked to an increase in .... in the atmosphere. This increase is mainly due to the burning of .... such as .... One way of reducing the problem may be to use biogas produced by micro-organisms kept in warm .... conditions. These micro-organisms convert .... into this renewable energy source.

Edexcel 1997   *(Total 5 marks)*

6 The whitefly, *Trialeurodes*, is a pest of glasshouse cucumber and tomato crops and can be controlled biologically using a minute parasitic wasp, *Encarsia*. In an experiment, adult *Encarsia* wasps were introduced to a glasshouse crop infested with *Trialeurodes* and the density of each species was monitored over twenty generations. The results are shown in the table below.

Generation number	Density of *Trialeurodes* /insects per unit area	Density of *Encarsia* /insects per unit area
0 (start of experiment)	28	10
5	20	8
10	3	26
15	21	5
20	10	22

(a) Describe the changes in the density of *Trialeurodes* over the course of this experiment. *(3 marks)*

(b) Comment on the relationship between the density of *Trialeurodes* and the density of *Encarsia*. *(3 marks)*

(c) Suggest *two* adverse effects on a crop of infestation by *Trialeurodes*. *(2 marks)*

(d) (i) Give *two* advantages of biological rather than chemical control of insect pests. *(2 marks)*

(ii) Give *one* disadvantage of biological rather than chemical control of insect pests. *(1 mark)*

Edexcel 1997   *(Total 11 marks)*

16 Gene technology

In gene technology DNA is altered to produce a desired product. For instance in insulin production the human gene for the hormone insulin is isolated and inserted into a host bacterium for replication. The mass-produced insulin can then be used by sufferers of diabetes to reduce their blood glucose level. Gene technology is also used in a variety of other ways including the genetic modification of plant crops, gene therapy for human illness and genetic fingerprinting.

Gene technology, in the widest sense, is used to refer to a number of procedures involving the manipulation of DNA. One application involves changing the genetic make-up and therefore the properties of an organism. Usually genes are taken from one organism and introduced into another. Other uses of gene technology, such as **genetic fingerprinting**, do not involve producing new combinations of genes. The terms **genetic engineering** and **recombinant DNA technology** are often used in a similar way to the term **gene technology**.

16.1 Stages

There are a number of stages and techniques which are common to many of the uses of gene technology. One well-known application is the production of human insulin by genetically modified bacteria. This will be used as a case study to illustrate some of these main stages and techniques. (See Figure 16.1).

Bacteria are used to produce human insulin. The required tasks are to:

1. *isolate* (separate) the human insulin gene from the rest of the human DNA

2. *insert* the gene into a suitable host bacterium using a **vector** (a delivery tool)

3. *produce* many copies of the modified bacteria which will all produce insulin

4. separate and purify the insulin (**downstream processing**) which can then be used by people with diabetes.

16.2 Stage 1: isolation of the required gene – method A

Two methods can be used. The first method involves cutting the gene out from the complete chromosome; the second method uses reverse transcription to make a copy of the gene.

Use of restriction endonuclease enzymes to cut the gene out of a chromosome
Starting from the complete chromosomes of the donor, the required gene has to be located. One way is to use **electrophoresis** (see Box 16.6, page 498) and **DNA probes**. Once its position has been identified, the gene is cut out using restriction endonuclease enzymes.

Restriction endonucleases act as **molecular scissors**, cutting DNA at a specific base sequence. Different restriction enzymes cut at different base sequences because only these bases are the right shape to fit into their active site. By choosing a particular restriction enzyme (out of the hundreds available) the DNA may be cut at exactly the right place to **isolate** (remove) the gene.

This chapter includes:
- methods of isolating the required gene
- the use of vectors to insert a gene into a host cell
- the function of the enzymes restriction endonuclease, DNA ligase and reverse transcriptase
- applications of gene technology including: insulin manufacture; genetically modified animals and plants; gene therapy; genetic fingerprinting
- the social and ethical implications of gene technology.

Remember

Gene technology refers to procedures involving the manipulation of DNA. The terms genetic engineering and recombinant DNA technology usually mean the same thing

Definition

Restriction endonucleases are enzymes which act as **molecular scissors**, cutting DNA at a specific base sequence. Different restriction enzymes cut at different base sequences

Figure 16.1 *The use of micro-organisms to produce human protein – the production of human insulin by bacteria*

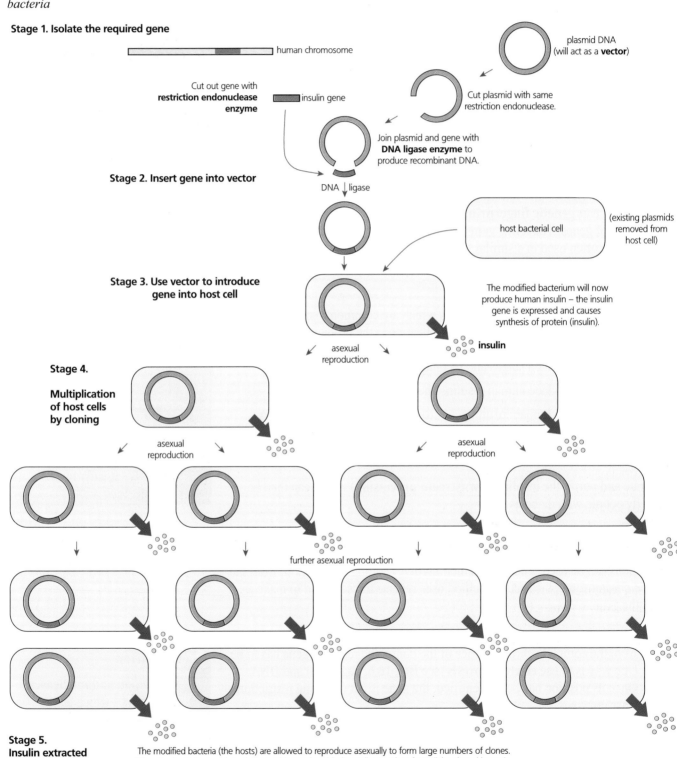

Stage 1. Isolate the required gene

human chromosome

plasmid DNA (will act as a **vector**)

Cut out gene with **restriction endonuclease enzyme**

insulin gene

Cut plasmid with same restriction endonuclease.

Join plasmid and gene with **DNA ligase enzyme** to produce recombinant DNA.

Stage 2. Insert gene into vector

DNA ↓ ligase

host bacterial cell

(existing plasmids removed from host cell)

Stage 3. Use vector to introduce gene into host cell

The modified bacterium will now produce human insulin – the insulin gene is expressed and causes synthesis of protein (insulin).

asexual reproduction

insulin

Stage 4.

Multiplication of host cells by cloning

asexual reproduction

asexual reproduction

further asexual reproduction

Stage 5. Insulin extracted and purified. (downstream processing)

The modified bacteria (the hosts) are allowed to reproduce asexually to form large numbers of clones. When the bacteria reproduce the recombinant plasmid *also* replicates. Therefore *all* the cloned bacteria contain the human insulin and they can all produce insulin.

?

1 Given just one restriction endonuclease enzyme, explain why this cannot be used to cut out all the genes on a chromosome. *(2 marks)*

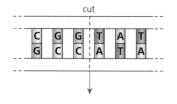

Figure 16.2 *Restriction endonuclease enzymes and sticky ends – the action of restriction enzyme Hind III.*

Some restriction endonuclease enzymes cut **evenly**. This produces **even** or **blunt** ends.

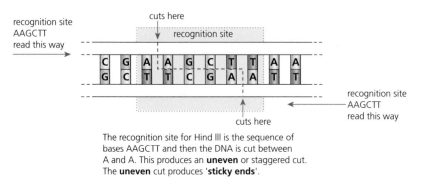

recognition site
AAGCTT
read this way

cuts here

recognition site

recognition site
AAGCTT
read this way

cuts here

The recognition site for Hind III is the sequence of bases AAGCTT and then the DNA is cut between A and A. This produces an **uneven** or staggered cut. The **uneven** cut produces '**sticky ends**'.

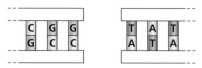

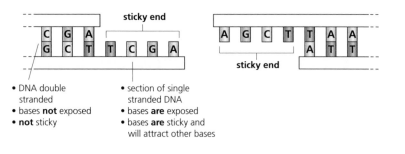

sticky end

sticky end

- DNA double stranded
- bases **not** exposed
- **not** sticky

- section of single stranded DNA
- bases **are** exposed
- bases **are** sticky and will attract other bases

- blunt ends
- **no** exposed bases
- **no** sticky ends

Cutting with the **same** restriction enzyme will always produce the **same** sticky ends with the **same** bases.

Many restriction enzymes produce an uneven or staggered cut. This leaves single-stranded ends with exposed bases (**sticky ends**). Because these bases are exposed (unpaired) they are 'sticky' – they will attract and stick to the exposed bases of complementary **sticky ends**. (See Section 5.2, page 120.)

Other restriction enzymes produce straight cuts with blunt rather than sticky ends (no exposed bases). See Figure 16.2.

Restriction endonucleases are found naturally in bacteria where they help protect against invasion by viruses by cutting up viral DNA. About 400 different types have now been obtained. Restriction enzymes are also important in electrophoresis (see Box 16.6, page 498).

Definition

Sticky ends are sections of single-stranded DNA produced by the staggered cut of some restriction endonuclease enzymes. They will attract and join with complementary sticky ends

Definition

Reverse transcription is the reverse of normal transcription. A particular sequence of DNA is copied from a messenger RNA template.

Reverse transcriptase is an enzyme which catalyses reverse transcription

Use of reverse transcription to make a copy of the gene

Reverse transcription is the reverse of normal transcription, as in this process a sequence of DNA is copied from a messenger RNA template. The process is catalysed by the enzyme **reverse transcriptase**, making **copy DNA** (cDNA) or a copy gene. (See Figure 16.3)

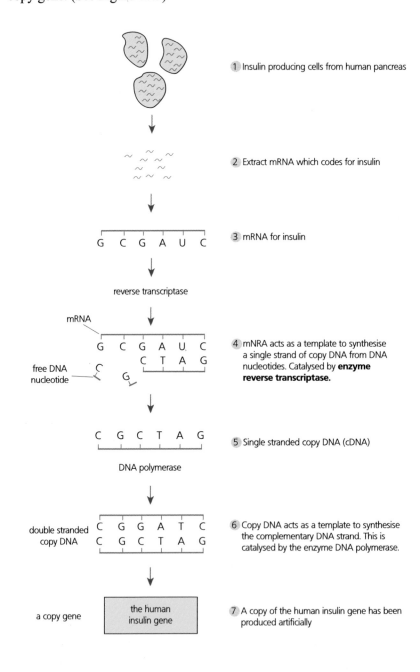

Figure 16.3 Isolation of the required gene by reverse transcription – the required DNA is made from messenger RNA, e.g. in the production of the insulin gene

Messenger RNA (mRNA) is obtained from cells where the gene is actively synthesising protein. This mRNA is used as a template to produce a complementary single strand of DNA from free DNA nucleotides. This process is catalysed by the enzyme **reverse transcriptase**. The single strand of DNA is now made double stranded using free DNA nucleotides and the enzyme **DNA polymerase**. A **copy gene** has been made. The usual process of transcription (see Section 5.9, page 134) has been *reversed*. DNA has been made from mRNA – hence reverse transcription. Reverse transcriptase enzymes are found naturally in retroviruses – the group which includes HIV, the AIDS virus.

There are two advantages to this method. Firstly, each active cell will have *many* copies of the mRNA so it should be easier to find than the *single* copy of the DNA gene in each cell. Secondly, the *length* of the mRNA strand exactly corresponds to the length of the DNA gene – it does not have to be *cut out* of a longer piece as with DNA.

2 Suggest one disadvantage of storing genetic information as RNA (as in retroviruses) rather than as DNA. *(1 mark)*

Isolation of the required gene: some difficulties
Method A was used in 1982 to produce the first human insulin, Humulin, made using gene technology. (See Figure 16.26, page 503). However, it is difficult to use method A to obtain genes from eukaryotic cells, e.g. from humans, for use in prokaryotic hosts, e.g. bacteria. One reason is the presence of introns (see Box 5.5, page 138) in eukaryotic genes which are normally edited out when proteins are made. Prokaryotic cells cannot edit out the introns so that the wrong polypeptide may be synthesised. Secondly, the regulatory genes (see Box 16.1, page 487) for eukaryotic genes and prokaryotic genes are different.

Method B overcomes the intron problem as the introns are removed at the transcription stage of protein synthesis. The messenger RNA used for method B has had the introns already removed. Method B is now much more commonly used to isolate eukaryotic genes for insertion into the prokaryotic hosts.

Alternatively, eukaryotic microorganisms, e.g. yeast, are used as hosts instead of prokaryotes such as bacteria. Both methods A and B can be used with yeast.

16.4 Stage 2: inserting the gene into a vector

A **vector** is a molecule of DNA which is used to carry a foreign gene into a host cell. The most commonly used vectors are bacterial plasmids and phage viruses.

Plasmids are circular pieces of double-stranded DNA found naturally in bacteria. They are found in addition to the main DNA of the bacteria. Plasmids may contain genes which can be useful to the bacterium, e.g. genes which provide resistance to antibiotics. Plasmids can enter bacteria and the plasmid DNA replicates (divides) when the bacteria reproduce. These last two features make them suitable as vectors.

The insertion of the gene into a plasmid vector is shown in Figure 16.4. The enzyme **DNA ligase** helps to join the DNA of the plasmid and the gene.

Definition
Vectors are molecules of DNA which are used to carry foreign genes into a host cell. They act as molecular *lorries*.

Plasmids are circular pieces of double-stranded DNA found naturally in bacteria. They are found in addition to the main DNA of the bacteria. They are used as vectors in gene technology

Definition
DNA ligase is an enzyme used to join pieces of DNA. It causes the sugar phosphate backbones to join. It acts as *molecular glue*

Figure 16.4 *Inserting the required gene into the vector – the importance of sticky ends*

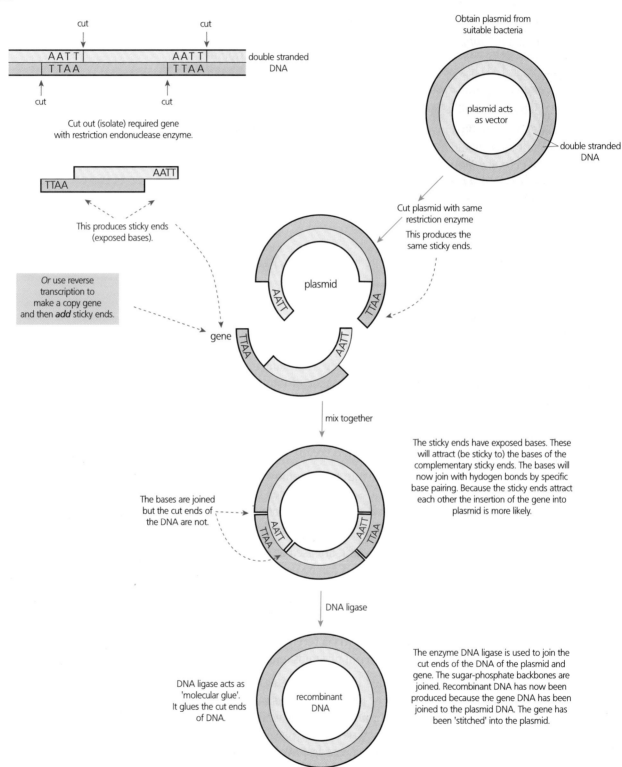

Extension

Box 16.1 Switching on genes

Genes are *expressed* when their base sequence is being transcribed into mRNA for protein synthesis. Many genes have to be *activated* (switched on) before they can be expressed. This prevents protein being produced (and wasted) at the wrong time or in the wrong place. Other sections of DNA are involved in this switching on, including **promoters**, **regulators** and **operators**. A division is sometimes made between *structural* genes which code for actual functional protein and *regulatory* genes which control the activities of other genes, e.g. operator genes. One structural gene together with the regulatory genes which control it are known as an **operon**. The initial research on this was done by Jacob and Monod in 1961. With gene technology the regulation of gene expression has to be taken into account. Inserting a human gene into a bacterium for example, on its own may not be sufficient. Appropriate regulatory genes, especially a promoter, may also have to be inserted, otherwise the bacterium will not express the human gene.

Extension

Box 16.2 The use of the bacterium *Agrobacterium tumefaciens* as a vector with plants

This is a bacterium which naturally infects plants, causing swellings called galls. To insert a gene into a plant the required gene is inserted into a plasmid and then the plasmid is inserted into *Agrobacterium*. *Agrobacterium* is then allowed to infect plant cells grown in culture. Here it transfers the plasmid into the plant cells. Plants grown from these genetically modified plant cells will all contain the inserted gene. This method was used in 1993 to produce genetically modified oilseed rape plants. These had a gene added to make them produce a different type of oil which could be extracted and used commercially to make detergents.

16.5 Stage 3: using the vector to insert the gene into a host

Plasmids are removed from the bacterial cells which are to act as the hosts, freeing the bacteria for the vector plasmids. Now the recombinant plasmids are mixed (*incubated*) with the host bacterial cells.

Various treatments may be used to make it easier for the plasmids to enter the host bacteria. These include calcium ions, temperature shock and electrical shock as they help to make the bacterial cell wall more permeable.

Getting the gene into the host is not an exact process. Thousands of bacteria and plasmids are involved and only a few bacteria will take up the plasmid with the human gene (the **recombinant plasmid**). These bacteria are said to be *modified* or *transformed*. Other bacteria will take up non-recombinant plasmids without the human gene.

The modified bacteria therefore have to be identified and separated (*screened*) from amongst the others. One method involves the use of **DNA probes** (see Figure 16.15, page 497). Another method involves the use of **genetic markers** such as genes for antibiotic resistance. Plasmids with a gene for antibiotic resistance are used as the

Before

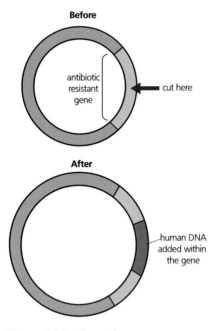

antibiotic resistant gene ← cut here

After

human DNA added within the gene

Figure 16.5 *Plasmids*

vectors. Cutting the plasmid and inserting the human DNA is done *within* the bases of the antibiotic gene. If the human DNA is inserted successfully the antibiotic gene cannot function because it has been *damaged*. (See Figure 16.5.)

Samples taken from the original cultures are grown on a medium containing the antibiotic. (These samples are obtained by **replica plating** – a process which allows the exact *location* of the different colonies of bacteria to be known and retained.) Non-modified bacteria which have taken up plasmids without the human DNA *will be able to grow* because their antibiotic resistance gene is not damaged. Modified bacteria which have taken up plasmids with the human DNA *will not grow* because their antibiotic resistance gene has been damaged by insertion of the human DNA. By going back to the original cultures the colonies of modified bacteria can be identified and only these are used for the rest of the stages.

16.6 **Stage 4: multiplication of the host cells by cloning**

The modified bacteria are now grown on a large scale in industrial fermenters by **cloning**. Large numbers of bacteria are required if insulin is to be produced in commercial quantities (see Box 16.3, page 490).

The bacteria are allowed to reproduce asexually by cell division. Asexual reproduction produces **clones**, new bacteria which are genetically identical to the parent cell. More importantly, each time the bacterial cell divides, the plasmid also replicates – producing an exact copy of itself, including the inserted human insulin gene. So, each new bacterial cell receives a copy of the plasmid including the insulin gene.

In this way, all the bacteria in the culture will have the human insulin gene. Inside the bacterium the insulin gene will be **expressed** – it will instruct the bacterium to produce insulin by protein synthesis. Because the DNA instructions of the insulin gene are for *human* insulin, the insulin produced by the bacteria will be chemically identical to the insulin produced normally by the human pancreas.

16.7 **Stage 5: downstream processing**

The insulin produced by the bacteria is secreted into the culture solution. The insulin is then extracted and purified so that it is safe for human use by people with diabetes. See also Box 16.3, page 490–491.

16.8 The applications of gene technology

Gene technology is used in a wide variety of applications. Genetically modified microorganisms are used to produce useful proteins. Genetically modified animals are also used to produce useful proteins. Genetically modified plant crops are used in farming as genetic modification can give commercial advantages. Gene technology is also used in gene therapy to treat human genetic disease. It is also used in genetic fingerprinting in which people can be identified from a sample of their DNA. The uses of gene technology are described in more detail in Sections 16.9 to 16.13 on the following pages.

Using genetically modified microorganisms to produce proteins

A wide range of proteins are now produced industrially from a variety of types of microorganism including bacteria, yeasts and moulds. This makes up the bulk of modern biotechnology. The useful proteins include: enzymes such as those used in biological washing powders; vaccines such as those against the Hepatitis B antigen; antibiotics such as penicillin; hormones such as human growth hormone and insulin.

Chymosin (rennin) is an enzyme produced by gene technology. It is produced from genetically modified yeast and is used in cheese-making to coagulate milk protein to produce solid curds. Chymosin produced this way has replaced the natural enzyme rennin (rennet) which used to be extracted from the stomachs of calves. (See box 16.3, page 490.)

Insulin

One of the first commercial uses of gene technology was in **insulin manufacture**. Insulin-dependent diabetes is a very common condition, with over two million people requiring daily insulin injections. Previously, cow or pig insulin was obtained from dead animals. These types of insulin are slightly different chemically to human insulin, causing an immune response in some people which destroyed the insulin. Using microorganisms for production has the advantage of providing human insulin with no risk of an immune response. Secondly, micro organisms can be grown in large quantities cheaply, which keeps down production costs.

One method for the production of insulin from bacteria was given earlier (Figure 16.1 on page 482). Different approaches are also used. Reverse transcription may be used to produce a copy of the insulin gene starting from messenger RNA. This copy gene is then introduced into the host. In another method, yeasts may be used as the host rather than bacteria.

Finally, it should be noted that insulin in fact consists of two polypeptide chains. These can be produced separately and then added together later.

However, nowadays insulin is usually produced as **pro insulin**. This consists of the two polypeptide chains joined by a third chain. This third chain is removed chemically to give a protein identical to human insulin.

3 Why are other types of organic molecule, e.g. lipids or sugars, not produced from genetically modified microorganisms in this way?   *(1 mark)*

Box 16.3 The commercial production of the enzyme chymosin

Chymosin (rennin) is an enzyme produced from genetically modified yeast or bacteria. It is used in cheese making to coagulate milk protein to produce solid curds. Originally the source of chymosin was rennet which was extracted from the stomachs of calves, but by the 1960s different sources of supply were being sought. Alternative enzymes were obtained from certain species of fungi and these are still used in about one-third of worldwide cheese production. By the 1980s gene technology was being used and today a number of different species of microorganism have been genetically modified to produce chymosin. These include the bacterium *Escherichia coli* and the yeast *Saccharomyces cerevisiae*. The chymosin produced by gene technology is identical to the 'natural' enzyme produced by calves. The advantages of the 'genetic' enzyme include fewer impurities and properties that are more predictable. For commercial production the gene for chymosin is inserted into yeast cells using a suitable vector. These genetically modified yeast cells are added to an industrial fermenter so that large numbers can be grown.

Growth in a fermenter

Fermenters are large vessels made of stainless steel and with a capacity of up to 500,000 dm³. Although they are historically referred to as fermenters, the term fermentation in this context is used for any large scale production of products from microorganisms and not just for processes involving anaerobic fermentation.

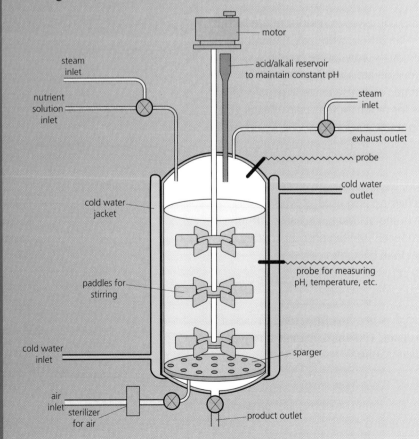

Figure 16.6 *A typical fermenter*

Box 16.3 The commercial production of the enzyme chymosin cont'd

Features of the fermenter

1. **Aseptic (sterile) conditions**: it is very important to prevent growth of other microorganisms which could compete with the yeast for nutrients or contaminate the product making it harmful. Before use the fermenter is sterilised with steam used under pressure and everything added to the fermenter such as the nutrients and the air is also sterilised.

2. **Nutrients**: the yeast must be provided with all the nutrients they need for growth in the form of a liquid media. Different microorganisms have different nutritional requirements so a nutrient media which is specific to yeast is used. This will contain an energy source such as a carbohydrate, a source of nitrogen for protein synthesis and a range of other minerals and ions such as phosphate and sulphur.

3. **Oxygen**: the yeast require oxygen for aerobic respiration so sterilised air is pumped in via a sparger which produces many small bubbles.

4. **Stirrer**: the contents of the fermenter are constantly stirred to maintain a thorough mixing of nutrient solution and yeast cells.

5. **Probes**: these are electronic sensors which constantly monitor conditions such as pH and temperature inside the fermenter.

6. **Water jacket**: respiration by the yeast produces a lot of heat which could harm the yeast or denature the enzyme product made by the yeast. The jacket has cold water flowing through it which removes excess heat to cool the fermenter.

Downstream processing

This is the extraction and purification of the product – in this case the chymosin enzyme.

Intracellular and extracellular enzymes: intracellular enzymes stay within the cell and if they are produced commercially the cells must first be broken open before the enzyme can be extracted. Extracellular enzymes are secreted from cells. Chymosin is an extracellular enzyme and so it is secreted by the yeast into the surrounding nutrient solution.

Stages of downstream processing: The fermenter is shut down and the mixture of nutrients and yeast cells (the culture solution) is drained off.

Solid particles, including the yeast cells are removed by filtration or centrifugation. The remaining solution contains a mixture of substances.

The chymosin is separated from the solution using a variety of techniques including solvent extraction and chromatography. Reverse osmosis, where hydrostatic pressure is used to move solutes against a concentration gradient may also be used. This separation is carefully regulated to ensure that the final product has a very high level of purity. The pure chymosin can now be packaged ready for sale.

16.9 Genetically modified (transgenic) animals

Human genes have been introduced into farm animals such as sheep and goats to give **transgenic animals** that can produce useful human proteins in their milk. The animals are milked and the proteins are extracted and purified. Examples of proteins which have been produced in this way include **blood factor IX** used to treat people with haemophilia and **ATT** (alpha-1-antitrypsin) used as part of the treatment for emphysema, cystic fibrosis and other lung conditions. The animals are used as living factories to manufacture human proteins. Research of this type led to Dolly, the first cloned sheep (see Section 6.8, page 165). Using animals in this way has been given the nickname '**pharming**'.

Research is also under way into the use of pigs to grow human organs such as kidneys. The human kidney would grow inside the living pig and then be removed for use in kidney transplants.

16.10 Genetically modified plant crops

Plant crops have been genetically modified in various ways. In many modified varieties the new genetic make-up is inherited by the offspring. The new variety is then self-perpetuating.

Some examples include the following:

- **Maize** has been modified to protect it against an insect pest, the corn borer. A gene from the bacterium *Bacillus thuringiensis* is introduced which causes the maize to produce a protein which is toxic to the insect pest but is harmless to humans eating the maize.

- **Flavr Savr tomatoes** are tomatoes that have been modified to slow down the ripening process, increasing the shelf life and reducing waste. Rather than stimulating production of a new protein, this method works by blocking synthesis of an enzyme involved in ripening. An **'antisense' gene** is introduced which blocks expression of the enzyme gene. Paste made from these tomatoes was the first genetically modified food to be sold in the UK in 1995.

- **Soya bean plants** have been made herbicide (weedkiller) resistant. Bacterial genes are added which make the plants resistant to a particular herbicide. The crop can then be sprayed with the herbicide to kill the weeds but the soya is not affected. Soya is added to a wide variety of processed foods.

- **Oilseed rape** (see Box 16.2, page 487).

There has been considerable public discussion both for and against genetically modified foods. Some of the issues are covered in Section 16.14, page 402.

Did You Know

It has been estimated that 2000 genetically modified sheep could produce enough of the medicine ATT to satisfy all the world's demand.

Did You Know

By 1998 thirty per cent of the soya bean crops in the USA were genetically modified

16.11 Gene therapy

Gene therapy describes the treatment of genetic disease by the introduction of healthy genes, to replace damaged ones that are causing disease. One example is gene therapy for cystic fibrosis. This is considered in detail in Box 16.5, below.

Extension

Box 16.4 Gene therapy for cystic fibrosis

Genetic disease of humans

About 4000 human disorders are due to the mutation of a single gene. However, most human disease is non-genetic, caused by bacteria, viruses, malnutrition etc.

Somatic and germ line therapy

Theoretically, genes may be added into **germ cells** (eggs or sperm) or into body or **somatic cells**. Germ cell therapy is banned at present in the UK because it involves making genetic changes which will be passed on to the next generation. Changing the genes of future generations is considered unethical.

Cystic fibrosis

This is caused by an autosomal recessive allele and therefore sufferers must inherit two copies of the allele. In the UK one person in 2000 has cystic fibrosis and one in 22 are carriers of one allele.

An affected person produces mucus that is too thick and unable to flow properly. This causes a variety of problems including the following. The respiratory pathways and lungs become partially blocked by mucus, making breathing difficult and gas exchange less efficient. The mucus normally helps to keep the lungs clean and sufferers are likely to have more lung infections. The pancreatic duct can become blocked with mucus so that enzymes from the pancreas do not reach the gut and food is not digested properly. Finally, in males the sperm duct can become blocked with mucus so that sperm cannot be released from the body. This can cause infertility in some male sufferers.

People with cystic fibrosis rarely live beyond thirty and sufferers require regular physiotherapy for their lung problems (see Figure 16.8).

The cystic fibrosis or CFTR gene

The CFTR gene is found on chromosome 7. It was first located in 1985 after a research effort by a number of centres that cost an estimated 150 million US dollars. Locating the gene was essential before gene therapy could be developed. The CFTR gene codes for a protein – a transmembrane regulator (TR) – that is essential for the transport of chloride ions across cell surface membranes (see Figure 16.9).

In the cystic fibrosis mutation three DNA bases are missing. It is a deletion gene mutation. After protein synthesis from the gene, one amino acid is missing from the polypeptide chain. Further details on the mutation are given in Section 5.13, page 143.

Definition

Gene therapy attempts to treat human genetic disease by introducing healthy genes to replace the damaged genes which are causing the disease.

Did You Know

The first successful gene therapy treatment was in 1990. Healthy genes were added to the blood cells of a three-year-old girl to treat SCID (severe combined immunodeficiency disease).

Children who have SCID have no effective immune system and cannot fight off infections. Without treatment they have to be protected from exposure to any germs by living in an isolation 'bubble' rather like a space suit (Figure 16.7).

Figure 16.7 *Baby who is receiving gene therapy for SCID*

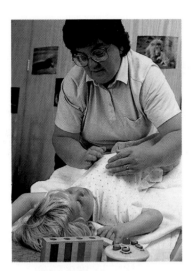

Figure 16.8 *Physiotherapist treating a child with cystic fibrosis*

Extension

Box 16.4 Gene therapy for cystic fibrosis cont'd

Detection

Because three DNA bases are missing the deletion can be identified using **electrophoresis** (Box 16.6, page 498). Only a short section (50 bases) of the DNA is compared. The DNA from a sufferer will be shorter in length and will travel further in electrophoresis than the healthy DNA.

Therapy

Healthy CFTR genes are obtained and cloned to give many copies. Two types of vector have been used to introduce the healthy genes into the cells of sufferers. In the first method, the genes were inserted into a harmless virus and the virus was used as a vector to insert the CFTR genes. This had some success but one volunteer became ill and there are some doubts about this method. The second approach was developed at St Mary's Hospital in London. Healthy genes are wrapped in lipid and sprayed down into the lungs of a patient. Many of these tiny lipid packages (**liposomes**) are absorbed into the epithelial cells lining the lungs. The lipid coat helps them pass through the phospholipid cell surface membrane.

The new genes may be expressed and allow the epithelial cell to produce normal runny mucus. Epithelial cells regularly die and are replaced and so the treatment has to be regularly repeated.

This treatment only helps the lung problems. The other problems have to be treated in other ways, for instance extra enzymes are taken as a medicine to help digestion.

Figure 16.9 *Epithelial tissues from the lungs of*
(a) healthy person
(b) person with cystic fibrosis

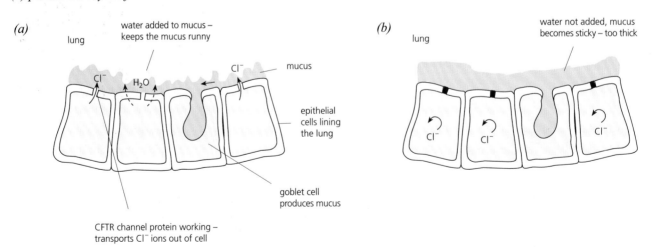

Healthy CFTR gene codes for normal CFTR protein. Transport of Cl⁻ ions out of cell allows water to follow by osmosis. This keeps the mucus runny.

CFTR channel protein not working – Cl⁻ ions not transported out of cell so water does not follow. There is a mutation in the CFTR gene. The correct CFTR protein is not synthesised and cannot function properly.

16.1 Genetic fingerprinting

Genetic fingerprinting is a method of comparing samples of DNA by producing a visible pattern rather like a bar code. The DNA of each person is different (apart from identical twins) and will produce a pattern unique to that individual.

Genetic fingerprinting was invented by Professor Alex Jeffreys of Leicester University in 1984.

In genetic fingerprinting samples of DNA are compared by using them to produce a visible pattern rather like a bar code. Each person (apart from identical twins) has a unique DNA giving a unique pattern. The technique is used in various ways: in police work to help identify criminals, in disputes concerning the parentage of a child and to investigate the evolutionary relationships between different species.

Not all the DNA codes for a particular protein (see Box 5.5, page 126). Some of this non-coding DNA consists of short sequences of bases called minisatellites. These sequences are repeated and the number of repeats varies between individuals. Genetic fingerprinting compares the banding pattern produced by these sequences. The distribution of these sequences is inherited so a child will share some bands in common with both parents (Figure 16.13b).

Figure 16.10 *Genetic fingerprinting*

> **! Did You Know**
>
> Genetic fingerprinting was used to identify a skeleton dug up in South America as being that of Dr Josef Mengele, the Nazi war criminal who had avoided capture after the war. DNA taken from the bones was compared with DNA taken from the blood of Mengele's still-living son.

Figure 16.12 *Josef Mengele*

The technique of genetic fingerprinting is shown in Figure 16.14. It includes the important techniques of **electrophoresis** and **DNA probes**.

Figure 16.11 *Professor Alex Jeffreys of Leicester University who invented genetic fingerprinting in 1984*

Figure 16.13 *Two uses of genetic fingerprinting*

(a) Use as criminal evidence

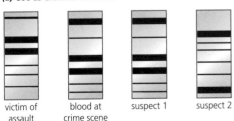

victim of assault | blood at crime scene | suspect 1 | suspect 2

This provides evidence that suspect 1 is guilty.

(b) Use as evidence of parentage (paternity cases)

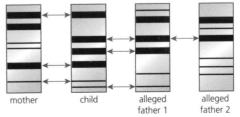

mother | child | alleged father 1 | alleged father 2

This provides evidence that father 1 is the true father as he shares 3 bands with the child compared to just 1 for father 2.

shared bands

Note that the child has its own unique banding pattern but that because this is inherited, it does share some bands with both parents.

Figure 16.14 *The technique of genetic fingerprinting*

① **Extract DNA from sample**

DNA extracted from a suitable sample, e.g. blood cells.

② **Cut up DNA**

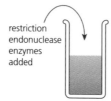

restriction endonuclease enzymes added

Restriction enzymes cut DNA into different sized fragments. Smaller fragments contain fewer repeat sequences of the indicator DNA (minisatellites)

short fragment – 2 sequences
longer fragment – 5 sequences

③ **Separate DNA fragments according to size using electrophoresis**

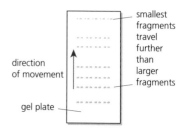

direction of movement

smallest fragments travel further than larger fragments

gel plate

The fragments of DNA are separated by **electrophoresis** on the basis of size. They are sieved through a gel plate. This produces a **banding pattern** – **not visible** at this stage.

④ **DNA made single stranded**

DNA bands treated to make them single stranded, e.g. heated.

⑤ **DNA fragments transferred to membrane**

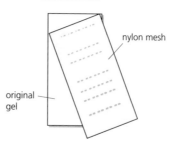

nylon mesh

original gel

The pattern of DNA bands is transferred to a nylon membrane by Southern blotting.

⑥ **Fragments labelled with DNA probes**

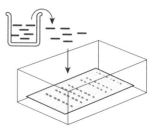

Radioactive DNA probes are washed over the membrane. These attach by base pairing to complementary bases on the DNA fragments.

⑦ **DNA made visible using autoradiography**

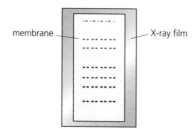

membrane — X-ray film

Autoradiography – place membrane with labelled DNA onto X-ray film. The radioactive probes '**fog**' the film producing a pattern of dark bands.

⑧ **Final visible DNA fingerprint available**

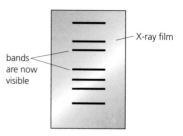

bands are now visible

X-ray film

A pattern of bands rather like a bar code. The pattern is unique to each individual (apart from identical twins).

① Section of DNA which contains the sought for base sequence. The location of this sequence is **not** known but the order of the bases is known.

double stranded DNA

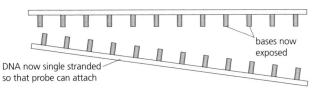

② Radioactive DNA probes are made. These are single stranded and have the complementary base sequence to the sought-for DNA.

radioactivity

single stranded i.e. bases are exposed

③ The sections of DNA are made single stranded, e.g. by heating.

bases now exposed

DNA now single stranded so that probe can attach

④ The radioactive DNA probes are mixed with the sections of single stranded DNA.

⑤ The DNA probes will only bind (hybridise) with the complementary bases of the sought-for DNA sequence due to base pairing.

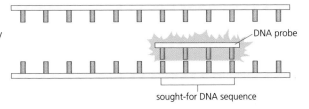

DNA probe

sought-for DNA sequence

⑥ Autoradiography. Sections of DNA with DNA probes attached placed on X-ray film.

X-ray film

radioactivity

⑦ The X-ray film is only exposed (fogged) at the location where the DNA probe has attached.

X-ray film 'fogged' – a black area

X-ray film

The position of the black area reveals the location of the sought-for DNA sequence.

Figure 16.15 *Use of DNA probes to locate a specific DNA sequence, e.g. as used in genetic fingerprinting*

Definition

DNA probes are short, single-stranded lengths of DNA which have been radioactively labelled. The probes are made so that the sequence of bases is complementary to the bases on the DNA being sought. The probe is mixed with the DNA where it binds with the bases of the sought-for DNA, identifying its location

(16) Gene technology

Extension

Box 16.5 Outline of electrophoresis

A sample of DNA is treated with a particular restriction endonuclease enzyme. If the same restriction enzyme is used with the same DNA then the same fragments will be produced every time. These fragments will be of different sizes (lengths) because the enzyme only cuts at specific sequences of bases called recognition sites. (See Figure 16.17.)

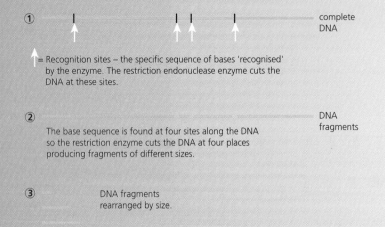

①   complete DNA

↑ = Recognition sites – the specific sequence of bases 'recognised' by the enzyme. The restriction endonuclease enzyme cuts the DNA at these sites.

②   DNA fragments

The base sequence is found at four sites along the DNA so the restriction enzyme cuts the DNA at four places producing fragments of different sizes.

③   DNA fragments rearranged by size.

Figure 16.17 *A sample of DNA is treated with a restriction endonuclease enzyme to give DNA fragments*

Electrophoresis is used to separate the fragments on the basis of their different sizes. The DNA fragments are placed at the cathode end of the gel (jelly) plate and an electric current is passed through the gel. The DNA fragments move through the gel towards the anode. The smaller fragments can pass through the gel easiest and so the smaller fragments travel faster and move furthest in a given time. (See Figure 16.18.)

The different-sized fragments move different distances producing *invisible* banding. The pattern of DNA bands can be *revealed* directly by staining the DNA. Alternatively the pattern of bands is transferred to a nylon membrane by Southern blotting. The DNA bands are made single stranded by heating, and radioactive DNA probes are washed over the membrane. The probes attach to the DNA bands by specific base pairing. The position of the probes and therefore the bands can now be revealed by **autoradiography**. An X-ray film is placed over the membrane and the film is fogged by the radioactive probes. This produces a '*fingerprint*' – a visible pattern of dark bands rather like a bar code. (See Figure 16.14, page 496.)

Figure 16.16 *A researcher preparing an electrophoresis gel.*

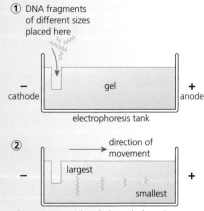

① DNA fragments of different sizes placed here

cathode −   gel   + anode

electrophoresis tank

②   direction of movement

−   largest   +   smallest

Fragments are 'sieved' through the gel. The smallest fragments travel faster and further.

Figure 16.18 *Electrophoresis is used to separate the DNA fragments*

Extension

Box 16.5 Outline of electrophoresis cont'd

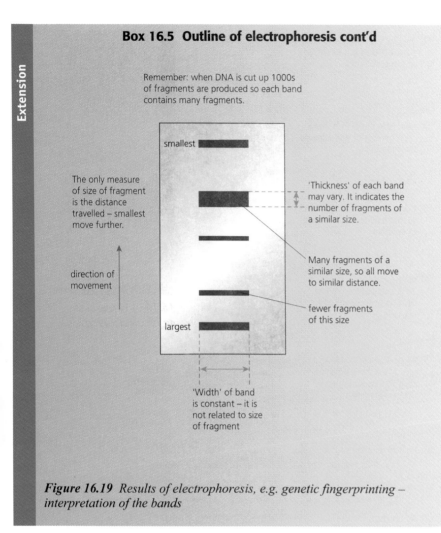

Remember: when DNA is cut up 1000s of fragments are produced so each band contains many fragments.

smallest

The only measure of size of fragment is the distance travelled – smallest move further.

direction of movement

largest

'Thickness' of each band may vary. It indicates the number of fragments of a similar size.

Many fragments of a similar size, so all move to similar distance.

fewer fragments of this size

'Width' of band is constant – it is not related to size of fragment

Figure 16.19 Results of electrophoresis, e.g. genetic fingerprinting – interpretation of the bands

Remember

Exam hint
Remember that electrophoresis is carried out *horizontally* not vertically like chromatography.

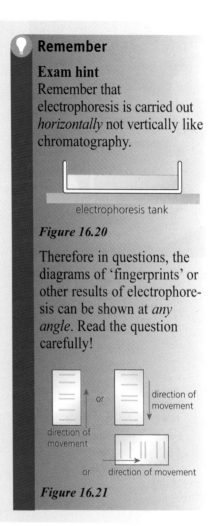

electrophoresis tank

Figure 16.20

Therefore in questions, the diagrams of 'fingerprints' or other results of electrophoresis can be shown at *any angle*. Read the question carefully!

direction of movement   or   direction of movement

or   direction of movement

Figure 16.21

16.13 The polymerase chain reaction (PCR)

Some procedures in gene technology, e.g. genetic fingerprinting, require large amounts of the same DNA but only a small sample may be available, e.g. blood at a crime scene. The polymerase chain reaction enables many identical copies of DNA to be made from a small sample (see Figure 16.23). The requirements for PCR are as follows:

● a thermocycler – an automated and computer-controlled piece of equipment

● a small sample of the double-stranded DNA to be copied

● the enzyme DNA polymerase

● primers – short pieces of DNA

● free DNA nucleotides.

Everything is placed in the thermocycler at 70°C. From now on the process is controlled automatically. The temperature is raised to 95°C, separating the original strands by breaking the hydrogen bonds. The temperature is reduced to 40°C and primers are added. These are short pieces of DNA complementary to the bases at the beginning of the DNA chains. The primers bind to the DNA and

Definition

The **polymerase chain reaction** allows many identical copies of DNA to be made from a small starting sample. In effect DNA replication is made to occur repeatedly and millions of copies can be made in a few hours. PCR is like biological photocopying

Figure 16.22 *PCR (Polymerase Chain Reaction) machine*

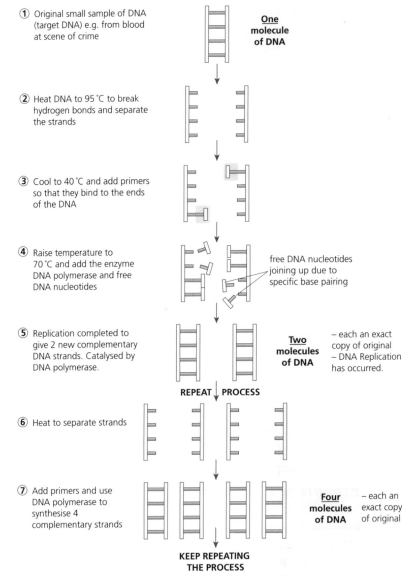

① Original small sample of DNA (target DNA) e.g. from blood at scene of crime

One molecule of DNA

② Heat DNA to 95 °C to break hydrogen bonds and separate the strands

③ Cool to 40 °C and add primers so that they bind to the ends of the DNA

④ Raise temperature to 70 °C and add the enzyme DNA polymerase and free DNA nucleotides

free DNA nucleotides joining up due to specific base pairing

⑤ Replication completed to give 2 new complementary DNA strands. Catalysed by DNA polymerase.

Two molecules of DNA
– each an exact copy of original
– DNA Replication has occurred.

REPEAT ↓ **PROCESS**

⑥ Heat to separate strands

⑦ Add primers and use DNA polymerase to synthesise 4 complementary strands

Four molecules of DNA
– each an exact copy of original

KEEP REPEATING THE PROCESS
to produce millions of copies of target DNA

Figure 16.23 *The polymerase chain reaction (PCR)*

> **Did You Know**
>
> PCR was invented in 1983 by the American biochemist Kary B. Mullis. It was supposedly thought up whilst driving. Years later the copyright to the PCR reaction was sold for 300 million US dollars

act as signals to the DNA polymerase. The temperature is raised to 70 °C and DNA polymerase and free DNA nucleotides are added. The DNA polymerase catalyses the formation of new DNA chains starting at the primers.

Replication of the DNA is completed and two identical molecules of the original DNA are now present. The thermocycler is pre-programmed for a certain number of cycles. The process is now repeated for the set number of times. Each of the two copies is replicated to give four copies. Four are copied to give eight and so on until many thousands of copies of the original DNA have been made.

PCR is also used to obtain the large quantities of DNA needed for **DNA sequencing**. This is where the exact sequence of bases is identified so as to build up a map of the DNA. It is an automated process which also involves electrophoresis and the labelling of the bases. The Human Genome Project (Box 16.6, page 501) is using PCR and DNA sequencing to map out the entire human genetic code.

4–11 Copy the table and complete the gaps labelled **4** to **11**. The first one is done for you.   *(8 marks)*

The genetic engineer's tool kit	
Tool	**Job (keep brief)**
polymerase chain reaction	copies DNA many times
vector	**4**
5	catalyses the copying of DNA from mRNA
6	locates a DNA sequence by labelling it
DNA ligase enzyme	**7**
8	compares DNA by producing a visible pattern of bands
restriction endonuclease enzyme	**9**
electrophoresis	**10**
11	single stranded ends of DNA which attract complementary bases

Remember

Exam hint: The genetic engineer's tool kit
Gene technology uses various techniques. It is important that you know about the following: reverse transcriptase enzyme; DNA probe; DNA ligase enzyme; electrophoresis; restriction endonuclease enzymes; polymerase chain reaction; vectors; sticky ends.
(See question's 4–11)
Use the completed table as a revision summary

Box 16.6 The Human Genome Project

On Monday June 26th 2000 a momentous discovery was announced to the world. The first draft of the human genetic blueprint was published. Some parts remain to be completed but the bulk of the work has been done.

This work is part of the **Human Genome Project** which involves mapping all of the approximately 3 billion bases found on the complete set of human chromosomes (the human genome). The 15-year project is a huge undertaking involving over one thousand scientists from fifty countries and with a cost estimated at between 3 and 6 billion US dollars. The mapping of the genome should be complete by 2003, in time for the 50th anniversary of Watson and Crick's original discovery of the structure of DNA.

The full 'text' of the genome will not be published on paper. It would take up half a million pages and fill a stack of books 31 metres high. Instead the data is being published on the Internet.

The information will be used to help treat and prevent human diseases influenced by our genes. Scientists believe there are 4000 hereditary diseases caused by faults in single genes. In addition, conditions such as heart disease, stroke and cancer are all influenced by heredity. The first chromosome to be mapped, chromosome 22, alone carries genes linked to leukaemia, schizophrenia, heart disease and breast cancer.

Identifying and locating disease-causing genes is the first essential stage in the development of gene therapies which might be able to treat or cure the disease (see Section 16.11, page 493).

Did You Know

98.4% of human DNA is identical to the DNA of a chimpanzee and 97.7% is identical to gorilla DNA

Extension

Box 16.6 The Human Genome Project cont'd

As with other aspects of gene technology, the Human Genome Project does raise social and ethical issues and it has generated a lot of debate. Some people are worried that this knowledge may make possible 'designer babies' with pre-selected genetic features such as IQ or height. See also Section 16.14 on the ethical implications of gene technology.

Another issue is concern over the 'ownership' of the information. Some private companies have applied for patents on specific lengths of human DNA. Researchers would have to pay the company to obtain the DNA base sequences. The companies argue that this is necessary to repay them for the costs of the original research. In contrast, the Human Genome Project is being funded by charities and public funds and is published on the Internet for anyone to use free of charge.

12 Six applications of gene technology are: gene therapy; genetic fingerprinting; genetically modified animals; genetically modified plants; PCR; use of modified microorganisms to produce proteins. Which one (or more) of these does *not* involve the production of recombinant DNA?

(1 mark)

16.14 The social and ethical implications of gene technology

Applications of gene technology such as genetically modified foods, gene therapy and the cloning of animals for 'pharming' raise many new ethical, moral and legal issues. The situation is being monitored by government committees and legal controls do exist, e.g. germ cell gene therapy and human cloning are both illegal in the UK.

However, this is a very complex area. Research is proceeding very rapidly and our knowledge has increased enormously in a very short time. Remember, it is less than 50 years since the structure of DNA was discovered by Watson and Crick. In addition, the ethical issues raised are particularly difficult, producing different points of view and with a clear-cut 'right' answer very hard to find.

In these circumstances it is particularly important that we all try and stay as fully informed as possible and that we attempt to evaluate the issues for ourselves. Public opinion can be very influential and the heated public debate on genetically modified foods does seem to have had an impact. For example:

- On May 1st 1998 Iceland became the first UK supermarket chain to remove all genetically modified ingredients from its own-brand foods. Other supermarkets have since followed.

- On June 5th 1999 the UK's first farm-scale trial of genetically modified crops was destroyed on the orders of the family trust which owned the land.
- On October 5th 1999 Monsanto, one of the largest biotechnology companies, publicly announced that it would stop developing 'terminator' seeds. These genetically modified seeds deliberately include sterility genes so that farmers have to buy fresh seeds every year.

Some of the social and ethical issues to consider are listed in Table 16.1.

?

13 "The role of the scientist is to break the laws of nature rather than to establish, let alone accept them."
Steen Willadsen as quoted in *Clone – the road to Dolly and the path ahead* by Gina Kolata, published by Allen Lane, page 143.
Briefly give one argument in support of this statement and one against.

(2 marks)

Key discovery raises spectre of designer children with high IQs

GENETIC SUPER BABIES STORM

Figure 16.24 *Public concern about gene technology*

Example	Potential benefits	Potential risks
use of modified microorganisms to produce proteins	cheaper production and wider availability of medically important proteins, e.g. hormones and vaccines. They may be purer than alternatives, e.g. human insulin	some of the microorganisms used, e.g. the bacterium *E. coli*, normally live in humans. Genetically modified bacteria could 'escape' from the laboratory and create a new strain of 'superbug' with a risk to human health
gene therapy	effective treatment of genetic diseases, e.g. cystic fibrosis, relieving suffering and prolonging life	there is concern that the techniques used for human genetic modification could eventually make possible 'designer babies' with pre-selected genetic features, e.g. height, IQ
genetically modified food	cheaper food for richer countries and reduction in food shortages in poorer countries	concerns include possible side-effects for humans, e.g. allergic reactions. Also the dangers of 'genetic pollution' with the spread of new genes from the modified crops to wild species, e.g. the risk of new 'superweeds'

Table 16.1 *The social and ethical implications of gene technology – some of the issues*

Figure 16.25 *Concern about GM foods.*

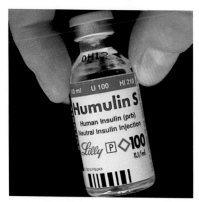

Figure 16.26 *Human insulin is produced by genetically modified microorganisms*

Summary – (16) Gene technology

- Gene technology (genetic engineering) involves changing the genetic make-up and therefore the properties of an organism.

- A major application is to genetically modify microorganisms, e.g. bacteria, so that they produce a useful protein, e.g. human insulin, as follows:

  - The donor gene is isolated by cutting it out with restriction endonuclease enzymes.

  - A vector, e.g. a plasmid, is used to deliver the gene into the host cell.

  - The plasmid is cut with the same restriction enzyme.

  - Both donor gene and plasmid now have complementary sticky ends (single-stranded sections with exposed bases).

  - This helps the gene to attach to the plasmid.

  - DNA ligase enzyme is used to join the DNA to produce recombinant DNA.

  - Recombinant plasmids are mixed with and enter the host cells.

  - Inside the host cells the donor gene is expressed, enabling the cells to produce the required protein.

  - Large numbers of the modified microorganisms are cloned, allowing bulk production.

  - The protein is extracted and purified.

- Copy genes can also be made from mRNA by reverse transcription.

- There are many other applications of gene technology, as follows:

- Animals and plants can be genetically modified to improve the productivity of farmed species, e.g. plant crops can be made pest resistant.

- Farm animals can be modified to produce human proteins in their milk.

- Gene therapy involves treating human genetic disease, e.g. cystic fibrosis, by adding healthy genes.

- Genetic fingerprinting uses gene technology to compare DNA samples, e.g. for criminal investigations.

- DNA fragments can be separated using electrophoresis and their profile revealed as a 'bar code' using radioactive DNA probes.

- Gene technology raises many ethical and social issues, and public awareness and debate are very important.

- See also Figure 16.27 for a summary of this chapter.

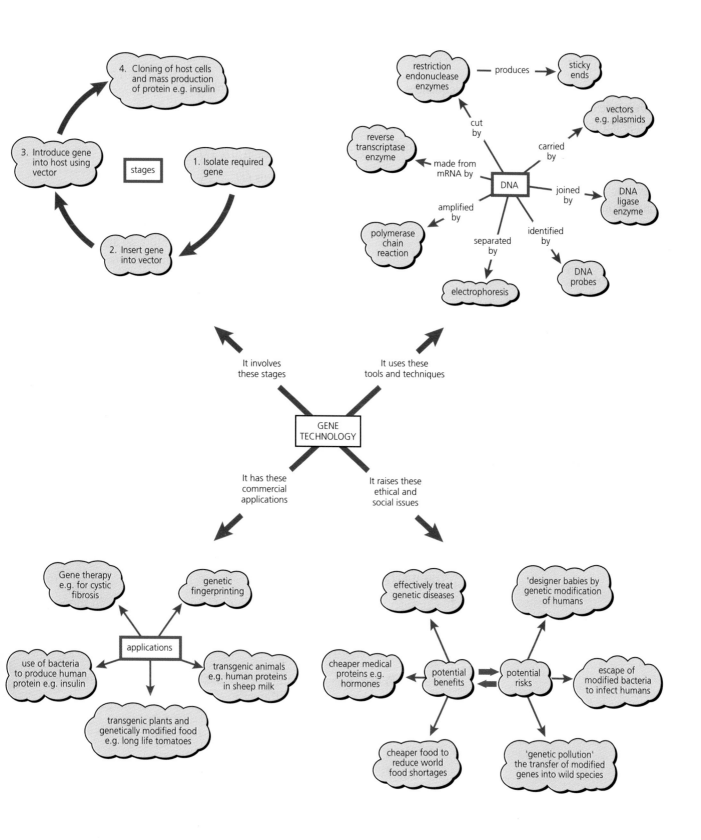

Figure 16.27 *Summary of gene technology*

1 Different genes have different base sequences on either side of them. One restriction enzyme only cuts at one particular base sequence *(2)*.

2 RNA is single stranded; the bases are exposed; bases more likely to get damaged *(1)*.

3 Because DNA/genes only code for the synthesis of protein and not for sugars or lipids *(1)*.

4 Carries the DNA/gene into the host cell *(1)*.

5 Reverse transcriptase enzyme *(1)*.

6 DNA probe *(1)*.

7 Joins pieces of DNA *(1)*.

8 Genetic fingerprinting *(1)*.

9 Cuts DNA *(1)*.

10 Separates fragments of DNA on the basis of differences in size *(1)*.

11 Sticky ends *(1)*.

12 Genetic fingerprinting; PCR *(1)*.

13 For: nature causes genetic diseases, it is morally right to try to cure them and therefore go against nature. Against: we cannot be absolutely sure of the consequences of transferring genes in an unnatural way. There may be unpredictable and harmful consequences *(2)*.

End of Chapter Questions

1 Bacteria can be used to make human insulin. One method involves reverse transcription. Explain one precise role for each of the following in the above process:

   (a) Restriction endonuclease.   **(d)** Plasmid vector.

   (b) Copy DNA.   **(e)** Reverse transcriptase.

   (c) DNA ligase.   **(f)** Sticky ends.   *(12 marks)*

2 For any particular DNA probe:

   (a) Why is it a specific length?

   (b) Why is it single stranded?

   (c) Why is it radioactive?   *(6 marks)*

3 Consider the ethics of gene technology. Give two arguments in support and two arguments against gene technology. Give examples.   *(6 marks)*

4 Figure 16.27 shows the results of electrophoresis with DNA samples A, B, C and D.
The DNA used was linear and not circular. Each sample contained identical DNA but each was treated differently:

Sample A – no restriction enzymes were used (DNA not cut).

Sample B – incubated with restriction enzyme R3 which cuts at 3 sites.

Sample C – incubated with restriction enzyme T4 which cuts at 4 sites.

Sample D – incubated with both the enzymes (R3 and T4).

(a) Match the results with the samples. In each case explain your answer.

(8 marks)

(b) Sketch the diagram and add an arrow to show the direction travelled by the DNA – top to bottom or bottom to top. Give a reason for your answer.

(1 mark)

(c) Why do the results for enzyme R3 produce a different pattern from those for enzyme T4? *(2 marks)*

(Total 11 marks)

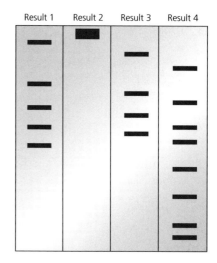

Figure 16.27 *Results of electrophoresis*

5 The flow chart below outlines stages in the process by which foreign DNA may be inserted into a bacterium.

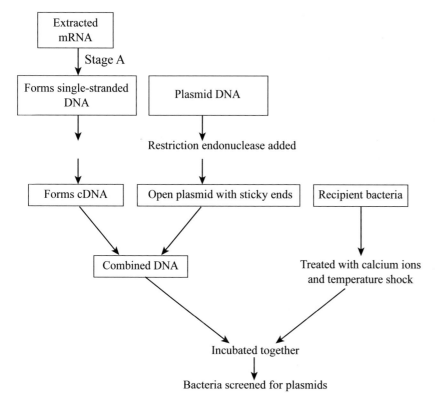

(a) (i) Name the enzyme used to make single-stranded DNA in stage A.

(1 mark)

(ii) The original mRNA contained the following base sequence:

U A A C U G C C G

Write the corresponding sequence of bases in the single-stranded DNA made in stage A. *(2 marks)*

(b) (i) Explain how the sticky ends allow a temporary link to be made between suitable pieces of DNA. *(2 marks)*

  (ii) Name the enzyme used to convert this temporary link into a permanent combined DNA. *(1 mark)*

  (iii) What name is usually given to this combined DNA? *(1 mark)*

(c) Suggest why the bacteria were treated with calcium ions and subjected to temperature shock. *(2 marks)*

(d) Describe *one* way in which bacteria can be screened for the presence of plasmids. *(3 marks)*

London 1997

(Total 12 marks)

6 The polymerase chain reaction is a technique used by biologists to make large amounts of DNA from very small samples. The process is explained in the diagram.

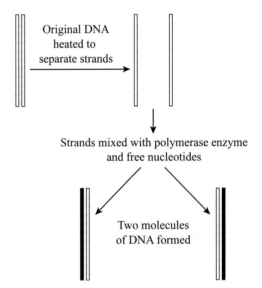

Original DNA heated to separate strands

Strands mixed with polymerase enzyme and free nucleotides

Two molecules of DNA formed

(a) Explain why the DNA produced in this reaction is exactly the same as the original DNA. *(2 marks)*

(b) At the end of the first cycle of this reaction, there will be two molecules of DNA. How many molecules of DNA will there be at the end of five cycles? *(1 mark)*

(c) Give **two** ways in which this process differs from transcription. *(2 marks)*

AEB 1997

(Total 5 marks)

17 Human health and disease

The World Health Organisation (WHO) defined health as 'a state of complete physical, mental and social well-being which is more than just the absence of disease'.

Disease occurs when symptoms show that part of the body is not able to function at maximum efficiency (there is dis-ease of the body). There are many, varied causes of such impairment of the working of the body.

17.1 Health and disease

It is extremely difficult to judge if someone is totally healthy, using this definition of health issued by WHO in 1958.

(a)

(b)

Figure 17.1 *It is easy to distinguish between the healthy and unhealthy child here – but it is not always so easy*

The following points, included in this definition, have to be considered:

- what is absence of disease?
- what is physical well-being?
- what is mental well-being?
- what is social well-being?

Definition

Disease is a disorder of the body, preventing it working at maximum efficiency. It produces special symptoms which are detectable. The disorder has a specific cause, even if this is not understood

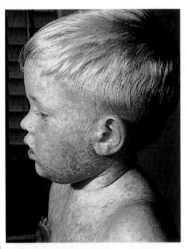

(a)

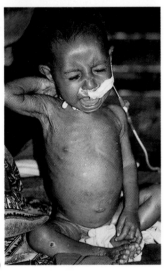

(b)

Figure 17.2 Different diseases have different symptoms
(a) Measles – a skin rash, Koplik's spots in the mouth and watery eyes
(b) Kwashiorkor – swollen abdomen and thin limbs

Absence of disease

Absence of disease means that a person shows no detectable symptoms, attributable to a certain cause, which prevent the body functioning as well as possible. However, symptoms may be too slight to detect. A person may have a slight, chronic (long-term) condition, which may be caused by malnutrition, a slight inherited disorder or a long-term infection. In this case, he or she may not even notice that she is not functioning as well as possible.

> **Remember**
>
> A **chronic** disease is one which lasts for a very long time; it is an on going condition. An **acute** disease is one from which a person may recover quite quickly. These terms do **not** refer to the severity of the disease. It is possible to have a very severe acute attack of meningitis while chronic indigestion may be very mild

Physical well-being

A person may be free from specific symptoms, but the body may not be performing to its maximum potential.

Aerobic exercise (see Section 10.7, page 289), taken regularly over a long period of time, can have a marked effect on the cardiovascular system. Heart muscle cells enlarge and their blood supply improves. The stroke volume increases so much that cardiac output can be maintained with a lower heart rate, either at rest or during physical activity. The cells of the body muscles also enlarge and their blood supply improves. It also makes the bones stronger. All this leads to the idea of physical fitness.

There are degrees of physical fitness, which make it difficult to judge physical well-being. A footballer can run about the Wembley pitch for an hour and a half (about six miles) in a temperature of 40 °C and then answer an interviewer's questions. A watching supporter may be breathless after running halfway up the pitch. The difference may be clear here, but where exactly does physical well-being start? Doctors recommend that everyone should undergo at least 3 to 5 half-hour sessions of aerobic exercise each week to maintain health. Such exercise may be brisk walking or swimming.

Mental well-being

This is more than the absence of mental disease, so what is it? It is very difficult to know, but it implies a balanced outlook and a certain degree of contentment and feeling of self-worth.

Social well-being

This is even more difficult to judge and possibly outside the scope of biology. However, it implies satisfactory integration into a society which is not deprived of basic needs.

17.2 Different types and causes of disease

Diseases are often put into categories according to which parts of the body are affected, the specific causes or whether or not they can be transmitted from one person to another. These categories may overlap. The most common categories of disease are discussed below.

Physical diseases
Here the symptoms are associated with the malfunction of any organ or system of the body apart from the higher centres of the brain. The cause may be any of those listed. For example, **pulmonary tuberculosis** is a disease of the lungs caused by bacteria while in **cystic fibrosis**, the mucous membranes, particularly of the lungs and alimentary canal, malfunction as a result of a genetic (inherited) disorder.

Mental diseases
In mental illness, the working of the higher centres of the brain is affected and the symptoms are usually behaviour patterns and responses which cannot be considered as 'normal'. A common symptom, such as memory loss, may indicate the degenerative disease such as **Alzheimer's disease**. **Huntington's chorea** is a distressing inherited mental condition which may appear in middle age. The symptoms are very severe, leading from memory loss and personality change to eventual death.

It is not always possible to separate mental and physical illnesses. Arterial disease such as atheroma may lead to a stroke causing death of some brain cells and eventual behavioural changes. On the other hand, memory loss may lead to someone not eating properly, resulting in stomach disorders such as food poisoning.

Social diseases
The meaning of this term can vary. On one hand it can refer to illnesses which are widespread in a society owing to shortage of food or poor hygiene. Undernutrition can lead to diseases such as **kwashiorkor**. (See Box 13.4, page 382.)

More usually, it is used to refer to infectious diseases which are transmitted during sexual behaviour. These sexually transmitted diseases include **gonorrhoea**, caused by bacteria, and **AIDS** which is usually believed to be caused by human immunodeficiency viruses.

Infectious diseases
These are disorders caused by **pathogens** or larger parasites which can be **transmitted** from one person to another. Pathogens are parasitic micro-organisms that harm part of the body of their host, leading to the symptoms of disease.

The transmission may be by direct contact (contagious diseases). Alternatively, transmission may be indirect through water droplets in the air, in food or drinking water or by **vectors**. Vectors are organisms that are also hosts of the pathogen or parasite and carry them from one human to another. For example, the pathogen for malaria is carried from one person to another by the female Anopheline mosquito which acts as a vector.

Some examples of infectious diseases are shown in Table 17.1.

Figure 17.3 *What is physical fitness?*

Figure 17.4 *A range of pathogens:*
(a) Adeno virus (TEM × 30 000)
(b) Salmonella enteroides
(c) Trypanosoma brucei *protoctistans among red blood cells(SEM × 1750)*
(d) Candida albicans – *the causative agent of thrush (SEM × 1200)*

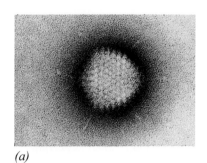

(a)

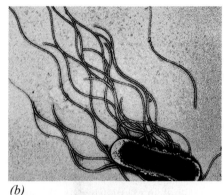

(b)

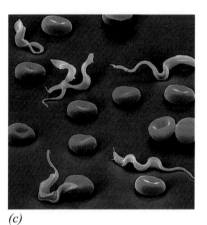

(c)

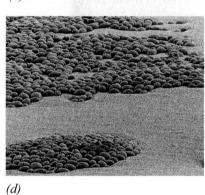

(d)

Table 17.1 *Infectious diseases*

Infectious disease	Type of pathogen
chicken pox, smallpox, influenza, colds, AIDS	viruses
tuberculosis, cholera, meningitis (B and C), botulism, tetanus	bacteria
malaria, sleeping sickness	single-celled organisms (Protoctista)
athlete's foot, ringworm, thrush	fungi

! Did You Know

Recently discovered types of protein molecules, known as prions, may be the infective agents responsible for causing BSE (Bovine Spongiform Encephalopathy) and the related new strain of CJD (Creutzfeldt-Jakob Disease) which affects the brain of humans. If this is so, then these behave in a similar way to the pathogens although they are not microorganisms.

Figure 17.5 *A model of prion molecule*

Larger parasitic organisms may also be pathogenic (lead to disease) and be transmitted from person to person. The most common ones are roundworms (nematodes) and flatworms (Platyhelminthes).

Elephantiasis is a very unpleasant condition caused by the nematode, a filaria worm called *Wuchereria bancrofti*, which blocks lymph vessels. This blocks the drainage of tissue fluid (see Figure 10.26, page 301) and the surrounding tissues grow, leading to enormous enlargement of the infected area, which may be the limbs, breasts or scrotum (Figure 17.6).

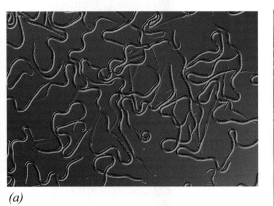

(a)

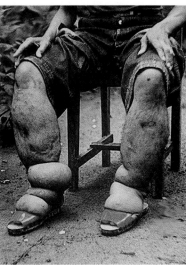

(b)

Figure 17.6
(a) Filaria worms (× 80)
(b) A case of elephantiasis

Non-infectious diseases

These are not caused by pathogens and cannot be transmitted. (Strictly, genetic diseases can be transmitted, but only by inheritance and these are not infectious.) There are four main types of cause of non-infectious diseases: inherited (genetic) diseases, degenerative diseases, self-inflicted diseases and deficiency diseases. These are explained below.

An **inherited (genetic) disease** may occur when a person suffers from a disorder as a result of inheriting a defective allele of a gene which does not carry the correct code. As a result the body is not able to make an essential protein for normal functioning. If the allele is recessive, one must be inherited from both parents for the condition to appear, for example **cystic fibrosis** (see Box 16.4, page 493). If the allele is dominant, then it need only be inherited from one parent, for example **Huntington's chorea**.

The Human Genome Project (see Box 16.6, page 501) has determined the location of all human genes. The vast amount of research in this field is leading to a greater understanding of the positions of faulty alleles and the possibility of gene therapy.

Alternatively, chromosome mutations can also lead to a genetic condition. **Down's Syndrome** results from faulty meiosis (see Section 6.10, page 169) and the consequent inheritance of an extra chromosome 21.

Degenerative diseases are diseases that usually appear as a person ages. Cells which die are not replaced quickly and efficiently. (Nerve cells and muscle cells are not replaced at all.) The tissues begin to malfunction and biochemical pathways may begin to change. **Alzheimer's disease** and other forms of **dementia** are the result of degenerative changes in the brain. **Osteoporosis** occurs when the bone is losing more calcium than it is gaining and cavities develop in the bone.

Sometimes auto-immunity, where the body develops an immune response to some of its own tissues (see Section 11.9, page 324), can cause degeneration. For example, **rheumatoid arthritis** is a degenerative disease which can appear at any age.

Why do some people suffer from degenerative diseases which do not occur in others? There may be a genetic cause. There may be a genetic link but the disease only appears if a particular environmental 'trigger' occurs, such as an infection.

Self-inflicted diseases result from abuse of the body. It may be chemical abuse. If chemicals which are known to harm and change body metabolism are deliberately taken into the body, then any resulting damage can be considered as self-inflicted. Such toxins (poisons), which may damage the body, include illegal drugs, alcohol and cigarette smoke. It is also possible to damage the body physically. Inappropriate and excessive exercise may lead to damage of the joints, leading to **osteoarthritis**. Behavioural problems, such as **anorexia nervosa** (see Box 13.4, page 382), can also damage the body. Prolonged undernutrition may have long-term effects.

Deficiency diseases are disorders which result from an inappropriate diet. They may be caused by general undernutrition or by malnutrition, where there is a particular deficiency of one or more elements of the diet. For example, **scurvy** is caused by lack of vitamin C.

17.3 Health statistics and their usefulness

Health statistics are an important tool for studying the patterns of distribution of diseases. This type of study is called **epidemiology**.

The overall aim of studying health and disease must be to promote health. This must involve the treatment and, better still, the prevention of disease. Epidemiological studies reveal where and under what conditions many diseases are more likely to occur. They can provide important pointers to possible causes, which can then be tested experimentally. They can also be useful in determining the effectiveness of treatments and preventative measures.

Statistics involves the collection of facts and treating them numerically. By using various statistical techniques, it is possible to determine whether there are significant relationships between various factors or whether any apparent relationship is just due to chance. For example, statistics have linked cigarette smoking with various diseases. This has been followed up by experimental studies which have confirmed that smoking can be the cause of some diseases or, at least, a contributing factor (see Box 17.1).

Extension

Box 17.1 Cigarette smoking and disease

Statistics show clear positive correlations between numbers of cigarettes smoked and the incidence of diseases such as coronary heart disease, lung and other cancers, bronchitis, emphysema and thrombosis.

For example, Figure 17.7 shows the relationship between the number of cigarettes smoked per day and the increased risk of dying of lung cancer and developing coronary heart disease.

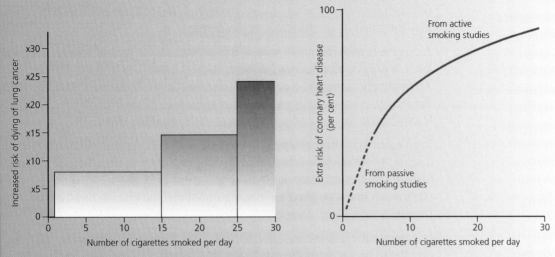

Figure 17.7 (a) Cigarette smoking and lung cancer deaths
(b) Cigarette smoking and coronary heart disease

Statistics must be assembled and interpreted carefully. Problems include:

● It may take many years for a heavy smoker to develop lung cancer, and so it is necessary to relate incidence of lung cancer to earlier smoking patterns.

● There may be other risk factors involved with these diseases, so results are only valid if the samples of people studied are large and chosen carefully, to eliminate the effects of other risk factors.

● Positive correlation between two factors does not necessarily imply that one causes the other. It could be that people with inborn tendencies to develop lung cancer or heart disease, also tend to smoke.

However, the experimental evidence has revealed:

● the presence of many carcinogens (chemicals which cause cancer) in cigarette smoke.

● nicotine in cigarette smoke increases the heart rate and causes some vasoconstriction, leading to increased blood pressure. There is also an increased tendency to deposit lipid substances in artery walls and for blood clots to form. All of these contribute to atheroma and coronary heart disease (see Box 10.5, page 289).

● carbon monoxide in cigarette smoke prevents the carriage of oxygen by haemoglobin (see Section 11.2, page 312). It also damages the linings of blood vessels.

Taken together, the epidemiological and experimental evidence show clearly that smoking is a causal factor in these diseases.

Further evidence has revealed many facts such as:

● About 90% of lung cancer cases are caused by smoking.

● About 80% of coronary death in men under 50 years is caused by smoking.

● Although the risk of lung cancer increases with number of cigarettes smoked, it is even more dependent upon the duration of smoking. Smoking 20/day for 40 years carries eight times the risk of smoking 40/day for 20 years.

● The risk of lung cancer is reduced by ceasing to smoke.

● On average, non-smoking partners of smokers have been shown to die four years earlier than non-smoking partners of non-smokers. (This suggests that passive smoking can be harmful.)

● 50% of all regular cigarette smokers will be killed by their habit.

Health statistics are also useful for studying the occurrence and importance of diseases in different parts of the world.

It is essential to use statistics with care; it is necessary to realise that the prevalence of infectious diseases can vary at different times. Sometimes an infectious disease may suddenly spread across an area where it has not been common for some time and many young children have no resistance to it. This may form part of an **epidemic** or **pandemic**.

A disease is **endemic** in an area, if it is present all the time at roughly the same level. It may be an infectious disease, such as malaria in tropical Africa. Alternatively, it may be a deficiency disease. Goitre, a disease caused by iodine deficiency, is endemic in mountainous areas such as the Himalayas, as iodine has leached from the soil and is not present in the drinking water.

In an **epidemic**, there is a sudden increase in the occurrence of an infectious disease, which spreads across a fairly large area such as the whole of Britain. Childhood diseases, such as chicken pox, commonly show epidemics every few years when many younger children have not met the disease and have no immunity to it.

In a **pandemic**, the increase and spread of the disease is worldwide. AIDS is proving to be a present-day pandemic. In the past, new strains of influenza, such as Asian 'flu in 1957, have produced pandemics.

17.4 Standards of health in developed and developing countries

Measuring health

Statistics enable valid, but very limited, comparisons to be made between the standards of health in different parts of the world. As health is difficult to define, and as statistics must record and count definite facts, only certain factors which indicate the state of health of a nation can be used for comparisons. There are many such factors. A few of these are:

- the **infant mortality rate**. This is the number of deaths during the first year of life per 1000 live births. It is often used as an index of health as there are frequently reasonable records of this in a country. Also, it changes quickly if public health measures help to prevent the spread of infectious childhood diseases.

- **life expectancy at birth**. In a given population, this is the average number of years which a newly born child may expect to live. It is difficult to calculate, especially in countries with poor health records. (Life expectancy changes with age. In many countries, if a child survives for the first five years then its life expectancy rises dramatically, as death rate is highest among young children.)

- the **prevalence of various diseases**. This indicates how commonly various diseases occur in a population.

- the **percentages of deaths caused by certain diseases**. This indicates the **importance** of certain diseases in a population.

Classifying countries

Any method of grouping countries together and giving the group a label is bound to be crude and not fully accurate. The United Nations Organisation ranks countries according to a 'Human Development Index' which includes life expectancy, educational attainment and a measure of income. The World Bank ranks countries upon the national income per person while the World Health Organisation ranks them according to standards of health. There is some correlation between these rankings (see Figure 17.8).

To produce the scattergram shown in Figure 17.8, 160 countries have been first ranked for Gross National Product (GNP) per head. GNP is a measure of the output of a national economy. It is a measure of a country's wealth. This figure has been divided by the number of people in the population to produce GNP/head. (The wealthiest country ranks 1 and the poorest ranks 160.) This rank has been plotted against the country's rank on the UN's Human Development Index. If a country's rank is the same for both development and wealth, it will be on the diagonal line. Countries below the line have a level of development below that which their wealth indicates should be possible, while those above the line have a level of development above that which could be predicted by their wealth. Such countries must be diverting resources very effectively into health and education.

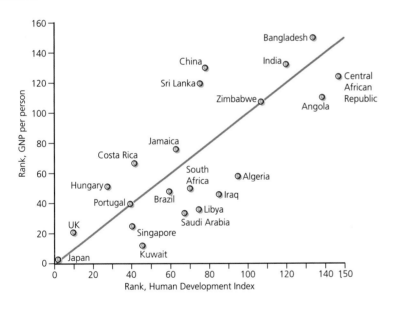

Figure 17.8 *Correlation between ranking by GNP and ranking by Human Development Index*

1 Using Figure 17.8, name
  (a) two countries which rank higher than 25th on GNP and Human Development Index.
  (b) two countries which rank lower than 100th on both indices.
  (c) one country which ranks higher than 20th on GNP but lower than 40th on the Human Development Index.   *(5 marks)*

The countries towards the top on *most* rankings are referred to as the **industrialised countries** or the **developed countries**. They include: all European countries, Russia, North America, Japan, Australia and New Zealand.

The countries towards the bottom on most rankings are referred to as the **developing countries** or the **third world**. These include the countries of Central and South America, Africa and Asia (although countries such as China, India and Brazil are industrialised in parts).

Differences between standards of health
Table 17.2 shows the infant mortality rates and life expectancy at birth for many countries in 1990.

2 Using the data from Table 17.2, calculate
  (a) the mean infant mortality rate for developing countries and the mean infant mortality rate for developed countries.
  (b) the mean life expectancy at birth for males in developing countries and the mean life expectancy at birth for males in developed countries.

(4 marks)

Table 17.2 Some health statistics for selected countries (1990)

Country	Population /millions	Infant mortality rate per 1000 live births	Expectation of life at birth/years Male	Female
Africa				
Central African Republic	3	100	44	47
Egypt	52	61	59	61
Mali	9	164	46	50
Zimbabwe	10	61	57	60
Americas				
Brazil	150	60	62	68
Cuba	11	11	73	76
Jamaica	2	16	71	77
USA	249	10	71	78
Europe				
Poland	38	16	67	76
Portugal	10	13	68	75
Sweden	8	6	74	80
UK	57	9	72	78
Asia				
Bangladesh	116	114	57	56
China	1139	30	68	71
India	853	94	52	52
Japan	124	4	75	81
Sri Lanka	17	26	68	72

Figure 17.9 shows the percentages of deaths from different causes in the developed and developing countries (calculated in the 1990s for figures in the late 1980s).

3 Using Figure 17.9, indicate
  (a) two types of disease which are responsible for a larger percentage of deaths in the industrial countries than in the developing countries.
  (b) three causes which are responsible for a larger percentage of deaths in the developing countries than in the industrial countries.
  (c) a cause of death with similar effects in both groups of countries. *(6 marks)*

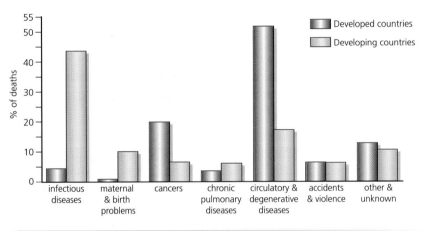

Figure 17.9 Causes of death

4 Although degenerative diseases (see Section 17.2, page 511) kill a higher percentage of people in the industrialised countries, the actual number of people dying from these causes is lower than in the developing countries. Using information from Table 17.2, explain why this is so. *(1 mark)*

A disease may be very common and affect the health of a population quite severely without actually being a main cause of death. For example, in developing countries, at any one time over half the population may be suffering from respiratory infections. However, only a quarter of the population die as a result of such complaints. On the other hand, tetanus and meningitis only affect a few people but they are often fatal. Any health programme must take this into account.

17.5 Health in developed and developing countries

In general, although there are many exceptions, these statistics seem to show that people in developing countries are more likely to die during the first year of life and are likely to die younger, on average, than people in developed countries. These two factors are linked, of course. Other studies show that even people surviving childhood are likely to live less long in developing nations.

The main causes of death in the developing countries are the infectious diseases and problems related to childbirth whereas in the developed countries the main causes of death are the degenerative diseases and cancer. Care must be taken when interpreting statistics, and situations change all the time. The recent pandemic of AIDS is now having a major effect.

The developed countries have eradicated or developed effective prevention and treatment programmes for infectious diseases. As a result people live long enough for the degenerative diseases of old age and cancer to be the major killers. After all, people must die of something!

Knowledge of methods of prevention and treatment of infectious diseases is worldwide so why are there still marked differences between the nations? The reasons are economic, environmental and social.

Economic reasons

The developed nations which have been industrialised in the past have often been the colonisers of other nations and have modified the economic activity of these nations to suit themselves rather than the colonised area. For example, during the eighteenth and nineteenth centuries, most of the fertile land in India was converted to produce crops such as tea for the industrialised coloniser, rather than allowing it to continue to supply the needs of the local populations. Meanwhile the traditional textile industry in India was almost totally destroyed as manufactured cotton products had to be bought from Britain.

Upon achieving independence, these countries have had to change their types of production and this has been difficult, leading to a low income for the country and poverty. Borrowing money and the necessity to pay it back with interest has added to the poverty. A poor nation cannot afford to have enough doctors, nurses, hospitals and mobile clinics in rural areas to carry out effective prevention and treatment programmes.

Poverty and the rural nature of much of the population also make the development of clean water supplies and good sanitation difficult to achieve. Good housing and shelter are also expensive.

Environmental reasons

Many of the developing countries are in the warmer regions of the Earth. Many pathogens, larger parasites and insects, which act as vectors for these pathogens, thrive in warm air and warm water and are more difficult to eradicate here than in cooler regions.

In some areas, such as the Southern Sahara, low rainfall has made it difficult to grow enough crops to sustain life and feed animals. This in turn leads to poverty, starvation and death from otherwise relatively harmless diseases.

Social reasons

In the developing countries, infant mortality is higher if children are born more closely together in a family, especially in areas where food is in short supply. Each child is breast fed for a shorter time and may then have to rely on a diet which is low in protein. This can lead to kwashiorkor and early death. However, the **fertility rate** is still higher in the developing countries than in the industrialised nations. The social reasons for this are many. They include religious beliefs, lack of education and effective family planning advice, custom and the fear of not having enough children survive to labour and care for the parent in old age.

Definition

The fertility rate of a country is the number of live births per thousand women of child-bearing age born in one year

Life style and diet variations between poorer and richer nations can lead to differences in the prevalence of particular diseases. For example, colon cancer is very rare among African people with a vegetarian diet. This is thought to be related to the quick passage through the gut of food rich in fibre when compared with the Western lower-fibre diet.

5 Coronary heart disease (see Box 10.5, page 289) is a more common cause of death in the developed countries than in the developing ones. Suggest three reasons why this is so. *(3 marks)*

17.6 Infectious disease — cholera

Cause and effects

Cholera is caused by the vibrio (comma-shaped) bacterium called *Vibrio cholerae* (see Figure 17.10 (a)). It is taken in by mouth and reproduces and secretes toxins in the alimentary canal, especially in the small intestine. These toxins affect the absorption of water and salts by the epithelial lining of the intestine. A few days after infection, copious watery, and highly infectious, diarrhoea (rice water diarrhoea) may begin. If the condition is untreated, death from dehydration can occur within two more days.

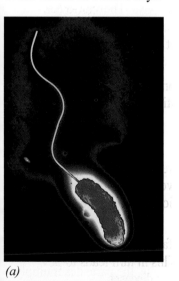
(a)

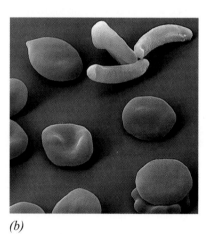
(b)

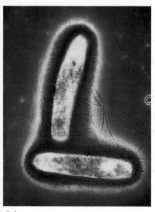
(c)

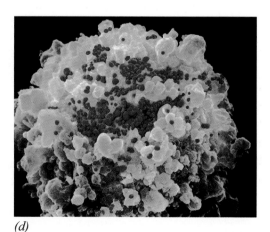
(d)

Figure 17.10
(a) Vibrio cholerae *(TEM × 10 000)*
(b) Plasmodium falciparum *with red blood cells (SEM × 2300)*
(c) Mycobacterium tuberculosis *(TEM × 18 500)*
(d) Human immunodeficiency viruses *(red) on an infected T lymphocyte (SEM × 6000)*

Transmission

A person can be infected if he ingests the bacteria. The most usual way this is done is by drinking water which has been contaminated by the faeces of a diseased person. The vibrios survive well in water. However, it is also possible to be infected by eating contaminated food. If shellfish have been growing in the contaminated water of river estuaries, they provide a rich source of infection if they are not cooked thoroughly. Also flies can spread the vibrios from faeces to food.

Prevention and control

It is possible to vaccinate (see Section 11.13, page 331) against cholera using a vaccine made from killed vibrios. However, it is only about 50% effective and only lasts a few months.

If cholera is treated very quickly using the very cheap and effective **oral rehydration therapy**, recovery can follow within about five days. This therapy consists of a mixture of glucose and salts which must be added to boiled water in the correct proportions to replace water and salts lost in the diarrhoea. Drinking this prevents dehydration and provides a source of energy while the body fights the bacteria. If a person is infirm or the condition is particularly serious, antibiotics can be used which destroy the bacteria.

Global importance

Cholera was once common throughout the populated world. The vibrio has often mutated, leading to pandemics, as there was no immunity to the novel forms. Before the discovery of effective treatments, the disease was often fatal. Its importance globally has now diminished. Good sanitation and health practices have prevented its spread throughout Europe and many parts of the world. Now it is found only in a few areas of the world, such as the Ganges valley.

17.7 Infectious disease – malaria

Cause and effects

Malaria is caused by a single-celled organism, a protoctistan parasite of the genus *Plasmodium* (Figure 17.10 (b)). There are four common species of *Plasmodium* which give rise to slightly different forms of malaria. For example, *P. vivax* gives a milder form of malaria than *P. falciparum*. The different forms are most common in different areas of the world.

Figure 17.11 *A mosquito feeding on human blood.*

Having been introduced into the blood by a mosquito bite, the parasites multiply inside liver cells before emerging to invade and multiply inside erythrocytes (red blood cells) (Figure 17.12). From then on, the parasites emerge from erythrocytes, releasing toxins in the blood, and invade more erythrocytes at regular intervals. The length of the cycles varies with the species of *Plasmodium*. Every time the toxins are released, the immune reactions of the body which destroy them are accompanied by severe fevers. These fevers with their bouts of chills and sweats can decrease in severity if the body slowly becomes immune to the toxins, and many people can carry malaria.

Bouts of fever can recur later on in life in such carriers. Such people may be weakened and succumb to other diseases. However, malaria kills many people directly. Some species can cause such widespread damage of red blood cells that

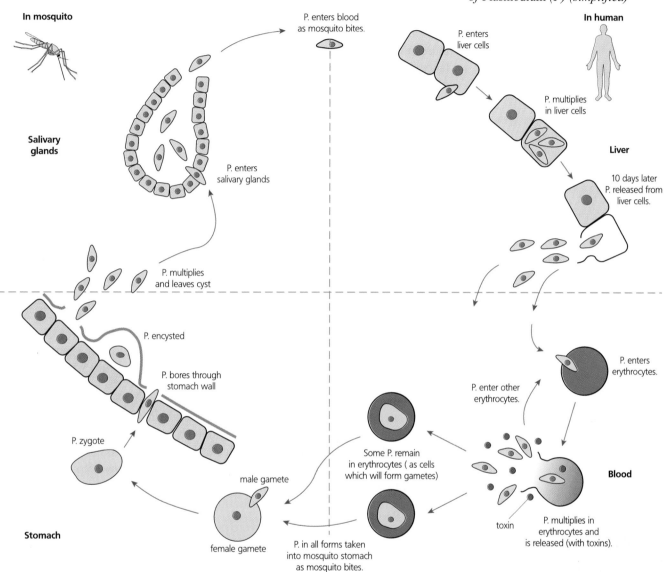

Figure 17.12 *Stages in the life history of* Plasmodium *(P) (simplified)*

In mosquito

P. enters blood as mosquito bites.

P. enters liver cells

In human

Salivary glands

P. enters salivary glands

P. multiplies in liver cells

Liver

10 days later P. released from liver cells.

P. multiplies and leaves cyst

P. encysted

P. bores through stomach wall

P. enters erythrocytes.

P. enter other erythrocytes.

P. zygote

Some P. remain in erythrocytes (as cells which will form gametes)

Blood

male gamete

Stomach

female gamete

P. in all forms taken into mosquito stomach as mosquito bites.

toxin

P. multiplies in erythrocytes and is released (with toxins).

they can clog capillaries of the brain, leading to coma. Haemoglobin may escape into the urine (blackwater fever) and kidney damage can also be fatal.

Transmission

Plasmodium is also a parasite of mosquitoes. If the female *Anopheles* mosquito 'bites' and takes in blood from an infected person, the *Plasmodium* parasites enter her body. The parasites undergo various stages of their life history inside the mosquito (Figure 17.12). The parasites may then be introduced into another person as the mosquito pours her saliva into a wound during a further biting action.

In this way, the mosquito acts as a **vector**, transmitting the parasite from one person to another.

Prevention and control

Treatment of malaria, which involves killing all forms of the parasite within the human body, is notoriously difficult. Considering the importance of the disease, there has not been a vast amount of money put into research to find drugs. Much more money has been invested in AIDS research. There are drugs which can be taken before infection occurs which are moderately successful at preventing the parasite form becoming established. Travellers are advised to take these before, during and after visiting malaria zones. However, there are no totally successful drugs which kill all the *Plasmodium* stages once the disease has taken hold. It is also difficult to find a vaccine which will trigger immunity to all stages of the parasite, as it changes the chemical nature of its surface during its life history. However, investment has now increased in vaccine development and recent results are encouraging.

Prevention of transmission involves eradication of the mosquito. As mosquitoes breed in stagnant water, much effort has been put into drainage projects. In Singapore, it is against the law to allow stagnant water to accumulate. Mosquitoes can breed in tiny amounts of water such as puddles in wheel ruts, so it is not easy to eliminate all breeding sites. Expanses of water can be sprayed with a cover of oil to prevent the larvae breathing, but this leads to pollution. Fish which eat the larvae have been introduced with some success. DDT has been a very effective insecticide spray and has eliminated the mosquitoes in some areas. However, some mosquitoes have evolved which are resistant to it. DDT is also persistent in the environment and causes serious pollution problems (see Section 15.12, page 449).

Global importance

The prevalence of malaria is immense and widespread. It is most common in sub-Saharan Africa, but it is also found widely in Latin America and Asia. Over 250 million people are thought to be affected by malaria to some degree (compared with 33.6 million with AIDS/HIV in 1999). It causes up to 2 million deaths each year, with over two-thirds of these occurring in Africa. Malaria is said to be endemic in these tropical and sub-tropical areas of the developing world.

Malaria has always been a more severe problem in warm countries where the high temperatures and humidity favour the survival of the *Anopheles* mosquito and its parasite. It has occurred in the UK, but only in certain localities. However, it has been more widespread in the past. In the 1950s and 1960s, WHO backed a mosquito eradication programme which drove malaria out of North America, Europe and parts of Asia. There are now about 1500 cases in the UK each year but almost all of these have been contracted abroad.

Figure 17.13 *Spraying insecticides on mosquito breeding sites*

Although there has been an overall decline in the numbers of malarial cases and deaths worldwide there has been a resurgence of the disease since the 1970s, particularly in sub-Saharan Africa. There are many reasons for this including:

● the emergence of strains of mosquito which are resistant to pesticides

● deforestation and building activity, which has created more breeding sites

● population growth, famine and civil wars, which have led to mass movements of people as refugees. Infected people have moved into previously malaria-free areas and the mosquitoes have become infected. Non-immune people from malaria-free zones have moved into infected areas and local epidemics result.

Figure 17.14 Mass movement of refugees escaping civil war in Africa.

17.8 Infectious disease – tuberculosis (TB)

Cause and effects

Tuberculosis (TB) is usually caused by a type of bacterium called *Mycobacterium tuberculosis* (Figure 17.10 (c)). It can also be caused by the related *Mycobacterium bovis*. Often the first (primary) infection may lead to few symptoms beyond a slight cough, as the bacteria are ingested by macrophages (see Section 11.8, page 324). It is possible for a healthy individual in a healthy environment to totally overcome the bacteria over a period of time. However, if a person is undernourished or unhealthy in some way, the bacteria can remain dormant for many years and suddenly break out again, leading to severe illness. They can affect many parts of the body although, most commonly, they destroy lung tissue (respiratory tuberculosis or 'consumption'). The main symptoms are high fever, severe coughing and loss of weight.

Transmission

The main form of transmission occurs when the bacteria are carried in the air, in droplets of water breathed out by an infected person, even one not showing any symptoms of illness. Other people can become infected by breathing in these droplets. The spread is favoured by damp, dimly lit and overcrowded conditions. The bacteria can withstand many disinfectants but are destroyed quickly on exposure to sunlight. Drinking unpasteurised milk from cattle infected with *M. bovis* can also cause disease.

Prevention and control

It has been seen that good nutrition and living conditions are very important in halting the progress of the disease. If the severe form of the disease develops, treatment involves the use of a mixture of antibiotics and more prolonged use of specialised drugs. It can take up to eighteen months to clear all the infection.

Less crowded and well-aerated, brightly lit conditions help to slow the spread of the disease.

(a)

(b)

(c)

Figure 17.15 *Working conditions can ve very varied even as recently as the 1990s*
(a) Boys working in the Olympian cotton mills, South Carolina, USA (1900)
(b) Production line on the shop floor, UK (1990)
(c) Workers in a Brazilian nut factory (1992)

A vaccination programme was initiated in the 1950s in the UK. The BCG (bacille Calmette-Guerin) vaccine which contains a living but attenuated (inactivated) form of the bacterium is injected. Usually this is offered to 14 year-olds and key workers. Vaccination is only given if a previous test shows that the person is not already immune to the disease.

A mass X-ray programme was also introduced in the UK in the 1950s. This helped with the early detection and, so, treatment of the disease. This mass X-ray programme has ceased since the prevalence of the disease has declined.

Pasteurisation of milk, which involves heating milk to 72°C for at least 15 seconds, is enough to kill the micro-bacteria in milk and prevent the spread of the disease from infected cattle to humans. However, much care is taken to keep herds of cattle free from the disease.

Global importance
TB was one of the most feared killers in the UK, as recently as the early part of the 20th century. In fact, it has been a serious disease all around the world, except in the Pacific regions. There has been a rapid decline in its occurrence and in numbers of deaths caused in many of the developed countries since 1850. In the 1990s, however, there was evidence of a slight rise of the incidence of the disease.

6 It is very difficult to be sure whether medical factors or social factors have been more important in bringing about the decline of tuberculosis in countries like the UK. Clearly, they have worked together very successfully.
(a) List three medical factors that have led to the decline of TB and its severity.
(b) List three social factors that have led to the decline of TB and its severity.
(6 marks)

The decline of TB has been much less in developing countries, such as India. Most of the factors which have been effective are very expensive. Treatment is long term and the drugs are costly. Overcrowded conditions and poor general health are also linked to poverty. Vaccination programmes are less expensive than treatment, but they are still difficult to administer in large, widespread populations.

The recent increase in incidence in the developed countries has been attributed to several causes:

- the spread of AIDS, which lowers a person's immunity to the bacteria.

- the evolution of forms of the bacteria which are resistant to antibiotics.

- the increase in worldwide travel and migration, introducing the bacteria from regions where there is a high incidence to other areas.

17.9 Infectious disease — acquired immune deficiency syndrome (AIDS)

Cause and effects

The cause of AIDS is generally considered to be a virus known as the **human immunodeficiency virus** (HIV) (Figure 17.10(d)), although it is possible to possess the virus, and for the blood to contain antibodies to it (HIV positive) without developing AIDS. There are a few varieties of this virus. The viruses parasitise very important cells of the immune system called helper T cells (see Section 11.11, page 327). The helper T cells not only assist killer T cells to destroy viruses and cancers, but also help some B cells to produce antibodies. The immune system is severely disrupted if the HIV becomes active and harms the effectiveness of their host cells. The main symptoms of full-blown AIDS include the development of other diseases to which healthy people would quickly develop immunity. These diseases include tuberculosis, Kaposi's sarcoma (a form of cancer rare in young people) and a rare form of pneumonia caused by *Pneumocystis carinii*. The victims usually die. It was the sudden increase of these diseases among the gay population of San Francisco, in 1981, which led to investigations and the final isolation of the virus in 1985. It was later discovered that similar symptoms had occurred in Central Africa three years earlier and that the virus may have been present in the population for as many as ten years. Slightly different strains of the virus were discovered in West Africa too. In Africa, the virus is common in the heterosexual population.

Transmission

Fortunately, the viruses do not survive in air and are quickly killed by hot water and detergent. They can only be passed from person to person by direct contact between body fluids, mainly blood. A person may be a source of infection if he or she possesses the virus, even if there are no symptoms of AIDS and even if it is too soon to register HIV positive in an AIDS test.

The most common ways in which transmission occurs are:

- during unprotected (without using condoms) homosexual or heterosexual intercourse. Globally, 70% of all transmission is via heterosexual intercourse.

- by using a needle for intravenous injection which has been used by an infected person.

- by receiving contaminated blood products, for example in the treatment for haemophilia or during a blood transfusion.

- a fetus may be infected by its mother, as the viruses can pass across the placenta. A baby can also be infected during the process of birth or by its mother's milk. (See Box 7.4, page 202.)

Figure 17.16 *AIDS – the modern pandemic*

In fact, any way that blood from an infected person makes contact with the blood of another person could lead to infection, even if it enters through a tiny abrasion. Less likely ways include the infection of dentists from bleeding gums and the infection of medical staff who accidentally prick themselves on a contaminated needle. There is so far no evidence that HIV has been transmitted via mosquito bites or via kissing (although saliva may contain a few viruses).

Prevention and control

There is, as yet, no cure for AIDS. Drugs are being developed all the time which can slow down the progression towards the development of full-blown AIDS in some cases. Mixtures of various drugs have also been found helpful. Some of these drugs have unpleasant side-effects. For example, AZT has been licensed for general use and has been shown to postpone the development of severe symptoms. However, at first, about half the patients taking it developed severe anaemia.

Clearly, prevention is important. Despite an enormous amount of money being put into research, there is still no effective vaccine. It is extremely difficult to develop a vaccine which will selectively target a variable virus which quickly 'hides' inside the cells of the immune system.

Education about ways of preventing transmission is of paramount importance. Although the rapid rise of the incidence of the disease has been slowed in some communities, such as the gay community, the disease is still increasing rapidly. The obvious ways of preventing transmission include:

- avoiding unprotected and promiscuous sexual intercourse. The use of condoms is vital

- avoiding the sharing of needles in drug abuse

- the screening or treatment of blood products

- testing pregnant women for HIV. Infected mothers should be treated with drugs, the babies should be delivered by Caesarean section and breastfeeding should be avoided.

Global importance

The disease was unrecorded before 1981 and yet in 1999, reports issued by the Joint United Nations Programme on HIV and AIDS contained the following facts:

- WHO estimate that, since the AIDS epidemic began, 50 million people have been infected worldwide and 33.6 million are still alive.

- More than 95% of the 33.6 million people estimated to be carrying the virus, are unaware that they are infected.

- There are estimated to be 30000 people in Britain who are infected with HIV. 10000 of these do not know that they are infected. This carries obvious risks to sexual partners.

- The epidemic is growing fastest in Eastern Europe and the former Soviet Union. In Russia, this is thought to be linked to the explosive increase of injecting drug users.

- In Africa, there are 12 infected women for every 10 infected men.

Cases of HIV/AIDS are found all around the world although they are unevenly distributed.

For example, in 1996, it was estimated that 63% of the total number of people carrying the virus lived in West and Central Africa although the population of the whole of Africa only made up between 12% and 19% of the world's population. On the other hand, only 3% were found in North America (with about 8% of the world's population) and 2% in Europe (with about 7% of the world's population).

7 Suggest two reasons why such a high proportion of people with HIV or AIDS are found in West and Central Africa. *(2 marks)*

Clearly AIDS is a present-day pandemic of enormous importance. At present, control relies mainly on prevention with some help from treatment. The care of people sick and dying with AIDS has an enormous impact, especially on the poorer countries. To care for people in Africa who are suffering from AIDS could take one third to one half of the national healthcare budgets. This is bound to affect the treatment of other serious diseases.

17.10 Vaccination programmes against infectious diseases

Programmes of mass vaccination are expensive to run and require efficient administration and public awareness. If a country can afford to run them, they are thought to be cost-effective, as treating the illnesses which might otherwise result would be even more expensive. In the UK, children are voluntarily vaccinated against a whole range of potentially serious diseases Table 17.3).

Table 17.3 Publication issued to mothers by the Department of Health in 1997 and 1998. In 1999, vaccination against Meningitis C was added to this published list.

When is the Immunisation due?	Which Immunisation	Type
At two months	polio	By mouth
	Hib	One injection
	Diphtheria	
	Tetanus	
	Whooping cough	
At three months	Polio	By mouth
	Hib	One injection
	Diphtheria	
	Tetanus	
	Whooping cough	
At four months	Polio	By mouth
	Hib	One injection
	Diphtheria	
	Tetanus	
	Whooping cough	
At 12 to 15 months	Measles	One injection
	Mumps	
	Rubella	
3 to 5 years (usually before the child starts school)	Measles Mumps Rubella	One injection
	Diphtheria	One injection
	Tetanus	
	Polio	By mouth
10 to 14 years (sometimes shortly after birth)	BCG (against tuberculosis)	Skin test followed by one injection if needed
School leavers 13 to 18 years	Diphtheria Tetanus	One injection
	Polio	By mouth

Produced by the Health Education Authority and the Department of Health

Box 17.2 The eradication of smallpox – a success story

An effective vaccine against smallpox was discovered (if not understood) by a country doctor, Edward Jenner, in 1796. However, the disease continued to remain a threat in various parts of the world for almost another 200 years.

In 1967, there were estimated to be ten million cases of smallpox distributed throughout thirty countries of the world. At this time WHO began a campaign to eradicate smallpox from the face of the Earth. The campaign included careful observation to detect cases. Transmission, which takes place by droplet infection or directly through skin wounds, was prevented by isolation of patients. All this was reinforced by vaccination programmes.

As a result, the last naturally occurring case of smallpox was diagnosed in Somalia in 1977.

There are now thought to be no surviving smallpox variola viruses left free in the environment. Some samples are, however, kept under tight security in a very few laboratories.

Figure 17.18 *Smallpox victims*

Study the information in Box 17.2, about the eradication of smallpox. It poses two major questions.

The first question is why did it take so long to begin an eradication programme if an effective vaccine had been available for such a long time? Possible answers include:

● Modern means of communication and sufficient resources had to be available in order to organise a worldwide programme.

● A heat-stable form of vaccine, suitable for tropical countries, was only developed in the 1950s.

The second question is why has it been possible to eradicate smallpox, but not other serious illnesses? Possible answers to this include:

● The smallpox virus has nowhere in the environment where it can survive long term outside the human body. It is transmitted directly from person to person. There are no second hosts, as in the case of malaria. It cannot survive in air, soil or water for long. Cholera, for example, can survive in water for long periods.

● The vaccine is very effective and gives long-term immunity against a rather stable virus. This contrasts with malaria, where an effective vaccine has still to be developed, and cholera, where the vaccine is only 50% effective and produces only short-term immunity.

● Smallpox is spread slowly and tends to appear in clusters of cases. There is a fairly long incubation period during which people at risk can be isolated as a precaution. They do not become infectious until the easily recognisable rash appears. This contrasts with the short incubation period and rapid spread of measles or cholera.

● An infected person will always develop the symptoms after a time. The virus is not carried by people who show no symptoms, but are nevertheless infectious. Carriers of TB make an eradication programme of this disease difficult.

It is thought that it might be possible to eradicate polio and measles in the future, if sufficient resources are made available.

17.11 The role of antibiotics against infectious diseases

Antibiotics are chemicals which are produced by saprobiontic bacteria and fungi. They destroy or halt the growth of competing saprobiontic species of bacteria and fungi, so leaving more resources for the species producing the antibiotic to use. The term antibiotics is now extended to include synthetic modifications of these original antibiotics as well.

Figure 17.19
(a) Sir Alexander Fleming
(b) A culture of Penicillium *prevents the growth of bacteria*
(c) Fleming's original notes

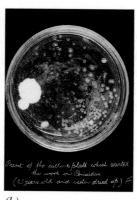
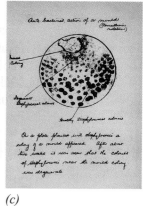

(a)

(b)

(c)

 Did You Know

During the post-war years, penicillin was in such short supply that it was recovered from patients' urine and used again!

 Remember

Antibiotics are usually only effective against bacterial and fungal diseases. A few, such as Flagyl, can suppress single-celled, protoctistan pathogens, such as some *Amoebae* (but unfortunately not the malarial parasite, *Plasmodium*). **They have no effect upon viruses**

In 1928, Alexander Fleming was observant enough to notice that a chemical produced by *Penicillium* mould, accidentally growing in a culture of pathogenic bacteria, stopped the bacteria multiplying. This began a medical revolution. In 1940, Ernst Chain and Howard Florey extracted and purified the active chemical, penicillin. They found that, while it was harmless to humans, if taken internally it could destroy the pathogenic bacteria within them. This first antibiotic was in great demand, immediately, during the Second World War. It was effective against many diseases including staphylococcal infections (blood poisoning). This prevented the development of infections following war wounds, which had caused so many deaths in the First World War.

Antibiotics have since been extracted from many species of bacteria and fungi and some have been modified, so that a whole range of effective antibiotics form important treatments. Some people are allergic to certain antibiotics and sometimes they produce unpleasant side-effects, but, in general, they have been of extreme importance in the fight against infectious diseases.

Originally, penicillin was destroyed by acid in the stomach and so had to be injected. It was excreted quickly by the kidneys and had to be given frequently. Chemical modifications have produced forms such as amoxycillin which can be taken by mouth and remain longer in the body.

Some antibiotics (broad spectrum) are effective against a wide range of bacterial diseases. Tetracycline, which was discovered in 1948, has a wide range of effectiveness and was used for many years in the treatment of respiratory infections. Other antibiotics (narrow spectrum) may be effective against fewer diseases but have particular uses.

The action of antibiotics on bacteria varies. For example, penicillin prevents the formation of some types of bacterial cell walls. The weakened walls allow the bacteria to burst when water is absorbed by osmosis. Tetracyclines act at the ribosomes, inhibiting protein synthesis. Drugs such as quinolone stop the coiling of DNA, preventing it from fitting within the bacterium.

Antibiotics have been of enormous importance in the treatment of infectious diseases. However, the development of **resistant bacteria** has reduced their effectiveness.

Random mutations occur in bacteria, as in all organisms. By chance, a mutation might occur which leads to a change in a bacterium's metabolism, preventing it being harmed by a particular antibiotic. In the absence of the antibiotic, this has no effect. However, if that antibiotic is present, the mutated bacteria are the only ones able to survive. The resistant bacteria are free from competition for resources and multiply rapidly, leading to a new strain of resistant bacteria. Clearly, the more the antibiotics are used, the more rapidly these strains are likely to arise.

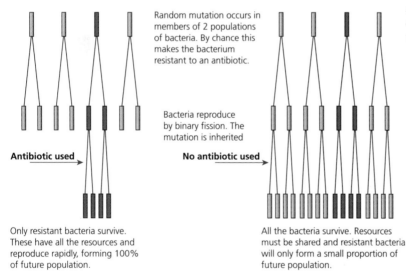

Random mutation occurs in members of 2 populations of bacteria. By chance this makes the bacterium resistant to an antibiotic.

Bacteria reproduce by binary fission. The mutation is inherited

Antibiotic used

No antibiotic used

Key

resistant bacterium

susceptible bacterium

Only resistant bacteria survive. These have all the resources and reproduce rapidly, forming 100% of future population.

All the bacteria survive. Resources must be shared and resistant bacteria will only form a small proportion of future population.

Figure 17.20 *Diagram to illustrate the emergence of a population of bacteria which is resistant to an antibiotic*

Staphylococcus aureus has now become resistant to penicillin. The effectiveness of tetracyclines has also been greatly reduced by the emergence of resistant strains. Discovery of new antibiotics has been trying to keep pace with the new strains, but some bacteria are now resistant to whole ranges of antibiotics. Unfortunately, these strains are most likely to arise where there is the greatest use of antibiotics – in hospitals!

In an attempt to slow down the emergence of resistant strains of bacteria, doctors are now reluctant to prescribe antibiotics unless they are really necessary. The public are being educated in the proper use of antibiotics and are being discouraged from demanding them to treat viral infections, against which they have no effect.

Summary – ⟨17⟩ Human health and disease

- **Disease** is a disorder of the body which displays particular symptoms and has a specific cause.

- **Health** is more than the absence of disease. To be healthy, a person must have a physically fit body and be mentally and socially well adjusted.

- **Physical** diseases may affect any organ of the body except the higher brain centres. In **mental** diseases, higher brain centres malfunction, leading to behavioural symptoms.

- **Social** diseases may be caused by social problems, but, more usually, the term applies to diseases transmitted during sexual behaviour.

- **Infectious** diseases are diseases caused by pathogens or parasites. They can be transmitted from one person to another.

- **Pathogens** are parasitic micro-organisms which cause disease in their hosts. Some viruses, bacteria, fungi and protoctista may act as pathogens. Larger parasites such as tapeworms and round worms also may be pathogenic.

- **Non-infectious** diseases are not caused by pathogens or parasites. They include **inherited (genetic)** diseases; **degenerative** diseases, where age or auto-immunity leads to destruction of some tissues; **self-inflicted** diseases which result from chemical or physical self-abuse; **deficiency** diseases which result from the lack of one or more essential nutrients.

- **Epidemiology** is the study of patterns of distribution of disease. It can reveal relationships between the incidence of certain diseases and particular factors. This can lead to understanding the causes and to methods of prevention of these diseases. **Health statistics**, in which facts are collected and treated numerically, are an important tool in epidemiology. They have been important in revealing the link between smoking and various diseases.

- Developing countries have **higher infant mortality** and a **lower life expectancy** than developed countries. More people die of infectious diseases and birth problems in developing countries, whereas in developed countries, more people die of cancer, circulatory and degenerative diseases. The reasons for the differences are economic, environmental and social.

- Four infectious diseases which are important worldwide are **cholera**, **malaria**, **tuberculosis** and **AIDS**.

- **Vaccination** programmes are an effective form of control for certain diseases. They have been a contributing factor to the eradication of smallpox. There are no really effective vaccines for diseases such as cholera, malaria and AIDS.

- **Antibiotics** have been an important treatment for infectious diseases caused by bacteria and fungi. They are *not* effective against viruses. The evolution of strains of bacteria which are resistant to antibiotics has reduced their usefulness, in spite of the discovery of new antibiotics.

Answers

1 **(a)** UK and Japan *(2)*.

  (b) Two of – India, Bangladesh, Central African Republic, Angola *(2)*.

  (c) Kuwait *(1)*.

2 **(a)** Developing countries – 67.0 per 1000 live births, Developed countries – 9.7 per 1000 live births *(2)*.

  (b) Developing countries – 59.7 years, Developed countries – 71.2 years *(2)*.

3 **(a)** cancers, circulatory and degenerative diseases *(2)*.

  (b) infectious diseases, maternal and birth problems, chronic pulmonary diseases *(3)*.

(c) accidents and violence *(1)*.

4 More people live in developing countries than in developed countries *(1)*.

5 People in developed countries: (i) have diets more rich in lipids/with higher energy value; (ii) take less exercise; (iii) are more likely to live long enough for such a disease to develop *(3)*.

6 **(a)** vaccination; antibiotics; overall better health *(3)*.

  (b) less overcrowding; drier, airy, light working conditions; better housing *(3)*.

7 Viruses have existed longest here; poverty restricts health education programmes *(2)*.

End of Chapter Questions

1 Give four reasons why it is almost impossible for a doctor to determine whether a patient visiting his surgery is completely healthy. *(4 marks)*

2 Give an example of each of the following:

  (a) A social, viral pandemic disease.

  (b) A physical, fungal disease.

  (c) A mental, degenerative disease.

  (d) A bacterial disease which has been responsible for pandemics in the past.

  (e) A disease caused by a multicellular parasite.

  (f) A self-inflicted, deficiency disease.

  (g) An inherited, physical disease. *(7 marks)*

3 Discuss three ways in which health statistics must be compiled and/or interpreted with care, if valid conclusions are to be made. *(3 marks)*

4 Vaccination, together with identification and isolation of infectious people, has helped to eradicate smallpox, but not measles, tuberculosis, malaria or cholera. Giving one reason for each of these four diseases, explain why each one is more difficult to eradicate than smallpox. *(4 marks)*

5 **(a)** In the United Kingdom vaccination against the following diseases is available through the National Health Service during the first few years of life:

measles	mumps	tetanus	whooping cough (pertussis)
polio	rubella	diphtheria	meningitis (Hib)

  (i) Give **three** diseases against which children may be vaccinated during the first six months by a single injection containing all three vaccines. *(1 mark)*

(ii) At what age is the MMR (measles, mumps and rubella) vaccination usually given? *(1 mark)*

(b) Outline the vaccination schedule against tuberculosis in the United Kingdom. *(2 marks)*

(c) The table shows the results of a number of surveys into the vaccination of children against whooping cough.

	Survey			
	A	**B**	**C**	**D**
percentage of children vaccinated	55	75	85	95
number of cases of disease	560	325	74	0

(i) Use the information in the table to explain the effectiveness of vaccination in preventing an epidemic of whooping cough. *(2 marks)*

(ii) Suggest **one** reason why parents may choose not to have their children vaccinated against whooping cough. *(1 mark)*

AQA (NEAB) 1997 *(Total 7 marks)*

6 Explain the meaning of the following terms as they apply to infectious disease.

Endemic Epidemic *(2 marks)*

Table 1.1

developing countries		developed countries	
disease	**percentage details**	**disease**	**percentage details**
diarrhoea	42	heart diseases	32
respiratory infections:		cancers	23
e.g. tuberculosis (TB)	25		
malnutrition	10	strokes	12
malaria	7	bronchitis	6
mealses	15	pneumonia	5
others	11	others	22

(b) With reference to Table 1.1,

(i) explain why infectious diseases are leading causes of death in developing countries. *(4 marks)*

(i) explain why degenerative diseases are leading causes of death in developed countries *(4 marks)*

(Total 10 marks)

7 The bacterium, *Vibrio cholerae*, is the causative agent of cholera. The El Tor strain of *V. cholerae* originally occurred only in Indonesia. In 1961, this strain began to spread replacing existing strains in other parts of Asia. El Tor is now widespread throughout Asia, the Middle East, Africa and parts of Eastern Europe, but has never established itself in Western Europe.

El Tor is hardier than the strain it replaced and the bacteria may continue to appear in the faeces for up to three months after patients have recovered. The bacteria may persist in water for up to fourteen days.

(a) State **two** ways in which *V. cholerae* is transmitted from infected to uninfected people. *(2 marks)*

Some people infected with cholera have mild symptoms, or none at all, and are carriers of the disease:

(b) Suggest how laboratory tests could identify carriers of cholera *(2 marks)*

(c) Suggest **four** reasons why El Tor has not become established in Western Europe. *(4 marks)*

The United Nations, recognising that most of the outbreaks of cholera were the result of polluted water supplies, set up a 'Decade of Water' in 1981. Its aim was to provide safe water for everyone. Over the decade 1981/1990, the number of people lacking a safe water supply in developing countries dropped from 1800 million to 1200 million.

(d) Explain why cholera continues to be worldwide problem, in spite of the 'Decade of Water' campaign.

(In this question, 1 mark is available for the quality of written communication.) *(8 marks)*

The antibiotic tetracycline is sometimes used as a treatment for cholera.

(e) **(i)** Suggest **two** ways in which tetracycline can affect *V. cholerae*. *(2 marks)*

(ii) Explain why tetracycline should not be used routinely for all cases of cholera. *(1 mark)*

(Total 19 marks)

Answers to End of Chapter Questions

Chapter 1, pages 32–35

1 (a) A: ribosome (or *rough* endoplasmic reticulum); B: Golgi apparatus; C: mitochondrion; D: nuclear envelope/nuclear membrane; E: nucleolus *(5)*.

(b) Ribosomes on the rough endoplasmic reticulum are the site of protein synthesis in the cell *(1)*. Vesicles containing this protein are 'pinched off' the rough ER to form the membrane-bound cisternae of the Golgi apparatus *(1)*. Inside the Golgi the proteins are modified, for example by the addition of carbohydrate to form glycoproteins *(1)*. Vesicles (X) bud off the Golgi cisternae containing these modified proteins *(1)*.

(c) The mitochondrion carries out the final stages of aerobic respiration *(1)*. This leads to the production of the compound adenosine triphosphate or ATP *(1)* on the inner membrane or cristae *(1)* of the mitochondrion. ATP is used as a source of chemical energy in cells *(1)*.

(Total 13 marks)

2 One mark per correct row in table:

Feature	Animal cell	Plant cell	Prokaryotic cell
Cell wall made of cellulose	✗	✔	✗
Cell membrane	✔	✔	✔
Endoplasmic reticulum	✔	✔	✗
Mesosome	✗	✗	✔
Cytoskeleton	✔	✔	✗
Ribosomes	✔	✔	✔
Golgi apparatus	✔	✔	✗
Chloroplasts	✗	✔	✗

(Total 8 marks)

3 (a) The resolving power of a microscope is the smallest distance between two objects where the microscope can still distinguish them as separate *(1)*.

(b) In a slide preparation, an artefact is a structure or appearance of the specimen which is a result of the preparation procedure *(1)* and is not present in the living cell or tissue *(1)*.

(c) A lysosome is a small, round, membrane-bound organelle *(1)* containing digestive enzymes *(1)*. It fuses with other membrane-bound vacuoles containing food particles or redundant organelles *(1)* and the enzymes break these down *(1)*.

(d) The middle lamella is a mixture of calcium and magnesium pectates *(1)* acting as an adhesive *(1)* between adjacent plant cell walls *(1)*.

(e) A plasmodesma is a cytoplasmic connection *(1)* between adjacent plant cells *(1)* passing through pores in the cell walls *(1)*. It allows for transport of materials between cells *(1)*.

(f) Thylakoids are flattened sack-like membranes inside chloroplasts *(1)*. Chlorophyll is located on these membranes *(1)* and so they are the place where light energy is trapped in photosynthesis *(1)*.

(g) Cell differentiation is a process which occurs during the development of an organism *(1)* where the structure of a cell changes to allow it to perform a particular function *(1)*.

(h) Plasmids are small loops of DNA present in the cytoplasm of (some) bacteria *(1)*. They contain non-essential genes *(1)* such as those giving resistance to antibiotics.

(Total 21 marks)

4 A: mitochondrion; B: nucleus; C: centriole/centrosome; D: smooth endoplasmic reticulum; E: microvilli *(5)*.

5 (a) A: cell wall; B: plasma/cell (surface) membrane; C: ribosomes/*rough* endoplasmic reticulum; D: chloroplast *(4)*.

(b) Homogenise tissue *(1)* in ice-cold *(1)* istonic solution *(1)* centrfuge *(1)*. *(max 3 marks)*

(Total 7 marks)

6 (a) A: flagellum; C: cell wall; D: DNA/chromosome *(3)*.

(b) B: location of (enzymes of) aerobic respiration; C: protection/maintains shape; E: carbohydrate storage *(3)*.

(Total 6 marks)

7 (a) A: plasma/cell (surface) membrane; B: centrioles/centrosomes; C: Golgi apparatus; D: ribosome/*rough* endoplasmic reticulum *(4)*.

(b) Length = 11 mm (11 000 μm) *(1)* so actual length = 11 000 ÷ 12 000 = 0.92 μm *(1)*

(Total 6 marks)

Chapter 2, pages 58–60

1 Substances can cross the membrane by simple diffusion, facilitated diffusion, active transport, osmosis and through gaps in the membrane which form during cytosis *(4)*.

2 Endocytosis is the entry of materials into the cell through gaps that form due to folding of the cell membrane *(1)*. Exocytosis is the release of substances out of the cell due to fusing of vesicles with the cell surface membrane *(1)*. The fluid nature of the membrane allows the breaking and reforming of the membrane, always with the phosphate 'heads' on the outside and the fatty acid 'tails' on the inside *(1)*.

(Total 3 marks)

3 At equilibrium, the water potential of adjacent cells is the same. The water molecules have the same amount of kinetic energy and will move equally from one cell to another. No net movement of water will take place and osmosis will cease *(2)*.

4 Water will move from cell A to cell B by osmosis as the water potential is higher in cell A. Eventually equilibrium is reached and their water potential will be the same. This is the average water potential of the two cells, −650 kPa *(2)*.

5 A soil with salt lowers the water potential of the soil water. Water moves from a higher water potential in the plant to a lower water potential in the soil. If the soil water potential is not higher than that in the plant, then water will not enter the plant *(3)*.

6 When starch is hydrolysed into sugar, this increases the number of solute particles present and lowers the water potential. Starch does not affect water potential as it is insoluble *(2)*.

7 Respiratory inhibitors stop the process of respiration and the production of energy. Phosphate ions enter root hair cells by active transport which requires energy, as the ions pass to a higher concentration in the roots. If a respiratory inhibitor is used, active transport ceases and phosphate ions can only enter by diffusion, so the concentration of ions inside the roots and in the soil will be the same *(3)*.

8 **(a)** There is a higher concentration of K^+ in solution and a lower concentration in the carrot. (diffusion is high to low concentration) Membrane must be permeable to K^+ *(2)*.

   (b) **(i)** At 20°C, 300 at 2 hours, 630 at 6 hours (up 330 in 4 hours).

   $$\frac{330}{4} = 82.5 \,mg\, g^{-1} \text{ per hour (approx)} \quad (3)$$

   (ii) Much higher rate of K^+ uptake at 20°C, 630 over 6 hours compared to 110 at 2°C. (nearly 6 times more at 20°C) *(3)*.

   (iii) At 20°C, higher temperature means more kinetic energy and molecules move faster. If K^+ ions move faster, they are more likely to cross the membrane, so greater uptake at higher temperatures. Higher temperature also increases the metabolic rate of plant tissue, K^+ ions will be used more quickly maintaining a greater difference in concentration between the solution and the carrot, increasing the rate of diffusion *(3)*

   (Total 11 marks)

9 **(a)** Osmosis is passive/does not require ATP/energy;
   Osmosis only relates to transport of water;
   Osmosis occurs along a concentration gradient;
   Osmosis does not use carrier (proteins); *(Max 2)*

   (b) **(i)** The water potential of the solution is higher/less negative than that of cells;
   water enters the blood cell;
   by osmosis;
   cells increase in volume/pressure; *(3)*

   (ii) Cells do not all have the same water potential; *(1)*

   (c) Onion cells have cell walls *(1)*

   (Total 7 marks)

Chapter 3, pages 96–99

1 Stir mixture into amylase solution and leave at 35–40°C for fifteen minutes. Filter so that only insoluble cellulose remains in filter paper. Wash several times with water before leaving to dry *(3)*.

2 **(a)** **(i)** Basis of cell membranes *(1)*

   (ii) Hydrophobic tail and hydrophilic head cause them to form bilayers *(1)*

   (b) **(i)** Structural component of animal bodies, e.g. blood vessel walls *(1)*

   (ii) Triple helix gives flexibility and strength *(1)*.

   (c) **(i)** Main component of plant cell walls *(1)*

   (ii) Inversion of alternate beta-glucose gives straight chains which form H-bonds with adjacent chains, giving tough fibres *(1)*

   (d) **(i)** Enzyme/carrier/receptor site/antibody *(1)*

   (ii) Specific shape of molecule causes it to 'fit' and react with only one specific compound *(1)*

   (Total 8 marks)

3 Primary – order of amino acids in each polypeptide chain
   Secondary – any folding into alpha-helix or beta-pleated sheet within each chain *(1)*
   Tertiary – any specific folding of each chain caused by bonds between R-groups *(1)*
   Quaternary – linking of four polypeptide chains and haem groups *(1)*
   (Total 4 marks)

4 **(a)** **(i)** Glucose, triglyceride, cellulose, sucrose, glycogen, starch *(1)*

   (ii) Cellulose, sucrose, glycogen, starch *(1)*

   (iii) Triglyceride, cellulose, globular protein, sucrose, conjugated protein, glycogen, phospholipid, fibrous protein, starch *(1)*

   (b) **(i)** The monomers are alpha-glucose *(1)*

   (ii) They act as energy stores *(1)*

   (iii) They are insoluble in water *(1)*

   (Total 6 marks)

5 **(a)** **(i)** A glycerol *(1)*
   B fatty acid *(1)*

   (ii) triglyceride *(1)*

   (iii) condensation *(1)*

   (b) **(i)** energy source or store/insulation/waterproofing/protection against blows *(1)*

   (ii) high energy value/insoluble/poor conductor of heat/hydrophobic *(1)*

   Answer to (ii) must relate to answer in (i)

   (Total 6 marks)

6 (a) starch present; no reducing sugar present; protein present *(3)*

(b) stain with chlor-zinc iodide; cellulose stains violet colour *(2)*

(Total 5 marks)

7 (a) solvent front *(1)*

(b) mixture of amino acids *(1)*

(c) $R_f = 0.54$; working *(2)*

(d) they have different solubilities in that solvent *(1)*

(Total 5 marks)

8

Statement	Triglyceride	Glycogen
Contains only carbon, hydrogen and oxygen	✔	✔
Glycosidic bonds present	✘	✔
Soluble in water	✘	✘
Provides storage of energy	✔	✔
Occurs in flowering plants and animals	✔	✘

(Total 5 marks)

Chapter 4, pages 114–117

1 activation / proteins / active site / *high* temperature / *extremes* of pH / non-reversible / competitive *(7)*

2 (a)

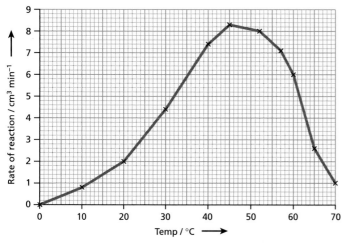

1 mark for each of:

● axes right way round, correctly labelled, with units

● reasonable size and scales

● points correctly plotted

● points joined with straight lines, not extrapolated.

(b) (i) Increasing temperature causes increased kinetic energy/movement of molecules *(1)* and therefore more collisions of enzyme and substrate/more enzyme–substrate complexes *(1)* so increasing the rate of reaction.

(ii) At high temperatures enzyme denatured/tertiary structure damaged *(1)* bonds maintaining shape of active site broken *(1)* therefore fewer enzyme-substrate complexes formed *(1)*.

(c) Between 40 °C and 52 °C. (Note that it is strictly impossible to state more accurately than this from the data, but any value between these figures accepted.) *(1)*

(d) pH of the mixture/concentration of enzyme/concentration of substrate *(1)*.

(e) Enzyme may not have had long enough at high temperatures for denaturing to take effect/enzyme may not be human in origin/may be bacterial etc. and therefore have a different optimum *(1)*.

(f) Measure light transmission through suspension/use a colorimeter *(1)*.

(Total 13 marks)

3 (a) Active site *(1)*

(b) Each enzyme has an active site of a particular shape *(1)* only one substrate fits into/is complementary with active site *(1)*

(c) Competitive inhibitor is similar shape to substrate *(1)* fits into active site *(1)* (temporarily) prevents entry of substrate *(1)*

(Max 3 marks)

4 (a) (i) High temperature denatures enzymes/destroys tertiary structure *(1)* by breaking bonds between polypeptide chains *(1)* alters hape of active site *(1)* substrate unable to fit/reaction cannot be catalysed *(1)*

(ii) Enzymes are proteins with a specific tertiary structure.shape *(1)* with specific shape of active site *(1)* into which only one substrate will fit *(1)*

(iii) Competitive inhibitors enter active site and temporarily prevent reaction *(1)* non-competitive inhibitors attach to places other than active site and alter its shape *(1)* preventing substrate from entering *(1)*

(Total 10 marks)

5 (a) Glucose diffuses through membrane *(1)* sensor contains enzyme glucose oxidase *(1)* glucose binds to enzyme *(1)* reaction produces (gluconic) acid/uses up oxygen *(1)* converted to electric current by transducer *(1)* size of current proportional to concentration of glucose *(1)* *(Max 5 marks)*

(b) (i) Enzymes (and receptors) are proteins *(1)* with specific shape/tertiary structure *(1)* only react with complementary molecule/substrate *(1)*

(ii) Enzyme reactions produce a different product/many products *(1)* which are detectable *(1)*

(c) Use a biosensor to measure a certain known reaction *(1)* concentration of heavy metal ions will be proportional to degree of inhibition of reaction *(1)*

(Total 12 marks)

Chapter 5, pages 148–154

1 (a) (i) sulphur = protein.

(ii) phosphorus = DNA *(2)*.

(b) Both the DNA and the protein would be labelled as they both contain carbon *(1)*.

(c) (i) DNA *(1)*

(ii) Only the bacteria in experiment 2 become radioactive so radioactive DNA must have entered the bacteria *(2)*.

(iii) The original radioactive phage DNA is used to replicate new DNA for the new phages. As replication is semi-conservative some of the new phages will also contain radioactive DNA *(3)*.

(Total 9 marks)

2 (a) Ser Gly Leu Ser *(1)*

(b) The second 'word' is a stop triplet – this would end the polypeptide, meaning that the last two amino acids would not be produced *(2)*.

(c) Four: Ser Leu Tyr Ile (AG and A will not code for an amino acid) *(2)*.

(Total 5 marks)

3 (a) Degenerate means one amino acid may be coded for by more than one mRNA codon. Plus any example from table, e.g. UUU and UUC both code for Phe *(2)*.
Triplet means a sequence of three bases code for each amino acid. Any example from table, e.g. UUU codes for the amino acid Phe *(2)*.
A codon is a sequence of three bases on mRNA which codes for one amino acid. Any example from table, e.g. UUU codes for the amino acid Phe *(2)*.

(b) TAC *(1)*

(c) 1 = deletion, 2 = substitution (U for C), 3 = substitution (G for C) *(3)*.

(d) 1 causes a frame shift and all four amino acids are changed *(2)*.

(e) 2 because the new codon still codes for the same amino acid (Leu) because the code is degenerate. The mutation has no effect on the protein *(2)*.

(f) Ser, Leu, Met, Ala *(1)*

(g) UCG, GAC, UAC, CGU *(1)*

(Total 16 marks)

4 organic; deoxyribose/pentose; phosphate; hydrogen; DNA helicase; thymine; uracil; ribose; ribosomal; nucleolus; messenger; ribosomes; transfer; amino acids *(7)*.

5 (a)
ademine   adenine
cytosine   cytosine
thymine   uracil
cytosine   cytosine
guanine   guanine
thymine   uracil *(2)*

(b) two *(1)*

(c) purine *(1)*

(d) transcription *(1)*

(e) RNA polymerase   DNA polymerase *(1)*

(f) 28% A   therefore 28% T
28 + 28 = 56   100 − 56 = 44% C and G
therefore cytosine = 22% *(2)*

(Total 9 marks)

6 (a) CUCG *(1)*

(b) this is the anticodon; it joins up with the matching codon on the mRNA by specific pairing so that the amino acids line up in the correct seqeuence. *(2)*

(c) see table 5.1 page 124 – any two differences *(2)*

(Total 5 marks)

7 (a) (i) TTCGCACCT

(ii) AAGCGU

(b) (i) CCU

(ii) anticodon

(c) (i) transcription

(ii) translation

(d) ribosome   *(Total 7 marks)*

8 (a) hydrogen bond *(1)*

(b) (i) transcription *(1)*

(ii) translation *(1)*

(c) (i) TGC AAT CGA *(1)*

(ii) UGC AAU CGA *(1)*   *(Total 5 marks)*

Chapter 6, pages 178–182

1 (a) (i) 20 units   12 chromosomes

(ii) 20 units   12 chromosomes

(iii) 10 units   12 chromosomes

(b) (i) 20 units   12 chromosomes

(ii) 20 units   12 chromosomes

(iii) 10 units   6 chromosomes

(iv) 5 units   6 chromosomes *(14)*

2 A = interphase; B = G^1; C = S; D = G^2; E = meiosis 1; F = meiosis 2; G = telophase 1; H = telophase 2 *(8)*

3 Both determine that chromosomes pass into daughter cells *(1)*. Mitosis gives genetic identity, meiosis gives genetic variety in daughter cells *(1)*.
Identity important: in growth as all cells need all genes *(1)*; in asexual reproduction to exploit favourable environment quickly *(1)*. Variety important to prevent whole species being wiped out by environmental change *(1)*.

(Total 5 marks)

4 (a) XYZ, X́ÝŹ, XYŹ, XÝZ, X́YZ, XÝZ, X́ÝZ, X́YŹ *(4)*

   (b) In crossing over, parts of chromatids are exchanged between homologous chromosomes *(1)* so one daughter cell can inherit a chromosome which contains maternal genes attached to paternal genes *(1)*.

(Total 6 marks)

5 (a) (i) anaphase *(1)*; **(ii)** interphase *(1)*

   (b) More cells in metaphase than anaphase *(1)*;

   (c) (i) 44 *(1)*; **(ii)** 11 *(1)*.

(Total 5 marks)

6

Statement	First division of meiosis	Second division of meiosis
pairing of homologous chromosomes occurs	✔	✘
chromosomes consist of pairs of chromatids during prophase	✔	✔
chiasmata are formed	✔	✘
chromatids are separated	✘	✔
independent assortment of chromosomes occurs	✔	✘

(Total 5 marks)

7 (a) This is a region where cells are dividing *(1)*

   (b) (i) So that chromosomes can be distinguished *(1)*

   (ii) To provide a thin layer of cells so that detail can be seen *(1)*

   (c) (i) Anaphase *(1)*

   (ii) Chromosomes do not appear as paired structures *(1)*

(Total 5 marks)

8 (a) (i) A homologous pair of chromosomes/four chromaids when they have come together/associated *(1)*

   (ii) the point where chromatids cross over each other *(1)*

   (b) metaphase – as chromosomes lined up on the equator *(1)*

(c) (i) 10 *(1)*

   (ii) 5 *(1)*

(Total 5 marks)

Chapter 7, pages 210–213

1 (a) 46; **(b)** 46; **(c)** 23; **(d)** 23 *(4)*

2 (a) Male gametes produced continuously after puberty, female gametes start before birth and complete development one per monthly cycle; Four male gametes produced from one primary spermatocyte, only one female gamete and three polar bodies formed from one primary oocyte; Male gametes complete formation in the testis, female gamete only completes formation after fertilisation *(3)*

   (b) Formation includes a multiplication phase involving mitosis/growth phase;
Formation includes a maturation phase involving meiosis;
Formation never complete before puberty *(3)*

(Total 6 marks)

3 (a) A corpus luteum is formed each time a female gamete is released from the ovary. Each female gamete may produce a fetus, if fertilised *(2)*

   (b) Not all female gametes may be fertilised. Some young embryos may not have implanted and may have died *(2)*

   (c) Some zygotes may have divided to produce twins *(1)*.

(Total 5 marks)

4 (i) (a) oestrogen; **(b)** FSH; **(c)** progesterone; **(d)** LH *(4)*

   (ii) Day 11. Progesterone rises soon afterwards as corpus luteum forms/peak in LH *(2)*

(Total 6 marks)

5 (a) FSH increases the size (as it stimulates their development).

   (b) LH decreases their size (as it promotes ovulation).

(Total 2 marks)

6 Made of part fetal tissue and part maternal tissue, bringing the two bloods close together for exchange of substances; Many fetal chorionic villi with branches giving large surface area for exchange; Each villus well supplied with fetal capillaries close to the surface; Maternal capillary walls not present, so maternal blood bathes the villi, keeping diffusion distance as short as possible; Microvilli on villi walls increase surface area for diffusion and active transport; Many mitochondria produce ATP, providing energy for active transport; Counterflow (explain if learned this). *(Max. 5)*

7 (a) (i) Corpus luteum *(1)*

   (ii) Outer follicle cells of Graafian follicle *(1)*

   (iii) To produce progesterone and oestrogen *(1)*

   (iv) It will degenerate *(1)*.

(b) (i) Follicle stimulating hormone (FSH) *(1)*

(ii) Anterior pituitary gland *(1)*.

(c) A gonadal hormone is produced in the gonads (ovary or testis). A gonadotrophic hormone is produced in the anterior pituitary and has an effect upon the gonads *(1)*.

(Total 7 marks)

8

Hormone	Secreted by ovaries	Reaches highest level in blood before ovulation
follicle stimulating hormone (FSH)	✗	✔
luteinising hormone (LH)	✗	✔
oestrogen	✔	✔
progesterone	✔	✗

(Total 4 marks)

9 (a) Formed as a result of mitosis *(1)*.

(b) Crossing over; independent assortment of chromosomes; mutation *(Max. 2)*

(c) Uneven division of cytoplasma leads to only one of the four cells produced by meiosis developing into a gamete *(1)*.

(d) Secretion of hormones *(1)*

(Total 5 marks)

10 (a) (i) 39 pairs/78 *(1)*

(ii) oestrogen *(1)*

(b) Secretion of progesterone and oestrogen; which maintains the endometrium allowing the embryo to implant *(2)*.

(c) A and D *(1)*

(d) Have haploid nucleus; can be fertilised by male gamete; remains in body *(2)*.

(Total 7 marks)

11 (a) 20 days; time from certain concentration of all hormones until those concentrations are repeated *(2)*.

(b) LH transported to ovary and stimulates ovulation; also stimulates formation of corpus luteum from outer follicle cells progesterone is secreted by corpus luteum *(Max. 3)*

(c) Figures would remain high; as corpus luteum remains, secreting progesterone maintaining endometrium for embryo *(2)*

(d) (i) Via blood *(1)* **(ii)** so that cow can be mated again next cycle; calf and produce milk as soon as possible for economic reasons *(2)*.

(e) Oestrogen; inhibits FSH production; so no ovulation
Progesterone; inhibits FSH and LH; makes vaginal mucus too thick for sperm passage
FSH; stimulates developing of follicles *(Min. 1) (Max. 4)*

(marks not awarded if answers not expressed in good English prose)

(Total 15 marks)

Chapter 8, pages 227–229

1 Similarity – Both involve mitosis and meiosis *(1)*.
Difference – The final division producing the gamete is mitosis in a plant (meiosis produces the microspore). The final division producing a gamete in mammals is meiosis *(1)*. *(Total 2 marks)*

2 (i) B, embryo sac *(1)*

(ii) C, integument *(1)*

(iii) I, female gamete (egg cell) *(1)*

(iv) J, polar nucleus *(1)*

(v) E, male gamete *(1)*

(vi) D, pollen tube *(1)*

(vii) A, nucellus *(1)* *(Total 7 marks)*

3 (a) Pollination is the transfer of pollen grains from anther to stigma *(1)* but fertilisation is the fusion of male and female gamete nuclei *(1)*.

(b) The pollen grain is a microspore containing two haploid nuclei *(1)*. One of these nuclei divides to give two haploid nuclei which are the male gametes *(1)*.

(c) The ovule is a structure made of many diploid cells and containing a megaspore which has eight haploid nuclei *(1)*. One of these nuclei will fuse with a male gamete. This nucleus is the female gamete *(1)*.

(Total 6 marks)

4 (a) D; G; *(2)*

(b) petals/no petals;
anthers in flower/anthers exposed;
loose anthers/fixed anthers;
small sticky stigma/feathery stigma;
may have nectary/no nectary *(Max. 2)*

(c) protandry; – anthers ripen before stigma;/protogyny; – stigma ripens before stamens;/dioecious; – male and female flowers on separate plants; self-sterility; pollen not grow on same plant's stigma;/description of a particular structure; *(Max. 2)*

(Total 6 marks)

5 (a) (i) G *(1)*

(ii) E *(1)*

(iii) B *(1)*

(b) large petals which attract/provide landing stage for insects; anthers inside flower in position where insects rub against them; stigmas in position to receive pollen from insect;*(Max. 2)*

(Total 5 marks)

Chapter 9, pages 268–269

1 (a) alveoli; **(b)** spongy mesophyll cells; **(c)** lamella or gill plate *(3)*.

2 All gas exchange surfaces show the following features: a large surface area; thin; permeable; moist; close to transport; ventilation mechanism. Any four of these *(4)*.

3 All gas exchange surfaces are moist, as membranes permeable to gases will also be permeable to water. Terrestrial organisms must expose their moist gas exchange surface to the air for gas exchange and inevitably some of this water will evaporate due to the drying action of the air. *(2)*

4 Large organisms have a small surface area to volume ratio and therefore not enough oxygen can enter through the outer surface to supply the cells. Extra surface for gas exchange is provided either by folds in the external surface, external gills, or having internal folded membranes. *(2)*

5 Plants have large, thin, flat leaves with many stomata, through which air enters and exits. The air spaces in the leaf are in contact with many widely spaced spongy mesophyll cells which provide the surface for gas exchange. These cells are moist, thin-walled and offer a large surface area for gas exchange. The removal of gases to other cells maintains a concentration gradient, so allowing continued diffusion. *(3)*

6 Alveolar epithelium is made of a thin layer of cells only one cell thick, called squamous or pavement epithelium. This reduces the diffusion distance for respiratory gases. The surface is folded to increase the surface area for diffusion, and moist, so indicating permeability to gases. *(3)*

7 (a) 15 breaths per minute, $\frac{60}{4} = 15$

(1)

(b) (i) Between 2 and 4 seconds *(1)*

(ii) Pressure in lungs is higher than atmosphere pressure *(1)*

(c) diaphragm muscle contracts and flattens; External intercostal muscles contract and pull rib-cage up and out, so increasing volume of chest cavity *(2)*

(Total 5 marks)

8 (a) (i) oxygen diffuses to cells *(1)*

(ii) CO_2 lost through tracheoles and spiracles (not carried in blood) in insects. CO_2 transported in blood in fish *(1)*.

(b) 100 cycles per minute *(1)*

(c) Water flows from high pressure to low pressure. Pressure is higher in buccal cavity than in opercular cavity, so water forced over gills *(2)*

(d) Floor of buccal cavity rises and mouth shuts. Volume of buccal cavity decrease so increasing the pressure *(2)*

(Total 7 marks)

Chapter 10, pages 306–308

1 Pressure falls through the capillary bed from the arteriole to the venule end due to: loss of fluid at arteriole end; increased friction of blood against narrow capillary wall; increasing distance from the heart. (Any two reasons) *(2)*

2 Heart sounds are produced when heart valves close. The closure of the atrioventricular valves causes the first heart sound and closure of the semilunar valves causes the second. *(2)*

3 Thicker muscle in the left ventricle means that the muscle can contract with greater force and push the blood under high pressure. This high pressure ensures that oxygenated blood is carried efficiently to the body cells. High hydrostatic pressure at the capillaries allows the formation of tissue fluid to bathe the cells for efficient exchange of materials. *(2)*

4 The smooth muscle in the arterioles can contract and relax. When the circular muscle contracts, it shortens and the lumen diameter is narrowed. This is called vasoconstriction and it reduces the blood flow to the adjacent capillaries. Relaxing of the muscle widens the lumen and more blood flows through. This is vasodilation. Therefore the smooth muscle controls blood flow. *(2)*

5 Capillaries are tiny blood vessels with walls only one cell thick, called squamous epithelium. This thin wall is permeable and allows diffusion of materials between the blood and the cells. The short diffusion distance and the numerous capillaries provide a huge surface area for maximising diffusion. The squamous epithelium combined with high hydrostatic pressure at the arteriole end, causes the formation of tissue fluid. Capillaries are found extending through all the organs, ensuring that all cells can be provided with nutrients and oxygen, and waste can readily be removed by diffusion. *(2)*

6 (a) Sinoatrial node, SAN *(1)*

(b) (i) Allows time for blood to fill ventricles from atria, before ventricles contract *(1)*

(ii) Blood pushed up to arteries, at top of heart *(1)*

(c) Impulse along sympathetic nerve to SAN, increasing the frequency of waves of excitation from SAN. Heart rate increases *(2)*

(d) (i) Elastic fibres in artery wall *(1)*

(ii) Blood flows in pulses, and elastic fibres help to smooth out blood flow and keep the pressure up *(2)*

(Total 8 marks)

7 (a) Right ventricle *(1)*

(b) (i) Ventricles contracting (systole) *(2)*

(ii) Atria contracting/heart in diastole, ventricles relaxed and filling with blood from atria, atrioventricular valve open *(2)*

(c) (i) High pressure in brachial artery as branch of aorta from left ventricle with thicker muscle. (pulmonary artery carries blood from right ventricle) *(1)*

(ii) Lower pressure to lungs means blood is moving slowly so maximising gas exchange and preventing lung damage *(1)*

(Total 7 marks)

8 (a) right ventricle *(1)*

(b) *(1)*

Valve	Open	Closed
1	no	yes
2	yes	no
3	no	yes
4	yes	no

(c) Line drawn with same pattern, peaks and troughs at same time as for pulmonary artery, but both at a higher pressure in the aorta *(2)*.

(Total 4 marks)

Chapter 11, pages 336–342

1 **A** red blood cell; **B** granulocyte e.g. neutrophil; **C** lymphocyte; **D** monocyte. *(4)*

2 (a) left; (b) right; (c) left; (d) right. *(4)*

3 (a) Equation 1 *(1)*

(b) Transport of carbon dioxide from respiring cells to the lungs so it can be breathed out. *(2)*

(c) Shift curve to right. *(1)*

(d) Red blood cells *(1)*

(Total 5 marks)

4 They are non-identical twins and therefore different genetically with different antigens on their cells. *(2)*

5 The first contact with the bacteria caused a primary immune response. This is slow and the person became ill. However, memory lymphocytes were also produced. Therefore the second contact with the bacteria produced the secondary response by the memory cells. This response is faster and kills off the bacteria before the person becomes ill. *(4)*

6 (a) Antibodies a and b present. *(1)*

(b) Person with group B has antigen B on red blood cells. Person with group A has antibodies b in plasma. Antibodies b attack antigens B causing agglutination. *(3)*

(c) Has no antibodies (a or b) in the blood plasma so can safely be given any type of blood with no risk of agglutination. *(1)*

(Total 5 marks)

7 (a) Angle of section when slide prepared *(1)*

(b) (i) line top right

(ii) 40 mm (length on drawing) = 7.5 μm actual size
therefore 1 mm = 0.19 μm
therefore 6 mm = 1.14 μm
therefore actual length of path = 1.14 μm *(2)*

(c) (i) Biconcave shape increases surface area to volume ration therefore faster rate of diffusion of oxygen into cell

(ii) Room for more haemoglobin therefore more oxygen can be carried. *(2)*

(d) Haemoglobin cannot be filtered out at kidneys *(1)*

(Total 6 marks)

8 (a) Has a high affinity for oxygen where oxygen partial pressure is high; has a low affinity for oxygen where oxygen partial pressure is low. *(2)*

(b) (i) 10.8 − 3.5 = 7.3 kPa *(2)*

(ii) Muscle cells which are actively respiring and therefore using up the oxygen *(2)*

(c) Curve shifts to right due to Bohr effect;
with more carbon dioxide, more hydrogen ions are produced and this causes more oxygen to be releated from haemoglobin; high carbon dioxide reduces the affinity of haemoglobin for oxygen; both loading tension and unloading tension are higher. *(4)*

(d) Fetal haemoglobin has a higher affinity for oxygen than mothers haemoglobin because it must be able to take up oxygen from the mother's blood. *(2)*

(e) In solution in plasma;
as hydrogen carbonte ions in plasma;
combined with haemoglobin as carbaminohaemoglobin. *(3)*

(Total 15 marks)

9 (a) (i) First graft produced a slow primary immune response; second graft produced a quicker secondary response because memory cells were present as a result of the first contact with the antigen. *(2)*

(ii) Blood serum does not contain memory cells and therefore the slower primary immune response occured. *(1)*

(iii) The lymphocytes included memory cells allowing the faster secondary immune response to occur. *(2)*

(b) The fluid in the eye contains no lymphocytes as these might block the light; therefore no immune response. *(1)*

(Total 6 marks)

10 (a) They have no nucleus and therefore can produce no proteins by protein synthesis. *(1)*

(b) Artificial blood is much smaller than red blood cells and get past the blockage. *(2)*

(c) It can carry a higher concentration of oxygen per volume because there are no other structures present e.g. white cells; it has no antigens and cannot cause agglutination – it can be given to people of any blood group without risk. *(2)*

(d) See section 11.3 page 315 *(7)*

(Total 12 marks)

11 ✗ ✗ ✔
  ✔ ✗ ✗
  ✗ ✔ ✗
  ✗ ✗ ✔
  ✗ ✗ ✔ *(5)*

Chapter 12, pages 369–372

1 Transpiration is the loss of water from a plant in the form of water vapour. Transpiration increases in hot, dry and windy conditions. *(2)*

2 Ions are found in root hairs at a higher concentration than in the soil, so they must have entered by active transport. *(2)*

3 (a) Potassium ions pass by active transport as they pass from a lower concentration in cell A, 295, to a higher concentration in the guard cell, 450 units. *(2)*

(b) A high concentration of ions lowers the water potential of a cell. *(1)*

(c) The higher concentration of ions in guard cells lowers the water potential there. This draws in water by osmosis from adjacent cells which have a higher water potential. The guard cells swell with the extra water and become turgid. Turgid guard cells bend apart, so opening the stoma. *(3)*

(Total 6 marks)

4 At midday, higher temperatures increase the rate of transpiration. The loss of water through the leaves creates a negative pressure, drawing up more water from the xylem. This transpiration pull or

suction pulling upwards, combined with gravity pulling the xylem downwards, causes tension, like pulling an elastic band in both directions. As a result each xylem vessel is narrowed, leading to a slight decrease in the branch diameter. This does not occur so much at midnight as the lower temperatures reduce the rate of transpiration and the stomata close. *(4)*

5 Leaves with equally large numbers of stomata on both upper and lower surfaces lose more water in transpiration than those with fewer on the upper surface. This will lead to excessive water loss in dry conditions and death. For this reason trees with this mutation will not reach maturity. *(2)*

6 A plant ringed at ground level has the phloem removed. Therefore sugar made in the leaves cannot be transported down to the roots. Without sugar, respiration and growth are not possible and the roots soon die. *(2)*

7 (a) Stomata open during daylight hours to allow CO_2 in for photosynthesis. Stomata close at night, when no light, which reduces transpiration *(2)*.

(b) (i) During day K^+ move into guard cells lowering the water potential and drawing in water by osmosis. Guard cells with swollen vacuoles pull apart and stomata open *(3)*.

(ii) K^+ pass from low to high concentration by active transport. An input of energy is required provided by ATP. Protein carriers are involved in active transport across a membrane *(2)*.

(Total 7 marks)

8 (a) A = sieve tube cell; B = companion cell *(2)*

(b) (i) Translocation of sucrose and amino acids *(1)*.

(ii) Decapitated feeding aphids have stylets penetrating into the phloem. Phloem contents ooze out under pressure and the sap can be analysed for content, speed and direction of movement, using radioactive CO_2. *(3)*

(Total 6 marks)

9 (a) Roots (shoot tips) *(1)*

(b) Many mitochondria in companion cells producing ATP/energy. Mass flow hypothesis is a passive process, no function for this energy *(2)*.

(c) Leaves in light photosynthesise and make sugar, lowering the water potential and drawing in water by osmosis to create high pressure. Therefore solutes pass to low pressure regions. In dark, no sugar, no build up of pressure and no translocation *(2)*.

(Total 5 marks)

Chapter 13, pages 408–412

1 (a) Small intestine/ileum *(1)*

(b) Because they *cannot* digest food themselves – they need a supply of food which has been digested already by the host. This is found in the small intestine. *(2)*

(c) *Two* of:
  (i) Digestive enzymes of host.
  (ii) Very acidic conditons in stomach.
  (iii) Lack of oxygen – anaerobic conditions.
  (iv) Peristalsis causing complete removal from gut.
  (Max 2)
  (Total 5 marks)

2 (a) attaches to gut wall preventing removal due to peristalsis *(2)*

  (b) (i) it is a parasite obtaining food from the living human host; food digested by the host is absorbed through the body wall *(2)*

  (ii) Rhizopus is a saprobiont digesting its own food by extracellular digestion. It feeds on dead organic matter. *(2)*
  (Total 6 marks)

3 (a) (i) 67 g, 51 g *(2)*

  (ii) Steady and constant increase up to day 9; levels off until day 11 when it reaches a maximum of 51 g; decreases until day 15; slight increase until day 18 *(2)*.

  (iii) group A grows faster when milk added than group B when milk added; both increase and then decrease when no milk given; both are the same mass at day 46; group A reaches a higher mass than group B; group B finishes with a higher mean mass than group A. *(3)*

  (b) milk contains vitamins; milk contains lactose for more energy; milk contains extra protein for growth; milk contains extra calcium needed for bones. *(2)*

  (c) needed for bones and teeth; needed for muscle contraction; needed for nerve activity; needed to help blood clotting. *(3)*
  (Total 12 marks)

4 Mouth; maltose; (salivary) amylase; pancreas; glucose; fructose. *(6)*

5 (a) (i) Vitamins are essential nutrients that are needed in small quantities for the healthy functioning of the body. *(1)*

  (ii) pellagra – B3; beri-beri – B1 *(2)*

  (b) Balanced diet – provides adequate amounts of all nutrients to maintain good health – not too much and not too little. protein – energy malnutrition involves a shortage of both protein and energy. This can cause disease such as kwashiorkor and marasmus *(4)*

  (c) (i) essential amino acids cannot be made in the body and must be obtained in the diet. *(1)*

  (ii) maize and soya bean *(1)*

  (iii) lack of the essential amino acids – lysine; phenylalanine and tyrosine; threonine *(2)*

  (d) Too much saturated fat raising cholesterol levels and causing atherosclerosis; energy intake greater than energy expenditure causing obesity; salt intake too high raising blood pressure. *(4)*
  (Total 15 marks)

6 (a) Pepsin is a protease and egg white contains protein whereas egg yolk contains lipid. *(1)*

  (b) Larger surface area for action of the pepsin enzyme *(1)*

  (c) Acts as a control with no active ingredients *(1)*

  (d) So that the total volumes are the same in each tube (20 cm³) *(1)*

  (e) (i) Digestion of the egg white protein because the conditions are acidic and this is the optimum pH for the action of pepsin. *(1)*

  (ii) Egg white not digested because conditions are alkaline so that the pepsin is denatured and is inactive. *(1)*

  (f) To test whether acidic conditions alone can break down the egg white *(1)*

  (g) Stomach *(1)*   *(Total 8 marks)*

7 (a) **A** mucosa; **B** sub mucosa; **C** circular and longitudinal muscle *(3)*

  (b) D columnar epithelial cell; E lacteal; F crypt of Lieberkühn *(3)*

  (c) Function of C is peristalsis. Function of E is removal of absorbed lipid. *(2)*

  (d) Two of: microvilli – increase surface area; lots of mitochondria – provide energy as ATP for active transport; the epithelial layer is only one cell thick, therefore a shorter distance for diffusion. *(4)*
  (Total 12 marks)

Chapter 14, pages 436–438

1 (a) A diagram showing the total biomass (weight) of organisms at each trophic level *(1)* in a particular ecosystem/habitat *(1)* (at any one time).

  (b) The rate of production of new biomass (or energy) by the plants/producers of a particular ecosystem *(1)*. It equals the gross primary production minus the respiratory losses of the plants/producers *(1)*.

  (c) All the organisms of different species *(1)* living in a particular ecosystem/habitat *(1)*.
  (Total 6 marks)

2 (a) Pyramid drawn to scale *(1)*, symmetrical *(1)* and in correct order *(1)*.

  (b)
  $$\frac{1790 - 225}{1790} \times 100 = 87.4\%$$ *(2)*

(c) Energy/mass lost as respiration by grass *(1)* and to decomposers *(1)*.

(d) Losses of biomass to decomposers not shown *(1)*, some organisms feed at more than one trophic level, i.e. omnivores *(1)*, method does not sample plankton/microscopic organisms *(1)*.

(Total 9 marks)

3 (a) A: *Clostridium/Rhizobium/Bacillus/Azotobacter/*etc.
B: *Nitrosomonas/Nitrococcus/*etc.
C: *Nitrobacter/*etc.
D: *Pseudomonas/Bacillus/Thiobacillus/*etc. *(4)*

(b) Anaerobic/no oxygen *(1)*; waterlogged soil/marsh/bog etc. *(1)*

(Total 6 marks)

4 (a) (i) Nitrate or ammonium ions *(1)*

(ii) *Rhizobium/*bacteria in root nodules fix atmospheric nitrogen *(1)* to ammonia/ammonium *(1)* combine with organic acids/make amino acids *(1)* *(Max. 2)*

(b) (i) No difference until day 36 *(1)* then amount of nitrogen fixed is greater in CO_2 enriched conditions *(1)* in CO_2 enriched no levelling off but in normal air remains at 20 mg from day 36 to 60 *(1)* in CO_2 enriched smaller increase after 90 days but in normal air little increase after 80 days *(1)* any calculation from figures, e.g. percentage change *(1)* *(Max. 3 marks)*

(ii) More CO_2 allows more photosynthesis *(1)*

(c) Greater yield *(1)* cereals grown on low nitrate soils *(1)* less/no fertiliser needed *(1)* less eutrophication (or equivalent) *(1)* *(Max. 2)*

(Total 9 marks)

5 Any of the following points *(1 mark each)*:
Energy from sunlight;
Absorbed by photosynthetic pigments/named pigment;
Converted to chemical energy;
In the form of organic compounds/carbohydrates/named example;
By photosynthesis in producers/green plants;
Explanation of GPP;
Used in respiration by plants;
Energy lost by plant respiration;
Explanation of NPP;
Energy passed on through food chains/through trophic levels;
Less energy at higher trophic levels;
Efficiency of transfer about 10%;
Energy lost due to locomotion;
Energy converted to indigestible material so not passed on through chain;
Energy lost in faeces;
Energy lost in excretory material;
Named excretory material, e.g. urea. *(Max. 10 marks)*

Chapter 15, pages 477–479

1 (a) Eutrophication is the over-enrichment of bodies of fresh water with mineral nutrients *(1)*. It can occur naturally, but is often the result of human activities, such as inorganic fertiliser runoff *(1)* or effluent from sewage treatment works *(1)*.

(b) Bioaccumulation is the gradual build-up in concentration *(1)* of a toxic substance along a food chain *(1)*. It often refers to pesticides *(1)*.

(c) Desertification is the process of conversion of fertile arid or semi-arid land into desert *(1)* as a result of human activities and climate change *(1)*.

(d) The greenhouse effect occurs when gases in the atmosphere *(1)* trap and re-radiate infra-red radiation *(1)* emitted by the Earth. This raises the surface temperature of the Earth *(1)*. (It is also more commonly used to mean an *increase* in this effect due to human activities.)

(Total 11 marks)

2 Any of the following points *(1 mark each)*
Contents of sewage (faeces/urine/detergents etc.);
Overproduction of sewage from increasing population;
Failure of sewage treatment/release of raw sewage/agriculturla spillage;
Sewage forms nutrients for bacterial/fungal growth;
Increases aerobic respiration of microorganisms/increases BOD;
Sewage contains pathogenic bacteria/viruses etc.;
Sewage contains toxic/heavy metals/other named chemicals (e.g. oestrogens). *(Max. 10 marks)*

3 (a) (i) Decreased *(1)* greater concentration needed each year to kill the same numbers of pest *(1)* mark for manipulation of figures, calculation of percentage change etc. *(1)* *(Max. 2 marks)*

(ii) Some insects are resistant *(1)* due to a mutant gene *(1)* these survive to breed *(1)* resistance passed to offspring *(1)* so fewer killed in next generation *(1)* *(Max. 4 marks)*

(b) (i) Insecticide is persistent/non-biodegradable *(1)* small amount absorbed by pest *(1)* stored/no excreted *(1)* many primary consumers eaten by secondary consumers so insecticide builds up *(1)* animals at the end of the food chain receive most *(1)* *(Max. 3 marks)*

(ii) Can be made specific/selective *(1)* non-persistent/biodegradable *(1)*

4 (a) (i) Soil is waterlogged/airspaces full of water *(1)* little/no oxygen present *(1)* root cells cannot respire *(1)*

(ii) Lack of oxygen means that cells respire anerobically *(1)* forming ethanol *(1)*

(b) Helps stem to float *(1)* allows oxygen to get to cells below water *(1)*.

(Total 7 marks)

5 Sulphur dioxide/carbon dioxide/nitrogen oxides *(1)* fossil fuels *(1)* coal/oil/gas/petrol *(1)* anaerobic *(1)* biomass/organic waste *(1)*

(Total 5 marks)

6 **(a)** Decrease for first 10 generations *(1)* rises again to 15 generations *(1)* falls between 15 and 20 generations *(1)*

(b) There is an inverse relationship *(1)* *Trialeurodes* provides food for *Encarsia (1)* More *Encarsia* means more *Trialeaurodes* killed *(1)* Fewer *Trialeurodes* means less breeding by *Encarsia (1)* *(Max. 3)*

(c) Decreased yield *(1)* spread of viruses/disease *(1)* spoilage of crop/decreased value *(1)* *(Max. 2)*

(d) (i) 1. No residues on crops/does not harm other organisms/non-toxic/etc.
　　2. Longer lasting effect/no need to re-apply/pests don't develop resistance *(2)*

(ii) Does not kill all *Trialeurodes*/takes longer to work/more dependent on environmental conditions/only controls one pest *(1)*

(Total 11 marks)

Chapter 16, pages 506–508

1 **(a)** An enzyme which cuts DNA at specific base sequences. In this example used to cut open plasmid to insert insulin gene. *(2)*

(b) A copy of a gene – the insulin gene. Made by reverse transcription from the messenger RNA which codes for insulin. *(2)*

(c) An enzyme used to join pieces of DNA. Here it is used to attach the insulin gene to the plasmid vector by joining the sugar-phosphate backbones. *(2)*

(d) A plasmid is a circular piece of DNA used as a vector. Here it is used to deliver the insulin gene into the host bacterial cells. *(2)*

(e) An enzyme which catalyses reverse transcription. Single-stranded DNA is copied from the mRNA for insulin. The single-stranded DNA is then made double stranded to give a copy insulin gene. *(2)*

(f) Many restriction enzymes cut DNA unevenly. The ends of the DNA are now single stranded with exposed bases. These ends are sticky because they will attract and stick to matching sticky ends. This helps the sticky ends of the insulin gene attach to the matching sticky ends of the plasmid. *(2)*

(Total 12 marks)

2 **(a)** The DNA to be located will be of a specific length. The probe must have the complementary bases to attach to the DNA, so it must be the same length. *(2)*

(b) The probe needs to have exposed bases to attach to the complementary bases of the sought-for DNA. If the probe was double stranded it would not be able to attach. *(2)*

(c) The probe is radioactive so that it can be located after it has attached to the sought-for DNA. The position of the probe and therefore the position of the DNA can be revealed by autoradiography. *(2)*

(Total 6 marks)

3 Take examples from Table 16.1, page 503. *(6)*

4 **(a)** Sample A with result 2 – only one fragment as it has not been cut. *(2)*
Sample B with result 3 – restriction enzyme will cut at three sites, producing four fragments of different lengths. *(2)*
Sample C with result 1 – five fragments produced by restriction enzyme cutting at four sites. *(2)*
Sample D with result 4 – both enzymes cut at different sites so a total of seven cuts, producing eight fragments of different lengths. *(2)*

(b) Arrow pointing downwards. The largest fragment, the uncut DNA (result 2), will travel the least distance, i.e. it will be nearest to the start. *(1)*

(c) Different restriction enzymes cut at different specific sequences of bases. This will produce fragments of different lengths – hence a different pattern of bands. *(2)*

(Total 11 marks)

5 **(a) (i)** Reverse transcriptase *(1)*

(ii) ATTGACGGC *(2)*

(b) (i) Sticky ends have exposed bases which will combine with complementary bases by hydrogen bonding *(2)*

(ii) DNA ligase *(1)*

(iii) recombinant DNA *(1)*

(c) Makes the cell wall/membrane more permeable so that the plasmids can enter *(2)*

(d) The plasmid has a gene for antibiotic resistance; the cells are grown on a medium containing the antibiotic; only cells which have taken up the plasmid will grow; other cells will be killed by the antibiotic. *(3)*

(Total 12 marks)

6 **(a)** One chain acts as a template for the copying of a new chain; only the complementary bases will attach and therefore the new chain will be identical to the original; each new DNA molecule will have one original chain and one new chain. *(2)*

(b) 32 *(1)*

(c) procedures a new strand of DNA and does not produce mRNA; the whole molecule is copied rather than just part of the DNA being copied; in this process adenine is copied to thymine, in transcription adenine is copied to uracil; in transcription heat is not used *(2)*.

(Total 5 marks)

Chapter 17, pages 534–536

1 Symptoms of some diseases may be too slight or long term to notice *(1)*. Although indicators of physical fitness may be measured (e.g. blood pressure), it is not possible in surgery conditions to be sure how fit someone is *(1)*. It is not possible to determine how mentally well adjusted someone is. The time is too short *(1)*. It is not possible to be sure how well a patient is integrated into society *(1)*.

(Total 4 marks)

2 (a) AIDS

(b) Thrush

(c) Alzheimer's disease

(d) cholera

(e) elephantiasis

(f) anorexia nervosa

(g) cystic fibrosis *(7)*

3 Samples of people studied must be large *(1)*. Care must be taken when choosing samples to eliminate any other factors which may affect the cause of the disease *(1)*. A positive relationship between a particular factor and the incidence of the disease does not necessarily mean that the factor is a cause of the disease unless supported by experimental evidence *(1)*.

(Total 3 marks)

4 Measles – incubation period shorter than smallpox, so it is more difficult to identify and isolate contacts before they become infectious *(1)*.
Tuberculosis – patients can carry pathogen and be infectious without showing symptoms, therefore they are difficult to identify and isolate *(1)*.
Malaria – no effective vaccine/ pathogen can exist in mosquitoes *(1)*.
Cholera – vaccine not very effective/ pathogen can survive in water *(1)*.

(Total 4 marks)

5 (a) (i) diphtheria, tetanus and whooping cough *(1)*

(ii) 1–2 years *(1)*

(b) 12–14 years, earlier if high risk;
skin test first;
one injection *(Max. 2)*

(c) (i) vaccination most effective if high percentage of children are vaccinated; fewer infected people means that spread of the disease is more difficult. *(2)*

(ii) fear of side effects/religious beliefs *(Max. 1)*

(Total 7 marks)

6 (a) endemic – disease always present in a population *(1)*
epidemic – spread of a disease through a town or country *(1)*

(b) (i) poor living conditions; water shortage; poor water purification; poor sewage treatment; malnutrition leading to poor immunity; few vaccination programmes; usually warm climates which favours insect vectors; any valid point developing any of the above ideas. *(Max. 4)*

(ii) fewer people die young as many infectious diseases controlled; live longer and degenerative diseases commoner in old age; many degenerative diseases take a long time to develop; any valid example developing the above ideas. *(Max. 4)*

(Total 10 marks)

7 (a) from faeces of infected person in drinking water and ingested by another person; carried by flies from infected faeces to food eaten by another person;
contamination of food by infected person not washing hands before preparing food;
eating seafood grown in contaminated water;
eating vegetables irrigated with contaminated water. *(Max. 2)*

(b) test blood for antibodies against *V. cholerae*;
test specimen of faeces or rectal swab for bacteria by growing on medium and identifying by microscopy/described method. *(Max. 2)*

(c) good sewage treatment;
good sanitation methods;
clean water supplies;
good food hygiene; any other valid point *(Max. 4)*

(d) Still 12 million people who have poor water supply;
so large pool of people to be infected and transmit cholera large populations in overcrowded conditions;
poor sanitation in overcrowded areas;
poverty menas facilities not maintained;
no effective vaccine;
wars damage/prevent the development of facilities;
any other valid points;
(Max. 7 + 1 for quality of communication)

(e) (i) stops the development of bacterial cell walls;
disrupts protein synthesis at transcription/translation phase disrupts DNA replication/cell division *(Max. 2)*

(ii) patient may recover with oral rehydration;
overuse of antibiotics may favour development of resistant strains *(Max. 1)*

(Total 19 marks)

Index

sorghum 258, 441
Southern blotting 495–6, 498
soya beans, transgenic 492
species-specific pest control 452
sperm count 196
spermatogenesis 183–7, 192
Sphagnum moss 468
sphincter muscles, arterioles 294
sphygmomanometers 278, 279
spindle fibres 14, 160, 172
spiracles 264–6
split genes 138
spongy mesophyll cells 25, 343–4
    gas exchange 236, 257–8
sporangia, fungi 400–1
squamous epithelium 23, 24, 45
    capillaries 296, 300
    gas exchange 240, 264
Stahl, F.W. 128–9
staining 2, 7
stalked particles, mitochondria 12, 13
stamens 216, 218, 219, 222, 226
standing crops 425
Staphylococcus 531–2
starch
    chemical test 76
    digestion 390–1
    fungal enzyme activity 402
    structure 68–9, 71, 75
statistics, health 514–21
stearic acid 77
stem cells, embryonic 199
steroids 76, 79, 81, 82
sticky ends, restriction endonucleases 483, 486
stigma 216, 218–21, 222, 224, 225
stomach
    human 383, 385, 390, 394
    ruminants 398–9
stomata
    gas exchange 235, 257–9
    transpiration 343–9
stop codons, mutations 142–3
stratified epithelium 23, 24
strawberry plant 163
stretch receptors 252–3
stroke volume, heart 286, 288
strokes 244, 290–2

stroma 17, 18
structural genes 487
style, flowers 216, 218, 219, 221, 224, 225
stylets 365
suberin 15, 354
submerged leaves 259
submucosa 384
subsistence agriculture 455
substitution mutations 140–2, 144
substrates, enzymes 101, 105
sucrose
    digestion 391
    structure 68, 75
    transport in plants 361–8
sugar-phosphate backbone 119–20
sugars 65–8
sulphur dioxide 465, 466, 468
sun 419
surface area to volume ratio 232–4
surface runoff 446
surfactant 250
sustainable agriculture 440, 454
sustainable forestry 457–8
sweet pea 218
symbiosis see mutualistic nutrition
sympathetic nerves, heart 282, 284
symplast pathway 353–6, 364
systemic circulation 271, 272–3
systemic herbicides 447
systemic insecticides 448
systole 276–81, 284, 293

T lymphocytes 312, 324–5, 327–9
    AIDS 521, 527
tadpoles, gas exchange 235
Taenia solium 403–4
Tansley, Sir Arthur 413
tapeworms 403–4
    gas exchange 233–4
tar (tobacco), lung cancer 243–4
Tatum, E.L. 126
TB *see* tuberculosis
teeth 390, 397
telomeres 164
telophase
    meiosis 172, 173
    mitosis 158, 160

temperature
    enzymes 104
    transpiration 345
    water 63, 64
tension, water transport 356–7
tertiary structure, proteins 47
tessellated membrane 24
testa 225
testis 184
testosterone 192
tetracycline 532
thermocyclers 499–500
Thiobacillus denitrificans 433
third world 518–21, 524–5, 526
thoracic duct 303
thoracic spiracles 265
thorax, human 238–9, 246–7
thrombus 290
thrush (disease) 512
thylakoids 17, 18
thymine 120–1
thymus gland 325
tidal flow, ventilation 238, 241
tidal volume, lungs 248–9
tissue fluid 272, 300–4
tomatoes, transgenic 492
tonoplasts 4, 16, 361
total lung capacity 249
totipotent genes 165
trachea
    cilia 15
    epithelium 3
    gas exchange 238–9
    insects 265
tracheids 359
tracheoles 265–6
transcription 133–7, 146
transfer cells, phloem 364
transfer RNA (tRNA) 123, 133–7, 152
transferases 107
transformation, genetic 487
transfusions, ABO blood groups 334–5
transgenic animals/plants 492
translation, protein synthesis 133–7, 139, 146
translocation, phloem 362–8
transmembrane regulator proteins 493–4

Photo Acknowledgements

We are grateful to the following for permission to reproduce photographic material:

Front cover:

top: Stone (Frans Lanting)
centre: Stone (Art Wolfe)
bottom: Science Photo Library (Andrew Syred)

Heather Angel /Natural Visions, pages 217(a), 217(f), 219 top, 400, 428 below, 453 top, 461(a), 461(d); Art Directors & TRIP, pages 187 (M Walker), 248 (Helene Rogers), 310, 455 (Eric Smith); Dr Glenn Baggott, page 3(a), 3(b), 3(d), 3(e), 3(f), 240; Bettmann/ Corbis, pages 284, 495 bottom left; Biophoto Associates, pages 15 bottom, 16,40, 170, 171, 172, 173, 387; Gareth Boden, pages 74(b), 76, 80, 91, 109; Colorific! /Jean-Claude Coutausse, page 525; Corbis, page 124(c); Dr Glenn L. Decker, School of Medicine, John Hopkins University, page 9; Dorling Kindersley/Dave King, page 218(b); Mary Evans Picture Library, page 526(a); GeoScience Features Picture Library, page 81(e), 161; Robert Harding Picture Library, pages 44 (Dr Dennis Kunkel), 218 top (Raj Kamal), 413(a) (Robert Francis), 433 (Carolina Biological Supp/Phototake NYC); Andrew Lambert, page 460; Life Science Images, pages 413(b), 429, 472(a), 472(b), 472 (c), 510(a), 512(b), 513(b); Paul Mulcahy, pages 194, 444(a), 444(b); NHPA, pages 74 top right (N A Callow), 81(f) (Stephen Dalton), 217(c) and 217(g) (Laurie Campbell), 221 top (Jany Sauvanet), 260 left (Agence Nature), 428 top right (Andy Rouse), 440(a) (G I Bernard), 440(c) (Joe Blossom), 453 bottom, 461(b) (Stephen Dalton), 461(c) (Lutra), 468 (David Woodfall), 472 below (E A Janes); Oxford Scientific Films, pages 22 bottom (David J Patterson), 73(a) (Scott Camazine), 217(d) (Terry Heathcote), 217(e) (Martyn Chillmaid), 224(c) (Dr C E Jeffree), 415(a) (Peter Cook), 422(b) (J A L Cooke), 22(c) (Richard Packwood), 422(d) (Mike Birkhead), 422(e), 422(f) (Peter Parks), 422(g) (Tony Bomford), 422(h) (Rodger Jackman), 440(b) (Scott Camazine), 443 (Colin Milkins), 459 (John McCammon); Panos Pictures, pages 509(a) (Sean Sprague), 509(b) (Betty Press), 524 (Clive Shirley); Planet Earth Pictures, page 64; Rex Features, pages 168 (J Sutton-Hibbert), 195; Science Photo Library, pages 3 (c) (Astrid & Hanns-Frieder), 5 (Dave Parker), 9 (Dr Don Fawcett), 13 top (Professors P Motta & T Naguro), 13 bottom (Francis Leroy, Biocosmos), 15(a) (CNRI), 15(b) (Dr Gopal Murti), 15 centre (Quest), 18 (Dr Jeremy Burgess), 22 top (Andrew Syred), 22 centre (Alex Rakosy, Custom), 26 (Dr Linda Stannard, UCT), 38 (K R Porter), 69 (Andrew Syred), 70 (Dr Don Fawcett), (72(a) (David Scharf), 72(b) (Dr Jeremy Burgess), 72(c) (Gca-CNRI), 73 (b) (William Ervin), (74 top left (David Scharf), 81(c) (John Beatty), 124 left (A Barrington Brown), 124 right, 144 (Dr Gopal Murti), 157 (CNRI), 164 (Dr E Walker), 176 (J L Carson, Custom Medical Stock Photo), 186 (Astrid & Hanns-Frieder Michler), 188 top (Biophoto Associates), 188 bottom (Professor P M Motta *et al*), 200 (P Saada/Eurel IOS), 217(b) (Dr Jeremy Burgess), 219 bottom left (Dr Jeremy Burgess), 219 bottom right (Dr Jeremy Burgess), 221 bottom (Leonard Lessin), 233 (Dr Morley Read), 279 (D Ouellette, Publiphoto Diffusion), 290, 332 (George Bernard), 386 (Eye of Science), 413 (c) (Simon Fraser), 422(a) (John Heseltine), 428 top left (Chris Knapton), 445 (John Heseltine), 446 left (BSIP Martin PL), 446 right (Novosti), 453 centre (David Scharf), 457 (Simon Fraser), 493 (Peter Menzel), 494 (Hattie Young), 495 bottom right (David Parker), 498 (Sinclair Stammers), 500 (Robert Longuehaye, NIBSC), 503 (Julia Kamlish), 512(a) (Murtz/Biozentrum, University of Basel), 512 (c) (Eye of Science), 512(d) (David Scharf), 512 bottom (Alfred Pasieka), 513(a) (Sinclair Stammers), 521(a) (Eye of Science), 521(b) (Eye of Science), 521(c) (CAMR/A B Dowsett), 521(d) (NIBSC), 522 (Claude Nuridsany & Marie Perennou), 527 (Hank Morgan), 530 (Bernard Pierre Wolff), 531(b) and 531(c) (St Mary's Hospital Medical School); Stone, pages 6 (David Burder), 81(a) (John Lawrence), 81(d) (Stuart Westmorland), 224(a) and 224(b) (S Lowry/Univ. Ulster), 260 right (Jeff Rotman), 526(c) (Joel Simon); Richard Summers, The Sanger Centre, page 501; Telegraph Colour Library, pages 81(b) (L Kuhn), 467, 495 top (L Lefkowitz), 526(b) (Rosenfeld); University of Massachusetts, Amherst, page 28; Wellcome Trust Photo Library, pages 111, 205 (Royal Veterinary College), 311 (D Gregory & D Marshall), 510(b), 531(a).

Other copyright material:

Iceland Foods Plc, page 503 centre